The Renaissance in Europe: An Anthology

The Renaissance in Europe

An Anthology

Edited by Peter Elmer, Nick Webb and Roberta Wood

Yale University Press
New Haven and London
in association with The Open University

First published 2000

Set in Adobe Garamond and Helvetica Condensed by Best-set Typesetter Ltd, Hong Kong
Printed in Great Britain by Biddles Ltd, Guildford and Kings Lynn

ISBN   0-300-082177   (hbk.)
          0-300-082223   (pbk.)

Library of Congress Cataloging-in-Publication Data

The Renaissance in Europe : an anthology / edited by Peter Elmer, Nick
    Webb, and Roberta Wood.
        p.   cm.
      Includes index.
      ISBN 0–300–08217–7   (cloth: alk. paper). – ISBN 0–300–08222–3
    (pbk.: alk. paper)
        1. Renaissance.   2. Europe – Civilization.   I. Elmer, Peter.   II. Webb, Nick,
    1959–   .   III. Wood, Roberta.
    CB361.R3862   2000
    940.2′1 – dc21   99–41077
                                                                                                              CIP

A catalogue record for this book is available from the British Library

10 9 8 7 6 5 4 3 2 1

Summary

Contents

Section Two **Politics and Humanism**

Section Three **The Renaissance Court**

Illustrations

Introduction

During the course of the fifteenth and sixteenth centuries, the cultural life of Europe was transformed by the widespread revival of interest in the classical past. Initially the preserve of scholars and poets, the rediscovery of antiquity, or the Renaissance, rapidly acquired an enthusiastic audience in the courts of discerning and powerful patrons, not just in Italy, but throughout the continent. One of the defining features of this movement of ideas and values was that it sought both to imitate and, ultimately, to emulate the classical tradition upon which it was based. Today, lively debate continues to surround every facet of this crucial episode in the cultural history of Europe. To what extent, for example, should we accept the view of some contemporary humanist scholars, as well as later commentators, that the Renaissance marked a definitive break with the past – a conscious rejection of the medieval inheritance? Was there in fact a distinctive period of European history which we can neatly define as the 'Renaissance'? What was the precise nature of the process whereby the initial enthusiasm for the classical revival in Italy was subsequently transmitted and received by scholars and patrons in other parts of Europe?

These, and many other questions, form the starting-point of the Open University course (*The Renaissance in Europe: A Cultural Enquiry*) for which this anthology of sources was specifically commissioned. Their apparent randomness is partly explained by this fact, although some attempt has been made to group them according to general themes. All, however, share the general aim of seeking to illustrate critical issues in current academic debates over the meaning and significance of the Renaissance in the cultural life of Europe. Thus, the anthology contains a vast range of sources for those interested in charting how a preoccupation with the classical past informed the artistic, literary, educational, religious and scientific life of this period. Interpretation of the sources, of course, is not problem free. In the three-volume series associated with this anthology, an attempt is made to contextualise the extracts with, in most cases, exercises followed by discussions to enable the reader to make their own judgements. For both the student and the general reader, the following caveats should be borne in mind when reading and analysing the texts.

In attempting to recover meaning in texts and documents from the past, it is useful to come prepared with a checklist of questions and queries: what was the nature of the original source (printed or manuscript) and how might this affect our judgement of its value? Who wrote the document, and why? What does the original style, genre or language in which the document was first written tell us about the source? Is the document likely to be representative of its type, or does it possess any features which hint at its exceptional status? What else does it unwittingly tell us about the author, its subject, or the purpose for which it was recorded for posterity? Texts can be read on a variety of levels and appeal to different readers for different reasons. Historians interested in the role of women in Renaissance society, for example, will undoubtedly approach texts such as the examination of Anne Askew (Text 51) or Pico's demonology (Text 90) from a very different perspective from that of an historian whose main concern lies in the field of religious history.

The texts selected for this anthology have been grouped into six central categories reflecting their sequential appearance in the course. In order that the general reader might better understand the rationale behind their selection, it might be helpful to say something more about the general features of the course and to relate them to some of the documents printed here. In the first part of the course, we focus on the role of humanism in various aspects of Renaissance life and thought, including the study of history, music, politics, religion and philosophy, as well as its impact on women. Many of the earlier selections are intended to equip the reader with a basic understanding of what was involved in the humanist pursuit of ancient learning and to illustrate something of the enthusiasm which men like Ciriaco of Ancona (Text 2) felt in unearthing and recording the remains of the classical past. This is followed by concrete examples of how the new learning might be adapted to present-day circumstances to critique and advance received wisdom. Lorenzo Valla, for example, neatly demonstrates how the new philological and rhetorical techniques helped to undermine the political authority of the papacy (Text 4). In like manner, religious debate was critically influenced by the adaptation of humanist methods to the scriptures (Text 5), as was the writing of history (Text 12). A common theme linking all these texts is the humanist reverence for classical and pagan authors and a willingness on the part of humanist commentators to appreciate the moral value of their teachings for a contemporary Christian audience. Renaissance humanists, it has to be said, were not uniformly successful in this respect, as the case of Machiavelli demonstrates (Texts 21 and 23–6).

In the second section of the course, we focus attention on the role of the court and the patron in promoting and disseminating Renaissance values. Case studies focus on three seigneurial courts (Urbino, Mantua and Milan) which are contrasted with what many consider to be the prototype for the patronage of classical culture, Republican Florence. In addition, we consider the court of Matthias Corvinus, king of Hungary (1458–90) as an example of how Renaissance art and culture were translated into an environment (monarchical, eastern Europe) which was very different from that of Italy. In the final section of this part of the course, Renaissance poetry and drama take centre stage in an in-depth study of the British Renaissance of letters. The selected extracts in this section offer a reappraisal of a wide variety of cultural forms in their courtly settings. These include the architectural interests of one of the most celebrated princely patrons of the fifteenth century, Federico da Montefeltro of Urbino (Text 33) as well as the poly-mathic concerns of that archetypal 'Renaissance man', Leonardo da Vinci (Text 31). In choosing such texts, the emphasis throughout has been to provide as much contextual background as possible, whether through the citation of the classical sources themselves (for example, Texts 42 and 44) or via the comments and critical analyses of those engaged in the production and consumption of Renais-sance texts and artefacts.

In the final section of the course, attention is focussed primarily on the six-teenth century and the interaction of Renaissance values with developments in other fields of thought and learning. A central objective here is to explore the relationship between the Renaissance and the Reformation, both in the period immediately prior to 1517, as well as in the impact of classical wisdom upon the establishment of the Protestant church in the German-speaking lands.

Extracts here illustrate a variety of historical issues ranging from the attempt to reform the Catholic Church from within (Texts 57–9) to the Lutheran Refor-mation (Texts 63–79). Divisions within the ranks of the reformers on these and other issues are fully explored and conclude with a reappraisal of the Radical Reformation (Texts 80–7). In addition to religious reform, the sixteenth century witnessed the beginnings of a new approach to science and the natural world cul-minating in the so-called 'Scientific Revolution' of the following century. Until fairly recently, historians of science were largely dismissive of the contribution of Renaissance scientists in this respect. That this is no longer the case is evident from the recent upsurge of scholarly interest in the science of the period which is reflected in some of the extracts cited here and in the *Reader* associated with this volume. One aspect of this scholarly revolt against traditional approaches to Renaissance science is a determination to explore the full range of meanings 'scientific' texts and ideas held for contemporaries. Rather than privileging those texts which seemed to prefigure the great advances of the seventeenth century (for example, Vesalius in anatomy), it is increasingly common to treat all manifestations of early modern science with an equal respect in line with contemporary thinking. Consequently the emphasis in such studies is upon a more empathetic, rather than judgemental, approach. This approach is reflected here in the specially commissioned translation of an early sixteenth-century demonology (Text 90) which forms the basis of an in-depth study in the third volume of the series associated with this reader.

With respect to all the texts, it has been editorial policy to keep notes to a minimum. This is also true of the headnotes which accompany each item, though it is hoped that these will assist in providing a little more context for the general reader and student. Editorial additions are enclosed in square brackets and dele-tions within the text are indicated by three ellipses within square brackets. We have not attempted to standardize spellings or other editoral insertions in the original texts. Throughout we have adopted the current usage of BCE to indicate Before Common Era in place of BC, and CE, Common Era, in place of AD.

Peter Elmer, Nick Webb and Roberta Wood edited this anthology on behalf of the course team who chose and assisted in the editing of the documents.

Members of the team were: Richard Brown, Lucille Kekewich, Susan Khin Zaw, Anne Laurence, Antony Lentin, David Mateer, Ceri Sullivan, Anabel Thomas, Keith Whitlock. We should also like to thank Rod Boroughs, Caryll Green, Dorigen Caldwell and Robert Goulding for their time and effort in translating original documents. Finally, we would like to thank Sam Horne for her patience and expertise in assisting with the preparation of the manuscript of the anthology.

Section One
Humanism

1   Giovanni Francesco Poggio Bracciolini *On the Inconstancy of Fortune* (*c.***1448**)

Giovanni Francesco Poggio Bracciolini (1380–1459) studied Greek in the 1390s
with Manuel Chrysoloras (*c.*1350–1414) and had a wide circle of humanist
friends and colleagues (with some of whom he later quarrelled) such as Coluccio
Salutati, Niccolò Niccoli and Leonardo Bruni. For most of his life he was
employed as a secretary to the papal *curia* (court) in Rome, and despite the
turbulence of his masters' lives, he enjoyed the freedom to study, write and travel
extensively. He was a prolific writer, producing moral essays (including *On the
Inconstancy of Fortune*), vituperative works aimed at contemporary humanists and
politicians, letters and a *History of Florence*. He undertook the latter in the 1440s
when he returned to a comfortable villa in Florence, full of his collection of
antiquities, a young wife and the prestigious office of chancellor of the republic.

   His companion in the walk round Rome in this document was Antonio Loschi,
a humanist from Viterbo who had also been in papal employment and was
chancellor to the Visconti of Milan from 1398–1402.

Source: Giovanni Francesco Poggio Bracciolini, *De Varietate Fortunae*, 1, ed. O.
Merisalo, Suomorlainen Tiedeakatemia toimituksia, *Annales Academiae Scientiarum
Fennicae*, Sar B, nide 265, Helsinki, 1993, pp. 91–7, translated for this edition by
Caryll Green

The Book of Poggio the Florentine on the Inconstancy of Fortune to Pope
Nicholas V (1447–55), begins:

In the recent past, when Pope Martin (1417–1431) had withdrawn from Rome to
the Tuscan countryside due to ill-health, just before his death, the distinguished
Antonio Loschi and I, when freed from business and public duties, used to make
fairly frequent visits to the wastelands of the city. Our minds marvelled at the
former greatness of the fallen buildings and the desolate ruins of the ancient city.
We also reflected on both the remarkable overthrow of so great an empire,
astounding indeed, and the lamentable inconstancy of fortune.

   One day when we had climbed some way up the Capitoline Hill, Antonio and
I were a little wearied by riding, and sought a moment's rest. Dismounting from
our horses, we sat down together in the very ruins of the Tarpeian citadel[1] behind
the huge marble sill of some doorway, apparently of a temple, with many broken
columns scattered about. From this point a very wide view of the city lay revealed.
Having cast his eyes here and there upon the prospect for some while, Antonio,
looking stunned, sighed and said: 'Oh, how different these temples and citadels
are, Poggio, from those which our Virgil celebrated in verse:

> *Aurea nunc, olim silvestribus horrida dumis*
> [Now glittering like gold, once bristling with woody brambles,
> *Aeneid*, VIII.348]

'Indeed that line could be deservedly rephrased:

Aurea quondam, nunc squalida spinetis vepribusque referta
[Gilded once, neglected now, massed with thorn–thickets and briars.]

'Marius, who once held supreme power in Rome, comes to mind. They say that having landed in Africa, an exile and destitute driven from his homeland, he sat down above the ruins of Carthage, pondering his own changed situation and that of Carthage, while comparing the fortune of each of them and in doubt as to which of their fates was the greater wonder.[2] Truly, for myself, I cannot compare the boundless destruction of this city to any other. The disaster here certainly exceeds that of all other cities, either which the nature of things has produced, or which the hand of man has brought about.

'Though you peruse all the volumes of history, study all the written records, though you scrutinise all the annals of past deeds, fortune has never preferred a greater example of its own mutability than the city of Rome, once the most beautiful and magnificent of all cities which have existed or will exist. Libanius, a most learned Greek author, when writing to his friend who wanted to see Rome, described it not as a city but as if it were some part of heaven.[3]

'How much more amazing is it to relate and bitter to see the extent to which the cruelty of fortune has changed the appearance and nature of this actual city, so that now it lies prostrate and stripped of all its splendour, like a giant corpse with every part corrupted and eaten away. This city is to be mourned indeed, at one time the mother of so many illustrious men and emperors, of so many military commanders, the nurse of most distinguished rulers, the parent of so many and such great virtues, the procreator of so many good arts. From Rome flowed military discipline, the sanctity of customs and of life, the ordinance of laws, examples of all the virtues and the art of right living. Once she was the mistress of affairs, now through the unfairness of fortune which transforms all things, not only is she dispoiled of her authority and majesty, but delivered up to the meanest servitude, unsightly and degraded, and by her ruins alone revealing her past grandeur and greatness.

'Let us pass over dominion swept away, kingdoms divided, provinces lost, in the giving and taking away of which, according to her own law, fortune exercises her sovereignty. What seems much more to be deplored is that fortune's mounting wantonness so ran riot within the walls of the city to Rome's complete undermining and overthrow, that if any of those former citizens of the ancient city should be restored to life he would firmly assert that he was looking upon other men and inhabiting another city far away. Its appearance and even the ground itself were so derelict that he would recognize almost nothing which represented the former city. Yet powers are replaced, sovereignties transferred, nations split off, people (for the mind of men ever seeking novelty is fickle) are set in motion at the nod of fortune, so that it seems an everyday occurrence that Rome should submit to fortune's whim.

'But in truth, these buildings of the city, which seemed to rival with immortality itself, were believed to be beyond the powers of fortune. Of these, some are wholly destroyed, some collapsed and overturned, just a few remain which preserve their former greatness. Awful indeed is the force and inconstancy of

1 General view over the site of the Forum Romanum, from the Victor Emmanuel Memorial, with the Colosseum in the background. Photo: A. F. Kersting.

fortune, which has completely demolished the very foundations of buildings. Their builders considered those structures to be beyond the grasp of fate, but of such great achievements fortune has allowed almost nothing to remain. For what greater thing has the world ever seen than the numerous buildings of Rome, temples, porticoes, baths, theatres, aqueducts, wharves, palaces, claimed by their own destiny, and out of such a great profusion of magnificent structures nothing, or virtually nothing, has survived?'

Then I answered, 'You are right to wonder, Antonio, at the injustice fortune has stirred up against this disgracefully maltreated mother of cities. I myself, as I daily traverse Rome to explore it, am compelled not only to marvel but also to lament that scarcely anything remains intact, except for a few relics from that former city, and those half worn away and spoiled. For out of all the buildings, either public or private, of a city state at one time independent, only some small, broken, piecemeal vestiges can be seen.

'On the Capitoline hill, incorporated into new buildings now serving as a store for the public salt supply, there are extant a double row of arched vaults on which are inscribed in extremely old lettering much eaten away by the moisture of the salt, a statement that Quintus Lutatius Cutalus, son of Quintus and grandson of Quintus Consul, took it upon himself to have the substructure and *Tabularium* [record office] built – a work which is worthy of veneration on the grounds of its age alone.

'Hard by the Capitol as well there is the tomb of Gaius Publicius Bibulus, in which he and his descendants are interred. The tomb was granted by senatorial decree and by order of the populace to honour his reputation and excellence. Similarly there is a bridge of very ancient stonework over the Tiber leading to the island of Tiberina. The inscription [for the bridge] attests that Lucius Fabricius (son of Gaius), the Keeper of the Highways, arranged for its construction, and the Consul Marcus Lepidus (son of Marcus) gave his approval. Furthermore, there is a Tiburtine stone arch over the road between the Aventine Hill and the Tiber bank and from the letters carved upon it we learn that it was set up and approved in accordance with a Senate decree by Publius Lentulus Scipio and Titus Quintius Crispinus.

'In addition, there are some ancient remains, which today are known as the Cimbrian Temple [also known as the Temple of Honour and Virtue], which was erected by Gaius Marius with the proceeds from his Cimbrian War spoils, and in which his trophies can still be seen. Also there is the pyramid near the Ostian Gate, set into the city walls, the noble funeral monument of Gaius Cestius, member of the College of the Priests responsible for supervising the banquet of the gods. The inscription tells us that this work was completed as instructed by Pontius Clamela in three hundred and thirty days. As this inscription is still extant, the more I wonder why Francesco Petrarch, that most erudite of men, writes in one of his letters that it is the tomb of Remus.[4] I believe, following a commonly held view, that he did not go to a great effort in carefully examining an inscription hidden by vegetation. Those less learned who have followed after-wards have shown more diligence in reading these inscriptions.'

'I certainly applaud your care and attention about this, Poggio,' said Antonio. 'You have searched in many places both within the city and outside it and having gathered together those same inscriptions [found] on both public and private buildings in a small volume, you have bequeathed them to be read by scholars.'

'However other people may receive it,' I replied, 'it surely is to the public benefit to seek them all out carefully in their obscurity – quite a lot of them actu-ally hidden by the scrub and brambles – and for them to be transcribed word for word so that they can be accessible to others in their entirety. In this way, even if the people of Rome destroy them, at least a record of the inscriptions will survive. Only these, therefore, out of so many ornaments of a city which is still free, have endured down to our own day through the carelessness of fortune.

'What shall I say about the successive ages in which disaster has put paid to the grandeur of the buildings? A large number of remarkable buildings for private and public use are mentioned as having been constructed at great expense for various emperors and private individuals who were leading figures at the time. The divine Augustus used to say that the city he had taken over in brick, he was handing back in marble. Notwithstanding that Agrippa his son–in–law, Asinius Pollio, Plantius, Cornelius Balbus and the rest of his friends had embellished the city with various works of architecture at his instigation, he himself also had added not a few buildings in his own right. Apart from the Pantheon, the notable work of Marcus Agrippa, with its portico comprised of roof beams of bronze instead of wood and the rather inconspicuous arch in Tiburtine stone between the Palatine and the Tiber, on which is carved the name of the divine Augustus, the rest suffered the depredation of annihilistic fortune.

'This was a city crammed with temples, shrines, and the dwelling places of gods and goddesses whom the citizens used to worship, of which a few fragments survive. I have noticed that of the Temple of Peace built long ago by the divine Vespasian, only three arches stand virtually intact over the massive ruin. There used to be six. Out of its many marble columns of amazing size you can see only one still remaining upright, the rest are either in pieces or buried among the ruins of the temple. Behind it, facing the Capitol, was a temple of Romulus, which even today offers us the extraordinary spectacle of a very ancient section of wall in square–cut masonry. This temple is now consecrated to the Saints Cosmas and Damian.[5] Next to this was the temple of the divine Antonius and the divine Faustina, today dedicated to the blessed Lawrence [the church of San Lorenzo], from the rubble of whose portico many marble columns have disappeared.

'Moreover, the twin temples of Castor and Pollux survive in place in an elevated position on the Via Sacra [Holy Way], one facing west and the other east, and today they are known as Santa Maria Nova [also known as San Francesco Romana]. This was the famous place where the Senate used to assemble, now largely fallen down saving a few traces.[6] I often go there and am overwhelmed by a kind of revery, I cast my mind back to those times when formal senatorial opinions were delivered there, imagining Lucius Crassus or Hortensius or Cicero putting forward their arguments to me. [. . .][7]

'Adjacent to the Capitol and facing the Forum the portico of the Temple of Concord still stands. When I first came to the city I saw this almost whole and completely radiant with marble. The Romans have since demolished the whole temple for lime, as well as part of the portico, and the columns lie dashed to pieces. The letters S.P.Q.R.[8] up to the present day on the portico have been consumed by fire and are to be re-instated. Opposite was the Temple of Tellus, of which no traces remain. Today they call this [the church of] Salvator in Tellune, a corruption of the word Tellure. Some people like to conjecture – and they may not be far from the truth – that there was a Temple of Saturn near the Forum which was known to the ancient Romans as the Aerarium [Treasury], which is now consecrated to Pope Hadrian.[9] Where the fishmarket is now, there still stands the noble portico of the Temple of Mercury, which our religion has transferred to the Archangel Michael. Preserved by our religion and transferred to the worship of God is the Temple of Apollo in the Vatican, close to the basilica of Saint Peter. [. . .][10]

'To the best of my knowledge, no historical account has been published as to the number of triumphal arches that existed, but judging by the large number of emperors and others to whose glory they were set up I should think that there were very many. Still standing virtually intact, with their inscriptions preserved, are those of: Septimius Severus, Titus Vespasian and Constantine. A fragment of that of Nerva Trajanus, an extraordinary work, is left close to the Comitium [to the north of the Forum]. The letters carved on it tell us that it was the Arch of Trajan. Over the Via Flaminia [the Flaminian Way] there are two: on one of which the inscription is completely worn away and on the other it is damaged. Regarding the one which is near San Lorenzo in Lucina, where there are quite a few marble statues, older people often used to report that according to the ancient inscription it had been erected on account of the victory of the three cities. Today, they also call it the Arch of Tripolis. The name of another has completely worn away (a very few letters and some ancient carved marble tablets still survive, and

I am often struck that these have escaped the frenzy of the demolishers). And then another was dedicated to the Emperor Galienus, as indicated on an inscription in the Via Nomentana. I have also read the inscription on that arch in the Circus Maximus where there are now vegetable gardens, which his relations dedicated to Titus Vespasianus after the Jews had been conquered and Jerusalem destroyed [64 CE].

'Julius Frontinus records that there were nine aqueducts. I myself discovered this little book stashed away and lost to sight in the monastery of Monte Cassino a while ago. These were the Appian, the old Anienan, the Martian, the Tepulan, the Julian, the Virgo, the Alsietan, the Claudian, and the new Anienan. So costly was their workmanship and so marvellous their construction that the same Julius Frontinus, who writes that he was made keeper of the water supply under the divine Nerva, ranked them on a par with the pyramids of Egypt. [. . .][11]

'The city used to be crowded with theatres and amphitheatres for the purpose of laying on spectacles for the populace. Vast and the most beautiful of all was, so they say, the one commonly called the Colosseum. Built in Tiburtine stone, it is almost in the middle of the city and was the commission of the divine Vespasian. Now it has been in large measure destroyed thanks to the folly of the people of Rome. There is a portion of a second amphitheatre between the Tarpeian Hill and the Tiber where meat is now displayed for sale, which was established by Gaius Julius Caesar, as we read, long ago.[12] Over against it, on the same street, are several marble columns, part of the portico of a temple, they say of Jupiter, of which the round section is occupied by new buildings, but on the inside there is a little garden.[13] A third, in baked brick, is next to the church they call Santa Croce in Gerusalemme. With these new walls grafted on to it, it forms part of the encircling fortifications of the city.[14]

'These days they call the Circus Agonale[15] the huge open space set aside for the people as a gathering place for wild beast hunts and shows. Even now, the Romans annually engage in certain idiotic diversions here. The passage of time has left us little enough to be seen of the Circus Maximus, once packed with spectators, but now filled up with gardens. We read that here there used to be both a mighty obelisk as well as the triumphal arch of Titus Vespasian. [. . .]'

NOTES

1   The Tarpeian rock was to the south-west of the Capitoline Hill.
2   Gaius Marius (c.157–86 BCE) fled to Africa after his defeat by Sulla in 89 BCE. His life story is recounted by Plutarch.
3   This reference cannot be found in the works of Libanius (314–93 CE), a Greek orator, but it does correspond with the general content of the *Eis Roomen* (*On Rome*) of the Greek writer, Aelius Aristides (117–81 CE).
4   Francesco Petrarch (Petrarca) (1304–74), *Rerum familiarum libri* (*Books on personal matters*), VI.2, 5–14, a letter to Giovanni Colonna. Remus, together with his brother Romulus, was the legendary founder of Rome who was killed for jumping the boundary wall newly built by Romulus. There appears to be confusion here with the

double pyramid formerly in the Borgo, which was traditionally thought to house the tombs of Romulus and Remus.

5   Attached to the early Christian church, the temple was dedicated to Romulus, son of the Emperor Valerius Maximus, who died in 309.

6   Poggio is here merging the Temple of the Dioscuri with the church of Santa Maria Nova occupying the area of the Palatine Vestibule to the south and the senatorial *curia* on the other side of the Forum to the north-west.

7   Lucius Licinius Crassus (140–91 BCE) was a famous orator celebrated by Cicero, *Brutus*, 38.143; Quintus Hortalus Hortensius (114–50 BCE) was considered an expert in 'asiatic' oratory, in Cicero, *Brutus*, 64.228–230; Marcus Tullius Cicero (106–43 BCE), was a Roman orator, statesman and man of letters.

8   *Senatus Populusque Romanus*: 'The Roman Senate and People'.

9   This was one of the oldest temples in Rome, founded between 509 and 493 BCE.

10   No temple to Apollo is recorded on the site of St Peter's but nearby is the mausoleum of Hadrian associated with the sun-god Helios.

11   Sextus Julius Frontinus (*c*.30–103 CE), governor of Britain and writer on military theory and engineering. His 'little book' was *De aquis urbis Romae* (*On the Waters of the City of Rome*). The Benedictine monastery of Monte Cassino was a major repository of classical literature.

12   This is the Theatre of Marcellus, named after the son-in-law of the Emperor Augustus, but started under Gaius Julius Caesar (*c*.100–44 BCE).

13   Probably a reference to the Temple of Jove, founded around 510–509 BCE.

14   Poggio is here conflating the Sessorian Palace with the Castrense amphitheatre to the south.

15   The circus Agonale, first century CE, is now the Piazza Navona.

2   Ciriaco of Ancona **Journeys in the Propontis (1444)**
(i) The ruins of Cyzicus (ii) Ciriaco's letter to John Hunyadi

Ciriaco of Ancona (*c*.1390–1455) was a merchant who travelled extensively in Italy and the Near East. He used his contacts in the Church and with princes and diplomats to visit a large number of classical sites, where he drew the remains and copied ancient inscriptions. He described what he found in numerous letters and also made two collections: the *Itinerary* and *Commentaries*. He also purchased coins and statuary both for himself and his humanist friends.
He was employed by several princes as an intermediary in diplomatic and commercial transactions. The first extract is an example of Ciriaco's activity as an antiquarian; the Propontis is the classical term for the area around the Sea of Marmora. The second extract shows him involved in diplomatic exchanges connected with the 'crusade of Varna', when the Hungarian general, John Hunyadi, with the help of various Christian princes, was seeking to save Constantinople. This attempt ended swiftly in the Christians' defeat at the battle of Varna in 1444 and the death in battle of Wladyslaw (Ladislav), king of Poland and Hungary.

Source: (i) *Cyriacus of Ancona's Journeys in the Propontis and the Northern Aegean*, ed. E. W. Bodnar and C. Mitchell, American Philosophical Society, Philadelphia, 1976, pp. 27–31, translated for this edition by Chris Emlyn-Jones. (ii) J. Colin, *Cyriaque d'Ancone: le voyageur, le marchand, l'humaniste*, Maloine, Paris, 1981, pp. 358–9, translated for this edition by Lucille Kekewich

(i) The ruins of Cyzicus

Perinthus to Erdek, 31st July; arrival in Cyzicus, 2 August.

On the day before the Kalends of August (31st July), on our way from Perinthus to the island of Proconnesus and Cyzicus, we reached Artace (Erdek), an ancient village of the Cyzicans, where many remains of Antiquity are to be seen, fragments of columns and statues, and I learned about this very beautiful colossal marble statue, standing ruined amid vines.

Indeed, it was for the sake of this statue that I had made the journey, and we crossed the Propontine sea, when I thought of revisiting that wonderful and most noble temple of Proserpina,[1] and while I gazed at its huge size, the exceptional richness of its execution, and the living faces constructed from marble, I acknowledged that the poet of Sulmo had not unfairly expressed it:

> Then I came to Cyzicus clinging to the Propontine shores –
> Cyzicus, noble creation of the Haemonian race.
> (Ovid, Tristia I.10, 29–30)

And Pliny too, that most diligent author of the *Natural History*, in that part of his writing where he recalls the natural and nobler creations of the world, among which he considered this work preeminent, in his introduction says: 'at Cyzicus too there survives a shrine, in which the architect has inserted gold thread[2] in all the joints of the polished stonework' [*Natural History*, XXXVI. 98] and other details. We actually saw the width and concavity of these constructed pipes and we took care that this feature and many other remarkable details of this exceptional building, when they had been carefully inspected and measured as far as this was permitted, should be described and drawn with a pen.

But alas! what a degradation it was which we now revisited compared with what we had seen twice seven years previously; for then we had seen thirty-one columns standing upright, but now, indeed, I saw that only twenty-nine remained and those had partly lost their architraves. But also the glorious walls, which had almost all then stood intact, now seemed for the most part to have been reduced by the barbarians and fallen to the ground. But in its remarkable and wonderful frontal aspect, those special and most famous statues of marble, with Jupiter Optimus[3] himself as protector and guardian of his exalted majesty, are kept safe, unharmed and remain intact in their almost primeval splendour. The dimensions of this very large temple are established from the width of the spaces between the columns: length 240 cubits [cubit: 46–56 centimetres], width actually 110, with the highest walls and the gigantic columns measuring 70 feet [21.3 metres] in height.

On the fourth day before the Nones of August [2nd August], a Sunday, an auspicious day, we came to Cyzicus, a noble and most powerful city, once the metropolis of Asia.

But when I looked around the city everywhere ruined, and I had learned that within days it would be utterly destroyed by the barbarians, I was sorely grieved; and, drawing the conclusion that those bringing calamity on the human race should in their turn be punished by human rulers, I exclaimed: 'O Augustus Caesar, divine restorer of the cities of Asia'.

We saw nevertheless very many noble monuments of that most revered antiquity, standing up to our own day as witnesses to such greatness, and in particular we saw surviving a section of its extraordinary, primeval walls, constructed of Propontine stone, huge statues and, scattered here and there on the ground, massive marbles and ingeniously fashioned rocks. But – a most potent testimony to the extraordinary size of the city of Cyzicus – there survive, at the fourth and sixth milestone from the city, both Artace (this is what the inhabitants under the Byzantine emperor call it) and other towns which lie nearer to the city, neglected but fashioned with marble walls, of which a not inconsiderable part seems to have been constructed with towers.

When I had examined more closely the size of that wonderful temple and decided to make a more precise measurement, we learned that the dimensions of the walls situated in front of the side of the temple were: 140 feet [42.67 metres] in length, 70 feet [21.34 metres] in width, and fixed at the same height. The columns on each side added up to 30 in number, of the same height as the walls, distant 13 feet [3.96 metres] from each other and the same distance from the walls themselves. And with large-sized stones between the columns and the clearly visible walls, a noble pavement provides here and there wide walkways for promenaders. Further, before the façade of the temple, as decoration for the *pronaos* [front hall of a temple], columns are seen standing out against the sides, four each in rows of five, twenty in number, covered with a very ornamental panelled entablature. But in the rear part of the shrine we saw that the temple also had, besides those columns which were standing against the sides, also four each in rows of three, making twelve. From which we deduced that all the columns of this huge temple added up to 62, besides ten very ornate smaller columns situated inside in rows of five, attached to the walls.

In the shrine at Cyzicus, on a half-broken marble stone these names of the religious magistrates of the temple are disclosed, in very ancient and polished lettering:

> To the gods
> in the archonship [chief minister of Athens]
>   of Hermodoros in Cyzicus
> religious magistrates
> Pleistalotos son of Polykles
> Herarores son of Mousokles
> Anthemis son of Eualkis
> Apollodoros son of Apollonios
> Diphilos son of Dionysid[oros]
> Makareus son of Poseidonios
> Artemidoros son of Hierotias
> Agesilas son of Kerykis
> Iphikrates son of Metriketes
> private citizens

Apollodoros son of Athenos
Demetrios son of Apollodoros
Agelles son of Menodoros
Dion son of Diokles
Agathinos son of Apollonis
Hipponax son of Akesaios
Mantikles son of Xenothemis
Proteas son of Apollodoros

(ii) Letter to John Hunyadi

We have written to you of those matters from Adrianople, most Christian Prince, and we have spoken of the barbarians [Turks] with the greatest possible moderation to avoid a cruel death at their hands. Without such constraint I will speak more frankly about the situation and the peace to which they have been forced: since we have learnt (and you have been fully informed by your emissaries) that the Trojans [those in Asia Minor] and the Turks, terrified and dismayed, are constantly repairing their walls and their ramparts, and that the soldier prepares for flight rather than combat.

On the other hand, Amurath, the proud tyrant, has learnt that the prince [Ibrahim] of Caramania has revolted against him in Asia, devastating and ruining his territories and towns. Infuriated, he has left his son Cialaby⁴ in Thrace with Chalil Pacha, his right arm, and many companies of soldiers, and had decided to cross Hellespont and lead a considerable force into Asia.

In this manner you could, excellent Christian Prince, vainly observe his shameful and harmful peace, despite the fact that it could immediately be dismantled, dismissed or, in some way, led into entanglement with the prince of Caramania. Conversely, he [the Sultan] will strengthen his companies in Asia as much as he can; he could cross Hellespont, he could make every effort to return to Thrace with a more formidable army to penetrate Mesia [Serbia] and Pannonia [Hungary] with all his force to avenge the disasters which you have inflicted on him.

If, on the contrary, as is more likely, as we already know that he dreads it, he hears that you mistrust a harmful peace and that you have thrown your invincible and spirited soldiers into Thrace, that they are already prepared to march against him and that the Hellespont will be occupied by our fleet; fearing to be surrounded in Europe, he will consider it to be less ignominious to remain in Asia.

Therefore, excellent princes, go forward: declare a war which is worthy of the Christian religion and, since a very holy and glorious campaign has started under happy auspices, never think of abandoning it before the achievement of the desired object.

From Byzantine Pera [a district of Constantinople], the day of our arrival, 8ᵗʰ of the kalends of July, the happy and most venerated day of the Forerunner or Baptist (24ᵗʰ June 1444).

NOTES

1   Proserpina, Queen of Hades, and wife of Pluto.
2   Or narrow golden-coloured pipes running through stonework.
3   Literally 'Jupiter the most excellent, chief of the gods'.
4   Amurath is the Sultan Murad II; Carmania refers to the region of the Dalgari mount-
     ains in Turkey; Cialaby is the future Mohammed II (1451–81), founder of the Ottoman
     empire.

3   Giovanni Francesco Poggio Bracciolini **Two letters about classical manuscripts (1416 and 1427)**

(i) Poggio to Guarino of Verona from the Council of Constance (1416)
Poggio and his friends were attending the Council in the service of Pope John
XXIII, who was deposed there and replaced by Martin V. None of this affected
Poggio who remained in papal service and used his mission to continue his
energetic pursuit of classical texts. Guarino of Verona (1370–1460) was a
humanist whose school in his native city was renowned throughout Europe. He
was one of the first humanists to acquire a good knowledge of Greek. Details of
Poggio's career are given in Text 1.

(ii) Poggio to Niccolò Niccoli from Rome (1427)
Niccolò Niccoli (1363–1437) was a Florentine book collector who copied many
of the classical manuscripts which were being circulated by Poggio and other
humanists. Poggio had already arranged with the unnamed monk of Hersfeld in
Germany for one shipment of books to be made via Nuremberg. They would then
either be purchased or copied and sent to bibliophiles like Niccolò and Cosimo
de'Medici, another of Poggio's friends and patrons. They would often be copied
again and circulated for discussion and comment amongst fellow humanists,
enabling knowledge of new finds to be circulated rapidly. Some have queried
whether Poggio's letters were really written at the dates he gave or whether they
were exercises intended to display his rhetorical skills and learning. Gordon, the
editor of the collection from which this translation is taken, believes them to be
genuine, while acknowledging Poggio polished them when he collected them for
wider circulation.

Source: *Two Renaissance Book Hunters: The letters of Poggius Bracciolini to
Nicolaus Niccolis*, ed. and trans. Phyllis Walter Goodhart Gordan, Records of
Civilization: sources and studies, 91, Columbia University Press, New York and
London, 1974, Appendix: Letter III, pp. 193–6, Letter XL, pp. 99–100.
Copyright © 1974 Columbia University Press. Reprinted with the permission of the
publisher.

i) To Guarino of Verona from the Council of Constance

Although I know well that no matter how busy you are each day, your kindness
to all and your affection for me in particular always make the arrival of my letters

a pleasure to you, I ask you especially to pay most particular attention to this one; not that there is anything in me which would have any claim even on a person who was completely at leisure, but because of the interest of the subject of which I am about to tell you. I know it will bring the utmost pleasure to you, who have long been an expert, and to other learned men. For what, for Heaven's sake, is there that could be more delightful, more pleasant, and more agreeable to you and the rest of the learned world than the knowledge of those things whose acquaintance makes us more learned and, what seems even more important, stylistically more polished. When Mother Nature gave the human race mind and reason, two wonderful guides to a righteous and happy life, she could think of nothing finer to give. Then she gave us one thing that perhaps may be the greatest gift of all, the use and understanding of speech, without which mind and reason would not have been of any use to us. For it is speech alone which we use to express the power of our mind and which separates us from the other beings. And so we must be deeply grateful to the pioneers in the other liberal arts and especially to those who by their concern and efforts have given us rules for speaking and a pattern of perfection. They have made it possible for us to excel other men in the ability in which all men excel beasts.

You know that while there were many writers in the Latin tongue who were renowned for elaborating and forming the language, there was one outstanding and extraordinary man, M. Fabius Quintilian, who so cleverly, thoroughly, and attentively worked out everything which had to do with training even the very best orator that he seems in my judgment to be perfect in both the highest theory and the most distinguished practice of oratory.[1] From this man alone we could learn the perfect method of public speaking, even if we did not have Cicero, the father of Roman oratory. But among us Italians, he so far has been so fragmentary, so cut down, by the action of time I think, that the shape and style of the man has become unrecognizable. So far you have seen the man only thus:

> Whose face and limbs were one continued wound,
> Dishonest, with lopp'd arms, the youth appears,
> Spoil'd of his nose, and shorten'd of his ears.
> [Virgil, *Aeneid*, VI. 495–97]

Surely we ought to feel sorrow and anger that we have done so much damage to the practice of oratory by our careless destruction of a man so eloquent. But the more we regret and blame ourselves for the damage that was formerly done to him, the more we should congratulate ourselves that by our energetic search he has now been restored to us in his original appearance and grandeur, whole and in perfect condition. For if Marcus Tullius rejoiced so fervently when Marcus Marcellus was returned from exile, and that at a time when Rome had a great many able and outstanding men like Marcellus both at home and abroad, what should men do now in learned circles, and especially men who devote themselves to oratory, when the one and only light of the Roman name, except for whom there was no one but Cicero and he likewise cut to pieces and scattered, has through our efforts been called back not only from exile but from almost complete destruction?[2] By Heaven, if we had not brought help, he would surely have perished the very next day. There is no question that this glorious man, so elegant,

so pure, so full of morals and of wit, could not much longer have endured the
filth of that prison, the squalor of the place, and the savage cruelty of his keepers.
He was sad and dressed in mourning, as people are when doomed to death; his
beard was dirty and his hair caked with mud, so that by his expression and appearance it was clear that he had been summoned to an undeserved punishment. He
seemed to stretch out his hands and beg for the loyalty of the Roman people, to
demand that he be saved from an unjust sentence, and to feel it a disgrace that
he who had once preserved the safety of the whole population by his influence
and his eloquence could now not find one single advocate who would pity his
misfortunes and take some trouble over his welfare and prevent his being dragged
off to an undeserved punishment. But how often things turn out spontaneously
which you dare not hope, as Terence says.[3]

For by good luck, as much ours as his, while we were doing nothing in Constance, an urge came upon us to see the place where he was being kept prisoner.
This is the monastery of St. Gall, about twenty miles from Constance. And so
several of us went there, to amuse ourselves and also to collect books of which
we heard that they had a great many. There amid a tremendous quantity of books
which it would take too long to describe, we found Quintilian still safe and
sound, though filthy with mold and dust. For these books were not in the Library,
as befitted their worth, but in a sort of foul and gloomy dungeon at the bottom
of one of the towers, where not even men convicted of a capital offense would
have been stuck away. As I know for certain, if there ever had been any other
men who explored these prison houses of the barbarians where they confine such
men as Quintilian and if they had recognized them after the custom of our ancestors, they would have found a treasure like ours in many cases where we are now
left lamenting. Beside Quintilian we found the first three books and half of the
fourth of C. Valerius Flaccus' *Argonauticon*, and commentaries or analyses on
eight of Cicero's orations by Q. Asconius Pedianus, a very clever man whom
Quintilian himself mentions.[4] These I copied with my own hand and very
quickly, so that I might send them to Leonardus Aretinus and to Nicolaus of Florence; and when they had heard from me of my discovery of this treasure they
urged me at great length in their letters to send them Quintilian as soon as possible.[5] You have, my dearest Guarinus, all that a man who is devoted to you can
send you just now. I wish I could send you the book itself but I had to satisfy
Leonardus; but you know where it is, so that if you want it and I expect that you
will want it as soon as possible, you can get it easily. Farewell and love me as I
do you. At Constance, 15 December, A.D. 1416.

ii) To Niccolò Niccoli from Rome

I have found out from your two letters to me about Antonius' books.[6] What a
stupid thing to do, to thrust that treasure into a place where it will do no good.
I cannot think what his purpose was to establish Greek books among those two-
legged donkeys who do not even know a word of Latin. He did not dedicate
them to the Muses but to dust and worms; I believe he was afraid that someone

might enjoy them. Yet unless he forbade the sale of them in his will, they will I think have an auction soon for reasons of avarice or ignorance. You write that you have found the tragedies for sale, you think for seven gold pieces, and the *De officiis*. Indeed I have long wanted the tragedies myself, and so if it seems to you that the money would be well spent on them, please buy them for me. But try to get the *De officiis*[7] for Bartholomeus, who wrote some time ago to Cosmus or rather to his bankers to give you the money which you were asking for; ask Nicolaus for the money for the tragedies. See about the Lactantius too and what can be done about it; and if anything else comes to hand which you think would be nice for us, attend to it yourself and do not wait for another order.[8]

Some time we shall dig Julius Frontinus from that field at Cassino, but it is hard to rouse our barbarians to take an interest in anything except money.[9] If I had been alert when the man who brought us the Severus was going there, he would have brought us both authors, for he was that brother who was with the Cardinal of Piacenza and he did not tell me he was going before he went. This kind of man is rarely seen, unless he needs something or is begging. But I am stirring Angelottus and I do not give up the hope that we shall get the book shortly.[10] A man from the Monastery of Cluny will leave the Curia very shortly; he has become a friend of mine through my own efforts and promised to take care to have the Tertullian copied and undertook to do it.[11] I have hopes that he will do something because he needs my help; still he is a monk but he does not seem in the least bad; he has some education and knows the book. When I discussed the payment and promised that it would be at hand wherever he wished he said that he did not want money at all; for he has undertaken the whole job and indeed apparently willingly. Time will show what he is like. I am waiting for the parchment; see that I get it even if it is bad, provided that it is soon. I am writing to my mother to see to the Trebiano [wine] which you ask for. See that she gets the letters quickly before she leaves, for she is coming to visit me after the vintage, and so send her the letters and at the same time see to the wine. Farewell, at Rome, the twenty-eighth of September.

NOTES

1   Marcus Fabius Quintilianus (Quintilian *c.*35–*c.*100 CE), was a teacher of rhetoric. He is most famous for his *Institutiones oratoriae* (*Training in Oratory*).

2   Marcus Tullius Cicero, 106–43 BCE, *Pro Marcello*, I. 1–2.

3   Publius Terentius Afer (Terence *c.*190–159 BCE), *Phormio*, line 787; Latin poet, dramatist and former slave.

4   Quintilian, *Institutionaes oratoriae* (*Training in Oratory*), v.10.9. Gaius Valerius Flaccus was a first-century CE poet who wrote an epic on Jason and the Argonauts. Quintus Asconius Pendianus was a Latin grammarian from Padua, living in the first century CE, whose commentaries on the speeches of Cicero became popular after their rediscovery by Poggio Bracciolini.

5   Leonardus Aretinus is Leonardo Bruni (1370–1444); Nicolaus is Niccolò Niccoli (1364–1437), both Florentine humanists.

6   Antonio Corbinello (*c.*1377–1425), distinguished humanist.

7   Lucius Annaeus Seneca (4 BCE–65 CE), first minister to the Emperor Nero, a

philosopher and author of the *Tragedies* which were reworkings of Greek drama. Cicero (see note 2 above) wrote *De officiis* (*On Duties*) as a moral guide to his son.

8   Bartolomeo de Bardis, (*c.*1397–1429), the head of the Roman branch of the Medici Bank; Cosmus is Cosimo de'Medici, (1389–1464); Nicolaus is Niccolò de'Medici, (1385–1454), an unsuccessful banker; Lucius Caecilius Firmianus Lactantius (*c.*240–320) was a Christian apologist who was frequently cited by Christian humanists. See also below, Text 15.

9   Sextus Julius Frontinus, (*c.*30–103 CE); the monastery of Monte Cassino was a major repository of classical texts.

10   Sulpicius Severus (*c.*365–425), French monk and historian, who was responsible for a *Life* of St Martin of Tours and a universal chronicle. The Cardinal of Piacenza was Branda Castiglione (1350–1443), an important figure at the papal court. He had a fine library; Angelottus was Cardinal Angelotti Fusco who was murdered in 1444.

11   Cluny was a Benedictine monastery in France, noted for its library and book-copying. Quintus Septimus Florens Tertullianus (Tertullian, *c.*160–*c.*240 CE), Patristic writer.

4   Lorenzo Valla *The Treatise on the Donation of Constantine* (1440)

Lorenzo Valla (*c.*1405–57) was born and educated in Rome and became a priest. He gained a great reputation as a scholar who used humanist methods in his criticism of ancient texts. While he was employed by the king of Naples, Alfonso I of Aragon, he applied these methods in order to disprove the *Donation of Constantine.* It was a forgery of the eighth century CE first appearing in the ninth century collection of *Decretals*, or laws of the Church. These purported to record that the Emperor Constantine, in the fourth century CE, had given Pope Sylvester I great possessions in, and wide powers over, the Church and the Empire. Valla's Neapolitan master was in dispute with the papacy when this treatise was produced and, not surprisingly, offered him protection. Accordingly he was able to deploy his formidable rhetorical skills to demonstrate the vulnerability of the document on the grounds of historical anachronism, philological impurity and logical improbability. Seven years later he went to Rome and was received into the service of the new pope, Nicholas V, a patron of humanists. He remained there for the rest of his life.

Source: *The Treatise of Lorenzo Valla on the Donation of Constantine*, ed. and trans. C. B. Coleman, Yale University Press, New Haven, 1922, pp. 11–19, 24–9, 63–7, 115–17, 177–83

(i) The Donation of Constantine As Given in Part One Division XCVI, Chapters 13 and 14 of Gratian's Decretum, or Harmony of the Canons.

CHAPTER 13 'THE EMPERORS MUST BE UNDER THE PONTIFFS, NOT OVER THEM'

The Emperor Constantine yielded his crown, and all his royal prerogatives in the city of Rome, and in Italy, and in western parts to the Apostolic [See]. For in the Acts of the Blessed Sylvester (which the Blessed Pope Gelasius in the Council of the Seventy Bishops recounts as read by the catholic, and in accordance with ancient usage many churches he says follow this example) occurs the following.[1]

CHAPTER 14 CONCERNING THE SAME

The Emperor Constantine[2] the fourth day after his baptism conferred this privilege on the Pontiff of the Roman church, that in the whole Roman world priests should regard him as their head, as judges do the king. In this privilege among other things is this: 'We – together with all our satraps [governors], and the whole senate and my nobles, and also all the people subject to the government of glorious Rome – considered it advisable, that as the Blessed Peter is seen to have been constituted vicar of the Son of God on the earth, so the Pontiffs who are the representatives of that same chief of the apostles, should obtain from us and our empire the power of a supremacy greater than the clemency of our earthly imperial serenity is seen to have conceded to it, choosing that same chief of the apostles and his vicars to be our constant intercessors with God. And to the extent of our earthly imperial power, we have decreed that his holy Roman church shall be honored with veneration, and that more than our empire and earthly throne the most sacred seat of the Blessed Peter shall be gloriously exalted, we giving to it power, and dignity of glory, and vigor, and honor imperial. And we ordain and decree that he shall have the supremacy as well over the four principal seats, Alexandria, Antioch, Jerusalem, and Constantinople, as also over all the churches of God in the whole earth. And the Pontiff, who at the time shall be at the head of the holy Roman church itself, shall be more exalted than, and chief over, all the priests of the whole world, and according to his judgment everything which is provided for the service of God and for the stability of the faith of Christians is to be administered. *And below*: §. 1. On the churches of the blessed apostles Peter and Paul, for the providing of the lights, we have conferred landed estates of possessions, and have enriched them with different objects, and through our sacred imperial mandate we have granted him of our property in the east as well as in the west, and even in the northern and the southern quarter; namely, in Judea, Greece, Asia, Thrace, Africa, and Italy and the various islands: under this condition indeed, that all shall be administered by the hand of our most blessed father the supreme Pontiff, Sylvester and his successors. *And below*: §. 2. And to our Father, the Blessed Sylvester, supreme Pontiff and Pope universal, of the city of Rome, and to all the Pontiffs, his successors, who shall sit in the seat of the Blessed Peter even unto the end of the world, we by this present do give our imperial Lateran palace, then the diadem, that is, the crown of our head, and at the same time the tiara and also the shoulder-band, – that is, the strap that usually surrounds our imperial neck; and also the purple mantle and scarlet tunic, and all the imperial raiment; and also the same rank as those presiding over the imperial cavalry, conferring also even the imperial scepters, and at the same time all the standards, and banners, and the different ornaments, and all the pomp of our imperial eminence, and the glory of our power. §. 3. We decree moreover, as to the most reverend men, the clergy of different orders who serve that same holy Roman church, that they have that same eminence, distinction, power and excellence, by the glory of which it seems proper for our most illustrious senate to be adorned; that is, that they be made patricians and consuls, and also we have proclaimed that they be decorated with the other imperial dignities. And even as the imperial militia is adorned, so also we decree that the clergy of the holy Roman church be adorned. And even as the imperial power is adorned with different offices, of chamberlains, indeed, and door-keepers, and all the guards, so we wish the holy Roman church also to be decorated. And in order that the pontifical glory may shine forth most fully, we decree this also; that the horses of the clergy of this same holy Roman church be decorated with saddle-cloths and linens, that is, of the whitest color, and that they are to so ride. And even as our senate uses shoes with felt socks, that is, distinguished by white linen, so the clergy also should use them, so that, even as the celestial orders, so also the terrestrial may be adorned to the glory of God. §. 4. Above all things, moreover, we give permission to that same most holy one our Father Sylvester and to his successors, from our edict, that he may make priest whomever he wishes, according to his own pleasure and counsel, and enroll him in the number of the religious clergy [i.e., regular, or monastic, clergy; [. . .]], let no one whomsoever presume to act in a domineering way in this. §. 5. We also therefore decreed this, that he himself and his successors might use and bear upon their heads – to the praise of God for the honor of the Blessed Peter – the diadem, that is, the crown which we have granted him from our own head, of purest gold and precious gems. But since he himself, the most blessed Pope, did not at all allow that crown of gold to be used over the clerical crown which he wears to the glory of the Blessed Peter, we placed upon his most holy head, with our own hands, a glittering tiara of dazzling white representing the Lord's resurrection, and holding the bridle of his horse, out of reverence for the Blessed Peter, we performed for him the duty of groom, decreeing that all his successors, and they alone, use this same tiara in processions in imitation of our power. §. 6. Wherefore, in order that the supreme pontificate may not deteriorate, but may rather be adorned with glory and power even more than is the dignity of an earthly rule; behold, we give over and relinquish to the aforesaid our most blessed Pontiff, Sylvester, the universal Pope, as well our palace, as has been said, as also the city of Rome, and all the provinces, places and cities of Italy and the western regions, and we decree by this our godlike and pragmatic sanction that they are to be controlled by him and by his successors, and we grant that they shall remain under the law of the holy Roman church. §. 7. Wherefore we have perceived it to be fitting that our empire and the power of our kingdom should be transferred in the regions of the East, and that in the province of Byzantia, in the most fitting place, a city should be built in our name [Constantinople], and that our empire should there be established, for where the supremacy of priests and the head of the Christian religion has been established by the heavenly Emperor, it is not right that there an earthly emperor should have jurisdiction. §. 8. We decree, moreover, that all these things, which through this our sacred imperial [charter] and through other godlike decrees we have established and confirmed, remain inviolate and unshaken unto the end of the world. Wherefore, before the living God who commanded us to reign, and in the face of his terrible judgment, we entreat, through this our imperial sanction, all the emperors our successors, and all the nobles, the satraps also, the most glorious senate, and all the people in the whole world, now and in all times still to come subject to our rule, that no one of them in any way be allowed either to break these [decrees], or in any way overthrow them. If any one, moreover, – which we do not believe – prove a scorner or despiser in this matter, he shall be subject and bound over to eternal damnation, and shall feel the holy ones of God, the chief of the apostles, Peter and Paul, opposed to him in the present and in the future life, and he shall be burned in the lower hell and shall perish with the devil and all the impious. The page, moreover, of this our imperial decree, we, confirming it with our own hands, did place above the venerable body of the Blessed Peter, chief of the apostles. Given at Rome on the third day before the Kalends of April, our master the august Flavius Constantine, for the fourth time, and Gallicanus, most illustrious men, being consuls.' [A date between 314 and 336 CE]

ii) Lorenzo Valla, *On the Falsely-Delivered and Forged Donation of Constantine. A Commentary*

EXTRACT I

[. . .]

Scio iamdudum exspectare aures hominum quidnam pontificibus Romanis criminis impingam. Profecto ingens, sive supinae ignorantiae, sive immanis avaritiae quae est idolorum servitus, sive imperandi vanitatis cuius crudelitas semper est comes. Nam aliquot iam saeculis aut non intellexerunt donationem Constantini commenticiam fictamque esse, aut ipsi finxerunt, sive posteriores in maiorum suorum dolis vestigia imprimentes pro vera quam falsam cognoscerent defenderunt, dedecorantes pontificatus maiestatem, dedecorantes veterum pontificum memoriam, dedecorantes religionem Christianam, et omnia caedibus, ruinis, flagitiisque miscentes. Suam esse aiunt urbem Romam; suum regnum Siciliae Neapolitanumque; suam universam Italiam, Gallias, Hispanias, Germanos, Britannos; suum denique occidentem; haec enim cuncta in ipsa donationis pagina contineri. Ergo haec omnia tua sunt, summe pontifex? Omnia tibi in animo est recuperare? Omnes reges ac principes occidentis spoliare urbibus, aut cogere ut annua tibi tributa pensitent, sententia est? [This paragraph in Latin corresponds with the first paragraph of the following translation.]

[. . .] I know that for a long time now men's ears are waiting to hear the offense with which I charge the Roman pontiffs. It is, indeed, an enormous one, due either to supine ignorance, or to gross avarice which is the slave of idols, or to pride of empire of which cruelty is ever the companion. For during some centuries now, either they have not known that the Donation of Constantine is spurious and forged, or else they themselves forged it, and their successors walking in the same way of deceit as their elders have defended as true what they knew to be false, dishonoring the majesty of the pontificate, dishonoring the memory of ancient pontiffs, dishonoring the Christian religion, confounding everything with murders, disasters and crimes. They say the city of Rome is theirs, theirs the kingdom of

Sicily and of Naples, the whole of Italy, the Gauls, the Spains, the Germans, the Britons, indeed the whole West; for all these are contained in the instrument of the Donation itself. So all these are yours, supreme pontiff? And it is your purpose to recover them all? To despoil all kings and princes of the West of their cities or compel them to pay you a yearly tribute, is that your plan?

I, on the contrary, think it fairer to let the princes despoil you of all the empire you hold. For, as I shall show, that Donation whence the supreme pontiffs will have their right derived was unknown equally to Sylvester and to Constantine.

But before I come to the refutation of the instrument of the Donation, which is their one defense, not only false but even stupid, the right order demands that I go further back. And first, I shall show that Constantine and Sylvester were not such men that the former would choose to give, would have the legal right to give, or would have it in his power to give those lands to another, or that the latter would be willing to accept them or could legally have done so. In the second place, if this were not so, though it is absolutely true and obvious, [I shall show that in fact] the latter did not receive nor the former give possession of what is said to have been granted, but that it always remained under the sway and empire of the Caesars. In the third place, [I shall show that] nothing was given to Sylvester by Constantine, but to an earlier Pope (and Constantine had received baptism even before that pontificate), and that the grants were inconsiderable, for the mere subsistence of the Pope. Fourth, that it is not true either that a copy of the Donation is found in the Decretum [of Gratian][3] or that it was taken from the History of Sylvester; for it is not found in it or in any history, and it is comprised of contradictions, impossibilities, stupidities, barbarisms and absurdities. Further, I shall speak of the pretended or mock donation of certain other Caesars. Then by way of redundance I shall add that even had Sylvester taken possession, nevertheless, he or some other pontiff having been dispossessed, possession could not be resumed after such a long interval under either divine or human law. Last [I shall show] that the possessions which are now held by the supreme pontiff could not, in any length of time, be validated by prescription [the possession of a right over a long period] [. . .].

EXTRACT II

[. . .] Indeed, we must suspect not so much that Sylvester refused the grants as that he tacitly disclosed that neither could Constantine legally make them nor could he himself legally accept.

O avarice, ever blind and ill-advised! Let us suppose that you may be able to adduce even genuine documents for the assent of Sylvester, not tampered with, authentic: even so, were the grants actually made which are found in such documents? Where is any taking possession, any delivery? For if Constantine gave a charter only, he did not want to befriend Sylvester, but to mock him. It is likely, you say, that any one who makes a grant, gives possession of it, also. See what you are saying; for it is certain that possession was not given, and the question is whether the title was given! It is likely that one who did not give possession did not want to give the title either.

Or is it not certain that possession was never given? To deny it is the sheerest impudence. Did Constantine ever lead Sylvester in state to the Capitol amid the shouts of the assembled Quirites [Roman citizens], heathen as they were? Did he place him on a golden throne in the presence of the whole Senate? Did he command the magistrates, each in the order of his rank, to salute their king and prostrate themselves before him? This, rather than the giving of some palace such as the Lateran, is customary in the creation of new rulers. Did he afterwards escort him through all Italy? Did he go with him to the Gauls? Did he go to the Spains? Did he go to the Germans, and the rest of the West? Or if they both thought it too onerous to traverse so many lands, to whom did they delegate such an important function, to represent Caesar in transferring possession and Sylvester in receiving it? Distinguished men, and men of eminent authority, they must have been: and nevertheless we do not know who they were. And how much weight there is here in these two words, *give* and *receive!* To pass by ancient instances, I do not remember to have seen any other procedure when any one was made lord of a city, a country, or a province; for we do not count possession as given until the old magistrates are removed and the new ones substituted. If then Sylvester had not demanded that this be done, nevertheless the dignity of Constantine required that he show that he gave possession not in words but in fact, that he ordered his officers to retire and others to be substituted by Sylvester. Possession is not transferred when it remains in the hands of those who had it before, and the new master dares not remove them.

But grant that this also does not stand in the way, that, notwithstanding, we assume Sylvester to have been in possession, and let us say that the whole transaction took place though not in the customary and natural way. After Constantine went away, what governors did Sylvester place over his provinces and cities, what wars did he wage, what nations that took up arms did he subdue, through whom did he carry on this government? We know none of these circumstances, you answer. So! I think all this was done in the nighttime, and no one saw it at all!

Come now! Was Sylvester ever in possession? Who dispossessed him? For he did not have possession permanently, nor did any of his successors, at least till Gregory the Great,[4] and even he did not have possession. One who is not in possession and cannot prove that he has been disseized certainly never did have possession, and if he says he did, he is crazy. You see, I even prove that you are crazy! Otherwise, tell who dislodged the Pope? Did Constantine himself, or his sons, or Julian,[5] or some other Caesar? Give the name of the expeller, give the date, from what place was the Pope expelled first, where next, and so in order. Was it by sedition and murder, or without these? Did the nations conspire together against him, or which first? What! Did not one of them give him aid, not one of those who had been put over cities or provinces by Sylvester or another Pope? Did he lose everything in a single day, or gradually and by districts? Did he and his magistrates offer resistance, or did they abdicate at the first disturbance? What! Did not the victors use the sword on those dregs of humanity, whom they thought unworthy of the Empire, to revenge their outrage, to make sure of the newly won mastery, to show contempt for our religion, not even to make an example for posterity? Did not one of those who were conquered take to flight at all? Did no one hide? Was no one afraid? O marvellous event! The Roman Empire, acquired by so many labors, so much bloodshed, was so calmly, so quietly both won and lost by Christian priests that no bloodshed, no war, no uproar took place; and not less marvellous, it is not known at all by whom this was done, nor when, nor how, nor how long it lasted! You would think that Sylvester reigned in sylvan shades, among the trees, not at Rome nor among men, and that he was driven out by winter rains and cold, not by men! [. . .]

But since you cannot [prove anything], I for my part will show that Constantine, to the very last day of his life, and thereafter all the Caesars in turn, did have possession [of the Roman Empire], so that you will have nothing left even to mutter. But it is a very difficult, and, I suppose, a very laborious task, forsooth, to do this! Let all the Latin and the Greek histories be unrolled, let the other authors who mention those times be brought in, and you will not find a single discrepancy among them on this point. [. . .]

EXTRACT III

[. . .] Which shall I censure the more, the stupidity of the ideas, or of the words? You have heard about the ideas; here are illustrations of his words. He says, 'It seems proper for our Senate to be adorned' (as though it were not assuredly adorned), and to be adorned forsooth with 'glory.' And what is being done he wishes understood as already done; as, 'we have proclaimed' for 'we proclaim': for the speech sounds better that way. And he puts the same act in the present and in the past tense; as, 'we decree,' and 'we have decreed.' And everything is stuffed with these words, 'we decree,' 'we decorate,' 'imperial,' 'imperial rank,' 'power,' 'glory.' He uses 'extat' for 'est,' though 'extare' means to stand out or to be above; and 'nempe' for 'scilicet' [that is, 'indeed' for 'to wit']; and 'concubitores' [translated above, bed-watchers] for 'contubernales' [companions or attendants]. 'Concubitores' are literally those who sleep together and have intercourse; they must certainly be understood to be harlots. He adds those with whom he may sleep, I suppose, that he may not fear nocturnal phantoms. He adds 'chamberlains'; he adds 'door-keepers.' [. . .]

And when he had said nothing about the garb of senators, the broad stripe, the purple, and the rest, he thought he had to talk about their shoes; nor does he specify the crescents [which were on their shoes], but 'socks,' or rather he says 'with felt socks,' and then as usual he explains, 'that is, with white linen,' as though socks were of linen! I cannot at the moment think where I have found the word 'udones' [socks], except in Valerius Martial, whose distich inscribed 'Cilician Socks' runs:

> Wool did not produce these, but the beard of an ill-smelling goat.
> Would that the sole in the gulf of the Cinyps might lie.
>
> [Martial, XIV, 140]

So the 'socks' are not linen, nor white, with which this two-legged ass says, not that the feet of senators are clad, but that senators are distinguished.

And in the phrase 'that the terrestrial orders may be adorned to the glory of God, just as the celestial,' what do you call celestial, what terrestrial? How are the celestial orders adorned? You may have seen what glory to God this is. But I, if I believe anything, deem nothing more hateful to God and to the rest of humanity than such presumption of clergy in the secular sphere. But why do I attack individual items? Time would fail me if I should try, I do not say to dwell upon, but to touch upon them all.

EXTRACT IV

But why need I say more in this case, absolutely self-evident as it is? I contend that not only did Constantine not grant such great possessions, not only could the Roman pontiff not hold them by prescription, but that even if either were a fact, nevertheless either right would have been extinguished by the crimes of the possessors, for we know that the slaughter and devastation of all Italy and of many of the provinces has flowed from this single source. If the source is bitter, so is the stream; if the root is unclean, so are the branches; if the first fruit is unholy, so is the lump. And *vice versa*, if the stream is bitter, the source must be stopped up; if the branches are unclean, the fault comes from the root; if the lump is unholy, the first fruit must also be accursed. Can we justify the principle of papal power when we perceive it to be the cause of such great crimes and of such great and varied evils?

Wherefore I declare, and cry aloud, nor, trusting God, will I fear men, that in my time no one in the supreme pontificate has been either a faithful or a prudent steward, but they have gone so far from giving food to the household of God that they have devoured it as food and a mere morsel of bread! And the Pope himself makes war on peaceable people, and sows discord among states and princes. The Pope both thirsts for the goods of others and drinks up his own: he is what Achilles calls Agamemnon, Δημοβόρος βασιλεύς, 'a people-devouring king.'[6] The Pope not only enriches himself at the expense of the republic, as neither Verres nor Catiline[7] nor any other embezzler dared to do, but he enriches himself at the expense of even the church and the Holy Spirit as old Simon Magus[8] himself would abhor doing. And when he is reminded of this and is reproved by good people occasionally, he does not deny it, but openly admits it, and boasts that he is free to wrest from its occupants by any means whatever the patrimony given the church by Constantine; as though when it was recovered Christianity would be in an ideal state, – and not rather the more oppressed by all kinds of crimes, extravagances and lusts; if indeed it can be oppressed more, and if there is any crime yet uncommitted!

And so, that he may recover the other parts of the Donation, money wickedly stolen from good people he spends more wickedly, and he supports armed forces, mounted and foot, with which all places are plagued, while Christ is dying of hunger and nakedness in so many thousands of paupers. [. . .]

But if the Roman people through excess of wealth lost the well-known quality of true Romans; if Solomon likewise fell into idolatry through the love of women; should we not recognize that the same thing happens in the case of a supreme pontiff and the other clergy? And should we then think that God would have permitted Sylvester to accept an occasion of sin? I will not suffer this injustice to be done that most holy man, I will not allow this affront to be offered that most excellent pontiff, that he should be said to have accepted empires, kingdoms, provinces, things which those who wish to enter the clergy are wont, indeed, to renounce. Little did Sylvester possess, little also the other holy pontiffs, those men whose presence was inviolable even among enemies, as Leo's presence over-awed and broke down the wild soul of the barbarian king, which the strength of Rome had not availed to break down nor overawe.[9] But recent supreme pontiffs, that is, those having riches and pleasures in abundance, seem to work hard to make themselves just as impious and foolish as those early pontiffs were wise and holy, and to extinguish the lofty praises of those men by every possible infamy. Who that calls himself a Christian can calmly bear this?

However, in this my first discourse I do not wish to urge princes and peoples to restrain the Pope in his unbridled course as he roams about, and compel him to stay within bounds, but only to warn him, and perhaps he has already learned the truth, to betake himself from others' houses to his own, and to put to port before the raging billows and savage tempests. But if he refuses, then I will have recourse to another discourse far bolder than this. If only I may sometime see, and indeed I can scarcely wait to see it, especially if it is brought about by my counsel, if only I may see the time when the Pope is the vicar of Christ alone, and not of Caesar also! If only there would no longer be heard the fearful cry, 'Partisans for the Church,' 'Partisans against the Church,' 'The Church against the Perugians,' 'against the Bolognese'! It is not the church, but the Pope, that fights against Christians; the church fights against 'spiritual wickedness in high places.'[10] Then the Pope will be the Holy Father in fact as well as in name, Father of all, Father of the church; nor will he stir up wars among Christians, but those stirred up by others he, through his apostolic judgment and papal prerogative, will stop.

NOTES

1   Sylvester I, pope 314–35; Gelasius I, pope 492–96; both canonized.

2   Flavius Valerius Aurelius Constantinus (Constantine the Great *c.*274–337 CE), who divided the Roman Empire in two, with the east governed from Byzantium or Con-stantinople. He established Christianity as the Empire's official religion at the Council of Nicaea in 325.

3   The *Decretum* or *Decretals* were a collection of ecclesiastical laws assembled by Gratian, a twelfth-century professor of law.

4   Gregory I, 'the Great', pope 590–604.

5   Emperor Julian, nicknamed 'the Apostate', (*c.*331–63), nephew of Constantine the Great. Under him the Empire temporarily reverted to paganism.

6   Homer, *Iliad*, I.231. Agamemnon was king of Mycenae.

7   Gaius Verres (d. 43 BCE) was a Roman governor in Sicily who was charged with extortion. In the ensuing legal and oratorical battle he was defended by Quintus Hort-ensius and accused by Cicero, both formidable rhetoricians. Cicero won and Verres retired from public life. Lucius Sergius Catalina (d. 62 BCE) was a disreputable gover-

nor of Africa who planned a revolt against the Roman State. His plot was exposed by
Cicero.

8   Simon Magus was a magician of Samaria mentioned in *Acts* 8:9–24.

9   Leo I (pope 440–61). The 'barbarian king' is Attila (*c.*406–53). In 452 he invaded Italy
     and devastated cities such as Milan and Padua. Rome was saved by the personal inter-
     vention of Leo.

10   Paul, *Ephesians* 6:12.

5   Desiderius Erasmus **Annotations on St Paul's Epistle to the Romans 1:1–3 (1535)**

In the Annotations, ER refers to Erasmus's version, VG to the Vulgate.

Desiderius Erasmus (*c.*1466–1536) was probably born in Rotterdam in the duchy
of Burgundy. A poor orphan, he entered the order of Augustinian canons with
some reluctance, but this did not impede his classical scholarship or his career
as a professional humanist. He was supported by several patrons and earned fees
as a teacher. He travelled widely in Europe and visited England on several
occasions, where he enjoyed the company of humanists such as John Colet
(1467–1519) and Thomas More (1478–1535), who was then a rising young
lawyer. Erasmus's lighthearted works, the *Adages, Colloquies* and *The Praise of
Folly* (for this, see Text 17) were very popular, but he achieved his greatest
distinction as a scholar and a theologian as the translator of a new Latin version
of the New Testament. This was the first major revision since St Jerome produced
the Vulgate in the early days of Christianity. Erasmus also produced lengthy
Annotations on the Latin New Testament. He followed a tradition established by
the Fathers of the Church and continued by scholars in the Middle Ages, but
went beyond his predecessors in applying the latest humanist teaching in his
works, for example, he sought the most precise equivalents for Greek texts.
This kind of scholarship had appealed to humanists such as Lorenzo Valla,
who also wrote some (much briefer) *Annotations on the Epistles to the
Romans*.

Source: (i) St Paul's Epistle to the Romans, The Authorised Version of the Bible,
British and Foreign Bible Society, London, 1:1–3. (ii) *Collected Works of Erasmus*,
56, *Annotations on the Epistle to the Romans*, ed. R. D. Sider, trans. and annotated J.
B. Payne, A. Rabil, R. D. Sider, W. S. Smith, New Testament Scholarship, University
of Toronto Press, Toronto and London, 1994, pp. 3–8

(i) St Paul's Epistle to the Romans. 1:1–3

1. Paul, a servant of Jesus Christ, called to be an apostle, separated unto the gospel
of God.

2. (Which he had promised afore by his prophets in the holy scriptures.)

3. Concerning his son Jesus Christ our Lord, which was made of the seed of
David according to the flesh:

2 After Hans Holbein the Younger, *Portrait of Erasmus*, 1523, oil on panel, 42 × 32 cm, Louvre. Photo © R.M.N. – Arnaudet.

(ii)

1:1 [ER VG] *Paulus* '**Paul.**' There are those who think that Saul's name had been changed following his conversion; among these is Ambrose.[1] St Jerome, however, commenting on the Epistle to Philemon, supposes that he began to be called Paul instead of Saul because of the proconsul Sergius Paulus, the first of all the gentiles whom this apostle gained for Christ, as we read in the thirteenth chapter of the Acts of the Apostles. Chrysostom thinks his name was changed by the divine will, like that of the chief of the apostles, who was called Cephas or Peter instead of Simon. There are those who think he had two names; and this in my opinion is closer to the truth, though I believe that the Hebraic name Saul was originally given to Paul, who was first a Hebrew. For by that name Christ addresses him on the road: Σαοὺλ Σαοὺλ τί με διώκεις, that is, 'Saul, Saul, why do you persecute me?' Then, since for the most part by that time Egypt, Cilicia, and the part of Syria that bordered it spoke Greek – a result of Alexander the Great's empire and the later Roman administration – the Hebrew word was changed to a Greek form. For Greeks have no word ending in λ [*l*], so that Saul became Saulus, as even today Latin speakers say Adamus for Adam, Abrahamus for Abraham, and Josephus for Joseph. Finally, since the name Paul was equally familiar to Greeks and Romans, Saulus was further changed to Paulus, so that they whose teacher he claimed to be would with even greater pleasure recognize his name, and in this, too, he would be all things to all men. Certainly he himself used this name constantly in his writings.

Saul in Hebrew is שָׁאוּל meaning 'sought,' a passive from שָׁאַל, for he had been admitted into apostolic service. Ambrose points out that Saul means 'tribulation' or 'restlessness.' Elsewhere likewise people give interpretations of all kinds for Hebrew names that have only a tenuous play on words; I shall not analyse these closely as it is not part of this enterprise. But the Greek word σαῦλος, if the υ is removed, becomes σάλος, which means 'agitation' and 'disturbance,' properly of the sea and the waves; whereas Paul in Greek means 'at rest' – from the verb παύομαι [pauomai 'I cease, rest from'], whence also the name παῦλα [Paula] 'rest.' To the Romans [paulus] means 'paltry.' Now as to Jerome's point, that in Hebrew Paul means 'wonderful' – it is a wonder to me that he commits the very fault he elsewhere criticizes in others who sought the etymologies of words from a different language. Since, indeed, it is clear that Paulus is a Latin word, or at least Greek, it was not appropriate to derive its etymology from Hebrew. I have pointed this out in passing, so that what saintly expositors in their commentaries discuss concerning the explanation of names – or the puns they make – might be understood more easily.

1:1 [ER] *vocatus ad munus apostolicum* 'called to apostolic service' [VG] *vocatus apostolus* 'called an apostle'; κλητὸς ἀπόστολος. 'Called' in this passage is not the participle 'said' or 'named' – as today certain men for the sake of modesty commonly write 'called a bishop,' indicating not so much with modesty as with truth that they are bishops in name more than in fact. Even St Bernard [of Clairvaux, 1090–1153], in general a man of Christian learning, holy eloquence, and devout geniality, falls into this κακόζηλος [affectation]: he qualifies his own title by writing 'called an abbot.' The designation is a substantive – [he is], as an apostle, κλητός [a 'called one'], not κληθείς or κεκλημένος [was, or has been, called (an apostle)]. So also a little below the 'called of Jesus Christ,' κλητοί, and just afterwards κλητοῖς ἁγίοις, that is, 'to those called, to the saints.' So 'called' is a term with a sense complete in itself – just as long ago among the Romans those who were summoned to war as friends were said to be 'the ones called forth,' and today as well in France some who are close to senatorial dignity are called 'the elect.' The word has virtually the same force as though you said 'an apostle with a calling,' or 'an apostle by calling,' and 'to those who are saints by calling.'

At the outset, in the very preface to the Epistle, Paul looks to his own interest and secures trustworthiness and authority for himself. First, with his very name he sets in sharp relief his altered mode of life. Then, by calling himself a 'servant' he indicates that he is attending to the interest not of himself, but of him who had sent him. When to this he adds 'of Jesus Christ' he excludes Moses, who had become so deeply fixed in the minds of the Jews that there was a danger that the gentiles too might be led away into the servitude of the law of Moses. This clearly would have happened if Paul had not most vehemently resisted with might and main, so that the gospel of Christ can appear as revived through this champion. Then he adds 'apostle,' which means 'envoy' or 'one sent by another.' And since at that time there were many pseudo-apostles who were thrusting themselves into this office for the sake of glory and gain, he adds κλητός 'called,' which has a double meaning: either that he was called, that is, 'summoned,' to this office by Christ himself, and had not claimed for himself the work of an apostle – indeed, he had assumed this obligation not from men but from Christ himself; or that with this word he is excluding the merit and works of the Law and declaring the grace of the gospel, which is given to all, not from the ceremonies of the Mosaic law, in which the Jews trusted, not from human wisdom, on which the Greeks relied, but at the call of deity. For the blessed Paul's chief concern in this letter is to take away from both groups their pride: to deprive the Jews of their confidence in the law of Moses and the Greeks of their security in philosophy, and consequently to unite both groups on an equal basis in Christ. The apostles have certain special words of their own – grace, calling, election, foreknowledge, destination, and predestination – and these are virtually always opposed to trust in the Law, a danger, paramount at that particular time, that seemed to threaten. I am not unaware that Origen, using the opportunity afforded by this word, discourses – with shrewdness and erudition, no doubt – concerning those who are indeed called, but who fall short of the reward of their service. It is not my intention to reject such an interpretation; but in divine literature the simplest and the least forced interpretations are more satisfactory. Yet I would certainly not deny that this word κλητός [called] is sometimes used in a way not much different from a participle, as in Matthew: 'Many are called, but few are chosen' [22:14], where ἐκλεκτοί [chosen] and κλητοί [called] are read. This word belongs especially to Paul, who is eager to remove from everyone trust in human works, and to transfer all the glory to the God who calls. Whoever heeds God when he calls is saved. Thus Paul soon obeyed after he had been called from heaven.

1:1 [ER VG] *segregatus in evangelium dei* 'set apart for the gospel of God'; ἀφωρισμένος. With an admirably increasing emphasis he commends his own position as one who not only has been called to perform the service of an apostle, but, as a chosen vessel, has also been selected and separated for the duty of preaching the gospel. For ἀφωρίζειν [aphōrizein] not only means 'to separate' but also 'to distinguish and select with judgment.' Thus physicians call rules stated briefly and complete in themselves ἀφορισμοί [aphorismoi 'aphorisms'], as the ἀποφθέγματα [apophthegmata] of the wise are called.

This expression does not have a simple significance. For in the first place, he seeks to avert the charge of inconstancy, because he appeared to be deserting the law of Moses. He says 'called' and 'set apart,' as though he were some chosen and special instrument; Christ himself bears witness: 'He is my chosen vessel, to bear my name before the gentiles.' Second, he makes an allusion to the party to which he adhered in Judaism, playing on its name. For the Jewish people, although they embraced the same Law, were divided into various schools; Josephus, in the second chapter of the eighteenth book of *Antiquities*, mentions the chief of these

– Essenes, Sadducees, and Pharisees.[2] Paul belonged to the Pharisaic sect, which receives its name from the Hebrew word פָּרַס, *pharas* [separate], because they wanted to appear separated and removed from the common people due to their noteworthy holiness of life and their superior doctrine. Paul therefore began to be in the gospel what he had been in Judaism, but in a different way. Under Judaism his title was one of pride; in the gospel he had been marvellously separated from Moses unto Christ, from the letter unto the spirit, from trust in works unto grace.

1:3 [ER *qui genitus fuit* 'who was begotten']

[VG] *qui factus est ei* 'who was made to him'; τοῦ γενομένου. Lorenzo Valla prefers 'begotten' [*genitus*] or 'born' [*natus*] rather than 'made'; in the present case, I neither approve nor disapprove his opinion. It would certainly be 'begotten' if the Greek were γεννηθείς or γεννόμενος. Augustine,[3] in the eleventh book *Against Faustus*, chapter 4, testifies that some Latin manuscripts read 'born' instead of 'made.' And yet elsewhere the same author explains why the Apostle preferred to say 'was made' rather than 'was born,' namely, because he was conceived and born not from the seed of a man, but from the work of the Holy Spirit. Nevertheless, this reason does not prevent the word 'born' from being used elsewhere. [. . .]

NOTES

1   Ambrosiaster wrote the Commentaries on the Pauline Epistles used by Erasmus, although Erasmus attributed them to St Ambrose of Milan (*c*.339–97).
2   Flavius Josephus (*c*.37–*c*.100 CE) was a writer on Jewish history and religion.
3   Aurelius Augustinus, known as St Augustine of Hippo (354–430), was a major Christian theologian and commentator, whose *City of God* was one of the most influential texts in the Middle Ages and the Renaissance.

6   Thomas More **Dedicatory letter to Thomas Ruthall on his translation of the *Dialogues* of Lucian of Samosata (1505–6)**

Sir Thomas More (1478–1535) was born in London. As a student, he spent some time in Oxford where Thomas Linacre (1460–1524) taught him Greek. He then studied law to please his father and became a successful barrister. At the same time he continued to maintain a circle of humanist friends including John Colet and Desiderius Erasmus. His best-known work, the *Utopia*, was first published in 1516 (see Text 18). Henry VIII sent him on diplomatic missions, gave him a knighthood and, in 1529, made him Lord Chancellor, after the fall of Cardinal Wolsey. He was obliged by his conscience to resign the post three years later, when it became clear that the king would divorce Catherine of Aragon and marry Anne Boleyn. He evaded attempts to incriminate him as a traitor for some time, but in 1535 he was finally convicted and executed. He was canonized by the Roman Catholic church in 1935.

3 Hans Holbein the Younger, *The Family of Sir Thomas More*, 1527, ink, 38.9 × 52.4 cm,
Öffentliche Kunstsammlung Kupferstichkabinett. Photo: ÖKB, Martin Bühler.

More made his Latin translations of some of the satirical Greek *Dialogues* of
Lucian (second century CE) at a time when Erasmus, who was staying in his
household, was engaged in similar work. Both versions proved to be very popular
and were printed many times during the first half of the sixteenth century. The wit
and irony of Lucian made the translation of his work a congenial exercise for
Renaissance Greek scholars.

Source: C. R. Thompson, *The Translations of Lucian by Erasmus and St. Thomas
More*, Vail-Ballou Press, Ithaca, New York, 1940, pp. 24–7

To the most distinguished and learned Thomas Ruthall, Royal Secretary, Thomas
More sends greeting:
   If, most learned sir, there was ever anyone who fulfilled the Horatian precept
and combined delight with instruction, I think Lucian certainly stood *primus
inter pares* [first among equals] in this respect. Refraining both from the arrogant
teachings of the philosophers and the more dissolute dallyings of the poets, he
everywhere remarks and censures, with very honest and at the same time very
amusing wit, the shortcomings of mortals. And this he does so cleverly and so

effectively that although no one pricks more deeply, yet there is no one of impartial mind who would not allow his stings of sarcasm. Although he always does it excellently, he seems to me nevertheless to have done it rather exceptionally well in these three dialogues, which chiefly for that reason I have chosen from so great a number of exceedingly merry ones to translate; though perhaps other persons might much prefer other dialogues. For just as all men do not love the same maiden, but one prefers and loves a certain one, nor can he easily tell precisely why, but she simply suits his taste, so of the most agreeable dialogues of Lucian one man likes a certain one best, another prefers another; these ones have particularly struck my fancy, nor that merely by accident, I trust, nor they alone.

To begin with the shortest one, which is entitled *Cynicus*, and which might appear to be unacceptable on account of its brevity, did not Horace remind us that the greater strength is often to be found in a slight body; and we ourselves see that even the smallest gems are greatly prized.[1] St. John Chrysostom, a man of the most acute judgment, nearly the most Christian of all the Doctors and (as I surely think) the most learned of Christians, has supported my choice of it with his estimable opinion: whom this dialogue so delighted that he introduced a good part of it into that *Homily* which is a commentary on St. John's Gospel.[2] Nor was it undeserving of that. For what should have pleased that grave and truly Christian man more than this dialogue, in which, while the severe life of the Cynics and their contented existence with few possessions is defended, the soft and enervating luxury of voluptuaries is denounced? In the same work the simplicity, temperance, and frugality of the Christian life, and finally that strait and narrow way that leads to life are commended.

Then *Necromantia* [*Menippus*] (for that is the title of the second dialogue), although not quite happy in the title yet most happy in its matter, does it rebuke at all falsely the jugglery of magicians or the silly figments of poets or the fruitless contendings of the philosophers among themselves on any question?[3]

There remains *Philopseudes*, which, not without Socratic irony, exposes to ridicule and reproof (as its title indicates) the inordinate love of lying: a dialogue which is I know not whether more amusing or more instructive.[4] It does not greatly disturb me that in this dialogue he appears to have been disposed to doubt immortality, and that he was in the same error as Democritus, Lucretius, Pliny, and many others likewise were. For why should it concern me what a pagan thinks about those matters that are contained in the peculiar mysteries of the Christian faith? Surely this dialogue will bring us this lesson: that we should not put trust in tricks and that we should eschew superstition, which here and there obtrudes under the guise of religion; that we should live a life less disturbed by anxiety, fearing the less, that is, the gloomy and superstitious untruths that often are related with such great confidence and authority that some crafty fellow, I know not who, even prevailed upon the most blessed Father Augustine, a most sober man and an ardent foe of lies, so that as a result he told for true as a thing that occurred in his own lifetime that tale of two soothsayers, one coming to life and the other departing from it, which in this dialogue Lucian, with only the names changed, made fun of so many years before Augustine was born.[5] Wherefore you should wonder the less if with their inventions they influence the minds of the more stupid vulgar, they who think indeed that they have done a great thing and have obligated Christ to them perpetually if they have feigned a story of some saint or a tragedy of hell, which some old or silly woman cries at or is terrified by. And so there is scarcely a martyr's or a virgin's life which they have passed over and in which they have not inserted some falsehoods of this kind – piously, of course, for otherwise there was danger lest the truth be insufficient in itself, insufficient unless it be supported by lies! They have not feared to corrupt by their inventions that very religion which Truth itself instituted and wished to consist of truth unadorned, nor have they perceived to what degree their fables fail to contribute anything of this kind; so that as a result nothing more perilous obstructs it. Surely, as the Father Augustine mentioned above affirms, when he detects an untruth mixed with it, the authority of truth is immediately diminished and weakened.[6] Whence the suspicion often arises within me that a large portion of the fables of this sort has been concocted by some sly and wicked rascals and heretics whose object was partly to gain amusement from the reckless credulity of persons more simple than careful, partly to take away belief in the true histories of Christians by associating them with feigned stories; who in fact frequently fable certain things so closely resembling those contained in Holy Writ that they easily reveal themselves to have mocked by their jesting. On this account unquestioning faith should be placed in those stories that the divinely inspired Scripture commends to us. Testing the others by the doctrine of Christ, as by the rule of Critolaus,[7] we should either accept cautiously and with judgment or reject, if we wish to be free from foolish trust and superstitious dread. [. . .]

NOTES

1   The *Cynicus* is a humorous portrait of a begging cynic philosopher.
2   St John Chrysostom (*c.*347–407), whose *Homilies on the Gospel of St John*, contains references to the Lucianic dialogue.
3   The *Necromantia* [*Menippus*] was a satire on philosophy, wealth and power presented through the imaginary descent into Hell of Menippus and his conversations with the inhabitants of the Underworld. He had previously visited heaven in the *Icaromenippus*.
4   *Philopseudes* concerns lying and credulity in respect of accounts of the supernatural.
5   Possibly there is confusion here with Gregory the Great, who records a similar story in his *Dialogues* IV.36. It is not identifiable in the works of Augustine.
6   Augustine, *De mendacio* (*On Lying*), 17.
7   Cicero, *Tusculan Disputations*, V.17.51. Critolaus of Phanetis was a leading Peripatetic philosopher of the second century BCE who claimed that the goods of the soul could be shown to outweigh the goods of the body or the external world.

7   John Barclay *Euphormio's Satyricon* (1603–7)

John Barclay (1582–1621) was born in France where his father, a Scottish Catholic, held a chair in civil law at Pont-à-Mousson. He was educated by the

Jesuits and developed a strong dislike for them. He divided his adult life between England and France: his Scottish origin seems to have commended him to James I of England (VI of Scotland) who patronized him. In return the king received the dedication of one of Barclay's major works, *Euphormio's Satyricon*. It is an account of a journey undertaken by Euphormio and is modelled on the *Satyricon* of Petronius Arbiter, a Roman patrician who lived in the time of the emperor Nero in the first century CE. Barclay used it as a means of expressing his dislike of the hypocrisy and decadence of life in Europe; Jesuits, puritans and smoking were singled out for particular censure. The characteristics of Catharinus in this extract are meant to be typical of puritan behaviour. It ends with fulsome praise of Barclay's benefactor, King James (Tessaranactus). The work belongs to the genre of satire which included the Lucianic *Dialogues* (Text 6).

Source: *Euphormio's Satyricon*, trans. and ed. D. A. Fleming, Nieuwkoop, B. de Graef, 1973, pp. 339–47, 349–51

CHAPTER THIRTY

At length we sailed off from Boeotia in most favorable winds and reached our appointed goal more quickly than we had even hoped. I did not want to go to Tessaranactus [James I] together with Trifartitus, for I thought it beneath my dignity to rely on the support of this Legate. I had heard that Tessaranactus was an admirer of virtue, and was himself a miracle of virtue, greater than the heroes of antiquity that we read about in Xenophon's empty tales.[1] In accord with a vanity shared by nearly all the learned, I considered myself the favorite of the Muses. Moreover, the name of Themistius had not yet been forgotten among those people. So I took leave of Trifartitus, using some vague excuse; and together with a traveler from Icoleon who was also on his way to Tessaranactus, I set off at an easy traveling pace.

It happened to be a feast-day, and we lightened the labor of the journey by innocent pleasantries. When the Sun started burning quite warmly, we sat down under some trees which surrounded the buildings of a country estate with a delightful shade. There we also indulged our laughter and sought for joy to banish our troublesome worries.

Our joviality had already gotten as far as song when we saw some servants from the nearby house, clothed in pure-white togas, approaching us with marvelous gentleness. Their heads were all bowed, their eyes cast down in girlish modesty. They entreated us to come into the house, and they attested in their very gentle speech that they had been sent by the master of the estate for this reason. We accepted so welcome a kindness on the part of this man and followed the servants into their hospitable dwelling. In a moment, we were led into an inner chamber and found ourselves in the presence of the father of the household. He was seated in a semicircular settee, after the fashion of Cicero's majestic Scaevola.[2] His face was sanctimonious and severe, his eyes were lowered and gazing at his flowing beard. He was clothed in a pure white garment, and we saw nothing about him which was not scrupulously free from all filth. Indeed you would have judged him to be a virtuous man, the kind who would not have been attacked of old by the licentious Gauls, if he had sat in the ruling seat when the city was captured.[3]

As we entered his room and approached him, he received us with a perfunctory greeting. Then he began to pour forth such a flood of tears that we were quite afraid we had renewed the memory of some old bitter grief by our arrival. We were horrified and amazed by this new kind of politeness, which consisted in ruining the pleasure of one's guests by so much grief. I approached the settee, composed my face to appear as confused as possible, and inquired after the cause of so sudden a sorrow. He beat his chair with his fists, nodded his head up and down, and answered that he was moved not by any personal cause, but rather by our danger: for (he said) 'no one can vex the patience of heaven with crimes and expect them to remain unavenged.' We were horrified at being overwhelmed by so dreadful and confused an accusation. We stopped short in mutual amazement, looking now at each other, now at the old man, who kept on groaning. Above all, we started examining our innocent consciences.

I did not hesitate to ask him what cause he had found to suspect us of crime. He was sad and his eyes were wet, but his face changed somewhat into anger, and he cried out: 'Do you even ask this, as if you had been educated in Scythian ferocity, and in total barbarousness and ignorance of the divine law? Is it possible that you do not know what an inexpiable crime it is to undertake a journey on a feast day? And besides (I hate even to describe it), you have been celebrating your travels, not in serious remembrance of the Divinity but in all licentious joviality and in lax remissness. You have even polluted my innocent home by your ill-timed jocoseness; when you were tired along the way, you sat down nearby, and my roofs provided an unhappy shade for your sacrilege.'

We were totally stupefied at this outburst, and we adored him as a prophet of the heavenly divinities. We begged his pardon for the rash error of our youth. Having calmed down now that due honors had been rendered, he assured us that we should in no way despair of the gentleness of heaven; if our tears were genuine in promising amendment, the Gods above had already forgotten all our failings.

We were refreshed by the blessedness of so wondrous a hope. At this point, it occurred to my companion to ask this sanctimonious old man his name. He held his breath a bit as he considered. Then he replied: 'I would indeed prefer for you to hear it from others; but, lest I offend you, my inquisitive guests, by troublesome taciturnity, I will tell you that I am Catharinus. I have received this pure name in the course of religious controversies. And if I dare speak of myself, I can say that I am among the greatest men living when it comes to uprightness of morals, and I have no competitors in religiosity.'

I was struck by so proud an uprightness; I inquired further about his religious observance and his manner of life, doubting whether it was vain ambition or sincere piety that had christened Catharinus with so haughty a name. The old man noisily coughed a few times, giving a signal to his household. With wondrous alacrity all hastened to listen to his oration. They also brought in upholstered chairs for us, where we could comfortably receive the authority of the heavenly oracles. My predictions of misery have never been in vain: by now I could prophesy, seeing so much religious finery, that we were going to pay for the favor of hospitality by listening to a troublesome oration from the old man.

CHAPTER THIRTY-ONE

Once the noise of those who entered had calmed down, when the eyes and faces of everyone were expectantly turned to him, he began to speak, in approximately the following words: 'At the beginning of time, when the progeny of the stars had not yet perished from the human race, and when it was not virtue but the place of habitation that made the difference between the heavenly race and mortal men – in that age a path was open from here below to the stars, for those who deserved it; mortality passed on almost unchallenged to heaven. Examples of this are Hercules and Bacchus [respectively the heroic embodiment of strength and god of wine in Roman mythology], whose reputation is sacred to their progeny, and such numerous forms of human bodies, who went on living while they were added to the number of the stars. But then lust took the place of virtue's own reward, and men began to believe that nothing was good unless it promised plea-sure. The gods turned aside from so corrupt a humanity, and they feared to burden their aether any longer with such heavy crimes.

'So it was that, once the path to eternity had been lost, the following centuries went about their labors unhappily. People solicited the anger of the gods still more by inventing new kinds of sacred rites. Finally, shortly before my lifetime, a few spurned such inadequate cults, snatched the masks away from false super-stitions, or – to put it better – they tried to snatch them away. For they stopped short in their attempt, as if they were awed by the magnitude of the undertak-ing. They were content to cut away little weeds from the field of religion, but they feared to touch the most harmful roots.

'Finally I came along, dear guests, born under greater fates. Once age drew me away from my lax teachers and pure heavenly doctrine flowed into me, I could no longer restrain my groans at such a calamity for mortal men. For I realized that everyone who had lived in the past twelve centuries had fallen deeply, as if it were dark night and they had slipped into precipices and measureless chasms. One thing especially moved me: the thought that in that whole stretch of time not a single person had entered this world and remained unstained. The common crime of all had propelled them all into perpetual punishments, once death had overtaken them. No one, I insist, prepared for himself by the help of the religion which was then prevalent any other eternal dwelling than the torture-chamber of the impious, where dying is the most pleasant hope of all. Indeed God will see to the whole matter, but he neither should nor could have spared any of them without staining his integral reputation for justice. He will not be angered at this frank saying; for I have often dared to utter things more serious, and yet he has willed that I might live unto this age which you see in me.

'I hate with equal bitterness those patchwork reformers of our age, who have spared superstitions, who have far too easily found a place for Poimenarchs (as they call them), for seasons and vigils, for priestly ornaments of linen and all the rest of the insanities of antiquity. As far from them as from those who still lie entirely asleep in their ancient errors, I have insisted on another way of reform. I have laid my hand to the task more thoroughly, and I have removed the most tenuous threads of superstition, even the very image of it. I began by condemning whatever the age of our grandfathers approved; and, believe me, I nearly came to doubt whether I should believe in the existence of the Divinity, since inept antiquity had given its consent to him.

'My diligence has certainly yielded me a great reward. I have seen innocence revive in my household, just as the Divinity infused it in the first mortals at the beginning of the world. My prayers are simple, my religion pure, corrupted by none of the foul odors of vain ceremonies. On the sacred day it is not allowed for us to take a journey of any length, nor to indulge in the pleasure of public spectacles or private games. We have a most holy love of equality; and believe me, I give commands more by the good will of my family than by any authority proper to me. The moderation of good men must be maintained by modesty and by the virtues; they are not to be compelled by severe evils and punishments. Consider the imaginings of the Poets who describe the blessedness of the golden age: then, they say, no force subjected one intelligence to another of the same strength, and there were no tribunals from which severity could mete out fear and terror to those who were summoned before them. But I am afraid that before I can persuade this proud world of my truth, while the fates are still hesitating over these beginnings of something better, disease and old age may pour out my strength and my soul to the four winds.' He spoke *and his face grew moist with flowing tears.*

It seemed to me that I was listening to Pythagoras, spewing forth the whole charter of his laws in the pages of some Poet.[4] If tears had not conveniently interrupted the old man, we would have been in danger of passing the whole night listening to him. He quickly wiped his eyes and seemed about ready to bring forth a new plot on his stage, when his charming wife sealed his wandering lips with a few kisses. She was a woman of praiseworthy beauty, with a very fine face. Her eyes, neither protruding nor too deep-set, tingled with a slightly melancholy sauciness. She was about twenty years old. As she drank in Catharinus' flowing tears and mixed her lovely face in among her husband's wrinkles, she gently interceded with him to spare his jaws and his heart. By now supper was ready and waiting for them to eat; and the guests, already bettered by his exhortations, would be further enticed by the delight of the banquet. I loved the woman after she had said all this, and I thought that she was more potent than all of Catharinus' precepts.

As we took our places for supper and were regaled with many platters, we started forgetting our pre-supper piety; and even Catharinus encouraged us to proceed to cheerfulness and toasting. I kept turning my eyes to him; now he was much calmer and his sad severity was disappearing. He kept his eyes so constantly fixed on the face of his beautiful wife that you would have thought some magnet was hidden there, forcing the iron face of the old man in its direction. I could not restrain my laughter, and I nodded at my companion to call his attention to the scene.

But nothing was more amazing to me than what happened at the end of the banquet. Some strange instruments were borne in; they were light and polished, but made out of clay. Each of them consisted of a cup of small capacity attached to a small, straight hollow tube. Catharinus emptied something out of a paper pouch, cut it up into tiny particles, stuffed it into the cup, and lit it with a flame. A bit of smoke billowed out and disappeared in the air. Catharinus inserted the far end of the tube into his mouth, sucked in the smoke by inhaling it through the hollow chambers of the instrument, and held it for a while in his cheeks, until the dreadful vapor had taken full possession of the dwelling-place of his mind. Eventually, by some marvelous prodigy, it was released through nearly all of his sense-organs. His eyes conceived a cloud of tears, but they were still flashing and lively; his nostrils poured forth volumes of smoky air; and his mouth was an excellent likeness of a furnace when its flame has not yet conquered and expelled the humidity of its kindling. A huge and filthy river poured forth while the bodily humors, which were either set in motion or conceived by this plague, rolled out through all his pores. And lest anything be lacking to this filthy spectacle, so pestilential a stink invaded the dining-room that I was soon wishing that Catharinus had dragged his oration on until that hour.

Then we too were invited to this same sweet medicinal practice: the plant was said to be marvelously effective against all noxious humors, and doubtless valid for treating all diseases. But neither I nor my companion was yet tired of life and desirous of death. Rather, we conjectured that the man, in addition to the gifts which he had mentioned to us, was also a Psyllan,[5] for otherwise he would never have endured so dreadful a poison.

> O harmful plant, O plant that spews out deadly smoke,
> Once nature kind did keep you far from all our climes;
> O harmful plant, what madman now begins to bear
> You in his dreary ship and bring you to our lands?
> Already cursed Mars would snatch, devour our times –
> There's formless famine, sickness drear, and failing age.
> Alas! Our savage hags go gathering poisons sure –
> Alas! Must this fate too bring forth our total ruin?
> What tongue can tell your filth, your crime, your vapors dire,
> What tongue describe the rising clouds of sordid smoke?
> 'Tis like Avernus vapors dread that spoil the air,
> Rise to the stars; they smother soon the dying seeds,
> And strike the nearby flocks and stop the winging fowl.
> 'Tis like the evils at the gates of hellish realms
> Where stinks propel the ghosts, where flits Erinnys sad,
> Puts out the lamps, where torches smoke when battle's o'er.
> O harmful plant, O plant that spews out deadly smoke,
> Had Cacus thrown you cruelly at his foe's fierce nose,
> Alcides would have yielded to the stink of old;
> Had early ages known your power, they'd have preferred
> You to hemlock; they would have told your birth in song,
> And said Cerberean foam had brought you forth.

Had someone then in slaughter raged 'gainst parents dear,
They would have thought mere flames too meek, and drowning slow;
They would have made him swallow clouds from smoking pipes.[6]

After the smelly discomfort of this supper and some more discourses on the
part of Catharinus, we were satiated no less with the vanity of the man than with
his banquet, and we retired. I considered it all at greater remove – both what I
had just seen in the household of Catharinus and what I had once known among
the Acignians, as well as whatever I had learned from the priests of various religions. I was filled with bitter pain, for I realized that the contentiousness of mortal
men commits as many abuses in divine ceremonies as in human conflicts. People
are driven to great lengths by vain zeal and cruel curses, and yet they blame one
another for their lack of charity. The learned are propelled by ambition and the
powerful by factiousness; as for the weak, they merely follow authority, either
that of a doctrine or that of the more powerful forces. How many are there, I
asked myself, either among the Acignians or in the household of Catharinus, who
were not lured into their party either by an education impressed on them by their
parents, or by the attitude of their race, or by some enthusiasm without rational
basis? How few are led by the decision of a mature mind! And yet we battle one
another in these hatreds; you can easily see that everyone thinks himself wise. O
proud mortality! O merciless ingenuity of superstition! As if those whose opinions are true did not owe more to blessedness than to their own wise decision;
or as if those who have been deceived on a way confused with such a maze of
paths were committing something worthy of anger rather than of pity!

Falling asleep amid such thoughts, I lost my cares for the public welfare
together with my senses. The next morning I approached Catharinus, having
prayed Jove, patron of hospitality, to repay his gracious kindness, and I set out
on my appointed journey to Tessaranactus, together with my companion.

Scolimorrhodia [Britain] is the most beautiful of countries; now it swells up in
little hills, now it stretches out into fertile, grain-filled plains; everywhere it exults
in joyous green. Along the public roads stand full-grown trees, and hedges
precisely mark off one field from another. Everywhere the traveler has the
impression of moving through a forest. Flocks of cattle and sheep are so
numerous that you could consider this the scene for the fables of Geryon and
the children of the Atlantic.[7] The river which our path constantly paralleled
delightfully reflected our regular motions in its correspondingly regular waves.
Here and there it was laden with huge boats, and it was so frequently beaten by
skiffs and oars that Xerxes never plied the Hellespont more heavily.[8]

CHAPTER THIRTY-TWO

I was in wonder at this happy region, and I fell in love with its fields, which were
so like those of Lusinia. But the people (as happens often) were fattened by excessive fortune and had replaced the resourceful initiative that results from poverty
by a proud laziness. We foreigners were particularly considered a bother; and had
I not known from the example of Catharinus that so uncouth a crime infected

only the meaner sort, I would already have begun to be disgusted by Scolimor-rhodian pride. Yet whenever we relaxed with the great of the land, I found that even the politeness of my Lusinia suffered by comparison.

Their furniture is splendid, the floor itself is swept daily. Their gardens, divided according to the different natures of the plants, delightfully relax eyes that are tired from traveling. When I considered the conversation of the great men and the good-breeding of their daughters, they somehow seemed to me more blessed than heaven itself. Then there were their banquets, filled with every richness, and their tables groaning under the burden of the platters. The decoration of their dining couches and their precise cleanliness in everything softened my soul even more than Themistius' prophecies had led me to expect.

When we first came to the dwelling of Tessaran[a]ctus, on seeing the vener-able majesty of his numerous household, the wealth of so many salons, so many halls glowing with the splendor of his servants, I thought the place was almost too fine for Jupiter's habitation. But once I had gazed on Tessaranactus himself, I came to the conclusion that any splendor, no matter how august, would be inferior to his exalted worth.

Eager to gain access to him, I directed myself to Amphiaraus, the principal of his friends. No one is closer to Tessaranactus in intimate friendship; nor could a worthier friend be born for any of the gods. Even Jupiter in heaven has no Mercury like him. I immediately came to know him because of his affability; led by him to Tessaranactus, I quickly began to enjoy the favor of the better gods. Before long Tessaranactus, having enriched me in no small way, even introduced me into his sanctuary, where, among his chosen servants, he dines on ambrosia. Snatched up by the enthusiasm of a sacred inspiration, I have expressed this benefit of his in the following spontaneous verses:

> So great and powerful Phaeton was
> In seeking his great father's home –
> If only he had been content
> To see, not mount the fated car!
> So blessed am I, on entering now
> Your heaven, yes, your private rooms,
> Your beauteous chambers – you who are
> Both son and father of the gods,
> Who honor scepter, robes, and crown,
> The purple signs of your great rule.
> Nor are you less than blazing Sun,
> From whom proud Phaeton claimed his birth;
> You're our Apollo, Titan bright,
> A new Osiris, harvest-god,
> And Mitra, Paean, whate'er else
> The Sun has been through all the world.
> The Sun rules mid encircling stars;
> So you rule kings; your treaties great.
> Bind all the world in your sure law. [. . .]⁹

NOTES

1   Xenophon (c.435–354 BCE) was a Greek historian, essayist and military commander.
2   Quintus Mucius Scaevola (d.c.88 BCE), Stoic and lawyer, was mentioned by Cicero in
     his *De amicitia* among other works.
3   387 BCE; Livy, *Histories*, V.41.
4   Publius Ovidius Naso (Ovid, 43 BCE–17 CE); Ovid, *Metamorphoses*, XV.60.
5   Psyllans were protected from snake bites by a special antidote in their bodies.
6   Avernus was the lake at the entrance to the Underworld; Erinnys, one of the Furies;
     Hercules (Alcides) killed Cacus for having stolen part of his herd, Virgil, *Aeneid*, 8, 192;
     Cerberus, Pluto's dog, the watchdog of the Underworld.
7   The three-headed, or -bodied, Geryon was the owner of a mythical herd of enormous
     cattle. He lived on an island in the far west. The children of the Atlantic inhabited the
     Fortunate Isles, which were famous for their fertility; see Pliny, *Natural History*.
8   This refers to Xerxes I, King of Persia (486–465 BCE) and his expedition against the
     Greeks. As part of this massive expedition he built a bridge across the Hellespont made
     of a double line of boats.
9   Phaeton, son of Apollo, who drove his father's chariot too close to the sun; Osiris,
     Egyptian god of rebirth; Mitra or Mithras, a Persian and Roman god of the sun; Paean
     was an epithet for the Greek sun-god Apollo.

8   Isotta Nogarola *Of the Equal or Unequal Sin of Adam and Eve* (1451–3)

Isotta (1418–66) and Ginevra Nogarola (1417–61/8) were sisters and natives of Verona, who both achieved a good knowledge of Latin and Greek. Isotta seems to have aspired to enter the circle of humanists surrounding Guarino of Verona. She wrote to him but he failed to answer, so she wrote again reproaching him for humiliating her in learned circles. He then replied, praising her attainments and encouraging her studies. It was perhaps this episode that made her decide to live a celibate life within her family rather than to marry, enter a convent or continue to try to practice humanist studies in public. For a time she conducted an intense correspondence with Ludovico Foscarini, a Venetian nobleman, the character who appears with Isotta in this extract. Apart from that, her studies were private and dedicated to religion. Her sister Ginevra married and apparently abandoned any aspirations to be a humanist. The experience of these women illustrates the difficulties in pursuing humane studies when success was defined by public recognition, something which the male authors of other documents in this section enjoyed. The number of references in this speech to philosophical and theological authorities as well as to the Bible provide ample evidence of Isotta's erudition.

Source: *Her Immaculate Hand: Selected Works By and About Women Humanists of Quattrocento Italy*, ed. and trans. M. L. King and A. Rabil, SUNY Binghamton, 1983, pp. 59–67, 69

LUDOVICO BEGINS: If it is in any way possible to measure the gravity of human sinfulness, then we should see Eve's sin as more to be condemned than Adam's [for three reasons]. [First], she was assigned by a just judge to a harsher punishment than was Adam. [Second], she believed that she was made more like God, and that is in the category of unforgiveable sins against the Holy Spirit. [Third], she suggested and was the cause of Adam's sin – not he of hers; and although it is a poor excuse to sin because of a friend, nevertheless none was more tolerable than the one by which Adam was enticed.

ISOTTA: But I see things – since you move me to reply – from quite another and contrary viewpoint. For where there is less intellect and less constancy, there is less sin; and Eve [lacked sense and constancy] and therefore sinned less. Knowing [her weakness] that crafty serpent began by tempting the woman, thinking the man perhaps invulnerable because of his constancy. [For it says in] *Sentences* 2:[1] Standing in the woman's presence, the ancient foe did not boldly persuade, but approached her with a question: 'Why did God bid you not to eat of the tree of paradise?' She responded: 'Lest perhaps we die.' But seeing that she doubted the words of the Lord, the devil said: 'You shall not die,' but 'you will be like God, knowing good and evil.' [*Genesis* 3:4–5]

[Adam must also be judged more guilty than Eve, secondly] because of his greater contempt for the command. For in Genesis 2 it appears that the Lord commanded Adam, not Eve, where it says: 'The Lord God took the man and placed him in the paradise of Eden to till it and to keep it,' (and it does not say, 'that they might care for and protect it') '. . . and the Lord God commanded the man' (and not 'them'): 'From every tree of the garden you may eat' (and not 'you' [in the plural sense]), and, [referring to the forbidden tree], 'for the day you eat of it, you must die,' [again, using the singular form of 'you'; *Genesis* 2:15–17]. [God directed his command to Adam alone] because he esteemed the man more highly than the woman.

Moreover, the woman did not [eat from the forbidden tree] because she believed that she was made more like God, but rather because she was weak and [inclined to indulge in] pleasure. Thus: 'Now the woman saw that the tree was good for food, pleasing to the eyes, and desirable for the knowledge it would give. She took of its fruit and ate it, and also gave some to her husband and he ate,' [*Genesis* 3:6] and it does not say [that she did so] in order to be like God. And if Adam had not eaten, her sin would have had no consequences. For it does not say: 'If Eve had not sinned Christ would not have been made incarnate,' but 'If Adam had not sinned.' Hence the woman, but only because she had been first deceived by the serpent's evil persuasion, did indulge in the delights of paradise; but she would have harmed only herself and in no way endangered human posterity if the consent of the first-born man had not been offered. Therefore Eve was no danger to posterity but [only] to herself; but the man Adam spread the infection of sin to himself and to all future generations. Thus Adam, being the author of all humans yet to be born, was also the first cause of their perdition. For this reason the healing of humankind was celebrated first in the man and then in the woman, just as [according to Jewish tradition], after an unclean spirit has been expelled from a man, as it springs forth from the synagogue, the woman is purged [as well].

Moreover, that Eve was condemned by a just judge to a harsher punishment is evidently false, for God said to the woman: 'I will make great your distress in childbearing; in pain shall you bring forth children; for your'husband shall be your longing, though he have dominion over you.' [*Genesis* 3:16] But to Adam he said: 'Because you have listened to your wife and have eaten of the tree of which I have commanded you not to eat' (notice that God appears to have admonished Adam alone [using the singular form of 'you'] and not Eve) 'Cursed be the ground because of you; in toil shall you eat of it all the days of your life; thorns and thistles shall it bring forth to you, and you shall eat the plants of the field. In the sweat of your brow you shall eat bread, till you return to the ground, since out of it you were taken; for dust you are and unto dust you shall return.' [*Genesis* 3:17–19] Notice that Adam's punishment appears harsher than Eve's; for God said to Adam: 'to dust you shall return,' and not to Eve, and death is the most terrible punishment that could be assigned. Therefore it is established that Adam's punishment was greater than Eve's.

I have written this because you wished me to. Yet I have done so fearfully, since this is not a woman's task. But you are kind, and if you find any part of my writing clumsy you will correct it.

LUDOVICO: You defend the cause of Eve most subtly, and indeed defend it so [well] that, if I had not been born a man, you would have made me your champion. But sticking fast to the truth, which is attached by very strong roots, I have set out [here] to assault your fortress with your own weapons. I shall begin by attacking its foundations, which can be destroyed by the testimony of Sacred Scripture, so that there will be no lack of material for my refutation.

Eve sinned from ignorance and inconstancy, from which you conclude that she sinned less seriously. [But] ignorance – especially of those things which we are obligated to know – does not excuse us. For it is written: 'If anyone ignores this, he shall be ignored.' [*I Corinthians* 14:38] The eyes which guilt makes blind punishment opens. He who has been foolish in guilt will be wise in punishment, especially when the sinner's mistake occurs through negligence. For the woman's ignorance, born of arrogance, does not excuse her, in the same way that Aristotle and the [lawyers], who teach a true philosophy, find the drunk and ignorant deserving of a double punishment.[2] Nor do I understand how in the world you, so many ages distant from Eve, fault her intellect, when her knowledge, divinely created by the highest craftsman of all things, daunted that clever serpent lurking in paradise. For, as you write, he was not bold enough to attempt to persuade her but approached her with a question.

But the acts due to inconstancy are even more blameworthy [than those due to ignorance]. For to the same degree that the acts issuing from a solid and constant mental attitude are more worthy and distinct from the preceding ones, so should those issuing from inconstancy be punished more severely, since inconstancy is an evil in itself and when paired with an evil sin makes the sin worse.

Nor is Adam's companion excused because Adam was appointed to protect her, [contrary to your contention that] thieves who have been trustingly employed by a householder are not punished with the most severe punishment like strangers or those in whom no confidence has been placed. Also, the woman's frailty was not the cause of sin, as you write, but her pride, since the demon promised her knowledge, which leads to arrogance and inflates [with pride], according to the apostle. [*I Corinthians* 1:27–29] For it says in Ecclesiasticus: 'Pride was the beginning of every sin.'[3] And though the other women followed, yet she was the first since, when man existed in a state of innocence, the flesh was obedient to him and [did not struggle] against reason. The first impulse [of sin], therefore, was an inordinate appetite for seeking that which was not suited to its own nature, as Augustine wrote to Orosius: 'Swollen by pride, man obeyed the serpent's persuasion and disdained God's commands.' For the adversary said to Eve: 'Your eyes will be opened and you will be like God, knowing good and evil.' [*Genesis* 3:5] Nor would the woman have believed the demon's persuasive words, as Augustine says [in his commentary] on Genesis, unless a love of her own power had overcome her, which [love is] a stream sprung from the well of pride.[4] [I shall continue to follow Augustine in his view that at the moment] when Eve desired to capture divinity, she lost happiness. And those words: 'If Adam had not sinned, etc.' confirm me in my view. For Eve sinned perhaps in such a way that, just as the demons did not merit redemption, neither perhaps did she. I speak only in jest, but Adam's sin was fortunate, since it warranted such a redeemer.

And lest I finally stray too far from what you have written, [I shall turn to your argument that Adam's punishment was more severe than Eve's and his sin, accordingly, greater. But] the woman suffers all the penalties [inflicted on] the man, and since her sorrows are greater than his, not only is she doomed to death, condemned to eat at the cost of sweat, denied by the cherubim and flaming swords entry to paradise, but in addition to all these things which are common [to both], she alone must give birth in pain and be subjected to her husband. [Her punishment is thus harsher than Adam's, as her sin is greater].

But because in such a matter it is not sufficient to have refuted your arguments without also putting forward my own, [I shall do so now]. Eve believed that she was made similar to God and, out of envy, desired that which wounds the Holy Spirit. Moreover, she must bear responsibility for every fault of Adam because, as Aristotle testifies, the cause of a cause is the cause of that which is caused. Indeed, every prior cause influences an outcome more than a secondary cause, and the principle of any genus, according to the same Aristotle, is seen as its greatest [component]. In fact, [it] is considered to be more than half the whole. And in the *Posterior Analytics* he writes: 'That on account of which any thing exists is that thing and more greatly so.'[5] Now [since] Adam sinned on account of Eve, it follows that Eve sinned much more than Adam. Similarly, just as it is better to treat others well than to be well-treated, so it is worse to persuade another to evil than to be persuaded to evil. For he sins less who sins by another's example, inasmuch as what is done by example can be said to be done according to a kind of law, [and thus justly]. For this reason it is commonly said that 'the sins that many commit are [without fault].' [Thus Eve, who persuaded her husband to commit an evil act, sinned more greatly than Adam, who merely consented to her example]. And if Adam and Eve both had thought that they were worthy of the same glory, Eve, who was inferior [by nature], more greatly departed from the mean, and consequently sinned more greatly. Moreover, as a beloved companion she could deceive her husband [vulnerable to her persuasion because of his love for her] more easily than the shameful serpent could deceive the woman. And she persevered longer [in sin] than Adam, because she began first, and offenses are that much more serious (according to Gregory's decree) in relation to the length of time they hold the unhappy soul in bondage.[6] Finally, to bring my discourse to a close, Eve was the cause and the example of sin, and Gregory greatly increases the guilt in the case of the example. And Christ, who could not err, condemned more severely the pretext of the ignorant Jews, because it came first, than he did the sentence of the learned Pilate, when he said: 'They who have betrayed me to you have greater sin, etc.'[7] All who wish to be called Christians have always agreed with this judgment, and you, above all most Christian, will approve and defend it. Farewell, and do not fear, but dare to do much, because you have excellently understood so much and write so learnedly.

ISOTTA: I had decided that I would not enter further into a contest with you because, as you say, you assault my fortress with my own weapons. [The propositions] you have presented me were so perfectly and diligently defended that it would be difficult not merely for me, but for the most learned men, to oppose them. But since I recognize that this contest is useful for me, I have decided to obey your honest wish. Even though I know I struggle in vain, yet I will earn the highest praise if I am defeated by so mighty a man as you.

Eve sinned out of ignorance and inconstancy, and hence you contend that she sinned more gravely, because the ignorance of those things which we are obligated to know does not excuse us, since it is written: 'He who does not know will not be known.' I would concede your point if that ignorance were crude or affected. But Eve's ignorance was implanted by nature, of which nature God himself is the author and founder. In many people it is seen that he who knows less sins less, like a boy who sins less than an old man or a peasant less than a noble. Such a person does not need to know explicitly what is required for salvation, but implicitly, because [for him] faith alone suffices. The question of inconstancy proceeds similarly. For when it is said that the acts which proceed from inconstancy are more blameworthy, [that kind of] inconstancy is understood which is not innate but the product of character and sins.

The same is true of imperfection. For when gifts increase, greater responsibility is imposed. When God created man, from the beginning he created him perfect, and the powers of his soul perfect, and gave him a greater understanding and knowledge of truth as well as a greater depth of wisdom. Thus it was that the Lord led to Adam all the animals of the earth and the birds of heaven, so that Adam could call them by their names. For God said: 'Let us make mankind in our image and likeness, and let them have dominion over the fish of the sea, and the birds of the air, the cattle, over all the wild animals and every creature that crawls on the earth,' [*Genesis* 1:26] making clear his own perfection. But of the woman he said: 'It is not good that the man is alone; I will make him a helper like himself.' [*Genesis* 2:18] And since consolation and joy are required for happiness, and since no one can have solace and joy when alone, it appears that God created woman for man's consolation. For the good spreads itself, and the greater it is the more it shares itself. Therefore, it appears that Adam's sin was greater than Eve's. [As] Ambrose [says]: 'In him to whom a more indulgent liberality has been shown is insolence more inexcusable.'[8]

'But Adam's companion,' [you argue], 'is not excused because Adam was appointed to protect her, because thieves who have been trustingly employed by a householder are not punished with the most severe punishment like strangers or those in whom the householder placed no confidence.' This is true, however, in temporal law, but not in divine law, for divine justice proceeds differently from temporal justice in punishing [sin].

[You argue further that] 'the fragility of the woman was not the cause of sin, but rather her inordinate appetite for seeking that which was not suited to her nature,' which [appetite] is the product, as you write, of pride. Yet it is clearly less a sin to desire the knowledge of good and evil than to transgress against a divine commandment, since the desire for knowledge is a natural thing, and all men by nature desire to know. And even if the first impulse [of sin] were this inordinate appetite, which cannot be without sin, yet it is more tolerable than the sin of transgression, for the observance of the commandments is the road which leads to the country of salvation. [It is written]: 'But if thou wilt enter into life, keep the commandments;' and likewise: 'What shall I do to gain eternal life? Keep the commandments.' [*Matthew* 19:16–17] And transgression is particularly born of pride, because pride is nothing other than rebellion against divine rule, exalting oneself above what is permitted according to divine rule, by disdaining the will of God and displacing it with one's own. Thus Augustine [writes] in *On Nature and Grace*: 'Sin is the will to pursue or retain what justice forbids, that is, to deny what God wishes.'[9] Ambrose agrees with him in his *On Paradise*: 'Sin is the transgression against divine law and disobedience to the heavenly commandments.'[10] Behold! See that the transgression against and disobedience to the heavenly commandments is the greatest sin, whereas you have thus defined sin: 'Sin is the inordinate desire to know.' Thus clearly the sin of transgression against a command is greater than [the sin of] desiring the knowledge of good and evil. So even if inordinate desire be a sin, as with Eve, yet she did not desire to be like God in power but only in the knowledge of good and evil, which by nature she was actually inclined to desire.

[Next, as to your statement] that those words, 'if Adam had not sinned,' confirm you in your view [of Eve's damnability], since Eve may have so sinned that, like the demons, she did not merit redemption, I reply that she also was redeemed with Adam, because [she was] 'bone of my bone and flesh of my flesh.' [*Genesis* 2:23] And if it seems that God did not redeem her, this was undoubtedly because God held her sin as negligible. For if man deserved redemption, the woman deserved it much more because of the slightness of the crime. For the angel cannot be excused by ignorance as can the woman. For the angel understands without investigation or discussion and has an intellect more in the likeness of God's – to which it seems Eve desired to be similar – than does man.

Hence the angel is called intellectual and the man rational. Thus where the woman sinned from her desire for knowledge, the angel sinned from a desire for power. While knowledge of an appearance in some small way can be partaken of by the creature, in no way can it partake in the power of God and of the soul of Christ. Moreover, the woman in sinning thought she would receive mercy, believing certainly that she was committing a sin, but not one so great as to warrant God's inflicting such a sentence and punishment. But the angel did not think [of mercy]. Hence Gregory [says in the] fourth book of the *Moralia*: 'The first parents were needed for this, that the sin which they committed by transgressing they might purge by confessing.'[11] But that persuasive serpent was never punished for his sin, for he was never to be recalled to grace. Thus, in sum, Eve clearly merited redemption more than the angels.

[As to your argument] that the woman also suffers all the penalties inflicted on the man, and beyond those which are common [to both] she alone gives birth in sorrow and has been subjected to man, this also reinforces my earlier point. As I said, the good spreads itself, and the greater it is the more it shares itself. So also evil, the greater it is the more it shares itself, and the more it shares itself the more harmful it is, and the more harmful it is the greater it is. Furthermore, the severity of the punishment is proportional to the gravity of the sin. Hence Christ chose to die on the cross, though this was the most shameful and horrible kind of death, and on the cross he endured in general every kind of suffering by type. Hence Isidore writes concerning the Trinity: 'The only-born Son of God in executing the sacrament of his death, in himself bears witness that he consummated every kind of suffering when, with lowered head, he gave up his spirit.'[12] The reason was that the punishment had to correspond to the guilt. Adam took the fruit of the forbidden tree; Christ suffered on the tree and so made satisfaction [for Adam's sin]. [As] Augustine [writes]: 'Adam disdained God's command' (and he does not say Eve) 'accepting the fruit from the tree, but whatever Adam lost Christ restored.'[13] [For Christ paid the penalty for sin he had not committed, as it says in] Psalm 64: 'For what I have not taken, then I atoned.' Therefore, Adam's sin was the greatest [possible], because the punishment corresponding to his fault was the greatest [possible] and was general in all men. [As the] apostle [says]: 'All sinned in Adam.'

'Eve,' [you say], 'must bear responsibility for every fault of Adam because, as Aristotle shows, whatever is the cause of the cause is the cause of the thing caused.' This is true in the case of things which are, as you know better [than I], in themselves the causes of other things, which is the case for the first cause, the first principle, and 'that on account of which anything is what it is.' But clearly this was not the case with Eve, because Adam either had free will or he did not. If he did not have it, he did not sin; if he had it, then Eve forced the sin [upon him], which is impossible. For as Bernard says: 'Free will, because of its inborn nobility, is forced by no necessity,'[14] not even by God, because if that were the case it would be to concede that two contradictories are true at the same time. God cannot do, therefore, what would cause an act proceeding from free will and remaining free to be not free but coerced. [As] Augustine [writes in his commentary] on Genesis: 'God cannot act against that nature which he created with a good will.'[15] God could himself, however, remove that condition of liberty from any person and bestow some other condition on him. In the same way fire cannot, while it remains fire, not burn, unless its nature is changed and suspended for a time by divine force. No other creature, such as a good angel or devil can do this, since they are less than God; much less a woman, since she is less perfect and weaker than they. Augustine clarifies this principle [of God's supremacy] saying: 'Above our mind is nothing besides God, nor is there anything intermediary between God and our mind.' Yet only something which is superior to something else can coerce it; but Eve was inferior to Adam, therefore she was not herself the cause of sin. [In] Ecclesiasticus 15 [it says]: 'God from the beginning created man and placed him in the palm of his counsel and made clear his commandments and precepts. If you wish to preserve the commandments, they will preserve you and create in you pleasing faith.' [*Ecclesiasticus* 15:14–16] Thus Adam appeared to accuse God rather than excuse himself when he said: 'The woman you placed at my side gave me fruit from the tree and I ate it.' [*Genesis* 3:12]

[Next you argue] that the beloved companion could have more easily deceived the man than the shameful serpent the woman. To this I reply that Eve, weak and ignorant by nature, sinned much less by assenting to that astute serpent, who was called 'wise,' than Adam – created by God with perfect knowledge and understanding – in listening to the persuasive words and voice of the imperfect woman.

[Further, you say] that Eve persevered in her sin a longer time and therefore sinned more, because crimes are that much more serious according to the length of time they hold the unhappy soul in bondage. This is no doubt true, when two sins are equal, and in the same person or in two similar persons. But Adam and Eve were not equals, because Adam was a perfect animal and Eve imperfect and ignorant. [Therefore, their sins were not comparable, and Eve, who persevered longer in sin, was not on that account more guilty than Adam].

Finally, if I may quote you: 'The woman was the example and the cause of sin, and Gregory emphatically extends the burden of guilt to [the person who provided] an example, and Christ condemned the cause of the ignorant Jews, because it was first, more than the learned Pilate's sentence when he said: "Therefore he who betrayed me to you has greater sin."' I reply that Christ did not condemn the cause of the ignorant Jews because it was first, but because it was vicious and devilish due to their native malice and obstinacy. For they did not sin from ignorance. The gentile Pilate was more ignorant about these things than the Jews, who had the law and the prophets and read them and daily saw signs concerning [Christ]. For John 15 says: 'If I had not come and spoken to them, they would have no sin. But now they have no excuse for their sin.' [*John* 15:22] Thus they themselves said: 'What are we doing? for this man is working signs.' [*John* 11:47] And: 'Art thou the Christ, the Son of the Blessed One?'[16] For the [Jewish] people was special to God, and Christ himself [said]: 'I was not sent except to the lost sheep of the house of Israel. It is not fair to take the children's bread and cast it to the dogs.' [*Matthew* 15:24, 15:26] Therefore the Jews sinned more, because Jesus loved them more.

Let these words be enough from me, an unarmed and poor little woman. [. . .] [Ludovico then continues]

I have explained my views with these few words, both because I was ordered not to exceed the paper [you] sent me, and because I speak to you who are most learned. For I do not wish to be a guide on such a road to you for whom, because of your great goodness, all things stand open in the brightest light. I, indeed – a single man and a mere mortal, as it were, a reflection of the celestial life – have only pointed a finger, so to speak, in the direction of the sources. And although others may find that my writings suffer from the defect of obscurity, if you, most brilliant, accept them and join them to what you and I have already written, our views will become very evident and clear, and will shine amid the shadows. And if what I have written is clumsy, by your skill you will make it worthy of your mind, virtue, and glory. For you march forward to new battles to the sound of sacred eloquence (as do soldiers to the clamor of trumpets), always more learned and more ready. And you march forward against me, who has applied the whole sum of my thinking to my reading, all at the same time, and to my writing, that I might present my case and defend myself against yours, although the many storms and floods of my obligations toss me about at whim. Farewell.

NOTES

1   Peter Lombard, Italian theologian, (*c.*1100–64), *Sententiae in IV libris distinctae* (*Separate Judgements in Four Books*), Book 2, distinction 21, chapter 5, par. 2.
2   Aristotle (384–22 BCE) Greek philosopher and scientist, *Nichomachean Ethics* III.5.
3   Loosely based on *Ecclesiasticus* 10:14.
4   Augustine, *De Genesi ad litteram* (*On the Literal Meaning of Genesis*) 11.30.
5   Aristotle, *Posterior Analytics* II.11 (94a20), 12 (96a19), 13 (96a24).
6   Gregory, *Curia Pastoralis* (*The Pastoral Care*) II, 32, I.2 respectively.
7   This is possibly taken from an apocryphal source.
8   Ambrose, *De Paradiso (On Paradise)*, 14.70, 15.73.
9   Augustine, *De natura et gratia (On Nature and Grace)*, 67.
10   Ambrose, *De Paradiso (On Paradise)*, 8.39.
11   Gregory, *Moralium libri in Job (On Morals)*, IV.36–62.
12   Isidore of Seville, *Etymologiae*, VII, possibly confusing passages in chapters 2 and 7.
13   Augustine, *De Genesi ad litteram* (*On the Literal Meaning of Genesis*), 11.9–6.
14   Bernard of Clairvaux, *De Gratia et libero arbitrio* (*On Grace and Free Will*), 1.2, 4, 9.
15   Augustine *De Genesi ad litteram* (*On the Literal Meaning of Genesis*), 11.9–16.
16   *Mark* 14:61 but also *Matthew* 26:63, *Luke* 22:67, 22:70.

9   Cassandra Fedele **Oration to the University of Padua (1487)**

Cassandra Fedele (1465–1558) belonged to the citizen class of Venice where several of her relatives held public office. Her father, himself a man of learning, employed a humanist to teach her Latin and Greek. She was regarded as something of a curiosity and, very unusually, was encouraged by the state to deliver public orations. As she aged, interest in her dwindled and she was married off to an obscure physician. After his death she lived in poverty and produced no humanist works. But at the age of ninety-one, in 1556, she delivered a speech of welcome to the queen of Poland, when her great age seems once again to have made her a celebrity. The speech printed here was delivered in honour of Bertucio Lamberto; he is otherwise unknown but appears to have been related to Cassandra Fedele.

Source: *Her Immaculate Hand: Selected Works By and About Women Humanists of Quattrocento Italy*, ed. and trans. M. L. King and A. Rabil, SUNY Binghamton, 1983, pp. 70–3

If I were permitted to be afraid as I bravely start to speak, honorable fathers, governors of the university, and most illustrious gentlemen, then faced with these ranks of learned men I would falter, bow and bend. But it behooves me, I know, to be brave. And so I shall contain my timidity – although I know it might seem to many of you audacious that I, a virgin too young to be learned, ignoring my sex and exceeding my talent, should propose to speak before such a body of learned men, and especially in this city where today (as once in Athens) the study of the liberal arts flourishes. However, the bond of duty and blood which joins me to Bertucio has forced me to undertake this task against my will, since I prefer to be called too bold rather than, by shirking my duty to a relative to whom I owe loyalty, diligent service and respect, to be too hard. There are other considerations which almost discouraged me from beginning; now, however, they in particular incite and impel me to undertake this task. So relying on your singular kindness and your rare courtesy, I dare to advance to speak. I knew that your kindness would absolve me if, in the course of my speech, I said something inelegant or unlearned. Indeed, I believe that you are endowed not only with this virtue but all others. Of these I would gladly speak if I were not afraid that needlessly to detain you with a long oration would be wearisome and unwise and that it would be exceedingly rash to judge that I could praise your virtues as much as I ought. So I will not assume that task, though I will touch on the matter, since it would be more difficult for me to end your praises than to begin them. So with this encouragement, I shall set my sails on a new course. I must speak of my [cousin], or appear to shirk my duty. I shall speak briefly.

I have chosen as the subject of my praise the threefold tradition of Cicero, Plato, and the Peripatetics [followers of Aristotle], who believed that men derived true honor from the goods of the soul, the goods of the body, and from those goods which some prominent philosophers ascribed to fortune. Therefore, I beseech you, illustrious gentlemen, to pay close attention, although I know that you expect no profound insights from me. Lest you think that I speak ostentatiously (which I am striving particularly not to do), I shall use humble, everyday words, which I am sure will please you. However brilliant one's origin, it is granted highest praise, as you know, only when the record of one's virtues achieves the level of one's nobility. These virtues alone add glory to one's family name and make people truly noble and truly famous. For what is the point of praising my relative's [Bertucio's] origin more than his character and learning, his quick, versatile, and receptive disposition, his tenacious memory or his remarkable love of the good arts? It would mean little, indeed, to have been born among the Venetians in the most celebrated marketplace of the whole world, if there were not added [to that merit] an education inferior to none with respect to religion and piety. And he has many friends, many admirers, many supporters of his glory. [Yet] the more he is praised, the less is he arrogant and overbearing. Look upon his skillfulness and dignity of form: how innocently and piously he has spent his youth is clearly evident. A youth more obedient to his parents does not exist, nor ever did. In all, to sum up, to that degree that he seems to be green in age, he is ripe, you will discover, in virtue. All this is obvious, or I would not have dared to mention it before so great an assembly. But now I shall turn to more serious matters.

Riches, bodily strength, and other such things pass away in a brief time. Deeds of genius, by contrast, are immortal, as is the soul, while goods of the body and of fortune [are snatched away]: the end is like the beginning. Neither money nor, I believe, magnificent houses nor wealth nor other pleasures of that kind which many pursue, should be counted as good things. Never, indeed, is such hungry craving satisfied, never filled. For who can deny that our weak and changeable flesh is fleeting? Yet where now is magnificent Thebes, adorned with such a luxuriance of buildings? Where is the splendor of the Persians and their Cyrus? Where is Darius? Where are the Macedonians with their kings Philip and Alexander? Where are the Spartans with their Lycurgus? Where is the strength of invincible Hercules? It was not beauty preserved which made Spurina famous, but beauty ruined, [his] face [scarred] by wounds for the sake of chastity. Who can possess these [fleeting goods] securely? Necessity appoints [their fate] equally to the greatest and the least. Was not even Croesus, king of the Lydians, deprived of an immense treasure of wealth and riches by Cyrus? Then a cheap little woman [Tomyris, queen of the Massagetae] robbed Cyrus in turn of both kingdom and life. And Xerxes,[1] who roared across land and sea with a great fleet of ships, fled back to his kingdom, content with the wood of one little ship, his whole army lost. I could go on and on. Where is Rome, that tamer of barbarians and ruler of the Greeks? Clearly, all these things have withered away. Terrible death attends all fleeting things. But those things which are produced by virtue and intelligence are useful to those who follow.

In the same way now here our Bertucio, having with keen mind and excellent memory devoted all his attention and studies to eloquence from his earliest years, now flourishes, [possessed of a] fluency and singular grace in speech. These very studies also add much honor and ornament to the advantages of fortune and of the body. For it is in speech that men excel beasts. What is so uncultivated, so unpolished, so unintelligible, so base, that it cannot be set aglow and, so to speak, ennobled by a carefully wrought oration? What is more praiseworthy than eloquence, more outstanding, or more lovely, whether [greeted] by the admiration of listeners or the hope of those in need or the thanks of those who have been defended? Nothing, moreover, is so incredible or difficult that it cannot become acceptable and easy through speaking. And how much more humane, praiseworthy and noble do those states and princes become who support and cultivate these studies! Certainly for this reason this part of philosophy has laid claim for itself to the sweet name of 'humanity,' since those who are rough by nature become by these studies more civil and mild-mannered. But I am here to praise the youth [Bertucio], pursuing the study of philosophy, which [branch of] knowledge has always been thought divine among the wisest men, and rightly so. For the other disciplines deal with matters related to man; this one teaches clearly what man himself is, what he must strive for, what he must flee. There is no understanding of life, no outstanding principle, and, finally, nothing which pertains to living well and happily, which does not result from the study of philosophy. Has anyone ever plunged into error who was imbued with philosophy? These studies refine the mind, intensify and strengthen the force of reason. The minds of men who have lapsed into error are set straight by this rudder. For this reason Stratonicus[2] rightly calls philosophy the true security. Our minds striving, by means of philosophy, we are able to discover truth and to know hidden things; she is the perfect craftsman and teacher of happiness. For what is more fruitfully useful? What [contributes] more to dignity, what more happily to righteous pleasure, or more aptly to the glory of cities than the branches of philosophy? For this reason Plato, a man almost divine, wrote that republics are blessed when their administrators have been trained in philosophy or when men trained in philosophy have undertaken to administer them. [. . .][3]

It is not easy to describe the careful diligence with which [Bertucio] has spent a lifetime in these studies. As much time as others are accustomed to devote to celebrating festive days, to the pleasures of the spirit, to the repose of the body, so much time has he devoted to the cultivation of these studies. Now indeed the reward, the dignity, he has earned by means of these labors and vigils, I need not mention to you, most worthy men, since you, in your wisdom, have judged that he should be awarded the insignia of philosophy; although it must not be doubted that he will attain still higher rewards in the future.

I would speak at greater length if I did not know that Johannes Regius,[4] whom you heard a little while ago, had spoken with greater elegance. Since that is so, distinguished gentlemen, lest by a longer speech I turn your joy to boredom, I shall pass over the rest. I attend instead to my particular duty, to extend thanks particularly to you, illustrious magistrates of this city, and to you, excellent fathers and distinguished men, because you have deigned to lend your welcome presence in a distinguished assembly to honor my relative. For no one is so ungrateful or insensitive or crude that he would neglect to praise you for this recent favor. But, to tell the truth, there could hardly be an orator so consummate and with such discerning judgment who could – I do not say recount all your merits (for this cannot be done) – but even touch lightly upon them. Happy, therefore, are you, Cassandra, that you happened to be born into these times! Happy this age and this excellent city of Padua, overbrimming with so many learned men. Now let everyone cease, cease, I say, to marvel at the ancients! The highest and greatest God has wished the studies of all peoples to flourish in this place, and to be commended and consecrated to eternity. For age will exhaust and devour all things, but your divine studies will flourish daily more and more and will free themselves from all danger of oblivion.

But I return to what I set out to say, that I thank you abundantly for being present today in such great numbers for my speech and for Bertucio, my kinsman, and for seeing fit to honor both of us with your illustrious presence. I promise that our unfailing loyalty and respect will never flag for you distinguished men as long as we both live.

NOTES

1 Thebes: either the Mycenean city in central Greece or the capital of Egypt; Cyrus the Great (559–529 BCE), founder of the Persian Empire; Darius I, king of Persia (521–486 BCE), defeated at the battle of Marathon; Philip II, king of Macedon and his son Alexander the Great (390–323 BCE), rulers of the Macedonian Empire; Lycurgus, legendary lawgiver of Sparta (c.600 BCE); Hercules, Greek demi-god, famous for his 'Labours'; Spurina, a beautiful young Etruscan man who mutilated his own face to preserve his chastity; being 'as rich as Croesus' remains an epithet still in circulation today; Xerxes I, king of Persia defeated at Salamis and Plataea by the Greeks.
2 Stratonicus, Athenian musician and wit, fourth century BCE.
3 Plato, *The Republic*, V.471C–474.
4 This is possibly a reference to Johannes Regiomontanus (1436–76) a celebrated German astronomer who travelled and taught throughout Europe.

10 Marguerite of Navarre **Novel XXX from *The Heptameron* (1558)**

Marguerite of Angoulême (1492–1549) was the sister of Francis I of France. By 1527, when she married Henry, King of Navarre, she had become the centre of a group of humanist Catholic reformers which included Jacques Lefèvre d'Etaples and the poet Clément Marot. She produced several devotional works and is credited with the authorship of the *Heptameron*, which was first published nine years after her death: other members of her family and entourage may also have contributed to it. According to the prologue, these stories were told to pass the time by a group of five men and five women who were stranded in a monastery in the Pyrenees. They all took assumed names, some of which seem to be anagrams, and probably included Marguerite herself as well as her husband and courtiers.

Source: *The Heptameron: Tales of Marguerite, Queen of Navarre*, trans. W. M. Thompson, The Temple Company, London, 1896, pp. 190–5

MARVELLOUS EXAMPLE OF HUMAN FRAILTY, WHEREIN A LADY, TO SHIELD HER HONOUR, GOES FROM BAD TO WORSE

In the time of Louis XII [1498–1515] a member of the house of Amboise, the nephew of the legate of France, whose name was George, being then legate in Avignon, there was a lady in Languedoc (whose name I shall not mention out of respect for her family) who had an income of more than four thousand ducats. She was left a widow with one son, whilst she was still very young; and partly out of regret for her husband, partly out of love for her child, she determined not to marry again, and in order to avoid all opportunity of doing so, she only went into the society of devout people, as she knew that sin creates the opportunity. The young widow, therefore, gave herself up wholly to the service of God, shunning all worldly society, insomuch that she had scruples of conscience at being present at a wedding, or at hearing the organ played in church. When her son was seven years old she engaged a man of very saintly life to be his tutor, so that he might be instructed in all things pertaining to piety and devotion; but when he was between fourteen and fifteen, nature, who is a very secret schoolmaster, finding that he was too well fed and very lazy, taught him another lesson to that which his instructor did, for he began to look at and to desire what he considered beautiful, and amongst others a young lady who slept in his mother's room – but nobody had any suspicion of this, for he was looked upon as a child, and nothing was ever talked about in the house but God or holy matters.

This young man, however, began secretly to make love to this girl, who went and told her mistress; but she loved her son so much and thought so highly of him that she regarded it as a trumped-up story to get him into disgrace, but the girl persisted so strongly on the truth of her statement, that her mistress told her she would find out whether it was correct or not, and that she would punish him if she found out that it was as she said; but, on the other hand, if she had accused him falsely, she should suffer the punishment. To test the matter, she instructed her to make an assignation with her son, to come at midnight and sleep with her in her room in a bed close to the door, where the girl slept all by herself; and the girl having done as she was told, at night the lady took the girl's place, having made up her mind that, if what she had been told were true, she would punish him so severely that he would never lie with another woman without remembering it. Whilst she was in this angry state of mind her son actually came to bed to her, but as she would not believe that he had any improper intentions, she waited in order to speak to him to have some plainer sign of his designs, for she could not imagine that he really had any criminal desires; but she waited so long, and nature is so frail, that her anger was turned into an abominable pleasure and she forgot the name of mother. And just as water which is dammed back is all the more impetuous when it is let loose, than when flowing in its ordinary current, thus this poor lady placed all her pride in the restraint she put upon her body. When she had descended the first step from her chastity, she suddenly found herself at the very bottom one, and that same night she became pregnant by him whom she wished to prevent from getting others with child. As soon as the sin was committed, remorse of conscience set in, her repentance lasted all her life, and it was so keen at first that, rising from beside her son, who thought the whole time that it was the young lady, she went into a closet, and there calling to mind her good resolutions, and how badly she had carried them out, she spent the whole night in tears and sobs. But instead of humbling herself, and recognising the fact that our flesh is so weak that without the grace of God it must sin, she wished to make up for the past of herself by her tears, and avoid evil for the future by her prudent conduct, always imputing her sin to the occasion and not to wickedness, for which there is no remedy but the grace of God.

The next morning, however, as soon as it was daylight, she sent for her son's tutor and said to him: 'My son is growing up rapidly, and it is time that he should leave this house. One of my relations, who is on the other side of the Alps with the Grand-Master of Chaumont, will be very glad to take charge of him; therefore set out with him at once, and so that I may not have the pain of parting with him, do not let him come and take leave of me.' She then gave him the necessary money for his journey, and that morning they started, at which the young man was very pleased, for having enjoyed his mistress (as he thought) he wished nothing better than to go to the wars. The lady remained for a long time in a state of profound sorrow and melancholy, and but for the fear of God, she would have wished that the unhappy fruit of her womb might perish, and pretended to be ill so as to conceal her fault. When she was near her confinement, she sent for a bastard brother of hers in whom she trusted more than in any man living, and whom she had helped very much with money, and told him her misfortune, but did not tell him that her son was the cause of it, and begged him to save her honour, which he did, and a few days before her confinement he advised her to go to his house for change of air, where she would be more likely to recover than at home. She accordingly went thither with a very small retinue, and found a midwife there who had come for her brother's wife, and who, without knowing her, delivered her one night of a fine little girl. The gentleman gave her to a nurse and had her brought up as his own, and the lady, having stayed there a month, returned home quite alone, where she lived more strictly than ever, fasting and disciplining herself constantly.

When her son was grown up, and as there did not happen to be any war in Italy just then, he wrote to ask his mother to be allowed to return home; but as she was afraid of relapsing into the same sin, she would not allow it, but he pressed her so much, that as she had no valid reason for refusing, at last she agreed, but she told him that he must never appear before her until he was married to a wife whom he loved dearly, and that he need not look after wealth, but that it would be enough if she were of noble birth. During this time the bastard brother, seeing that the daughter of whom he had charge had grown up into a very tall handsome girl, thought of sending her into some noble family at a long distance off where she would not be known, and by the mother's advice he sent her to the Queen of Navarre. This girl, whose name was Catherine, was so handsome and well-bred at about thirteen, that the Queen of Navarre got very fond of her, and wished to get her well married to some man of high rank, but as she was poor, she found plenty of lovers but no husband. The gentleman, her unknown father, visited the Queen of Navarre's Court on his way back from Italy, where he fell in love with his own daughter as soon as he saw her, and as he had his mother's permission to marry any woman he pleased, he only inquired whether she were of noble birth, and on receiving a reply in the affirmative, he asked the queen for her hand, which she very willingly bestowed on him, for she knew that he was rich, handsome and well-bred.

After the marriage had been consummated, the gentleman wrote to his mother, that she could not refuse to let him come home now, as he was bringing her a daughter-in-law who was perfect in every respect. When she inquired whom he had married, and found that it was their own daughter, she was so shocked and grieved that it nearly killed her. Not knowing what else to do, she went to the Legate of Avignon, to whom she confessed the enormity of her sin, and asked him to advise her what to do. In order to satisfy her conscience he consulted several Doctors of Divinity, to whom he related the matter, without mentioning any names, and their decision was that the lady must never disclose anything about the affairs to her children, as they had not sinned, but that she must do penance all her life, without appearing to do so. So that unhappy lady returned home, where soon afterwards her son and daughter-in-law arrived, who loved each other as much as it was possible for husband and wife to do, and she was his daughter, his sister and his wife, and he was her father, her brother and her husband. This love lasted all their life, and the unfortunate lady was so penitent that she could never see any acts of endearment between them without weeping.

'This is what happens, ladies, to those of your sex who think they can vanquish love and nature, and all the faculties which God has given them, by their own strength and virtue, but the best thing would be, if they knew their own weakness, not to expose themselves to such an enemy, but to take refuge in a real friend and say with David: "Answer for me, O Lord."

'I never heard a stranger case than that,' Oisille said, 'and I think that all of us here, men and women, ought to bow the head in the fear of God, seeing how the hope of doing a good action was productive of so much mischief.'

'Certainly,' said Parlamente, 'as soon as any one begins to trust in himself, he at once begins to lose his trust and confidence in God.'

'He is a wise man,' Guebron continued, 'who knows no enemy but himself, and who is constantly on the watch to guard against his own will and counsel, however good or even holy they may appear to be.'

'Nothing,' said Longarine, 'can possibly justify a woman in running the risk of going to bed with a man, however closely related they may be, for it is dangerous to bring fire and tow too nearly together.'

'Devout as she was,' Emarsuitte answered, 'she nevertheless was a conceited fool, who thought herself so holy that she could not sin, as some would make silly people believe of them, which is a very great error.'

'It is hardly possible,' said Oisille, 'that there are any persons so foolish as to believe this.'

'They go even further than that,' Longarine answered her, 'for they say that one must accustom oneself to the virtue of chastity, and to try their strength, they speak with the handsomest women they can find, and those whom they love best, and by kissing and handling them, they try whether all lust of the flesh is dead in them, and when they find that this pleasure excites them, they leave the women, and fast and discipline themselves thoroughly, and when they have mortified their flesh, that neither talking nor kissing excite the slightest emotion in them, they voluntarily expose themselves to the most foolish temptation, that is of going to bed together, and embracing without any lustful feelings. But where one escapes, so many fall, that the Archbishop of Milan, where this peculiar form of devotion found particular favour, found it necessary to separate them and to put the men into the monasteries and the women into the nunneries.'

'Really,' Guebron said, 'it is the height of folly, for any one to think himself impassible, and safely to seek occasions for sinning.'

'There are others,' Saffredant answered, 'who do just the contrary, and although they avoid temptation as much as possible, yet concupiscence seems to follow them everywhere. Even holy St. Jerome, after he had soundly scourged himself and hidden himself in the desert, confessed that he could not escape from the fiery lust which burnt in his very marrow. The only thing to do, then, is to commend ourselves to God; for if his power and goodness hold us not up, we are apt to take pleasure in falling.'

'You do not seem to see what I do,' said Hircan, 'that as long as we were telling our stories, the monks behind the hedge did not hear the vesper-bell, but as soon as we began to talk of God away they went, and now the second bell is going.'

They all got up and went to church, where they devoutly heard vespers, and during supper talked about the stories that had been related, and thought over events of which they were cognisant, to see which were most worthy of being retained in their memory for reproduction. After they had spent a very pleasant evening, they all went to bed, hoping that nothing would occur the next day to interrupt their agreeable occupation. And thus the third day ended.

11   Giovanni Villani *The Florentine Chronicle* (1348)

Giovanni Villani (*c.*1275–1348) was born in Florence and belonged to a merchant family. His early career was spent travelling on business in western Europe. He later held a number of offices in Florence and was sent on diplomatic missions. His *Florentine Chronicle* begins in biblical times and ends in the year of his death in 1348, the year of the Black Death. It was stylistically influential and was used extensively by most of the city's later historians. Villani's contemporary Dante Alighieri (1265–1321) used the manuscript when writing his *Divine Comedy*.

In the *Divine Comedy* Boniface VIII (Benedetto Caetani, pope 1294–1303), the 'prince of pharisees', was seen as responsible through his alliance with France for the expulsion of the White Guelf faction (which included Dante) from Florence. The king of France is Philip IV 'the Fair' (1285–1314).

Source: *Villani's Chronicle: being selections from the first nine books of the 'Chroniche Fiorentine' of Giovanni Villani*, trans. R. E. Selfe and P. H. Wicksteed, Archibald Constable and Co. Ltd., London, 1906, pp. 344–6

BOOK VIII, SECTION 62. – HOW THERE AROSE STRIFE AND ENMITY BETWEEN POPE BONIFACE AND KING PHILIP OF FRANCE

[. . .] The king of France had become angered against Pope Boniface by reason of the promise which the said Pope had made to the king, and to M. Charles of Valois, his brother, to make him Emperor, when he sent for him, as afore we made mention; which thing he did not fulfil, be the cause what it might. Nay, rather in the same year he had confirmed as king of the Romans Albert of Austria

[Duke Albert I *c.*1250–1308], son of King Rudolf, for the which thing the king of France held himself to be greatly deceived and betrayed by him, and in his wrath he entertained and did honour to Stefano della Colonna[1] his enemy, which was come to France on hearing of the discord which had arisen; and the king to the best of his power favoured him and his followers. And beyond this, the king caused the bishop of Pamiers, in the district of Carcassone, to be taken prisoner on charge of being a Paterine [heretic]; and he spent the revenues of every vacant bishopric, and would confer the investitures himself. Wherefore Pope Boniface, which was proud and disdainful, and bold in doing all great things, of high purposes and powerful, as he was and as he held himself to be, beholding these outrages on the part of the king, added indignation to ill-will, and became wholly an enemy to the king of France. And at first, to establish his rights, he caused all the great prelates of France to be invited to his court; but the king of France opposed them, and would not let them go, wherefore the Pope was the more greatly incensed against the king, and would have it, according to his privilege and decrees, that the king of France, like other Christian princes, ought to acknowledge the temporal as well as the spiritual sovereignty of the Apostolic Chair; and for this he sent into France as his legate a Roman priest, archdeacon of Narbonne, that he might protest against and admonish the king under pain of excommunication to comply thereto, and acknowledge him; and if he would not do this, he was to excommunicate him and leave him under an interdict. And when the said legate came to the city of Paris, the king would not allow him to publish his letters and privileges, nay rather they were taken from him by the king's people, and he himself was dismissed from the realm. And when the said papal letters came before the king and his barons in the temple, the Count d'Artois, which was then living, threw them into the fire and burnt them in despite, whence great judgment came upon him; and the king ordered that all the entrances to his kingdom should be guarded, so that no message nor letter from the Pope should enter into France. When Pope Boniface heard this, he pronounced sentence of excommunication against the said Philip, king of France; and the king of France to justify himself, and to make his appeal, summoned in Paris a great council of clerics and prelates and of all his barons, excusing himself, and bringing many charges against Pope Boniface of heresy, and simony [sale of benefices] and murders, and other base crimes, by reason whereof he ought to be deposed from the papacy. But the abbot of Citeaux would not consent to the appeal, rather he departed, and returned into Burgundy in despite of the king of France. In such wise began the strife between Pope Boniface and the king of France, which had afterwards so ill an end; whence afterwards arose great strife between them, and much evil followed thereupon, as hereafter we shall make mention.

In these times there came to pass a very notable thing in Florence, for Pope Boniface having presented to the commonwealth of Florence a fine young lion, which was confined by a chain in the court of the palace of the Priors, there came in thither an ass laden with wood, which when it saw the said lion, either through the fear he had of him or through a miracle, straightway attacked the lion fiercely, and so struck him with his hoofs that he died, notwithstanding the help of many men which were there present. This was held for a sign of great changes to come, and such like, which certainly came to pass to our city in these times. But certain of the learned said that the prophecy of the Sibyl was fulfilled where she said: 'When the tame beast shall slay the king of beasts, then will begin the destruction of the Church'; and this was shortly made manifest in Pope Boniface himself, as will be found in the chapter following.[2]

NOTES

1   Stefano della Colonna, self-appointed Roman tribune (c.1265–1349).
2   The Sibyls were ancient prophetesses, whose Oracles circulated as forgeries in the Middle Ages after the destruction of their authentic sayings in late Antiquity; in March 1303 the minister of Philip IV, Guillaume Nogaret, captured Boniface at Anagni.

12 Leonardo Bruni **Preface to *The History of the Florentine People*** (1444)

Leonardo Bruni (c.1370–1444) was born in Arezzo and is sometimes known as 'Leonardo Aretino'. He learned Greek from Manuel Chrysoloras (c.1350–1414) in the 1390s and won renown as one of the most accomplished humanists of his time, translating many Greek texts into elegant Latin. Initially he worked for the papacy but in 1415 he settled in Florence and entered the service of the republic. He became Chancellor in 1427, a post he retained until his death. He has been identified by some scholars as a leading exponent of 'civic humanism'. He was conscious of the republican heritage of ancient Rome and wished to see the best of its conduct and institutions flourishing in states such as Florence. He started *The History of the Florentine People*, which encapsulates this approach, in 1415 and had not finished it when he died in 1444.

Source: *The Humanism of Leonardo Bruni, Selected Texts,* ed. and trans G. Griffiths, J. Hankins, D. Thompson, Medieval and Renaissance Texts and Studies, 46, Binghampton, New York, 1987, pp. 190–2

I have been debating for a long time—with the verdict favoring one side as often as the other—whether I should try to write a book about the deeds of the people of Florence: their foreign and domestic struggles, and their notable achievements in peace and war. On the one hand I was impressed by the magnitude of the resources that enabled this people, after coping successfully, first with civil and other conflicts among themselves, and then against their neighbors, now in our own time, with greatly increased power, to stand up to the powerful duke of Milan and to the bellicose King Ladislas in a fashion that caused all Italy, from the Alps to Apulia, to tremble under the clash of arms, and also brought in kings and great armies from across the Alps out of France and Germany. On top of these events came the capture of Pisa which, whether because its spirit is so different, or because it was a rival power, or because of the outcome of the war, I think I could rightly call a second Carthage. The siege and final conquest, fought with equal obstinacy by victors and vanquished, includes deeds that are so worthy of memory that they appear in no way inferior to the greatest deeds of the ancients that we read about.

Such things seemed to me worthy of record and of a book, and I thought a knowledge of them would be of great profit to the public as well as to the private citizen. For if men of more advanced age are held to be wiser by virtue of their having seen more of life, how much more will history, if we read it right, be able to furnish us that wisdom, by which we may sift the achievements and counsels of many ages (so that you easily learn what to follow and what to avoid), and to stimulate us to virtue by accounts of the glory of great men?

On the other hand I was put off by the enormous labor, by the obscure or interrupted record of dates and names, whose harshness makes it hard to introduce any kind of stylistic elegance, and by many other difficulties. Finally, however, after thinking over these problems a great deal and for a long time, I have come to this conclusion: to regard any rationalization for writing as preferable to dull silence.

I have therefore set about writing this, not unaware of my own limitations nor unmindful of what a burden I was assuming. But I hope that God will assist me in what I have undertaken, and that, since I am engaged in a good cause, he will see that it turns out well, or if my powers are not sufficient for the task I have ventured upon, that he will nevertheless look with favor upon the endeavor and effort. Would that they of an earlier age, whatever their education or fluency, had written down what had happened in their own times instead of remaining silent. For it is in my opinion a first duty of learned persons at least to make known their own age and so try to rescue it from oblivion and fate and consecrate it to immortality. I think there were various reasons for their silence: that for fear of the labor involved in some cases, or for lack of ability in others, they turned their minds to other kinds of writing instead of to history. For if you try a little, you can easily complete a little booklet or letter. But history, in which such a long and continuous account must be kept of so many things at the same time, and the causes of every action must be explained, and in the course of which a judgment must be rendered on every matter, is a subject on which, since its almost infinite bulk threatens to crush one's pen, it is as risky to embark as it is difficult to succeed. Thus, because each man gave himself up to his own peace and quiet, or remained silent out of regard for his reputation, the public utility was neglected, and the memory of eminent men and of important things has been almost obliterated.

I have, however, decided to recall the history of this city not only in my own times, but in earlier ones as far as the record permits. A knowledge of it must, however, involve the rest of Italy, for nothing worth recalling has occurred in Italy for a long time in which some of this people were not participants. To explain why embassies were sent or received, moreover, considerable notice will have to be taken of other peoples. But before coming to the times that are our proper concern, I wanted – following the path of those who have written about the beginnings and origin of this city, but rejecting common and fabulous interpretations – to offer what I believe to be the most accurate account, so that the whole subsequent story may be more intelligible.

13 Plato **Socrates' second speech from *Phaedrus*, (*c*.415 BCE)**

Plato (*c*.429–*c*.347 BCE) was an Athenian philosopher influenced by the personality and ideas of Socrates, who figures as the principal speaker in his dialogues. *The Republic* set out an ideal programme for a form of government which would enable citizens to achieve a good life. However, Plato's one practical attempt to advise a ruler, the tyrant of Syracuse, ended badly. He founded the Academy in Athens *c*.387 for the pursuit of philosophical research. Its deliberations proved influential both on contemporaries such as Aristotle and on subsequent generations in classical, medieval and modern times. Phaedrus, a beautiful young man who participates in this dialogue, was a favourite pupil of Plato. The main subject is the use of rhetoric and a refutation of the sophists (paid teachers of oratory and philosophy) who believed that it was not important to be truthful as long as the speaker was eloquent and persuasive. Plato, on the other hand, claimed that good rhetoricians must understand the nature of the soul through contemplation of eternal truth and service to the gods. This could be achieved by an intellectual ascent from the world of the senses to some knowledge of the Forms, in comparison to which the things of this world were mere shadows. One of the means by which this could be achieved was love; for it could elevate sensuous passion to a pure reverence for the beauty of the beloved. This idea, expressed through the myth of the charioteer, is the subject of these extracts.

Source: Plato, *Phaedrus; and the seventh and eighth letters*, trans. with intro. W. Hamilton, Penguin Classics, Harmondsworth, 1973, pp. 46–58, 61–3, 65. Copyright © Walter Hamilton, 1973. Reproduced by permission of Penguin Books Ltd

SOCRATES' SECOND SPEECH, TYPES OF DIVINE MADNESS. THE IMMORTALITY OF SOUL[1]

SOCRATES: Well then, my handsome lad, you must realize that the previous speech was the work of Phaedrus, son of Pythocles, a man of Myrrhinus, whereas this which you are about to hear comes from Stesichorus, son of Euphemus, a native of Himera.[2] This is how it must go. 'False is the tale' which says that because the lover is mad and the non-lover sane the non-lover should be given the preference when one might have a lover. If it were true without qualification that madness is an evil, that would be all very well, but in fact madness, provided it comes as the gift of heaven, is the channel by which we receive the greatest blessings. Take the prophetess at Delphi and the priestesses at Dodona,[3] for example, and consider all the benefits which individuals and states in Greece have received from them when they were in a state of frenzy, though their usefulness in their sober senses amounts to little or nothing. And if we were to include the Sibyl [prophetess] and others who by the use of inspired divination have set many inquirers on the right track about the future, we should be telling at tedious length what everyone knows. But this at least is worth pointing out, that the men of old who gave things their names saw no disgrace or reproach in madness; otherwise they would not have connected with it the name of the noblest of all arts, the art of discerning the future, and called it the *manic* art. [. . .]

In the next place, when ancient sins have given rise to severe maladies and troubles, which have afflicted the members of certain families, madness has appeared among them and by breaking forth into prophecy has brought relief by the appropriate means: by recourse, that is to say, to prayer and worship. It has discovered in rites of purification and initiation a way to make the sufferer well and to keep him well thereafter, and has provided for the man whose madness and possession were of the right type a way of escape from the evils that beset him.

The third type of possession and madness is possession by the Muses. When this seizes upon a gentle and virgin soul it rouses it to inspired expression in lyric and other sorts of poetry, and glorifies countless deeds of the heroes of old for the instruction of posterity. But if a man comes to the door of poetry untouched by the madness of the Muses, believing that technique alone will make him a good poet, he and his sane compositions never reach perfection, but are utterly eclipsed by the performances of the inspired madman.

These are but some examples of the noble effect of heaven-sent madness. Intrinsically there is nothing in it to frighten us, and we must not allow ourselves to be alarmed and upset by those who say that the friendship of a man in his sober senses is preferable to that of one whose mind is disturbed. They will prove their case only if they can demonstrate in addition that love sent from heaven is not a blessing to lover and loved alike. It is for us to prove the opposite, and to show that this type of madness is the greatest benefit that heaven can confer on us. Our argument will carry conviction with the wise, though not with the merely clever. First of all we must form a true notion of the nature of soul, divine and human, by observing it in both its passive and its active aspects. And the first step in our demonstration is this.

All soul is immortal; for what is always in motion is immortal. But that which owes its motion to something else, even though it is itself the cause of motion in another thing, may cease to be in motion and therefore cease to live. Only what moves itself never ceases to be in motion, since it could not so cease without being false to its own nature; it is the source and prime origin of movement in all other things that move. Now a prime origin cannot come into being; all that comes into being must derive its existence from a prime origin, but the prime origin itself from nothing; for if a prime origin were derived from anything, it would no longer be a prime origin.

Moreover, since it does not come into being, it must also be indestructible; for since all things must be derived from a prime origin, if the prime origin is destroyed, it will not come into being again out of anything, nor any other thing out of it. So we see that the prime origin of motion is what moves itself, and this can neither be destroyed nor come into being: otherwise the whole universe and the whole creation would collapse and come to a stop, and there would be nothing by which it could again be set in motion and come into existence. Now, since it has been proved that what moves itself is immortal, a man need feel no hesitation in identifying it with the essence and definition of soul. For all body which has its source of motion outside itself is soulless; but a body which moves itself from within is endowed with soul, since self-motion is of the very nature of soul. If then it is established that what moves itself is identical with soul, it inevitably follows that soul is uncreated and immortal.

THE MYTH. THE ALLEGORY OF THE CHARIOTEER AND HIS HORSES

SOCRATES: This must suffice concerning soul's immortality; concerning its nature we must give the following account. To describe it as it is would require a long exposition of which only a god is capable; but it is within the power of man to say in shorter compass what it resembles. Let us adopt this method, and compare the soul to a winged charioteer and his team acting together. Now all the horses and charioteers of the gods are good and come of good stock, but in other beings there is a mixture of good and bad. First of all we must make it plain that the ruling power [reason] in us men drives a pair of horses, and next that one of these horses is fine and good and of noble stock [spirit] and the other the opposite in every way [appetite]. So in our case the task of the charioteer is necessarily a difficult and unpleasant business.

Now we must try to tell how it is that we speak of both mortal and immortal living beings. Soul taken as a whole is in charge of all that is inanimate, and traverses the entire universe, appearing at different times in different forms. When it is perfect and winged it moves on high and governs all creation, but the soul that has shed its wings falls until it encounters solid matter. There it settles and puts on an earthly body, which appears to be self-moving because of the power of soul that is in it, and this combination of soul and body is given the name of a living being and is termed mortal. [. . .] Let us pass on to consider the reason which causes a soul to shed and lose its wings; it is something like this.

The function of a wing is to take what is heavy and raise it up into the region above, where the gods dwell; of all things connected with the body, it has the greatest affinity with the divine, which is endowed with beauty, wisdom, goodness and every other excellence. These qualities are the prime source of nourishment and growth to the wings of the soul, but their opposites, such as ugliness and evil, cause the wings to waste and perish. [. . .]

Now many glorious sights meet the eyes of the blessed gods on the journeys to and fro beneath the vault of heaven which they take in pursuit each of his allotted task, and they are followed by whoever is able and willing to follow them. [. . .] But when they go to the celebration of their high feast day, they take the steep path leading to the summit of the arch which supports the outer heaven. The teams of the gods, which are well matched and tractable, go easily, but the rest with difficulty; for the horse with the vicious nature, if he has not been well broken in, drags his driver down by throwing all his weight in the direction of the earth; supreme then is the agony of the struggle which awaits the soul.

Now the souls that are termed immortal, when they reach the summit of the arch, go outside the vault and stand upon the back of the universe; standing there they are carried round by its revolution while they contemplate what lies outside the heavens. [. . .] The region of which I speak is the abode of the reality with which true knowledge is concerned, a reality without colour or shape, intangible but utterly real, apprehensible only by intellect which is the pilot of the soul. So the mind of a god, sustained as it is by pure intelligence and knowledge, like that of every soul which is destined to assimilate its proper food, is satisfied at last with the vision of reality, and nourished and made happy by the contemplation of truth, until the circular revolution brings it back to its starting-point. And in the course of its journey it beholds absolute justice and discipline and knowledge, not the knowledge which is attached to things which come into being, nor the knowledge which varies with the objects which we now call real, but the absolute knowledge which corresponds to what is absolutely real in the fullest sense. And when in like manner it has beheld and taken its fill of the other objects which constitute absolute reality, it withdraws again within the vault of heaven and goes home. And when it comes home the charioteer sets his horses at their manger and puts ambrosia before them and with it a draught of nectar to drink.

Such is the life of the gods. But of the other souls that which is likest to a god and best able to follow keeps the head of its charioteer above the surface as it makes the circuit, though the unruly behaviour of its horses impairs its vision of reality. A second class sometimes rises and sometimes sinks, and owing to the restiveness of its horses sees part, but not the whole. The rest, in spite of their unanimous striving to reach the upper world, fail to do so, and are carried round beneath the surface, trampling and jostling one another, each eager to outstrip its neighbour. Great is the confusion and struggle and sweat, and many souls are lamed and many have their wings all broken through the feebleness of their charioteers; finally, for all their toil, they depart without achieving initiation into the vision of reality, and feed henceforth upon mere opinion, [as opposed to true knowledge].

The reason for their extreme eagerness to behold the plain of truth is that the meadow there produces fit pasturage for the best part of the soul, and that the wings by which the soul is borne aloft are nourished by it. And it is decreed by fate that any soul which has attained some vision of truth by following in the train of a god shall remain unscathed till the next great circuit, and if it can continue thus for ever shall be for ever free from hurt. But when a soul fails to follow and misses the vision, and as the result of some mishap sinks beneath its burden of forgetfulness and wrong-doing, so that it loses its wings and falls to earth, the law is this. In its first incarnation no soul is born in the likeness of a beast; the soul that has seen the most enters into a human infant who is destined to become a seeker after wisdom or beauty or a follower of the Muses and a lover [. . .]

The lot which befalls a man between two incarnations corresponds to the goodness or badness of his previous life. The individual soul does not return whence it came for ten thousand years; so long does it take for a soul to grow its wings again, except it be the soul of one who has sought after wisdom without guile or whose love for a boy has been combined with such a search. These souls, if they choose the life of the philosopher three times successively, regain their wings in the third period of a thousand years, and in the three-thousandth year win their release. The rest at the end of their first life are brought to judgement, and after judgement some go to expiate their sins in places of punishment beneath the earth, while others are borne aloft by justice to a certain region of the heavens to enjoy the reward which their previous life in human form has earned. [. . .] It is impossible for a soul that has never seen the truth to enter into our human shape; it takes a man to understand by the use of universals, and to collect out of the multiplicity of sense-impressions a unity arrived at by a process of reason. Such a process is simply the recollection of the things which our soul once perceived when it took its journey with a god, looking down from above on the things to which we now ascribe reality and gazing upwards towards what is truly real. That is why it is right that the soul of the philosopher alone should regain its wings; for it is always dwelling in memory as best it may upon those things which a god owes his divinity to dwelling upon. It is only by the right use of such aids to recollection, which form a continual initiation into the perfect mystic vision that a man can become perfect in the true sense of the word. Because he stands apart from the common objects of human ambition and applies himself to the divine, he is reproached by most men for being out of his wits; they do not realize that he is in fact possessed by a god.

This then is the fourth type of madness, which befalls when a man, reminded by the sight of beauty on earth of the true beauty, grows his wings and endeavours to fly upward, but in vain, exposing himself to the reproach of insanity because like a bird he fixes his gaze on the heights to the neglect of things below; [. . .] it is when he is touched with this madness that the man whose love is aroused by beauty in others is called a lover. As I have said, every human soul by its very nature has beheld true being – otherwise it would not have entered into the creature we call man – but it is not every soul that finds it easy to use its present experience as a means of recollecting the world of reality. [. . .]

LOVE IS THE REGROWTH OF THE WINGS OF THE SOUL. THE DIFFERENT
TYPES OF LOVER

SOCRATES: So much by way of tribute to memory, whose revival of our yearning for the past has led us far afield. But beauty, as we were saying, shone bright in the world above, and here too it still gleams clearest, even as the sense by which we apprehend it is our clearest. For sight is the keenest of our physical senses, though it does not bring us knowledge. What overpowering love knowledge would inspire if it could bring as clear an image of itself before our sight, and the same may be said of the other forms which are fitted to arouse love. But as things are it is only beauty which has the privilege of being both the most clearly discerned and the most lovely.

Now the man who is not fresh from his initiation or who has been corrupted does not quickly make the transition from beauty on earth to absolute beauty; so when he sees its namesake here he feels no reverence for it, but surrenders himself to sensuality and is eager like a four-footed beast to mate and to beget children, or in his addiction to wantonness feels no fear or shame in pursuing a pleasure which is unnatural. But the newly initiated, who has had a full sight of the celestial vision, when he beholds a god-like face or a physical form which truly reflects ideal beauty, first of all shivers and experiences something of the dread which the vision itself inspired; next he gazes upon it and worships it as if it were a god, and, if he were not afraid of being thought an utter madman, he would sacrifice to his beloved as to the image of a divinity. Then, as you would expect after a cold fit, his condition changes and he falls into an unaccustomed sweat; he receives through his eyes the emanation of beauty, by which the soul's plumage is fostered, and grows hot, and this heat is accompanied by a softening of the passages from which the feathers grow, passages which have long been parched and closed up, so as to prevent any feathers from shooting. As the nourishing moisture falls upon it the stump of each feather under the whole surface of the soul swells and strives to grow from its root; for in its original state the soul was feathered all over. So now it is all in a state of ferment and throbbing; in fact the soul of a man who is beginning to grow his feathers has the same sensations of pricking and irritation and itching as children feel in their gums when they are just beginning to cut their teeth.

When in this condition the soul gazes upon the beauty of its beloved, and is fostered and warmed by the emanations which flood in upon it – which is why we speak of a 'flood' of longing – it wins relief from its pain and is glad [. . .] his whole effort is concentrated upon leading the object of his love into the closest possible conformity with himself and with the god he worships. This is the aspiration of the true lover, and this, if he succeeds in gaining his object in the way I describe, is the glorious and happy initiation which befalls the beloved when his affections are captured by a friend whom love has made mad. Now the manner of his capture is this.

THE CHARIOTEER ALLEGORY RESUMED. THE SUBJUGATION OF APPETITE, TYPIFIED BY THE BAD HORSE, AND THE AWAKENING OF LOVE FOR THE LOVER IN THE BELOVED

SOCRATES: Let us abide by the distinction we drew at the beginning of our story, when we divided each soul into three elements, and compared two of them to horses and the third to their charioteer. One of the horses, we say, is good and one not; but we did not go fully into the excellence of the good or the badness of the vicious horse, and that is what we must now do. The horse that is harnessed on the senior side is upright and clean-limbed; [. . .] The other horse is crooked, lumbering, ill-made; [. . .] Now when the charioteer sees the vision of the loved one, so that a sensation of warmth spreads from him over the whole soul and he begins to feel an itching and the stings of desire, the obedient horse, constrained now as always by a sense of shame, holds himself back from springing upon the beloved; but the other, utterly heedless now of the driver's whip and goad, rushes forward prancing, and to the great discomfiture of his yokefellow and the charioteer drives them to approach the lad and make mention of the sweetness of physical love. At first the two indignantly resist the idea of being forced into such monstrous wrong-doing, but finally, when they can get no peace, they yield to the importunity of the bad horse and agree to do what he bids and advance. So they draw near, and the vision of the beloved dazzles their eyes. When the driver beholds it the sight awakens in him the memory of absolute beauty; he sees her again enthroned in her holy place attended by chastity. At the thought he falls upon his back in fear and awe, and in so doing inevitably tugs the reins so violently that he brings both horses down upon their haunches; the good horse gives way willingly and does not struggle, but the lustful horse resists with all his strength. When they have withdrawn a little distance the good horse in shame and dread makes the whole soul break into a sweat, but the other no sooner recovers from the pain of the bit and of his fall than he bursts into angry abuse, reproaching the driver and his fellow horse for their cowardice and lack of spirit in running away and breaking their word. After one more attempt to force his unwilling partners to advance he grudgingly assents to their entreaty that the attempt should be deferred to another time. When that time comes they pretend to forget, but he reminds them; forcing them forward, neighing and tugging, he compels them to approach the beloved once more with the same suggestion. And when they come near he takes the bit between his teeth and pulls shamelessly, with head down and tail stretched out. The driver, however, experiences even more intensely what he experienced before; he falls back like a racing charioteer at the barrier, and with a still more violent backward pull jerks the bit from between the teeth of the lustful horse, drenches his abusive tongue and jaws with blood, and forcing his legs and haunches against the ground reduces him to torment. Finally, after several repetitions of this treatment, the wicked horse abandons his lustful ways; meekly now he executes the wishes of his driver, and when he catches sight of the loved one is ready to die of fear. So at last it comes about that the soul of the lover waits upon his beloved in reverence and awe.

Thus the beloved finds himself being treated like a god and receiving all manner of service from a lover whose love is true love and no pretence, and his own nature disposes him to feel kindly towards his admirer. [. . .]

If the higher elements in their minds prevail, and guide them into a way of life which is strictly devoted to the pursuit of wisdom, they will pass their time on earth in happiness and harmony; by subduing the part of the soul that contained the seeds of vice and setting free that in which virtue had its birth they will become masters of themselves and their souls will be at peace. Finally, when this life is ended, their wings will carry them aloft; they will have won the first of the three bouts in the real Olympian Games, the greatest blessing that either human virtue or divine madness can confer on man. [. . .]

Such, my son, are the divine blessings which will accrue to you from the friendship of a lover. [. . .]

NOTES

1   Socrates compares the madness or divine possession of lovers with that of prophecy, the demonic affliction of the accursed and artistic inspiration. In order to prove that love is a form of divine madness Socrates first had to show that the soul is immortal.

2   Fragments of his poems survive.
3   In Epirus, the site of a grove of oak trees sacred to Zeus. Oracles were deduced from the rustling of their leaves.

14   Marsilio Ficino **Commentary on Plato's *Phaedrus* (1466–1468?)**

Marsilio Ficino (1433–1499) was a priest and Florentine philosopher who was patronized by the Medici. He translated all the works of Plato from Greek and some treatises by his later followers, providing most of them with his own commentaries. This laid the foundations for the school of Neoplatonism which influenced the thinking of many later humanists. He is sometimes presented as the founder of an academy where men of letters discussed philosophy, but his informal gatherings appear to have little correspondence with the intellectual clubs hosted by the dukes of Tuscany in the sixteenth century. There is no conclusive evidence for when he translated the *Phaedrus* and wrote this commentary, but it is likely to date from between 1466 and 1468. It first appeared in Ficino's *Complete Works of Plato* which was published in Florence in 1484. Unlike earlier translators, Ficino did not attempt to bowdlerize or Christianize the content.

Source: *Marsilio Ficino and the Phaedran Charioteer*, ed. and trans. M. J. B. Allen, Center for Medieval and Renaissance Studies, University of California, Los Angeles, 1981, pp. 82–6 (English text only)

CHAPTER 4. THE POETIC MADNESS AND THE REST OF THE MADNESSES;
THEIR ORDER, AFFINITY, AND USEFULNESS

[i] Next it seems worthwhile to explain some of this book's principal mysteries a little more fully. Let me first say something about poetry and the other madnesses that I have neglected in the *Phaedrus* and not dealt with elsewhere. To achieve poetic madness (the madness that may instruct men in divine ways and sing the divine mysteries), the soul of the future poet must be so affected as to become almost tender and soft and untouched too. The poet's province is very wide, and his material is varied; so his soul (which can be formed very easily) must subject itself to God. This is what we mean by becoming 'soft' and 'tender.' If the soul has already received alien forms or blemishes because of its ability to be formed so easily, then it certainly cannot be formed in the meantime by the divine forms; and this is why Socrates added that the soul must be completely 'untouched,' that is, unblemished and clear.

[ii] Why did Socrates put poetry third in the degrees of madness – for he reminded us that prophecy was first, the hieratic art second, poetry third, and love fourth. It's because prophecy pertains mainly to knowing, the hieratic art to volition (so it succeeds prophecy), but poetry already declines to hearing.[1] The ancient poets did not compose divine hymns until, admonished by the prophets and priests, they had first thought to celebrate the gods, to pray to them, to intercede, and to give thanks. The amatory madness, however, will be placed fourth; for it is usually excited through sight, which we naturally use after hearing.

Besides, through prophecy and priestly mysteries we know God as the good, so we immediately worship divine things and sing [of them] poetically. We have not yet conceived of the amatory madness. After we have gazed at sensible beauty more attentively, however, and known the divine beauty, then we finally love God as the beautiful, having long ago cherished him as the good. In [commenting on] the *Symposium* and *Ion* I arranged the four madnesses in the order pertaining to the soul's restoration; here I have arranged the order insofar as it looks to the actual origin of madness.[2]

[iii] But it is pleasant to indulge the poets a little more. Whoever experiences any kind of spiritual possession is indeed overflowing on account of the vehemence of the divine impulse and the fullness of its power: he raves, exults, and exceeds the bounds of human behavior. Not unjustly, therefore, this possession or rapture is called madness and alienation. But no madman is content with simple speech: he bursts forth into clamoring and songs and poems. Any madness, therefore, whether the prophetic, hieratic, or amatory, justly seems to be released as poetic madness when it proceeds to songs and poems. And since poetic song and verse demand concord and harmony and every harmony is entirely included in the scale of nine (as I show in the *Timaeus* with music), the number nine seems rightly to have been consecrated to the Muses.[3]

[iv] Finally, having already described three species of madness, Socrates added that divine madness has further remarkable results, namely the wonderful effects of the amatory madness; for the remaining madness was love. Indeed, only love restores us to our celestial homeland and joins us with God, as will be apparent subsequently. The apostle Paul absolutely and incontrovertibly confirms this when he puts charity before all the divine gifts, however great [1 *Corinthians*, 13:13]. But before Socrates can affirm that love restores us to heaven, he has to examine a number of things concerning the condition of the soul, both divine and human. He must show first that the rational soul is sempiternal in order to prove that it gazed at one time upon the divine beauty along with the heavenly host, and that here it recalls the divine beauty through sensible beauty, and that, excited by love, it is recalled hence to sublimities and beatified.

NOTES

1   Note that the form of divine possession which leads to the ritual cleansing is here called the 'hieratic art' and is equated with the role of the priest.
2   Plato's dialogue, the *Symposium*, discussed the nature of love, while the *Ion* was concerned with the ethical value of poetry.
3   The *Timaeus* considered, among other metaphysical topics, the origin of the world and the cosmological harmony of the universe.

15 Lorenzo Valla *Of the True and the False Good* (1431)
(i) Book I (ii) Book II (iii) Book III

When Valla first wrote this treatise in 1431 he called it *On Pleasure* and it was only in a later version that it became known as *Of the True and the False Good*. It seeks to debate the question of how humanity can achieve the good: by following the precepts of the ancient philosophical schools, notably Epicureanism and Stoicism, or by accepting the guidance of Christian teachings. The matter is debated by a number of eminent orators, poets and clerics and, at the end, it is agreed that Christianity provides the best way of achieving the good life. In choosing to prefer the arguments of the Epicureans over those of the Stoics, he was being deliberately provocative. The ideas of the latter, who advocated virtue for its own sake, were clearly more compatible with conventional Christian teachings than those of the former, who argue in favour of pleasure as the guiding principle of moral behaviour. The imaginary discussion takes place in the porch of a church in Milan and the garden of one of the speakers. Text 4 gives details of Valla's life.

Source: Lorenzo Valla, *On Pleasure: De Voluptate* (*Of the True and the False Good*), ed. M. Lorch, trans. A. Kent Hiett and M. Lorch, Albaris Books Inc., New York, 1977, pp. 49–65, 73–7, 91, 121–3, 133–7, 167, 235–7, 259–65, 267–9, 279, 297–301, 305 (English text only)

i) Book I

HERE BEGINS THE PROEM OF THE FIRST BOOK OF LORENZO VALLA'S *ON THE TRUE AND THE FALSE GOOD*

When I undertook the discussion of the cause of the true and the false good, which is dealt with in the three following books, it seemed best to follow a most compelling division of the subject according to which we are to believe that only two goods exist, one in this life, one in the next. Necessarily, I shall have to deal with both of them, but in such a way that I shall seem to have gradually moved from the first to the second. All of my treatise is directed to the matter of this second good, which, as tradition holds, we reach through two means: religion and virtue. However, it is not my purpose to speak of religion, since others, especially Lactantius and Augustine, have dealt with it sufficiently and fully: one of them, as the earlier, appears to have confuted the false religions; and the other to have confirmed the true one with greater distinction.[1] I have been seized instead with the desire of dealing as far as is humanly possible with those true virtues through which we reach the true good. [. . .]

There are quite a few people and (even more shamefully) learned men with whom I have often talked, who ask and inquire: Why is it that many of the ancients and of our contemporaries as well, who either did not know or did not venerate God as we do, are said not only to be excluded from the celestial city but also to be cast out into hellish night? They ask: Are such great honesty, justice, faith, piety, and the chorus of their other virtues in no way able to aid them so that they should not be consigned to the company of the impious, the impure, and the evil, and thrust down into eternal torture – these men (O impious words!) who were not inferior in virtue and wisdom to many whom we call saintly and blessed? It is difficult to count all whom those questioners rank above the latter. They bring forth philosophers and many others about whom philosophers and writers talk, to whose irreproachable lives, say these people, almost nothing could be added. Why continue? These questioners imitate those whom they praise, and at the same time (most unbearable of all), they most actively induce others to accept their opinion, not to say their madness. What can this be, I ask, but the claim that Christ came into the world in vain? Or indeed that he did not come at all? For my part, not being able to bear this abuse and the offense committed against the name of Christ, I have taken it upon myself to restrain or to cure these men. And since the arguments of my predecessors, although certainly very powerful, are not completely accepted, I have instituted a new method of reasoning. Whereas those I mention attribute so much to antiquity – I mean, to pagans – asserting that these pagans are endowed with every virtue, I on the contrary shall make plain, with the arguments not of our side but of these same philosophers, that paganism has done nothing virtuously, nothing rightly. This is truly a great and difficult task, and I am not sure whether it is not more audacious than that of any of my predecessors. [. . .]

Since the Stoics assert more bitterly than all others the value of virtue, it seems to me sufficient to single out the Stoics as our adversaries and to assume the defense of the Epicureans. [. . .] While all three of these books aim to destroy the race of the Stoics, the first book shows that pleasure is the only good, the second that the virtue of philosophers is not even a good, and the third distinguished the true good from the false. In this third book, it will not be irrelevant to compose a kind of eulogy of Paradise in the most splendid possible manner, in order to recall the souls of the listeners to the hope of the true good, as far as it is within my power. I must add that this last book derives a kind of dignity from the subject matter itself. In Books I and II, and especially in Book I, I have interspersed gayer and almost (I would say) licentious material, for which no one will blame me if he considers the character of the matter, and if he listens to the reason for my enterprise. In fact, as for the character, what would be further from defending the cause of pleasure than a sad, severe style and the behavior of a Stoic when I am taking the part of the Epicureans? Instead, it was necessary to exchange the rude, strong, and excited style that I often use in favor of this other more relaxed and agreeable way of speaking. Certainly, an orator's greatest strength is in pleasing, and this expedient has been followed here expressly (to speak of my intentions) in order to reproach more strongly those ancients who professed any religion whatever that differed from ours. For not only do I prefer the Epicureans, despised and rejected men, to the custodians of what is virtuous [*honestum*], but I also prove that the aforementioned followers of wisdom have followed not virtue but the shadow of virtue, not honor but vanity, not duty but vice, not wisdom but folly; for they would have done better had they worked for the cause of pleasure, if they did not indeed do so. I introduce as interlocutors on the subject very eloquent men who are also my good friends, assigning to each a discourse according to his character and position and consistent with the conversations they recently held among themselves. [. . .]

THE STOIC OPENS THE DISCUSSION:

Fixing his gaze upon the ground for a while and then lifting it to his audience, Catone[2] began in the following way: [. . .]

I often ask myself with astonishment about the wickedness of mind or weakness common to almost all men, qualities that are evident in many things, but most clearly in this: that men, as I see it, are strongly inclined to acquire things that are not by nature good or certainly are not to be matched from any point of view with virtue; on the other hand, the true and noble qualities – the only good ones – are, I see, not only desired by very few but are also ignored or despised or hated. And what are these goods? They are, indeed, those pertaining to right behavior [honestas], such as justice, fortitude, temperance. For, if the countenance of virtue could be seen with the corporeal eye, as Socrates says in the Phaedrus, it would incite an incredible love for wisdom.[3] Truly, that countenance is too noble and divine to become visible and subject to our eyes. Instead, we must contemplate it with the mind and with the soul, and each of us will see the countenance of virtue as the face of the sun, the more perfectly the more he is gifted with a penetrating mind. [. . .]

Here is what comes to my mind after having thought at length and deeply on this problem. Here is my opinion. As far as I can judge, I find only two causes for this human perversity, and both derive from Nature herself. One is that the army of the vices is more numerous than that of virtue, so that, even if we wanted to, we could not win the fight against such forces. The other cause (and it seems monstrous) is that we do not want to conquer these most troublesome and dangerous enemies, not even if we could. Nature has engendered in us a certain calamitous love of delighting in our own sickness, and the vices that are the plagues of our minds are a source of our pleasure. On the other hand, Virtue [honestas], who teaches and participates in the divine blessings, seems to most to be harsh, sour, and bitter. But more of this later.

Now, pray, let us consider what we pointed out before, that is, let us talk about the disproportionate number of enemies. [. . .]

Fortitude has its antitheses, cowardice and temerity. Prudence has guile and folly. Civility has scurrility and rusticity. And so on, successively, with all the other qualities with which Aristotle has dealt, as usual with the greatest care, in those books entitled Ethics, although he does not mention prudence among the moral virtues but relegates it to the intellectual virtues. I pass over philosophers who have assigned to each virtue as its contraries not merely two vices but many. I beg you to observe and to consider how unjust it is that this multitude of vices has been created. For there is no color contrary to white but black, no sound contrary to a sharp one but a dull one, no taste contrary to sweet but bitter. All other colors, sounds, or tastes are said to be not contrary but various, not opposite but diverse.[4]

However, a virtue like diligence is placed between two contraries, curiosity and negligence; and it is so placed that when you withdraw your foot from one, you are in danger of falling into the other, as the proverb says, 'When I flee from Scylla I am dragged into Charybdis.'[5] The same circumstance occurs in what I was saying about solitary philosophers and in what Cicero says: 'While, O judges, you avoid the one censure (which you did not deserve at all) of being considered cruel, you meet with the other of being thought timid and slothful.'[6] We are provided with a thousand and more examples of this kind.

Nor am I indignant because a great many kinds of vices have been found (I am willing to ignore the fact, I endure it, I bear it); rather am I angered because too few kinds of virtues have been discovered, and – most shamefully – because the vices, although dissenting among themselves, still make common cause against us as though by treaty, assemble against us and, as it were, encircle us, who, not having enough to do to avoid one sin, are also in danger of yielding to another, not of a dissimilar variety (such as falling from avarice into cowardice), but of the very same sort (like falling from the avarice that I have mentioned into prodigality, both of which vices are the contrary of liberality). And how great a task will that be? How much prudence, vigilance, and diligence must we employ against this enemy that falls upon us on both sides, and actually in front of us and to our rear as well? [. . .]

Let us now move to the second cause of human perversity. Should we not deplore what has been deplored by many, namely that we have absorbed with our mother's milk the love of vices? That we have done so should be blamed in no way on us but on Nature, if we wish to admit the truth. To be sure, we can see children from infancy turning toward the vices of gluttony, games, and luxury, more than toward virtue and honor; they hate punishment and love caresses; they flee instruction and seek out lasciviousness. I pass over in silence with what pain good habits are inculcated. Not only children but some adults, and indeed most people in general, take punishment badly, although they should be happy to be corrected and to be informed of the cause of their sins. Moreover, and worst of all, they are enraged at the very persons from whom they have received the benefit of correction.

So that no one may be led astray by an empty argument, I affirm that what is good by nature is desired spontaneously, and, contrariwise, that what is bad is naturally avoided. Hence brute animals, to which nothing better than a body has been given, flee from hunger, thirst, cold, heat, fatigue, and death. For us, however, who possess the power of reason and are thus allied with the immortal gods, virtue is the sole good, and vice the only evil. Things being thus, why do we evade what is virtuous and desire and love vices? It is one thing to fall into error, to succumb, to be urged on by some expectation (although this partakes of evil); it is another thing to delight in sin itself. As Quintilian with his usual brilliance says, 'There is a certain wretched love of committing outrage, and the most intense pleasure of shameful action is in defiling virtue.'[7] And Cicero says, 'There was in this man such a desire for sinning that the sin itself delighted him even if there was no cause for it.'[8]

Must I go on with this subject, or is the truth not more than sufficiently self-

evident? Why should we delight so in defiling women who are chaste, virginal, pure, and respectable; and why are we more quickly inflamed by the desire to dishonor them than to possess prostituted, depraved, lascivious, and base women, even when these are more beautiful? Certainly Sextus Tarquinius was induced to ravish Lucretia not so much by her beauty (for he had seen her several times before) as by her austere way of life, of which he had previously been ignorant.[9]
[. . .]

[The Epicurean poet, Maffeo Vegio, then replies:] Truly, the excuse that the wickedness of man derives from Nature seems to me to incriminate Nature (however unjustly) more than it exculpates man. If indeed you are a wise man (as you persuade yourself, and as I grant, considering your labors and your vigils), why don't the others follow wisdom, especially when they have you for an example and teacher? Being wise is denied no one. You have been deceived and led into this censure by the Stoic heresies, which, not in words but in deeds (since the two things always differ from each other), accord no honor to gods or men. The Stoics do indeed cast many a stone at Nature, as if she could be reformed. And they do attempt to reform her, for example, in the case of perturbations of the human mind, which are the passions, and which they believe could be rooted out of us completely; or when they contend that there can be no man not demented, or mad, or possessed of whatever other qualities of the most offensive nature that can be uttered. And being of such an opinion, they nevertheless claim to be not accusers but witnesses. For what concerns myself, therefore, although I agree with you in other matters, I am taking up the defense of Nature together with that of the human race, which cannot be separated from its first cause, as I shall show. [. . .]

To begin with, what you have said about Nature can be answered piously, religiously, and without offending the ears of man: what Nature created and shaped cannot be anything but holy and praiseworthy, like this heaven that revolves above us, adorned with lights for both day and night, and disposed with such rationality, beauty, and utility. Why need I mention the seas, the earth, the air, the mountains, the fields, the rivers, the lakes, the springs, even the clouds and the rain? Why domestic animals, wild beasts, the birds, the fish, the trees, the crops? You will not be able to find anything that is not perfected, furnished, and adorned to the highest degree with rationality, or beauty, or usefulness. Even the structure of our own bodies can be shown to prove this fact, as Lactantius, a man of keen and eloquent genius, most clearly shows in the book that he entitled De opificio [On the Handiwork of God], although many more points could be mentioned that would not be less important than what he says.

And you should not be surprised if I, who seem to defend Epicurus (because, like him, I identify the highest good with pleasure), do not deny that all things have been created in accordance with the providential care of Nature – a point that he repudiated. [. . .]

Now, to go back to your argument, Catone, the primary reason that it dissatisfies is that you Stoics, unhappy and inflexible as you are, desire that nothing should exist that is not wicked and vile; you measure everything by a hollow wisdom that is in all respects fixed and complete. Thus, while you take joy in flying prodigiously and in striving toward the higher regions, your wings melt (not being natural to you but artificial and made of wax), and like the foolish Icarus [who flew too close to the sun] you fall into the sea. Truly, what kind of farfetched subtlety is it to describe the wise man in such a way that, by your own admission, no example can be found among us men, and to declare that he alone is happy, that he alone is friendly, good, and free? I would gladly endure this if your law did not deem that anyone who is not a wise man is by necessity a fool, a reprobate, an exile, an enemy, and a deserter, 'anyone' meaning all of us, since no one has yet possessed this wisdom. And lest by chance someone could become wise, you barbarians have made vices more numerous than virtues, and have invented an infinity of the most minute kinds of sins so that there are not more diseases of the body, which you say are hardly known adequately by the doctors themselves. If only one of these maladies were to affect the body, its health would not be completely lost; but if even a minimal spiritual evil exists in a man (as is necessarily the case), you pretend not only that this man completely lacks the honor belonging to wisdom but that he is also deformed by every shame and infamy. By Hercules, it is amazing that, when the doctors say there is only one state of health and many illnesses, you do not also affirm that virtue is also single, although this is the same as declaring that whoever has one virtue possesses them all.

What shall I say? You surpass the doctors in all respects. Even more than I should wish. You believe not that there is one virtue but that there is none. Whoever has one virtue has all virtues; since no one has all of them, therefore no one has any. [. . .]

That pleasure is a good I perceive not only to have been agreed on by many eminent authors but to be the testimony of general opinion, which commonly speaks of goods of our souls, goods of the body, goods of fortune. Of these, the last two are believed by those solemn men, the Stoics, not to contain any element of good, as though, indeed, they were evil. Since the Stoics cannot deny that these things have been produced by Nature and granted to the choice of man, I do not understand why, if we use them well, they should not be numbered among the goods, unless we are everywhere to blame Nature herself and slander her as foolish and unjust. [. . .]

You say, 'But pleasure is very often the cause of evils. Because of pleasure we often grow ill, because of pleasure we cannot recover, because of pleasure we even die.'

You are wrong, believe me, you are wrong. For someone suffering from fever, for example, what is harmful is not the pleasure found in drinking cold water but the quality of the water, which would have harmed him even without the pleasure. I remember having drunk water without any pleasure at all (for sometimes the water at hand is disagreeable); I also remember that a most delicious water, drunk to satiety and with much pleasure, against the doctor's orders and in the very heat of fever, was good for me, so that no blame can be attached to the pleasing taste of the water. Thus, every kind of pleasure is good. [. . .]

ii) Book II

IN WHICH IT IS SHOWN THAT CONDUCT BASED ON VIRTUE AS ADVOCATED BY
PHILOSOPHERS IS NOT EVEN A GOOD PROEM

Among all the merits of eloquence, which are surely innumerable, by far the most
important to my way of thinking is 'fullness in expression,' [. . .] This power is
the one that makes a matter clear and places it before our eyes. This quality reigns
in demonstrations and refutations, influences the minds of men, and displays all
the ornaments, splendors, and riches of eloquence. It carries the listener away
and then brings him back to himself, and it gathers around itself almost all other
merits of oratory. But we must remember that whatever is of highest excellence
is usually not only most difficult but also most dangerous. It is in fact plain that
not a few who admire and would imitate what in the greatest writers I call 'fullness in expression' actually achieve an abominable loquacity.

Such is the persistent urging of arguments pro or con, the superfluity of illustrations, repetition, and windings and turnings of the arguments so as to attach
itself, like a vine, to whatever it meets, until I cannot tell whether the futility of
the performance or its shamefulness is the greater. A diffuse and wandering
discourse of this kind is difficult to commit to memory and is an annoyance to
listeners' ears, which ought above all to be protected from boredom. It should be
added that with the greatest copiousness the greatest attention to order is
demanded, as we see in the well-known proverb: The companion of a multitude
of things is confusion. How harmful such confusion can be is evident, for
example, in warfare, for disordered armies are an impediment to themselves;
those who are almost at battle with each other cannot conquer an enemy.

Thus, whoever wishes to appear eloquent must achieve two most difficult
things: first, he should say only what is useful, lest along with his soldiers he
should bring into battle the grooms, camp followers, and cooks; second, he
should put everyone in his proper place (the infantry of the main line here, the
horsemen there, the light infantry in another position, the slingers in yet another,
and the archers elsewhere), and he should dispose his host according to the location, the occasion, and the condition of the enemy – an ability that is by far the
most admirable part of generalship. [. . .]

I concerned myself as much with carefully arranging the material which I
lighted upon as I did with producing that material copiously in the first place,
although order itself is the best teacher of both invention and copiousness. Unless
we set forth our material carefully, we run an even greater risk. For unnecessary
points are heard with tedium, and arguments that are badly arranged are not
understood; they get in each other's way, as I said. In just the same way, a general
who is ignorant of how to dispose an army and who leads his troops into battle
pell-mell, with each man occupying the position he fancies, errs more grievously
than the one who stations all the camp rabble among the ranks of his soldiers.
If I have not been able to avoid these two vices as I wished, blame it partly on
my inexperience, partly on the difficulty of the task. In crossing the unfamiliar
Alps even Hannibal, the greatest general of the Carthaginians, could not avoid

losing many of his troops and most of his elephants and even one of his eyes because of the difficulty of that territory. [. . .]

[Vegio the Epicurean undertakes to show that courage is not a good:] Let us therefore first speak of courage, or fortitude, and then of the other virtues if the matter calls for it. Courage seems indeed to offer the broader scope for the exercise of virtue, and a kind of acknowledged opportunity for exercise against pleasures. We are agreed that the men [Roman heroes] whom we mentioned have exercised themselves, more than all others, in this virtue. You exalt these people to heaven, as I said, but I do not, by Hercules, see any cause for us to say that they did well and offered us a good example. If I, for instance, were not to shun hardships, losses, hazards, and at last death, what reward or goal would you set before me? You reply, 'The safety, the dignity, and the greatness of your country!' Are you really offering this to me as a good? Do you reward me at this price? Do you exhort me to face death in the hope of achieving this? And if I did not obey, would you say that I deserved badly of my country?

But consider how far this error of yours goes, if it ought to be called an error and not just a piece of malice: you set before us illustrious and splendid words as my rewards – 'safety,' 'freedom,' 'greatness'; and then you don't give these things to me. In dying I am so far from obtaining these promised rewards that, if I had already possessed some of them, I should now lose them too. For what is left to the man who has given himself to death? 'But,' you will say, 'wasn't the death of those men for the good of their country?' Certainly. 'Then,' you will ask, 'isn't the safety of one's country a good?' I do not see that this is true unless you can explain it to me. 'Because a state freed from danger enjoys peace, freedom, quiet, and wealth,' you say? You are right, you speak truly, I agree with you. Here is the reason why virtue is so greatly praised and exalted to the stars: it gains the things of which the greatest pleasure consists. But those men themselves displayed the courage, while their country got the resulting security and greatness. Is it not the case, then, that those who gave their country security and greatness were alone excluded from these goods? Oh, you fools – Codrus, Curtius, Decius, Regulus, and all you other most courageous men – what you have obtained from your godlike virtue is to die and be defrauded of the things which are the rewards of bravery and toil![10] You are like the vipers, which, when they bear, give the light of day to their young, and they themselves lose it [by going blind], so that they would have done far better not to bear young at all. Similarly, you encounter death of your own accord so that others may not die, while they, on their side, would not think of undergoing any hardships for the sake of your merit. [. . .]

Nevertheless, the Stoics do not really seek fame by way of mute solitude or of their consciences. In fact, when they cannot obtain it in the right way, they seek it crookedly. [. . .]

And now let us add that this fame that we are discussing aspires not only to pleasure for the ears and, so to speak, to a harvest of poetic praise, but also to something further. Why are we glad to be considered good, just, active? Surely so as to obtain authority and trust. In what way? By having others say this of us:

'He is brave and vigorous; let us make him our leader in war. He is careful, hard-working, and honest in administrative affairs; how can we do better than to assign the administration of our state to him? He is full of good ideas and eloquence; let us elect him to our body to be both a support and an ornament for us.' It is with this aim in mind, I say, that people desirous of glory will take pains. Not merely many, but almost infinite, examples are at hand. But I offer only one as being needed. Caesar ran after eloquence and popularity harder than anyone else. What was he thinking of? Of being virtuous in protecting the rights of the Roman people? Not this at all (the result proves it), but of attaining the highest rank and power, which he succeeded in doing. The point can also be proved in a contrary fashion. No one shudders at infamy and dishonor for fear of moral disgrace, but for fear of becoming an object of ridicule to others, of being hated, of losing people's trust, of becoming universally suspect, and, finally, of losing his life. [. . .] As Quintilian wisely says, 'No one is so evil as to wish to appear evil.' From all this it is to be concluded that all fame aims at pleasure, as all avoidance of infamy has as its goal the escape of mental pain.

iii) [Book III]

THE CHRISTIAN REPRESENTATIVE ANTONIO DA RHO, A MONK AND THEOLOGIAN,
NOW ADJUDICATES BETWEEN CATONE AND VEGIO

I say that both sides of the argument – that of virtue and the right and that of pleasure – ought to be both approved and disapproved. They ought to be approved because the virtuous and pleasure are both excellent things; they ought to be disapproved because they should be understood differently from the ways that your arguments intended. Although I trust that you both agree with me, my business will be mainly with you, Catone, who began the argument. As for Vegio, I hope to satisfy him with an oration as short as his was long.

For what concerns the first part of the argument, Catone, where you bewail the lot of mankind, who cannot, even if they wish, overcome the great number of their enemies with the few resources at their command, I approve of your complaint and praise it. I remind you that anyone who feels pain for the troubles of others is of a gentle, good character. As to your attack on Nature for having treated us badly, I boldly accept and subscribe to the accusation, if only you will make clear what crime it is that you reproach her with. You do not really prove what you consider manifest and take for granted, namely that the number of the vices is greater than that of the virtues. Your bringing in of Aristotle, with his enormous genius, as an authority, does not immediately make us agree. In fact, Aristotle did not discover this idea for himself but borrowed it from his master, Plato, from whom he usually likes to dissent. You see that I am helping your side: we have not only the authority of Aristotle but, what is more, that of Plato, which in my opinion has always been, and ought to be, of greater value. But remember that we do not always have to take the authorities' word. Although they were right many times, yet, being human, they erred. I therefore consider anyone most foolish who entrusts himself entirely to books and does not examine them carefully to see whether they tell the truth; and although it is necessary to do this in all cases, it is particularly important in reference to the virtues, on which the whole design of our life depends. This being so, let us see whether your Aristotle was right to establish a greater number of vices than of virtues. You agree with him in this, but I do not at all, since it can be shown by the plainest reasoning that each individual vice is confronted by an individual virtue; it can be shown further that the theory is false according to which excess stands on one side, deficiency on the other, with virtue in the middle, defined as a certain point of moderation between too much and too little, and that it is useless to argue about which of the two extremes is more contrary to the mean.

For example, take a man who fears and flees from what ought to be fled from. Does he seem to you to possess fortitude? Certainly he should not be called timid. Again, take a man who embraces certain licit pleasures. Will he be called temperate on that account? Not at all. Someone is said to possess fortitude not because he flees from dangers, but because he does not flee; someone is said to be temperate not because he embraces pleasures, but because he sets himself limits in their use. [. . .]

Let us now return to the matter of judging your debate and to the description of the true good. One of you defines the sole and highest good as virtue; the other, as pleasure: between two schools of philosophers, one contrary to the other, each one defends his own. That you should have spoken like some of the ancient philosophers came at the right time, and I took it without objections. With this method, the error common to all of them will be apparent. And what you have done has turned out the more happily because you have debated, as if with set intent, on what I think are the two noblest of all the philosophical schools. Among many other indications of this preeminence, there is one in the Acts of the Apostles, where only the Epicureans and Stoics are remembered; at that time they seem to have flourished more than all other philosophical schools in Athens, home of studies and nurse of philosophy.

Yet, Catone and Vegio, you would have done better to assert God's doctrine rather than the Stoic one or the Epicurean one, and not to have chosen, for the sake of exercise and novelty, to delight in reproducing the ancients' material and habits in debating. Vegio, although your speech was more adapted to the perversion of souls (I am not yet judging between you), yet which of us doubts that you have not been yourself, since usually not only do you live but also speak differently from the way you have just spoken? To omit other things, you said that after the death of man's body nothing more remained, which many philosophers have said and also thought. But do you really call this matter into doubt, being as you are a soldier, and wanting to be known as a soldier of the Christian religion, properly called the Christian faith? I am not so ignorant of your ideas, or so far from them, as to be able to persuade myself that you think what you have been saying. I suspect you of having spoken not seriously but playfully (as you usually do) in the manner of Socrates. [. . .] Why do I say 'I suspect'? You have confessed the fact by word and even by deed, so that unless I knew you were speaking under false pretenses I could reproach you for speaking and acting against your own argument. You said, as though you had forgotten you were defending pleasure, that very often you are exhausted, weakened, and tormented by your studies, and nearly made ill in mind and body. Besides, I saw nothing in your banquet today that could not be praised: splendid, indeed, as is required by your standing, but also sober, moderate, and virtuous.

Therefore, as I said, you spoke under false pretenses. You would certainly not have done this, or would not have been right in doing it, before a different audience. You did not have to fear just now that you would corrupt such men as these with your oration, all the more because it was not out of place to reply in kind to Catone, who had begun according to the custom of the ancients. I myself have followed your procedure as best I could. But so as not to seem to be confuting the thought of Epicurus more by your confession than by logic, I ask you to accept à propos of the animals a better analogy for our purpose than the one you have used. You say that men's souls are like those of brutes. What is more similar than the light of the stars to that of a lantern? Yet the latter is mortal, the former eternal. Thus the soul, which the ancients said has the energy of a flame, differs between men and animals. You compared act with act; I am comparing substance with substance.

I have said these things not against you but against the philosophers. You, as I said, were a simulator or an ironist – more Socrates than Epicurus; but Catone, whose speech seemed to come closer to the truth, no doubt spoke seriously and did not begin the debate as a joke. What shall we say then? That he erred? By no means; what is less likely than that to happen to Catone? Instead he wanted to show himself as an admirer of the ancient world. To that world I concede humane letters, the study of doctrines, and – always most important – eloquence; I deny, however, that the ancients arrived at wisdom and the knowledge of true virtue.

But, Catone, I don't wish to debate with you as a defender of the Stoics, because I know you to be a most scrupulous defender of the faith, no less than of your arguments; I once heard you say that you had gone through all the books relating to our religion that are worth reading in order to dare to compare them and to say what was best in each of them. Why then do I need to contradict you when you agree with me, even though you have spoken otherwise? If anyone else had spoken as you have done, thinking differently from you, and if he had really assumed the role of a Stoic although he was a Christian, I would have answered him thus:

Why have you spoken as though you were not a Christian when you are one? Why is there in your speech such a surprising silence concerning our religion, as if it were something superfluous, created and shaped out of the teachings of the philosophers? Why have you preferred to call upon Nature rather than God, the author of all? I am not concerned about your talking of the immortal gods. The angels are immortal gods, as Augustine plainly declared, and not only the angels but also men who have been consecrated to the angelic city, although I do not know whether you were talking of these.[11] Why, finally, did you turn your discourse toward Nature rather than toward Jesus Christ, who can appear anywhere and stand forth before our eyes, who is always present, and is present in this gathering, and who is always ready to help those who call upon him, as he is at this very moment? Not, then, the Nature whom you have placed before us, which is nothing, but God himself, creator of the things of nature, whom you have affronted, replies through me or commands me to reply. It is manifest that all things holy are commanded by him. [. . .]

To give my decision finally, I pronounce thus: since the philosophers who praised the principle of virtue claimed that there were no rewards, or only uncertain and empty ones, after this life in which we are living, and defined the highest good as virtue, and since the Epicureans defined it as pleasure, therefore, although I disapprove of both sides, I make my decision in favor of the Epicureans (not in favor of you, Vegio, nor against you, Catone, who are each bound by your faith to another army) and against the Stoics, whom I condemn for two reasons: one, because they say virtue is the highest good; the other because they were guilty of dishonesty, living a different life from the one they professed – praisers of the virtues and lovers of pleasures (if less so than others) and surely of fame, which they followed after with their hands and their feet. If anyone does not believe me, let him believe our wise men, who did not hesitate to say, 'A philosopher is an animal that wants fame.'[12] [. . .]

If anyone asked me about the origin and cause of that false goodness and the false virtues, I should say that, because there was from the beginning one set of criteria for observing divine requirements and another for earthly ones, men called the former the 'rightful' and the 'virtues,' and the latter 'expediency.' But with the irruption of false religions and the prevalence of the vices, the science of things divine fell into oblivion or was confined to very few people. Only the names of the virtues remained, preserving something of their pristine majesty because the memory of praiseworthy ancient deeds and sayings had not completely faded away. Yet the memory was like a shadow without substance.

Since later generations were ignorant of what these virtues depended on, some people, moved by the splendor of the virtues themselves, said that these should be desired for their own sake, being alien to all earthly things; these people were for the most part the Stoics. Other people, unconscious of any other possible end or goal, said that the virtues ought to be desired for their profit to one's own interest; these people are chiefly the Epicureans, with whom the majority of nations agreed, believing that it was for personal advantage that the gods ought to be worshipped. Virtuous behavior as we Christians understand it, however, is the same as I have said it was in the first place, before the other conceptions of it: virtue is not to be desired for itself, as something severe, harsh, and arduous, nor is it to be desired for the sake of earthly profit; it is to be desired as a step toward that perfect happiness which the spirit of soul, freed from its mortal portion, will enjoy with the Father of all things, from whom it came.

Who would hesitate to call this happiness 'pleasure,' or who could give it a better name? I find it called by this name, as in Genesis, 'paradise of pleasure' and in Ezekiel, 'fruit and tree of pleasure,' and the like, when the goods associated with the divine are spoken of. We find in Psalms, 'Thou shalt make them drink of the torrent of pleasure,' although in Greek the meaning is rather 'of joy,' or 'of delights' than 'of pleasure.'[13] [. . .]

From all of which it is to be understood that not virtue but pleasure must be desired for itself by those who wish to experience joy, both in this life and in the life to come.

This experience is twofold: one pleasure now on earth, the other hereafter in the heavens (I say 'heavens' according to our usage, not that of the ancients, who thought there was only one heaven); one pleasure is the mother of vices, the other, of virtues. Let me speak more plainly. Whatever is done without hope of the later pleasure and in hope of the present pleasure is a sin: not only in major matters, as when we build a house, buy property, enter trade or get married, but also in the least important, as when we eat, sleep, move about, talk, and wish for something. In all these things both a reward and a punishment are offered to us. Therefore we must abstain from the pleasure here below if we want to enjoy the one above. We cannot enjoy both of them, because they differ from each other as do heaven and earth, soul and body. Our pleasure here is more uncertain and deceptive; that pleasure above is certain and stable. Indeed a kind of probable pleasure is not lacking in this life, and the greatest such comes from the hope of future happiness, when the mind, which is aware of right action, and the spirit, which unceasingly contemplates divine things, consider themselves a kind of candidate for the heavenly, represent to themselves the promised honors, and in a way make them present – the more happily and zestfully, the more candidates and competitors it has seen. Thus it is said: 'He who gives up earthly things for God shall receive much more here below, and eternal life in the time to come,' by which is signified the joy of him who hopes in God. Nothing is done rightly without pleasure, nor is there any merit in serving in the army of God only with patient endurance and not with a good will. 'God loves a cheerful giver,' [Psalms 36:4] [. . .]

But beyond doubt the main condition for obtaining happiness is the possession of a sense of virtue, by which I mean Christian virtue, not the virtue of the philosophers. I do not deny that many things in their writings are fruitful and salutary, but these things acquired value and began to bear fruit only after Christ, the deliverance of the quick and the dead, being sent by his Father, cleansed the face of the earth of the thorns and weeds with which it was filled and made it ready to bear fruit. [. . .]

I have now confuted or condemned both the Epicurean and Stoic dogmas, and have shown that the highest good, or the good that ought to be desired, is not found in either school or among any philosophers, but does exist in our religion, being attainable not on earth but in the heavens. However, it is not enough to have shown what this good is, and where it is, unless we also explain to the best of our ability what sort of thing it is, and what is its extent. [. . .]

Since we are dealing with the exchange of earthly goods for divine ones, let us consider whether there will be pleasures up above that are the equal of all those that we have felt here below and have repudiated; thereafter we shall return to the agreed order of this discourse. Many, in fact (including those whom, as I said, we are trying to recall to the faith), can be only painfully detached from these earthly pleasures, partly because no greater pleasures than these seem to such people to be discoverable (we carefully dissuade them from this), and partly because they believe that once the body is dead, the pleasures of the body will never return. It thus happens that they do not abstain from delights of the senses but indulge in them even more, like those who fill themselves with food before setting out on a trip through desert places. [. . .]

Here the questioners may object: 'But if that is the way it is, and if, as is true, body comes before spirit (for the animal nature is said to be prior to the spiritual one), then why don't the rewards of the body come first – the pleasures that we experience here? For those pleasures of the soul are very unfamiliar; not knowing them, we can't love them.' [. . .] Aren't you by what you say putting a higher value on physical goods than on spiritual ones? If you have come into possession of infinitely better goods, why, stupid men, do you continue to tickle yourselves with the desire for trifles? When you are already dowered with such marvelous goods, why don't you wait a little for the rest? I swear by those eternal joys of the souls that you would not think in this way if you had reached that spiritual happiness. Are those who have been received into the eternal tabernacles not completely happy, or do people live better on earth than they do in heaven? But you talk in this way because you have very little faith; that impels you to make such shameless demands. For what do you want with this request of yours unless it is to see angels carrying the corpses on high or devils dragging them to hell as the earth gapes open to receive them? Is this faith? Is this hope? Even if these things could be seen, may it never happen that they will be seen! No one would sin if the punishment and the reward were so evident to him. Do you perhaps not know that a ground for your being given rewards is that you should believe of those whom you see dead that they have a life elsewhere, and that the parts now reduced to dust will be returned to their former state?

[I]n order to satisfy you, let us imagine that the soul's goods are corporeal, and let us assign to the soul what will be the body's goods, and let us bring it about that these goods will arrive immediately, although they will really come later. [. . .]

Our body, then, will be more brilliant than the noonday sun, yet not so as to have so lovely a fragrance, can we doubt that many more of the kind will be found there? Even our very bodies, as can be discerned from the bones and powdery remains of the saints, exhale a certain odor of immortality. I said 'our' bodies, meaning the bodies of individual persons, for as do the appearance and the speech of the bodies of the blessed, so also their fragrance will delight themselves and each other. Also concerning food and drink, many things can be conjectured. But this pleases me more than all the rest (and let it be said with your goodwill): that the body and blood of our Lord and King, Jesus Christ, will be ministered to us, even from his very hands, in that most honorable, celebrated, and in truth Godly banquet. This food and drink will be of such sweetness that I might almost say the sense of taste will conquer the other senses. We shall never be satiated with this nourishment; it will not permit hunger and thirst to return, but will leave a continuous sweetness in our mouths – not only a sweetness in our mouths but also its power and suavity in all our parts. And this suavity will be so intimately diffused through all the body, even to the marrow of our bones, that even if all other things were lacking, yet you could be satisfied with this. How much pleasure there is, each time that we are restored and refreshed by shade or breeze during the hottest summer, or by a fire when we have been pinched and nipped by snow and wind! To my way of thinking this is the most gratifying of all the kinds of pleasure. With the others, individual parts of the body are given pleasure as the palate by food, the nostrils by the rose and the violet; but with this kind, the whole body is partner to the pleasure. It is a kind of joy, also, that is felt by not one but many senses; let it be touched upon only most briefly here because it relates to formerly mentioned matters, like your banquets, dances, and games, Maffeo Vegio; in the state of eternal felicity that kind of pleasure will be much richer and more plentiful. [. . .]

We should not, therefore, fear to renounce the affairs of man. Rather, we must take good hope: nothing of us will perish; all things will be restored that we have entrusted to God here, and be restored a hundred for one, of the same kind or of another, and yet always better and more sanctified, whatever its kind, as I have said. So that whatever honor, praise, fame, delight, gaiety, or pleasure attract us, from which our spiritual health might in any way take harm, let us then promptly turn the eyes of our mind to the future reward, and let us always remember (it delights me to repeat these words, and the delight is a holy one) – let us always remember, I say, that for each thing we renounce, we shall be repaid a hundred times and more. I do not yet say what I think: every time that we are attracted by something delightful, we shall be all the more strongly drawn toward the hope of heavenly things, and we shall marvel, sometimes at the power and wisdom of God in these present things, sometimes at his loving kindness toward us, who promises us things a thousand times more excellent than these things that it hardly seems possible to exceed, and invites us through these present goods to partake of the future ones. [. . .]

NOTES

1   Lucius Caecilius Firmianus Lactantius made a defence of Christianity against pagan philosophy in his *De opificio Dei* (*On the Handiwork of God*) and the *Divine Institutes*. Augustine, Bishop of Hippo (354–430) juxtaposed pagan and Christian Rome, together with their accompanying ethical values, in his *De civitate Dei* (*On the City of God*).

2   Catone Sacco of Padua, an orator whose name recalls a famous Roman Stoic, Cato.

3   Plato, *Phaedrus* 250D.

4   Aristotle, *Nicomachean Ethics* II.7; VI.13.1–8.

5   Scylla was a six-headed sea monster and Charybdis an adjacent whirlpool which caused difficulties for seafarers.

6   Cicero, *Verrine Orations*, I.5.

7   Quintilian, *Institutiones oratoriae*, III.4.18.

8   Cicero, *Verrine Orations*, II.53.

9   Lucretia, the wife of the first Roman consul, was raped by Sextus Tarquinius, the son of the last king of Rome. She informed her husband and friends and then committed suicide. This led to the expulsion of the Tarquin kings.

10   Codrus was the legendary founder of Athens who died winning a battle against the Dorians; Marcus Curtius saved Rome by riding into a deep pit that appeared in the Forum in accordance with an oracle; Decius Mus sacrificed himself to ensure a Roman

victory; Regulus was rolled to death in a spiked barrel because he refused to persuade
the Romans to surrender to the Carthaginians.
11   Augustine, *De civitate Dei* (*On the City of God*), IX.23.
12   Tertullian, *De anima* (*On the Soul*) I; Jerome, *Epistles*, 118:5.
13   *Genesis* 2:8, 2:15, *Ezekiel* 31:9; *Psalms* 35:9.

16 Baldassare Castiglione *The Courtier* (1528)

Baldassare Castiglione (1478–1529) was born near Mantua and educated in
Milan where he entered the service of duke Ludovico (il Moro) Sforza. After the
overthrow of the Sforza regime he served as a diplomat for the marquis of
Mantua and the dukes of Urbino. Subsequently he was seconded to the Vatican
and died whilst he was the papal ambassador at the Hapsburg court in Spain. A
published poet in Latin and the vernacular, he probably began *The Courtier* in the
eight years between the death of duke Guidobaldo da Montefeltro in 1508 and the
temporary exile of his successor in 1516. The setting is the ducal palace at
Urbino during the time of Guidobaldo, and more specifically, the occasion of a
visit by members of the papal court in March 1507. As an invalid, Guidobaldo left
the conduct of the social gatherings at court to his duchess, Elizabetta Gonzaga,
and her companion, Emilia Pia. The treatise is in the form of a series of after-
dinner conversations. The other major participants in these extracts are Ottaviano
Fregoso, sometime Doge of Genoa; his brother, Federigo Fregoso, archbishop of
Salerno and later cardinal; Count Ludovico Pio, the brother of Emilia, a papal
captain who died in 1512; and Pietro Bembo (1470–1547), a distinguished
neoplatonist and poet, who later became a cardinal. They discuss initially how
courtiers should attempt to exert a good influence on their princes in order that
they might behave in accordance with the Aristotelian ethical code. Later, Bembo
delivers an eloquent eulogy on platonic love and the means by which the soul
attains knowledge of the good. This section bears a close resemblance to
Bembo's own *Gli Asolani* (*The Lovers of Asolo*), published in 1505.

Source: Baldassare Castiglione, *The Courtier*, trans. and intro. G. Bull, Penguin
Classics, London, 1967, pp. 288–9, 291–5, 301–2, 324–8, 333–40. Copyright ©
George Bull, 1967. Reproduced by permission of Penguin Books Ltd

(i) Reason and moral virtues

SIGNOR OTTAVIANO: 'I maintain, [. . .] that since nowadays rulers are so corrupted
by evil living, by ignorance and by false conceit, and it is so difficult to give them
an insight into the truth and lead them to virtue, and since men seek to win their
favour through lies and flattery and other wicked means, the courtier easily can
and should seek to gain the goodwill of his prince by means of the noble qualities
given to him by Count Lodovico and Federico. Through these, he should so win
over the mind of his prince that he may go to him freely whenever he wishes to
discuss any subject without hindrance. And, if he is as has been described, he will
succeed in this purpose without great effort and thus he will always be able to

reveal the true facts on any subject very promptly. Moreover, he will gradually be able to instil virtue into his mind, to teach him continence, fortitude, justice and temperance, and enable him to relish the sweet fruit which lies under the slight bitterness first tasted by one who is struggling against his vices, which are always as harmful, offensive and notorious as the virtues are beneficial, agreeable and universally praised. And he will be able to incite his prince to virtue by the example of those famous captains and other outstanding men of whom it was customary in the ancient world to make statues of bronze and marble, and sometimes of gold, and to erect them in public places, both to honour the great and to inspire others to work to achieve the same glory through worthy emulation.

'In this way, the courtier will be able to lead his prince along the stern path of virtue, adorning it, however, with shady fronds and strewing it with gay flowers to lessen the tedium of an arduous journey for one whose endurance is slight; and so now with music, now with arms and horses, at other times with verse or with conversations about love, and with all the means these gentlemen have suggested, he will be able to keep the prince continually absorbed in innocent pleasures, while also, as I have said, always accompanying these beguilements with emphasis on some virtuous habit, and in that way practising a healthy deception like a shrewd doctor who often spreads some sweet liquid on the rim of a cup when he wants a frail and sickly child to take a bitter medicine. Thus, under the cloak of pleasure, no matter what the time, or place, or pursuit, the courtier will always achieve his objective, and for this he will deserve far greater praise and reward than for any other good work he could possibly do. For there is nothing so advantageous to mankind as a good prince, and nothing so harmful as an evil one; and it follows that no matter how cruel and atrocious, no punishment can be enough for those courtiers who turn gentle and charming manners and noble qualities to evil ends, and by these means seek to ingratiate themselves with their prince in order to corrupt him and make him stray from the path of virtue into vice. For of these it can be said that they contaminate with deadly poison not a single cup used by one person but the public fountain at which everyone must drink.'

Signor Ottaviano fell silent, as if he were unwilling to add to what he had said. But then signor Gaspare remarked:
    'It does not seem to me, signor Ottaviano, that this goodness of mind and the continence and other virtues in which you wish the courtier to instruct his lord can be learned; rather, I think that the men who possess them have been given them by Nature and by God. [. . .]'
    [Ottaviano replies:] '[I]t would be too wicked and foolish to punish men for defects that proceed from Nature through no fault of our own. This would be an error on the part of the laws, which do not inflict punishment on wrong-doers for what they have done in the past (for what is done cannot be undone) but have regard for the future, so that the one who has erred may err no more, nor cause others to do so through his bad example. So we see that the laws accept that the virtues can be learned, and this is certainly true; for we are born capable

of acquiring virtues, and similarly vices, and therefore we become habituated to the one or the other through the behaviour we adopt, first of all practising the virtues or the vices, and then becoming virtuous or vicious. But the opposite is the case with qualities that are given us by Nature, which we first of all have the potentiality to practise, and then we actually practise, as in the case of the senses. For first we have the capacity to see and hear and touch and then we do see and hear and touch; although many of these faculties too are enhanced by education. For this reason, good masters not only teach children their letters but also polite manners and correct bearing in eating, drinking, speaking and walking.

'Therefore, as with other arts and skills so also with the virtues, it is necessary to have a master who by his teaching and precepts stirs and awakens the moral virtues whose seed is enclosed and buried in our souls and who, like a good farmer, cultivates and clears the way for them by removing the thorns and tares of our appetites which often so darken and choke our minds as not to let them flower or produce those splendid fruits which alone we should wish to see born in the human heart. Thus in this way justice and self-respect, which you say Jove sent on earth to all men, are natural in each one of us. But just as however robust it is a man's body may fail when seeking to accomplish some task, so, although the potentiality for these virtues is rooted within our souls, it often fails to develop unless helped by education. For if it is to pass to actuality and to its full realization, it cannot, as I said, rely on Nature alone but needs the assistance of skilful practice and reason to purify and enlighten the soul by removing from it the dark veil of ignorance, which is the cause of most human errors, since if good and evil were easily recognized and understood everyone would always choose good and eschew evil. Thus virtue may be defined more or less as prudence and the knowledge of how to choose what is good, and vice as a kind of imprudence and ignorance, which leads us into making false judgements. This is because men never choose evil deliberately but are deceived by a certain semblance of good.'

Then signor Gaspare replied: 'Yet there are many who fully understand that they are doing evil, and still do it; and this is because, like thieves and murderers, they are more conscious of the pleasures of the moment than of the punishment they fear in the future.'

Signor Ottaviano remarked: 'True pleasure is always good, and true suffering always evil; therefore these men deceive themselves when they take false pleasures for true and true suffering for false. And so their false pleasures often earn them genuine pain. It follows that the art that teaches us to distinguish the true from the false can certainly be learned; and the virtue which enables us to choose what is genuinely good and not what wrongly appears to be so may be called true knowledge, which is more advantageous in life than any other kind, because it rids us of the ignorance which, as I said, is the cause of all the evils there are.'

At this, Pietro Bembo said: 'I do not understand, signor Ottaviano, why signor Gaspare should have to concede that all evils spring from ignorance and that there are few who realize what they are doing when they sin and do not at all deceive themselves regarding true pleasure or suffering. It is certain that even men who are incontinent form their judgement reasonably and logically, and are fully aware of the evil and sinful nature of what they desire. So they use their reason to oppose and resist their desires, and this causes the battle of pleasure and pain against judgement. Then eventually the desires prove too strong for reason, which abandons the struggle, like a ship which for a time resists the storm but finally, battered by the overwhelming fury of the winds, with anchor and rigging smashed, lets herself be driven by the tempest, unresponsive either to helm or compass. So the incontinent commit their follies with a certain hesitant remorse, as if despite themselves. And this they would not do if they did not know that what they were doing was evil; on the contrary, without any resistance from reason they would abandon themselves utterly to their desires, and in this case would not be incontinent but simply intemperate. And this is far worse, since reason plays a part in incontinence, which is therefore a less serious vice; just as continence is an imperfect virtue, since it is influenced by the emotions. In consequence, it seems to me that one cannot ascribe the follies of the incontinent to ignorance or say that they are merely deceiving themselves without sinning, when they know full well what they are doing.'[1]

'Well,' answered signor Ottaviano, 'your argument sounds very fine. Nevertheless, I don't think that it is really valid. For although the incontinent sin in that hesitant manner, and their reason does struggle with their desires, and they realize what evil is, yet they lack full knowledge and do not understand evil as well as they need to. Possessing only a vague notion rather than any certain knowledge of evil, they allow their reason to be overcome by emotion. But if they enjoyed true knowledge there is no doubt that they would not fall into error. For reason is always overcome by desire because of ignorance, and true knowledge can never be defeated by the emotions, which originate in the body rather than the soul. And if the emotions are properly governed and controlled by reason, then they become virtuous, and if otherwise, then vicious. However, reason is so potent that it always makes the senses obey it, insinuating itself by marvellous ways and means, provided what it ought to possess is not seized by ignorance. In this manner, though a man's faculties, nerves and bones do not possess reason, when the mind begins to stir within us it is as if thought were shaking the bridle and spurring our faculties on, so that all the parts of the body prepare themselves: the feet to run, the hands to grasp or to do what the mind suggests. This is shown by what often happens when someone unknowingly eats food that tastes delicious but is really foul and disgusting; for when he finds out what it was, his mind is revolted and dismayed, and then the body responds so quickly to his judgement that he has to vomit.'

Signor Ottaviano was going on to say more, but he was then interrupted by the Magnifico Giuliano who remarked:
'If I have heard aright, you said that continence is not a perfect virtue because it is influenced by the emotions. Yet it seems to me that when there is conflict in our minds between reason and desire, the virtue which fights and

gives the victory to reason ought to be considered more perfect than that which conquers when no lust or emotion opposes it. For in the latter case the person concerned does not refrain from evil out of virtue but because he has no wish to do it.'

Then signor Ottaviano said: 'Who would you think the more admirable: a commander who runs the risk of open confrontation with the enemy, and yet conquers him, or one who uses his skill and knowledge to sap the enemy's strength and render him powerless and so conquers without risk or bloodshed?'

The Magnifico replied: 'The one who conquers by less dangerous means is certainly the more praiseworthy, provided that his inevitable victory is not brought about by the enemy's ineptitude.'

'You have judged aright,' said signor Ottaviano. 'And so I tell you that continence can be compared to a commander who fights manfully and who, when the enemy is strong and powerful, conquers all the same, though not without great difficulty and risk. But unruffled temperance is like the commander who conquers and rules without opposition; and when it has not only subdued but totally extinguished the fires of lust in the mind which possesses it, like a good ruler in time of civil war, temperance destroys all seditious enemies within and hands over to reason the sceptre of absolute power. Thus this virtue does no violence to the soul, but gently infuses it with a powerful persuasion that turns it to honest ways, renders it calm and full of repose, in all things even and well-tempered, and informed in all respects with a certain harmony that adorns it with serene and unshakeable tranquillity; and so in all things it is ready to respond completely to reason and to follow wherever reason may lead with the utmost docility, like a young lamb that runs and walks alongside its mother, stops when she does, and moves only in response to her. This virtue of temperance, therefore, is wholly perfect and especially appropriate for men who rule, for it gives rise to many other virtues.' [. . .]

Said signor Gaspare: 'I think that if you lack any of the accomplishments attributed to the courtier, they are music and dancing and such things of little importance rather than those which concern the education of the ruler and this aspect of courtiership.'

To this, signor Ottaviano replied: 'They are none of them of little importance, all those things that help the courtier gain the favour of his prince, which he must do, as we have said, before he may venture to teach him the virtue of true knowledge; and this I think I have demonstrated can be learned and is as beneficial as ignorance (from which all faults stem, and especially the sin of false conceit) is harmful. However, I am sure I have now said enough, and perhaps more than I promised.'

Then the Duchess replied: 'The more you exceed your promise, so much the more we shall be indebted to you for your courtesy. So I hope you will be happy to say what you think in answer to signor Gaspare's question, and, please, to tell us also everything you would teach your prince if he needed instruction and assuming you had completely won his favour and could therefore speak your mind freely.'

Signor Ottaviano smiled and said: 'If I had the favour of some of the rulers I know, and were to speak my mind freely, I imagine I would soon lose it again. However, since you wish me to answer this question of signor Gaspare's as well, in my opinion princes should lead both kinds of life, though especially the contemplative since for them there are two aspects to this. The first entails clear insight and judgement; the other, issuing lawful commands in the proper manner, concerning things that are reasonable and within their authority, and having these carried out at appropriate times and places by those who have cause to obey. Of this Duke Federico was speaking when he said that the man who knows how to command is always obeyed. Giving commands, then, is the chief duty of a ruler, who very often, however, also has to be present and see them being carried out himself, and in certain circumstances sometimes has to perform himself. All these are concerned with action; but the active life should be designed to lead to the contemplative life, just as war is meant to lead to peace, and toil to rest. [. . .]

(ii) Love, beauty and the courtier

Thereupon, Pietro Bembo remained quiet for a little while. Then, having composed himself for a moment as if to speak of important things, he began as follows:

'Gentlemen, to show that old men can love not only blamelessly but sometimes more happily than the young, it will be necessary for me to enter upon a little discourse in order to make it clear what love is and what is the nature of the happiness that lovers experience. So I beg you to listen attentively, because I hope to make you realize that there is no man to whom it is unbecoming to be in love, even though he should be fifteen or twenty years older than signor Morello.'

After there was some laughter at this, Pietro Bembo continued:

'I say, therefore, that as defined by the philosophers of the ancient world Love is simply a certain longing to possess beauty; and since this longing can only be for things that are known already, knowledge must always of necessity precede desire, which by its nature wishes for what is good, but of itself is blind and so cannot perceive what is good. So Nature has ruled that every appetitive faculty, or desire, be accompanied by a cognitive faculty or power of understanding. Now in the human soul there are three faculties by which we understand or perceive things: namely, the senses, rational thought and intellect. Thus the senses desire things through sensual appetite or the kind of appetite which we share with the animals; reason desires things through rational choice, which is, strictly speaking, proper to man; and intellect, which links man to the angels, desires things through pure will. It follows that the sensual appetite desires only those things that are perceptible by the senses, whereas man's will finds its satisfaction in the contemplation of spiritual things that can be apprehended by intellect. And then man, who is rational by his very nature and is placed between the two extremes of brute matter and pure spirit, can choose to follow the senses or to aspire to the intellect, and so can direct his appetites or desires now in the one direction, now in the other. In either of these two ways, therefore, he can long for beauty, which is the quality possessed by all natural or artificial things that are composed in the good proportion and due measure that befit their nature.[2]

'However, I shall speak of the kind of beauty I now have in mind, which is that seen in the human body and especially the face and which prompts the ardent desire we call love; and we shall argue that this beauty is an influx of the divine goodness which, like the light of the sun, is shed over all created things but especially displays itself in all its beauty when it discovers and informs a countenance which is well proportioned and composed of a certain joyous harmony of various colours enhanced by light and shadow and by symmetry and clear definition. This goodness adorns and illumines with wonderful splendour and grace the object in which it shines, like a sunbeam striking a lovely vase of polished gold set with precious gems. And thus it attracts to itself the gaze of others, and entering through their eyes it impresses itself upon the human soul, which it stirs and delights with its charm, inflaming it with passion and desire. Thus the mind is seized by desire for the beauty which it recognizes as good, and, if it allows itself to be guided by what its senses tell it, it falls into the gravest errors and judges that the body is the chief cause of the beauty which it enshrines, and so to enjoy that beauty it must necessarily achieve with it as intimate a union as possible. But this is untrue; and anyone who thinks to enjoy that beauty by possessing the body is deceiving himself and is moved not by true knowledge, arrived at by rational choice, but by a false opinion derived from the desire of the senses. So the pleasure that follows is also necessarily false and deceptive. Consequently, all those lovers who satisfy their impure desires with the women they love meet with one of two evils: either as soon as they achieve the end they desire they experience satiety and distaste and even begin to hate what they love, as if their desire repented of its error and recognized the way it had been deceived by the false judgement of the senses, which had made it believe that evil was good; or else they are still troubled by the same avidity and desire, since they have not in fact attained the end they were seeking. Admittedly, confused by their short-sighted view of things, they imagine that they are experiencing pleasure, just as sometimes a sick man dreams that he is drinking from a clear fountain. Nevertheless, they enjoy neither rest nor satisfaction, and these are precisely what they would enjoy as the natural consequences of desiring and then possessing what is good. On the contrary, deceived by the resemblance they see, they soon experience unbridled desire once more and in the same agitation as before they again find themselves with a raging and unquenchable thirst for what they hope to possess utterly. Lovers of this kind, therefore, are always most unhappy; for either they never attain their desires, and this causes them great misery, or if they do attain them they find themselves in terrible distress, and their wretchedness is even greater. For both at the beginning and during the course of this love of theirs they never know other than anguish, torment, sorrow, exertion and distress; and so lovers, it is supposed, must always be characterized by paleness and dejection, continuous sighings and weepings, mournfulness and lamentations, silences and the desire for death.

'We see, therefore, that the senses are the chief cause of this desolation of the spirit; and they are at their full strength in youth, when they are stimulated by the urges of the flesh which sap a man's powers of reason in exact proportion to their own vigour and so easily persuade the soul to yield to desire. For since it is sunk in an earthly prison and deprived of spiritual contemplation, the soul cannot of itself clearly perceive the truth when it is carrying out its duties of governing the body. So in order to understand things properly it must appeal to the senses for its first notions. In consequence it believes whatever they tell it and respects and trusts them, especially when they are so vigorous that they almost compel it; and because the senses are deceptive they fill the soul with errors and mistaken ideas. As a result, young men are invariably absorbed by this sensual kind of love and wholly rebellious against reason, and so they make themselves unworthy of enjoying the blessings and advantages that love gives to its true devotees; and the only pleasures they experience in love are the same as those enjoyed by unreasoning animals, though the distress they suffer is far more terrible than theirs. Therefore on this premise, which I insist is the absolute truth, I argue that lovers who are more mature in age experience the contrary; for in their case the soul is no longer so weighed down by the body and their natural ardour has begun to cool, and so if they are inflamed by beauty and their desire for it is guided by rational choice, they are not deceived and they possess completely the beauty they love. Consequently its possession brings them nothing but good, since beauty is goodness and so the true love of beauty is good and holy and always benefits those in whose souls the bridle of reason restrains the iniquity of the senses; and this is something the old can do far more easily than the young.

'So it is not unreasonable to argue also that the old can love blamelessly and more happily than the young, accepting that by old we do not mean those who are senile or whose bodily organs have grown so feeble that the soul cannot perform its operations through them, but men whose intellectual powers are still in their prime. I must also add this: namely, that in my opinion although sensual love is bad at every age, yet in the young it may be excused and perhaps in some sense even permitted. For although it brings them afflictions, dangers, exertions and all the unhappiness we have mentioned, yet there are many who perform worthy acts in order to win the favour of the women whom they love, and though these acts are not directed to a good end they are good in themselves. And so from all that bitterness they extract a little sweetness, and the adversities they endure finally teach them the error of their ways. So just as I think those young people who subdue their desires and love in a rational manner are truly heroic, I excuse those who allow themselves to be overcome by the sensual love to which human weakness inclines them, provided that they then display gentleness, courtesy, worthiness and all the other qualities these gentlemen mentioned, and that when they are no longer young they abandon it completely and leave sensual desire behind them, as the lowest rung of the ladder by which we can ascend to true love. But no blame is too severe for those who when they are old still allow the fires of passion to burn in their cold hearts and make strong reason obey their feeble senses; for they deserve the endless shame of being numbered like idiots among the animals which lack reason, because the thoughts and ways of sensual love are wholly unbecoming to men of mature years.' [. . .]

Bembo was [. . .] determined to say no more, but the Duchess begged that he should do so, and therefore he continued:

'It would be too unfortunate for humanity if our soul, in which such ardent desire can so easily arise, were forced to find nourishment only in what it has in common with the animals and could not direct its desire to its nobler element. So, as this is your wish, I will not refuse to discuss this noble theme. And since I know that I am unworthy to speak of Love's sacred mysteries, I pray him so to inspire my thoughts and words that I can teach this excellent courtier of ours how to love in a manner beyond the capacity of the vulgar crowd. And because I have since boyhood dedicated my life to him, may my words now conform to this intention and redound to his credit. I maintain, then, that since in youth human nature is so inclined to the senses, while the courtier is young he may be allowed to love in a sensual manner; but if in more mature years he should be inflamed with this amorous desire, he must proceed with circumspection and take care not to deceive himself or let himself experience the distress which in young men deserves compassion rather than blame but in old men blame rather than compassion.

'Therefore when he sets eyes on some beautiful and attractive woman, with charming ways and gentle manner, and being skilled in love recognizes that his spirit responds to hers, as soon as he notices that his eyes fasten on her image and carry it to his heart and his soul begins to take pleasure in contemplating her and feels an influx that gradually arouses and warms it, and those vivacious spirits shining from her eyes constantly add fresh fuel to the fire, then he should at the very beginning procure a swift remedy and alert his reason in order to defend with its help the fortress of his heart, and so close the passes to the senses and to desire that they cannot enter either by force or deception. If the flame is extinguished, so is the danger. But if it perseveres or grows, then in the knowledge that he has been captured the courtier should determine to eschew all the ugliness of vulgar passion and guided by reason set forth on the path of divine love. Then first he must reflect that the body in which beauty shines is not the source from which it springs, and on the contrary that beauty, being incorporeal and, as we have said, a ray of the supernatural, loses much of its nobility when fused with base and corruptible matter: for the more perfect it is, the less matter it contains, and it is most perfect when completely separated from matter. He must also reflect that just as a man cannot hear with his palate or smell with his ears, beauty can in no way be enjoyed nor can the desire it arouses in our souls be satisfied through the sense of touch but solely through what has beauty for its true object, namely, the faculty of sight. So he should ignore the blind judgement of these senses and enjoy with his eyes the radiance, the grace, the loving ardour, the smiles, the mannerisms and all the other agreeable adornments of the woman he loves. Similarly, let him use his hearing to enjoy the sweetness of her voice, the modulation of her words and, if she is a musician, the music she plays.

In this way, through the channels of these two faculties, which have little to do with corporeal things and are servants of reason, he will nourish his soul on the most delightful food and will not allow desire for the body to arouse in him any appetite that is at all impure. Next, with the greatest reverence the lover should honour, please and obey his lady, cherish her even more than himself, put her convenience and pleasure before his own, and love the beauty of her soul no less than that of her body. He should, therefore, be at pains to keep her from going astray and by his wise precepts and admonishments always seek to make her modest, temperate and truly chaste; and he must ensure that her thoughts are always pure and unsullied by any trace of evil. And thus, by sowing virtue in the garden of her lovely soul, he will gather the fruits of faultless behaviour and experience exquisite pleasure from their taste. And this will be the true engendering and expression of beauty in beauty, which some say is the purpose of love. In this manner, our courtier will be most pleasing to his lady, and she will always be submissive, charming and affable and as anxious to please him as she is to be loved by him; and the desires of both will be very pure and harmonious, and consequently they will be perfectly happy.'

Then signor Morello remarked: 'In reality, this engendering of beauty in beauty must mean the begetting of a beautiful child in a beautiful woman; and it would seem to me a far clearer sign that she loved her lover if she pleased him in this than if she treated him merely with the affability you mention.'

Bembo laughed and replied: 'You mustn't go beyond the bounds, signor Morello; nor indeed does a woman grant just a token of affection when she gives her lover her beauty, which is precious to her, and along the paths into her soul, namely, sight and hearing, sends the glances of her eyes, the image of her face, her voice and her words, which penetrate her lover's heart and convey the proof of her love.'

Signor Morello then said: 'Glances and words can be false witnesses, and often are. So anyone who has no better pledge of love is in my opinion most uncertain; and truly I was expecting you to make this lady of yours a little more courteous and generous towards the courtier than the Magnifico made his. However, I think both of you are acting in the same way as those judges who pronounce sentence against their own people in order to seem wise.'

'I am perfectly willing,' Bembo continued, 'for this lady to be far more courteous to my elderly courtier than signor Magnifico's lady is to the young courtier. And this is with good reason, for my courtier will wish only for seemly things, all of which she may therefore concede to him quite innocently. But the Magnifico's lady, who is not so certain of the young courtier's modesty, should concede him only what is seemly and deny him what is not. Therefore my courtier, who obtains all he asks for, is happier than the other, who is granted some of his requests but refused others. And to help you understand even better that rational love is happier than sensual love, I say that sometimes the same things should be denied in sensual love and granted in rational love, because in the former context they are unseemly, and in the latter, seemly. Thus to please her gracious lover, besides granting him pleasant smiles, intimate and secret conversations, and the liberty to joke and jest and touch hands, the lady may very reasonably and innocently go so far as to grant a kiss, which in sensual love, according to the Magnifico's rules, is not permitted. For as a kiss is a union of body and soul, there is a risk that the sensual lover may incline more to the body than the soul; but the rational lover knows that although the mouth is part of the body nevertheless it provides a channel for words, which are the interpreters of the soul, and for the human breath or spirit. Consequently, the rational lover delights when he joins his mouth to that of the lady he loves in a kiss, not in order to arouse in himself any unseemly desire but because he feels that this bond opens the way for their souls which, attracted by their mutual desire, each pour themselves into the other's body in turn and so mingle that each of them possesses two souls, and it is as if a single spirit composed of the two governs their two bodies. So the kiss may be called a spiritual rather than physical union because it exerts such power over the soul that it draws it to itself and separates it from the body. For this reason, all chaste lovers desire a kiss as a union of souls; and thus when inspired to love Plato[3] said that in kissing the soul comes to the lips in order to leave the body. And because the separation of the soul from things that are perceptible to the senses and its complete union with spiritual things can be signified by the kiss, in his inspired book of the *Song of Songs* Solomon says: 'let him kiss me with the kiss of his mouth', in order to express the wish that his soul be transported by divine love to the contemplation of celestial beauty and by its intimate union with this beauty might forsake the body [*Song of Songs*, 1].

All were listening very attentively to what Bembo was saying; and then, after a moment's pause, he added:

'Since you have made me begin to teach the courtier who is no longer young about love that is truly happy, I want to lead him a little further still. For to stop at this point is very dangerous, because, as we have said several times already, the soul is strongly inclined towards the senses; and although reason may choose well in its operation and recognize that beauty does not arise from the body, and therefore act as a check to impure desires, yet the constant contemplation of physical beauty often perverts true judgement. And even if no other evil resulted from this, absence from the person one loves causes much suffering. This is because when beauty is physically present, its influx into the lover's soul brings him intense pleasure, and by warming his heart it arouses and melts certain hidden and congealed powers which the warmth of love nourishes and causes to flow and well up round his heart and send through his eyes those spirits or most subtle vapours, composed of the purest and brightest part of the blood, to receive the image of her beauty and embellish it with a thousand varied adornments. In consequence, the soul is filled with wonder and delight; it is frightened and yet it rejoices; as if dazed, it experiences along with its pleasure the fear and reverence invariably inspired by sacred things, and it believes it has entered into its Paradise.

'Therefore the lover who is intent only on physical beauty loses all this good and happiness as soon as the woman he loves by her absence leaves his eyes deprived of their splendour and, consequently, his soul widowed of its good. For, since her beauty is far away, there is no influx of affection to warm his heart as it did when she was there, and so the openings of his body become arid and dry; yet the memory of her beauty still stirs the powers of his soul a little, so that they seek to pour those spirits forth. Although their paths are blocked and there is no exit for them, they still strive to depart, and thus tormented and enclosed they begin to prick the soul and cause it to suffer bitterly, as children do when the teeth begin to grow through their tender gums. This causes the tears, the sighs, the anguish and the torments of lovers, because the soul is in constant pain and turmoil and almost raging in fury until its cherished beauty appears once more; and then suddenly it is calmed and breathes again, and wholly absorbed it draws strength from the delicious food before it and wishes never to part from such a ravishing vision. Therefore, to escape the torment caused by absence and to enjoy beauty without suffering, with the help of reason the courtier should turn his desire completely away from the body to beauty alone. He should contemplate beauty as far as he is able in its own simplicity and purity, create it in his imagination as an abstraction distinct from any material form, and thus make it lovely and dear to his soul, and enjoy it there always, day and night and in every time and place, without fear of ever losing it; and he will always remember that the body is something altogether distinct from beauty, whose perfection it diminishes rather than enhances. In this way the courtier of ours who is no longer young will put himself out of reach of the anguish and distress invariably experienced by the young in the form of jealousy, suspicion, disdain, anger, despair and a certain tempestuous fury that occasionally leads them so much astray that some not only beat the women they love but take their own lives. He will do no injury to the husband, father, brothers or family of the lady he loves; he will cause her no shame; he will not be forced sometimes to drag his eyes away and curb his tongue for fear of revealing his desires to others; or to endure suffering when they part or during her absence. For he will always carry the treasure that is so precious to him safe in his heart; and by the power of his imagination he will also make her beauty far more lovely than it is in reality.

'However, among all these blessings the lover will find one that is far greater still, if he will determine to make use of this love as a step by which to climb to another that is far more sublime; and this will be possible if he continually reflects how narrowly he is confined by always limiting himself to the contemplation of a single body. And so in order to escape from this confinement, he will gradually add so many adornments to his idea of beauty that, by uniting all possible forms of beauty in his mind, he will form a universal concept and so reduce all the many varieties to the unity of that single beauty which sheds itself over human nature as a whole. And thus he will come to contemplate not the particular beauty of a single woman but the universal beauty which adorns all human bodies: and then, dazzled by this greater light, he will not concern himself with the lesser; burning with a more perfect flame, he will feel little esteem for what he formerly prized so greatly. Now this stage of love, although so noble that few attain it, still cannot be called perfect. For the human imagination is a corporeal faculty and acquires knowledge only through the data supplied to it by the senses, and so it is not wholly purged of the darkness of material things. Thus although it may consider this universal beauty in the abstract and simply in itself, yet it perceives it not at all clearly nor within a certain ambiguity because of the affinities that the images it forms have with the body itself; and so those who reach this stage of love are like fledglings which on their feeble wings can lift themselves a little in flight but dare not stray far from the nest or trust themselves to the winds and the open sky.

'Therefore when our courtier has arrived at this stage, even though he can be called most happy in comparison with those lovers who are still sunk in the miseries of sensual love, I wish him not to be satisfied but to move boldly onwards along the sublime path of love and follow his guide towards the goal of true happiness. So instead of directing his thoughts to the outward world, as those must do who wish to consider bodily beauty, let him turn within himself to contemplate what he sees with the eyes of the mind, which begin to be penetrating and clear-sighted once those of the body have lost the flower of their delight; and in this manner, having shed all evil, purged by the study of true philosophy, directed towards the life of the spirit, and practised in the things of the intellect, the soul turns to contemplate its own substance, and as if awakened from deepest sleep it opens the eyes which all men possess but few use and perceives in itself a ray of that light which is the true image of the angelic beauty that has been transmitted to it, and of which in turn it transmits a faint impression to the body. Thus, when it has become blind to earthly things, the soul opens its eyes wide to those of heaven; and sometimes when the faculties of the body are totally absorbed by assiduous contemplation, or bound to sleep, no longer hindered by their influence the soul tastes a certain hidden savour of the true angelic beauty, and ravished by the loveliness of that light it begins to burn and to pursue the beauty it sees so avidly that it seems almost drunk and beside itself in its desire to unite with it. For the soul then believes that it has discovered the traces of God, in the contemplation of which it seeks its final repose and bliss. And so, consumed in this most joyous flame, it ascends to its noblest part, which is the intellect; and there, no more overshadowed by the dark night of earthly things, it glimpses the divine beauty itself. Even so, it does not yet enjoy this perfectly, since it contemplates it only in its own particular intellect, which cannot comprehend universal beauty in all its immensity. And so, not even satisfied with bestowing this blessing, love gives the soul greater happiness still. For just as from the particular beauty of a single body it guides the soul to the universal beauty of all bodies, so, in the last stage of perfection, it guides the soul from the particular intellect to the universal intellect. And from there, aflame with the sacred fire of true divine love, the soul flies to unite itself with the angelic nature, and it not only abandons the senses but no longer has need of reason itself. For, transformed into an angel, it understands all intelligible things and without any veil or cloud it gazes on the wide sea of pure divine beauty, which it receives into itself to enjoy the supreme happiness the senses cannot comprehend.[4] [. . .]

NOTES

1   Cf. Aristotle, *Nicomachean Ethics*, VII.3.3–14.
2   Pietro Bembo, *Gli Asolani* (*The Lovers of Asolo*), II.13.
3   This section paraphrases Plato's *Symposium*.
4   Pietro Bembo, *Gli Asolani* (*The Lovers of Asolo*), III.6, III.12.

17   Desiderius Erasmus *The Praise of Folly* (1511)

(i) *The Praise of Folie* was first translated into English by Sir Thomas Chaloner (1520–65) in 1549. He was a man of letters, soldier and diplomat who served every Tudor monarch from Henry VIII to Elizabeth I. This first edition was printed by Thomas Berthelet, the king's printer. Chaloner's Introduction provides evidence of the reception of the works of Erasmus in England and of one man's approach to the challenge of translating a famous example of humanist wit. It was entirely in keeping with the Erasmian approach to translation that Chaloner should make the overall sense rather than the literal meaning the main aim of his rendition.

(ii) Erasmus wrote *The Praise of Folly* or *Moriae Encomium* (a pun on the surname of Sir Thomas More), in 1510 while he was recovering from illness in More's house in London. It was printed in Paris in the following year; the many later editions, some revised by Erasmus himself, reflected its wide popularity. Its publication coincided with a climate of opinion which was critical of the authority of the Catholic Church, the work itself combining a humanist programme of religious and educational reform. The figure of Lady Folly preaching a sermon in praise of herself was the means by which Erasmus held up many religious and scholarly traditions to ridicule. The text contains a large number of Erasmus's *Adages*. His compilation of such classical proverbial sayings and quotations was extremely popular throughout Europe. Details of Erasmus' life are given in the headnote to Text 5.

Source: (i) Desiderius Erasmus, *The Praise of Folie*, translated into English by Sir Thomas Chaloner, ed. C. H. Miller, Oxford University Press, 1965, pp. 3–6. With grateful acknowledgment to The Council of the Early English Text Society. (ii) Desiderius Erasmus, *The Praise of Folly*, ed. and trans. C. H. Miller, Yale UP, New Haven and London, 1979, pp. 17–23, 87–93, 136–8

(i) Sir Thomas Chaloner's Introduction to his English translation

TO THE READER

A folie it maie be thought in me to haue spent tyme in englisshyng of this boke, entitled *the praise of Folie*, wheras the name it selfe semeth to set foorth no wisedome, or matter of grauitee [seriousness]: vnlesse perhappes **Erasmus**, the autour therof, delited to mocke men, in callyng it one thyng, and meanyng an other. To this I answeare, that Folie in all poinctes is not (as I take it) so strange vnto vs, but that hir [her] name maie well be abidden [persisting], aslong as will we or

4 Hans Holbein the Younger, drawing of a teacher chastising a pupil, from *Laus stultitiae (The Praise of Folly)* by Erasmus, Öffentliche Kunstsammlung, Kupferstichkabinett, Basel. Photo: Martin Bühler.

nill we [whether we like it or not], she will be sure to beare a stroke in most of our dooynges: how so euer a certaine secte of faulte finders condemne all thinges, that fully square not with theyr owne rules, yea twyse [twice] blinde in this, that amonges the commen errours and infyrmitees of mortall men, they will beare nothyng with their bretherne, as who saieth, they were demigoddes, and not more than one or two waies [ways] lynked in Folies bandes [Folly's companies].

I haue therfore bestowed an englisshe liuerey [livery] vpon this latine boke, as well as I coulde: not so muche to please all men, as rather to shew how euin this Foly toucheth all men. Wherin I woulde not be noted as a carper of any man particulerly (for what more vnsittyng than in bokes or plaies to touche men by name?) nor that herein I seke to haue any kinde of men noted for theyr trade of lyfe, otherwyse than the abuse thereof deserueth, but onely my meanyng is suche, as **Erasmus** in this booke shall expresse for vs bothe. He of his modestee is content to set no great face vpon it, nor woulde be noted to haue spent great labour in makyng therof: sauyng as in pastime to haue essaied, whether ought might be spoken in praise of Folie, wheras wysedome the vertue can praise it selfe.

And therfore he imagineth, that Folie shoulde be a Goddesse, who before all kyndes of men assembled as to a sermon, shoulde declare how many benefites they receiue at hir handes: and how without hir accesse, nothyng in this life is delectable, commodious, or tollerable vnto vs, no not our owne life. This braue bost myght well come from Folie: and seyng that wyser men are wont to take in woorth what is saied by a foole, therfore is **Erasmus** also the bolder to put that tale in Folies mouth, whiche vnder an other person he woulde haue made more curtesie [courtesy] to haue spoken. So what excuse he maketh, the same I requyre maie serue for me: that thynges spoken foolisshely, by Folie, maie be euin so taken, and not wrested to any bitter sence or ernest applicacion. For surely if the crabbedst [most fractious] men that be, are wont to take a fooles woordes as in sporte, for feare lest others myght recken they would not wynche [relent] without a galled [cowed] backe: Than how muche more is a domme [dumb] booke written generally to be borne withall? namely where the title pretendeth no grauitee, but rather a toye to stirre laughter, without offence in the boke, if the reader bringe none offence with hym. For than truely he maie chaunce to see his owne image more liuely described than in any peincted table. But if that waies he mislike the deformitee of his countrefaicte, let hym muche more mislyke to be suche one in deede.

And seeyng the vices of our daies are suche as can not enough be spoken against, what knowe we, if **Erasmus** in this booke thought good betweene game and ernest [jest and seriousness] to rebuke the same? And chiefely to persuade (if it myght be) a certaine contentacion in euerie man, to holde hym agreed with suche lotte and state of liuyng [living], as ariseth to hym. For whiche purpose was I also soonest moued to englisshe it, to the end that meane men of baser wittes and condicion, myght haue a maner coumfort and satisfaction in theim selfes. In as muche as the hiegh god, who made vs all of one earth, hath natheles chosen some to rule, and more to serue. Wherat so muche lacketh that the inferiours shoulde repine, as rather, set in the meaner degree, they should thanke god the more: without aspyryng to thinges aboue theyr reache, whiche should draw more trouble and perilles, than if they absteigned therfro, and gaue place to others, who had greater giftes of God, and were called by auctoritee of theyr prince or countrey to welde [wield] the same. For surely, if a man of the poorer sorte, whose eies is dased in beholdyng the fayre glosse of wealth and felicitee, whiche the state of a great lorde or counsailour in a commen wealth dooeth outwardly represent, did inwardly marke the trauailes, cares, and anxietees, whiche suche one is driuen to susteigne [sustain] (doyng as he ought to dooe) in seruyng his maister and countrey, wherby he is nothyng lesse than his owne man: now I beleue he would not muche enuie his state, nor chose to chaunge condicions of life with hym. But this were euin the chiefest poincte of wysedome, though fooles (as Folie calleth theim) that is to saie vulgare folke, are those that, vnwittyng of their treasure, dooe in deede enioie this sweete quietnesse, and greatest good tourne.

And waiyng [weighing] this foolishe boke, after this sence, I wene a profite also maie arise therethrough to the readers, besides the delectacion, beyng so pithilie pleasaunt as it is. For as **Erasmus** in all his woorkes sauoureth of a liuelie quicknesse, and spareth not sometyme in graue mattiers to sprincle his style, where he maie snache oportunitee with meerie conceited sentences: so in this booke, treatyng of suche a **Theme**, and vnder suche a person, he openeth all his bowget: So farfoorth as by the iudgement of many learned men, he neuer shewed more arte, nor witte, in any the grauest boke he wrote, than in this his praise of Folie. Whiche the reader hauyng any considerance, shall soone espie, how in euery mattier, yea almost euery clause, is hidden besides the myrth, some deaper sence and purpose.

In deede I againe saie not, but he maketh Folie to speake at randon, without sparyng of any estate of men: but yet indifferent eares will heare their faultes paciently, aslong as they maie chose, whether they will take the faulte vppon theim or not: or be aknowne to be those, whom Folie noteth. But euin this frankenesse of Folies taunting I haue presumed in some poinctes to ytche [to change slightly] to the beste: namely in two or thre places, whiche the learned reader comparyng with the latine boke, maie easely perceiue, how either I haue slipped ouer a line or two, or eased the sowre [sour] sence of the latine with some manerlier englishe worde. Wherin I chose rather to be counted a skante true interpretour, than otherwise to touche thynges, whiche were better vnsaied, aslong as it hurted not the grace of the boke though they were omitted. Likewise in all my translacion I haue not peined my selfe to render worde for woorde, nor prouerbe for prouerbe, wherof many be greke, such as haue no grace in our tounge: but rather markyng the sence, I applied it to the phrase of our englishe. And where the prouerbes woulde take no englishe, I aduentured to put englisshe prouerbes of like waight in their places, Whiche maie be thought by some cunnyng translatours a deadly sinne. But I sticke not for all that, in this foolishe booke to vse mine owne foolishe caste. And if it be misliked, I passe not greatly though I lose the praise of my Folie.

(ii) Extracts from *The Praise of Folly*. First extract

Now, lest my claim to divinity should seem unsubstantiated, listen carefully and I will show you how many benefits I bestow on gods and men alike and how widely my divine power extends. Consider, if that author (whoever he was) was not far from the mark when he wrote that the essence of divinity is to give aid to mortals, and if the persons who taught mortals how to produce wine or grain or some other commodity have been justly elevated to the senate of the gods, why should I not rightly be considered and called the very *alpha* [the best] of all the gods, since I alone bestow all things on all men?

First, what can be sweeter or more precious than life itself? But to whom should you attribute the origin of life if not to me? For it is not the spear of *stern-fathered* Pallas[1] or the aegis of *cloud-gathering* Zeus[2] which begets and propagates the human race. No, Jupiter himself, father of the gods and king over men, whose mere nod shakes all Olympus, even he must put aside that three-forked light-ning bolt of his; he must dispense with that fierce Titanic countenance (with which he can, at his pleasure, terrify all the gods); clearly, he must change his role like an actor and play a humble part whenever he wants to do what in fact he is forever doing – that is, *make a baby.*[3] To be sure, the Stoics rank themselves only a little lower than the gods. But give me a man who is a Stoic three or four times over, a Stoic to the nth degree, and he too, though he may not have to shave off his beard – the sign of wisdom (though goats also have one) – he certainly will have to swallow his pride; he will have to smooth out his frowns, put aside his iron clad principles, and indulge just a bit in childish and fantastic trifles. In short, I am the one that wise man must come to – I repeat, he must come to me – if he ever wants to be a father.

But let me take you into my confidence even more candidly, as is my fashion. I ask you, is it the head, or the face, or the chest, or the hand, or the ear – all considered respectable parts of the body – is it any of these which generates gods and men? No, I think not. Rather, the human race is propagated by the part which is so foolish and funny that it cannot even be mentioned without a snicker. That is the sacred fount from which all things draw life, not the Pythagorean tetrad.[4] Come now, would any man ever submit to the halter of matrimony if he followed the usual method of these wisemen and first considered the drawbacks of that state of life? Or what woman would ever yield to a man's advances if she either knew about or at least called to mind the perilous labor of childbirth, the trials and tribulations of raising children? So, if you owe your life to matrimony, and you owe matrimony to my handmaid *Anoia* [Incomprehension], you can easily see how much you owe to me. Then again, what woman who has once had this experience would ever consent to go through it again if it were not for the divine influence of *Lethe* [Forgetfulness]? Even Venus herself (in spite of what Lucretius says)[5] would never deny that her power is crippled and useless without the infusion of our divine influence. Thus, this game of ours, giddy and ridiculous as it is, is the source of supercilious philosophers (whose place has now been taken by so-called monks), and kings in their scarlet robes, and pious priests, and pope-holy pontiffs and, finally, even that assembly of poetic gods, so numerous that Olympus, large as it is, can hardly accommodate the crowd.

But it would be little enough for me to assert my role as the fountain and nursery of life, if I did not also show that all the benefits of life depend completely on my good offices. After all, what is this life itself – can you even call it life if you take away pleasure? . . . Your applause has answered for you. I was certain that none of you is so wise, or rather foolish – no, I mean wise – as to be of that opinion. In fact, even these Stoics do not scorn pleasure, however diligently they pretend to – ripping it to shreds in their public pronouncements for the very good reason that when they have driven others away from it they can enjoy it all the better by themselves. But for god's sake, I wish they would tell me, is there any part of life that is not sad, cheerless, dull, insipid, and wearisome unless you season it with pleasure, that is, with the spice of folly? To this fact Sophocles, a poet beyond all praise, offered ample testimony when he paid us that most elegant compliment: '*Never to think, that is the good life.*'[6] Nevertheless, let us examine (if you please) everything point by point.

First of all, who can deny that everyone finds the first age of man most charming and delightful? What is it about babies that makes us hug and kiss and coddle them, so that even an enemy would assist them at that age? Nothing but the allurement of folly, which Nature in her wisdom purposely provided to newborn babes so that by giving a recompense (as it were) of pleasure they might lighten the burden of rearing them and wheedle their way into the good graces of their guardians. Then the next age, adolescence, how charming everyone finds it, how generously they take care of teenagers, how eagerly they further their careers, how solicitously they extend a helping hand! Now I ask you, where do adolescents get this youthful charm? Where but from me? By my favor they know very little and hence are very easy to get along with: naiveté is not snappish. Before long, when they have grown up a bit and through experience and study have begun to think more maturely, call me a downright liar if the fine flower of their beauty does not suddenly wilt. Their energy slackens, their gracefulness stiffens, their vigor withers away. The further they are withdrawn from me, the less they are alive, until they finally reach τὸ χαλεπὸν γῆρας, that is, burdensome old age, hateful not only to others but even to itself. Clearly, no mortal could tolerate the pains of age if I did not take pity on them and offer my help: just as the gods of mythology help the dying by some metamorphosis, so I too bring those who already have one foot in the grave, back once more as close as possible to childhood. Thus, the widespread notion of *second childhood* is quite accurate. Now, if someone wants to know how I change them, I will not withhold that either: I bring them to the spring of our handmaid Lethe, which has its origin in the Isles of the Blest (the Lethe in the underworld is only a rivulet flowing from the main spring), so that they may drink large drafts of oblivion and thus by gradually dissipating their cares grow young once again.

But then they have lost their grip on reality, someone may say; their minds are wandering. True enough, but that's what it means to return to childhood. Isn't childhood distinguished by a weak grasp of reality and a wandering mind? Isn't the principal charm of childhood the fact that it knows nothing? Aren't we put off by the child who has the knowledge of a grown man? Don't we avoid such precocious prodigies like the plague? That we do so is confirmed by the widespread proverb: a child wise beyond his years is a pest. On the other hand, who would want any contact or association with an old man who added to his wealth of experience a corresponding vigor of mind and sharpness of judgment?

And so through my favor an old man loses contact with reality. But at the same time he is relieved of all those wretched worries that torment the wise man. He is also an entertaining drinking companion. He never feels that 'taedium vitae' [boredom with life] which even younger, stronger men can hardly bear. Sometimes, like the old man in Plautus, he regresses to those three letters (a m o) – then, if he had any wisdom at all, he would be miserable beyond belief. But now, through my favor, he is happy, well-liked by his friends, a hale fellow well met. [. . .] In this respect old age even surpasses childhood: infants are sweet indeed, but speechless, deprived of one of the chief blessings of this life, namely gossiping. Also keep in mind that old men are immoderately fond of children, and, conversely, children are delighted by old men – 'so birds of a feather flock together.' After all, what difference is there between them, except that an old man has more wrinkles and has had more birthdays? Otherwise they agree exactly: both have whitish hair, toothless gums, a small bodily frame, and a liking for milk; both stutter and babble and engage in tomfoolery; both are forgetful and thoughtless; in short, they resemble each other in every respect. And the older they get the nearer they come to childhood, until like children, without being bored by life or afraid of death, they depart from this life.

Now anyone who likes can go and compare this benefit of mine with the sort of metamorphosis bestowed by the other gods. No need to mention what they do when they are angry: those whom they favor most, they have a habit of turning into a tree, a bird, a locust, or even a snake – as if to become something else were not in itself a kind of death. But I, on the other hand, restore the same man to the happiest part of his life. In fact, if mortals would refrain completely from any contact with wisdom and live their entire lives with me, there would not be any old age at all. Instead, they would enjoy perpetual youth and live happily ever after.

You see, don't you, how these grave and sober personages who devote themselves to philosophical studies or to serious and difficult tasks seem to enjoy hardly any youthful years at all; they grow old before their time because they are forever worrying and beating their brains out about knotty problems, so that their vital spirits gradually dry up, leaving them exhausted and juiceless, as it were. My fools, on the other hand, are plump and rosy, with a very well-preserved complexion; they are *as fit as a fiddle*, as the saying goes. In fact, they would never feel the slightest discomfort of old age, except that they are occasionally infected with a bit of wisdom by contagion. So it is that nothing in man's life can be absolutely flawless.

These arguments are also confirmed by the authority (not to be taken lightly) of the proverb which asserts that Folly is the only means of preserving youth, otherwise so evanescent, and of keeping harsh old age at a distance. Not without reason do people bandy about the vernacular saying that, whereas other men usually grow wiser with age, the people of Brabant [a province in Flanders] grow more and more foolish the older they get. And yet no other nationality is more cheerful in the ordinary affairs of everyday living or less subject to the gloom of old age. Close to the Brabanters not only in geographical location but also in their way of life are those Dutchmen of mine – and why shouldn't I call them mine, since they promote my cult so eagerly that they are proverbially described by a well-deserved epithet taken from my name. And so far are they from being ashamed of the label 'foolish' that they boast of it as one of their chief claims to fame. [. . .]

(iii) Second extract

As for the theologians, perhaps it would be better to pass them over in silence, '*not stirring up the hornets' nest*' and 'not laying a finger on the stinkweed, since this race of men is incredibly arrogant and touchy. For they might rise up en masse and march in ranks against me with six hundred conclusions and force me to recant. And if I should refuse, they would immediately shout 'heretic.' For this is the thunderbolt they always keep ready at a moment's notice to terrify anyone to whom they are not very favorably inclined.

Certainly, though no one is less willing than they are to recognize my good will toward them, still these men are also obliged to me for benefits of no little importance. They are so blessed by their Selflove as to be fully persuaded that they themselves dwell in the third heaven, looking down from high above on all other mortals as if they were earth-creeping vermin almost worthy of their pity. They are so closely hedged in by rows of [magistral definitions,] conclusions, corollaries, explicit and implicit propositions, they have so many '*holes they can run to,*' that Vulcan[7] himself couldn't net them tightly enough to keep them from escaping by means of distinctions, with which they cut all knots as cleanly as the fine-honed edge of 'the headsman's axe' – so many new terms have they thought up and such monstrous jargon have they coined. Moreover, they explicate sacred mysteries just as arbitrarily as they please, explaining by what method the world was established and arranged, by what channels original sin is transmitted to Adam's posterity, by what means, by what proportion, in how short a period of time Christ was fully formed in the virgin's womb, how accidents subsist in the eucharist without any domicile. But such questions are run-of-the-mill. There are others which they think worthy of great and 'illuminated' theologians, as they say. If they ever encounter these, then they really perk up. Whether there is any instant in the generation of the divine persons? Whether there is more than one filial relationship in Christ? Whether the following proposition is possible: God the Father hates the Son. Whether God could have taken on the nature of a woman, of the devil, of an ass, of a cucumber, of a piece of flint? And then how the cucumber would have preached, performed miracles, and been nailed to the cross? And what Peter would have consecrated [if he had consecrated] during the time Christ was hanging on the cross? And whether during that same time Christ could be called a man? And whether it will be permissible to eat and drink after the resurrection? – taking precautions even now against hunger and thirst.

There are numberless *petty quibbles* even more fine-spun than these, concerning notions, relations, instants, formalities, quiddities, ecceities – things to which no eyesight could ever penetrate, unless it were an 'x-ray vision' so powerful it could perceive through the deepest darkness things that are nowhere. Also throw in those *sententiae* [opinions] of theirs, so *paradoxical* that those oracular sayings which the Stoics called paradoxes seem downright crude and commonplace by comparison – such as this, for example: it is a less serious crime to murder a thousand men than to fix just one shoe for a poor man on the Lord's day; or it would be better to let the whole world be destroyed – 'lock, stock, and barrel,' as they say – than to tell just one, tiny, little white lie. And then these most subtle subtleties are rendered even more subtle by the various 'ways' or types of scholastic theology, so that you could work your way out of a labyrinth sooner than out of the intricacies of the Realists, Nominalists, Thomists, Albertists, Occamists, Scotists – and I still haven't mentioned all the sects, but only the main ones[8].

In all of these there is so much erudition, so much difficulty, that I think the apostles themselves would need to be inspired by a different spirit if they were forced to match wits on such points with this new breed of theologians. Paul could provide a living example of faith, but when he said 'Faith is the substance of things to be hoped for and the evidence of things not seen,' his definition was not sufficiently magisterial. So too, he lived a life of perfect charity, but he neither distinguished it nor defined it with sufficient dialectical precision in the first epistle to the Corinthians, chapter 13. Certainly the apostles consecrated the eucharist very piously, but still if they had been asked about the 'terminus a quo' and the 'terminus ad quem,' about transubstantiation, about how the same body can be in different places, about the difference between the body of Christ as it is in heaven, as it was on the cross, and as it is in the eucharist, about the exact point at which transubstantiation takes place (since the speech through which it is accomplished is a divisible quantity which takes place in a flowing period of time), I don't think they would have responded with a subtlety equal to that of the Scotists when they discuss and define these points. They knew Jesus' mother, but which of them has shown how she was preserved from the stain of Adam's sin as philosophically as our theologians have done it? Peter received the keys, and received them from one who would not have committed them to someone unworthy of them, but still I don't know whether he understood – certainly he never attained sufficient subtlety to understand – how even a person who does not have knowledge can still have the keys of knowledge. They baptized everywhere, but nowhere did they teach what are the formal, material, efficient, and final causes of baptism, nor do they even so much as mention the delible and indelible marks of the sacraments. Certainly they worshiped God, but they did so in the spirit, following no other directive than the one given in the gospel: 'God is a spirit and those who worship him should worship him in the spirit and in truth.' But it is hardly clear that it was also revealed to them that a charcoal sketch drawn on a wall should be worshiped with the same worship as Christ himself, provided that the picture has two fingers extended, long hair, and three rays in the halo stuck on the back of the skull. For who could perceive these things unless he had spent thirty-six whole years in studying the physics and metaphysics of Aristotle and the Scotists? So too, [the apostles] preach grace very forcefully, but nowhere do they distinguish between grace 'gratis data' [freely given by God] and grace 'gratificans' [grace showing gratitude to God]. They exhort us to good works, without distinguishing 'opus operans' [the work operating in the giving or receiving of Holy Communion] from 'opus operatum' [the work done by the sacraments of bread or wine]. Everywhere they inculcate charity, without separating infused from acquired charity or explaining whether charity is an accident or a substance, a created or an uncreated thing. They detest sin, but I would stake my life they couldn't define scientifically what it is that we call sin, unless perchance they had been instructed by the spirit of the Scotists. Nor can I bring myself to believe that Paul, from whose learning we may judge that of the others, would so often have condemned questions, disputes, genealogies, and (as he calls them) λογομαχίαι (quarrels about words), if he had been so expert in subtle argumentation, especially since all the quarrels and disputes of that time were coarse and crude by comparison with the supersubtleties of our doctors of theology. [. . .][9]

Not in these matters only, which I have given simply as examples but in absolutely every activity of life, the [pious man] flees from whatever is related to the body and is carried away in the pursuit of the eternal and invisible things of the spirit. Hence, since these two groups [the pious and the ordinary people] are in such utter disagreement on all matters, the result is that each thinks the other is insane – though that word applies more properly to the pious than to ordinary men, if you want my opinion. This will be much clearer if, according to my promise, I devote a few words to showing that their supreme reward is no more than a certain insanity.

First, therefore, consider that Plato had some glimmer of this notion when he wrote that the madness of lovers is the height of happiness. For a person who loves intensely no longer lives in himself but rather in that which he loves, and the farther he gets from himself and the closer to it, the happier he is. Moreover, when the mind is set on leaving the body and no longer has perfect control over the bodily organs, no doubt you would rightly call this condition madness. Otherwise what is the meaning of such common expressions as 'he is out of his wits,' 'come to your senses,' and 'he is himself once more.' Also, the more perfect the love, the greater and happier is the madness. What, then, is that future life in heaven for which pious minds long so eagerly? I'll tell you: the spirit, stronger at last and victorious, will absorb the body. And it will do so all the more easily, partly because it is in its own kingdom now, partly because even in its former life it had purged and refined the body in preparation for such a transformation. Then the spirit will be absorbed by that highest mind of all, whose power is infinitely greater, in such a way that the whole man will, be outside himself, and will be happy for no other reason than that he is located outside himself, and will receive unspeakable joy from that Highest Good which gathers all things to Himself.

Now, although this happiness is not absolutely perfect until the mind, having received its former body, is endowed with immortality, nevertheless it happens that, because the life of the pious is nothing but a meditation and a certain shadow (as it were) of that other life, they sometimes experience a certain flavor or odor of that reward. And this, even though it is like the tiniest droplet by comparison with that fountain of eternal happiness, nevertheless far surpasses all pleasures of the body, even if all the delights of all mortals were gathered into one. So much beyond the body are the things of the spirit; things unseen, beyond what can be seen. This, indeed, is what the prophet promises: 'Eye has not seen, nor ear heard, nor has the heart of man conceived what things God has prepared for those who love him.' [I *Corinthians* 2:9; *Isaiah* 64:4] And this is Folly's part, which shall not be taken from her by the transformation of life, but shall be perfected. Those who have the privilege of experiencing this (and it happens to very few) undergo something very like madness: they talk incoherently, not in a human fashion, making sounds without sense. Then the entire expression of their faces vacillates repeatedly: now happy, now sad; now crying, now laughing, now sighing – in short, they are completely beside themselves. Soon after, when they come to themselves, they say they do not know where they have been, whether in the body or out of it, whether waking or sleeping. They do not remember what they heard or saw or said or did except in a cloudy way, as if it were a dream. All they know is that they were never happier than while they were transported with such madness. Thus, they lament that they have come to their senses and want above all else to be forever mad with this kind of madness. And this is only a faint taste, as it were, of that future happiness.

But I have long since forgotten myself and '*have gone beyond the pale.*' If you think my speech has been too pert or wordy, keep in mind that you've been listening to Folly and to a woman. But also remember that Greek proverb '*Often a foolish man says something to the point*' – unless, perhaps, you think it doesn't apply to women.

I see that you are waiting for an epilogue, but you are crazy if you think I still have in mind what I have said, after pouring forth such a torrent of jumbled words. The old saying was '*I hate a drinking-companion with a memory.*' Updated, it is '*I hate a listener with a memory.*' Therefore, farewell, clap your hands, live well, drink your fill, most illustrious initiates of Folly.

Finis

NOTES

1	Pallas Athene, the goddess of wisdom and just war.
2	Zeus, ruler of the gods.
3	Zeus was famous for his amorous exploits with mortals, which usually required some change in his appearance. They are recounted in Ovid's *Metamorphoses*.
4	'tetrad': the intervals found in the first four numbers.
5	Titus Lucretius Carus (Lucretius, 94–55 BCE), an Epicurean philosopher and poet, whose *De rerum natura* (*On the Nature of Things*) I. 17–23, contains a long eulogy to Venus as the goddess of love and prime mover of the Universe.
6	Sophocles (*c.*496–405 BCE), *Ajax*, 554. Ajax was a Greek hero in the Trojan War who went mad and committed suicide.
7	Vulcan, god of fire. He forged a net to catch his wife Venus in adultery with Mars.
8	Medieval Scholasticism was riven by the debate over 'realism' and 'nominalism'. Realists believed in the existence of abstract concepts ('Universals') such as whiteness. Nominalists, on the other hand, maintained that such categories were mere words and argued instead that philosophers should focus exclusively on 'particulars'. Realism dominated the early period of scholasticism (up to about 1350), its chief exponents being Thomas Aquinas (1225–74) and Johannes Duns Scotus (*c.*1265–1308). After about 1350, Nominalism succeeded Realism and was the dominant force in scholastic circles, particularly under the influence of the writings of the Franciscan scholar, William of Ockham (Occam) (*c.*1285–1347/9).
9	The argument is taken from Thomas Aquinas, *Summa theologica*, I:2.3.aa.1.4.

18 Thomas More *Utopia* (1516) (i) Beliefs (ii) Human relations

Utopia was probably conceived on a trip to Antwerp in 1515 where More spent some time on a diplomatic mission and met Peter Giles (*c.*1486–1533), who figures in the narrative. It was printed in the following year at Louvain, under the supervision of another friend, Desiderius Erasmus. *Utopia* ('nowhere' in Greek) belongs to a tradition of political writings about the ideal commonwealth which extends back to Plato's *Republic* and Aristotle's *Politics*. In traditional humanist fashion, it proffers advice about how the good might be achieved by political means. More, however, does not offer the conventional solution. Instead he suggests a radical re-ordering of the social structure which would enforce a strict moral code and the abolition of private property. The style is ironic and scholars have not been able to agree whether More was seriously proposing the social order of Utopia or simply using it as a means to castigate contemporary abuses of power. The marginalia here were added either by Giles or Erasmus with More's approval. Details of More's life are given in the headnote to Text 6.

Source: *Utopia*, Latin text and English translation, ed. G. M. Logan, R. M. Adams, C. H. Miller, Cambridge University Press, Cambridge 1995, pp. 159–69, 185–97 (English text only)

i) Book II: Beliefs

Ethics

Higher and lower goods

Supreme goods

The Utopians consider honest pleasure the measure of happiness

First principles of philosophy to be sought in religion

Utopian theology

The immortality of the soul, about which nowadays no small number even of Christians have their doubts

Not every pleasure is desirable, neither is pain to be sought, except for the sake of virtue

This is like Stoic doctrine

[. . .] In matters of moral philosophy, they carry on the same arguments as we do. They inquire into the goods of the mind and goods of the body and external goods. They ask whether the name of 'good' can be applied to all three, or whether it refers only to goods of the mind. They discuss virtue and pleasure, but their chief concern is what to think of human happiness, and whether it consists of one thing or of more. On this point, they seem rather too much inclined to the view which favours pleasure, in which they conclude that all or the most important part of human happiness consists. And what is more surprising, they seek support for this comfortable opinion from their religion, which is serious and strict, indeed almost stern and forbidding. For they never discuss happiness without joining to the rational arguments of philosophy certain principles drawn from religion. Without these religious principles, they think that reason by itself is weak and defective in its efforts to investigate true happiness.

The religious principles they invoke are of this nature: that the soul is immortal, and by God's beneficence born for happiness; and that after this life, rewards are appointed for our virtues and good deeds, punishments for our sins. Though these are indeed religious principles, they think that reason leads us to believe and accept them.[1] And they add unhesitatingly that if these beliefs were rejected, no one would be so stupid as not to feel that he should seek pleasure, regardless of right and wrong. His only care would be to keep a lesser pleasure from standing in the way of a greater one, and to avoid pleasures that are inevitably followed by pain. They think you would have to be actually crazy to pursue harsh and painful virtue, give up the pleasures of life, and suffer pain from which you can expect no advantage. For if there is no reward after death, you have no compensation for having passed your entire existence without pleasure, that is, miserably.[2]

To be sure, they think happiness is found, not in every kind of pleasure, but only in good and honest pleasure. Virtue itself, they say, draws our nature to pleasure of this sort, as to the supreme good. There is an opposed school which declares that virtue is itself happiness.[3]

They define virtue as living according to nature; and God, they say, created us to that end. When an individual obeys the dictates of reason in choosing one thing and avoiding another, he is following nature. Now above all reason urges us to love and venerate the Divine Majesty to whom we owe our existence and our capacity for happiness. Secondly, nature prescribes that we should lead a life as free of anxiety and as full of joy as possible, and that we should help all others – because of our natural fellowship – toward that end. The most hard-faced eulogist of virtue and the grimmest enemy of pleasure, while he invites you to toil and sleepless nights and mortification, still admonishes you to relieve the poverty and distress of others as best you can. It is especially praiseworthy, they think, when we provide for the comfort and welfare of our fellow creatures. Nothing is more humane (and humanity is the virtue most proper to human beings) than to relieve the misery of others, remove all sadness from their lives, and restore them to enjoyment, that is, pleasure. Well, then, why doesn't nature equally invite all of us to do the same thing for ourselves? Either a joyful life (that is, one of pleasure) is a good thing, or it isn't. If it isn't, then you should not help anyone to it – indeed, you ought to take it away from everyone you can, as being harmful and deadly to them. But if you are allowed, indeed obliged, to help others to such a life, why not first of all yourself, to whom you owe no less favour than to anyone else? For when nature prompts you to be kind to your neighbours, she does not mean that you should be cruel and merciless to yourself. Thus, they say, nature herself prescribes for us a joyous life, in other words, pleasure, as the goal of all our actions; and living according to her rules is to be defined as virtue. But as nature bids mortals to make one another's lives cheerful, as far as they can – and she does so rightly, for no one is placed so far above the rest that he is nature's sole concern, and she cherishes equally all those to whom she has granted the same form – so she repeatedly warns you not to seek your own advantage in ways that cause misfortune to others.

But now some people cultivate pain as if it were the essence of religion, rather than incidental to performance of a pious duty or the result of natural necessity – and thus to be borne, not pursued

Consequently, they think that one should abide not only by private agreements but by those public laws which control the distribution of vital goods, such as are the very substance of pleasure. Any such laws, when properly promulgated by a good king, or ratified by the common consent of a people free of tyranny and deception, should be observed. So long as they are observed, to pursue your own interests is prudent; to pursue the public interest as well is pious; but to pursue your own pleasure by depriving others of theirs is unjust. On the other hand, to decrease your own pleasure in order to augment that of others is a work of humanity and benevolence, which never fails to reward the doer over and above his sacrifice. You may be repaid for your kindness, and in any case your consciousness of having done a good deed, and recalling the affection and good will of those whom you have benefited, gives your mind more pleasure than your

Contracts and laws

Mutual assistance

body would have drawn from the things you forfeited. Finally, as religion easily persuades a well-disposed mind to believe, God will requite the loss of a brief and transitory pleasure here with immense and never-ending joy in heaven. And so they conclude, after carefully considering and weighing the matter, that all our actions, including even the virtues exercised within them, look toward pleasure as their happiness and final goal.

What pleasure is   By pleasure they understand every state or movement of body or mind in which we find delight according to the behests of nature. They have good reason for adding that the desire is according to nature. By following our senses and right reason we may discover what is pleasant by nature: it is a delight that does not injure others, does not preclude a greater pleasure, and is not followed by pain. But all pleasures which are against nature, and False pleasures   which men agree to call 'delightful' only by the emptiest of fictions (as if one could change the real nature of things just by changing their names), do not, they have decided, really make for happiness; in fact, they say such pleasures often preclude happiness. And the reason is that once they have taken over someone's mind, they leave no room for true and genuine delights, and they completely fill the mind with a false notion of pleasure. For there are a great many things which have no genuine sweetness in them but are for the most part actually bitter – yet which, through the perverse enticement of evil desires, are not only considered very great pleasures but are even included among the primary reasons for living.

Mistaken pride in   Among the pursuers of this false pleasure, they include those fancy dress   whom I mentioned before, the people who think themselves finer folk because they wear finer clothes. On this one point, these people are twice mistaken: first in supposing their clothes better than anyone else's, and then in thinking themselves better. As far as a garment's usefulness goes, why is fine woollen thread better than coarse? Yet they strut about and think their clothes make them more substantial, as if they were exalted by nature herself, rather than their own fantasies. Therefore, honours they would never have dared to expect if they were plainly dressed they demand as rightfully due to their fancy suit, and they grow indignant if someone passes them by without showing special respect.

Foolish honours   Isn't it the same kind of stupidity to be pleased by empty, merely ceremonial honours? What true or natural pleasure can you get from someone's bent knee or bared head? Will the creaks in your own knees be eased thereby, or the madness in your head? The phantom of false pleasure is illustrated by others who are pleasantly mad with delight over their own blue blood, flatter Empty nobility   themselves on their nobility, and gloat over all the long line of rich ancestors they happen to have (and wealth is the only sort of nobility these days), and especially over their ancient family estates. Even if these ancestors have left them no estates to inherit, or if they've squandered all of their inheritance, they don't consider themselves a bit less noble.

In the same class they put those people I described before, who are captivated by jewels and gemstones, and think themselves divinely happy if they get a good specimen, especially of the sort that happens to be fashionable in their country at the time – for not every country nor every era values the same kinds. But collectors will not make an offer for a stone till it's taken out of its gold setting, and even then they will not buy unless the dealer guarantees and gives security that it is a true and genuine stone. What they fear is that their eyes will be deceived by a counterfeit. But why should a counterfeit give any less pleasure, if, when you look at it, your eyes cannot distinguish it from a genuine gem? Both should be of equal value to you – no less so, by heaven, than they would be to a blind man. [. . .]

The silliest pleasure of all: gemstones

Popular opinion gives gems their value or takes it away

ii) Book II: Human Relations

The only prisoners of war the Utopians keep as slaves are those captured in wars they fight themselves. The children of slaves are not born into slavery, nor are any slaves obtained from foreign countries. They are either their own citizens, enslaved for some heinous offence, or else foreigners who had been condemned to death in their own cities; the latter sort predominate. Sometimes the Utopians buy them at a low price; more often they ask for them, get them for nothing, and bring them home in considerable numbers. These kinds of slaves are not only kept constantly at work, but are always fettered. The Utopians, however, deal more harshly with their own people than with the others, feeling that they are worse and deserve stricter punishment because they had an excellent education and the best of moral training, yet still couldn't be restrained from wrongdoing. A third class of slaves consists of hard-working penniless drudges from other nations who voluntarily choose slavery in Utopia. Such people are treated with respect, almost as kindly as citizens, except that they are assigned a little extra work, on the score that they're used to it. If one of them wants to leave, which seldom happens, no obstacles are put in his way, nor is he sent off empty-handed.

The wonderful fairness of these people

As I said before, they care for the sick with great affection, neglecting nothing whatever in the way of medicine or diet which might restore them to health. Everything possible is done to mitigate the pain of those suffering from incurable diseases; and visitors do their best to console them by sitting and talking with them. But if the disease is not only incurable, but excruciatingly

The sick

and unremittingly painful, then the priests and public officials come and remind the sufferer that he is now unequal to any of

Deliberate death life's duties, a burden to himself and others; he has really outlived his own death. They tell him he should not let the pestilence prey on him any longer, but now that life is simply torture he should not hesitate to die but should rely on hope for something better; and since his life is a prison where he is bitterly tormented, he should escape from it on his own or allow others to rescue him from it. This would be a wise act, they say, since for him death would put an end not to pleasure but to agony. In addition, he would be obeying the counsel of the priests, who are the interpreters of God's will; thus it would be a pious and holy act.

Those who have been persuaded by these arguments either starve themselves to death of their own accord or, having been put to sleep, are freed from life without any sensation of dying. But they never force this step on a man against his will; nor, if he decides against it, do they lessen their care of him. The man who yields to their arguments, they think, dies an honourable death; but the suicide, who takes his own life without approval of priests and senate, him they consider unworthy of either earth or fire, and they throw his body, unburied and disgraced, into a bog.

Marriages   Women do not marry till they are eighteen, nor men till they are twenty-two. Clandestine premarital intercourse, if discovered and proved, brings severe punishment on both man and woman; and the guilty parties are forbidden to marry for their whole lives, unless the governor by his pardon remits the sentence. Also both the father and mother of the household where the offence was committed suffer public disgrace for having been remiss in their duty. The reason they punish this offence so severely is that they suppose few people would join in married love – with confinement to a single partner and all the petty annoyances that married life involves – unless they were strictly restrained from promiscuous intercourse.

In choosing marriage partners they solemnly and seriously follow a custom which seemed to us foolish and absurd in the

Not very modest, extreme. Whether she be widow or virgin, the woman is shown
but not so naked to the suitor by a responsible and respectable matron; and
impractical either similarly, some honourable man presents the suitor naked to the woman. We laughed at this custom, and called it absurd; but they were just as amazed at the folly of all other peoples. When men go to buy a colt, where they are risking only a little money, they are so cautious that, though the animal is almost bare, they won't close the deal until saddle and blanket have been taken off, lest there be a hidden sore underneath.[4] Yet in the choice of a mate, which may cause either delight or disgust for the rest of their lives, men are so careless that they leave all the rest of the woman's body covered up with clothes and estimate her attractiveness from a

mere handsbreadth of her person, the face, which is all they can see. And so they marry, running great risk of bitter discord, if something in either's person should offend the other. Not all people are so wise as to concern themselves solely with character; and even the wise appreciate the gifts of the body as a supplement to the virtues of the mind. There's no doubt that a deformity may lurk under clothing, serious enough to alienate a man's mind from his wife when his body can no longer lawfully be separated from her. If some disfiguring accident takes place after marriage, each person must bear his own fate; but beforehand everyone should be legally protected from deception.

There is extra reason for them to be careful, because in that part of the world they are the only people who practise monogamy, and because their marriages are seldom terminated except by death – though they do allow divorce for adultery or for intoler- Divorce ably offensive behaviour. A husband or wife who is the aggrieved party in such a divorce is granted leave by the senate to take a new mate; the guilty party suffers disgrace and is permanently forbidden to remarry. But they absolutely forbid a husband to put away his wife against her will and without any fault on her part, just because of some bodily misfortune; they think it cruel that a person should be abandoned when most in need of comfort; and they add that old age, since it not only entails disease but is a disease itself, needs more than a precarious fidelity.

It happens occasionally that a married couple have incompatible characters, and have both found other persons with whom they hope to live more harmoniously. After getting approval of the senate, they may then separate by mutual consent and contract new marriages. But such divorces are allowed only after the senators and their wives have carefully investigated the case. Divorce is deliberately made difficult because they know that conjugal love will hardly be strengthened if each partner has in mind that a new marriage is easily available.

Violators of the marriage bond are punished with the strictest form of slavery. If both parties were married, both are divorced, and the injured parties may marry one another if they want, or someone else. But if one of the injured parties continues to love such an undeserving spouse, the marriage may go on, provided the innocent person chooses to share in the labour to which the slave is condemned. And sometimes it happens that the repentance of the guilty and the devotion of the innocent party so move the governor to pity that he restores both to freedom. But a relapse into the same crime is punished by death.

No other crimes carry fixed penalties; the senate decrees a spe- Assignment of cific punishment for each misdeed, as it is considered atrocious punishments left
to the magistracy or venial. Husbands chastise their wives and parents their children, unless the offence is so serious that public punishment is called for. Generally, the gravest crimes are punished with slavery, for they think this deters offenders just as much as getting rid of them by immediate capital punishment, and convict labour is more beneficial to the commonwealth. Slaves, moreover, contribute more by their labour than by their death, and they are permanent and visible reminders that crime does not pay. If the slaves rebel against their condition, then, since neither bars nor chains can tame them, they are finally put to death like wild beasts. But if they are patient, they are not left altogether without hope. When subdued by long hardships, if they show by their behaviour that they regret the crime more than the punishment, their slavery is lightened or remitted altogether, sometimes by the governor's prerogative, sometimes by popular vote.

The penalty for soliciting to lewdness   Attempted seduction is subject to the same penalty as seduction itself. They think that a crime clearly and deliberately attempted is as bad as one committed, and that failure should not confer advantages on a criminal who did all he could to succeed.

Pleasure derived from fools   They are very fond of fools, and think it contemptible to insult them. There is no prohibition against enjoying their foolishness, and they even regard this as beneficial to the fools. If anyone is so solemn and severe that the foolish behaviour and comic patter of a clown do not amuse him, they don't entrust him with the care of such a person, for fear that one who gets not only no use from a fool but not even any amusement – a fool's only gift – will not treat him kindly.

To deride a person for being deformed or crippled is considered ugly and disfiguring, not to the victim but to the mocker, who stupidly reproaches the cripple for something he cannot help.

Artificial beauty   Though they think it a sign of weak and sluggish character to neglect one's natural beauty, they consider cosmetics a disgraceful affectation. From experience they have learned that no physical attractions recommend a wife to her husband so effectually as an upright character and a respectful attitude. Though some men are captured by beauty alone, none are held except by virtue and compliance.

Citizens to be encouraged by rewards to do their duty   They not only deter people from crime by penalties, but they incite them to virtue by public honours. Accordingly, they set up in the marketplace statues of distinguished men who have served their country well, thinking thereby to preserve the memory of their good deeds and to spur on citizens to emulate the glory of their ancestors.

Running for office condemned   Any man who campaigns for a public office is disqualified for all of them. They live together in a friendly fashion, and their public officials are never arrogant or unapproachable. They are *Magistrates held in honour* called 'fathers', and that indeed is the way they behave. Because officials never extort respect from the people against their will,

the people respect them spontaneously, as they should. The gov- Dignity of the governor
ernor himself is distinguished from his fellow citizens not by a
robe or a crown but only by the sheaf of grain he bears, as the
sign of the high priest is a wax candle carried before him.

They have very few laws, for their training is such that very few Few laws
suffice. The chief fault they find with other nations is that even
their infinite volumes of laws and interpretations are not adequate. They think it completely unjust to bind people by a set of
laws that are too many to be read or too obscure for anyone to
understand. As for lawyers, a class of men whose trade it is to The useless crowd of lawyers
manipulate cases and multiply quibbles, they exclude them
entirely. They think it practical for each man to plead his own
case, and say the same thing to the judge that he would tell his
lawyer. This makes for less confusion and readier access to the
truth. A man speaks his mind without tricky instructions from a
lawyer, and the judge examines each point carefully, taking pains
to protect simple folk against the false accusations of the crafty.
This sort of plain dealing is hard to find in other nations, where
they have such a mass of incomprehensibly intricate laws. But in
Utopia everyone is a legal expert. For the laws are very few, as I
said, and they consider the most obvious interpretation of any law
to be the fairest. As they see things, all laws are promulgated for
the single purpose of advising every man of his duty. Subtle
interpretations admonish very few, since hardly anybody can
understand them, whereas the more simple and apparent sense of
the law is open to everyone. If laws are not clear, they are useless;
for simple-minded men (and most men are of this sort, and must
be told where their duty lies), there might as well be no laws at
all as laws which can be interpreted only by devious minds after
endless disputes. The dull mind of the common man cannot
understand such laws, and couldn't even if he studied them his
whole life, since he has to earn a living in the meantime. [. . .]

NOTES

1   The immortality of the soul was accepted as the official dogma of the Church by the
     Lateran Council of 1513, but it was subject to much philosophical debate during the fif-
     teenth and sixteenth centuries.
2   The idea of 'higher' and 'lower' pleasures is derived from Epicurean philosophy.
3   This statement and the paragraph which follows reflect Stoic doctrines.
4   The reference to looking out for 'a hidden sore' may refer here to one means of trying
     to curb the spread of syphilis.

Section Two

Politics and Humanism

19 Francesco Guicciardini *The History of Italy* (1540)

Francesco Guicciardini (1483–1540) was a member of a Florentine patrician
family. As a young man he supported the republic but, at the restoration of the
Medici in 1512, he entered the service of the Medici popes, Leo X and Clement
VII, as governor of several of the papal states. He was exiled from Florence by the
anti-Medici rising of 1527 but returned with them in 1530. He wrote histories of
Florence (1509) and Italy (1537–40) and a number of political commentaries
including the *Maxims and Reflections* (see Text 27). Some contemporaries
regarded him as an unprincipled time-server, but his commitment to the ideal of
a patrician republic organised on the Venetian model seems to have been
consistent, as does his pessimism about human nature.

Source: *The History of Italy*, trans. and ed. S. Alexander, Macmillan, New York and
London, 1969, pp. 4–8

[BOOK I]

Many factors kept her [Florence] in that state of felicity which was the consequence of various causes. But it was most commonly agreed that, among these,
no small praise should be attributed to the industry and skill of Lorenzo de'
Medici, so eminent amongst the ordinary rank of citizens in the city of Florence
that the affairs of that republic were governed according to his counsels. Indeed,
the power of the Florentine Republic resulted more from its advantageous location, the abilities of its citizens and the availability of its money than from the
extent of its domain. And having recently become related by marriage to the
Roman Pontiff, Innocent VIII [1484–92], who was thus induced to lend no little
faith in his advice, Lorenzo's name was held in great esteem all over Italy, and his
authority influential in deliberations on joint affairs.[1] Realizing that it would
be most perilous to the Florentine Republic and to himself if any of the
major powers should extend their area of dominion, he carefully saw to it that
the Italian situation should be maintained in a state of balance, not leaning more
toward one side than the other. This could not be achieved without preserving
the peace and without being diligently on the watch against every incident, even
the slightest.

Sharing the same desire for the common peace was the King of Naples,
Ferdinand of Aragon [ruled 1495–96], undoubtedly a most prudent and highly
esteemed prince, despite the fact that quite often in the past he had revealed
ambitions not conducive toward maintaining the peace, and at this time he was
being greatly instigated by his eldest son Alfonso, Duke of Calabria. For the
Duke tolerated with ill grace the fact that his son-in-law, Giovan Galeazzo Sforza,
Duke of Milan, already past twenty, although of very limited intellectual
capacity, kept his dukedom in name only, having been suppressed and supplanted
by Lodovico Sforza, his uncle [1452–1508]. More than ten years before, as a result
of the reckless and dissolute behavior of Donna Bona, the young prince's mother,
Lodovico Sforza had taken tutelage over his nephew and, using that as an excuse,

had little by little gathered into his own hands all the fortresses, men-at-arms, treasury and foundations of the state, and now continued to govern, not as guardian or regent but, except for the title of Duke of Milan, with all the outward trappings and actions of a prince.

Nevertheless, Ferdinand, more immediately concerned with present benefits than former ambitions, or his son's grievances, however justified, desired that Italy should not change. Perhaps he feared that troubles in Italy would offer the French a chance to assail the kingdom of Naples, since he himself, a few years earlier, had experienced amidst the gravest perils the hatred of his barons and his people, and he knew the affection which many of his subjects held toward the name of the house of France in remembrance of things past. Or perhaps he realized that it was necessary for him to unite with the others, and especially with the states of Milan and Florence, in order to create a counterbalance against the power of the Venetians, who were then formidable in all of Italy.

Lodovico Sforza, despite the fact that he was restless and ambitious, could not help but incline toward the same policy, since the danger of the Venetian Senate hung over those who ruled Milan as well as over the others, and because it was easier for him to maintain his usurped authority in the tranquility of peace rather than in the perturbations of war. And although he always suspected the intentions of Ferdinand and Alfonso of Aragon, nevertheless, since he was aware of Lorenzo de' Medici's disposition toward peace, as well as the fear that Lorenzo also had of their grandeur, Sforza persuaded himself that, in view of the diversity of spirit and ancient hatred between Ferdinand and the Venetians, it would be foolish to fear that they might set up an alliance between them, and decided that it was most certain that the Aragonese would not be accompanied by others in attempting against him what they could not achieve by themselves.

Therefore, since the same desire for peace existed among Ferdinand, Lodovico and Lorenzo, in part for the same reasons and in part for different reasons, it was easy to maintain an alliance contracted in the names of Ferdinand, King of Naples, Giovan Galeazzo, Duke of Milan, and the Republic of Florence, in defense of their states. This alliance, which had been agreed upon many years before and then interrupted as a result of various occurrences, had been adhered to in the year 1480 by practically all the minor Italian powers and renewed for twenty-five years. The principal aim of the pact was to prevent the Venetians from becoming any more powerful since they were undoubtedly stronger than any of the allies alone, but much weaker than all of them together. The Venetians continued to follow their own policies apart from common counsels, and while waiting for the growth of disunion and conflicts among the others, remained on the alert, prepared to take advantage of every mishap that might open the way for them toward ruling all of Italy. The fact that they aspired toward Italian hegemony had been very clearly shown at various times; especially, when taking advantage of the death of Filippo Maria Visconti, Duke of Milan, they had tried to become lords of that state, under the pretext of defending the liberty of the Milanese; and more recently when, in open war, they attempted to occupy the duchy of Ferrara.

This alliance easily curbed the cupidity of the Venetian Senate, but it did not unite the allies in sincere and faithful friendship, insofar as, full of emulation and jealousy among themselves, they did not cease to assiduously observe what the others were doing, each of them reciprocally aborting all the plans whereby any of the others might become more powerful or renowned. This did not result in rendering the peace less stable; on the contrary, it aroused greater vigilance in all of them to carefully stamp out any sparks which might be the cause of a new conflagration.

NOTE

1   Pope Innocent's illegitimate son, Francesco Cibo, had married Maddalena de'Medici, the daughter of Lorenzo the Magnificent.

20 Thomas Aquinas **Commentary on the *Sentences* of Peter Lombard (1254)**

Thomas Aquinas (1225–74) (the 'Angelic Doctor') came from Aquino in the kingdom of Naples. He studied at the abbey of Monte Cassino and later entered the order of Dominican friars. While a student he was strongly influenced by the renowned scholastic commentator on Aristotle, Albertus Magnus (c.1200–80). Aquinas soon gained a reputation for his wide-reaching learning and his grasp of the intellectual traditions both of classical antiquity and Christianity. In an attempt to settle controversies within the Western church and with the Greek theologians of the East, he showed in a series of works, notably the *Summa theologica*, which drew on Aristotle and the Christian fathers, that reason and faith could be reconciled. Despite criticisms from within the Catholic hierarchy during his lifetime, he was canonized in 1323 and his works came to be regarded as a fundamental source of orthodox Catholic theology.

Source: *Aquinas: Selected Political Writings*, ed. A. P. D'Entreves, trans. J. G. Dawson, Blackwell, Oxford, 1954, pp. 181, 183, 185 (English text only)

BOOK II

Dist. 44, Quest. 2, Art. 2. *The Obedience owed by Christians to the Secular Power and in particular to Tyrants*

1. It would seem that Christians are not bound to obey the secular powers, and particularly tyrants. For it is said, *Matthew* XVII, 25: 'Therefore the children are free.' And if in all countries the children of the reigning sovereign are free, so also should the children of that Sovereign be free, to whom all kings are subject. But Christians have become the sons of God as we read in the *Epistle to the Romans* (VIII, 16). 'For the Spirit himself giveth testimony to our spirit, that we are the sons of God.' Christians then are everywhere free, and are thus not bound to obey the secular powers.

   2. Furthermore: as we have already shown, servitude began in consequence of

sin. But men are cleansed from sin by baptism. Therefore they are freed from servitude. So we have the same conclusion.

3. Furthermore: a greater bond absolves from a lesser, as the new law absolved from observance of the old. But man is by baptism bound to God: and this obligation is a greater bond than that by which one man is bound to another by servitude. Therefore man is freed from servitude by baptism.

4. Furthermore: Any one is permitted, if opportunity offers, to take back what has been unjustly taken from him. But many secular princes have possessed themselves tyrannically of the lands they rule. Therefore when the opportunity of rebelling occurs, their subjects are not bound by obedience to them.

5. Furthermore: there can be no duty of obedience towards a person whom it is permissible or even praiseworthy to kill. But Cicero in the *De Officiis* (I, 26) justifies those who killed Julius Caesar, even though he was their friend and relative, because he usurped the imperial powers like a tyrant. To such, then, no obedience is owed.

But against the above arguments there is the text of the first *Epistle of St. Peter* (II, 18): 'Servants, be subject to your masters': and that of the *Epistle to the Romans* (XIII, 2): 'He that resisteth the power, resisteth the ordinance of God.' Now it is not permissible to resist the ordinance of God; neither, therefore, is it permissible to resist the secular power.

Solution. We must observe that, as has been stated already, in the observance of a certain precept, obedience is connected with the obligation to such observance. But such obligation derives from the order of authority which carries with it the power to constrain, not only from the temporal, but also from the spiritual point of view, and in conscience; as the Apostle says (*Romans* XIII): and this because the order of authority derives from God. [. . .] For this reason the duty of obedience is, for the Christian, a consequence of this derivation of authority from God, and ceases when that ceases. But, as we have already said, authority may fail to derive from God for two reasons: either because of the way in which authority has been obtained, or in consequence of the use which is made of it. There are two ways in which the first case may occur. Either because of a defect in the person, if he is unworthy; or because of some defect in the way itself by which power was acquired, if, for example, through violence, or simony or some other illegal method. The first defect is not such as to impede the acquisition of legitimate authority; and since authority derives always, from a formal point of view, from God (and it is this which produces the duty of obedience), their subjects are always obliged to obey such superiors, however unworthy they may be. But the second defect prevents the establishment of any just authority: for whoever possesses himself of power by violence does not truly become lord or master. Therefore it is permissible, when occasion offers, for a person to reject such authority; except in the case that it subsequently became legitimate, either through public consent or through the intervention of higher authority. With regard to abuse of authority, this also may come about in two ways. First, when what is ordered by an authority is opposed to the object for which that authority was constituted (if, for example, some sinful action is commanded or one which is contrary to virtue, when it is precisely for the protection and fostering of virtue that authority is instituted). In such a case, not only is there no obligation to obey the authority, but one is obliged to disobey it, as did the holy martyrs who suffered death rather than obey the impious commands of tyrants. Secondly, when those who bear authority command things which exceed the competence of such authority; as, for example, when a master demands payment from a servant which the latter is not bound to make, and other similar cases. In this instance the subject is free to obey or to disobey.

So, to the first objection we may reply that authority which is instituted in the interests of those subject to it, is not contrary to their liberty; so there is no objection to those who are transformed into sons of God, by the grace of the Holy Spirit, being subject to it. Or again we can say that Christ speaks of Himself and of His disciples, who were neither of servile condition nor had they any temporal possessions for which to pay tribute to temporal lords. So it does not follow that all Christians should enjoy such liberty, but only those who follow the apostolic way of life, without possessions and free from servile condition.

With regard to the second objection we must note that baptism does not take away all the penalties which derive from the sin of our first parents, as for instance the inevitability of death, blindness, and other such evils. But it regenerates in the living hope of that life in which we shall be free from such penalties. Therefore, from the fact that a man is baptized it does not necessarily follow that he should be freed from servile condition, even though this is a consequence of sin.

To the third objection we reply that the greater bond does not absolve from the lesser, unless the two be incompatible, since error and truth cannot be found together; therefore with the coming of the truth of the Gospel the darkness of the Old Law passed away. But the bond with which one is bound in baptism is compatible with the bond of servitude, and does not in consequence absolve from it.

To the fourth objection we reply that those who attain power by violence are not truly rulers; therefore their subjects are not bound to obey them except in the cases already noted.

With regard to the fifth objection it must be noted that Cicero was speaking of a case where a person had possessed himself of power through violence, either against the will of his subjects or by compelling their consent, and where there was no possibility of appeal to a higher authority who could pass judgement on such action. In such a case, one who liberates his country by killing a tyrant is to be praised and rewarded.

21 Niccolò Machiavelli **Reports on a mission to Cesare Borgia (1502)**

Niccolò Machiavelli (1469–1527) was a Florentine statesman and writer. He came from a family of minor citizens which owned some small estates, his father being employed as a jurist. His education gave him a good knowledge of Latin and the classical authors and provided a qualification for office in the administration. In

1494 the Medici domination of Florence ended and four years later Machiavelli became Second Chancellor of the Republic. He was sent on numerous missions. The extracts given below relate to Cesare Borgia (1476–1507), the son of Pope Alexander VI, whose expansionist policies in the Romagna were threatening Florentine security. Borgia established himself as the Duke of Romagna until the death of Alexander VI in 1503. Cultured, politically adroit and a competent soldier, his notorious cruelty was not unusual for this period. Machiavelli's reports provide excellent evidence about diplomatic exchanges during the fourteen years of his chancellorship, and also insights into Machiavelli's thinking which was later to be expressed in his four major works: *The Prince, The Discourses, The Art of War* and *The History of Florence* (Texts 24–26). These were written between 1513 and 1525, while Machiavelli was without an official post. He had been disgraced on the return of the Medici in 1512 and only gradually managed to regain their favour. His writings may have been instrumental in this process, not perhaps through his best known work, *The Prince*, but by bawdy comedies like the *Mandragola* (*The Mandrake Root*) and *The History of Florence*, which was commissioned by the Medici. He had just received his major appointment in 1526, as administrator of the fortifications, when another political upheaval again expelled the Medici from Florence and ended his career. He died on 20 June 1527 and was buried in the church of Santa Croce.

Source: Niccolò Machiavelli, *The Chief Works and Others*, trans. A. H. Gilbert, Duke University Press, Durham, North Carolina, 1965, vol 1 (3 vols) pp. 121–4, 128–9. Copyright 1965, Allan H. Gilbert. Reprinted by permission of Duke University Press. All rights reserved

LEGATION II. AN OFFICIAL MISSION TO DUKE VALENTINO [*CESARE BORGIA*] IN ROMAGNA

[*All the dispatches are directed to the Ten of Liberty and* Balía]

7 October 1502 10 a.m., from Imola.

. . . His Excellency Cesare Borgia said he had always wished alliance with Your Lordships, and that he had not attained it more through the malice of others than through cause of his own, saying that he was going to tell me in detail what he never had told anybody about his coming with his army to Florence. And he said that having taken Faenza and made an attempt on Bologna, the Orsini and Vitelli were at him, urging him to decide to return to Rome by way of Florence. This he refused because the Pope, by a Brief, instructed him otherwise. Vitellozzo [one of the Vitelli, a *condottiere* or mercenary commander], weeping, threw himself at his feet to beg him to take that road, promising him that he would not do any violence to the country or to the city. When he would not consent to this, they nevertheless kept at him with similar prayers, so that he yielded as to the coming, but under the condition that the country should not be injured and that the Medici should not be considered.

But still wishing to get some profit from his approach to Florence, he

5 The cipher of Niccolò Machiavelli. Photo: Paolo Dalmasso, Florence, from Sergio Bertelli and others, *Le corti Italiane del Rinascimento*, 1985, Milan, Mondadori.

determined within himself to try to make an alliance with Your Lordships, and to avail himself of that opportunity. This is proved by his saying little or nothing of the Medici in any of the parleys that were held – as the commissioners who dealt with him know – and by his never allowing Piero to come into his camp. And many times, when he was at Campi, the Orsini and the Vitelli asked him for permission to attack either Florence or Pistoia, showing him possibilities for success. But he never consented; on the contrary, with a thousand declarations he made them understand that he would oppose them. After the truce was made, the Orsini and Vitelli felt that he had gained his own wish and not theirs, and that their march had been to his profit and their loss. As a result, they set about destroying the truce with lies and did all that damage in order to vex Your Lordships and upset the agreement. And never has he been able to make atonement to you, both because he cannot be everywhere and because Your Lordships have not made him the loan which had been arranged, or rather indicated. [. . .]

He added then that it was now time, if Your Lordships wished to be his allies, to make pledges, because without regard to the Orsini he could make alliance with you. . . . He does not see how Your Lordships can turn away from a plan on which there is agreement by His Majesty the King and His Holiness Our Lord the Pope. [. . .]

9 October 1502 4 p.m., from Imola.

. . . His Excellency the Duke sent for me . . . and showed me a letter from Monseigneur d'Arles, the Pope's ambassador in France . . . in which he wrote how much the King and Rouen incline to please him; and as soon as they understood his wish to have soldiers for the expedition against Bologna, they ordered Monsieur de Chaumont at Milano to send the Duke, without making any objection, Monsieur de Lanques with three hundred lances, and if he were asked by the Duke, to go in person toward Parma with three hundred more lances. . . . And His Excellency had me look at Arles's signature . . . which I recognized on account of my experience in France and in Florence. . . . And His Excellency said: 'Now you see, Secretary, that this letter is written in answer to the question I asked about attacking Bologna, and you see how vigorous it is; imagine what I can get to defend myself from those men, the greater part of whom His Majesty the King believes are his violent enemies, because they have always tried to move chessmen in Italy for his injury. Believe me that this thing is to my advantage, and the Vitelli cannot reveal themselves at an hour when it will damage me less, nor can I, to strengthen my states, wish for a thing that will be more useful to me; because I shall know this time against whom I have to protect myself, and I shall recognize my friends. And if the Venetians reveal themselves in this matter, which I do not expect, I shall be the better pleased; nor could the King of France be more eager for it. I tell you this, and shall tell it to you on the day when it happens, so that you can write it to those Signors of yours, and they can see that I am not about to give up or to be without friends, among whom I wish to number Their Lordships, if they let me know soon; but if they do not do it now, I shall put them aside; if the water were up to my neck, I should not talk any more about friendship, even though it would always pain me to have a neighbor and not be able to do him good and receive it from him.' . . . And again he reminded me when I left him to remind Your Lordships that, if you remain neutral, you will lose under any conditions, but if you join with him you can win.

I cannot express with pen with how much show of love for you he spoke, and with how much justification of things past. . . .

Five days ago he reviewed six thousand infantry selected from his cities, which in two days he can get together. . . . He has as much artillery, and in good order, as almost all the rest of Italy. . . . On the other side, we see his enemies armed and in a position to make a sudden conflagration, and these people are still all Romagnoles, and have not been very well treated because this lord has always shown more favor to his soldiers than to them. . . .

12 October 1502, from Imola.

. . . When I came into the presence of His Excellency, he said to me: 'From all sides we have good news.' And he related to me how much had been offered him by the Venetians, . . . saying happily that this year there is a planet hostile to anyone who rebels. [. . .]

27 October 1502, from Imola.

. . . Anybody who examines the qualities of one side and the other recognizes this Lord as a man courageous, fortunate, and full of hope, favored by a pope and by a king, and injured by the other side [*i.e., the Vitelli, etc.*], not merely in a state that he hoped to conquer, but in one that he had conquered. Those others are suspicious about their states; they were fearful of his greatness before they injured him, and now they are much more so, having done him this injury. And it does not appear how he can forgive the injury and those can abandon their fear, nor as a result how they can yield one to the other in the expedition against Bologna and in the Dukedom of Urbino. It is reasonable that they can agree only if they can act in union against a third, in such a way that neither the Duke nor the confederates will have to decrease their forces, but rather each of the parties will grow in reputation and profit. And if this should happen, they can turn nowhere except against Your Lordships or against the Venetians. An expedition against Your Lordships is judged easier as to you, but harder as to the King; that against the Venetians easier as to the King, but harder as to them. The first would be more acceptable to this Duke, and the second more pleasing to the confederates. Nevertheless neither one nor the other is believed in, but they are talked of as things possible. And so I do not meet a person competent to decide on the method of agreement between the parties. And anybody who does decide believes that this Duke will detach from the group some one of these confederates, and when he has defeated the others he will no longer need to fear them and can carry out his designs. I rather believe this, having heard something brief said on it by some of his chief ministers. . . . Now Your Lordships, knowing what is said here, can decide about it best, as much more prudent and of greater experience. I think it good to write you all I hear. . . .

3 November 1502, from Imola.

. . . I have not tried to speak with the Duke, not having anything to tell him that is new, and the same things would bore him. You must recall that nobody speaks with him except three or four of his ministers and some foreigners who have to deal with him about matters of importance, and he does not come out of an antechamber except at eleven or twelve at night or later; for this reason there is no opportunity to speak with him ever, except through an audience appointed; and when he knows that a man brings him nothing but words, he never gives him an audience. This I have said that Your Lordships may not wonder at this decision of mine not to speak with him, and also may not wonder if in the future I write to you about not getting an audience.

22 Francesco Guicciardini **The Sack of Prato and the return of the Medici to Florence (1540)**

The sack of Prato in 1512 was momentous for the Florentines as it ended their hopes of enjoying an independent republic and enabled the Medici to return to their old, dominant position. It also demonstrated how ineffectual a citizen militia was against professional soldiers such as those employed by the king of Spain, Ferdinand. The devastation of Prato, together with the capture of Brescia and the sack of Rome, became a byword for the tactics of total war employed during the Italian campaigns in this period. On Guicciardini, see Text 19.

Source: *The History of Italy*, trans. and ed. S. Alexander, Macmillan, New York and London, 1969, pp. 261–7

Nothing flies away faster than opportunity, nothing more dangerous than to judge other people's intentions, nothing more harmful than immoderate suspicion. All the leading citizens wanted an agreement, accustomed by the example of their forefathers to often defend their liberty against iron with gold. Therefore, they urgently requested that the ambassadors chosen should immediately depart, charged among other things, to see to it that provisions be made available from Prato to the Spanish army, so that the Viceroy [of Naples, Raimondo de Cardona] might quietly wait if the treaty being negotiated should be drawn up. But the Gonfaloniere,[1] either because he persuaded himself against his natural timidity that the enemy despaired of victory and therefore would have to depart by themselves in any case, or fearing that the Medici might return to Florence by some device, or fate leading him on to be the cause of his own ruin and of the calamity of his country, guilefully delayed dispatching the ambassadors so that they did not depart on the day when they were supposed to go according to the decision.

Hence the Viceroy, pinched by the want of provisions and uncertain if the ambassadors would come any more, shifted camp on the following night from the gate of the Mercatale to the gate called del Serraglio, from which one goes toward the mountains, and there he began to batter the nearest wall with his two cannon; he chose this place because a high turret was joined to the wall from which one could easily climb up to the breach in the wall above that was being bombarded; and this advantage from without became a hindrance from within because the breach that was being made above the turret remained from within very high above the ground. One of the two cannon shattered at the very first salvo, and the other, which they continued to fire alone, had lost so much of its strength because it had been shot off so frequently that the shots reached the walls with weak velocity and to little effect. Nevertheless, after they had, over a period of many hours, made an opening of somewhat more than twelve cubits, some of the Spanish infantry mounted the turret to assail the breach and from there they got up to the top of the wall where they killed two of the footsoldiers who were guarding it. The death of these caused the others to begin to withdraw and the Spaniards were already climbing up the scaling ladders; and although within, near the wall there was a squadron of footsoldiers with pikes and grenades under orders not to permit any of the enemy to stay on the wall and to attack any of those who foolhardily jumped within or got down in any way, yet as soon as they began to see the enemies on the walls, they fled and abandoned the defense. The Spaniards, amazed that military men as well as humble inexpert civilians should show such cowardice and so little skill, broke into the wall without any opposition for the most part, and began to race through the town, where there was no longer any resistance, but only cries, flight, violence, sack, blood and killing, the terrified Florentine footsoldiers casting away their weapons and surrendering to the victors. And nothing would have been spared the avarice, lust and cruelty of the invaders had not the Cardinal de' Medici[2] placed guards at the main church and saved the honor of the women, all of whom had taken refuge there. More than two thousand men died, not fighting (for not one fought) but fleeing or crying for mercy; all the others together with the Florentine representatives were taken prisoner. Once Prato was lost, the Pistoiese [people of Pistoia] agreed to provide the Viceroy with provisions, and received from him a promise that they would not be harmed. But only in this instance did the Pistoiese depart from Florentine rule.

But as soon as the Florentines heard about the defeat of Prato (so that the ambassadors who were coming to the Viceroy turned back, halfway there), there was great perturbation in the minds of men. The Gonfaloniere, regretting his vain counsels, terrified and having almost completely lost his reputation and prestige, ruled rather than ruling, and irresolute, allowed himself to be led by the will of others, and did not attend to anything, neither protecting himself nor the safety of the citizenry. Others who were looking forward to a change in government waxed bold and publicly laid blame on the present state of affairs: but most of the citizens, unaccustomed to arms and having the miserable example of Prato before their eyes, although they warmly preferred a popular form of government, were exposed because of their fear, as easy prey of anyone who wished to oppress them.

Because of this, Paolo Vettori and Antonio Francesco degli Albizi, young noblemen, seditious and eager for innovations, became more audacious. Many months earlier these two had already secretly conspired with several others in favor of the Medici, and had secretly met and spoken with Giulio de' Medici[3] in a villa within Florentine territory near Siena, for the purpose of working out a means to restore this family to power. These young men now resolved to get the Gonfaloniere out of the municipal palace by force. Having apprised Bartolomeo Valori of their plans, a young man of the same rank and, like Paolo, deeply in debt because of his excessive expenditures, on the morning of the second day after the loss of Prato, which was the last day of August, they went with a small company to the palace, where they found no guard or resistance whatever, since the Gonfaloniere had surrendered everything to the will of chance and fortune; and entered his chamber and threatened to take his life if he should not leave the palace; in which case they promised to give him their pledge that he would go unharmed. The Gonfaloniere yielded to this, and now there was a tumultuous uprising all over the city, many persons revealing themselves opposed to him and no one in his favor. Having at their orders caused the magistrates immediately to convene, who according to the law had the widest authority over the *gonfalonieri* [municipal officials], the conspirators demanded that Soderini be legally removed from the magistracy, under the threat that otherwise they would take his life. Fearing he would be killed, he was removed from office against his will, and taken for safety to the house of Paolo Vettori whence, on the following night, carefully guarded, he was led to Sienese territory, and from there, pretending to go to Rome with the safe-conduct obtained from the Pope, he secretly took the road to Ancona and went by sea to Ragusa, because his brother the Cardinal had advised him that the Pope would break his promise to him, either out of hatred or greed to plunder his money since he was reputed to be very rich. Once the Gonfaloniere had been removed from the magistracy, the city immediately sent ambassadors to the Viceroy with whom they easily came to an agreement, the Cardinal de' Medici serving as intermediary. The Cardinal was satisfied that with regard to his own interests there should be no mention other than restitution of his family and all their followers within the country as private citizens, with the right to buy back, within a certain time, their properties which had been expropriated by taxation, but restoring the money spent and the [cost of] improvements made by those to whom they had been transferred. [. . .]

The Gonfaloniere having been cast out and the dangers of war having been removed by the agreement, the citizens now began to work to correct the government in certain matters in which the previous organization was considered to be useless, but with a universal intention (except for very few, and these either youths or almost all people of low rank), to maintain liberty and the Grand Council. Therefore they decided by new legislation that the Gonfaloniere should no longer be chosen in perpetuity but only for one year, and that in addition to the Council of the Eighty, which was changed every six months and which had the authority to determine the most serious matters, in order that the best-qualified citizens might participate in its councils, there should be added in perpetuity all those who had administered up to that day the chief offices, either at home or abroad: at home those who had been either Gonfaloniere of Justice or of the Ten of the Balìa,[4] of great prestige in that Republic; abroad all those who had been chosen by the Council of Eighty as either ambassadors to princes or general commissioners in war, leaving the organization of the government unchanged in all other respects.

Having established these things, the gonfaloniere elected for the first year was Giovan Battista Ridolfi, a noble citizen reputed to be very wise; the people having respect (as occurs in disturbed times) not so much for those who were more pleasing to them because of their popular touch, but rather those who could hold the trembling Republic firm by their own virtues, and by their great authority in the city, especially among the nobility.

But things had already gone too far, and the commonweal had too many powerful enemies – in the bowels of the domain a distrustful army, within the city the most audacious youth eager to oppress it. And although he demonstrated the contrary with words, the Cardinal de' Medici wanted the same thing. From the very beginning he would not have considered the restitution of his family as private citizens worthy reward for so much toil; furthermore, considering that now especially not even this would prove to be long-lasting, because together with his name, they would be deeply hated by everyone, the other citizens being always goaded by the suspicion that the house of Medici would lay ambush against their freedom, and much more because of the hatred felt against the Medici who had led the Spanish army against their country and been the cause of the most cruel sack of Prato, and because the city out of terror of arms had been forced to accept such base and iniquitous terms. Those who had previously conspired with him had spurred him on, as well as several others who had no honorable position in a well-ordered republic. But the consent of the Viceroy was necessary, who still remained at Prato waiting for the first payment, which the city was having difficulties in meeting because of conditions within Florence. And whatever might be his reason, the Viceroy was not inclined toward any change of government within the city.

Nevertheless, when the Cardinal demonstrated to him (and saw to it that he was seconded by the Marquis della Palude and Andrea Caraffa, Count of Santa Severina, condottiere [mercenary commander] in the army) that the very name of Spaniard could not help but be most odious to a city where they had caused so much harm; and that on any occasion whatever the Florentines would always support the enemies of the Catholic King (indeed there was danger that once the army withdrew, they would summon back the Gonfaloniere, whom they had been forced to expel), the Viceroy finally consented to the Cardinal's demands. He was also influenced thereto by the fact that the Florentines were having so much difficulty in raising the money which they had promised. Indeed, had they been more prompt in their payments, a firmer foundation for a free government would have been laid down.

As soon as the Cardinal had settled his affairs with the Viceroy, he immediately went to his palace in Florence; and many condottieri and Italian soldiers entered the city, some with the Cardinal and some separately, since the magistrates, for fear of the closeness of the Spaniards, did not dare forbid them to enter.

On the following day, a council of many citizens convened at the public palace to discuss affairs, Giuliano de' Medici[5] being present at the meeting, when suddenly soldiers assaulted the gate and then climbed the stairs and occupied the palace, pillaging the silver which was kept there for the use of the Signoria. The Signori, together with the Gonfaloniere, were forced to yield to the will of those who could do more with weapons than the magistrates could achieve by respect and unarmed authority; and so as Giuliano de' Medici proposed, the Signori immediately summoned the people to a parliament in the Piazza Signoria, by ringing the great bell. Those who appeared were surrounded by armed soldiers and young men within the city, who had seized arms for the Medici; and thus they agreed that power over public affairs should be turned over to about fifty citizens chosen according to the Cardinal's will, and that these citizens should have the same authority as had the entire people (which broad form of power the Florentines called Balìa). Now by the decree of these men, the government was reduced to that form which it used to have before the year 1494, and a garrison was set up within the palace, and the Medici seized once again that same position of grandeur, but governed much more imperiously and with much more absolute power than had their forefathers.

Thus the liberty of the Florentines was oppressed by arms, but the Florentines had been led to that situation primarily as a result of the disagreements among the citizens; and it was believed that they would not have fallen to such a state (I pass over the neutrality which they had so unwisely maintained, and the fact that the Gonfaloniere had permitted the enemies of popular government to become too confident) if they had not, also in recent times, so neglected public affairs. For the King of Aragon had not at first so great a desire to subvert liberty as to turn the city away from its loyalty to the King of France and get some money out of it to pay his army. Therefore, as soon as the French had abandoned the duchy of Milan, he commissioned the Viceroy that, when things made it necessary for him to turn to other enterprises, or for whatever other reason he might realize that the restitution of the Medici would prove difficult, he should make his decision according to conditions of the times, and should deal or not deal with the city according as it seemed opportune to him. [. . .] If, after the French had been evicted, the Florentines had carefully seen to it, by means of an agreement, that their situation was strengthened; or if they had fortified themselves with arms and trained soldiers, then either the Viceroy would not have marched against them or, finding it difficult to defeat them, would easily have been brought to an agreement with money. But it was destined that they should not act in that fashion, despite the fact that, besides what might have been understood by human reason, they had not also been forewarned of imminent perils by celestial signs: for, a little while earlier, a thunderbolt had struck the Prato gate and knocked the golden lilies, insignia of the King of France, off an ancient marble shield; another lightning bolt had hit the top of the palace and, entering into the Gonfaloniere's chamber, had struck nothing except the great silver box in which votes of the supreme magistracy had been gathered, and then flashing down to the lowest part of the palace, had struck a great stone which held up the whole weight of the building at the foot of the stairs, so that the stone was pushed out of its place unharmed and looked as if it had been drawn out of there by the most skillful architectural experts.

NOTES

1   *Gonfaloniere di Giustizia* (Standard bearer of Justice) was the official title of the head of
     the Florentine communal government, who in this instance was Piero Soderini.
2   Cardinal Giovanni de'Medici, pope Leo X 1513–21.
3   Giulio de'Medici, cousin of Cardinal Giovanni, Pope Clement VII 1523–34.
4   *Balìa* were short-term executive committees called together at times of crisis.
5   Giuliano de'Medici, the older brother of Cardinal Giovanni, and later Duke of Nemours
     (d.1516).

23 Niccolò Machiavelli **Letter to Francesco Vettori (1513)**

Francesco Vettori (1474–1539) was a Florentine patrician who had become
friendly with Machiavelli while they were both on an embassy during the time of
the republic. He was, however, instrumental in the return of the Medici in 1512
and was employed by them as an ambassador and counsellor. He helped
Machiavelli during his difficulties with the new regime, but could not manage to

get him a new job. This letter is of great importance as it shows that *The Prince* had been composed by 1513. It also provides an ironic but graphic picture of Machiavelli's enforced rural existence. Although it was to be some years before he was re-employed, he soon resumed semi-public life by participating in the discussions in the Orti Oricellari (Oricellari gardens). They were owned by the Rucellai family (Vettori was one of this circle and was related to the Rucellai). They were frequented by patrician republicans, some fervent supporters of the Medici and some, like Machiavelli, nostalgic for a more inclusive regime. The ideas aired in this circle stimulated Machiavelli's thinking and the books which he wrote during the next twelve years.

Source: Niccolò Machiavelli, *The Prince*, ed. M. L. Kekewich, Wordsworth Classics of World Literature, Ware, Hertfordshire, 1997, Appendix C, pp. 126–9.

10 December 1513, Florence

Magnificent ambassador – 'Never late were favours divine.'[1] I say this because I seemed to have lost – no, rather mislaid – your good will; you had not written to me for a long time, and I was wondering what the reason could be. And of all those that came into my mind I took little account, except of one only, when I feared that you had stopped writing because somebody had written to you that I was not a good guardian of your letters, and I knew that, except Filippo and Pagolo, nobody by my doing had seen them.[2] I have found it again through your last letter of the twenty-third of the past month, from which I learn with pleasure how regularly and quietly you carry on this public office, and I encourage you to continue so, because he who gives up his own convenience for the convenience of others, only loses his own and from them gets no gratitude. And since fortune wants to do everything, she wishes us to let her do it, to be quiet, and not to give her trouble, and to wait for a time when she will allow something to be done by men; and then will be the time for you to work harder, to stir things up more, and for me to leave my farm and say: 'Here I am.' I cannot however, wishing to return equal favours, tell you in this letter anything else than what my life is; and if you judge that you would like to swap with me, I shall be glad to.

I am living on my farm, and since I had my last bad luck, I have not spent twenty days, putting them all together, in Florence. I have until now been snaring thrushes with my own hands. I got up before day, prepared birdlime, went out with a bundle of cages on my back, so that I looked like Geta when he was returning from the harbour with Amphitryon's books.[3] I caught at least two thrushes and at most six. And so I did all September. Then this pastime, pitiful and strange as it is, gave out, to my displeasure. And of what sort my life is, I shall tell you.

I get up in the morning with the sun and go into a grove I am having cut down, where I remain two hours to look over the work of the past day and kill some time with the cutters, who have always some bad-luck story ready, about either themselves or their neighbours. And as to this grove I could tell you a thousand fine things that have happened to me, in dealing with Frosino da Panzano and others who wanted some of this firewood. And Frosino especially sent for a number of cords [a measurement of wood] without saying a thing to me, and on payment he wanted to keep back from me ten lire, which he says he should have had from me four years ago, when he beat me at *cricca* at Antonio Guicciardini's. I raised the devil, and was going to prosecute as a thief the waggoner who came for the wood, but Giovanni Machiavelli came between us and got us to agree. Batista Guicciardini, Filippo Ginori, Tommaso del Bene and some other citizens, when that north wind was blowing, each ordered a cord from me. I made promises to all and sent one to Tommaso, which at Florence changed to half a cord, because it was piled up again by himself, his wife, his servant, his children, so that he looked like Gabburra when on Thursday with all his servants he cudgels an ox. Hence, having seen for whom there was profit, I told the others I had no more wood, and all of them were angry about it, and especially Batista, who counts this along with his misfortunes at Prato. [He was in command there when it was taken by the Spanish in 1512.]

Leaving the grove, I go to a spring, and thence to my aviary. I have a book in my pocket, either Dante or Petrarch, or one of the lesser poets, such as Tibullus, Ovid and the like. I read of their tender passions and their loves, remember mine, enjoy myself a while in that sort of dreaming. Then I move along the road to the inn; I speak with those who pass, ask news of their villages, learn various things, and note the various tastes and different fancies of men. In the course of these things comes the hour for dinner, where with my family I eat such food as this poor farm of mine and my tiny property allow. Having eaten, I go back to the inn; there is the host, usually a butcher, a miller, two furnace tenders. With these I sink into vulgarity for the whole day, playing at *cricca* and at trich-trach, and then these games bring on a thousand disputes and countless insults with offensive words, and usually we are fighting over a penny, and nevertheless we are heard shouting as far as San Casciano. So, involved in these trifles, I keep my brain from growing mouldy, and satisfy the malice of this fate of mine, being glad to have her drive me along this road, to see if she will be ashamed of it.

On the coming of evening, I return to my house and enter my study; and at the door I take off the day's clothing, covered with mud and dust, and put on garments regal and courtly; and reclothed appropriately, I enter the ancient courts of ancient men, where, received by them with affection, I feed on that food which only is mine and which I was born for, where I am not ashamed to speak with them and to ask them the reason for their actions; and they in their kindness answer me; and for four hours of time I do not feel boredom, I forget every trouble, I do not dread poverty, I am not frightened by death; entirely I give myself over to them.

And because Dante says it does not produce knowledge when we hear but do not remember,[4] I have noted everything in their conversation which has profited me, and have composed a little work *On Princedoms*, where I go as deeply as I can into considerations on this subject, debating what a princedom is, of what kinds they are, how they are gained, how they are kept, why they are lost. And if ever you can find any of my fantasies pleasing, this one should not displease you; and by a prince, and especially by a new prince, it ought to be welcomed.

Hence I am dedicating it to His Magnificence Giuliano [de'Medici]. Filippo Casavecchia has seen it; he can give you some account in part of the thing in itself and of the discussions I have had with him, though I am still enlarging and revising it.

You wish, Magnificent Ambassador, that I leave this life and come to enjoy yours with you. I shall do it in any case, but what tempts me now are certain affairs that within six weeks I shall finish. What makes me doubtful is that the Soderini we know so well are in the city, whom I should be obliged, on coming there, to visit and talk with. I should fear that on my return I could not hope to dismount at my house but should dismount at the prison, because though this government has mighty foundations and great security, yet it is new and there-fore suspicious, and there is no lack of wiseacres who, to make a figure, like Pagolo Bertini, would place others at the dinner table and leave the reckoning to me. I beg you to rid me of this fear, and then I shall come within the time mentioned to visit you in any case.

I have talked with Filippo about this little work of mine that I have spoken of, whether it is good to give it or not to give it; and if it is good to give it, whether it would be good to take it myself, or whether I should send it there. Not giving it would make me fear that at the least Giuliano will not read it and that this rascal Ardinghellis[5] [. . .] will get himself honour from this latest work of mine. The giving of it is forced on me by the necessity that drives me, because I am using up my money, and I cannot remain as I am a long time without becom-ing despised through poverty. In addition, there is my wish that our present Medici lords will make use of me, even if they begin by making me roll a stone; because then if I could not gain their favour, I should complain of myself; and through this thing, if it were read, they would see that for the fifteen years while I have been studying the art of the state, I have not slept or been playing; and well may anybody be glad to get the services of one who at the expense of others has become full of experience. And of my honesty there should be no doubt, because having always preserved my honesty, I shall hardly now learn to break it; and he who has been honest and good for forty-three years, as I have, cannot change his nature; and as a witness to my honesty and goodness I have my poverty.

I should like, then, to have you also write me what you think best on this matter, and I give you my regards. Be happy.

Niccolò Machiavelli

NOTES

1   Francesco Petrarch (1304–74), *Triumph of Eternity*, V.13.
2   Filippo Casavecchia and Paolo Vettori were both close friends of Machiavelli and had worked with him in the Florentine chancellery. Pagolo is a variant spelling of Paolo. He was the younger brother of Francesco Vettori. The family owned a villa in nearby San Casciano (mentioned in the letter).
3   A reference to the Roman play by Plautus, *Amphitrio*.
4   Dante, *Paradiso*, V.41–2.

5   Piero Ardinghelli (1470–1526) originally sided with the Florentine Republic and then switched to the Medici.

24 Niccolò Machiavelli *The Discourses (c.1513–19)*
(i) How many Kinds of State there are (ii) That it is necessary to be the Sole Authority (iii) That it is very easy to manage Things in a State

The first ten books of the *History* of Titus Livius (59 BCE–17 CE) cover the years of the Roman republic. Machiavelli believed that this was the time when standards of good civic conduct (*virtù*) and the institutions of government were at their highest. These should be emulated by his contemporaries, particularly the Florentines, although it might be necessary, as in ancient Rome, for one man to enjoy absolute authority for a time to strengthen the state and protect it from its enemies. This long treatise has been thought by some to contradict the advice given in *The Prince* about how an individual could achieve supreme and effective power. This hinges on a remark in the second chapter of that treatise to the effect that Machiavelli had written about republics elsewhere. This must mean either that it was inserted later than 1513, when we know that a version had been completed, or that he worked on both books simultaneously. This second possibility is only problematic if it is thought that Machiavelli had become so disillusioned with the Medici by the middle of the decade that he wrote *The Discourses* in praise of republics. Yet they do allow for the possibility of princely rule in certain circumstances. They must have been completed by 1519 as they were dedicated to Zanobi Buondelmonte and Cosimo Rucellai who died in that year.

Source: *The Discourses,* ed. B. Crick, trans. L. J. Walker, Routledge, 1950, pp. 104–9, 111, 131–8, 243–8

i)

HOW MANY KINDS OF STATE THERE ARE AND OF WHAT KIND WAS THAT OF ROME

I propose to dispense with a discussion of cities which from the outset have been subject to another power, and shall speak only of those which have from the outset been far removed from any kind of external servitude, but, instead, have from the start been governed in accordance with their wishes, whether as republics or principalities. As such cities have had diverse origins, so too they have had diverse laws and institutions. For either at the outset, or before very long, to some of them laws have been given by some one person at some one time, as laws were given to the Spartans by Lycurgus; whereas others have acquired them by chance and at different times as occasion arose. This was the case in Rome.[1]

Happy indeed should we call that state which produces a man so prudent that men can live securely under the laws which he prescribes without having to emend them. Sparta, for instance, observed its laws for more than eight hundred years without corrupting them and without any dangerous disturbance. Unhappy, on the other hand, in some degree is that city to be deemed which, not having chanced to meet with a prudent organizer, has to reorganize itself. And, of such, that is the more unhappy which is the more remote from order; and that is the more remote from order whose institutions have missed altogether the straight road which leads it to its perfect and true destiny. For it is almost impossible that states of this type should by any eventuality be set on the right road again; whereas those which, if their order is not perfect, have made a good beginning and are capable of improvement, may become perfect should something happen which provides the opportunity. It should, however, be noted that they will never introduce order without incurring danger, because few men ever welcome new laws setting up a new order in the state unless necessity makes it clear to them that there is need for such laws; and since such a necessity cannot arise without danger, the state may easily be ruined before the new order has been brought to completion. The republic of Florence bears this out, for owing to what happened at Arezzo in [15]02 it was reconstituted, and owing to what happened at Prato in [15]12 its constitution was destroyed.

It being now my intention to discuss what were the institutions of the city of Rome and what events conduced to its perfection, I would remark that those who have written about states say that there are to be found in them one of three forms of government, called by them *Principality*, *Aristocracy* and *Democracy*, and that those who set up a government in any particular state must adopt one of them, as best suits their purpose.

Others – and with better judgement many think – say that there are six types of government, of which three are very bad, and three are good in themselves but easily become corrupt, so that they too must be classed as pernicious. Those that are good are the three above mentioned. Those that are bad are the other three, which depend on them, and each of them is so like the one associated with it that it easily passes from one form to the other. For *Principality* easily becomes *Tyranny*. From *Aristocracy* the transition to *Oligarchy* is an easy one. *Democracy* is without difficulty converted into *Anarchy*. So that if anyone who is organizing a commonwealth sets up one of the three first forms of government, he sets up what will last but for a while, since there are no means whereby to prevent it passing into its contrary, on account of the likeness which in such a case virtue has to vice.[2]

These variations of government among men are due to chance. For in the beginning of the world, when its inhabitants were few, they lived for a time scattered like the beasts. Then, with the multiplication of their offspring, they drew together and, in order the better to be able to defend themselves, began to look about for a man stronger and more courageous than the rest, made him their head, and obeyed him.

It was thus that men learned how to distinguish what is honest and good from what is pernicious and wicked, for the sight of someone injuring his benefactor evoked in them hatred and sympathy and they blamed the ungrateful and respected those who showed gratitude, well aware that the same injuries might have been done to themselves. Hence to prevent evil of this kind they took to making laws and to assigning punishments to those who contravened them. The notion of justice thus came into being.

In this way it came about that, when later on they had to choose a prince, they did not have recourse to the boldest as formerly, but to one who excelled in prudence and justice.

But when at a yet later stage they began to make the prince hereditary instead of electing him, his heirs soon began to degenerate as compared with their ancestors, and, forsaking virtuous deeds, considered that princes have nought else to do but to surpass other men in extravagance, lasciviousness, and every other form of licentiousness. With the result that the prince came to be hated, and, since he was hated, came to be afraid, and from fear soon passed to offensive action, which quickly brought about a tyranny.

From which, before long, was begotten the source of their downfall; for tyranny gave rise to conspiracies and plots against princes, organized not by timid and weak men, but by men conspicuous for their liberality, magnanimity, wealth and ability, for such men could not stand the dishonourable life the prince was leading. The masses, therefore, at the instigation of these powerful leaders, took up arms against the prince, and, when he had been liquidated, submitted to the authority of those whom they looked upon as their liberators. Hence the latter, to whom the very term 'sole head' had become odious, formed themselves into a government. Moreover, in the beginning, mindful of what they had suffered under a tyranny, they ruled in accordance with the laws which they had made, subordinated their own convenience to the common advantage, and, both in private matters and public affairs, governed and preserved order with the utmost diligence.

But when the administration passed to their descendants who had no experience of the changeability of fortune, had not been through bad times, and instead of remaining content with the civic equality then prevailing, reverted to avarice, ambition and to seizing other men's womenfolk, they caused government by an aristocracy to become government by an oligarchy in which civic rights were entirely disregarded; so that in a short time there came to pass in their case the same thing as happened to the tyrant, for the masses, sick of their government, were ready to help anyone who had any sort of plan for attacking their rulers; and so there soon arose someone who with the aid of the masses liquidated them.

Then, since the memory of the prince and of the injuries inflicted by him was still fresh, and since, having got rid of government by the few, they had no desire to return to that of a prince, they turned to a democratic form of government, which they organized in such a way that no sort of authority was vested either in a few powerful men or in a prince.

And, since all forms of government are to some extent respected at the outset, this democratic form of government maintained itself for a while but not for long, especially when the generation that had organized it had passed away. For anarchy quickly supervened, in which no respect was shown either for the individual or for the official, and which was such that, as everyone did what he liked, all sorts of outrages were constantly committed. The outcome was inevitable. Either at the suggestion of some good man or because this anarchy had to be got rid of somehow, principality was once again restored. And from this there was, stage by stage, a return to anarchy, by way of the transitions and for the reasons assigned.

This, then, is the cycle through which all commonwealths pass, whether they govern themselves or are governed. But rarely do they return to the same form of government, for there can scarce be a state of such vitality that it can undergo often such changes and yet remain in being. What usually happens is that, while in a state of commotion in which it lacks both counsel and strength, a state becomes subject to a neighbouring and better organized state. Were it not so, a commonwealth might go on for ever passing through these governmental transitions.

I maintain then, that all the forms of government mentioned above are far from satisfactory, the three good ones because their life is so short, the three bad ones because of their inherent malignity. Hence prudent legislators, aware of their defects, refrained from adopting as such any one of these forms, and chose instead one that shared in them all, since they thought such a government would be stronger and more stable, for if in one and the same states there was principality, aristocracy and democracy each would keep watch over the other.

Lycurgus is one of those who have earned no small measure of praise for constitutions of this kind. For in the laws which he gave to Sparta, he assigned to the kings, to the aristocracy, and to the populace each its own function, and thus introduced a form of government which lasted for more than eight hundred years to his very great credit and to the tranquillity of that city. [. . .]

[In Rome] tribunes of the plebs came to be appointed, and their appointment did much to stabilize the form of government in this republic, for in its government all three estates now had a share. And so favoured was it by fortune that, though the transition from Monarchy to Aristocracy and thence to Democracy, took place by the very stages and for the very reasons laid down earlier in this discourse, none the less the granting of authority to the aristocracy did not abolish altogether the royal estate, nor was the authority of the aristocracy wholly removed when the populace was granted a share in it. On the contrary, the blending of these estates made a perfect commonwealth; [and since it was friction between the plebs and the senate that brought this perfection about, in the next two chapters we shall show more fully how this came to be.]

ii)

THAT IT IS NECESSARY TO BE THE SOLE AUTHORITY IF ONE WOULD CONSTITUTE A REPUBLIC AFRESH OR WOULD REFORM IT THOROUGHLY REGARDLESS OF ITS ANCIENT INSTITUTIONS

To some it will appear strange that I have got so far in my discussion of Roman history without having made any mention of the founders of that republic or of either its religious or its military institutions. Hence, that I may not keep the minds of those who are anxious to hear about such things any longer in suspense, let me say that many perchance will think it a bad precedent that the founder of a civic state, such as Romulus, should first have killed his brother, and then have acquiesced in the death of Titus Tatius, the Sabine, whom he had chosen as his colleague in the kingdom. They will urge that, if such actions be justifiable, ambitious citizens who are eager to govern, will follow the example of their prince and use violence against those who are opposed to *their* authority. A view that will hold good provided we leave out of consideration the end which Romulus had in committing these murders.

One should take it as a general rule that rarely, if ever, does it happen that a state, whether it be a republic or a kingdom, is either well-ordered at the outset or radically transformed *vis-à-vis* its old institutions unless this be done by one person. It is likewise essential that there should be but one person upon whose mind and method depends any similar process of organization. Wherefore the prudent organizer of a state whose intention it is to govern not in his own interests but for the common good, and not in the interest of his successors but for the sake of that fatherland which is common to all, should contrive to be alone in his authority. Nor will any reasonable man blame him for taking any action, however extraordinary, which may be of service in the organizing of a kingdom or the constituting of a republic. It is a sound maxim that reprehensible actions may be justified by their effects, and that when the effect is good, as it was in the case of Romulus, it always justifies the action. For it is the man who uses violence to spoil things, not the man who uses it to mend them, that is blameworthy.

The organizer of a state ought further to have sufficient prudence and virtue not to bequeath the authority he has assumed to any other person, for, seeing that men are more prone to evil than to good, his successor might well make ambitious use of that which he had used virtuously. Furthermore, though but one person suffices for the purpose of organization, what he has organized will not last long if it continues to rest on the shoulders of one man, but may well last if many remain in charge and many look to its maintenance. Because, though the many are incompetent to draw up a constitution since diversity of opinion will prevent them from discovering how best to do it, yet when they realize it has been done, they will not agree to abandon it.

That Romulus was a man of this character, that for the death of his brother and of his colleague he deserves to be excused, and that what he did was done for the common good and not to satisfy his personal ambition, is shown by his having at once instituted a senate with which he consulted and with whose views his decisions were in accord. Also, a careful consideration of the authority which Romulus reserved to himself will show that all he reserved to himself was the command of the army in time of war and the convoking of the senate. It is clear, too, that when the Tarquins were expelled and Rome became free, none of its ancient institutions were changed, save that in lieu of a permanent king there were appointed each year two consuls. This shows that the original institutions of this city as a whole were more in conformity with a political and self-governing state than with absolutism or tyranny. [. . .]

All things considered, therefore, I conclude that it is necessary to be the sole authority if one is to organize a state, and that Romulus' action in regard to the death of Remus and Titus Tatius is excusable, not blameworthy.

THOSE WHO SET UP A TYRANNY ARE NO LESS BLAMEWORTHY THAN ARE THE FOUNDERS OF A REPUBLIC OR A KINGDOM PRAISEWORTHY

Of all men that are praised, those are praised most who have played the chief part in founding a religion. Next come those who have founded either republics or kingdoms. After them in the order of celebratees are ranked army commanders who have added to the extent of their own dominions or to that of their country's. With whom may be conjoined men of letters of many different kinds who are each celebrated according to their status. Some modicum of praise is also ascribed to any man who excels in some art and in the practice of it, and of these the number is legion. On the other hand, those are held to be infamous and detestable who extirpate religion, subvert kingdoms and republics, make war on virtue, on letters, and on any art that brings advantage and honour to the human race, i.e. the profane, the violent, the ignorant, the worthless, the idle, the coward. Nor will there ever be anyone, be he foolish or wise, wicked or good, who, if called upon to choose between these two classes of men, will not praise the one that calls for praise and blame the one that calls for blame.

And yet, notwithstanding this, almost all men, deceived by the false semblance of good and the false semblance of renown, allow themselves either wilfully or ignorantly to slip into the ranks of those who deserve blame rather than praise; and, when they might have founded a republic or a kingdom to their immortal honour, turn their thoughts to tyranny, and fail to see what fame, what glory, security, tranquillity, conjoined with peace of mind, they are missing by adopting this course, and what infamy, scorn, abhorrence, danger and disquiet they are incurring. [. . .]

Let he who has become a prince in a republic consider, after Rome became an Empire, how much more praise is due to those emperors who acted, like good princes, in accordance with the laws, than to those who acted otherwise. It will be found that Titus, Nerva, Trajan, Hadrian, Antoninus and Marcus, had no need of soldiers to form a praetorian guard, nor of a multitude of legions to protect them, for their defence lay in their habits, the goodwill of the people, and the affection of the senate.[3] It will be seen, too, in the case of Caligula, Nero, Vitellius and other bad emperors, how it availed them little to have armies from the East and from the West to save them from the enemies they had made by their bad habits and their evil life.

If the history of these emperors be pondered well, it should serve as a striking lesson to any prince, and should teach him to distinguish between the ways of renown and of infamy, the ways of security and of fear. For of the twenty-six emperors from Caesar to Maximinus, sixteen were assassinated and only ten died a natural death. And, if some of those who were killed were good men, as Galba and Pertinax were, their death was due to the corruption which their predecessors had introduced among the troops. While, if among those who died ordinary deaths, there was a wicked man, like Severus, it must be put down to his great good luck and to his 'virtue', two things of which few men enjoy both. It will be seen, too, from a perusal of their history on what principle a good kingdom should rest; for all the emperors who acquired imperial power by inheritance were bad men, with the exception of Titus; those who acquired it through adoption, were all good, like the five counting from Nerva to Marcus; and when it fell to their heirs a period of decadence again ensued.[4]

Let a prince put before himself the period from Nerva to Marcus, and let him compare it with the preceding period and with that which came after, and then let him decide in which he would rather have been born, and during which he would have chosen to be emperor. What he will find when good princes were ruling, is a prince securely reigning among subjects no less secure, a world replete with peace and justice. He will see the senate's authority respected, the magistrates honoured, rich citizens enjoying their wealth, nobility and virtue held in the highest esteem, and everything working smoothly and going well. He will notice, on the other hand, the absence of any rancour, any licentiousness, corruption or ambition, and that in this golden age everyone is free to hold and to defend his own opinion. He will behold, in short, the world triumphant, its prince glorious and respected by all, the people fond of him and secure under his rule.

If he then looks attentively at the times of the other emperors, he will find them distraught with wars, torn by seditions, brutal alike in peace and in war, princes frequently killed by assassins, civil wars and foreign wars constantly occurring, Italy in travail and ever a prey to fresh misfortunes, its cities demolished and pillaged. He will see Rome burnt, its Capitol demolished by its own citizens, ancient temples lying desolate, religious rites grown corrupt, adultery rampant throughout the city. He will find the sea covered with exiles and the rocks stained with blood. In Rome he will see countless atrocities perpetrated; rank, riches, the honours men have won, and, above all, virtue, looked upon as a capital crime. He will find calumniators rewarded, servants suborned to turn against their masters, freed men to turn against their patrons, and those who lack enemies attacked by their friends. He will thus happily learn how much Rome, Italy, and the world owed to Caesar.

There can be no question but that every human being will be afraid to imitate the bad times, and will be imbued with an ardent desire to emulate the good. And, should a good prince seek worldly renown, he should most certainly covet possession of a city that has become corrupt, not, with Caesar, to complete its spoliation, but, with Romulus, to reform it. Nor in very truth can the heavens afford men a better opportunity of acquiring renown; nor can men desire anything better than this. And if in order to reform a city one were obliged to give up the principate, someone who did not reform it in order not to fall from that rank would have some excuse. There is, however, no excuse if one can both keep the principate and reform the city.

In conclusion, then, let those to whom the heavens grant such opportunities reflect that two courses are open to them: either so to behave that in life they rest secure and in death become renowned, or so to behave that in life they are in continual straits, and in death leave behind an imperishable record of their infamy.

iii)

THAT IT IS VERY EASY TO MANAGE THINGS IN A STATE IN WHICH THE MASSES ARE
NOT CORRUPT; AND THAT, WHERE EQUALITY EXISTS, IT IS IMPOSSIBLE TO SET UP
A PRINCIPALITY, AND, WHERE IT DOES NOT EXIST, IMPOSSIBLE TO SET UP A
REPUBLIC

Though what is to be feared and what is to be hoped for in states that are corrupt has been sufficiently discussed elsewhere, it does not seem to me irrelevant to consider here a decision made by the senate in regard to the vow which Camillus[5] had made to give a tenth part of the booty taken from the Veientes [a tribe of Etruscan people in Italy] to Apollo. This booty had come into the hands of the Roman plebs; and, since there was no other way of obtaining an account of it, the senate made an edict requiring everyone to bring to the public treasury a tenth part of what he had seized. This decision was not carried into effect since the senate later adopted other ways and means of rendering to Apollo the satisfaction which was due from the plebs. It is apparent, none the less, from this decision what trust the senate had in the goodness of the plebs in that it felt sure that no one would fail to bring forth immediately all that the edict prescribed. It shows, too, that the plebs had no thought of acting fraudulently in regard to the edict by handing over less than was due. What they did, instead, was to get rid of the edict by showing plainly how indignant they were with it.

This example, and many others which have already been cited, show how great was the goodness and the respect for religion which then prevailed among the Roman people, and how much could be expected of them. For where such goodness prevails one cannot but anticipate good conduct. It cannot, on the other hand, be expected in these days in territories which are obviously corrupt, as is Italy above all other lands. France and Spain, too, share in this corruption; and if in these countries disorders are apparently not so great as those that occur daily in Italy, this is not so much due to the goodness of the people there – for in goodness they are noticeably lacking – as to their having a king who keeps them united, not merely by his personal virtues, but by constitutional methods, which in those kingdoms as yet are not corrupt.

In the province of Germany it is quite clear that goodness and respect for religion are still to be found in its peoples, with the result that many republics there enjoy freedom and observe their laws in such a way that neither outsiders nor their own inhabitants dare to usurp power there.

And that it is true of these republics that in them there still prevails a good deal of the goodness of ancient times, I propose to make clear by giving an example similar to that related above of the Roman senate and people. When these republics have need to spend any sum of money on the public account, it is customary for their magistrates or councils, in whom is vested authority to deal with such matters, to impose on all the inhabitants of a town a tax of one or two per cent of the value of each one's property. The decision having been made, each person presents himself to the tax-collectors in accordance with the constitutional practice of the town. He then takes an oath to pay the appropriate sum, and throws into a chest provided for the purpose the amount which he conscientiously thinks that he ought to pay; but of this payment there is no witness save the man who pays. This is an indication of how much goodness and how much respect for religion there still is in such men; for presumably each pays the correct sum, since, if he did not do so, the tax would not bring in the amount estimated on the basis of previous collections made in the customary way, and failure to realize it would reveal any fraud, and in that case some other method of collecting the tax would have been adopted.

This goodness is the more to be admired in these days in that it is so rare. Indeed, it seems to survive only in this province. This is due to two things. In the first place the towns have but little intercourse with their neighbours, who seldom go to visit them, or are visited by them, since they are content with the goods, live on the food, and are clothed with the wool which their own land provides. The occasion for intercourse, and with it the initial step on the road to corruption, is thus removed, since they have no chance of taking up the customs either of the French, the Spaniards or the Italians, nations which, taken together, are the source of world-wide corruption.

The second reason is that those states where political life survives uncorrupted, do not permit any of their citizens to live after the fashion of the gentry. On the contrary, they maintain there perfect equality, and to lords and gentry residing in that province are extremely hostile; so that, should any perchance fall into their hands, they treat them as sources of corruption and causes of trouble, and kill them.

To make it clear what is meant by the term 'gentry', I would point out that the term 'gentry' is used of those who live in idleness on the abundant revenue derived from their estates, without having anything to do either with their cultivation or with other forms of labour essential to life. Such men are a pest in any republic and in any province; but still more pernicious are those who, in addition to the aforesaid revenues, have castles under their command and subjects who are under their obedience. Of these two types of men there are plenty in the kingdom of Naples, the Papal States, the Romagna and Lombardy. It is owing to this that in these provinces there has never arisen any republic or any political life, for men born in such conditions are entirely inimical to any form of civic government. In provinces thus organized no attempt to set up a republic could possibly succeed. To reconstitute them, should anyone want to do so, the only way would be to set up a monarchy there. The reason for this is that, where the material is so corrupt, laws do not suffice to keep it in hand; it is necessary to have, besides laws, a superior force, such as appertains to a monarch, who has such absolute and overwhelming power that he can restrain excesses due to ambition and the corrupt practices of the powerful.

This argument is borne out by the case of Tuscany, in whose territory, small as it is, one finds that there have long been three republics, Florence, Siena and Lucca; and that the other cities of this province, though in a way servile, yet are of such a mind and have such a constitution that either they maintain their freedom, or would like to do so. All of which is due to there being in Tuscany no baronial castles, and either none or very few gentry, and to the presence there of so great an equality that a wise man, familiar with ancient forms of civic government, should easily be able to introduce there a civic constitution. But, so great has been Tuscany's misfortune that up to the present she has come across nobody with the requisite ability and knowledge.

From this discussion the following conclusion may be drawn: (i) that, where the gentry are numerous, no one who proposes to set up a republic can succeed unless he first gets rid of the lot; and (ii) that, where considerable equality prevails, no one who proposes to set up a kingdom or principality, will ever be able to do it unless from that equality he selects many of the more ambitious and restless minds and makes of them gentry in fact and not in name, by giving them castles and possessions and making of them a privileged class with respect both to property and subjects; so that around him will be those with whose support he may maintain himself in power, and whose ambitions, thanks to him, may be realized. As to the rest they will be compelled to bear a yoke which nothing but force will ever be able to make them endure. Between force and those to whom force is applied a balance will thus be set up, and the standing of every man, each in his own order, will be consolidated. But, since to convert a province, suited to monarchical rule, into a republic, and to convert a province, suited to a republican regime, into a kingdom, is a matter which only a man of outstanding brainpower and authority can handle, and such men are rare, there have been many who have attempted it but few who have had the ability to carry it through. For the magnitude of an undertaking of this kind is such that it breaks down at the very beginning, partly because men get terrified and partly because it hampers them.

With my thesis that where there are gentry it is impossible to set up a republic, the experience of the Venetian republic may, perhaps, appear to be incompatible, for in that republic no man may hold any office unless he be a 'gentleman'. To which the answer is that this case in no way conflicts with my thesis, since 'gentlemen' in this republic are so in name rather than in point of fact; for they do not derive any considerable income from estates: their great wealth is based on merchandise and movable goods. Moreover, none of them have castles, nor have they any jurisdiction over men. The name 'gentleman' in their case is but a title, indicative of their standing. It is not based on any of the grounds which lead other cities to call people 'gentlemen'. Just as in other republics different classes go by different names, so in Venice the population is divided into 'gentlemen' and 'commoners'; and it has decided that of these the former alone shall hold, or be eligible for, office, from which the latter are wholly excluded. Why this does not cause disorder in that town has already been explained.

Let, then, a republic be constituted where there exists, or can be brought into being, notable equality; and a regime of the opposite type, i.e. a principality, where there is notable inequality. Otherwise what is done will lack proportion and will be of but short duration.

NOTES

1   Lycurgus and Numa were respectively the founding legislators of Sparta and Rome. They
     are compared by the Greek author Plutarch (*c*.46–*c*.120) in his *Parallel Lives of the Greeks
     and Romans*.

2   This is a summary of arguments for good and bad government from book four of the
     Politics of the Greek philosopher Aristotle.

3   These Roman emperors span the reigns of Titus Flavius Vespasianus (Vespasian 79–81)
     to Marcus Aurelius Antoninus (160–180). The intervening period is often referred to as
     the *Pax Romana*.

4   The range of rulers considered here extends from Gaius Julius Caesar (102–44 BCE)
     to Gaius Julius Maximinus (235–238), including the brief rules of Galba (68–9) and
     Pertinax (193). Presumably Lucius Septimius Severus (193–211) is the emperor who 'died
     an ordinary death' although he seems here to have been tarnished with the less laudable
     reputation of his later namesake, Severus Alexander, who was murdered. Marcus Coc-
     ceius Nerva (96–8) was morally upright in office, despite the fact that he had previously
     suppressed the Pisonian conspiracy against the notorious emperor Nero. The 'Marcus'
     here is the Stoic emperor, Marcus Aurelius.

5   Marcus Furius Camillus, a Roman general of the fourth century BCE.

25   Niccolò Machiavelli *The Art of War* (1520)

This was completed in 1520 and dedicated to Lorenzo Strozzi, a member of a
prominent Florentine patrician family. After it was published in the following year
it rapidly became one of the recognized European authorities on the subject. The
treatise took the form of a discussion set in the Orti Oricellari (Oricellari gardens).
The main speaker was Fabrizio Colonna, a well-known soldier and military expert.
Drawing heavily on classical authorities and showing little liking for modern
inventions such as artillery, Machiavelli discussed various aspects of warfare. His
principal theme was the superiority of citizen soldiers or militia to mercenaries,
an argument he had already presented in *The Prince* and *The Discourses*.

Source: *The Art of War*, in *The Chief Works and Others*, trans. A. H. Gilbert, Duke
University Press, Durham, North Carolina, 1965, Vol 2 (3 vols), pp. 568–70, 636–9.
Copyright 1965 by Allan H. Gilbert. Reprinted by permission of Duke University Press

THE ART OF WAR, BOOK I. THE CITIZEN SOLDIER

Cosimo Rucellai

Because I believe that without censure every man can be praised after his death,
since all cause and suspicion of flattery have disappeared, I shall not hesitate to
praise our Cosimo Rucellai, whose name I shall never remember without tears,
since I have observed in him those qualities strongly desired in a good friend by
his friends and in a citizen by his native city. I do not know what possession was
so much his (not excepting, to go no further, his soul) that for his friends he
would not willingly have spent it; I do not know of any undertaking that would
have frightened him, if in it he had perceived the good of his native land. And

I confess, freely, that I have never met, among all the men I have known and dealt with, a man whose spirit was more on fire for things grand and magnificent. At his death he complained to his friends of nothing except that he was born to die young in his own house, and unhonored, without according to his desire having assisted anyone, because he knew that nothing else could be said of him than that he died a good friend. It does not for that reason follow, however, even though deeds did not appear, that we, and any others who like ourselves knew him, cannot put faith in his praiseworthy qualities. Still it is true that to him Fortune was not so hostile that he did not leave some short record of his active intelligence, which appears in some love poems of his; for though he was not in love, yet in order not to waste his time until Fortune should lead him on to higher activities, in his youth he exercised himself in such writings. From these we learn with certainty how aptly he would have set forth his conceptions, and how much fame he would have won in poetry if he had practiced it as his chief interest. Since, then, Fortune has deprived us of association with so able a friend, I know we can find no other recourse than as much as possible to enjoy his memory and to repeat whatever he said with keenness or discussed with wisdom.

THE DISCUSSION IN COSIMO'S GARDENS

Because there is nothing of his fresher than the discussion which in very recent times Lord Fabrizio Colonna carried on with him in his gardens (for that gentleman held forth at length on military affairs and Cosimo keenly and wisely asked a great many questions), it has seemed good to me, since I, with some other friends, was present, to put it on record. Thereby the friends of Cosimo who were there assembled can, as they read, refresh their recollection of his excellent qualities. Any others will on the one hand have to regret that they were not there; on the other, they can learn many things useful not merely in military but in civilian life – sagely discussed by a very sagacious man.

FABRIZIO AND HIS AUDIENCE

I say, then, that when Fabrizio Colonna returned from Lombardy, where he had long been campaigning for the Catholic King [of Spain] with great glory to himself, he decided, as he was passing through Florence, to rest some days in that city in order to visit His Excellency the Duke and to see again some gentlemen with whom in the past he had been acquainted. Hence Cosimo thought it proper to invite him to a banquet in his gardens, not so much to exercise his own liberality as to have a reason for speaking with him at length, and from him hearing and learning various things such as from a man of that sort can be hoped for, since it seemed to Cosimo a chance to spend a day in talking about those matters that brought satisfaction to his own spirit. So Fabrizio came as Cosimo wished and was received by him along with other faithful friends, among whom were Zanobi Buondelmonti, Batista della Palla and Luigi Alamanni, all young men loved by him and zealous in the same studies, whose good qualities, because every day and every hour they are their own praise, we shall omit. Fabrizio, then, according to the times and the place, was by all of them honored with the greatest possible honors.

THE ANCIENTS TO BE IMITATED IN VIGOR

But when the pleasures of the banquet were over, and the tables were cleared and every sort of festivity had been concluded – something that in the presence of noble men whose minds are intent on honorable thoughts is concluded quickly – since the day was long and the heat great, Cosimo thought that in order better to satisfy his desire it would be well, using the excuse of escaping the heat, to go to the most secluded and shady part of his garden. When they had arrived there and taken seats, some on the grass, which is very fresh in that place, some on the seats arranged in those spots under the shade of very tall trees, Fabrizio praised the spot as delightful, and observing the trees closely and failing to recognize some of them, he was puzzled. Observing this, Cosimo said: 'You perhaps do not know some of these trees; but do not think it strange, because some of them were more renowned by the ancients than today they are by common custom.' And having told him their names and how Bernardo his grand-father had busied himself with such cultivation, he was answered by Fabrizio: 'I was thinking that it might be as you say, and this place and this avocation were making me remember some princes of the Kingdom, to whom these ancient plantings and shades give pleasure.' And pausing in his remarks at this point and sitting for a while as though inwardly intent on something, he added: 'If I thought I should not give offense, I would tell you my opinion of it, but I do not believe I shall offend, since I am speaking with friends, and in order to discuss things and not in order to censure them. How much better they would have done (be it said with due respect to all) to seek to be like the ancients in things strong and rough, not in those delicate and soft, and in those that are done in the sun, not in the shade, and to take their methods from an antiquity that is true and perfect, not from that which is false and corrupt, because as soon as activities of this sort satisfied my Romans, my native land went to ruin.' To which Cosimo replied – But to escape the bother of having to repeat so many times *He said* and *The other answered*, I shall give only the name of him who speaks, without repeat-ing anything else.

[. . .] [Luigi Alamanni speaking] I have heard many speak with contempt of the arms and the array of the ancient armies, arguing that today they could do little, rather would be wholly useless through the artillery's violence, because this breaks ranks and pierces armor in such a way that it seems to them madness to form ranks that cannot be kept and to suffer fatigue in wearing armor that cannot protect you.

RAPID ATTACK A PROTECTION AGAINST ARTILLERY

FABRIZIO: This question of yours, because it has several heads, needs a long answer. It is true that I did not make the artillery shoot more than once, and even of this once, I was in doubt. The reason is that it is more important for anyone to keep himself from being hit than to hit the enemy. You must understand that if artillery is not to damage you, of necessity it is where it cannot reach you, or you put yourself behind a wall or behind a bank. Nothing else can hold it off; moreover, such walls must be very strong. Yet generals who go out to fight a battle cannot remain behind walls or banks or where they cannot be reached. They must, then, since they cannot find a means for protecting themselves, find a means by which they will be least damaged. They can find no other way than quickly to seize the artillery beforehand. The method of seizing it beforehand is to go to attack it rapidly and in loose order, not slowly and in a mass, because when speed is used, the discharge cannot be repeated, and when the order is loose, it harms a smaller number of men. A band of men in close order cannot do this; if it moves rapidly, it loses its order; if it goes in loose formation, the enemy does not have much trouble in breaking it; indeed it has broken itself. Therefore I arranged the army in such a way that it could do both one thing and the other, because when I put on its flanks a thousand *velites* [lightly armed foot soldiers], I arranged that after our artillery had fired, these *velites* go out with the light cavalry to take the hostile artillery. Therefore I did not have my artillery shoot again, in order not to give time to that of the enemy, because I could not both give myself time and take it from others. For the very reason why I did not have it fire a second time, I considered not having it fire the first time, so that the enemy could not shoot even once. For in order to make the hostile artillery useless, there is no other means than to attack it; if the enemy abandon it, you take it; if they decide to defend it, they have to leave it in their rear; hence, taken by enemies or by friends, it cannot fire.

CLASSICAL PARALLELS

I should think that without examples these reasons would satisfy you; yet, since I can give some from the ancients, I wish to do so. Ventidius [one of Caesar's generals], coming to a battle with the Parthians, whose strength consisted for the most part in bows and in arrows, let them come almost up to his tents before he led his army out; this he did only that he could engage them quickly and not give them time to shoot. Caesar relates that in a battle in France, the enemy attacked him with such speed that his men did not have time to throw their javelins according to the Roman custom. Hence you see that if you wish anything shooting from a distance not to harm you when you are in the field, you have no other remedy than the utmost speed in taking it.

ARTILLERY SMOKE OBSTRUCTS THE VISION

Another cause also moved me to omit firing the artillery; perhaps you will laugh at it but I think it not to be despised. There is nothing that makes greater confusion in an army than to obstruct its view; many strong armies have been routed when their vision has been obstructed by the dust or the sun. There is nothing that more obstructs the view than the smoke artillery makes in firing; hence I believe it more prudent to let the enemy blind himself than for you, when blind, to attack him. Therefore either I would not fire or (because that would not be approved because of the artillery's reputation) I would put the artillery on the wings of the army; then when it fired its smoke would not blind the army's front; this is the important thing for my soldiers. That to obstruct the enemy's view is useful can be shown by Epaminondas'[1] example: to blind a hostile army about to fight a battle with him, he had his light cavalry gallop before the front of the enemy to raise the dust high and obstruct their view; this gave him victory in that battle.

THE LIMITATIONS OF ARTILLERY; DEVICES AGAINST IT

As to your saying that I directed the shots of the artillery according to my own will by making them pass over the heads of the infantry, I reply to you that there are many more times, beyond comparison, when the heavy guns do not strike the infantry than when they do strike them. For the infantry is so low and the guns are so hard to manage that, if you raise them a little, they fire over the heads of the infantry, and if you lower them, they hit the earth and the shot does not reach the troops. The infantry are protected also by the unevenness of the land, because every little thicket or bank between them and the guns is a protection. The horses, and especially those of the men-at-arms, because they have to stand closer together than the light horses and, being taller, are more easily hit, can be kept in the rear until the artillery has fired. It is true that much more harm is done by the harquebuses [muskets on stands] and the light artillery than by the heavy, against which the chief protection is to come to close quarters quickly; if in the first attack they kill somebody, in such conditions somebody always is killed. A good general and a good army do not fear an individual harm but a universal one; they imitate the Swiss, who never avoid a battle because they are dismayed by the artillery; on the contrary, they inflict capital punishment on those who for fear of it either leave their rank or with their bodies give any sign of fear. I had the artillery, as soon as it had fired, retire into the army that it might give free passage to the battalions. I made no further mention of it because it is useless in combat at close quarters.

NOTWITHSTANDING THE FURY OF ARTILLERY, ANCIENT METHODS ARE STILL USED

You have also said that because of the fury of this instrument, many consider the ancient arms and methods useless; this speech of yours suggests that the moderns have found methods and weapons that against artillery are effective. If you know any, I should be glad to have you explain them to me, because up to now I have never seen any of them nor do I believe any can be found. Indeed I should like to ask for what reasons the foot soldiers in our times wear the breastplate and the corselet of steel, and men on horseback are completely covered with armor, because those who condemn the ancient wearing of armor as useless against artillery, ought to give up modern armor too. I should like to know for what reason the Swiss, imitating ancient methods, form a close-packed brigade of six or eight thousand infantrymen and for what reason all other infantry imitates them, since this order is exposed to the same danger, with respect to artillery, to which are exposed all others that might be imitated from antiquity. I believe a champion of artillery would not know what to answer; but if you should ask soldiers who have some judgment, they would answer, first, that they go armored because, though that armor does not protect them from artillery, it does protect them from arrows, from pikes, from swords, from stones and from every other injurious thing that comes from the enemy. They would also answer that they go drawn up in close order like the Swiss so as to be able more easily to charge infantry, to resist cavalry better, and to give the enemy more difficulty in break-ing them. Evidently soldiers need to fear many things besides artillery; from these they protect themselves with armor and with good order. From this it follows that the better armored an army is and the more its ranks are locked together and strong, the more secure it is. Hence any who think artillery all-important must be either of little prudence or must have thought very little on these things. If we see that a very small part of the ancient method of arming that is used today, namely, the pike, and a very small part of their organization, namely, the brigades of the Swiss, do us so much good and give our armies so much strength, why are we not to believe that other arms and other customs that have been given up are useful? Besides, if we do not consider the artillery in putting ourselves in close formation like the Swiss, what other methods can make us fear it more? For evidently no arrangement can make us fear it so much as those that crowd men together. In addition, the artillery of the enemy does not frighten me off from putting myself with my army near a city where it can harm me with full security, since I cannot take it because it is protected by walls which permit it to repeat its shots at pleasure; indeed I can only hinder it, in time, with my artillery. Why, then, am I to fear it in the field where I can quickly take it? Hence I con-clude with this: artillery, in my opinion, does not make it impossible to use ancient methods and show ancient vigor. If I had not spoken with you another time of this instrument, I should here be more lengthy; but I wish to rest on what I then said about it.

NOTE

1   Epaminondas (c.418–362 BCE), Theban general and statesman.

26 Niccolò Machiavelli **The Pazzi Conspiracy from _The Florentine History_ (1525)**
(i) Machiavelli's Introduction (ii) The Pazzi Conspiracy

In 1520 Machiavelli received a commission for a regular salary from Pope Leo X (Giovanni de'Medici 1513–21) to write the *History*. By 1525 he had completed eight books on the history of the city to 1492, the year of the death of Lorenzo the Magnificent, when he presented them to pope Clement VII (Giuliano de'Medici). Machiavelli drew on earlier historians for much of the first part of the work, which extended from the late classical period to 1434, when Cosimo de'Medici assumed a leading role in the government. The last four books provided detailed accounts of the complex interplay of internal and external factors in the government of Florence from 1434 to the end of the century. Throughout, Machiavelli aired many of his favourite themes, especially the excellence of citizen militias as opposed to mercenary armies. He was also surprisingly frank about the pros and cons of Medici rule, although we know from a letter he wrote to a friend that he felt constrained by the fact that they had commissioned the book. The second extract gives an account of the Pazzi Conspiracy against the Medici of 1478. The long speech by Lorenzo the Magnificent which concludes the second extract may be a fabrication. This would be a typical rhetorical device employed by humanist historians when they wished to stress a point, in this case the strength and popularity of the Medici regime.

Source: *Florentine History*, trans. W. K. Marriott, J. M. Dent, London, 1912, pp. 1–3, 317–18, 321–9

i) Machiavelli's Introduction

It was in my mind when I first thought of writing the history of the Florentine people that I would commence my story with the year of the Christian religion 1434, at which time the family of the Medici, through the abilities of Cosimo and of his father Giovanni, had acquired more power than any other house in Florence. Because I thought to myself that Messer Lionardo [Bruni] d'Arezzo and Messer Poggio [Bracciolini], two most excellent historians, had related in great detail all the events which had happened before that date.[1] But after having diligently read their writings in order to see what plan and method they had adopted, that our history might profit by their example to the benefit of the readers, I found that in the descriptions of the wars waged by the Florentines against foreign princes and peoples they had been most exact, but upon the subject of civil discord and internal strifes and their consequences they had been entirely silent, or had written far too briefly concerning them; so that these historians have failed to convey anything either instructive or pleasing to their readers. I believe they did this, either because such incidents appeared to them so insignificant that they judged them unworthy of commemoration, or because they feared to offend the descendants of those whom in the course of their story they might have to condemn. Now – if they will allow me to say so – these two reasons are, it seems to me, quite unworthy of great men, because if anything teaches or pleases in history it is that which is described in detail, and if any reading can be profitable to citizens who may be called upon to govern republics, it is that which reveals the causes of hatreds and dissensions in a state, so that, learning wisdom from the perils of others, they may maintain themselves in unity. And if the history of any republic can exercise an influence upon us, then the example of our own will instruct us more, and to our greater advantage. For if ever the dissensions in a

6 Bertoldo di Giovanni, Medal celebrating the escape of Lorenzo de' Medici, il Magnifico, and Giuliano I de' Medici from the Pazzi conspiracy, 1478, bronze, diameter 6.6 cm. Obverse: bust of Lorenzo above the choir of the Duomo. Reverse: bust of Giuliano above the choir of the Duomo. Samuel H. Kress Collection © 1999 Board of Trustees, National Gallery of Art, Washington.

republic were remarkable, those of Florence have been the most remarkable, for most other republics of which we have any knowledge have been content with one division, with which, according to circumstances, they have either strengthened, or ruined their state; but Florence, not content with one, has had many. In Rome, as every one knows, after the kings were driven out, there arose the strife between the patricians and plebeians which lasted until Rome fell. Thus, also, it happened in Athens and in other republics which flourished in those days. But in Florence the dissensions were at first among the nobility themselves, afterwards between the nobles and the citizens, and finally between the citizens and the plebeians, and many times it has happened that one of these parties, having prevailed over the other, would divide and become two parties. From these dissensions there occurred more deaths, and banishments, and general extinction of families, than ever happened in any city of which we have knowledge. And truly, according to my judgment, nothing could have so well demonstrated the vitality of our city as these dissensions, which were fierce enough to have destroyed the greatest and most powerful city. Nevertheless our republic has always seemed to thrive, the ability of its citizens, and their skill and success in aggrandising their country and themselves, being so great that those who have survived these misfortunes have been able to bring far more advantage to the republic than the untoward circumstances, which diminished their numbers, could work it evil. And doubtless had Florence been fortunate enough after she had freed herself from the empire to have adopted a form of government that would have kept her united, I know of no republic, either ancient or modern, that would have been superior to her, with such capacity and valour was she replete. After the republic had expelled the Ghibellines in such numbers that Tuscany and Lombardy were full of them, the Guelfs,[2] with those who remained, drew from the city alone 1200 cavalry and 12,000 infantry during the war against Arezzo and a year before the battle of Campaldino. Afterwards in the war against Filippo Visconti, Duke of Milan, when, their own forces being exhausted, they were driven to rely on mercenaries, it is a matter of common knowledge that during the five years which the war lasted the Florentines raised 3,500,000 florins; and, to show the resources of the state, when that war was over they took the field against Lucca, being unable to rest satisfied with the peace. I cannot, therefore, understand by what reasoning these dissensions are deemed unworthy of commemoration. And if these noble authors were restrained by the fear of wounding the memory of those about whom they had to write, they are deceived, and show that they know little of the ambition of men and their desire to perpetuate their ancestors' names and their own. Nor has it occurred to them that many who have not had the opportunity of securing fame by praiseworthy deeds have gained it by infamous ones. Nor have they considered that actions intrinsically great, as are those of government and statecraft, however they may be handled, or to whatever end they may come, seem always to bring more honour than blame to men. These considerations have caused me to alter my plan and to commence my history with the foundation of our city. And as it is not my intention to occupy the place of other writers until 1434, I shall particularly describe those events only which occurred within the city, and of outside affairs I shall write only that which may be needful for a right understanding of those events which took place within. After the year 1434, I shall describe both in detail. Furthermore, before I shall treat of Florence, in order that this history shall be the better understood to all time, I shall describe the means by which Italy came under the sway of the rulers of those times. All these events, Italian as well as Florentine, will be contained in four books. The first will relate briefly the events which occurred in Italy from the decline of the Roman Empire until the year 1434. The second will commence with the story of the foundation of the city of Florence until the war against the pope, which arose after the expulsion of the Duke of Athens. The third will finish with the death of Ladislao, the King of Naples, in the year 1414. And with the fourth book we shall again reach 1434, from which time until the present the events which occurred both within and without the city will receive particular attention.

ii) The Pazzi Conspiracy

Nevertheless Lorenzo, in the hey-day of his youth and power, wished to have the decision of everything, and desired that the people should recognise his hand in everything; but the Pazzi, with all their wealth and pride of race, would not sit still under such injuries, and began to think of revenge. The first to make any move against the Medici was Francesco. This gentleman was very sensitive and high spirited, and he determined either to regain the position of which he had been deprived or to lose all he had in the attempt. As he was on bad terms with the government of Florence he resided in Rome, and having plenty of means, traded from there after the manner of Florentine merchants. He was very friendly with the Count Girolamo,[3] and together they often discussed the Medici. After having deplored the situation of affairs they came to the conclusion that the only way in which the one could enjoy his government and the other be restored to his country was to overturn the government of Florence, and this they considered they were unable to accomplish without the death of Lorenzo and Giuliano. They believed also that the pope [Sixtus IV, 1471–84] and the King of Naples would assent when it was proved how easily the murders could be perpetrated. Having come to this determination they communicated their plans to Francesco Salviati, the Archbishop of Pisa, who being an ambitious man, and having been only a short time previously injured by the Medici, willingly agreed. They debated between themselves how to accomplish it, and decided to draw Messer Jacopo Pazzi into their schemes in order to ensure success, as without it they feared they would fail. Francesco de' Pazzi went to Florence with a view to securing this aid, whilst the count and the archbishop remained in Rome to secure the pope to their side, when the time should arrive for communicating their designs to him. Francesco found Messer Jacopo very cautious, and far more difficult than was expected; he therefore let the friends in Rome know that more influence would be needed to bring Jacopo into their plans. Whereupon the archbishop and count communicated the whole affair to Giovanni Batista da Montesecco, the condottiere of the pope. This soldier was highly esteemed and under many obligations to the pope and the count, but he at once pointed out that the affair was one of extreme difficulty and danger; the archbishop strove to minimise these difficulties, and to assure him of the aid which the pope and king would give to the enterprise, of the hatred which the people of Florence bore to the Medici, of the number of relatives which the Salviati and Pazzi would influence, of the ease with which the two Medici could be killed when walking with their companions in the city and quite unconscious of danger, and of the ease with which the government could be changed when they were killed. Giovanni Batista did not place much faith in these assurances, because he had heard something entirely different from other Florentines. [. . .]

The conspirators having now completed their arrangements the design was communicated to the priest who was to celebrate High Mass, and their plans were also completed for the seizure of the palace by the archbishop and his men, who with Messer Jacopo Poggio were to compel the signoria to declare in their favour, either willingly or by force, as soon as the two brothers were killed.

Everything being now prepared the conspirators repaired to the church,[4] where the cardinal and Lorenzo had already arrived. The church was crowded with people, and the sacred office had already commenced although Giuliano had not arrived. Whereupon Francesco de' Pazzi and Bernardo [Bandini], who had been told off to kill him, ran to his house to find him and by prayer and guile brought him to the church. It is indeed to be noted that Francesco and Bernardo were inspired by such feelings of hatred and the lust of murder, and pursued their object with such callousness and resolution, that as they led Giuliano to the church, and even within it, they amused him with droll and jovial stories. Francesco even, under pretence of embracing him, took him in his arms and pressed him with his hands, to see if he were wearing a cuirass or other defensive armour. Although both Lorenzo and Giuliano were perfectly well aware of the resentment of the Pazzi and their desire to deprive them of the government, they had never gone in fear of their lives, as they always believed that when anything was attempted against them it would be by civil process and not by violence; so having no fears for their personal safety the Medici had always appeared friendly to the Pazzi. The murderers being now quite ready, those at the side of Lorenzo, having approached with ease owing to the crowd, and the others having reached their destination with Giuliano, Bernardo Bandini struck Giuliano in the stomach with a short dagger. Giuliano fell to the ground and Francesco covered him with wounds whilst he lay there, indeed with such rage did he strike that he wounded himself seriously in the thigh. Lorenzo was at the same time attacked by Messer Antonio and Stefano Sacerdote, who made many strokes at him, but only slightly wounded him in the throat. Either by their own lack of ability, or the courage of Lorenzo, who, finding himself attacked, defended himself with his sword, or by the aid of those around him, the efforts of his assailants were in vain. They becoming alarmed fled and endeavoured to hide themselves, but being discovered were killed and their bodies dragged through the city. Lorenzo and his friends retreated to the sanctuary, and shut themselves up. Bernardo Bandini, finding that he had killed Giuliano, turned on Francesco Neri, a great friend of the Medici, and killed him, either because of some old feud or because he had tried to save Giuliano. Nor was Bernardo content with these two murders, but he ran in search of Lorenzo, that with his own courage and swiftness he might make amends for the slowness and cowardice of others. But he found Lorenzo had taken refuge in the sanctuary and defied his attempts. In the midst of these terrible deeds it seemed as if the church would fall in upon the people; the cardinal clung to the altar, and with difficulty was saved by the priests; when the tumult was appeased he was taken by the signori to the palace where he remained until his liberation.

At this time there were residing in Florence some men of Perugia, who had been driven out of that city by the dominant faction, and whom the Pazzi had induced to join their conspiracy by promising to restore them to their city. When the archbishop with Jacopo, the son of Messer Poggio, and their friends and relations reached the palace [Palazzo Vecchio] which they were to seize, the archbishop left a number of his followers below, with instructions that when they heard a disturbance upstairs they were to hold the door. The archbishop and the greater number of the Perugians then mounted the stairs and found the signori at dinner as it was now getting late. However, after a short time he was admitted by Cesare Petrucci, the gonfaloniere of justice [the chief magistrate]. When the archbishop had entered with a few of his company, the greater number of his followers who were left outside shut themselves up in the Record room, the door of which was constructed in such a way that it could be opened neither from the inside nor the outside without a key. The archbishop had been admitted by the gonfaloniere into the council chamber under the pretence that he had something of importance from the pope to communicate; but when he commenced to speak in a hesitating manner, and to show some excitement, the suspicions of the gonfaloniere were aroused, and in a moment with a great shout he thrust him out of the chamber; at the same time he seized Jacopo Poggio by the hair and handed him over to the serjeants. He then raised the alarm among the signori, who seizing such arms as they could find fell upon the followers of the archbishop who had come upstairs, all of whom were either killed and thrown from the windows of the palace or locked up; whilst the archbishop, the two Jacopo Salviatis, and Jacopo Poggio were hanged. Those men who had been left downstairs had overpowered the guard, forced the doors of the palace, and occupied the lower part of the palace, so that those citizens who heard the tumult and came running to the defence of the palace could render no assistance whatever.

Francesco de' Pazzi and Bernardo Bandini lost heart when they found that Lorenzo had escaped them, and that one of themselves, and he the mainstay of the enterprise, was very grievously wounded. Thereupon, seeing that all was lost, Bernardo devoted himself to his own safety with the same ardour he had shown in his attack upon the Medici, and fled; Francesco de' Pazzi returned to his house, where he found that his wound would not allow him to mount his horse. The arrangement had been that he should ride through the city with armed men and call the people to arms and to liberty, but this he was unable to do because of his terrible wound and loss of blood. He undressed and threw himself naked upon his bed, and prayed Messer Jacopo to take his place, and do what he was to have done. Although Messer Jacopo was old and quite unaccustomed to such tumultuous scenes, he mounted his horse and made a last bid for success. With about 100 armed men who had been prepared for this service he sallied out in the direction of the Piazza of the palace calling the people to liberty and to his standard. But he obtained no response, for the liberality and success of the Medici caused the people to turn a deaf ear to him, besides which the name of liberty was hardly known in Florence. The signori, who were masters of the upper part of the palace, saluted him with stones and menaced him with threats. Whilst Messer Jacopo was hesitating what to do he encountered his relative, Giovanni Serristori, who reproached him for all the trouble which had arisen and advised him to go home, for the care of the people and of liberty was close to the hearts of many other citizens besides himself. Thus Messer Jacopo lost courage, for he found the palace hostile to him, Lorenzo still alive, Francesco disabled, and the people indifferent. Not knowing what else to do he determined to save his life if that were still possible by flight, and with some friends who had followed him to the Piazza he left Florence for Romagna.

By this time the city was thoroughly aroused, and Lorenzo de' Medici accompanied by a great escort of armed men had returned to his house. The palace had been recaptured by the people, and most of the rebels either killed or taken prisoners. Already the streets were re-echoing with the name of Medici, and the limbs of the dead were being borne aloft on pikes, or dragged along the ground, and all who bore the name of Pazzi were persecuted with rage and cruelty. Their houses were in possession of the mob, and Francesco, all naked, was dragged from his bed and led to the palace where he was hanged by the side of the archbishop and the others. Neither on the way to the palace, nor elsewhere, was it possible by word or deed to make him speak a word, but keeping a fixed look he breathed his last in silence. Guglielmo de' Pazzi, the brother-in-law of Lorenzo, because of his innocence, was saved by the aid of his wife in the house of his relative. In this emergency there was not a citizen who, whether armed or unarmed, did not go to the house of Lorenzo and place himself and his substance at the disposal of the Medici, such was the goodwill which this family had won by its prudence and liberality. Rinato de' Pazzi had retired to his villa before the above events happened, but when he heard of them he attempted to escape; he was, however, recognised, captured and led back to Florence. Messer Jacopo was also taken when crossing the mountains by the mountaineers who, noticing the speed with which he was travelling, and having heard of the events in Florence, arrested him and sent him back to the city. Although he entreated them to kill him rather than take him back to Florence, he could not induce them to do so. After a trial lasting four days, Messer Jacopo and Rinato were condemned to death. Among the many persons who were put to death during that time, and there were so many that the streets were strewn with their limbs, none excited any compassion but that of Rinato dei Pazzi, for he had none of the haughtiness of the other members of the family, but was considered a wise and honest man. In order that an extraordinary example should be made of the fate of these conspirators, Messer Jacopo was first buried in the sepulchre of his ancestors, afterwards he was treated as one excommunicated, taken thence and reburied under the walls of the city; he was dug up from there and dragged naked round the city by the halter with which he was hanged; then, as if earth was not to be allowed to give him a resting-place, those who had dragged him round cast him into the river Arno, which was then in great flood. To see a man so rich and powerful fall to such depths of misery amid ruin and disgrace was indeed a signal example of the mutability of fortune. Some men have spoken of his vices, among which were gambling and cursing, more fitting to a damned soul than to any other; but such vices were overbalanced by his countless charities to all in need, as well as to sacred places. One can also say this good thing of Messer Jacopo, on the Saturday previous to the Sunday chosen for the assassination he paid all his creditors and most scrupulously handed over to its owners all merchandise which happened to lie in his house or warehouses belonging to them, in order that others should not be involved in any reverse of his fortunes. Giovanni Batista da Montesecco was beheaded after a long trial. Napoleone Franzezi escaped punishment by flight. Guglielmo de' Pazzi was banished to Volterra, where with such of his cousins who were alive he was confined in the dungeons beneath the fortress. The tumults being now quieted and the conspirators punished, the obsequies of Giuliano were celebrated, accompanied by the lamentations of the whole city, for he was a man of more gentleness and liberality than is usually found in one of his position. He had one natural son, named Giulio, who, however, was born a few months after the death of his father. He possessed those virtues and acquired that high fortune by which he is known to-day to all the world, and which shall be set forth at length when I come to deal with the present events, if God only spares me for the task. The armies under Lorenzo da Castello in the Val da Trevere, and under Giovanni Francesco da Tolentino in Romagna, had united and were moving on Florence to the assistance of the Pazzi when they learned that the rebellion had failed, and at once turned back.

Seeing that no change of government had followed these disturbances in Florence, as had been desired by the pope and king, they determined to effect by open war what they had failed to accomplish by treachery, and both assembled their forces with the utmost despatch in order to attack the government of Florence, at the same time declaring they had no intentions against the city itself but the removal of Lorenzo, who alone of all Florentines was their enemy. When the army of the king had passed the Tronto, and that of the pope had reached Perugia, the pope desiring to give the Florentines a taste of the spiritual power as well as the temporal, excommunicated them and laid them under a malediction. The Florentines, finding that armies were gathering against them, began to prepare for defence with great vigour. As common report gave it out that the war was only against Lorenzo, he assembled the signori with many of the leading citizens at the palace and addressed to them the following words: –

'I cannot say, my lords and gentlemen, whether I should rejoice or mourn with you over what has occurred. When I call to mind the treachery and ferocity with which my brother has been slain and myself wounded, I cannot fail to be saddened and to grieve with my whole soul. But when I remember, on the other hand, with what readiness and earnestness, and with what sympathy and unity, the whole city has risen to avenge my brother and defend me, I am disposed not only to rejoice, but to feel honoured and exalted. And if my experience has now taught me that I had more enemies in this city than I supposed, it has also proved to me that I have far more fervent friends than I could have believed possible. I am therefore compelled to condole with you upon the wickedness of some, whilst I can congratulate myself upon your wonderful kindness to me; yet I am constrained to remember our wrongs, inasmuch as they are unparalleled, and totally undeserved by us. Let us for a moment, gentlemen, consider the evil fortune which has overtaken our family, that even among friends and relatives, nay in the very church itself, we are not safe. Those who fear murder are accustomed to fly for protection to their friends and relatives, but it was these whom we found armed for our destruction; whilst those who are persecuted for public or private reasons fly to the church for safety. Thus the Medici are killed by those who should have defended them, and where parricides and assassins find sanctuary the Medici found murderers. But God, who has never abandoned our family, has once more saved us, and has taken upon Himself our just defence. What injuries have we done to anyone to inspire such a thirst for vengeance? But in truth these men, who have shown such hostility against us, have never been injured by us in private life, for had we wronged them, we should have taken care to have put it beyond their power to retaliate. If on the other hand they attribute public injuries to us, by saying that you by our means have injured citizens, – and I do not know of any who have been wronged, – then they insult you, and the majesty of this palace of justice and the government of this city, rather than our family. But this statement is far from the truth, for we would not have done so had we had the power, and you would not have permitted us had we had the will. The man who seeks to find the truth of this matter will find that our family have always been held in the highest estimation by you for no other reason but that we have gained the goodwill of all by our kindliness and liberality. If we have conferred benefits upon strangers, is it likely that we should have reserved injuries for those who are nearer to us? But if our enemies have been incited to this crime by a thirst for dominion, as it would appear they have been by their seizure of the palace and the invasion of the Piazza with an armed force, then such a cause is ambitious, reprehensible, and brutal, and as soon as its object was discovered it was universally condemned. If they have entered upon this course out of envy and hatred of our authority, they have passed a censure upon you, because it was you who conferred all such authority upon us. Of a truth, for power to deserve hatred it must be usurped, not conferred for public spirit, generosity, and good-will. You know well that this family has never assumed any authority but that which has been conferred upon it by the united voice of this council. My grand-father Cosimo did not return from exile by force and violence, but by the call of the whole people. My father, old and infirm, did not defend the government by himself against so many enemies, but it was you, who with your power and loyalty defended it. After the death of my father, whilst a mere child, so to speak, I could not have maintained the position of my house if it had not been for your help and counsel. Therefore I cannot say what is the reasonable cause of the hatred or envy they have displayed against us. Let them rather execrate the memory of their ancestors who by their arrogance and avarice lost that reputation which ours by far different conduct knew how to gain. But let us concede that the injuries they received from us were very great, and demanded nothing less than our destruction, why then should they seize the palace? Why should they make a league with the pope and the king against the liberties of this republic? Why should they break the peace which has prevailed for so long in Italy? To these charges they have no reply, for they ought to have punished those who injured them, and not have confused private enmity with public injury. Although our enemies may have been destroyed the evil they committed still lives, because for their sake the pope and the king are advancing with their armies against us, declaring that the war is only upon me and my family. Would to God this were the truth, for then the remedy should be swift and certain, because I am not such a bad citizen as to value my own safety more than your peril, and willingly would I put an end to your troubles by my own destruction. But the injuries which the powerful inflict are always disguised under some specious pretence. Should you, however, believe otherwise, I am in your hands. You have to support me or abandon me. You, my fathers! You, my defenders! You have only to command me and I will obey. I will not refuse, nay I will do it willingly, if you will but say one word, and as this war was commenced with the death of my brother, so it shall be ended with mine.'

Lorenzo was listened to with so much sympathy by the citizens they could not keep back their tears whilst he was speaking, and when he had finished one of them was commissioned to speak for the rest. He bade Lorenzo be of good courage, that the citizens recognised in him and his family such merit that they would defend his life with the same readiness they had shown in revenging the murder of his brother, and that they would fight for him and his government, and before he should lose either they would lose their country. In order that their deeds should correspond with their words, they committed the care of his person to a body of armed men to defend him against domestic enemies.

After this they prepared for war, enlisting as many men as possible and, in virtue of their treaties, sending for aid to the Duke of Milan and the Venetians. As the pope had proved himself a wolf rather than a shepherd, the Florentines filled all Italy with the story of the treatment their government had received, and they took all means in their power to justify themselves, so that it should not be as a guilty people the pope should destroy them. They pointed out the impiety and iniquity of the pope, the frauds he had practised in obtaining the pontificate, and that he had wickedly abused his power. He had sent those whom he had elevated to the prelacy in company with murderers and traitors to commit perfidious deeds during the celebration of the sacrament in the midst of divine service. And afterwards, when he could not succeed in killing their citizens, or overturning their government, or putting the city to the sack, as he had wished, he had laid them under the pontifical malediction. But if God is a just God, and if violence is hateful to him, then He must be angry with His Vicar here on earth, and anxious that injured men, who can no longer find a place of refuge here, should have recourse to Him. The Florentines would not accept the interdict, but disobeyed it and compelled the priests to celebrate divine service. They also called a meeting of all Tuscan prelates who owed obedience to them, and appealed against the wrongs the pope had committed to the forthcoming general council. Neither did the pope fail to attempt his justification by maintaining that it was the duty of a pope to drive out tyrants, to punish wicked men, and to reward the good, and this he ought to do on every occasion; that it did not appertain to secular princes to put cardinals under restraint, to hang archbishops, to put to death and dismember priests, and drag them through the streets, or to kill without distinction the innocent and the guilty. [. . .]

NOTES

1   See Texts 1 and 12 above.
2   The Ghibellines were supporters of the emperor, the Guelfs supporters of the papacy.
3   Girolamo Riario, a nephew of the Pope.
4   The church of Santa Reparata, also known as Santa Maria dei Fiori, the cathedral church of Florence.

27 Francesco Guicciardini *Maxims and Reflections* (1528–30)

Some of this collection of maxims dates from early in Guicciardini's career, but he copied out the originals and added new ones between 1528 and 1530. This was a period when he had lost his position after the temporary fall of the Medici. Like Machiavelli in the previous decade, he at last had the leisure to write down his political ideas. The Italian text was first published in a Paris edition of 1576. Details of Guicciardini's career are given in the headnote for Text 19.

Source: *Maxims and Reflections of a Renaissance Statesman (Ricordi)*, trans. M. Domadi, intro. N. Rubinstein, Harper Torchbooks, New York, 1965, pp. 45–7, 49. Translation and Preface copyright © by 1965 by Mario Domandi. Reprinted by permission of Harper Collins Publishers, Inc.

19. Conspiracies cannot be hatched without the complicity of others, and for that reason they are extremely dangerous. For most men are either stupid or evil, and to take up with such people involves too great a risk.

20. Nothing works against the success of a conspiracy so much as the wish to make it ironclad and almost certain to succeed. Such an attempt always requires many men, much time, and very favorable circumstances. And all these in turn heighten the risk of being discovered. You see, therefore, how dangerous conspiracies are! All these factors that would add security to any other enterprise add danger to this one. I think the reason may be that Fortune, who plays such a large role in all matters, becomes angry with those who try to limit her dominion.

21. On several occasions, I have said and written that the Medici lost control of the state in [15]27 because they respected so many republican institutions; and that I was afraid the people would lose their liberty because they exercised such tight control of the state. The reasoning behind these two conclusions is this: the Medici regime, being odious to most of the citizens, needed solid support among devoted partisans if it was to maintain itself. These would have had to be men who not only stood to gain a great deal from the government, but who also recognized that they would be ruined and could not remain in Florence if the Medici were expelled. But such supporters were hard to find! For the Medici, trying hard to seem fair to everyone and not wishing to show any partiality towards friends and relatives, were in the habit of distributing the highest as well as the lower offices widely and generously.

If the Medici had done the contrary, they would certainly be worthy of censure. But even so, they did not gain many adherents to their regime. For although the majority of people were satisfied with the way the Medici conducted themselves, they were not completely won over. The desire to return to the Grand Council[1] was so rooted in the hearts of men that it could not be eradicated by any acts of kindness, mildness, or favor. The friends of the Medici liked the regime, but were not so attached as to run any risk for it. In case of a crisis, they hoped that, by behaving well, they could save themselves as they had done in '94; and thus they were disposed to let things take their course rather than try to withstand an onslaught.

A popular government must take a completely opposite course from the one that would have been favorable to the Medici. Generally, the people of Florence love popular government. It is not a machine guided by one or by a few toward a definite end, but rather changes its direction every day because of the number and the ignorance of those who run it. And therefore, a popular government must keep the favor of the people if it wishes to maintain itself. It must do all it can to stay out of the quarrels among its citizens lest they, having no other recourse, open the way to revolution. In short, popular government must tread the path of justice and equality. From these are born the security of all and, as a rule, general satisfaction. More, they will provide the basis for preserving popular government – not through a few partisans, which it could not tolerate, but through numerous friends. To continue tight control of the state is impossible, for it transforms popular government into another kind. And that does not preserve liberty but destroys it.

22. How often is it said: if only this had been done, that would have happened; or, if only that had not been done, this would not have happened. And yet, if it were possible to test such statements, we should see how false they are.

23. The future is so deceptive and subject to so many accidents, that very often even the wisest of men is fooled when he tries to predict it. If you look very closely at his prognostications, especially when they concern details – for often the general outcome is easier to guess – you will see little difference between them and the guesses of those who are considered less wise. Therefore, to give up a present good for fear of a future evil is, most of the time, madness – unless the evil is very certain, very near, or very great compared to the good. Otherwise, quite often a groundless fear will cause you to lose a good thing you could have kept.

24. Nothing is more fleeting than the memory of benefits received. Therefore, rely more on those whose circumstances do not permit them to fail you than on those whom you have favored. For often they will not remember the favors, or they will suppose them to have been smaller than they were, or they will even claim that you did them almost because you were obliged. [. . .]

30. If you consider the matter carefully, you cannot deny that fortune has great power over human affairs. We see these affairs constantly being affected by fortuitous circumstances that men could neither forsee nor avoid. Although cleverness and care may accomplish many things, they are nevertheless not enough. Man also needs good fortune.

NOTE

1   The Grand (or Great) Council was a republican body introduced after the fall of the Medici in 1494.

28 Innocent Gentillet *Against Nicholas Machiavell* (1576)

Innocent Gentillet (1535–88) was a prominent Huguenot pamphleteer. His *A Discourse upon the Means of Well Governing and Maintaining in Good Peace, a Kingdome, or other Principalitie, divided into three parts, namely the Counsell, the Religion, the Policie, which a Prince ought to hold and follow. Against Nicolas Machiavell the Florentine* was published in Geneva in 1576 and translated into English by Simon Patericke in 1602. As the title suggests, the work was partly intended to reaffirm the three bridles upon absolute rule of counsel, religion and policy. The main purpose was to draw fifty maxims out of Machiavelli's writings, especially *The Prince* and the *Commentary on the Discourses of Livy*, and show the evil consequences of their application.

Source: *A Disourse upon the Means of Well Governing. Against Nicholas Machiavell the Florentine.* Reprinted in *Culture and Belief in Europe, 1450–1600*, ed. D. Englander, D. Norman, R. O'Day, W. R. Owens, Blackwell, Oxford, 1990, pp. 416–18, spelling modernised by David Englander

15 MAXIME

A virtuous tyrant,[1] *to maintain his tyranny, ought to maintain partialities and factions amongst his subjects, and to slay and take away such as love the commonwealth.*

It most commonly happeneth (sayeth Machiavell) in countries governed by princes, that that which is profitable to him, is damageable to subjects, and that which is profitable to his subjects, is damageable unto him: Which causeth oftentimes princes to become tyrants, better loving their profit, than their subjects: As also the contrary makes subjects often arise against their prince, not able to endure his tyranny and oppression. To keep subjects then, that they do not conspire and agree together to a rise against his tyranny, he must nourish and maintain partialities and factions amongst them: For, by that means shall you see, that distrusting one another, and fearing that one will accuse and disclose another, they will not dare to enterprise any thing: But herewithall he must cause all them to be slain, which love liberty, and the commonwealth and which are enemies to tyranny. If Tarquin, the last king of Rome, had well observed this Maxim, and had caused Brutus to be slain,[2] no man would have been found, that durst have enterprised any thing against him, and then might he always after, have exercised his tyranny at his pleasure without controlment.

Here before Machiavell hath showed, how a prince should best become a tyrant; namely, by exercising all manner of cruelty, impiety, and injustice, after the examples of Cesar Borgia, of Oliver de Ferme, and of Agathocles.[3] Now he shows how he in his tyranny, may maintain and conserve himself, that is, by feeding and maintaining partialities and divisions amongst his subjects, and in causing such to die, as appear to be curious lovers of the common weale, because none can love the good and utility of the common weale, but he must be an enemy of tyranny: as contrary, none can love tyranny, but he must needs be an enemy to the common weale: For, tyranny draweth all to himself, and dispoileth subjects of their goods and commodities, to appropriate all to himself, making his particular good of that which belongs to all men, and applying to his own private profit and use, that which should serve to all men in general: So that it followeth, that whosoever loveth the profit of a tyrant, by consequent hateth the profit of his subjects, and he that loveth the common good of subjects, hateth also the particular profit of a tyrant. But thus speaking, I do not mean of tributes, which are lawfully levied upon subjects: for the exaction of taxes, may well

be the work of a prince, and of a just ruler, but we speak of the proper and particular actions of tyrants.

Surely indeed if there be any proper and meet mean to maintain a tyranny, it
seems well, that that which Machiavell teacheth is one. To maintain subjects in
partialities and divisions: For as Quintius sayeth (when he exhorted the towns
of Greece, to accord amongst themselves), Against a people which are in a good
unity amongst themselves, tyrants can do nothing, but if there be discord
amongst them, an overture is straight made, for him to do what he will: I freely
then confess (and if I would deny it, experience proves it) that in this point
Machiavell is a true doctor, who well understands the science of tyranny, and no
man can set down more proper precepts, for so wicked a thing, than such as this
Maxim containeth; namely, to slay all lovers of the commonwealth, and amongst
other subjects to maintain partialities. Surely if anything serve to maintain a
tyranny, these seem most proper and convenable: for they are made from the
same mould that tyranny itself is, and drawn from one same spring, of most
execrable wickedness and impiety.

An excellent wise man affirmeth [meaning Plato] that if tyrants' souls might
be seen uncovered, a man should see them torn and wounded with blows of
cruelty, riotousness, and wicked counsel, as we see bodies ulcerated with rods and
cudgels. What pleasure could Denis the tyrant of Sicily have,[4] who trusted none?
Also when one day a certain philosopher told him, that he could not be but
happy, who was so rich, so well served at his table, and had so goodly a palace
to dwell in, and so richly furnished: he answered him: Well, I will show you how
happy I am: and withall he led that philosopher into a chamber gallantly hanged
with tapestry, and caused him to be laid on a gilded rich bed to repose himself;
there were also brought him exquisite and delicate viands, and excellent wines:
but whilst certain servants made these provisions for Monsieur the philosopher,
who was so desirous of a tyrannical felicity, another varlet [servant] fastened by
the hilts to the upper bed [. . .] a bright shining sharp sword, and this sword was
hung only in a horse hair, the point of it right over the philosopher's face so newly
happy, who incontinent as he saw the sword hang by so small a thread, and so
right over his visage, lost all his appetite to eat, drink, or to muse at, or contemplate the excessive riches of the tyrant, but continually cast his sight upon
that sword: And in the end he prayed Denis, to take him from the supposed
beatitude [state of supreme blessedness or happiness], wherein he was laid: saying,
that he had rather be a poor philosopher, than in that manner to be happy: Did
not I then say well to thee (answered the tyrant) that we tyrants are not so happy
as men think, for our lives depend always upon a small thread?

What repose could Nero also have?[5] who confessed, that often the likeness of
his mother (whom he slew) appeared to him, which tormented and afflicted him;
and that furies beat him with rods, and tormented him with burning torches?
. . . And indeed it is one of the greatest wisdoms that can be in a tyrant, to take
a good course for his death, when it is necessary and expedient for him: for they
are often troubled, and do come short therein: as we see of Nero, who in his need
could find no man that would slay him, but he was forced to slay himself: True
it is, that his secretary held his hand, that with more strength and less fear he

might dash the dagger into his throat, yet neither his secretary nor any other person would of themselves attempt it. If this secretary had been one of Machiavell's scholars, it is likely he would have proved more hardy. [. . .]

Lastly, here would not be omitted altogether this wickedness of Machiavell, who confounding good and evil together, yieldeth the title of Virtuous unto a tyrant: Is not this as much as to call darkness, full lightsome and bright, vice, good and honourable, and ignorance, learned? But it pleaseth this wicked man thus to say, to pluck out of the hearts of men, all hatred, horror, and indignation, which they might have against tyranny, and to cause princes to esteem tyranny, good, honourable and desirable.

NOTES

1   Machiavelli used 'virtue' (*virtù*) in the sense of 'strong rule' and 'civic virtue' rather than of 'goodness' or 'morality'.
2   Lucius Brutus, who in the semi-legendary period of the sixth century BCE led the Romans against the tyrannical rule of king Tarquin the Proud. Later, as consul, he condemned his own two sons to death for plotting to destroy Tarquin.
3   Cesare Borgia, Duke of Valentino, infamous for his ruthless campaign to secure himself a principality; Oliver (Otto) da Ferm(o), an Italian *condottiere* (mercenary commander) who was murdered by Cesare Borgia; Agathocles (361–289 BCE), a tyrant of Syracuse.
4   Dionysius (*c.*432–367 BCE), a tyrant of Syracuse. The story of the sword of Damocles is recounted in Cicero's *Tusculan Disputations*, vi.21. 61–2.
5   Nero Claudius Caesar (37–68 CE), Emperor of Rome, notorious for his cruelty and extravagance.

Section Three

The Renaissance Court

29 A Sforza banquet menu (1491)

This list of courses and their formal presentation at an unknown banquet survives
as a fragmentary document in the Milanese Sforza archives. Besides illustrating
the range of food and drink consumed at a large feast, it indicates the sculptural
and theatrical presentation of each course. Several of the dishes are presented by
servants in costume. An hors d'oeuvre course of pastries, poultry and fish is
followed by a main course alternating between fish and heavier meats; it ends
with a course of sweet desserts and oysters. Formal dining is one aspect of court
life which underwent little change from the Middle Ages: a menu for a very
similar banquet survives for a Milanese court marriage in 1368. The Sforza menu
is comparatively light. Among the 'performance' banquets reported by the papal
chef, Bartolomeo Scappi (c.1500–80), was a meal for two hundred different plates
which a cardinal held in honour of Charles V.

Source: *Ludovico il Moro: La sua città e la sua corte (1480–1499),* Archivio di Stato
di Milano, Como, New Press, 1983, pp. 171–3, translated (with footnotes) for this
edition by Dorigen Caldwell

Food

Three swans with their skins, decorated with gold and mottoes; two roasted
reared geese per plate with bowls of grape juice on the side; one large golden
pastry of game per plate.

[Wine:] From Calabria

Presentation

The lids of the said game pies are to be in the form of three very high and ornate
mountains with forts on top and decorated with gold and mottoes.

Food

Large boiled pikes covered with black pepper sauce; one large whole boiled *tori*[1]
without sauce per plate, with bowls of blue sauce on the side; and salted fish, i.e.
two large *dentali*[2] per plate.

Wine: from the Marches

Presentation

The covers of the plates holding the salted fish should consist of a model of the
Colosseum lavishly decorated with gold and mottoes.

Food

A course of large boiled meats: two whole calves; four whole heifers; four whole
kids; two whole roe-deer; eight hares; pigs, and two wild boar, all served in three
large biers – that is to say, in one bier the two calves, in another the four heifers,
and in the other bier the four kids, two roe-deer and the eight hares. On large
platters should be served six large capons; six geese; six pheasants; six ducks;
twelve pigeons, and ten partridges. On other large platters should go the large

golden cured meats, i.e. the eight hams; two salami; six large sausages; six tongues; six *soppressate*.[3] The broth made from these boiled meats is flavoured with cinnamon.

Wine: Red S. Severino

Presentation
A centrepiece with a laurel tree which is cut open and spurts blood; a small boy comes out on horseback reciting apposite verses and mottoes with much grace and skill.

Food
Large pastries containing three capons and six pigeons stuffed with veal and their own stock; one pie containing four pigeons each; three pastries with conserved pigeon, and one pie each with two pigeons.

Wine: White from Rome

Presentation
The covers of these pastries should each have three forts, elaborately decorated with gold and other colours, with appropriate mottoes; another large castle, with two infants inside who are different according to their birth but both resolved on their own honour.

Food
A course of large fish: four fried *fraulini*[4] without sauce per plate; four fried John Dorys per plate in a sauce with olives and lemons; four fried sea bass covered with 'salsa verde' per plate with sugar-coated aniseed.

Wine: Cima de Cio

Presentation
A centaur made of sugar, carrying a woman dressed elaborately in vegetable leaves, crosses a river, as he runs from another figure made of sugar who appears to be following him and defeating him.

Food
One large whole roasted capon per plate, stuffed with good things; twelve *copiete*[5] turned inside out and stuffed per plate; braised rabbits and hares in other plates in a sauce in the French manner.

Wine: White Lambrusco

Presentation
A bull is presented by Indians and brought in by slaves of the Sultan in a most elaborately decorated procession of gold and silver with two little moors who sing very elaborately and an ambassador with an interpreter, who translates the words of the embassy.

Food

Game covered in black pepper; pies of wild boar decorated with gold – one per plate; whole roasted wild pig in yellow pepper sauce with pomegranates.

Presentation

The covers of the plates show three devils in caves who bring in black pepper, with mottoes.

Food

Large whole boiled octopus – one per plate: large boiled and stuffed cuttlefish – four per plate; squid in broth – one bowl each, with cinnamon and gold sprinkled over it.

Wine: Racese

Presentation

A large ornate temple, with fishes accompanied by mottoes and verses explaining their meaning.

Food

A course of roasted meats: two whole calves; four whole heifers; four whole kids; two large whole deer; eight hares, and two whole wild boar, brought in on enormous biers, with six men carrying each; on large platters six capons; six reared geese; six pheasants; six ducks; twelve pigeons; twelve partridges with wild cherry sauce in bowls; large roe-deer pies – two per plate; basins of apples and lemons.

Wine: sweet wine from Corsica and wine from Grandoli

Presentation

Three golden cows which search for their offspring and, finding them on the table, recite verses and mottoes on the subject.

Food

Fish jelly on large plates; saffron jelly on others; white jelly which looks like snow on others.

Wine: Red Roman wine

Presentation

The plate covers are three different forts made out of jelly with drawbridges over a moat in which live fish swim, surrounded by golden cuttlefish with flowers all around.

Food

Pies of sour apples; and other kinds of pies; black tarts with sour apples in basins and mashed pears in bowls.

Wine: White Roman wine

Presentation

Three large ships loaded with apple jam adorned lavishly with mottoes and carried by sailors from under the sea.

Food

Oysters in large basins with little bowls of pepper on the side; truffles in little plates or cups; giant roast chestnuts with fennel and pepper.

Wine: Cima de Cio

Presentation

A galleon full of oysters presented with other marine creatures adorned with mottoes.

Food

Large golden sponges; large golden marzipans; large *colisoni* of icing; and other things made out of sugar in the Roman manner and decorated with gold.

Presentation

A large ship from the Fortunate Isles bearing Moors with mottoes, full of sugar and gold.

Food

Giant wafers in large basins; round, low multicoloured mousses, sprinkled with icing sugar in the Roman manner.

Wine: Heppocrate

Presentation

Twenty-four plates of objects made of sugar paste, in all sorts of shapes, such as pockets and gloves.

Food

Basins of boiled coriander seeds; vases of open vanilla pods covered in sugar; vases of pinenuts covered in icing.

Wine: Moscatello

Presentation

Large and small castles held by Messer Facio with lids and mottoes in gold.

Food

Aniseed covered in sugar; *fulignati*[6] in icing sugar; golden, sugar-coated fennel seeds in other vases.

Presentation

Ornate lids in gold, in the Royal manner, depicting Rome triumphant with an ox, who together vow never to part, and this represents justice, temperance and great friendship, and many verses testifying to this are recited.

NOTES

1   *Toro* probably a kind of fish.
2   *Dentale* another variety of fish, probably sea bream.
3   *Soppressate* Another variety of meat, made up of large chunks.
4   *Fraulini* some type of fish.
5   *Copiete* are presumably some kind of small animal.
6   *Fulignati* are presumably a type of sweet or seed.

30 Aristotle *Nicomachean Ethics*, IV. 2–3

Many ideas of the ethical system of the Greek philosopher, Aristotle (384–322 BCE), were established as commonplace themes in European culture after the translation into Latin of his *Nicomachean Ethics* in the thirteenth century. The Golden Mean between opposed extremes, the distinction between art and practical reasoning, the idea that ethics and the arts contributed towards the collective art of politics were all notions derived from Aristotle. His version of the supreme good of philosophical contemplation was not so far from Christianity and one of his attractions for a feudal society was that he made the ideal type of the active life look much like a member of their own nobility, by placing the highest premium on 'greatness of soul', magnanimity or virtuous pride. The aristocratic person was best in behaviour and in rank. Artistic patronage was an obvious means for their self-advertisement, but Aristotle insists that even here, indeed especially here, a mean had to be found between frugality and extravagance. Magnificence is therefore the virtue of self-presentation that stems from a well-balanced 'greatness of soul'. At the end of his account of the magnanimous man Aristotle says he likes to own beautiful and useless things, since that displays his independence.

Source: *The Nicomachean Ethics* trans. W. D. Ross, revised by J. O. Urmson, in *The Complete Works of Aristotle. The Revised Oxford Translation*, ed. J. Barnes. Bollingen Series, LXXI. 1–2, 2 vols, Princeton University Press, Princeton NJ. 1984, vol. II, pp. 1771–3. Copyright © 1984 by Princeton University Press

It would seem proper to discuss magnificence next. For this also seems to be an excellence concerned with wealth; but it does not like liberality extend to all the actions that are concerned with wealth, but only to those that involve expenditure; and in these it surpasses liberality in scale. For, as the name itself suggests, it is a fitting expenditure involving largeness of scale. But the scale is relative; for the expense of equipping a trireme is not the same as that of heading a sacred embassy. It is what is fitting, then, in relation to the agent, and to the circumstances and the object. The man who in small or middling things spends according to the merits of the case is not called magnificent (e.g. the man who can say 'many a gift I gave the wanderer'), but only the man who does so in great things. For the magnificent man is liberal, but the liberal man is not necessarily magnificent. The deficiency of this state is called niggardliness, the excess vulgarity, lack of taste, and the like, which do not go to excess in the amount spent on right objects, but by showy expenditure in the wrong circumstances and the wrong manner: we shall speak of these vices later.

The magnificent man is like an artist: for he can see what is fitting and spend large sums tastefully. For, as we said at the beginning, a state is determined by its activities and by its objects. Now the expenses of the magnificent man are large and fitting. Such, therefore, are also his results; for thus there will be a great expenditure and one that is fitting to its result. Therefore the result should be worthy of the expense, and the expense should be worthy of the result, or

should even exceed it. And the magnificent man will spend such sums for
the sake of the noble; for this is common to the excellences. And further
he will do so gladly and lavishly; for nice calculation is a niggardly thing. And
he will consider how the result can be made most beautiful and most becoming
rather than for how much it can be produced and how it can be produced most
cheaply. It is necessary, then, that the magnificent man be also liberal. For the
liberal man also will spend what he ought and as he ought; and it is in these
matters that the greatness implied in the name of the magnificent man – his
bigness, as it were – is manifested, since liberality is concerned with these matters;
and at an equal expense he will produce a more magnificent result. For a
possession and a result have not the same excellence. The most valuable possession is that which is worth most, e.g. gold, but the most valuable result is that
which is great and beautiful (for the contemplation of such a thing inspires
admiration, and so does magnificence); and the excellence of a result involves
magnitude. Magnificence is an attribute of expenditures of the kind which we
call honourable, e.g. those connected with the gods – votive offerings, buildings,
and sacrifices – and similarly with any form of religious worship, and all those
that are proper objects of public-spirited ambition, as when people think they
ought to equip a chorus or a trireme, or entertain the city, in a brilliant way.
But in all cases, as has been said, we have regard to the agent as well and ask
who he is and what means he has; for the expenditure should be worthy of
his means, and suit not only the result but also the producer. Hence a poor
man cannot be magnificent, since he has not the means with which to spend
large sums fittingly; and he who tries is a fool, since he spends beyond what
can be expected of him and what is proper, but it is *right* expenditure that is
excellent. But great expenditure is becoming to those who have suitable means
to start with, acquired by their own efforts or from ancestors or connexions,
and to people of high birth or reputation, and so on; for all these things bring
with them greatness and prestige. Primarily, then, the magnificent man is of this
sort, and magnificence is shown in expenditures of this sort, as has been said:
for these are the greatest and most honourable. Of *private* occasions of expenditure the most suitable are those that take place once for all, e.g. a wedding
or anything of the kind, or anything that interests the whole city or the people
of position in it, and also the receiving of foreign guests and the sending of
them on their way, and gifts and countergifts; for the magnificent man spends
not on himself but on public objects, and gifts bear some resemblance to votive
offerings. A magnificent man will also furnish his house suitably to his wealth
(for even a house is a sort of public ornament), and will spend by preference
on those works that are lasting (for these are the most beautiful), and on every
class of things he will spend what is becoming; for the same things are not
suitable for gods and for men, nor in a temple and in a tomb. And since each
expenditure may be great of its kind, and what is most magnificent absolutely
is great expenditure on a great object, but what is magnificent *here* is what is
great in *these* circumstances, and greatness in the work differs from greatness in
the expense (for the most beautiful ball or bottle is magnificent as a gift to a
child, but the price of it is small and mean). – therefore it is characteristic of the

7 Rinaldo Piramo de Monopoli, detail of a page from Aristotle's *Nicomachean Ethics, c.*
1495, illustrated for Duke Andrea Maria di Acquaviva of Naples. Cod. Phil.graec.4, fol 52r:
Österreichische Nationalbibliothek, Vienna.

magnificent man, whatever kind of result he is producing, to produce it magnificently (for such a result is not easily surpassed) and to make it worthy of the
expenditure.

Such, then, is the magnificent man; the man who goes to excess and is vulgar
exceeds, as has been said, by spending beyond what is right. For on small objects
of expenditure he spends much and displays a tasteless showiness; e.g. he gives a
club dinner on the scale of a wedding banquet, and when he provides the chorus
for a comedy he brings them on to the stage in purple, as they do at Megara.
And all such things he will do not for the sake of the noble but to show off his
wealth, and because he thinks he is admired for these things, and where he ought
to spend much he spends little and where little, much. The niggardly man on

the other hand will fall short in everything, and after spending the greatest sums will spoil the beauty of the result for a trifle, and whatever he is doing he will hesitate and consider how he may spend least, and lament even that, and think he is doing everything on a bigger scale than he ought.

These states, then, are vices; yet they do not bring *disgrace* because they are neither harmful to one's neighbour nor very unseemly.

Pride[1] seems even from its name to be concerned with great things; what sort of great things, is the first question we must try to answer. It makes no difference whether we consider the state or the man characterized by it. Now the man is thought to be proud who thinks himself worthy of great things, being worthy of them; for he who does so beyond his deserts is a fool, but no excellent man is foolish or silly. The proud man, then, is the man we have described. For he who is worthy of little and thinks himself worthy of little is temperate, but not proud; for pride implies greatness, as beauty implies a good-sized body, and little people may be neat and well-proportioned but cannot be beautiful. On the other hand, he who thinks himself worthy of great things, being unworthy of them, is vain; though not every one who thinks himself worthy of more than he really is worthy of is vain. The man who thinks himself worthy of less than he is really worthy of is unduly humble, whether his deserts be great or moderate, or his deserts be small but his claims yet smaller. And the man whose deserts are great would seem *most* unduly humble; for what would he have done if they had been less? The proud man, then, is an extreme in respect of the greatness of his claims, but a mean in respect of the rightness of them; for he claims what is in accordance with his merits, while the others go to excess or fall short.

If, then, he deserves and claims great things, and above all the greatest things, he will be concerned with one thing in particular. Desert is relative to external goods; and the greatest of these, we should say, is that which we render to the gods, and which people of position most aim at, and which is the prize appointed for the noblest deeds; and this is honour; that is surely the greatest of external goods. Honours and dishonours, therefore, are the objects with respect to which the proud man is as he should be. And even apart from argument it is with honour that proud men appear to be concerned; for it is honour that they chiefly claim, but in accordance with their deserts. The unduly humble man falls short both in comparison with his own merits and in comparison with the proud man's claims. The vain man goes to excess in comparison with his own merits, but does not exceed the proud man's claims.

Now the proud man, since he deserves most, must be good in the highest degree; for the better man always deserves more, and the best man most. Therefore the truly proud man must be good. And greatness in every excellence would seem to be characteristic of a proud man. And it would be most unbecoming for a proud man to fly from danger, swinging his arms by his sides, or to wrong another; for to what end should he do disgraceful acts, he to whom nothing is great? If we consider him point by point we shall see the utter absurdity of a proud man who is not good.

NOTE

1   The Greek word for 'pride' is *megalopsuxia*, 'greatness of soul'. For Aristotle 'pride' in
       this positive sense carries meanings related to self-respect. Over-weening pride for the
       Greeks is *hubris*. The connotations of magnanimity for generosity of spirit were intro-
       duced by Christian theologians.

31   Leonardo da Vinci **Extracts from his *Notebooks***
(i) The Science of Art (ii) Perspective (iii) Proportion
(iv) Studio practice

The following selection from the writings of Leonardo da Vinci (1452–1519)
shows why this famous Renaissance polymath considered painting a science, or
a branch of knowledge associated with the *quadrivium* of the higher liberal arts:
mathematics, geometry, astronomy and music. According to Leonardo, in the first
extract perspective and proportion are clearly related to these disciplines. For
him, painting, and by implication, drawing, could serve as tools to understand
and interpret nature. He presents the conventional features of Renaissance picture
construction, such as linear definition or the description of light effects, as if they
had a microcosmic ability to reproduce sensory impressions. In the second
extract, Leonardo sets out the basic principles of artificial perspective and then
proceeds to point out some of the anomalies in natural perspective when
recorded on a two-dimensional surface. In the short summary at the end of this
section Leonardo explains what he means by *sfumato* or a smoky finish. Ideal
figurative forms are perceived through the harmony of their proportions, as
shown in the anecdote about the artistic judgement of Matthias Corvinus. Like
perspective, this is an artificial construct for the scale of people and objects,
based on the synthesis of observed examples. Leonardo was indebted to
Vitruvius whom he names in the third extract. The fourth extract provides
summary advice for the would-be painter about the value of individual research
and collaborative work. Leonardo's approach presents an alternative to the
conventional training based on the workshop and guild membership.

Source: *Leonardo on Painting*, ed. and trans. M. Kemp and M. Walker, Yale
University Press: New Haven and London, 1989, pp. 13–15, 32–4, 37–8, 49–55, 57,
59–61, 63–4, 87, 24, 26, 119–20, 122, 205

i) The Science of Art

HE WHO DESPISES PAINTING LOVES NEITHER PHILOSOPHY NOR NATURE

If you scorn painting, which is the sole imitator of all the manifest works of
nature, you will certainly be scorning a subtle invention, which with philosophical and subtle speculation considers all manner of forms: sea, land, trees,
animals, grasses, flowers, all of which are enveloped in light and shade. Truly this

is science, the legitimate daughter of nature, because painting is born of that nature; but to be more correct, we should say the granddaughter of nature, because all visible things have been brought forth by nature and it is among these that painting is born. Therefore we may justly speak of it as the granddaughter of nature and as the kin of god.

WHY PAINTING IS NOT NUMBERED AMONGST THE SCIENCES

Because writers had no access to definitions of the science of painting, they were not able to describe its rank and constituent elements. Since painting does not achieve its ends through words, it is placed below the . . . sciences through ignorance, but it does not on this account lose its divinity. And in truth it is not difficult to understand why it has not been accorded nobility, because it possesses nobility in itself without the help of the tongues of others – no less than do the excellent works of nature. If the painters have not described and codified their art as science, it is not the fault of painting, and it is none the less noble for that. Few painters make a profession of writing since their life is too short for its cultivation. Would we similarly deny the existence of the particular qualities of herbs, stones or plants because men were not acquainted with them? Certainly not. We should say that these herbs retained their instrinsic nobility, without the help of human language or writings.[1]

WHETHER PAINTING IS A SCIENCE OR NOT

The mental discourse that originates in first principles is termed science. Nothing can be found in nature that is not part of science, like continuous quantity, that is to say, geometry, which, commencing with the surfaces of bodies, is found to have its origins in lines, the boundary of these surfaces. Yet we do not remain satisfied with this, in that we know that line has its conclusion in a point, and nothing can be smaller than that which is a point. Therefore the point is the first principle of geometry, and no other thing can be found either in nature or in the human mind that can give rise to the point. [. . .][2]

No human investigation may claim to be a true science if it has not passed through mathematical demonstrations, and if you say that the sciences that begin and end in the mind exhibit truth, this cannot be allowed, but must be denied for many reasons, above all because such mental discourses do not involve experience, without which nothing can be achieved with certainty.

Those sciences are termed mathematical which, passing through the senses, are certain to the highest degree, and these are only two in number. The first is arithmetic and the second geometry, one dealing with discontinuous quantity and the other with continuous quantity. From these is born perspective, devoted to all the functions of the eye and to its delight with various speculations. From these three, arithmetic, geometry and perspective – and if one of them is missing nothing can be accomplished – astronomy arises by means of the visual rays. With number and measure it calculates the distances and dimensions of the heavenly bodies, as well as the terrestrial ones. Next comes music, which is born of

8 Leonardo da Vinci, *Self portrait*, red chalk on paper, 33.3 × 21.4 cm, Palazzo Reale, Turin. Photo: Anderson-Alinari.

continuous and discrete quantities and which is dedicated to the ear, a sense less noble than the eye. Through the ear, music sends the various harmonies of diverse instruments to the *sensus communis*. Next follows smell, which satisfies the *sensus communis* with various odours, but although these odours give rise to fragrance, a harmony similar to music, none the less it is not in man's power to make a science out of it. The same applies to taste and touch.[3]

[PRINCIPLES OF THE SCIENCE OF PAINTING]

The principle of the science of painting is the point; second is the line; third is the surface; fourth is the body which is enclosed by these surfaces. And this is just what it is to be represented, that is to say, the body which is represented, since in truth the scope of painting does not extend beyond the representation of the solid body or the shape of all the things that are visible.

Point is said to be that which cannot be divided into any part. Line is said to be made by moving the point along. Therefore line will be divisible in its length, but its breadth will be completely indivisible. Surface is said to be like extending the line into breadth, so that it will be possible to divide it in length and breadth. But it has no depth. But body I affirm as arising when length and breadth acquire depth and are divisible. Body I call that which is covered by surfaces, the appearance of which becomes visible with light. Surface I call the outer skin of a body, which defines the forms of a body and its boundary. Boundary I call the surrounding edge of each seen surface, the termination of which marks the division [between one body and another].

The second principle of the science of painting is the shadow of bodies, by which they can be represented. We shall give the principles of shadow, with which we must proceed if we wish to model in three dimensions on the aforesaid surface.[4]

The first intention of the painter is to make a flat surface display a body as if modelled and separated from this plane, and he who most surpasses others in this skill deserves most praise. This accomplishment, with which the science of painting is crowned, arises from light and shade, or we may say *chiaroscuro*. Therefore, whoever fights shy of shadow fights shy of the glory of art as recognised by noble intellects, but acquires glory according to the ignorant masses, who require nothing of painting other than beauty of colour, totally forgetting the beauty and wonder of a flat surface displaying relief.

There are two principal parts into which painting is divided: firstly the outlines which surround the shapes of solid bodies – and these outlines require draughtsmanship; and secondly what is called shading. But draughtsmanship is of such excellence that it not only investigates the works of nature but also infinitely more than those made by nature . . . On this account we should conclude that it is not only a science but a goddess which should be duly accorded that title. This deity repeats all the visible works of almighty God. [. . .][5]

AN ARGUMENT OF THE POET AGAINST THE PAINTER

You say that a science is correspondingly more noble to the extent that it embraces a more worthy subject, and accordingly, that a spurious speculation about the nature of god is more valuable than one concerned with something less elevated. In reply we will state that painting, which embraces only the works of God, is more worthy than poetry, which only embraces the lying fictions of the works of man.

The poet may say, 'I will make a story which signifies great things'. The painter can do the same, as when Apelles painted the *Calumny*.[6] The poet says that his science consists of invention and measure, and this is the main substance of poetry – invention of the subject-matter and measurement in metre – which is subsequently dressed up in all the other sciences. The painter responds that he has the same obligation in the science of painting, that is, invention and measure – invention of the subject that he must depict and measurement of the things painted, so that they should not be ill-proportioned.

Painting does not dress itself up in the three other sciences. On the contrary, these others dress themselves up largely by means of painting, as does astronomy, which can achieve nothing without perspective, the principal element of painting – I mean mathematical astronomy, not that false prophecy which is (if you will forgive me for saying so) the means by which fools live.

If poetry embraces moral philosophy, painting is natural philosophy. If poetry describes the operation of the mind, painting considers the action of the mind in bodily motions. If poetry terrifies people with fictional hells, painting can do likewise by presenting in reality the same thing. Supposing that the poet, like the painter, depicts beauty, fierceness, an evil or ugly thing, or something monstrous, by transforming objects in whatever manner he wishes, then the painter will give greater satisfaction. Have we not seen painting which had such a conformity with the imitated object that they have deceived both men and animals?

I once saw a painting which deceived a dog by means of the likeness of the painting to its master. The dog made a great fuss of it. And in a similar way I have seen dogs barking and trying to bite painted dogs, and a monkey did an infinite number of stupid things in front of a painted monkey. I have seen swallows fly and perch on iron bars which have been painted as if they are projecting in front of the windows of buildings.[7]

Here the poet answers, and concedes the above arguments, but adds that he is superior to the painter because he can make men talk and argue about diverse fictions in which he depicts things that do not exist; because he can induce men to take up arms; because he will describe the heavens, the stars, nature and the arts and everything. To this one replies that none of these things of which he speaks belongs within his real profession. But if he wishes to make speeches and orations, he must be persuaded that he will be conquered by the orator, and that if he wishes to speak of astronomy, he has stolen it from the astronomer, and philosophy from the philosopher. The only true office of the poet is to invent words for people who talk to each other. Only these words can he represent naturally to the sense of hearing, because they are in themselves the natural things that are created by the human voice. But in all other respects he is bettered by the painter. [. . .]

CONCLUDING ARGUMENTS OF THE POET, PAINTER AND MUSICIAN

There is the same difference between the representation of corporeal things by the poet and painter as between dismembered and intact bodies, because the poet in describing the beauty or ugliness of any figure shows it to you bit by bit and over the course of time, while the painter will permit it to be completely seen in an instant. The poet is not able to present in words the true configuration of the elements which make up the whole, unlike the painter, who can set them before you with the same truth as is possible with nature. The poet may be regarded as equivalent to a musician who sings by himself a song composed for four choristers, singing first the soprano, then the tenor, and following with the contralto and then the bass. Such singing cannot result in that grace of proportioned harmony which is contained within harmonic intervals. Alternatively, something made by the poet may be likened to a beautiful face which is shown to you feature by feature, and, being made in this way, cannot ever satisfactorily convince you of its beauty, which alone resides in the divine proportionality of the said features in combination. Only when taken together do the features compose that divine harmony which often captivates the viewer.

Yet music, in its harmonic intervals, makes its suave melodies, which are composed from varied notes. The poet is deprived of this harmonic option, and although poetry enters the seat of judgement through the sense of hearing, like music, the poet is unable to describe the harmony of music, because he has not the power to say different things at the same time. However, the harmonic proportionality of painting is composed simultaneously from various components, the sweetness of which may be judged instantaneously, both in its general and in its particular effects – in general according to the dictates of the composition; in particular according to the dictates of the component parts from which the totality is composed. And on account of this the poet remains far behind the painter with respect to the representation of corporeal things, and, with respect to invisible things, he remains behind the musician.

But if the poet borrows assistance from the other sciences, he may be compared to those merchants at fairs who stock varied items made by different manufacturers. The poet does this when he borrows from other sciences, such as those of the orator, philosopher, cosmographer and suchlike, whose sciences are completely separate from that of the poet. Thus the poet becomes a broker, who gathers various persons together to conclude a deal. If you wish to discover the true office of the poet, you will find that he is nothing other than an accumulator of things stolen from various sciences, with which he fabricates a deceitful composition – or we may more fairly say a fictional composition. And in that he is free to make such fictions the poet parallels the painter, although this is the weakest part of painting. [. . .][8]

PAINTING AND ITS DIVISIONS AND COMPONENTS

Light, shade, colour, body, shape, position, distance, nearness, motion and rest – of these ten parts of the functions of sight, painting has seven, of which the first is light, then shade, colour, shape, position, distance and nearness. I omit body and motion and rest. Light and shade are included, or we may wish to say shadow and illumination, or lightness and darkness. I do not include body because painting in itself is a thing of surface, and surface has no body as is defined in geometry.[9]

Amongst all the studies of natural phenomena, light most delights its students. Amongst the great things of mathematics, the certainty of its demonstrations most conspicuously elevates the minds of investigators. Perspective must therefore be preferred to all the human discourses and disciplines. In this field of study, the radiant lines are enumerated by means of demonstrations in which are found not only the glories of mathematics but also of physics, each being adorned with the blossoms of the other. Analysis of these has been conducted with great circumlocutions, but I will constrain myself with decisive brevity, treating them according to the nature of the material and its mathematical demonstrations. Sometimes I will deduce effects from causes and at other times causes from effects, adding also my own conclusions, some of which do not arise in this way but may nonetheless be formulated – if the Lord, light of all being, deigns to illuminate my discourse on light.[10]

ii) Perspective

INTRODUCTION TO PERSPECTIVE, THAT IS TO SAY, THE FUNCTION OF THE EYE

Now, take note reader, something about which we cannot believe our ancient predecessors, who have wished to define the nature of the soul and life – things beyond proof – whereas those things which at any time can be clearly known and proved by experience have for so many centuries been unknown or falsely conceived. The eye, the function of which is thus clearly shown by experience, has, until my own time, been defined by innumerable writers in one way; I find by experience that it is different.

In the eye the shapes, the colours, all the images of the parts of the universe are reduced to a point, and this point is such a marvellous thing! O wonderful, O marvellous necessity, you constrain with your laws all the effects to participate in their causes in the most economical manner! These are miracles . . . In so small a space the image may be recreated and recomposed through its expansion. In this way, clear and immediate effects can arise from confused origins, like the images which have passed through the aforesaid natural point. Describe in your anatomy what ratios exist between the diameters of all the spheres of the eye and what distance there is between them and the crystalline sphere. [. . .][11]

ON THE ERRORS OF THOSE WHO RELY ON PRACTICE WITHOUT SCIENCE

It is a very great vice found in many painters that they make the houses of men and other surrounding buildings in such a way that the gates of the city do not come up to the knees of the inhabitants even though they are closer to the eye of the observer than the man who indicates that he wishes to enter therein. We have seen porticos laden down with men, and the supporting column like a thin cane in the fist of the man who leans on it. Other similar things are to be disdained.

Those who are in love with practice without science are like the sailor who boards a ship without rudder and compass, who is never certain where he is going. Practice must always be built on sound theory, of which perspective is the signpost and gateway, and without perspective nothing can be done well in the matter of painting. The painter who copies by practice and judgement of eye, without rules, is like a mirror which imitates within itself all the things placed before it without any understanding of them.

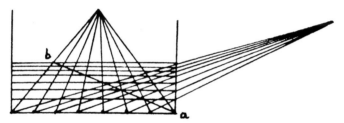

9 Standard perspective construction of a tiled floor (with confirming diagonal. *ab*), based on MS A 541r.

DISCOURSE ON PAINTING

Perspective, with respect to painting, is divided into three principle parts, of which the first is the diminution in the size of bodies at various distances; the second part is that which deals with the diminution in colour of these bodies; the third is the diminution in distinctness of the shapes and boundaries which the bodies exhibit at various distances. Of these three perspectives, the first has its foundation in the eye, while the other two are derived from the air interposed between the eye and the objects seen by the eye.[12]

Their rules will permit you to acquire an unfettered and good judgement, since good judgement is born of good understanding, and good understanding derives from rationality – drawn from good rules – and good rules are the daughters of good experience, common mother of all the sciences and arts. Hence, once you have my precepts in your mind, your rectified judgement will on its own enable you to judge and recognise every ill-proportioned work, whether with respect to perspective or figures or anything else.

Perspective is a rational demonstration by which experience confirms that all things send their semblances to the eye by pyramidal lines. Bodies of equal size will make greater or lesser angles with their pyramids according to the distances between one and the other. By pyramidal lines I mean those which depart from the surface edges of bodies and travelling over a distance are drawn together towards a single point.

All the instances of perspective are expounded through the five terms of the mathematicians, namely point, line, angle, surface and body. The point is unique of its kind: the point has neither height nor breadth nor length or depth, and, hence, it is to be concluded that it is indivisible and occupies no space. Line is of three types, namely straight, curved and sinuous, and has neither breadth nor height or depth, and, hence, is indivisible except in its length; its ends are two points. Angle is the termination of two lines at a point. [. . .]

THE PRINCIPLE OF PERSPECTIVE

All things send their semblances to the eye by means of pyramids. The image of the original object will be smaller to the extent that the pyramid is intersected nearer the eye (fig. 10). [. . .]

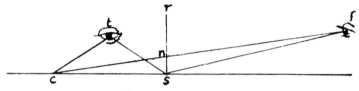

10 A square viewed in perspective.[13]

The eye *f* and the eye *t* are one and the same thing; but the eye *f* denotes the distance, that is to say how far away you are when looking at the object, and the eye *t* demonstrates the orientation, that is to say whether you are situated centrally or to the side or at an angle to the thing you are looking at. Remember that the eye *f* and the eye *t* should always be placed at the same height as each other. For example, if you lower or raise the eye *f*, which denotes the distance, you must do the same with the eye *t*, which denotes the orientation. The point *f* shows how far the eye is distant from the square plane and does not show in which way it is orientated, and similarly the point *t* provides this orientation and does not show the distance. Therefore, to know both distance and orientation, you must identify the eyes with each other, so that they may be the same thing.

If the eye *f* looks at a perfect square, in which all the sides are equal to the length between *s* and *c*, and if at the base of the side which is towards the eye is placed a staff or other straight object which stands perpendicularly, as is shown by *rs*, I say that if you look at the side of the square which is nearest to you it will appear at the base of the intersection *rs*. And if you look at the second side, opposite, it will appear higher up on the intersection at point *n*. Therefore, by this demonstration, you can understand that if the eye is above an infinite number of things placed on a plane one behind the other they will accordingly be located progressively higher, as far as the point which denotes the height of the eye. But they will appear no higher, providing the objects are placed on the plane on which your feet are located and the plane is flat. Even if this plane extends infinitely, it will never pass higher than the eye, because the eye has in itself that point towards which are directed and towards which converge all the pyramids that carry the images of the objects to the eye. And this point always coincides with the point of diminution that appears at the limit of everything we see . . . In the [fig. 11] above, let *ab* be the intersection, *r* the point of the pyramids ending in the eye, *n* the point of diminution. This point is always seen by the visual point in the eye along a straight axis and always moves with it, just as when a rod is moved its shadow moves and travels with it, no differently from the way a shadow travels with a solid body. And both points are the vertices of the pyramids that make a common base on the intervening intersection. Although their bases are equal, they make different angles, because the point of diminution is the apex of a smaller angle than that of the eye. If you should ask me, by what experience can you demonstrate these points to me, I will say to

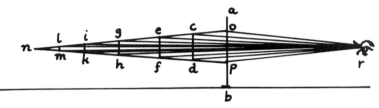

11 Points of the visual pyramid and the pyramid of diminution.

you that the extent to which the point of diminution travels with you will be apparent when you walk beside a ploughed plot of land with straight furrows, the ends of which reach down to the road on which you are walking. You will always see each pair of furrows in such a way that it seems to you that they are trying to press inwards and join together at their distant ends.

If the eye is in the middle between the tracks of two horses which are running towards their goal along parallel tracks, it will seem to you that they are running to meet each other. This happens because the images of the horses which impress themselves on the eye are moving towards the centre of its surface, that is, the pupil of the eye. [. . .]

Linear perspective embraces all the functions of the visual lines, proving by measurement how much smaller the second object is than the nearest, and how much the third is smaller than the second, and so on by degrees, as far as the objects can be seen. I have found by experiment that when the second object is as far from the first as the first is from the eye that, although they are the same size, the second will appear as half as small as the first. And if the third object is of equal size to the second, and the third is as far distant from the second as the second is from the eye, it will appear half the size of the second, and so on by degrees. At equal distances the second will always diminish by a half compared to the first, and so on. [. . .]

The practice of perspective is divided into [two] parts. The first represents all the objects to the eye at their distances and shows how the eye sees them diminished. The observer is not obliged to remain in one place rather than another, providing that the wall on which it is represented does not foreshorten it a second time. But the second practice is a mixture of perspective made in part by art and in part by nature, and a work undertaken according to this rule does not exhibit any elements that are not subject to a mixture of natural perspective and accidental perspective. By natural perspective I mean that in which the perspectival projection is produced on a flat intersection, and on this intersection, although it has parallel horizontal and upright sides, we are required to diminish the remoter parts more than the nearest, and this conforms to the first of the divisions mentioned above, in which the diminution of objects will be natural.[14]

Accidental perspective, that is to say, that made by art, acts in a contrary manner, because the size of bodies that are in themselves equal appears larger on the foreshortened intersection to the extent that the eye is naturally closer to the

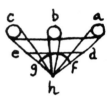

12 Problems of natural and artificial perspective preventing uniform vision.

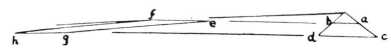

13 Problems of perspective distortion.

intersection and to the extent that some parts of the intersection on which it is represented are more distant from the eye.

Let the intersection be *de* on which are represented three equal circles, which are behind *de*, that is to say the circles *a b c* [fig. 12]. Now you can see that the eye *h* will see the intersections of the images on the rectilinear intersection as larger at greater distances or smaller when closer. But this invention requires that the observer should situate himself with his eye at a small aperture, and then through this hole the perspective will be well displayed. But because many spectators will strive to see at the same time the one work made in this manner – and as only one can see well how such perspective functions – all these other people will find it confusing. It is well therefore to avoid such compound perspective and to limit yourself to simple perspective, which does not see the intersection as itself foreshortened, but as much in its actual shape as is possible. In this simple perspective, the intersection cuts across the pyramids carrying the images to the eye at equal distances from the seat of vision, and these images are experienced on the curved surface of the transparent part of the eye, on which these pyramids are intersected at equal distances from the seat of vision.

The cause of accidental perspective lies with the wall on which the demonstration is performed, which is at unequal distances from the eye at various places along its length. The diminution of the wall arises naturally, but the perspective represented on it is accidental, because in no part does it accord with the actual diminution of the aforesaid wall. Thus it comes about that when the eye is removed from the station point for viewing the perspective, all the objects represented appear monstrous ... Let us say that the four-sided body *abcd* represented above is a foreshortened square, seen by the eye located opposite the middle of the side which is at the front [fig. 13]. Accidental perspective mixed with natural perspective will be found in the four-sided body known as a paral-lelogram, that is to say *efgh*, which must appear to the eye looking at it as similar to *abcd* when the eye remains fixed at its original place in relation to *cd*; and this will be seen to good effect, because the natural perspective arising from the wall will conceal the defects of this monstrous form.

WHY OBJECTS PORTRAYED PERFECTLY FROM NATURE DO NOT APPEAR TO POSSESS THE SAME RELIEF AS APPEARS IN AN OBJECT IN NATURE

It is impossible that a picture copying outlines, shade, light and colour with the highest perfection can appear to possess the same relief as that which appears in an object in nature, unless this natural object is looked at over the long distance and with a single eye. This is proved as follows: let the eyes be *a* and *b*, looking at an object *c*, with the converging central axes of the eyes as *ac* and *bc*, which converge on the object at the point *o* [fig. 14]. The other axes, lateral to the central one, see the space *gd* behind the object, and the eye *a* sees all the space *fd*, and the eye *b* sees all the space *ge*. Hence the two eyes see behind the object and all the space *fe*. On this account, this object *c* acts as if transparent, by the definition of transparency, according to which nothing behind it is concealed. This cannot happen with someone who looks at an object with one eye, if the object is bigger than the eye, although the same does not apply when this eye sees an object somewhat smaller than its pupil, as is demonstrated in the diagram. And from what has been said we can arrive at a conclusion to this question, because something painted interrupts our view of all the space behind it, and in no way is it possible to see any part of the background behind it within the circumferential outline of the object. [. . .]

PRECEPTS FOR PAINTING

That object, or rather its shape, is shown with more distinct and sharp bound-aries which is nearer to the eye. And on this account, painter, when in the name of dexterity you represent the view of a head seen at a short distance with abrupt brushstrokes and rough and harsh handling, you should realise that you are

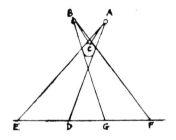

14 Binocular vision of an object.

deceiving yourself, because at whatever distance you represent your shape, it will always have a finished appearance appropriate to the degree of distance at which it is found. Although at a long distance the definition of the boundaries is lost, you should not on this account neglect to observe that a smokey finish is to be seen, and not boundaries and profiles that are sharp and harsh. Thus it is to be concluded that in a work to which the eye of the observer can approach closely, the parts of the picture should be finished with the greatest diligence at all degrees of distance, and in addition to this the nearest objects will be bounded by evident and sharp boundaries against the background, while those more distant will be highly finished but with more smokey boundaries, that is to say more blurred, or we may say less evident. It is to be observed at successively greater distances ... that firstly the boundaries are less evident, then the component parts and finally the whole object is less evident in shape and colour.

iii) Proportion

[The opinion of King Matthias Corvinus concerning the relative merits of painting and poetry]

On King Mathias's birthday, a poet had brought him a work made to commemorate the day on which the King was gifted to the world, when a painter presented him with a portrait of his beloved lady.[15] Immediately the King closed the book of the poet and turned to the picture, fixing his gaze upon it with great admiration. Whereupon the poet very indignantly said, 'Read, O King! Read and you will discover something of greater consequence than a dumb painting'. The King, on hearing the accusation that he was giving credence to dumb objects said, 'Be silent, O poet. You do not know what you are saying. This picture serves a greater sense than yours, which is for the blind. Give me something I can see and touch, and not only hear, and do not criticise my decision to tuck your work under my arm, while I take up that of the painter in both hands to place it before my eyes, because my hands acted spontaneously in serving the nobler sense – and this is not hearing. For my part I judge that there is an equivalent relationship between the science of the painter and that of the poet as there is between the senses to which they are subject. Do you not know that our soul is composed of harmony, and that harmony cannot be generated other than when the proportions of the form are seen and heard instantaneously? Can you not see that in your science, proportionality is not created in an instant, but each part is born successively after the other and the succeeding one is not born if the previous one has not died?[16] From this I judge that your invention is markedly inferior to that of the painter, solely because it cannot compose a proportional harmony. It does not satisfy the mind of the listener or viewer in the same way as the proportionality of the very beautiful parts composing the divine beauty of this face before me, and which by contrast are conjoined instantaneously, giving me such delight with their divine proportions. I judge that there is nothing on earth made by man which can rank higher.' [. . .]

[PRINCIPLES]

The configuration of bodies is divided into two parts, that is to say, the proportionality of the parts amongst themselves, which will correspond to the whole, and the movement appropriate to the occurrences in the mind of the living being that moves the body . . . The proportion of the limbs is also divided into two parts, that is to say, quality and motion. By quality I mean that, in addition to making the measurements correspond to the whole, you should not mix limbs of the young with those of the old, nor those of the stout with those of the lean, and besides this you should not make men with feminine limbs, nor mix graceful limbs with clumsy ones. By motion I mean that the gestures or movements of the old should not be made with the same vivacity as is suitable for the movement of a youth, nor that of a small child like that of a youth, nor that of a woman like that of a man.

Every part of the whole must be proportionate to the whole. Thus if a man has a thick and short figure, he must be the same in all his limbs, that is to say, with short and thick arms, with wide, thick hands, and short fingers, with their joints in the aforesaid manner, and so on with the remainder. And I intend to say the same about animals and plants universally, reducing or increasing them proportionately according to their diminution or increase in size. All the parts of any animal will correspond to the whole . . . and it is my intention to say the same about trees – those which have not been maimed by man or by winds, because these renew their youth above the old parts and thus disrupt the natural proportionality.[17]

Among the praiseworthy and marvellous things which are apparent in the works of nature, it happens that none of the productions of any species in themselves precisely resemble in any of their details those of any other. Thus, imitator of nature, observe and pay attention to the variety of the lineaments of things. I will be well pleased if you avoid monstrous things, like long legs with short torsos, and narrow chests with long arms. Therefore take the measurements between the joints and you should vary their breadths, which differ considerably. And if you should wish to make your figures according to a single measure, you must know that one cannot be distinguished from another – something which is never observed in nature.

If nature had fixed a single rule for the relationships of the features, all the faces of men would resemble each other in such a way that it would not be possible to distinguish one from the other. But she has varied the five parts of the face in such a way that, although she has made an almost universal rule for their sizes, she has not observed it in the relationships to such a degree that it is impossible to recognise clearly one person from another.

Measure on yourself the proportion of the composition of your limbs, and if you find any discordant part, take note of it and make very sure that you do not adopt it in the figures that are composed by you, because it is a common vice of painters to take delight in making things similar to themselves.[18] This happens because our judgement is that which directs the hand in the creation of the delineations of figures in various configurations until it is satisfied. Because this judgement is one of the powers of our soul, through which it composes the form of the body in which it lives according to its will, when it has to reproduce with the hands a human body, it willingly reproduces that body of which it was the original inventor, and from this it arises that he who loves will eagerly fall in love with things similar to himself.

ON THE MEASUREMENTS OF THE HUMAN BODY

Vitruvius, the architect, has it in his work on architecture that the measurements of man are arranged by nature in the following manner: four fingers make one palm and four palms make one foot; six palms make a cubit; four cubits make a man, and four cubits make one pace; and twenty-four palms make a man; and these measures are those of his buildings.[19]

If you open your legs so that you lower your head by one-fourteenth of your height, and open and raise your arms so that with your longest fingers you touch the level of the top of your head, you should know that the central point between the extremities of the outstretched limbs will be the navel, and the space which is described by the legs makes an equilateral triangle.

The span to which the man opens his arms is equivalent to his height.

From the start of the hair [i.e., the hairline] to the margin of the bottom of the chin is a tenth of the height of the man; from the bottom of the chin to the top of the head is an eighth of the height of the man; from the top of the breast to the top of the head is a sixth of the man; from the top of the breast to the start of the hair is a seventh part of the whole man; from the nipples to the top of the head is a quarter part of the man; the widest distance across the shoulders contains in itself a quarter part of the man; from the elbow to the tip of the hand will be a fifth part of the man; from this elbow to the edge of the shoulder is an eighth part of this man; the whole hand is a tenth part of the man; the penis arises at the middle of the man; the foot is a seventh part of the man; from the sole of the foot to below the knee is a quarter part of the man; from below the knee to the start of the penis is a quarter part of the man; the portions which are to be found between the chin and the nose and between the start of the hair and . . . the eyebrows are both spaces similar in themselves to the ear and are a third of the face.

iv) Studio Practice

ON THE LIFE OF THE PAINTER IN HIS STUDIO

Lest bodily prosperity should stifle a flourishing talent the painter or draughtsman should be solitary, especially when intent on those speculations and reflections which continually appear before his eyes to provide subjects for safe-keeping in the memory. If you are alone you belong entirely to yourself. If you are with just one companion you belong only half to yourself and less so in pro-portion to the intrusiveness of his behaviour. And the more of your companions there are, the more you will fall into the same trouble. If you should say 'I will go my own way, and draw apart – the better to be able to speculate upon the forms of natural objects', then I say this could be harmful to you because you will not be able to prevent yourself from often lending an ear to their idle chatter. And since you cannot serve two masters you will perform badly in the role of companion and there will be an even worse consequence for the speculative study of your art. And if you say I shall withdraw so far apart that their words will not reach me, and will cause me no disturbance, I for my part would say that you would be held to be mad. But consider: by doing it you would at least be alone. And if you must have company choose it from within your studio. This would enable you to reap the benefit of a variety of discussions. All other company could be extremely detrimental to you.

The painter needs such mathematics as pertain to painting. He must forego companions who are disinclined to his studies, and have a brain capable of react-ing to the different objects that present themselves before it, and removed from all other cares. And above all he must liken his mind to nature, giving it a surface like a mirror which is transformed into as many different colours as there are coloured objects placed before it. And the company he keeps should be like-minded towards those studies, and should such company not be found, he should keep his own during his contemplation, for in the end there will be no company more useful.

. . . To draw in company is much better than to do so on one's own for many reasons. The first is that you will be ashamed to be counted among draughtsmen if your work is inadequate, and this disgrace must motivate you to profitable study. Secondly a healthy envy will stimulate you to become one of those who are more praised than yourself, for the praises of others will spur you on. Another reason is that you will learn something from the drawings of those who do better than you, and if you become better than them you will have the advantage of showing your disgust at their shortcomings and the praises of others will enhance your virtue.[20]

NOTES

1   Note that painting was not regarded as a liberal art in antiquity, being considered a manual skill requiring a knack like cooking and gardening instead of the learned know-ledge of the liberal arts.

2   In the first book of his *Metaphysics*, Aristotle makes the claim that inventive artists are superior to mere reproductive craft workers just as reasoning about first principles is considered more important than experiential knowledge. Leonardo seems to be para-phrasing this source. He defines metaphysical existence in terms of dimensions.

3   Common sense was conceived of as an internal control which processed the informa-tion received from the external senses and transmitted it to the upper faculties of the mind according to the conventional psychology based on Aristotle.

4   This alludes to Leonardo's characteristic technique of *chiaroscuro*, 'light–dark': describ-ing the form through strong contrasts of lighting.

5   Leonardo refers to the Renaissance topos of art as the imitator or rival of nature.

6   This picture was described in a work of Lucian of Samosata. Leon Battista Alberti, in his treatise *On Painting*, cites it as a model for a varied pictorial composition in that the

allegory shows an interconnected group of figures. One of the earliest versions of this subject was a panel painting by Botticelli.

7   These occurrences are much like anecdotes recounted in Pliny's *Natural History*.

8   The comparison between painting and poetry was a Renaissance commonplace often referred to as *Ut pictura poesis* (*As in painting so in poetry*) from its discussion in a poem by the Roman Horace, the *Ars poetica*.

9   Most guides to the liberal arts explained them in terms of their component parts.

10   This paraphrases the opening of a popular book on medieval optics, John Peacham's *Perspectiva communis* (*Intergrated Perspective*).

11   Leonardo is here referring to the image recreated in the eye. Before the thirteenth-century influence of writings on optics by Arabic scholars, it was thought that the eye emitted visual rays rather than receiving the light via the cornea.

12   That is, perspective is determined by variation in size, colour and line.

13   This diagram shows how the grid floor served to determine the position not only of the recession back into space in single-point perspective but also where the viewer should be standing in order to view the image 'correctly'. The picture plane, that is, the actual surface of the picture rather than the imaginary space behind it, is represented in this diagram by the line 'r'—'s'. The following diagram shows how diminution will appear within a single-point perspectival scheme.

14   The distinction made here is between objects, preferably with flat sides, which lie parallel to the picture plane (called the 'intersection' by Leonardo) and recede back to a single vanishing point, with those which are more randomly placed and therefore appear to be distorted when visually depicted in foreshortened perspective. This is the visual phenomenon known as anamorphosis.

15   Leonardo da Vinci may have produced a religious painting for Ludovico Sforza which was given to King Matthias Corvinus of Hungary in the 1480s.

16   Leonardo's argument here is that the harmony of ideal proportions reflects the soul of the person depicted and affects the soul of the viewer since the soul is composed of a harmony.

17   Leonardo's argument here is that typical – less often ideal – proportions are observable in nature and show a regular scale of proportions between the parts and the whole of a normal living body.

18   Here Leonardo refers to a danger in figure painting to which he repeatedly alludes that 'every painter paints his self', meaning that painters have a tendency to depict their own features when painting other people.

19   Marcus Vitruvius Pollio lived between the first centuries BCE/CE. He discusses proportion in Book III, chapter 1 of his *De architectura*, where he compares the relative proportions of a temple with those of the human body.

20   The argument here is not as contradictory as it might seem: Leonardo maintains that the artist's inventive research should be conducted alone but that studio work in a group provides the stimulus for competition in technique. This idea became embedded in the founding of artistic academies.

32 Vespasiano da Bisticci **The *Life of Federico da Montefeltro***

A Florentine bookseller and book publisher serving a range of notable international clients, Vespasiano da Bisticci (1421–98) is most famous for his collection of vignette biographies of his own customers (notably English nobles and Hungarian clerics among the non-Italian contingent), his local associates and large-scale book collectors of the past. These memoirs were written during his retirement in the 1480s, once his own business had succumbed to competition from printing. The format of anecdotal biographical essays had long been familiar in Florence, having been initiated there by Villani (Text 11). Vespasiano's sources ranged from first-hand reports for the earlier lives and his own experience, supplemented by literary references. His somewhat moralising tone is in keeping with his other works, among them *A Book of Praise and Commendation of the Famous Women in the Bible, in Greek, Latin and Italian History*. The *Life* of Federico da Montefeltro was dedicated to the duke's son, Guidobaldo.

Source: *The Vespasiano Memoirs, Lives of Illustrious Men of the XVth Century*, ed. and trans. W. G. and E. Waters, George Routledge and Sons Ltd, London, 1926, pp. 99–102, 104–11, 113–14

[. . .] Hitherto I have written concerning some of the Duke's military exploits, leaving his greater deeds to be dealt with by those who will write his history; and now it seems meet to say something of his knowledge of the Latin tongue, taken in connection with military affairs, for it is difficult for a leader to excel in arms unless he be, like the Duke, a man of letters, seeing that the past is a mirror of the present. A military leader who knows Latin has a great advantage over one who does not. The Duke wrought the greater part of his martial deeds by ancient and modern example; from the ancients by the study of history, and from the moderns through nurture in warlike practices from early infancy under the discipline of Nicolo Piccinino [1386–1444], one of the worthiest captains of his age. But to return to letters, the Duke of Urbino was well versed therein, not only in history and in the Holy Scriptures, but also in philosophy, which he studied many years under a distinguished teacher, Maestro Lazzaro, afterwards for his merits made Bishop of Urbino. He was instructed by Maestro Lazzaro in the *Ethics* of Aristotle, with and without comments, and he would also dispute over the difficult passages. He began to study logic with the keenest understanding, and he argued with the most nimble wit that was ever seen. After he had heard the *Ethics* many times, comprehending them so thoroughly that his teachers found him hard to cope with in disputation, he studied the *Politics* assiduously, and during his stay in Florence, after the capture of Volterra [1472], he requested Donato Acciaiuoli [1429–78], who had already commented on the *Ethics*, to write comments also on the *Politics*. This he did and sent his work to the Duke who, having read these, wished next to read the *Natural History* and the *Physics*. Indeed, it may be said of him that he was the first of the Signori who took up philosophy and had knowledge of the same. He was ever careful to keep intellect and virtue to the front, and to learn some new thing every day.

After philosophy he was fain to study theology; that learning on which every Christian ought to frame his life. He read the first part of S. Thomas [Aquinas], and certain other works of his, thus acquiring a strong predilection for S. Thomas' doctrine, which seemed to him very clear and able to defend itself. He rated S. Thomas as clearer than Scotus though less subtle. Nevertheless he wished to know the works of Scotus, and he read the first of them. He knew the Scriptures well and the early Doctors, Ambrose, Jerome, Augustine and Gregory, whose works he desired to possess; likewise the works of the Greek Doctors, Basil, John

15 Baccio Baldini (attrib.), *Mercury*, *c.*1460, engraving, 32.4 × 22 cm., British Museum. The Florentine trades under this planet were associated with the visual arts.

Chrysostom, Gregory Nazianzen, Athanasius, Cyril and Ephrem, done into Latin, and works in poetry and history which he read and re-read; also Livy, Sallust, Quintus Curtius, Justin, the *Commentaries* of Cæsar, which he praised beyond measure; all the forty-eight lives of Plutarch, translated by various hands, Ælius Spartianus, together with certain other writers of the decadence of the Roman power. Æmilius Probus, Cornelius Tacitus, Suetonius, his lives of the Emperors, beginning with Cæsar and going on to other times. He read also Eusebius' *De Temporius* [*On the Chronologies*] with the additions of Girolamo Prospero and Matteo Palmieri.[1]

As to architecture it may be said that no one of his age, high or low, knew it so thoroughly. We may see in the buildings he constructed, the grand style and the due measurement and proportion, especially in his palace, which has no superior amongst the buildings of the time, none so well considered, or so full of fine things. Though he had his architects about him, he always first realised the design and then explained the proportions and all else; indeed, to hear him discourse [on the subject], it would seem that his chief talent lay in this art; so well he knew how to expound and carry out its principles. He built not only palaces and the like, but many fortresses in his dominions of construction much stronger than those of old time; for some, which were built too high, the Duke made much lower, knowing that the fire of the bombards would not then hurt them. He was a skilled geometrician and arithmetician, and with Master Paul,[2] a great philosopher and astrologer, with whom, just before his death, he read books on mathematics, discoursing thereon like one learned in them. He delighted greatly in music, understanding vocal and instrumental alike, and maintained a fine choir with skilled musicians and many singing boys. He had every sort of instrument in his palace and delighted in their sound, also the most skilful players. He preferred delicate to loud instruments, caring little for trombones and the like.

As to sculpture he had great knowledge, and he took much thought as to the work which he had made for his palace, employing the first masters of the time. To hear him talk of sculpture you would deem it was his own art. He was much interested in painting, and because he could not find in Italy painters in oil to suit his taste he sent to Flanders and brought thence a master[3] who did at Urbino many very stately pictures, especially in Federigo's study, where were represented philosophers, poets, and doctors of the Church, rendered with wondrous art. He painted from life a portrait of the Duke which only wanted breath. He also brought in Flemish tapestry weavers who wrought a noble set for an apartment, worked with gold and silk mixed with woollen thread, in such fashion as no brush could have rendered. He also caused other decorations to be wrought by these masters, and all the doors were enriched with works as fine as those within. One of his cabinets was adorned in a fashion so wonderful that no one could say whether it was done with a brush, or in silver, or in relief.[4]

Reverting to the study of letters, from the times of Pope Nicolas and King Alfonso[5] onward, letters and learned men were never better honoured and rewarded than by the Duke of Urbino, who spared no expense. There were few *literati* of that age who did not receive from him generous gifts. He gave Campano,[6] a learned man fallen into poverty, a thousand ducats or more. Many fine works were sent to him, and when he was in Florence he bestowed upon men of letters more than fifteen hundred ducats, and I can say naught of his gifts in Rome, Naples, and other places, for they are unknown to me. No one ever was such a defender of learned men, and when Pope Sixtus persecuted the Bishop of Sipontino the bishop would have fared badly if the Duke had not protected him.[7] He was always fain to have in his palace some learned man, and none ever came to Urbino who was not honoured or received at the palace.

We come now to consider in what high esteem the Duke held all Greek and Latin writers, sacred as well as secular. He alone had a mind to do what no one had done for a thousand years or more; that is, to create the finest library since ancient times. He spared neither cost nor labour, and when he knew of a fine book, whether in Italy or not, he would send for it. It is now fourteen or more years ago since he began the library, and he always employed, in Urbino, in Florence and in other places, thirty or forty scribes in his service. He took the only way to make a fine library like this: by beginning with the Latin poets, with any comments on the same which might seem merited; next the orators, with the works of Tully [Cicero] and all Latin writers and grammarians of merit; so that not one of the leading writers in this faculty should be wanted. He sought also all the known works on history in Latin, and not only those, but likewise the histories of Greek writers done into Latin, and the orators as well. The Duke also desired to have every work on moral and natural philosophy in Latin, or in Latin translations from Greek. [. . .][8]

Finding that he lacked a vast number of Greek books by various writers, he sent to seek them so that nothing in that tongue which could be found should be lacking; also whatever books which were to be had in Hebrew, beginning with the Bible and all those dealt with by the Rabbi Moses and other commentators. And besides the Holy Scriptures, there are books in Hebrew on medicine, philosophy and the other faculties.

The Duke, having completed this noble work at the great cost of thirty thousand ducats, beside the many other excellent provisions that he made, determined to give every writer a worthy finish by binding his work in scarlet and silver. Beginning with the Bible, as the chief, he had it covered with gold brocade, and then he bound in scarlet and silver the Greek and Latin doctors and philosophers, the histories, the books on medicine and the modern doctors, a rich and magnificent sight. In this library all the books are superlatively good, and written with the pen, and had there been one printed volume it would have been ashamed in such company. They were beautifully illuminated and written on parchment. This library is remarkable amongst all others in that, taking the works of all writers, sacred and profane, original and translated, there will be found not a single imperfect folio. No other library can show the like, for in all of them the works of certain authors will be wanting in places. A short time before the Duke went to Ferrara it chanced that I was in Urbino with His Lordship, and I had with me the catalogues of the principal Italian libraries: of the papal library, of those of S. Marco at Florence, of Pavia, and even of that of the University of Oxford, which I had procured from England. On comparing them with that of the Duke I remarked how they all failed in one respect; to wit, they possessed the same work in many examples, but lacked the other writings of the author; nor had they writers in all the faculties like this library.

I began by treating of his warlike deeds, then of his martial and literary merits combined; wishing to show that if anyone should be fain to produce so skilful a captain as the Duke without the aid of letters, the attempt to produce a man of such excellence must be vain without the conjunction of these two elements. I now bring forward a third quality, the faculty of wisely governing States and Lordships, a faculty rarely possessed by those endowed as richly as he was with the qualities I have already specified. In the ruling of his states and of his house, his age saw not his peer. First, in order that his rule might be conjoined with religion, he was before all things most devout and observant in his religious duties; for without this, and without a good example to others by his life, his rule would never have endured. Every morning he heard mass kneeling; he fasted on the vigils ordered by the Church, and throughout Lent, and the year before he died the Signor Ottaviano,[9] who loved him greatly and perceived that Lenten fast was hurtful to him, got a dispensation for him from Rome. One morning during Lent this dispensation was laid before him at table, whereupon he turned towards Ottaviano, laughing, and thanked him and said: 'If I am able to fast, why should you wish me to keep from so doing? What an example I should be giving to my own people!' And he continued from that day to fast as heretofore. Every morning with his household, and with whatever townsfolk might wish, he heard the sermon, and after this the mass; and on fast days he would cause to be read to him some holy book or work of S. Leo. When the reader came to a weighty passage he would bid him stop in order that it might be thoroughly considered, and every day he made Maestro Lazzaro read to him some passage of Holy Writ.

As to works of alms and piety he was most observant. He distributed in his house every day a good quantity of bread and wine without fail, and he gave freely to learned men and gentlefolk, to holy places, and to poor folk ashamed of their case, and he never forgot anyone of his subjects who might come to ask. Wherever he could he established Observant Friars in his dominions, allowing them alms to set the country in order at his charges. He introduced the friars of Monte Oliveto and the Jesuates and the friars of Scopeto, and was as a father to all.[10] The Duke never let a religious person approach him without doing him reverence, and taking him by the hand, and in conversation would always sit down beside him. He honoured these persons more than any man I ever saw. There was in Urbino a holy convent of nuns with some sixty inmates, and the Duke did much to the convent to make it suitable for their well-being. Once every week he would betake himself alone into the church, and sit by a grating that was therein. The Superior, a lady of years and authority, would speak to him, and he would ask if the nuns lacked anything. Indeed, he provided this convent and the Observant Friars with all they needed.

As to the ruling of his own palace, it was just the same as that of a religious society; for although he was called on to feed at his own expense five hundred mouths or more, there was nothing of the barrack about his establishment, which was as well ordered as any monastery. Here there was no romping or wrangling, but everyone spoke with becoming modesty. Certain noblemen committed their sons to the Duke for instruction in military science, and they would remain with him till they were efficient. These youths were under the charge of a gentleman of Lombardy of excellent character who had been trained by the Duke long time since, and now governed these youths as if they had been his own sons. They paid him the highest respect, keeping their actions well under restraint, as pupils in a school of good manners. The Duke had a legitimate son of singular worth, Count Guido, and other legitimate children born of Madonna Battista, the daughter of Signor Alessandro of Pesaro,[11] an illustrious lady. At her death she left her children very young, and to his son the Duke assigned, as tutors, two gentlemen of due age to teach him the course he ought to follow. Afterwards he put him under a learned young man who taught him Greek and Latin, and was expressly charged by the Duke to let him have no traffic with young folk, in order that he might at once assume the grave temperament which nature had given him. He had a marvellous memory, of which I can give numerous examples; for once, when Signor Ottaviano put Ptolemy before him, he knew how to point out all the regions of the earth so that, when he was asked for any place or district, he found it at once and knew the distance of one place from another. The Duke possessed a Bible with historical comments, the events of each book being narrated, and there was no name or place which the young prince did not know, even the unfamiliar names in Hebrew. He was educated to be worthy to follow his father, and the same training is still pursued. Another son of his, Signor Antonio, born to him when he was a young unmarried man, devoted himself to arms and was of excellent carriage. His daughters, attended by many noble and worthy ladies, occupied a wing of the palace whither went no one but the Signor Ottaviano and the young prince. When the prince came to the door of their apartments, those in attendance remained outside, going to the waiting-room till he should return. In his carriage he was most observant of what was becoming.

Having spoken of the governance of his house, let us now tell of that of his subjects. His treatment of them suggested that they were rather his children. He liked not that anyone should ever address him on behalf of any of them, seeing that everyone could speak to him at any hour of the day, when he would listen to all with the utmost kindness, remarking that this gave him no trouble. If there was anything he could do for them, he would see to it, so there might be no need for them to return, and there were few whose business could not be despatched on the same day, in order that no time might be lost. And should he mark that anyone amongst those who desired to address him might be shamefaced, he would call him up, and encourage him to say what he would. His subjects loved him so greatly for the kindness he showed to them that when he went through Urbino they would kneel and say, 'God keep you, my Lord,' and he would often go afoot through his lands, entering now one shop and now another, and asking the workmen what their calling was, and whether they were in need of aught. So kind was he, that they all loved him as children love their parents. The country he ruled was a wondrous sight: all his subjects were well-to-do and waxed rich through labour at the works he had instituted, and a beggar was never seen. If it happened that anyone, through misbehaviour or neglect of the laws, should be condemned, the Duke in clemency would intervene and settle the matter to the content of all. For all offences he showed a merciful spirit save one, to wit: blasphemy of God, or of the Madonna, or of His saints. For this he had no grace or forgiveness.

He was as benevolent to strangers as to those of his own state. Once I saw him go to the piazza on a market day, and ask of the men and women who were there, how much they wanted for the wares they were selling. Then, by way of joking, he added, 'I am the Lord and never carry any money: I know you will not trust me for fear you should not be paid.' Thus he pleased everybody, small and great, by his good-humour. The peasants he had spoken to went away so delighted that he could have done with them whatever he wished, and when he rode out he met none who did not salute him and ask how he did. He went about with few attendants; none of them armed. In summer he would ride out from Urbino at dawn with four or six horsemen and one or two servants, unarmed, at his stirrup and go forth three or four miles, returning when other folk were rising from bed. When they dismounted it would be the hour of Mass, which the Duke would hear, and afterwards go into a garden with the doors open and give audience to all who wished, till the hour of repast. When the Duke had sat down the doors would be left open, so that all might enter, and he never ate except the hall were full. Some one would always read to him; during Lent a spiritual work, and at other times the Histories of Livy, all in Latin. He ate plain food and no sweetmeats, and drank no wine save that made from such fruits as cherries, pomegranates or apples. Anyone who wished to address him might do so either between the courses or after the repasts, and a judge of appeal, a very distinguished man, would lay before him, one by one, the causes before the court which he would determine, speaking in Latin. This judge told me that the decisions of the Duke could not have been bettered if they had come before Bartolo or Baldo.[12] I saw a letter written on behalf of a physician who sought an appointment at Ancona. The Duke said, 'Put in this clause: that if they want a doctor they had better take him; if they do not, let them please themselves, for I have no mind that they should do what they do not wish, because of my letter.'

In summer, after rising from table and giving audience to all who desired, he went into his closet to attend to his affairs and to listen to readings, according to the season. At vespers he went forth again to give audience; and then, if he had time, to visit the nuns at S. Chiara in the monastery he had built, or to the convent of S. Francis, where there was a large meadow with a very fine view. There he would sit while thirty or forty of his young men, after stripping to their doublets, would throw the lance either at the apple or at the twigs in marvellous fashion. [. . .]

One day he remarked to me how every man, great or small, who might be at the head of any state ought to be generous, and he censured all those who acted otherwise; and, as to those who would apologise for their want of humanity through some defect of nature, it behoved all such persons to right themselves by strong measures, seeing that great men ought to cultivate humanity as an attribute before all others. Humanity can make foes into friends. It is long since Italy had known a prince so worthy of imitation in every respect as the Duke of Urbino. [. . .]

Some blamed the Duke for over-much clemency, but this quality is much to be praised, and few suppliants went away unforgiven, whatever their offence. He hated cruelty of every kind.

One admirable quality he possessed: to speak ill of no one. He praised rather than blamed, and he took it ill if one spoke evil of another before him, deeming such an action to be shameful. He loved not to hear those who praised their own deeds: indeed, on this score he was most modest, and he always preferred that others and not himself should speak of what he had done. Nature had given him a choleric temper, but he knew well how to moderate it, and he softened his temperament with the utmost prudence. He gave himself entirely to his state that the people might be content, and one of the greatest of his merits was that when he heard of a quarrel he would send for the parties, and give his wits no rest till peace should be made. [. . .]

After his death his body was borne with the highest possible honours to the Church of S. Donato, served by the Franciscan Observantists, according to the directions of his will. The greater part of what he left was at the disposition of Signor Ottaviano, his nephew, who had his full confidence, by reason of the great affection which subsisted between them; to him also he trusted the management of state affairs, as far as they concerned his son, indeed he had such love for Ottaviano that he desired him to succeed to the government of the state, if the Count Guido should die without heirs. There are many things worthy of note concerning the Duke, but these will be set down by those who write his life. [. . .]

NOTES

1   Many of these works were in Federico's personal library which is described in the text.
2   Paul von Middelburg (1445–1533) was one of several astrologers who were in contact with the Montefeltro court.
3   The 'master' was Justus van Gent, or van Wassenhove (active 1460–75) who entered the Painters' Guild in Antwerp and went to Urbino and Rome in the 1470s.
4   Vespasiano is here alluding to the *trompe l'oeil* effects created by the intarsia wood inlay on the doors and the studiolo panels in the ducal palace at Urbino.
5   Nicholas V (1446–55), and Alfonso, King of Aragon and Naples (1443–58).
6   Gianantonio Campano (1429–78) was a polymath humanist and bishop.
7   This was Niccolò Perotto (1429–80), a humanist and philologist.
8   Vespasiano then gives an author list of Greek and Latin books, many of which were supplied by this bookshop.
9   Ottoviano degli Ubaldini (1423–98), the son of Federico's sister Anna.
10 Olivetans (Reformed Benedictines), Hieronymites and another unspecified order of friars from Scopeto.
11 Guido is Guidobaldo, who ruled 1482–1508; Battista (1446–72), daughter of Alessandro Sforza, lord of Pesaro (1404–66).
12 These are Bartolo di Sassoferrato and Baldi de Baldeschi, two Italian jurists of the fourteenth century who were regarded as standard legal authorities.

33 Federico da Montefeltro *Letter Patent to Master Luciano Laurana* (1468)

Laurana, a Dalmatian, worked for Alessandro Sforza at Pesaro and for the Gonzaga at Mantua before he became involved in the expansion programme at Urbino. The first reference that we have to his activity there is a letter of 1465 describing Laurana taking measurements on the site. By 1466 Laurana had produced a model of the Urbinese ducal palace and in the following year he was involved in a dispute with a stone mason. The patent giving Laurana executive control over the project should therefore be seen as the confirmation rather than the inception of his role. Laurana went on to acquire property in Urbino, but left the city in the summer of 1472 and reappeared in Neapolitan financial records as a military engineer. He died at Pesaro in 1479. This document is not only informative about the relationship between architect and patron, but also tells us about some of the assumptions and objectives in Federico's project. In a way directly comparable to Leonardo's evaluation of painting (Text 31), Federico compares architecture to the liberal arts of arithmetic and geometry. He also assumes that Tuscany is the home of artistic innovation. The reason given for building the ducal palace is the honour which it will bring to Federico's family and to himself. The relationship between the architect and patron recalls the contemporary architect Filarete's metaphor of a building being the offspring of two parents.

Source: Federico da Montefeltro, Letter Patent to Luciano Laurana, 10 June 1468, reprinted in P. Rotondi, *The Ducal Palace of Urbino. Its Architecture and Decoration*, London: Alec Tiranti, 1969, pp. 11–12, translated for this edition by Dorigen Caldwell

Federico da Montefeltro, Count of Urbino and Castel Durante, Captain-General of the Serenissima and the League, etc.

We judge worthy of honour and praise those men who are endowed with ingenuity and are versed in certain skills, and particularly in those which have always been prized by both Ancients and Moderns. One such skill is architecture, founded upon the arts of arithmetic and geometry, which are the foremost of the seven liberal arts because they depend upon exact certainty. Architecture furthermore requires great knowledge and intellect and we appreciate and esteem it most highly. And we have searched everywhere, but principally in Tuscany, the font of architects, without finding anyone with real understanding and experience of this art. Recently, having first heard by report and then by personal experience seen and known, how much Master Luciano, the subject of this letter, is gifted and learned in this art, and having decided to make in our city of Urbino a beautiful residence worthy of the rank and fame of our ancestors and our own stature, we have chosen and deputed the said Master Laurana to be engineer and overseer of all the master workmen employed on the said work, such as masons, carpenters, smiths and any other person of whatever status, engaged in any kind of work in the said enterprise. And we thus order the said masters and workmen, and each of our officials and subjects who have to anything to do with the said project, to obey the said Master Luciano in all things and perform whatever they are ordered to do by him, as though by our own person. In particular we order Ser Andrea Cartoni, our Chancellor and Treasurer of the funds allotted for the said house, and Ser Mattio dall'Isola, appointed to provide all supplies for the said work, in the payments they have to make and the supplies they have to provide and order to do neither more nor less than is in accordance with Master Luciano's power and authority: to strike off and dismiss any master or workman who does not please or satisfy him in his own manner, and to be able to hire other masters and workmen to do piece-work or work by the day as he pleases, and to be able to punish, fine or hold back the wages and supplies of anyone who fails to perform his duty. And he may do all the other things pertaining to an architect and master of the works, and whatsoever we ourselves might do if we were present; and in faith of this we have had our present patent drawn up and sealed with our own great seal.

Dated at Pavia, 10 June 1468[1]

[Place and Seal]

I, Ser Antonio subscribed

NOTE

1   The location is explicable by Federico's service as a *condottiere* for Galeazzo Maria Sforza, Duke of Milan. The signature is that of a ducal secretary. The Sforza had a residence at Pavia.

34 Antonio Bonfini *Ten Books on Hungarian Matters*

Antonio Bonfini was born near Ascoli on the east coast of Italy. He made a reputation for himself as a public orator. At Reccanati, south of Pesaro, he was appointed head of the local school and spokesman for the commune. During the 1470s Bonfini was intermittently associated with the court of Federico da Montefeltro. Bonfini went to Buda some time after 1476. Around 1478, he may have encountered Cardinal Giovanni of Aragon (1427/34–1502), the brother of the new Queen Beatrice of Hungary and subsequently archbishop of Esztergom, who died in 1485. Thereafter, except for a brief return to Reccanati after the death of Matthias Corvinus, he remained in Buda and died there in 1502. Bonfini's literary work for Matthias included an account of the *Origins of the Hunyadi House*, a translation of Filarete's architectural treatise with an accompanying dedicatory preface to Matthias, and the *Ten Books on Hungarian Matters*. An illustrated copy of Filarete's *Treatise* was brought to Buda by Francesco Bandini de Baronecelli, a Florentine exile who served as an ambassador for the Hungarian court and who was also a close friend of both the Florentine philosopher, Marsilio Ficino (Text 14) and Bishop Miklós Báthory (*c.*1440–1506) (Text 33). The preface to the Filarete text by Bonfini was composed around 1487–8 and its descriptions of the Corvinian building projects were incorporated into the *Ten Books* with added details. This history was probably written over an extended period and not completed until 1496.

Source: R. Feuer-Tóth, *Art and Humanism in Hungary in the Age of Matthias Corvinus*, trans. G. Jakobi, Academic Press, Budapest, 1990, pp. 123–9, translated for this edition by Caryll Green

To escort Beatrice the king had sent ten nobles, who were to make the journey through Italy with unparalleled pomp and magnificence.[1] Whenever they reached a very important city, they all set out their display cabinets, every shelf loaded with jewel-encrusted goblets and vessels made of gold and silver. The leader of the delegation was the Archbishop of Varad, who was held in very high esteem by the king for his distinction, trustworthiness, eloquence and judgement, as well as for his readiness of intellect.[2] On being received by the Duke of Urbino [Federico da Montefeltro] with a hospitality that did him the highest honour, the prelate set forth on the table a salt cellar which excited the wonder of even that richest of princes. The base of it was a hill on the side of which grew a golden tree, overhanging the salt container. In place of fruit it was laden with jewels and very fine precious stones and instead of [casting] shade it glittered with a striking brilliance. On the hill hidden recesses ingeniously made concealed repositories for gems. There was also a golden pitcher, whose projecting lip was in the form of a panting dragon. Its body, made of mother-of-pearl, protruded [from the pitcher] with proudly elevated head. At its feet its tail was drawn back in golden coils. Above the handle set with jewels rose the lid, in the form of a ribbed dome, eighteen inches high. All the rest [of the pitcher] was made of gold. The massive work, three feet in height, stood upon a very lofty pedestal.

The other members of the group vied to match this display with their own treasures. I say nothing of the utter magnificence of their apparel, the refinement of the young men of the retinue, and their most distinguished mounted escort, which surpassed all the wonders of our time.

And when the queen arrived she formalized the dining arrangements and the style of living.[3] To houses that were disagreeably plain she introduced fine banqueting-halls, elegant reception rooms, gilded bedchambers. She restrained the king from over-familiarity. At the entrances [to royal houses] she stationed doorkeepers who were constantly present. She cut off easy rights of access and restored regal majesty so as to ensure an obsequious court protocol. She advised the king to proceed at fixed times into the hall of justice to give judicial decisions. She introduced to the Hungarians Italian customs and also entertained them with Latin banquets. Diverse arts, which had been lacking hitherto were hailed from Italy, together with master craftsmen at great expense. In this way painters, sculptors, moulders, medallists, joiners, cabinet makers and silversmiths, as well as stone carvers and architects, were hired from Italy and the salaries paid out for these were immense. From this time on the form of church worship was made more elaborate. The royal chapels were graced with singers brought from all over France and Germany. Furthermore specialists were summoned to design and tend both formal gardens and kitchen gardens, and farm overseers were fetched from Italy to produce even the cheeses by the Italian, Sicilian and French method. Actors and mime artists were included too. The queen was extremely keen on these. Then there were flute players, both soloists and others to play for the choral dances, bagpipers and singers who accompanied themselves on the cithara. Even the invited poets, orators and grammarians, who mistakenly believed that distant muses were more wretched than those they brought with them, returned to Italy bearing gifts. All these Matthias honored and fostered in an extraordinary manner in his attempt to make Pannonia [Hungary] a second Italy. He assiduously sought out from all parts the most pre–eminent men in whatever field and employed them, He held in high esteem astronomers,

16 Philostratus, *Works*, with
translation by Antonio Bonfini,
miniatures by Boccardino Vecchio,
1487–90, Oszágos Széchényi
Könyvtár, Budapest, Cod. Lat 417,
fol. IV.

physicians, mathematicians and lawyers, he did not even abhor magicians and necromancers; he never considered any art as unimportant.

Conversely, the Hungarians, lacking civil refinement and the niceties of life, bore all these things ill.[4] They condemned the senseless expenditure and daily found fault with the sovereign for being wanton with money and for disbursing taxes set up for better uses on things that were worthless and vain. They complained that he was departing from the frugality and temperance of the kings of former times, casting off old-established and austere practices, destroying ancient customs and was altogether defecting to Latin, or rather Catalan [i.e. troubadour] pleasures and effeminate ways. They grumbled also that he paid far too much attention to his wife and that the foreigners were not only plundering gold but day by day ruining the entire kingdom with the acquiescence of the ruler. There were many things with which they reproached him and they submitted to them with an ill grace. But for his part that divine ruler, a father of all the liberal arts, and patron of men of talent, openly condemned the Hungarians for their ways, and publicly reproached them for their Hunnish rusticity and uncultivated life. He utterly abhorred their barbarous customs. Gradually he introduced civil manners and encouraged the magnates to adopt a civilized way of life. He bid them build grand houses in proportion to their means, and entreated them to behave with much more courtesy and to be more tolerant of the ways of foreigners, which they had hitherto detested above all things. And so it was that, chiefly by the king's example, they were all attracted towards all these ideas.

He set in train the improvement of the citadel of Buda, where, apart from the magnificent buildings of Sigismund,[5] there was nothing worthy of regard. The inner courtyard of the palace was embellished beyond measure, inasmuch as he erected a chapel on the Danube side furnished with water organs, and also graced it with a double font made of marble and silver. He added a most distinguished college of priests, and beyond it established a library complete with an incredible supply [of books] in Greek and Latin. The books themselves were also ornamented in a most opulent style. In front of the library is a vaulted chamber where one can look upwards at the universe of the heavens, [painted as if you were] facing the southern sky. He built a palace of almost Roman splendour, with spacious dining-rooms, magnificent antechambers and bedchambers, and also coffered ceilings, all different, gilded and decorated with a great variety of devices. Then there are doors with outstanding inlay-work and remarkable fireplaces, in the upper parts of which four-horse chariots and many Roman allegories are sculpted. Stored below are documents and treasure. On the east side there are various dining-rooms and reception rooms, which are approached by an inner staircase and a loggia. There is a council chamber here and a private suite. Moving on further you come upon sundry high rooms with arched ceilings. There are many winter and summer rooms, balconies and gilded private apartments. In addition to this there are deep concealed alcoves and bedsteads and chairs made of silver. On the western side there is a much older building not yet restored; in the middle there is an open courtyard surrounded by an ancient colonnade. This court is crowned with galleries on two storeys, the higher one of these stretching in front of the new palace. You can ascend to the great hall by this gallery, which is remarkable for its ceiling decorated with the signs of the twelve planets. This is regarded with considerable wonder.

Everywhere you tread upon mosaic floors with illusionistic motifs; several floors are of encaustic [baked and glazed] tiles. Throughout there are hot and cold apartments.[6] The stoves in the dining-rooms are covered with tiles moulded in relief, which attract the attention not only by the beauty of their colours, but also by the variety of inventive animal forms.

In the courtyard three well-armed free-standing sculptures challenge those descending [from the raised area of the castle to the middle of the courtyard]. In the centre stands Matthias as a helmeted warrior, leaning on a spear and round shield, deep in thought; on the right is his father and on the left a somewhat sorrowful Ladislav. In the middle of the courtyard is a bronze fountain set in a marble basin, on top of which stands a helmeted and armed Minerva. At the entrance to this court, in the extremely wide front courtyard, two nude bronze statues of threatening warriors have been set up, equipped with shield, battleaxe and sword. Trophies in relief have been carved on their pediments. In this square space, in front of the hall built by Sigismund, Matthias had begun to repair the earlier palace at the side, and if he had been able to fulfil this plan he would have restored a great deal from proud antiquity.

He had added to this palace a twin flight of stairs in red marble, remarkable for its bronze lampholders. Over this he had constructed an entrance portal in the same stone, with double doors. This was embellished with wonderful door panels in bronze, skilfully fashioned with the labours of Hercules visible from the front as well as from the back. He ordered this epigram of Antonius Bonfini to be carved over the door:

> Palaces with doors and statues forged in bronze
> Record the genius of Corvinus the sovereign.
> After his many victories won from the enemy
> May valour, bronze, marble, written words
> Not allow Matthias to perish.

He had intended for this palace, at stupendous cost, timber ceilings whose panels would contain planets steering their way through the heavens, and their wandering courses would present a sight to marvel at. He had decided to place a band of triglyphs under the roof eaves and, as far as he was able, to execute a structure striking in its workmanship.

He had water drawn up to the palace fountain from almost a mile away in pitch-covered wooden pipes and lead conduits. He set about extending Sigismund's rampart walk, which virtually encompassed the whole citadel, at even greater expense. Sigismund built for eternity, but Matthias built for the present. He arranged long open stretches as well as many window panes. On projecting points of the walls a wooden hall was constructed, which he completed with a dining-room, bed-chamber, together with a dressing-room and a somewhat more secluded night study. But the layout seemed like a wild ruin tumbling into the Danube.

Outside the castle in a nearby valley lie delightful gardens and a villa built of marble. The entrance is set around with fluted columns covered in mosaic and these columns support bronze lampholders. The main door of the house is triumphal, and its dining-room and drawing-room with their windows and panelled ceilings are so remarkable that they closely resemble antiquity at its most splendid. Nearby is a covered walk which gives a view on to the gardens, and in the gardens a maze has been created with planted trees. Beside these there are aviaries full of foreign and native birds, and these are enclosed by wire-netting. There are also vines and fruit trees among the aviaries, and there is a grove and terrace walks arranged in tiers and surrounded with different species of trees. In addition there are covered walks, grassy areas, mosaics, fishponds; turrets, too, spread over with vine arbours, and upper storeys in which are dining-rooms with glazed windows. They are so delightful that you would think nothing more charming. The house is roofed with silver tiles. Moreover on the far side of the Danube in the Pest district, a mile from the town, he also had a suburban villa no less delightfully agreeable, where it was his custom to release himself from the cares of his mind. He had another suburban villa in the Buda district, three miles from the city, where wild animals were to be seen roaming loose in very spacious enclosures; here there was also a great herd of domesticated animals. There was a third not far from the city of Buda, near the salt-works.

But who could compare for grandeur what he initiated at Székesfehérvár in the church of the Holy Mother, where there are tombs of venerable kings? For not only was he endeavouring entirely to restore the building, but also to make it much more distinguished, and that excellent monarch would have fulfilled his purpose had not an untimely death taken him from the world. Among the first things he did was to set about laying the foundation of a great altar much larger than the former one, so that he could erect a mausoleum on this spot [for himself] and for his father. Here, in order to dedicate a sanctuary in this place for his parents and brother and for himself, he also transferred the body of Elizabeth his most gracious mother, who had not long since departed this life. This was to have been a domed structure in hewn stone, made with much art, but it was unfinished; it had already started to rise into a rounded vault and was built with so many arched openings all around that it exceeds even the most dazzling skill. It is sited on marshy ground and therefore it was laid on very deep foundations. So extravagantly did he build this edifice that with it alone he seems to render of no account all the works of the preceding kings.

At Visegrád, the one-time citadel of earlier monarchs, is situated in a very elevated position. Matthias enlarged the lower [part of] the castle to such an extent, and so embellished the gardens with enclosures for wild animals and with fishponds, that it also appears to surpass the others in the lofty pride of its buildings. Here you can see tapestry furnishings woven with gold, spacious dining-rooms, loggias in dazzling white stucco and magnificent windows. Here also are hanging gardens and fountains which are adorned with red marble and copper basins.

Further on you come upon Tata, which certainly in my judgement can, briefly, be said to take pride of place over all the other castles. For here the water, checked by a permanent and solid dam, has filled an enclosed valley and formed a lake measuring almost seven miles [11.3 kilometres] in land measures.[7] Where the water flows out there is a series of nine corn mills which are connected to the castle and can never be taken by force in war. The castle has a double ring wall and is fortified with a rampart and ditch; there is a small colonnaded court-yard which is surrounded by gilded banquet halls and magnificent reception rooms with coffered ceilings and carvings enhanced with much gold. The water flowing from the lake is stemmed at frequent points, resulting in innumer-able natural fishponds, in which there is a great abundance of pike and carp. There is a sizeable parkland area on either side, and two colonnades. Open wood-lands which support a considerable quantity of game surround the domain on all sides.

Not far from this place, beside the Danube, there still exist very many traces of a Roman legionary camp, which, moreover, was nominated as a colony of the Latin nation on account of the pleasantness of the location and the fertility of the soil. A little way beyond, on the tip of an island, Cumara comes into view. In scale it is certainly more extensive. Its ample loggias and very substantial dining halls with their varied coffered ceilings in every room were constructed, in truth, at very heavy expense. He had a state barge built of wood for sailing on the Danube. It is like his palaces, with a dining–room, anteroom, bedroom, men's and women's apartments all very neatly fitted in between the prow and the stern.

Moreover, after Vienna was taken, he created at the castle hanging gardens, loggias and marble fountains for which the water was drawn up from below. Hot and cold bathing rooms were built on the terraced ground. He created gardens lower down as well. There are cages for small birds and larger aviaries covered with wire mesh, and in a retired spot a little grove had been formed with glades for topiary work. There are paths under arched pergolas covered in vines. On top of the walls he created walkways which are ideal for taking a stroll.

He was considering the construction of a bridge over the Danube (and if time had been allowed him, perhaps he would have accomplished it). He was attracted to the ideal by the example of the emperor Trajan, who had thrown across the Ister [the lower part of the Danube] near Smederewo [Serbia] a marble bridge, of which several piles are still in existence. He was greatly interested in [a work on] architecture, which in the space of only three months Antonio Bonfini had translated from his maternal language [Italian] into Latin.[8] It would take too long to give proper explanation of all the other building works he carried out in castles, royal palaces and churches.

NOTES

1   These extracts come from the penultimate book of the incomplete treatise compiled by Bonfini. The marriage with Beatrice of Aragon took place in 1476.
2   Janós Filipecz was one of the Corvinian 'new men'.
3   Queen Beatrice is here presented as an important cultural influence on the King.
4   Compare the cultural animosity recounted in the next item by the Italian humanist, Galeotto Marzio.
5   Sigismund of Luxembourg, King of Hungary (1387–1437).
6   This possibly refers to the different forms of water-supply for bathrooms. The terminology is derived from Roman architectural sources.
7   The Öreg tó Lake, 69 kilometres west of Budapest. The fortress at Tata is still partially extant.
8   A reference to Filarete's *Treatise*. The illuminated presentation copy for Matthias Corvinus survives in the Biblioteca Nazionale Marciana, Venice.

35 Galeotto Marzio di Narni *Concerning the Famous, Wise and Amusing Words and Actions of King Matthias Corvinus*

Galeotto Marzio came from Narni in Umbria and was born around 1427. He first became acquainted with Hungary through his friendship with Jannus Pannonius, poet, court treasurer and nephew of Bishop Janos Vitéz, the archbishop of Esztergom, while both men were studying at the school of Guarino of Verona in Ferrara. A double portrait of the scholars was painted by Mantegna. Vitéz promoted Italian humanism in Hungary before his political downfall and death in 1472. Galeotto had dedicated an early work, *De homine*, to him. Several visits to the court of Matthias Corvinus followed and he probably wrote the text between 1484 and 1486. He later sought patronage from Lorenzo de'Medici in 1489 and by 1492 he was in France. The text here is modelled on a similar biographical collection drawn up for King Alfonso I of Naples and the popular series of classical exemplary lives retold by Valerius Maximus. The extract here begins with an account of the geographical locations of Buda and Pest, together with a typically humanist display of assorted asides about place-name derivations.

Source: Galeottus Martius Narniensis, *De egregie, sapiente, iocose dictis ac factis regis Mathiae ad ducem Iohannem eius filium liber*, ed. L. Juhász, Teubner, Leipzig, 1934, pp. 34–5, translated for this edition by Robert Goulding

A WISE SAYING

Buda is a city located on a mountain, around the base of which flows the Danube. There is some uncertainty over the origin of its name: either from the ancient Budalia, or from that godly man who was called Buddha – not because he founded the city, but because that man's name was applied to the city because of his excellence. Now Buddha (as St Jerome records) was the foremost teacher among the sophists of India, who are usually called the Gymnobrahmans. According to their tradition, a young girl gave birth to him out of her side. But I do not think it is very important to determine whether this story of his birth is true or false. One thing is most certain: that Buddha is the name of a very wise man, who formulated the learning of the Indians. This I did want to say: that Hungary has many place names which resemble those of famous men. For instance, the town of Sirmicum[1] retains a memory of the name of Sirmus, ancient king of the Triballi; and (not to go through every example) Strigonium[2] is found not only in Hungary,[3] likewise Pest, as when Virgil mentions Paestum[4] in his poem:

> I saw the rose-gardens, flourishing with Paestan care[5]

This city is in Italy, but the Hungarian Pest is on the Danube, facing Buda, and the Danube flows between them. Pest is in the plain, while Buda is placed on a mountain which gushes with hot springs and is planted with trees and vines; thus, in one direction, Buda looks out on hills lush with vines and, in the other, it takes in Pest and farmland. The descent from Buda to the river is so steep, that the stone stairway from the Cathedral of Mary to the Danube, which the kings built in their magnificence, stretches nearly three hundred feet.

Now, to return to our subject, when the general council of nobles gathered at Buda and were waiting to gain admittance to the king, among them was Miklós Báthory, a nobleman by birth and in rank the bishop of Vac. This city is twenty miles from Buda, but the journey from Vac to Buda is made downstream. This bishop Miklós was greatly endowed with virtue, spiritual nobility and a worthy demeanour. For he had studied the humanities in Italy, increasing his learning through application and diligence. He did not shun the hard work, late nights or any of the other discomforts which accompany learning; and so it was not long before the most learned and intelligent philosophers praised his learning and reading with the highest admiration.

17 Gian Cristoforo Romano, attrib. *Matthias Corvinus* and *Beatrice of Aragon*, 1485–90, marble with jasper background, each 55 × 38.5 cm Szépmüvészeti Museum, Budapest.

While the assembly of nobles was gathered, as a remedy against the tedium and long-windedness of the occasion he brought with him a book: Cicero's *Tusculan Disputations*, if my memory serves.[6] Many laughed at the unusual sight of this extraordinary young man reading books in such a place; it was a novelty to the Hungarians to see a bishop poring over a book, especially there, where speeches and discussions were the order of the day. But while they were laughing, King Matthias entered and, seeing Miklós holding his books, said to Galeotto: 'Miklós was, I believe, your former student and a beloved comrade in your reading and study. And quite rightly so. For the apostle, when he invested bishops, said that they should be teachers among others.[7] But no one can impart learning unless he himself is learned – and learning is either inspired from above or is acquired through study and hard work. Thus it is right that Miklós shuns laziness and idleness, and reads, studies and improves his mind.' Then Matthias turned to those princes, whose laughter he had heard, and said: 'Do not laugh at what you cannot understand out of ignorance. You made fun of bishop Miklós. Haven't you ever heard of that Roman, by the name of Cato, who was (as the histories tell us) very wise? When he died at Utica (which is a city in Africa), the great general Julius Caesar took it very badly, even though he had always been an enemy of Cato.[8] Now this Cato – a man of divine counsel and rare learning, and held in the highest repute by all – considered that inactivity was a fuel for vice, and so, when the Roman Senate was in session, always used to read something.'

When those who had laughed at Miklós heard this, they began instead to admire him. For they recognized his modesty, liberality and generosity; they marvelled at the antiquity of his family; with reverence they recalled his brother Stephen Báthory, and his massacre and slaughter of the Turks; they praised Miklós' graceful bearing and his gentle, charming and Ciceronian eloquence which they heard every day; they paid honour to the liveliness of his mind, his constancy, honesty, trustworthiness and the sincerity of his friendship, finding no traces of arrogance or flattery in his character; and they judged that he was, and had always been, a credit both to his ancestors (who were excellent, highly placed men) and to his brother Stephen. In one thing alone, out of their own ignorance, they condemned him: that he had been reading books in the palace, which was not the usual custom in his country. For they were well aware that he had, with great spirit and excellence of mind, borne and finally overcome the attacks of rivals and the envious. In the middle of a tumult of hatred and when threats to his livelihood and assaults from those who envied him were rife, he conducted himself in just the same way as they had seen him do on more favourable occasions.

I say nothing of the magnificence with which he built the cathedral, bringing over architects and builders from Italy at great expense, so that the church and the episcopal residence would befit his own personal generosity. There is, however, one thing which I shall not pass over. When I had been in Hungary for two years, I made a trip to see Miklós. He received me and looked after me with such humanity, that even I found his singular hospitality to be quite extraordinary. In addition, he urged me to write a history of the deeds of King Matthias, so that the actions of so great a king, which had adorned his country and made it great, would not fall into oblivion. I was also greatly pleased by the dignity and elegance of his household: for in his house there was always prayer, or study, or songs sung to a lyre, or honourable conversation; the place knew nothing of inactivity, or laziness, or time-wasting. The frequent strolls from the castle to the gardens (which he himself had laid out and furnished with ponds) and from the gardens back to the castle were not without the company of decent men and the companionship of books, with the result that even this journey was passed in conversation. Sometimes the bishop travelled in a carriage, revisiting that ring of pleasant and sunny hills, accompanied by reading and decent conversation, so that one might believe that Minerva and the Muses inhabited and frequented with joy those beautiful Bacchic hills.

NOTES

1	Actually ancient Sirmium (modern Serm Mitrovica, in Serbia).
2	Esztergom.
3	He is probably refering to the city of Stregona or Stragona in Northern Silesia, now Strzegom, Poland.

4   Ancient Posidonia or Paestum in southern Italy, where the famous Greek temples to
       Poseidon are found.
5   Not, in fact, from a poem by Virgil, but from the pseudo-Ausonian '*Ver erat . . .*'.
6   A copy of this work belonging to Miklós Báthory now survives as an illuminated
       manuscript in the Hungarian National Library.
7   *I Timothy* 3 : 2
8   The Stoic, Cato of Utica (95–46 BCE) fell on his sword after his defeat at the Battle of
       Thaspus in the Roman Civil War.

36 Luigi Gonzaga da Borgoforte **A report on the festivities at the Palazzo Te, Mantua, in honour of Charles V (1530)**

This chronicle of the Hapsburg emperor's tour of Italy is attributed to Luigi Gonzaga da Borgoforte, who died some time in the late 1530s. It survives in a sixteenth-century Pavian manuscript and was written within ten years of the tour. The circuit of Charles V followed the Treaty of Barcelona by which Spain's rule in Naples was confirmed and the French claim to Milan was revoked. The coronation of Charles V as Holy Roman Emperor by the Pope in Bologna in 1529 at once reasserted the medieval Ghibelline authority of the Emperor and reunited the contemporary spiritual and temporal powers. In addition to the temporary displays of triumphal entries and festivities which accompanied the entrance of the Emperor on his travels, several individual patrons used the events as opportunities to stimulate new building projects, sharing iconographic themes and even artists to some extent. The *Chronicle* is useful because of the detail it provides about the entertainments which accompanied Charles's progress. Luigi Gonzaga was a minor poet, genealogist, and counsellor-secretary at the duke of Mantua's court. For some of the events which he describes he was a first-hand witness.

Source: *Cronaca del soggiorno di Carlo V in Italia dal 26 Luglio al 25 Aprile 1530*, ed. G. Romano, Ulrico Hoepli, Milan, 1892, pp. 260–8, translated for this edition by Dorigen Caldwell

His Excellency saw that everything that could be done to honour the Emperor had been done, and that nothing remained but to invite his Majesty to dine with him so that he might show him his Palazzo Te;[1] and in the evening that they were in that place, he would give a wonderful party for him, and the event took place in this manner. First, on the morning of Thursday, the second of April,[2] the most Illustrious Marquis had certain rooms of the palazzo decked out very well with luxurious bed hangings so that nothing was lacking. And then his Excellency, being very well dressed, and having eaten with many princes and lords, mounted his horse, and proceeded to the Castle in order to collect the Emperor and take him to the aforementioned place of the Palazzo Te.

They found the Emperor at mass, and when that finished he dressed very elaborately, in white stockings, with white velvet shoes. And he wore a doublet of richly worked dark gold brocade matched with grey velvet embroidered most elegantly with little gold braids. On top of that he was wearing a cloak of dark grey velvet, lined completely in rich gold brocade on a dark background, with the aforementioned braids of gold thread embroidered on top, and a jacket of the said brocade of rich gold. And on his head he wore a black velvet hat bearing his personal device in gold, and by his side was a sword held in a belt. And all these objects were the work of a Spaniard called Messer Gualdalmo, who is possibly the best master of the art of 'azemina', that is to say casting gold with iron. And these were gifts from the Marquis to his Majesty, along with a most beautiful dagger worked in the same way, and these objects were judged to be among the most beautiful and exquisite things in the world. Thus dressed, his Majesty mounted onto a beautiful she-mule, all decked out in gold and silk; his whole guard was in attendance, and there were many princes, lords and gentlemen. And so they proceeded, with the Marquis by his side, and they chatted continuously about the beauty of the countryside and of many other things.

Once his Majesty had arrived at the Palazzo Te, and dismounted, he went into the beautiful 'Sala Grande' [Sala dei Cavalli], and stayed there a while to look around. Then he went into the 'Camarone' [Sala de Psiche], where he marvelled at the beauty of it and stayed a full half-hour to contemplate it, praising everything in it fully. From there he went into the room known as the 'Camera delli Pianeti et Venti' [the Room of the Planets and the Winds], where the said Marquis stays, and which was greatly admired by his Majesty. From there they proceeded to the room known as the 'Camera delle Aquile' [the Room of the Eagles], which is very beautiful and contains two wonderful doors of oriental jasper for use in the said room, and there is also a table of jasper, something which provoked much comment from his Majesty, and there were the fireplaces where they cook the most fine mixed game. And all of this his Majesty wanted to see most diligently.

They then passed into the loggia, which is yet to be decorated, but his Majesty was told of the plans for doing so. He then went into the garden, which he liked exceedingly, with all the works which were in progress around the place. His Majesty then returned inside to dine and ate in the main 'Camarone', next to the window on the lefthand side which looks out on the gardens. And that morning, the most Illustrious Marquis himself waited on the Emperor, giving him a towel to dry his hands with when he had finished eating; and the whole cost was met by the said Marquis. And in the 'Salotto Grande' there were tables laid out from one end to the other and covered with every kind of food for all the Emperor's courtiers to eat; and likewise in other smaller rooms there were tables laid out for the officials and for those who waited on his Majesty, so that everyone was honourably and abundantly catered for.

After spending some time discoursing on a variety of subjects with the Marquis, the Duke of Ferrara, the Prince of Besignano and the Marquis of Guasto, as well as with many other lords and princes, his Majesty expressed a wish to go and play real tennis in the Marquis's court, which was perfectly ordered and fitted out so that there was no shortage of balls and rackets. And his Majesty entered into the said court which he liked very much and very much enjoyed himself. After some discussion, his Majesty played a match with him and Monsignore di Balasone on one side, and the Prince of Besignano and a Spanish gentleman of his Majesty's household, Monsignore della Cueva, on the other. And they played the said game for perhaps four hours, and his Majesty played very well, being very skilled in the game. And they wagered twenty gold *scudi* for each round, his Majesty ending up losing sixty *scudi*. And, having satisfied himself thus, his Majesty went back to his own apartment accompanied only by his valets to change and to freshen up; and he stayed there for a while, resting.

Later the most Illustrious Marquis sent for Vincenzo Guerrero, his stable master and for Matteo Ratto, his groom, who arrived on two outstanding steeds bred by the Marquis; and these were dressed most wonderfully, in deep blue velvet, decorated all over; and every piece of velvet was trimmed with gold thread, and the effect was most impressive, with gold bows and deep blue silk. And the Marquis had them paraded in front of the emperor who was seated at the entrance to the gardens, on a platform set up there in order to view the horses, which were performing jumps as high as themselves. And the Marquis made a gift of the horses to his Majesty, with an appropriate speech, to which the emperor replied, thanking his Excellency and praising him most highly. And he said he wanted to leave them with the Marquis until he had to depart, and then take them with him, and this was done.

And then, a great party was begun for the entertainment of his Majesty, to which the Marquis had invited around sixty of the most beautiful ladies and gentlewomen to be found in Mantua, ordering them to come that evening to the Palazzo Te. And so, at eleven o'clock, everything was arranged in the 'Sala Grande', with all of its spaces, where the ladies were to be, and many torches were hung there, in such a way that was wonderful to behold. And then the carriages began to arrive, with the ladies all accompanied by princes and gentlemen. On coming into the hall, before going to the places assigned to them, they all paid homage to his Majesty the Emperor who stood opposite the entrance. And only when they were all inside the hall, which was hardly large enough to contain them all, did the festivities commence. People started to dance, while his Majesty, as ever, remained standing, his arms resting on a chair upholstered in rich golden cloth, positioned especially for him. The dancing continued in this way until three in the morning, and many young gentlemen of Mantua danced the galliard in front of the Emperor, as is our custom, and it pleased his Majesty greatly.

And when the dancing was over, it seemed to the Marquis that it was time to dine, and so he asked his Majesty if he were ready. The Emperor had thought to ask some ladies to dine with him at his table, but there were present two most reverend lord cardinals, Cibo and Medici, and so he invited them to dine with him and all three of them ate at the same table in the 'Camera Grande'. Tables were prepared around this central one for all the princes and gentlemen to eat at with their ladies; and this evening the illustrious Marquis wanted to carve the meat along with all the gentlemen who served at table, and his Excellency did this so that everything would proceed in the best possible way according to plan. And on guard at the door he put Count Nicola di Maffei and the Paduan gentleman Antonio Bagarotto, who is valet to his Imperial Majesty and a great servant of the Marquis. And the reason for this was because Antonio knew the whole of the imperial court and who is a gentleman and who is not. And the Marquis also placed on guard Carlo da Navulone, his own Chief of Guards, with his accompanying Taliani and Landesknecht guards.

Then the meal was begun; and there was such an array of different foods and such an abundance of things that the meal lasted more than three hours, and was conducted with such order that nothing was lacking. While everyone was still eating, his Majesty finished and retired with the aforementioned most reverend cardinals to the 'Camera dei Venti' and he spoke publicly for an hour with Cardinal Cibo, praising the rooms most highly, along with the Master and inventor of these things and of many others, and his Majesty wanted to understand them all.

When the dinner was over, the ladies returned to the 'Camerone Grande' [Sala dei Cavalli], in order to prepare the room for dancing. And while this was happening, his Imperial Majesty bestowed a particular favour on one lady present by summoning Lady Livia Cathabena da Gonzaga and her mother, Marchioness Isabella Benadusa, and for more than half an hour his Imperial Majesty conversed with Lady Livia. And since she did not understand what he was saying, the Most Reverend Cardinal Cibo acted as interpreter between the two of them, which greatly helped the young lady. Then the party started up, with his Majesty leading the ladies into the Hall, before taking his place, standing at his high-backed chair. Then the dancing commenced and continued until seven in the morning. At which point his Majesty considered that the party was over, and in a moment more than a thousand torches were extinguished by all those present, as night had given way to day. At which point, his Majesty took his leave of all those present, and was especially attentive to the said Lady Livia and her mother. This done, he mounted on his horse with his entire guard in attendance and, accompanied by all the princes and lords there present, the emperor made his way back to his lodgings at the castle in order to sleep. All the ladies were taken to their homes and thus ended the wonderful party that had taken place at the Palazzo Te.

NOTES

1   The Palazzo Te can also be referred to as the Palazzo del Te.
2   This is what the manuscript says, although April 2 was a Saturday.

37   Lorenzo de' Medici *Memorial*

Lorenzo the Magnificent (1449–92) had literary aspirations. He published poetry, wrote carnival songs and composed pageant plays. However, his private family records belong to a more informal genre of writing which was especially common among the merchants and bankers of Florence. Such memorials were often entered in account books or family bibles. They are useful historical documents because they represent private observations, even if the personals concerns and proud achievements are viewed in public terms. Their language reflects the commonplace conventions of the authors and in this respect at least, Lorenzo the republican seems to have much in common with the aristocracy of seigneurial regimes. Lorenzo closely identifies the family's prosperity with that of the Florentine state as a whole.

Source: *Lives of the Early Medici as told in their Correspondence*, trans. and ed. J. Ross, Chatto and Windus, London, 1910, pp. 152–5

[. . .] Cosimo our grandfather, a man of exceeding wisdom, died at Careggi on August 1, 1464, being much debilitated by old age and by gout, to the great grief not only of ourselves and of the whole city but of all Italy, because he was most famous and adorned with many singular virtues. He died in the highest position any Florentine citizen ever attained at any period, and was buried in S. Lorenzo. He refused to make a will and forbade all pomp at his funeral. Nevertheless all the Italian princes sent to do him honour and to condole with us on his death; among others H.M. the King of France [Louis XI, 1461–83] commanded that he should be honoured with his banner, but out of respect for his wishes our father would not allow it. By public decree he was named PATER PATRIAE [father of the fatherland] and the decree and the letters patent are in our house. After his death much sedition arose in the city, especially was our father persecuted out of envy. From this sprang the parliament and the change of government in 1466, when Messer Agnolo Acciaiuoli, Messer Diotisalvi, Niccolò Soderini, and others were exiled, and the State was reformed.

In the year 1465 H.M. King Louis of France, out of regard for the friendship between our grandfather, our father, and the House of France, decorated our escutcheon with three Lilies d'or on a field azure, which we carry at present. We have the patents with the royal seal attached, which was approved and confirmed in the Palace with nine beans [votes].

In July 1467 came the Duke Galeazzo [Maria Sforza] of Milan. He was fighting against Bartolomeo [Colleoni 1400–76] of Bergamo in the Romagna, who was vexing our State. By his own wish he lodged in our house, although the Signory had prepared everything for him in S. Maria Novella.

In February or in March of the same year Sarzana, Sarzanelle, and Castelnuovo were bought by the aid of our father Piero from M. Lorenzo and M. Tommasino da Campofregoso; notwithstanding that we were engaged in hot war the payment was made by Francesco Sassetti, our confidential agent, at that time one of the managers of the *Monte* [*Commune*, public debt].

I, Lorenzo, took to wife Clarice, daughter of the Lord Jacopo Orsini, or rather she was given [*i.e.* betrothed] to me in December 1468, and the marriage was celebrated in our house on June 4, 1469. Till now I have by her two children, a girl called Lucrezia, of [?] years, and a boy named Piero, of [?] months. Clarice is again with child. God preserve her to us for many years and guard us from all evil. Twin boys were born prematurely at about five or six months old, they lived long enough to be baptized.

In July 1469 I went to Milan at the request of the illustrious Duke Galeazzo to stand godfather as proxy for Piero our father to his firstborn child. I was received with much honour, more so than the others who came for the same purpose, although they were persons more worthy than I. We paid our duty to the Duchess by presenting her with a necklace of gold with a large diamond, which cost near 2000 ducats. The consequence was that the said Lord desired that I should stand godfather to all his children.

To do as others had done I held a joust in the Piazza S. Croce at great expense and with great pomp. I find we spent about 10,000 ducats *di suggello*, and although I was not highly versed in the use of weapons and the delivery of blows, the first prize was given to me; a helmet fashioned of silver, with Mars as the crest.[1]

Piero, our father, departed this life on July 2nd, aged [?] having been much tormented with gout. He would not make a will, but we drew up an inventory and found we possessed 237,988 scudi, as is recorded by me in a large green book bound in kid. He was buried in S. Lorenzo, and we are still at work to make his and his brother Giovanni's tomb as worthy to receive his bones as we can. God have mercy on their souls. He was much mourned by the whole city, being an upright man and exceedingly kindly. The princes of Italy, especially the principal ones, sent letters and envoys to condole with us and offer us their help for our defence.

The second day after his death, although I, Lorenzo, was very young, being twenty years of age, the principal men of the city and of the State came to us in our house to condole with us on our loss and to encourage me to take charge of the city and of the State, as my grandfather and my father had done. This I did, though on account of my youth and the great responsibility and perils arising therefrom, with great reluctance, solely for the safety of our friends and of our possessions. FOR IT IS ILL LIVING IN FLORENCE FOR THE RICH UNLESS THEY RULE THE STATE. Till now we have succeeded with honour and renown, which I attribute not to prudence but to the grace of God and the good conduct of my predecessors.

I find that from 1434 till now we have spent large sums of money, as appear in a small quarto note-book of the said year to the end of 1471. Incredible are the sums written down. They amount to 663,755 florins for alms, buildings, and taxes, let alone other expenses. But I do not regret this, for though many would consider it better to have a part of that sum in their purse, I consider that it gave great honour to our State, and I think the money was well expended, and am well pleased.

In the month of September 1471 I was elected to go as ambassador for the coronation of Pope Sixtus, and was treated with great honour. I brought back the two antique marble heads, portraits of Augustus and Agrippa, given to me by the said Pope Sixtus, and also our cup of chalcedony incised, and many other cameos which I then bought.

[The paragraph which follows is written on the fly-leaf of a small codex in the archive in Florence. It is not dated but is probably from 1483–5. It contains a list of letters written by Lorenzo to various people. The memorandum is entitled *Ricordi di Lorenzo de' Medici.*]

On the 19th day of September [1483] came the news that the King of France by his own free will had given to our Giovanni the Abbey of Fonte Dolce. On the 31st we heard from Rome that the Pope had ratified this and declared him capable of holding benefices, being seven years of age, and had created him a Protonotary. On the 1st June our Giovanni came from Poggio [a Caiano] and I with him. On his arrival he was confirmed by our Monsignore of Arezzo [Gentile Becchi] who gave him the tonsure, and thereafter he was called Messer Giovanni. These ceremonies took place in our own chapel, and in the evening we returned to Poggio.

NOTES

1   This was the joust held on 7 February 1469 to mark the conclusion of peace between Florence, Venice and Milan.

38   Leonardo da Vinci **Prospective letter of employment to Ludovico Sforza (*c*.1481–2)**

In this letter from Florence, Leonardo advertises his services to Ludovico Sforza as a prospective employer. He presents himself as a military engineer, with architecture, sculpture and painting as additional skills 'in time of peace'. The letter comes from the Leonardo notebook known as the 'Codex Atlanticus' in the Biblioteca Ambrosiana, Milan. However, it is not in Leonardo's handwriting.

Source: *Leonardo on Painting*, ed. and trans. M. Kemp and M. Walker, Yale University Press, New Haven and London, 1989, pp. 251–3

My Most Illustrious Lord, having now sufficiently seen and considered the achievements of all those who count themselves masters and artificers of instruments of war, and having noted that the invention and performance of the said instruments is in no way different from that in common usage, I shall endeavour, while intending no discredit to anyone else, to bring myself to the attention of Your Excellency for the purpose of unfolding to you my secrets, and thereafter offering them at your complete disposal, and when the time is right bringing into effective operation all those things which are in part briefly listed below:

1. I have plans for very light, strong and easily portable bridges with which to pursue and, on some occasions, flee the enemy, and others, sturdy and indestructible either by fire or in battle, easy and convenient to lift and place in position. Also means of burning and destroying those of the enemy.

2. I know how, in the course of the siege of a terrain, to remove water from the moats and how to make an infinite number of bridges, mantlets and scaling ladders and other instruments necessary to such an enterprise.

3. Also, if one cannot, when besieging a terrain, proceed by bombardment either because of the height of the glacis [a defensive slope] or the strength of its

situation and location, I have methods for destroying every fortress or other stronghold unless it has been founded upon a rock or so forth.

4. I have also types of cannon, most convenient and easily portable, with which to hurl small stones almost like a hail-storm; and the smoke from the cannon will instil a great fear in the enemy on account of the grave damage and confusion.

5. Also, I have means of arriving at a designated spot through mines and secret winding passages constructed completely without noise, even if it should be necessary to pass underneath moats or any river.

6. Also, I will make covered vehicles, safe and unassailable, which will penetrate the enemy and their artillery, and there is no host of armed men so great that they would not break through it. And behind these the infantry will be able to follow, quite uninjured and unimpeded.

7. Also, should the need arise, I will make cannon, mortar and light ordnance of very beautiful and functional design that are quite out of the ordinary.

8. Where the use of cannon is impracticable, I will assemble catapults, mangonels, trebuckets [siege catapults] and other instruments of wonderful efficiency not in general use. In short, as the variety of circumstances dictate, I will make an infinite number of items for attack and defence.

9. And should a sea battle be occasioned, I have examples of many instruments which are highly suitable either in attack or defence, and craft which will resist the fire of all the heaviest cannon and powder and smoke.

10. In time of peace I believe I can give as complete satisfaction as any other in the field of architecture, and the construction of both public and private buildings, and in conducting water from one place to another.

Also I can execute sculpture in marble, bronze and clay. Likewise in painting, I can do everything possible as well as any other, whosoever he may be.

Moreover, work could be undertaken on the bronze horse[1] which will be to the immortal glory and eternal honour of the auspicious memory of His Lordship your father, and of the illustrious house of Sforza.

And if any of the above-mentioned things seem impossible or impracticable to anyone, I am most readily disposed to demonstrate them in your park or in whatsoever place shall please Your Excellency, to whom I commend myself with all possible humility.

NOTE

1   This refers to a long-standing project for an equestrian monument to Francesco Sforza, which was subsequently developed by Leonardo both for the original subject and later as a statue in honour of the renegade general, Sforza enemy and sometime regent of Milan, Giangiacomo Trivulziano.

39 Bernardo Bellincioni *Il Paradiso*

Bernardo Bellincioni (1452–92) began his career as a court poet with Lorenzo de'Medici in Florence. In 1483 he served the Gonzaga and transferred to the

18 Messale
Arcimboldi,
*Coronation of Ludivoco
il Moro*, Library of the
Cathedral Chapter,
Milan. Photo: Luisa
Ricciarini, Milan.

Sforza court two years later. Among his sonnets there are eulogies to the Sforza, tirades against other poets and complaints about bad meals. This verse was written to celebrate the marriage of the heir to the duchy of Milan, Giangaleazzo Sforza, and Isabella of Aragon, the daughter of the King of Naples. The celebrations at the Castello di Porta Giovia comprised a series of fantastic scenes which culminated in the presentation of the poem to the nineteen-year-old Isabella by Apollo. In the poem, Isabella is associated with the Cardinal and Theological Virtues and the Liberal Arts. In 1490 Bellincioni was also involved in the celebrations of the marriage of Isabella d'Este to Gianfrancesco Gonzaga.

Source: *Le rime di Bernardo Bellincioni, scelta di curiosità lettararie inedite o rare dal secolo XIII al XVI*, ed. P. Fanfani, Gaetano Romagnoli, Bologna, 1876–1878, Vol II (2 vols), pp. 218–9. Translated for this edition by Nick Webb, with Tim Benton and Catherine King

Apollo presents the gift (of Bellincioni's poem) *and says to milady*:
Greetings, delightful, glorious and beautiful one,
Today such grace rains onto your lap;
O light of Aragon, o star of Sforza;
Great thundering Jove has sent me to you;[1]
And says that you are my sister,
Whence he shows me through your holy pledges,

That like me you were born with me on Delos,
You are the first lamp of the world, I am the first in heaven.
He who has made the heavens and the world and blind hell,
And who understands all things,
Who moves, guides, rules and has all things in his power,
Both meting out punishment and reward,
Descends from heaven to earth in his own form on your account;
And has not so much brought together gifts for you,
But rather rewards for your merits.
For to honour the high blood of Aragon,
And that noble Sforza stock,
For you such a festival is made, and heaven argues that
If the Duke and Ludovico both thus intend to honour you,
And Jove himself has come here in person
And similarly all the other gods have assembled for so great a spectacle
Then it can only be a miracle to see you with them.
And though he wishes to return to heaven with his divine throne:
Yet will he leave in your care these blessed ladies,
And they are here the three Graces and there the seven Virtues,
He now concedes to you in gift:
Hope, faith and charity,
Justice, Temperance with Prudence, Fortitude.
Accept the gift your Excellency.
Behold Justice, who rules all things;
Courage who makes man constant in doing good;
Prudence has a foot of lead for the person it corrects;
Temperance is a heavy bridle to the furies;
Hope raises to heaven the person who chooses the good;
Faith or peace holds their feet firm;
Behold Charity a divine treasure,
These are the three Graces which have been graciously bestowed on you.[2]
Apollo gives my ladyship a little book, in which were written all the verses of the festival . . .

NOTES

1   The masque as a whole contains a typically humanist medley of pagan and Christian references.
2   These are almost proverbial definitions of the virtues, as found in mottoes and personal *imprese* [devices].

40 Three accounts of the visit of Galeazzo Maria Sforza to the Medici Palace, Florence (1459)

i)   Letter from Galeazzo Maria Sforza to his parents.
ii) Diplomatic dispatch from Niccolò de'Carissimi da Parma.

iii) The *Terze Rime in Praise of Cosimo de'Medici and his sons and of the honour accorded in 1458 (sic) to the son of the Duke of Milan and to the Pope on their arrival at Florence [in] the year 1458 (sic).*

These three extracts contain reports of the impression made by the newly built Medici palace. The fifteen-year old Galeazzo Maria Sforza was ostensibly in Florence to conduct Pope Pius II to his Congress at Mantua. At the same time it provided Galeazzo Maria with the opportunity to reinforce the diplomatic ties between Florence and newly established Sforza Milan. His letter home to Francesco and Bianca Sforza confirmed that he had been treated as an honoured and familial guest. His stay at the Medici palace was paid for by the state. He returned again on pilgrimage with his wife in 1471. The magnificence of the palace reflected both on the status of the hosts and their guest: a point noted by a member of Galeazzo's escort, Niccolò de'Carissimi da Parma, who encourages his master, Francesco Sforza, to consider emulating the project as being the 'most signorial . . . the world has ever had'. The description given in the letter of Galeazzo Maria himself is a rhetorical exercise in word-painting – '*ekphrasis*'. The *Terze Rime* – rhyming triplets with eight syllables – was an anonymous praise poem in which Cosimo is compared with Christ guiding the people of Florence and reflects his endowment of religious foundations as well as his secular building programme. It seems likely that the frescoes of Benozzo Gozzoli in the Medici private chapel had not been started at the time of the visit.

Source: R. Hatfield, 'Some unknown descriptions of the Medici Palace in 1459', *The Art Bulletin*, 52 (1970), pp. 246, 232, 247–8. Translated by R. Hatfield with revisions for this edition by Anabel Thomas

i) Letter from Galeazzo Maria Sforza to his parents

I took leave of their lordships and finally, accompanied by the above mentioned crowd of gentlemen and people, all of whom were on holiday by public proclamation as if it were Easter Day, arrived here at the house of the magnificent Cosimo, where I discovered a house that is both in terms of the beauty of its ceilings, the height of its walls, the high finish of the entrances and windows, the number of bedchambers and reception rooms, the ornateness of the studies, the worth of the books, the neatness and gracefulness of the gardens, and in terms of the tapestry decorations, chests of inestimable workmanship and value, majestic sculptures, designs of infinite kinds as well as of priceless silver, the most beautiful I may ever have seen, or believe it possible to see [. . .]

I visited the esteemed Cosimo ['el magnifico Cosimo'] who I found in one of his chapels which lacked nothing of the ornateness and beauty of the rest of the house.

[. . .] On return to the house I dined in the garden of the esteemed ['magnifico'] Cosimo under a loggia. In fact it gave me the very greatest of pleasure to see this garden again. In my opinion it is the most beautiful and most ornate [garden] I have ever seen.

ii) Diplomatic dispatch to Francesco Sforza from Niccolò de'Carissimi da Parma

[. . .] the aforesaid count [Galeazzo Maria], together with the company, went round this palace, and especially the noblest parts, such as several studies, little chapels, reception rooms, bedchambers and the garden, all of which are constructed and decorated with admirable mastery, decorated throughout with gold and fine marbles, with intaglios and sculptures in relief, with pictures and intarsia work done in perspective by the most impressive and accomplished masters even down to the very benches and floors of the house; tapestries and household ornaments of gold and silk; endless silverware and bookcases; then the vaults or ceiling frameworks of the bedchambers and reception rooms, which are for the most part covered in fine gold with diverse and various forms; then a garden embellished with the finest of polished marbles with various plants, so that it seems painted rather than real. And among other things there is an adder in the form of Your Excellency's impresa [device], and beside it there is a shield with the arms of the aforementioned Cosimo. This adder and arms are formed out of grass planted in a plot of turf in such a way that the more the grass grows, the more the design itself will develop and whoever sees these things judges that they are more celestial than earthly. And everyone is agreed that this house is the most signorial and ornate that the world has ever had or may have now, and that it is without comparison. In sum, everyone believes that there is no other earthly paradise in the world other than this. If your Lordship were to see it, I am certain that it would result in your spending a good sum of money, because given your magnanimity and greatness of mind, you too would want to do something worthy – and not only equal to this but surpassing it if that were possible. I feel as if I am in a new world, and I believe that I shall never see anything worthier than what I have seen and am seeing for the first time. And I am not the only one of this opinion, but all the company here, who do nothing else but discuss it.

iii) The *Terze Rime*

> This is the palace full of marvels,
> that cost and is worth more than a city,
> which Cosimo lives in with his family.
> In it are bedchambers, loggias, courtyards and reception rooms,
> and so many rare and lovely appointments
> that there is no emperor or king who has their like.
> There are figures and carvings of serpentine
> and of alabaster and various kinds of porphyry and marbles,
> columns and capitals and fine dressed stone. [. . .]
>
> There is a ceiling that seems to me like a sky of stars,
> it is so decorated with blue, silver and gold
> that I couldn't recreate it with these odes.

I don't believe that the choir of seraphim
in the heavens shines more brightly
than do these carvings decorated with such artistry.
And there is such evidence of sculptural talent and expertise,
in various ironwork and wooden inlay,
of admirable architecture and paintwork, [. . .]

And there is also a chapel so ornate
that it has no equal in all the universe,
in its aptness for divine worship.
[. . .] it is so beautiful and decorous.
And this palace has a handsome garden
with courtyard, loggias, vault, and water and meadow,
and it was done and planted with flowers in a single morning.
And it is arranged in such a graceful manner
with laurel, myrtle, orange trees and box,
that one look reveals what is planted there. [. . .]

and it cost a hundred thousand florins net. [. . .]

Piero announced with prompt beneficence
'I will put my palace in order
to receive this illustrious and distinguished count.'
And he covered all the walls in tapestries,
and with rich hangings in gold, silver and silk,
and cast rugs over balconies and paving stones.
And Piero's genteel and welcoming bedchamber
was made ready for the guest [. . .]
in a manner worthy of an emperor and queen,
With a silken canopy of silk with fringed curtains,
and on the bed a precious velvet cover,
embroidered with silver and fine gold. [. . .]

His antechamber was decked out no less richly
with a bed and canopy,
and with a curtain and surrounding ornamentation. [. . .]

An intarsiated exit on one side
opens onto such a refined chapel
that no one ever tired of admiring it.
The altar there was furnished richly
with silver and gold and velvet and brocade, [. . .]

Likewise one sees on the other side
a door constructed with such artistry that I would say it
was real relief – yet it is flat intarsia –
Which gives into the glorious and lovely study,
that is full of such ingeniousness, order and harmony
that is seems to represent angelic dancing,

With its combination of inlays and painting,
perspective designs and sublime carvings,
and masterly architectural form.
There are a great number of highly ornate books
and vases of alabaster and chalcedony
etched in gold and silver.

Each takes his pleasure as he sees fit;
some admire the great ornamentation of the palace, [. . .]

And some the furnishings of the chapel,
some the bedchamber and study attentively admire,
some the reception rooms and some the gilded ceiling,
And all faces reveal wonder,
for when the torches are lit in the evening,
this ceiling appears like a sun of paradise.

41   Pope Pius II **On his visit to Florence and the hospitality of Cosimo de'Medici (1459)**

Enea Silvio Piccolomini (1405–64) came from a noble Sienese family. He trained as a humanist and was subsequently employed as a secretary and diplomat by the Holy Roman Emperor Frederick III and by several popes. He became a bishop and cardinal before being elected pope in 1458. His pontificate was distinguished by the renewed assertion of papal authority and by an attempt to organize a crusade six years after Constantinople had fallen to the Turks. Pius II built a miniature 'ideal city' at his home town Corsignano (renaming it Pienza), combining Gothic and *all'antica* features, which he describes in the *Commentaries.* In literature he acquired an early reputation as a writer and speaker of polished Latin, being a Poet Laureate of the comical and erotic; but he also wrote on history, biography, education and geography. All these interests are reflected in his autobiographical memoirs, whose candid style was offset by the adoption of the third-person and a descriptive, though by no means neutral, tone. He clearly had publication in mind since Gianantonio Campano, his secretary, was required to edit the work before his death. A second copy was commissioned from a German secretary in 1464. The text circulated in a number of sixteenth-century manuscripts before it was eventually printed at Siena in 1584.

Source: *The Secret Memoirs of a Renaissance Pope: The Commentaries of Pius II,* trans. F. A. Gragg with L. C. Gabel, George Allen and Unwin, London, 1960, pp. 105–10

[. . .] When Pius entered the Florentine territory, he was met at the town of Poggibonsi by ambassadors, the chief men of the city, who did honor to the Vicar

HIC AENEAS AFOELICE·V·ANTIPAPA LEGATVS AD FEDERICVM·III·
CAESAREM MISSVS LAVREA CORONA DONATVR ET INTER AMICOS
EIVS AC SECRETARIVS ANNVMERATVR ET PRAEFICITVR·

19 Pinturicchio, *The Life of Pius II*, fresco, 1503–8, Biblioteca Piccolomini, Siena Cathedral.

of Christ in glowing words. This town is in our time of slight importance and lies in the valley of the Elsa River, but was once built on the lofty mountain which overlooks its present site. It was large and populous and difficult to storm. But since it took the side of the Ghibellines and often gave the Florentines a great deal of trouble, they first destroyed its walls, then razed it and moved it to the site just described. Here the Pope spent the night and the next day was met at San Casciano by new ambassadors, more numerous and more distinguished, who escorted him to the beautiful estate of a private citizen not far from the town, where he passed that night. The following day on his way to the Carthusian monastery he was met by the lords of Faenza, Forlì, and Imola and soon after by Galeazzo Sforza, the eldest son of Francesco Sforza, Duke of Milan. This handsome youth was not yet sixteen, but his character, eloquence, and ability were such that he exhibited a wisdom greater than that of a grown man. In his expression and bearing there was the dignity befitting a prince; his extemporaneous speeches could hardly have been equaled by another after long preparation; there was nothing childish or trivial in his conduct. It was astounding to hear the sentiments of an old man issuing from the lips of a lad and to listen to a beardless boy giving utterance to the ideas of a graybeard.[1] His father had sent him with a splendid and magnificently accoutered escort of five hundred horsemen from Milan to Florence and thence to meet the Pope. Encountering Pius at the third milestone a little beyond the Certosa, Galeazzo dismounted and kissed the holy feet according to custom.

Luncheon was laid for the Pope in the monastery and after it he made haste toward the city, where he was met about two stades outside the gate by the chiefs of the Guelfs and at the gate itself by the Gonfalonier and many other magistrates, called the Lord Priors, who greeted the Pope humbly, kissed his feet, and commended to him the city and the people. The Pope because of his gout could not ride on horseback but was carried in a gold chair on the shoulders of his attendants. Just as he entered the city, after the priests carrying the sacred relics had received his blessing and had advanced to take their places at the head of the procession, Sigismondo Malatesta and the other vicars of the Church, whom I have mentioned above, raised the Pope's chair on their shoulders and carried their master some distance, *Sigismondo exclaiming indignantly, 'See to what we lords of cities have been brought!'* he could not help with the weight yet laid his hand on the chair as desiring to appear to be one of the bearers. The chief men of the city walked on either side. The bearers were changed at fixed intervals and the most distinguished citizens claimed a part in this service. When Galeazzo had walked a short distance, he remounted at the Pope's command and, soon after, the vicars of the Church did likewise. The city was full of people, both citizens and outsiders. From the neighboring towns and from the country they had gathered from all sides to see the new Pope. The women were richly dressed and there was a marvelous variety of costumes in both domestic and foreign style, *but their whitened faces clearly betrayed the use of cosmetics.* The Pope visited the church of the Reparata and the baptistery of San Giovanni and at both blessed the people. He was lodged at Santa Maria Novella, where Martin and Eugenius had been entertained before him.[2]

Florence, *once called Fluentia from the river Arno which 'flows' through it,* is now the capital of Tuscany. It was built on the ruins of Faesulae, which was destroyed by Totila, King of the Goths. The city subjugated Volterra, Pistoia, Arezzo, Cortona, and Pisa; deprived Lucca of much of her territory; inflicted great disasters on the Sienese, at whose hands she herself sometimes suffered. She often opposed the German emperors. Henry VII pitched his camp before her walls and laid strenuous siege to the city, which he would certainly have taken had he not been called to Naples to fight King Robert and on his way there with part of his forces died from poison at Buonconvento [as I have before related]. Charles IV advanced with an army up to the gates of Florence and restored the Ghibellines who had been expelled. The Dukes of Milan have cherished the bitterest hatred against the Florentines and have inflicted heavy losses upon them, though not without damage to themselves. Francesco Sforza made himself Duke of Milan with their help and was their fast friend. The kings of Naples were regarded by them now as friends, now as foes, and at one time were masters of the city, which was also once ruled by the Duke of Athens. When the latter was finally expelled, the people asserted their independence, though they first began to know real slavery when they believed themselves free, having driven out one master only to admit many. The city has often been racked by civil war, while the upper classes fought together for the mastery.

The most distinguished Florentines of our time have been thought to be Palla Strozzi, Niccolò Uzzano, and Rodolfo Peruzzi.[3] Palla surpassed all others in wealth, Niccolò in wisdom, Rodolfo in military prowess. Against these men Cosimo dei Medici stirred up a faction and as a result he was banished and remained for some time in exile. Uzzano was already dead. Then when Pope Eugenius was residing in Florence, amid the strife of the various parties Cosimo returned and in the general confusion cowed his opponents and regained his old prestige. He drove into exile Rodolfo and Palla together with numerous other citizens and they never returned, though Rodolfo, enlisting the services of Niccolò Piccinino against his country, raided and plundered the district of Mugellana. He afterward died in exile. Palla endured adversity cheerfully, occupying himself till he was very old in the study of philosophy at Padua, where he died when nearly ninety, a man who had not deserved banishment at the hands of his countrymen.

Cosimo, having thus disposed of his rivals, proceeded to administer the state at his pleasure and amassed such wealth as I should think Croesus could hardly have possessed. In Florence he built a palace fit for a king; he restored some churches and erected others; he founded the splendid monastery of San Marco and stocked its library richly with Greek and Latin manuscripts; he decorated his villas magnificently. It was beginning to look as if by these noble works he had overcome envy, but the people always hate superior worth and there were some who asserted that Cosimo's tyranny was intolerable and tried in every way to thwart his projects; *some also hurled insults at him.*

The time was now at hand for making a valuation of the property of each citizen. The Florentines call this process catasto; the Sienese, libra. By it the magistrates learn the resources of the citizens and can thus apportion the burdens fairly among them. Cosimo urged a new catasto; his opponents were against it. Therefore it was decided to call a parlamento. While it was assembling, armed men, gathered from all quarters at Cosimo's orders, surrounded the piazza and made it clear that any who objected to his plans would do so at their peril. The catasto was voted under fear of armed force and some of the citizens who had opposed it were banished, others fined. After this Cosimo was refused nothing. He was regarded as the arbiter of war and peace, the regulator of law; not so much a citizen as the master of his city. Political councils were held at his house;

the magistrates he nominated were elected; he was king in all but name and state. *Therefore when Pius once asked the Bishop of Orta what he thought about Florence and he replied that it was a pity so beautiful a woman had not a husband, the Pope said, 'Yes, but she has a paramour,' meaning that she had a tyrant instead of a king and referring to Cosimo, who like an unlawful lord of the city was grinding the people with cruel slavery.* During Pius's stay in Florence Cosimo was ill *or perhaps, as many believed, he pretended to be ill that he might not have to wait on the Pope.*

Cosimo's ancestors came to Florence from Mugello. His father Giovanni, *who became a client of the Medici, took the name of that family. He* had left a great fortune to his sons, Cosimo and Lorenzo, and Cosimo had increased it to an incredible degree, extending his business transactions over all Europe and *trading* even as far as Egypt. He was of fine physique and more than average height; his expression and manner of speech were mild; he was *more* cultured *than merchants usually are* and had some knowledge of Greek; his mind was keen and always alert; his spirit was neither cowardly nor brave; he easily endured toil and hunger and he often passed whole nights without sleep. Nothing went on in Italy that he did not know; indeed it was his advice that guided the policy of many cities and princes. Nor were foreign events a secret to him, for he had correspondents among his business connections all over the world, who kept him informed by frequent letters of what was going on around them. Toward the end of his life he suffered from gout, a disease which he lived to see passed on to his sons and grandsons. At the time the Pope was in Florence he was more than seventy years old. [. . .]

In former ages there have been many illustrious Florentines whose names are known even today, but most illustrious of all was Dante Alighieri, whose great poem with its noble description of Heaven, Hell, and Purgatory breathes a wisdom almost divine, though, being but mortal, he sometimes erred. Next to him was Francesco Petrarca, whose equal would be hard to find if his Latin works were comparable to those he wrote in Italian. The third place I should not go wrong in assigning to Giovanni Boccaccio, though he was *a little* more frivolous and his style was not highly polished. After him comes Coluccio, whose prose and verse suited his own age but seem rough to ours. He was Chancellor of Florence, and Galeazzo, Duke of Milan, used to say that Coluccio's pen did him more harm than thirty troops of the cavalry of the Florentines, who were then the enemies of Milan. For Coluccio was a shrewd man and, though his style lacked elegance, yet he had a thorough understanding of the general truths by which men are stirred and in his writing he handled them most skillfully. After several years he was succeeded in office by Leonardo, who was born in Arezzo but had been made a Florentine citizen. He was deeply versed in Greek and Latin *and his eloquence was almost Ciceronian.* He made a brilliant reputation by his many translations from Greek into Latin. Almost his equal in prose and his superior in verse was Carlo, who was also an Aretine by birth but a Florentine by courtesy. Poggio too was a famous citizen of Florence. After he had served for some time as papal secretary and had written several distinguished works, he finally returned to his native city, where he was made Chancellor and ended his days among his own kinsmen. A great many more men might be mentioned by whose abilities the power and prestige of Florence have been increased.[4]

The admirers of Florence call attention not only to her illustrious citizens but to the size of the city (*which is surpassed in all Italy by Rome alone*), the lofty and extraordinarily thick walls which encircle it, the elegance of the streets and squares which are not only wide but straight, the magnificent churches, and the splendid towering palaces, both public and private. But among all the buildings none is more deserving of mention than the church of the Reparata, the dome of which is nearly as large as that which we admire at Rome in the temple of Agrippa called the Pantheon.[5] Next comes the palace of the Priors and third that built by Cosimo. They admire too the sanctuary of St. John the Baptist and the church of San Lorenzo (also built by Cosimo). They mention the bridges which unite the city cut in two by the Arno and the numerous population and the costumes of both men and women and the shops of all sorts and the great estates and the splendid luxurious villas near the city erected at no less expense than the city itself, and finally the quick wits of the citizens, though they most excel in trade, *which philosophers think sordid. They seem too bent on making money, and therefore when the chief men of the city had collected 14,000 ducats from the people to honor the Pope, they kept the greater part for the city and used part to support Galeazzo and his retinue.* They spent very little on entertaining the Pope nor did they lay out much on lavish spectacles, though they brought lions into the piazza to fight with horses and other animals and arranged tournaments in which much more wine was drunk than blood spilled.

NOTES

1   In fact, Galeazzo Maria's speech was written by a Milanese humanist, Guiniforte da Barizza.
2   Pius II was in Florence between 25 April and 5 May 1459.
3   Palla Strozzi (1372–1462); Niccolò da Uzzano (d.1431); Rodolfo Peruzzi.
4   Dante Alighieri (1265–1321); Francesco Petrarch (1304–74); Giovanni Boccaccio (1313–75); Coluccio Salutati (1331–1406); Giangaleazzo Visconti (1378–1404); Leonardo Bruni (1369–1444); Carlo Marsuppini (d.1453); Giovanni Francesco Poggio Bracciolini (1380–1459).
5   This is the cathedral of Florence, also dedicated to Santa Maria dei Fiori. The cupola was executed by the architect Filippo Brunelleschi (1377–1446).

42 Pliny the Younger **A letter about his villa at Laurentium**

Gaius Plinius Caecilius Secundus (62–113 CE) was the nephew and adopted son of Pliny the Elder. He was a wealthy administrator within the Roman empire, owning property throughout Italy. This villa at Laurentium stood on the west coast of Italy, close to Ostia. Pliny's letters were known in the Middle Ages, but they became rich veins for humanists seeking to emulate the Ancients in their epistolary style. The descriptions of the architecture and layout of this villa, together with that on Lake Como, provided one of the antique models for Renaissance villas; others were supplied by Vitruvius and the remains of large sites such as the Emperor Hadrian's villa at Tivoli near Rome. The formal arrangement of the garden spaces, their integration with the overall architectural layout of the site, the choice of plants and the concern for good views are all features of Renaissance garden design which were derived from this source.

Source: *Letters and Panegyricus in two volumes*, ed. B. Radice, Letters, Books I–VII, Harvard University Press, Cambridge Mass. and London, 1969–1975, I, pp. 133, 135, 137, 139, 141, 143 (English text only)

TO CLUSINIUS (?) GALLUS

You may wonder why my Laurentine place (or my Laurentian, if you like that better) is such a joy to me, but once you realize the attractions of the house itself, the amenities of its situation, and its extensive seafront, you will have your answer. It is seventeen miles from Rome, so that it is possible to spend the night there after necessary business is done, without having cut short or hurried the day's work, and it can be approached by more than one route; the roads to Laurentum and Ostia both lead in that direction, but you must leave the first at the fourteenth milestone and the other at the eleventh. Whichever way you go, the side road you take is sandy for some distance and rather heavy and slow-going if you drive, but soft and easily covered on horseback. The view on either side is full of variety, for sometimes the road narrows as it passes through the woods, and then it broadens and opens out through wide meadows where there are many flocks of sheep and herds of horses and cattle driven down from the mountains in winter to grow sleek on the pastures in the springlike climate.

The house is large enough for my needs but not expensive to keep up. It opens into a hall, unpretentious but not without dignity, and then there are two colonnades, rounded like the letter D, which enclose a small but pleasant courtyard. This makes a splendid retreat in bad weather, being protected by windows and still more by the overhanging roof. Opposite the middle of it is a cheerful inner hall, and then a dining-room which really is rather fine: it runs out towards the shore, and whenever the sea is driven inland by the south-west wind it is lightly washed by the spray of the spent breakers. It has folding doors or windows as large as the doors all round, so that at the front and sides it seems to look out on to three seas, and at the back has a view through the inner hall, the courtyard with the two colonnades, then the entrance-hall to the woods and mountains in the distance.

To the left of this and a little farther back from the sea is a large bedroom, and then another smaller one which lets in the morning sunshine with one window and holds the last rays of the evening sun with the other; from this window too is a view of the sea beneath, this time at a safe distance. In the angle of this room and the dining-room is a corner which retains and intensifies the concentrated warmth of the sun, and this is the winter-quarters and gymnasium of my household for no winds can be heard there except those which bring the rain clouds, and the place can still be used after the weather has broken.[1] Round the corner is a room built round in an apse to let in the sun as it moves round and shines in each window in turn, and with one wall fitted with shelves like a library to hold the books which I read and read again. Next comes a bedroom-wing on the other side of a passage which has a floor raised and fitted with pipes to receive hot steam and circulate it at a regulated temperature. The remaining rooms on this side of the house are kept for the use of my slaves and freedmen, but most of them are quite presentable enough to receive guests.

On the other side of the dining-room is an elegantly decorated bedroom, and then one which can either be a large bedroom or a moderate-sized dining-room and enjoys the bright light of the sun reflected from the sea; behind is another room with an antechamber, high enough to be cool in summer and protected as a refuge in winter, for it is sheltered from every wind. A similar room and antechamber are divided off by a single wall. Then comes the cooling-room of the bath, which is large and spacious and has two curved baths built out of opposite walls; these are quite large enough if you consider that the sea is so near. Next come the oiling-room, the furnace-room, and the hot-room for the bath, and then two rest-rooms, beautifully decorated in a simple style, leading to the heated swimming-bath which is much admired and from which swimmers can see the sea. Close by is the ball-court which receives the full warmth of the setting sun. Here there is a second storey, with two living-rooms below and two above, as well as a dining-room which commands the whole expanse of sea and stretch of shore with all its lovely houses. Elsewhere another upper storey contains a room which receives both the rising and setting sun, and a good-sized wine-store and granary behind, while below is a dining-room where nothing is known of a high sea but the sound of the breakers, and even that as a dying murmur; it looks on to the garden and the encircling drive.

All round the drive runs a hedge of box, or rosemary to fill any gaps, for box will flourish extensively where it is sheltered by the buildings, but dries up if exposed in the open to the wind and salt spray even at a distance. Inside the inner ring of the drive is a young and shady vine pergola,[2] where the soil is soft and yielding even to the bare foot. The garden itself is thickly planted with mulberries and figs, trees which the soil bears very well though it is less kind to others. On this side the dining-room away from the sea has a view as lovely as that of the sea itself, while from the windows of the two rooms behind it can be seen the entrance to the house and another well-stocked kitchen garden.

Here begins a covered arcade nearly as large as a public building. It has windows on both sides, but more facing the sea, as there is one in each alternate bay on the garden side. These all stand open on a fine and windless day, and in stormy weather can safely be opened on one side or the other away from the wind. In front is a terrace scented with violets. As the sun beats down, the arcade increases its heat by reflection and not only retains the sun but keeps off the north-east wind so that it is as hot in front as it is cool behind. In the same way it checks the south-west wind, thus breaking the force of winds from wholly opposite quarters by one or the other of its sides; it is pleasant in winter but still more so in summer when the terrace is kept cool in the morning and the drive and nearer part of the garden in the afternoon, as its shadow falls shorter or longer on one side or the other while the day advances or declines. Inside the arcade, of course, there is least sunshine when the sun is blazing down on its roof, and as its open windows allow the western breezes to enter and circulate, the atmosphere is never heavy with stale air.

At the far end of the terrace, the arcade and the garden is a suite of rooms which are really and truly my favourites, for I had them built myself. Here is a sun-parlour facing the terrace on one side, the sea on the other, and the sun on both. There is also a bedroom which has folding doors opening on to the arcade and a window looking out on the sea. Opposite the intervening wall is a beautifully designed alcove which can be thrown into the room by folding back its glass doors and curtains, or cut off from it if they are closed: it is large enough to hold a couch and two arm-chairs, and has the sea at its foot, the neighbouring villas behind, and the woods beyond, views which can be seen separately from its many windows or blended into one. Next to it is a bedroom for use at night which neither the voices of my young slaves, the sea's murmur, nor the noise of a storm can penetrate, any more than the lightning's flash and light of day unless the shutters are open. This profound peace and seclusion are due to the dividing passage which runs between the room and the garden so that any noise is lost in the intervening space. A tiny furnace-room is built on here, and by a narrow outlet retains or circulates the heat underneath as required. Then there is an ante-room and a second bedroom, built out to face the sun and catch its rays the moment it rises, and retain them until after midday, though by then at an angle. When I retire to this suite I feel as if I have left my house altogether and much enjoy the sensation: especially during the Saturnalia when the rest of the roof resounds with festive cries in the holiday freedom, for I am not disturbing my household's merrymaking nor they my work.[3]

Only one thing is needed to complete the amenities and beauty of the house – running water; but there are wells, or rather springs, for they are very near the surface. It is in fact a remarkable characteristic of this shore that wherever you dig you come upon water at once which is pure and not in the least brackish, although the sea is so near. The woods close by provide plenty of firewood, and the town of Ostia supplies us with everything else. There is also a village,[4] just beyond the next house, which can satisfy anyone's modest needs, and here there are three baths for hire, a great convenience if a sudden arrival or too short a stay makes us reluctant to heat up the bath at home. The sea-front gains much from the pleasing variety of the houses built either in groups or far apart; from the sea or shore these look like a number of cities. The sand on the shore is sometimes too soft for walking after a long spell of fine weather, but more often it is hardened by the constant washing of the waves. The sea has admittedly few fish of any value, but it gives us excellent soles and prawns, and all inland produce is provided by the house, especially milk: for the herds collect there from the pastures whenever they seek water and shade.

And now do you think I have a good case for making this retreat my haunt and home where I love to be? You are too polite a townsman if you don't covet it! But I hope you will, for then the many attractions of my treasured house will have another strong recommendation in your company.

NOTES

1   Laurentium was primarily a winter residence.
2   This was an arched walkway covered by vines. Pliny's vineyards were in Tuscany.
3   Saturnalia was the Roman mid-winter festival of misrule.
4   Ostia was the main port for Rome.

Section Four
The Renaissance in Britain

43 Walter Raleigh 'The Nimphs reply to the Sheepheard'

Sir Walter Raleigh's (1552–1618) 'The Nimph's reply to the Sheepheard' was first printed in *England's Helicon* in 1600. This was a collection of pastoral poetry which showcased the most fashionable authors of the day. Raleigh was born in Devon and spent much of his life overseas, either attempting to gain territories in the Americas or in Ireland. He settled estates in Ireland and was governor of Jersey. He was arrested in July 1603 for allegedly conspiring against the new king of England, James I (1603–25), and was sentenced to death. The sentence was commuted to life imprisonment. While in the Tower of London he wrote a *History of the World* at the instigation of Henry, Prince of Wales (1594–1612). In 1616 King James released him to take part in an expedition to the Orinoco. The mission was a failure and Raleigh broke the terms of his release by razing a Spanish town. On his return the suspended death sentence was invoked and he was executed.

Source: Sir Walter Raleigh, 'The Nimphs reply to the Sheepheard', *England's Helicon*, ed. H. Macdonald, Routledge and Kegan Paul, London, 1949, p. 193

> If all the world and love were young,
> And truth in every Sheepheards tongue,
> These pretty pleasures might me move,
> To live with thee, and be thy love.
>
> Time drives the flocks from field to fold,
> When Rivers rage, and Rocks grow cold,
> And *Philomell*¹ becommeth dombe,
> The rest complaines of cares to come.
>
> The flowers doe fade, & wanton fieldes,
> To wayward winter reckoning yeeldes,
> A honny tongue, a hart of gall,
> Is fancies spring, but sorrowes fall.
>
> Thy gownes, thy shooes, thy beds of Roses,
> Thy cap, thy kirtle, and thy poesies,
> Soone breake, soone wither, soone forgotten:
> In follie ripe, in reason rotten.
>
> Thy belt of straw and Ivie buddes,
> Thy Corall claspes and Amber studdes,
> All these in mee no meanes can move,
> To come to thee, and be thy love.
>
> But could youth last, and love still breede,
> Had joyes no date, nor age no neede,
> Then these delights my minde might move,
> To live with thee, and be thy love.

NOTE

1   Philomel was raped by her brother-in-law, Tereus, King of Thrace, who cut out her
       tongue. She was later transformed into a swallow or nightingale.

44   Virgil **Eclogue V**

Virgil (70–19 BCE) was the most famous Roman poet of the classical period. His work in a variety of genres – especially pastoral (the *Eclogues*) and epic (the *Aeneid*) – became models for Renaissance poets to emulate and, if possible, surpass. The *Eclogues* were particularly influential on Elizabethan writers of pastoral like Edmund Spenser (*The Shepheardes Calender*) and Sir Philip Sidney (*Arcadia*).

Source: *The Eclogues*, the Latin text with a verse translation, G. Lee, Penguin Books, Harmondsworth, 1984, pp. 63, 65, 67 (English text only). Copyright © Francis Cairns (Publications) Ltd

Menalcas	Why don't we, Mopsus, meeting like this, good men both,
	You to blow the light reeds, I to versify,
	Sit down together here where hazels mix with elms?
Mopsus	You're senior, Menalcas; I owe you deference,
	Whether we go where fitful Zephyrs[1] make uncertain
	Shade, or into the cave instead. See how the cave
	Is dappled by a woodland vine's rare grape-clusters.
Menalcas	Only Amyntas in our hills competes with you.
Mopsus	What? He might just as well compete to outplay Phoebus.[2]
Menalcas	Then, Mopsus, you start first – with Phyllis' flames perhaps
	Or Alcon's praises or a flyting against Codrus.
	You start, and Tityrus[3] will watch the grazing kids.
Mopsus	No, I'll try out the song I wrote down recently
	On green beech bark, noting the tune between the lines:
	Then you can tell Amyntas to compete with me.
Menalcas	As surely as tough willow yields to the pale olive,
	Or humble red valerian to the crimson rose,
	So does Amyntas in our judgement yield to you.
	But no more talk, lad: we have come into the cave.
Mopsus	The Nymphs for Daphnis[4], cut off by a cruel death,
	Shed tears (you streams and hazels witness for the Nymphs),
	When, clasping her own son's poor body in her arms,
	A mother called both gods and stars alike cruel.
	In those days there were none who drove their pastured cattle
	To the cool rivers, Daphnis; no four-footed beast
	Would either lap the stream or touch a blade of grass.
	The wild hills, Daphnis, and the forests even tell

How Punic[5] lions roared in grief at your destruction.
Daphnis ordained to yoke Armenian tigresses
To chariots, Daphnis to lead on the Bacchic[6] rout
And twine tough javelins with gentle foliage.
As vines are glorious for trees, as grapes for vines,
As bulls for herds, and standing crops for fertile fields,
You are all glory to your folk. But since fate took you,
Apollo's self and Pales'[7] self have left the land.
From furrows we have often trusted with large barleys
Are born unlucky darnel and the barren oat.
For the soft violet, for radiant narcissus,
Thistles spring up and paliurus[8] with sharpened spines.
Scatter the ground with petals, cast shade on the springs,
Shepherds, (that such be done for him is Daphnis' will),
And make a mound and add above the mound a song:
Daphnis am I in woodland, known hence far as the stars,
Herd of a handsome flock, myself the handsomer.

Menalcas	For us your song, inspired poet, is like sleep
	On meadow grass for the fatigued, or in the heat
	Quenching one's thirst from a leaping stream of sweet water.
	You equal both your master's piping and his voice.
	Lucky lad! From now on you'll be second to him.
	Yet we, no matter how, will in return recite
	This thing of ours, and praise your Daphnis to the stars –
	Yes, to the stars raise Daphnis, for Daphnis loved us too.
Mopsus	What greater service could you render us than that?
	The lad himself deserved singing, and Stimichon[9]
	Some time ago spoke highly of your song to us.
Menalcas	Daphnis in white admires Olympus' strange threshold,
	And sees the planets and the clouds beneath his feet.
	Therefore keen pleasure grips forest and countryside,
	Pan also, and the shepherds, and the Dryad maids.
	The wolf intends no ambush to the flock, the nets
	No trickery to deer: Daphnis the good loves peace.
	For gladness even the unshorn mountains fling their voices
	Toward the stars; now even the orchards, even the rocks
	Echo the song: 'A god, a god is he, Menalcas!'
	O bless your folk and prosper them! Here are four altars:
	Look, Daphnis, two for you and two high ones for Phoebus.
	Two goblets each, frothing with fresh milk, every year
	And two large bowls of olive oil I'll set for you;
	And best of all, gladdening the feast with Bacchus' store
	(In winter, by the hearth; at harvest, in the shade),
	I'll pour Ariusian wine, fresh nectar, from big stoups.
	Damoetas and the Lyctian Aegon will sing for me;
	Alphesiboeus imitate the Satyrs' dance.

These offerings ever shall be yours, both when we pay
The Nymphs our solemn vows and when we purge the fields.
So long as fish love rivers, wild boar mountain heights,
So long as bees eat thyme, and the cicada dew,
Always your honour, name and praises will endure.
As farmers every year to Bacchus and to Ceres,
So they will vow to you; you too will claim their vows.

Mopsus   What can I give you, what return make for such song?
For neither does the whistling of Auster[10] coming
Sound so pleasant to me, nor beaches beaten by waves,
Nor rivers rushing down the valleys among rocks.

Menalcas We shall present you first with this frail hemlock pipe.
This taught us 'Corydon burned for beautiful Alexis';
This also taught us 'Whose flock? Meliboeus his?'

Mopsus   You take the crook, then, which Antígenes failed to get
For all his asking (lovable as then he was),
A handsome thing, with matching knobs and brass, Menalcas.

NOTES

1   Winds.
2   Apollo, god of the sun. He was also a superlative poet and musician.
3   Amyntas, Alcon, Codrus and Tityrus were names of other shepherds.
4   Daphnis was the son of the god Hermes, and was born in a sacred grove of bay-trees, from whence he gets his name ('daphne' is Greek for bay). He was famous for his good looks and musical ability, but died young because of the jealousy of a nymph who was in love with him. Virgil's praise of Daphnis draws on Theocrites, *Idyll* 1.
5   I.e. lions from Carthage, in North Africa.
6   Bacchic rout: followers of the god of wine, Bacchus.
7   A Roman goddess of agriculture.
8   A type of shrub.
9   Another fictional shepherd-poet.
10   A wind.

45 John Donne **'The Baite'**

John Donne's poem 'The Baite' was published posthumously in 1633 in an edition of his collected poems. A manuscript version of the poem exists but there are no details of its circulation before his death. Donne (*c.*1572–1631) was the son of a prosperous ironmonger and despite his early adherence to Catholicism was educated at Oxford and Lincoln's Inn. Before becoming secretary to Sir Thomas Egerton, the Keeper of the Great Seal, he took part in expeditions to Cadiz and the Azores. He was dismissed by Egerton when he secretly married Lady Egerton's niece, Anne More. He was unsuccessful in obtaining further office until he was ordained in 1614. He became Dean of St Paul's in 1621. His sermons were extremely popular.

Source: *The Complete English Poems of John Donne*, ed. C. A. Patrides, J. M. Dent and Sons, 1985, pp. 93–4

Come live with mee, and bee my love,
And wee will some new pleasures prove
Of golden sands, and christall brookes:
With silken lines, and silver hookes.

There will the river whispering runne
Warm'd by thy eyes, more than the Sunne.
And there the'inamor'd fish will stay,
Begging themselves they may betray.

When thou wilt swimme in that live bath,
Each fish, which every channell hath,
Will amorously to thee swimme,
Gladder to catch thee, than thou him.

If thou, to be so seene, beest loath,
By Sunne, or Moone, thou darknest both,
And if my selfe have leave to see,
I need not their light, having thee.

Let others freeze with angling reeds,
And cut their legges, with shells and weeds,
Or treacherously poore fish beset,
With strangling snare, or windowie net:

Let coarse bold hands, from slimy nest
The bedded fish in banks out-wrest,
Or curious traitors, sleavesilke flies[1]
Bewitch poore fishes wandring eyes.

For thee, thou needst no such deceit,
For thou thy selfe art thine owne bait,
That fish, that is not catch'd thereby,
Alas, is wiser farre than I.

NOTE

1   Sleavesilk flies were lures made of untwisted silk.

46 Francesco Petrarch **Sonnet 190, 'A white hind'**

Francesco Petrarch's *Rime Sparse* (*Scattered Rhymes*) were composed and polished throughout his life; they circulated widely throughout Italy in manuscript in the fifteenth century. Adaptations and partial translations of these and a further sequence, the *Trionfi* (*Triumphs*), which narrate a series of dream-visions of Petrarch's beloved Laura, who may have been a real person, became popular in the mid-sixteenth century in Britain.

Source: S. Minta, *Petrarch and Petrarchanism. The French and English Traditions*, Barnes and Noble, New York, 1980, pp. 68–9

> *Una candida cerva sopra l'erba*
> *verde m'apparve, con duo corna d'oro,*
> *fra due riviere, all'ombra d'un alloro,*
> *levando 'l sole a la stagione acerba.*
>
> *Era sua vista sì dolce superba*
> *ch'i' lasciai per seguirla ogni lavoro,*
> *come l'avaro che 'n cercar tesoro*
> *con diletto l'affanno disacerba.*
>
> *'Nessun mi tocchi' al bel collo d'intorno*
> *scritto avea di diamanti e di topazi*
> *'libera farmi al mio Cesare parve'*
>
> *Et era 'l sol già volto al mezzo giorno,*
> *gli occhi miei stanchi di mirar, non sazi,*
> *quand'io caddi ne l'acqua, et ella sparve.*

A white hind appeared to me on the green grass, with two horns of gold, between two rivers, in the shade of a laurel-tree, as the sun was rising in the youthful season.

Her look was so sweetly proud that I left all work to follow her, like the miser who, as he searches for treasure, sweetens his trouble with delight.

'Let no one touch me,' was written in diamonds and topazes around her lovely neck, 'it pleased my Caesar to make me free.'

And the sun had already turned to mid-day, my eyes weary with looking, but not satiated, when I fell into the water, and she vanished.

47 The Eton syllabus

The Eton syllabus details each hour's work for each class. It gives an idea of what sixteenth-century schoolboys studied on a day to day basis. The work undertaken by students is taken from both classical and contemporary texts. The contemporary references are to Juan Luis (Ludovico) Vives (1492–1540) a Spanish philosopher and humanist, whose works included a treatise on education, *De Disciplinis*; Johannes Sturm (1507–89), a German educationalist, who from 1536 reorganised education in the town of Strasbourg; Joannes Susenbrotus, the author of a hugely successful school primer *Epitome troporum ac Schematum et grammaticorum et rhetorum* [*A Compendium of tropes, schemes, grammar and rhetoric*] which was published in London in 1562; and Sir Thomas More.

20 *Petrarch in his Study*, manuscript illumination recording the composition of frescoes commissioned by Francesco da Carrara for the Sala Virorum Illustrium, Carrara Palace, Padua. Hessische Landes- und Hochschul-Bibliothek, Handschrifftenabteilung Codex 101, fol. v, Darmstadt, Germany.

Source: T. W. Baldwin, *William Shakespeare's Small Latine and Lesse Greeke*, University of Illinois Press, Urbana, 1944, vol. 1 (2 vols) pp. 353–8

Six o'clock

The usher enters and in the upper part of the school begins prayers on bended knees, which being finished, he descends to the first and lowest class, demanding from them both a part of speech and a verb, which on the preceding day he had given to be conjugated. From the first he turns to the second, from the second to the third, from the third, if it seems desirable, to the fourth, which sits in his part till seven o'clock, there to be examined if anything rather obscure should arise. Meanwhile one of the prepositors of school, going to the prepositors of each form in the part of the master as well as of the usher, brings from them the listed names of those absent from morning prayers, and gives them to the usher. Likewise another prepositor (who by himself always performs this duty) having inspected carefully the hands and face of each individual, if perchance any have come to school with unwashed hands; these he presents to the master immediately upon his entrance.

Seven o'clock

The fourth form transfers from the part of the usher to that of the master.

The master enters school. Here all the prepositors [monitors] of all forms report their absentees after seven o'clock; and also one of the prepositors of school reports the names of those who the day before were absent from school after six and seven in the evening, to the master his, likewise to the usher his. Then all forms render from memory what had been read to them, in such an order that the custos shall always begin and shall listen to the others as they recite.

Eight o'clock

The master assigns some *sententia*[1] to his, to the fourth class to be translated, to the fifth to be varied, to the sixth and seventh to be put in verses; from whose mouth the custos first receives it and first translates it. The usher likewise assigns some *sententia* to the third and to the second class to be translated, and to the first also, but a very short one. The vulgars produced by each are written down that morning, which they recite the next day in order and from memory.

Nine o'clock

Or thereabouts, first the custos of each form above recites and explains from memory the lecture of the class next below him; then the master reads the same lecture to his, and likewise the usher to his.

On Monday and Wednesday the four upper forms write in prose on a theme set for them; each one of the second, third, and first forms sets himself a *sententia* and translates it.

On Tuesday and Thursday the [two] upper forms put into verse the themes set them. The remaining two write the same in prose.

On Monday and Tuesday the master reads

    4th Terence.

To form 5th Justin the historian, *De Amicitia*, or others at his discretion.

    6th ⎱
    7th ⎰ Caesar's *Commentaries*, *Officia* of Cicero.

From which lectures the boys excerpt flowers, phrases, or locutions of speaking; likewise antithets, epithets, synonyms, proverbs, similitudes, comparisons, histories, descriptions of time, place, persons, fables, merry jests, schemes, and apothegms.

On the same days the usher reads

            ⎧ 3rd Terence.
To form   ⎨ 2nd Terence also.
            ⎩ 1st Vives.

On Wednesday and Thursday the master reads

    4th   Ovid, *De Tristibus*.

    5th   Ovid, *Metamorphoses*.

    6th ⎱
    7th ⎰ Virgil.

On the same days the usher reads

3rd Cicero's *Epistles* selected by Sturm.
2nd Lucian's *Dialogues.*
1st Ludovicus Vives.
At nine, when [the master and usher] have read, they go out of school.

Ten o'clock

The prepositor of school cries, 'Rise for prayers.'
Those standing erectly from both parts of the school follow the words, someone designated at the discretion of the prepositor leading.

Eleven o'clock

Thence two by two in a long row they all proceed into hall.
Dinner finished, they return to school in the same way they left.

Twelve o'clock

The usher enters, and those things which the master read to the fourth class before dinner, from the same now sitting in his part till one he demands them, and discusses each part of speech. To whom when he first enters the prepositors of the first four forms exhibit the names of their absentees.

One o'clock
[and two]

The fourth class migrates into its proper seat, and now the prepositors of each form turn over their absentees to the master when he enters. The master spends the time between one and three in examining the fifth, sixth, and seventh forms, and out of the assigned lecture makes vulgars for the practise of the Latin tongue; so that, however, half an hour before three the prepositors of the three upper forms hand in their own and their classmates themes, which he examines carefully.
The usher spends the same hours in examining his three forms.

There o'clock

Each goes out.

Four o'clock

Each returns.
At which time they render as much from these authors as has been assigned to them by the teacher, one assigned by the master requesting it.

⎧ 4th   From the figures in grammar and the system of versification.
⎪ 5th   Valerius Maximus, Lucius Florus, or Cicero's *Epistles*,
⎨   Susenbrotus.
⎪ 6th ⎫ The Greek grammar or something else at the discretion of
⎩ 7th ⎭ the teacher.

To the usher their absentees are exhibited, also the themes of the third form, as also the *sententiae* of the second which each one shall have set himself and shall have turned into Latin. Then each and everyone says from memory as much as had been assigned to him from the rules, then also the vulgars by which the grammar rules may be better understood are made by the boys, that thence Latin speech may in every way become more familiar.

Five o'clock

They go out and return in the same order as before dinner.

Six o'clock

Those who from the highest form have been designated by the master to teach other classes take up their duties, and exercise those committed to their faith in explaining lectures and in translating *sententiae* from the vernacular speech into Latin. Also, they recite and put in order those things dictated by the teacher that day. The prepositors of individual classes undergo this duty, so that the moderators of school may set their minds diligently on all for profit in letters and the forming of manners.

Seven o'clock

They are dismissed to drink. Returned after seven, they exercise themselves in the same way as after six, except at a certain time of the year, when they play after supper according to the discretion of the master and the custom.

Eight o'clock

They go to bed pouring out prayers.

Friday

On Fridays after the lecture recited which they had the day before, those who have committed any grave crime are accused.

They call them corrections, for they give the proper punishments of evil deeds.

Before dinner nothing is read.

The first hour after noon both enter and demand the lectures which they have given that week.

At three o'clock they go out.

At four they return and whatever they have taught between four and five that week is rendered to them.

Before five the master reads

To form
- 4th   Apophthegms, or Epigrams of Martial, Catullus, or Thomas More.
- 5th   Horace.
- 6th 7th } Lucan or some other at discretion.

And against seven o'clock in the morning of the next day he assigns some theme to the sixth and seventh in verses, but to be varied by the fifth in prose. And against the first hour in the afternoon of the same day to be explained more at large by the same again and by the fourth form also in prose.

Before five the usher reads

To form
- 3rd   Aesop's *Fables*.
- 2nd   Aesop's *Fables*.
- 1st   Cato.

Saturday

At seven o'clock, all forms render the things which had been read the day before.

The variations are turned over to the master.

The usher examines all he had read the day before.

At nine o'clock each goes out.

At one o'clock both enter school and hear the boys recite what they (the master and usher) had dictated that week.

The themes are also turned over to the teacher.

Here if there are any assigned that week by the teacher for the sake of exercising ability they declaim on a set original theme, and one inveighs against another in speeches. [. . .]

NOTE

1   *Sententia*: a quoted saying of some eminent person, an apoththegm. Also a pithy or pointed saying, an aphorism or maxim which had the status of a commonplace in the Renaissance.

48 Figures of diction **from *Rhetorica ad Herennium***

Part of a list of figures of diction from the *Rhetorica ad herennium* from the early first century BCE. In the Renaissance it was attributed to Cicero. The text was popular in Renaissance schools for language teaching. The ten figures of diction are tropes. Quintilian says a trope is 'an artistic change of a word or phrase from its proper signification to another' (8.6.1.).

Source: *Rhetorica ad Herennium* , trans. H. Caplan, William Heinemann, London, 1981, pp. 333, 335, 337, 339, 341, 343 (English text only). Copyright © Harvard University Press: Cambridge, Mass., 1954

XXXI. There remain also ten Figures of Diction, which I have intentionally not scattered at random, but have separated from those above, because they all belong in one class. They indeed all have this in common, that the language departs from the ordinary meaning of the words and is, with a certain grace, applied in another sense.

Of these figures the first is Onomatopoeia, which suggests to us that we should ourselves designate with a suitable word, whether for the sake of imitation or of expressiveness, a thing which either lacks a name or has an inappropriate name. For the sake of imitation, as follows: our ancestors, for example, said 'roar,' 'bellow,' 'murmur,' 'hiss;' for the sake of expressiveness, as follows: 'After this creature attacked the republic, there was a hullabaloo among the first men of the state.' This figure is to be used rarely, lest the frequent recurrence of the neologism breed aversion; but if it is used appropriately and sparingly, then the novelty, far from offending, even gives distinction to the style.

Antonomasia or Pronomination designates by a kind of adventitious epithet a thing that cannot be called by its proper name; for example, if some one speaking of the Gracchi should say: 'Surely the grandsons of Africanus did not behave like this!'; or again, if some one speaking of his adversary should say: 'See now, men of the jury, how your Sir Swashbuckler there has treated me.' In this way we shall be able, not without elegance, in praise and in censure, concerning physical attributes, qualities of character, or external circumstances, to express ourselves by using a kind of epithet in place of the precise name.

XXXII. Metonymy is the figure which draws from an object closely akin or associated an expression suggesting the object meant, but not called by its own name. This is accomplished by substituting the name of the greater thing for that of the lesser, as if one speaking of the Tarpeian Rock should term it 'the Capitoline'; . . . ; or by substituting the name of the thing invented for that of the inventor, as if one should say 'wine' for 'Liber,' 'wheat' for 'Ceres'; '. . . ;' or the instrument for the possessor, as if one should refer to the Macedonians as follows: 'Not so quickly did the Lances get possession of Greece,' and likewise, meaning the Gauls: 'nor was the Transalpine Pike so easily driven from Italy'; the cause for the effect, as if a speaker, wishing to show that some one has done something in war, should say: 'Mars forced you to do that'; or effect for cause, as when we call an art idle because it produces idleness in people, or speak of numb cold because cold produces numbness. Content will be designated by means of container as follows: 'Italy cannot be vanquished in warfare nor Greece in studies'; for here instead of Greeks and Italians the lands that comprise them are designated. Container will be designated by means of content: as if one wishing to give a name to wealth should call it gold or silver or ivory. It is harder to distinguish all these metonymies in teaching the principle than to find them when searching for them, for the use of metonymies of this kind is abundant not only amongst the poets and orators but also in everyday speech.

Periphrasis is a manner of speech used to express a simple idea by means of a circumlocution, as follows: 'The foresight of Scipio crushed the power of Carthage.' For here, if the speaker had not designed to embellish the style, he might simply have said 'Scipio' and 'Carthage.'

Hyperbaton upsets the word order by means either of Anastrophe or Transposition. By Anastrophe, as follows: 'Hoc vobis deos immortales arbitror dedisse virtute pro vestra' [This I deem the immortal gods have vouchsafed to you in reward for your virtue]. By Transposition, as follows: 'Instabilis in istum plurimum fortuna valuit. Omnes invidiose eripuit bene vivendi casus facultates.' [Unstable fortune has exercised her greatest power on this creature. All the means of living well chance has jealously taken from him]. A transposition of this kind, that does not render the thought obscure, will be very useful for periods, which I have discussed above; in these periods we ought to arrange the words in such a way as to approximate a poetic rhythm, so that the periods can achieve perfect fullness and the highest finish.

XXXIII. Hyperbole is a manner of speech exaggerating the truth, whether for the sake of magnifying or minifying something. This is used independently, or with comparison. Independently, as follows: 'But if we maintain concord in the state, we shall measure the empire's vastness by the rising and the setting of the sun.' Hyperbole with comparison is formed from either equivalence or superiority. From equivalence, as follows: 'His body was as white as snow, his face burned like fire.'[1] From superiority, as follows: 'From his mouth flowed speech sweeter than honey.'[2] Of the same type is the following: 'So great was his splendour in arms that the sun's brilliance seemed dim by comparison.'

Synecdoche occurs when the whole is known from a small part or a part from the whole. The whole is understood from a part in the following: 'Were not those nuptial flutes reminding you of his marriage?' Here the entire marriage ceremony is suggested by one sign, the flutes. A part from the whole, as if one should say to a person who displays himself in luxurious garb or adornment: 'You display your riches to me and vaunt your ample treasures.' The plural will be understood from the singular, as follows: 'To the Carthaginian came aid from the Spaniard, and from that fierce Transalpine. In Italy, too, many a wearer of the toga shared the same sentiment.' In the following the singular will be understood from the plural: 'Dread disaster smote his breasts with grief; so, panting, from out his lungs' very depth he sobbed for anguish.' In the first example more than one Spaniard, Gaul, and Roman citizen are understood, and in this last only one breast and one lung.[3] In the former the quantity is minified for the sake of elegance, in the latter exaggerated for the sake of impressiveness.

Catachresis is the inexact use of a like and kindred word in place of the precise and proper one, as follows: 'The power of man is short,' or 'small height,' or 'the long wisdom in the man,' or 'a mighty speech,' or 'to engage in a slight conversation.' Here it is easy to understand that words of kindred, but not identical, meaning have been transferred on the principle of inexact use.

XXXIV. Metaphor occurs when a word applying to one thing is transferred to another, because the similarity seems to justify this transference. Metaphor is used for the sake of creating a vivid mental picture, as follows: 'This insurrection awoke Italy with sudden terror'; for the sake of brevity, as follows: 'The recent arrival of an army suddenly blotted out the state'; for the sake of avoiding obscenity, as follows: 'Whose mother delights in daily marriages'; for the sake of magnifying, as follows: 'No one's grief or disaster could have appeased this creature's enmities and glutted his horrible cruelty'; for the sake of minifying, as follows: 'He boasts that he was of great help because, when we were in difficulties, he lightly breathed a favouring breath' [. . .].

NOTES

1   Cf. Homer *Iliad* 1.104: Agamemnon's eyes 'were like flashing fire'; in 10.437 the horses of Rhesus are 'whiter than snow'.
2   Homer *Iliad*, L.247–8, on Nestor, king of Pylos.
3   In ancient physiology the lungs were considered to be the right and left halves of one single organ.

49 Fulke Greville *The Life of the renowned Sir Philip Sidney*

Sir Fulke Greville, first Baron Brooke (1554–1628), went to Shrewsbury School (with Sir Philip Sidney) and Jesus College, Cambridge. He was an MP and held public office including secretary for Wales from 1583 to 1628 and Chancellor of the Exchequer (1614–21). His *Life of the renowned Sir Philip Sidney* was begun around 1610, though not published until 1652. Greville died in 1628 after being stabbed to death by a servant who thought he had been cut out of Greville's will.

Source: *Selected Writings of Fulke Greville*, ed. J. Rees, Athlone Press, London, 1973, p. 148

When my youth, with favour of court in some moderate proportion to my birth and breeding, in the activeness of that time gave me opportunity of most business, then did my yet undiscouraged genius most affect to find or make work for itself. And out of that freedom, having many times offered my fortune to the course of foreign employments as the properest forges to fashion a subject for the real services of his sovereign, I found the returns of those mis-placed endeavours to prove both a vain charge to myself and an offensive undertaking to that excellent governess over all her subjects' duties and affections. . . .

By which many warnings, I finding the specious fires of youth to prove far more scorching than glorious, called my second thoughts to council, and in that map clearly discerning action and honour to fly with more wings than one, and that it was sufficient for the plant to grow where his sovereign's hand had planted it, I found reason to contract my thoughts from those larger but wandering horizons of the world abroad, and bound my prospect within the safe limits of duty, in such home services as were acceptable to my sovereign.

In which retired view, Sir Philip Sidney, that exact image of quiet and action, happily united in him and seldom well divided in any, being ever in mine eyes, made me think it no small degree of honour to imitate or tread in the steps of such a leader. So that to sail by his compass was shortly (as I said) one of the principal reasons I can allege which persuaded me to steal minutes of time from my daily services, and employ them in this kind of writing.

50   Edmund Spenser **The Argument, Embleme and Glosse from 'Maye'**

Edmund Spenser (1552?–99) was educated at the Merchant Taylors' school and Pembroke Hall, Cambridge. *The Shepheardes Calender*, which includes 'Maye', was published in 1579. The *Calender* consists of twelve eclogues, combining political allegory and aesthetic competition. It is prefaced by a dedicatory epistle to Sir Philip Sidney signed by 'E. K.', and an anonymously written description of 'the general argument of the whole booke'. Each month has a woodcut representing its matter, a brief 'argument' about this, the verses themselves, a verbal emblem or motto summing up what the subject was, and an extensive annotation ('glosse') of the text. The identity of E. K., who produced this editorial material, is unknown and may even have been Spenser himself.

Source: *The Works of Edmund Spenser*, ed. E. Greenlaw, C. G. Osgood, F. M. Padelford, R. Heffner, The Johns Hopkins Press, Baltimore, 1943, pp. 46, 55–8

ARGVMENT

In this fift Æglogue, vnder the persons of two shepheards Piers and Palinodie, be rep-
resented two formes of pastoures or Ministers, or the protestant and the Catholique:
whose chiefe talke standeth in reasoning, whether the life of the one must be like the
other. [W]ith whom hauing shewed, that it is daungerous to mainteine any felow-
ship, or giue too much credit to their colourable and feyned goodwill, he telleth him
a tale of the foxe, that by such a counterpoynt of craftines deceiued and deuoured the
credulous kidde.

Palinodes Embleme.
Πὰς μὲν ἄπιστος ἀπιστεῖ.
Piers his Embleme.
Τὶς δ᾽ ἄρα πίστις ἀπίστω;

GLOSSE

1 Thilke) this same moneth.   It is applyed to the season of the moneth, when
all menne delight them selues with pleasaunce of fieldes, and gardens, and
garments.

5 Bloncket liueries) gray coates.   *6* Yclad) arrayed, Y, redoundeth,
as before.

9 In euery where) a straunge, yet proper kind of speaking.

10 Buskets) a Diminutiue .s. little bushes of hauthorne.

12 Kirke) church.   *15* Queme) please.

20 A shole) a multitude; taken of fishe, whereof some going in great companies,
are sayde to swimme in a shole.

22 Yode) went.   *25* Iouyssance) ioye.   *36* Swinck) labour.

38 Inly) entirely.   *39* Faytours) vagabonds.

54 Great pan) is Christ, the very God of all shepheards, which calleth himselfe
the greate and good shepherd.   The name is most rightly (me thinkes)
applyed to him, for Pan signifieth all or omnipotent, which is onely the
Lord Iesus. And by that name (as I remember) he is called of Eusebius in
his fifte booke de Preparat. Euang; who thereof telleth a proper storye to
that purpose. Which story is first recorded of Plutarch, in his booke of
the ceasing of oracles, and of Lauetere translated, in his booke of walking
sprightes. who sayth, that about the same time, that our Lord suffered his
most bitter passion for the redemtion of man, certein passengers sayling
from Italy to Cyprus and passing by certain Iles called Paxæ, heard a voyce
calling alowde Thamus, Thamus, (now Thamus was the name of an
Ægyptian, which was Pilote of the ship,) who giuing eare to the cry, was
bidden, when he came to Palodes, to tel, that the great Pan was dead:
which he doubting to doe, yet for that when he came to Palodes, there
sodeinly was such a calme of winde, that the shippe stoode still in the sea
vnmoued, he was forced to cry alowd, that Pan was dead: wherewithall
there was heard suche piteous outcryes and dreadfull shriking, as hath not

bene the like. By whych Pan, though of some be vnderstoode the great Satanas, whose kingdome at that time was by Christ conquered, the gates of hell broken vp, and death by death deliuered to eternall death, (for at that time, as he sayth, all Oracles surceased, and enchaunted spirits, that were wont to delude the people, thenceforth held theyr peace) and also at the demaund of the Emperoure Tiberius, who that Pan should be, answere was made him by the wisest and best learned, that it was the sonne of Mercurie and Penelope, yet I think it more properly meant of the death of Christ, the onely and very Pan, then suffering for his flock.

57 I as I am) seemeth to imitate the commen prouerb, Malim Inuidere mihi omnes quam miserescere.

61 Nas) is a syncope, for ne has, or has not: as nould, for would not.

69 Tho with them) doth imitate the Epitaphe of the ryotous king Sardanapalus, whych caused to be written on his tombe in Greeke: which verses be thus translated by Tullie.

" Hæc habui quæ edi, quæque exaturata libido
" Hausit, at illa manent multa ac præclara relicta.

which may thus be turned into English.

" All that I eate did I ioye, and all that I greedily gorged:
" As for those many goodly matters left I for others.

Much like the Epitaph of a good olde Erle of Deuonshire, which though much more wisedome bewraieth, then Sardanapalus, yet hath a smacke of his sensuall delights and beastlinesse. the rymes be these.

" Ho, Ho, who lies here?
" I the good Erle of Deuonshere,
" And Maulde my wife, that was ful deare,
" We liued together lv. yeare.
" That we spent, we had:
" That we gaue, we haue:
" That we lefte, we lost.

75 Algrind) the name of a shepheard.   76 Men of the Lay) Lay men.

78 Enaunter) least that.   82 Souenaunce) remembraunce.

91 Miscreaunce) despeire or misbeliefe.

92 Cheuisaunce) sometime of Chaucer vsed for gaine: sometime of other for spoyle, or bootie, or enterprise, and sometime for chiefdome.

111 Pan himselfe) God. [A]ccording as is sayd in Deuteronomie, That in diuision of the lande of Canaan, to the tribe of Leuie no portion of heritage should bee allotted, for GOD himselfe was their inheritaunce.

121 Some gan) meant of the Pope, and his Antichristian prelates, which vsurpe a tyrannical dominion in the Churche, and with Peters counterfet keyes, open a wide gate to al wickednesse and insolent gouernment. Nought here spoken, as of purpose to deny fatherly rule and godly gouernaunce (as some malitiously of late haue done to the great vnreste and hinderaunce of the Churche) but to displaye the pride and disorder of such, as in steede of feeding their sheepe, indeede feede of theyr sheepe.

130 Sourse) welspring and originall.   131 Borrowe) pledge or suertie.

142 The Geaunte) is the greate Atlas, whom the poetes feign to be a huge geaunt, that beareth Heauen on his shoulders: being in deede a merueilous highe mountaine in Mauritania, that now is Barbarie, which to mans seeming perceth the cloudes, and seemeth to touch the heauens. Other thinke, and they not amisse, that this fable was meant of one Atlas king of the same countrye, (of whome may bee, that that hil had his denomination) brother to Prometheus who (as the Grekes say) did first fynd out the hidden courses of the starres, by an excellent imagination, wherefore the poetes feigned, that he susteyned the firmament on hys shoulders. Many other coniectures needelesse be told hereof.

145 Warke) worke.   *147* Encheason) cause, occasion.

150 Deare borow) that is our sauiour, the commen pledge of all mens debts to death.   *158* Nought seemeth) is vnseemely.   *159* Wyten) blame.

160 Her) theyr, as vseth Chaucer.   *163* Conteck) strife contention.   *168* Han) for haue.   *168* Sam) together. [. . .]

Embleme

Both these Emblemes make one whole Hexametre. The first spoken of Palinodie, as in reproche of them, that be distrustfull, is a peece of Theognis verse, intending, that who doth most mistrust is most false. For such experience in falsehod breedeth mistrust in the mynd, thinking nolesse guile to lurke in others, then in hymselfe. But Piers thereto strongly replyeth with another peece of the same verse, saying as in his former fable, what fayth then is there in the faythlesse. For if fayth be the ground of religion, which fayth they dayly false, what hold then is there of theyr religion. And thys is all that they saye.

51 John Bale *The Examinations of Anne Askew*

Anne Askew (1521–46) came from Lincolnshire. She was well educated and well read in the Bible. In 1545 she was investigated in London for her heretical views about the sacraments, imprisoned in Newgate and the Tower of London and tortured. She was burned at the stake in 1546. The Protestant bishop of Ossory, John Bale (1495–1563), published two accounts of her examination and execution in 1546 and 1547. The account was incorporated in the hugely successful *Actes and Monuments* by John Foxe and first published in English in 1563. Bale was also author of several religious plays and polemical works in support of the Reformation.

Source: John Bale, *The Examinations of Anne Askew*, ed. E. Beilin, Oxford University Press, Oxford, 1996, pp. 110–13, 124–7

Anne Askewe.

The summe of the condempnacyon of me Anne Askewe, at yelde hawle [Guildhall].

They sayd to me there, that I was an heretyke and condempned by the lawe, if I wolde stande in my opynyon. I answered that I was no heretyke, neyther yet deserved I anye deathe by the lawe of God. But as concernynge the faythe whych I uttered and wrote to the counsell, I wolde not (I sayd) denye it, bycause I knewe it true. Then wolde they nedes knowe, if I wolde denye the sacrament to be Christes bodye and bloude: I sayd, yea. For the same sonne of God, that was borne of the vyrgyne Marie, is now gloriouse in heaven, and wyll come agayne from thens at the lattre daye [Day of Judgement] lyke as he went up, Acto. l. [*Acts* 1: 9] And as for that ye call your God, is but a pece of breade. For a more profe therof (marke it whan ye lyst) lete it lye in the boxe but iii. monthes, and it wyll be moulde, and so turne to nothynge that is good. Wherupon I am persuaded, that it can not be God.

Johan Bale.

Christ Jesus the eternall sonne of God, was condempned of thys generacyon for a sedicyouse heretyke, a breaker of their sabbath, a subverter of their people, a defyler of their lawes, and a destroyer of their temple or holye churche, Joan. 7. Luce 23. Mathei 26. Marci 14.[1] and suffered deathe for it at ther procurement, by the lawe than used. Is it than anye marvele, if hys inferiour subject here, and faythfull membre do the same, at the cruell callynge on and vyolent vengeaunce of their posteryte? No, no, the servaunt must folowe her mastre, and the fote her heade, and maye be founde in that poynte no frear than he, Joan. 13. Saynt Augustyne dyffynynge a sacrament, calleth it in one place, a sygne of an holye thynge. In an other place a vysyble shappe of an invysyble grace. Whose offyce is to instructe, anymate, and strengthen our faythe towardes God, and not to take it to it self, and so depryve hym therof. Christes bodye and bloude are neyther sygnes nor shaddowes, but the verye effectuall thynges in dede, sygnyfyed by those fygures of breade and wyne. But how that drye and corruptyble cake [communion wafer] of theirs shuld become a God, manye men wondre now a dayes in the lyght of the Gospell, lyke as they have done afore tyme also. And specyallye whye the wyne shuld not be accepted and set up for a God also so wele as the breade, consyderynge that Christ made so moche of the one as of the other.

Anne Askewe.

After that they wylled me to have a prest. And than I smyled. Then they asked me, if it were not good? I sayd, I wolde confesse my fawtes to God. For I was sure that he wolde heare me with faver. And so we were condempned without a quest.[2]

Johan Bale.

Prestes of godlye knowledge she ded not refuse. For she knewe that they are the massengers of the lorde, and that hys holye wordes are to be sought at ther mouthes, Mala. 2. Of them she instauntlye desyred to be instructed, and it was denyed her, as is written afore. What shuld she than els do, but returne unto her lorde God? in whome she knewe to be habundaunce of mercye for all them whych do from the hart repent, Deutro. 30. As for the other sort of prestes, she ded not amys to laugh both them and their maynteners to scorne. For so doth God also, Psalme 2. And curseth both their absolucyons and blessynges, Mala. 2. A thefe or a murtherer shuld not have bene condempned without a quest, by the lawes of Englande. But the faythfull members of Jesus Christ, for the spyght and hate that thys worlde hath to hys veryte, must have an other kynde of tyrannye added therunto, besydes the unryghtouse bestowynge of that lawe. Wo be unto yow (sayth the eternall God of heaven by hys prophete) or dampnacyon be over your heades, that make wycked lawes, and devyse cruell thynges for the poore oppressed innocentes. Esaie 10. Wo unto hym that buyldeth Babylon with bloude, and maynteyneth that wycked cytie styll in unryghtwysnesse, Abacuch 2. Nahum. 3. Ezech. 24.

Anne Askewe.

My beleve whych I wrote to the counsell was thys. That the sacramentall breade was left us to be receyved with thankes gevynge, in remembraunce of Christes deathe, the onlye remedye of our sowles recover[y]. And that therby we also receyve the whole benefyghtes and frutes of hys most gloryouse passion.

Johan Bale.

We reade not in the Gospell, that the materyall breade at Christes holye supper, was anye otherwyse taken of the Apostles, than thus. Neyther yet that Christ our mastre and saver requyred anye other takynge of them. If so manye straunge doubtes had bene therin, and so hygh dyffycultees, as be moved and are in controversye amonge men now a dayes both papystes and other, they coulde no more have bene left undyscussed of hym, than other hygh matters were. The dyscyples axed here neyther how nor what as doubtlesse they wolde have done, if he had mynded them to have taken the breade for hym. They thought it ynough to take it in hys remembraunce, lyke as he than playnelye taught them, Luce 22. The eatynge of hys fleshe and drynkynge of hys bloude therin, to the relevynge of their sowles thirst and hunger, they knewe to perteyne unto faythe accordynge to hys instruccyons in the vi. of Johan. What have thys godlye woman than offended, whych neyther have denyed hys incarnacyon nor deathe in thys her confessyon of faythe, but most firmelye and groundedlye trusted to receyve the frutes of them both. [. . .]

Anne Askewe.

Then commaunded they me to shewe, how I was maynteyned in the Counter [a prison], and who wylled me to stycke by my opynyon. I sayd that there was no creature, that therin ded strengthen me. And as for the helpe that I had in the Counter, it was by the meanes of my mayde. For as she went abroade in the stretes, she made to the prentyses [apprentices], and they by her ded sende me moneye. But who they were, I never knewe.

Johan Bale.

Joseph was in pryson undre Pharao the fearce kynge of Egypte, yet was he favourablye handeled and no man forbydden to consort [keep company with] hym, Gene. 39. Whan Johan Baptist was in stronge duraunce [imprisonment] undre Herode the tyraunt of Galile, hys dyscyples ded frelye vysytt hym, and were not rebuked for it, Math. 11. Paule beynge emprysoned and in cheanes at Rome, undre the most furyouse tyraunte Nero, was never blamed for sendynge hys servaunt Onesimus abroade, nor yet for writynge by hym to hys fryndes for socour, Philem. 1. Neyther yet was Philemon troubled for relevynge hym there by the seyd Onesimus, nor yet hys olde frynde Onesipherus, for personallye there vysytynge hym, and supportynge hym with hys moneye, lyke as he had done afore also at Ephesus. Now conferre these storyes and soch other lyke, with the present handelynge of Anne Askewe and ye shall wele perceyve our Englysh rulers and judges in their newe Christyanyte of renouncynge the pope, to excede all other tyrauntes in all crueltye, spyght and vengeaunce. But loke to have it no otherwyse, so longe as mytred prelates are of counsell [advisors]. Be ashamed cruell beastes, be ashamed, for all Christendome wondereth on your madnesse above all.

Anne Askewe.

Then they sayd, that there were dyverse gentylwomen, that gave me moneye. But I knewe not their names. Then they sayd that there were dyverse ladyes, whych had sent me moneye. I answered, that there was a man in a blewe coate, whych delyvered me ,x, shyllynges, and sayd that my ladye of Hertforde sent it me. And an other in a vyolet coate ded geve me viii. shyllynges, and sayd that my ladye Dennye sent it me.[3] Whether it were true or no, I can not tell. For I am not suer who sent it me, but as the men ded saye.

Johan Bale.

In the tyme of Christes preachynge what though the holye clergye wer than not pleased therwith, but judged it (as they do styll to thys daye) most horryble heresye, yet serten noble women, as Marye Magdalene, Joanna the wyfe of Chusa Herodes hygh stewarde, Susanna, and manye other folowed hym from Galile, and mynystred unto hym of their substaunce, concernynge hys bodylye nedes Luce 8. These with other more, after he was by the seyd clergye done to most cruell deathe for the veryte preachynge, both prepared oyntmentes and spyces to anoynte hys bodye, Luce 24. and also proclamed abroade hys gloryouse resurreccyon to hys Apostles and other, Joan. 20 contrarye to the Byshoppes inhybycyon, Acto. 4. Yet reade we not that anye man or woman was racked for the accusement of them. A woman amonge the Macedonyanes, dwellynge in the cytie of Thyatira, and called Lydia by name, a purple seller verye rytche in mer-chaundyse, receyved Paule, Sylas, and Timothe with other suspected bretherne in to her howse and habundauntly releved them there. Act. 16. yet was she not troubled for it. In lyke maner at Thessalonica, a great nombre of the Grekes and manye noble women amonge them, beleved Paules forbydden doctryne, and resorted boldelye both to hym and to Sylas, Acto. 17. yet were they not cruellye handeled for it.

Be ashamed than ye tyrauntes of Englande, [. . .]

Anne Askewe.

Then they sayd, there were of the counsell that ded maynteyne me. And I sayd, no. Then they ded put me on the racke, bycause I confessed no ladyes nor gentyllwomen to be of my opynyon, and theron they kept me a longe tyme. And bycause I laye styll and ded not crye, my lord Chauncellour and mastre Ryche, toke peynes to racke me their own handes, tyll I was nygh dead.[4] [. . .]

NOTES

1   John Bale's biblical references are not given in this text. The chapter numbers he pro-
      vides are the sources for the biblical examples he cites.
2   According to law, presentment by a jury (a quest) should have preceded Anne Askew's
      condemnation.
3   Anne Seymour, Countess of Hertford (d.1587) and Joan, Lady Denny. Both were wives
      of leading Protestant members of Henry VIII's court. Edward Seymour, Earl of Hert-
      ford (c.1506–52) was the brother of Jane Seymour and therefore brother-in-law to the
      king and uncle of the Prince of Wales. He was Lord Great Chamberlain. Sir Anthony
      Denny (1501–49) was chief Gentleman of the Privy Chamber and keeper of the Palace
      of Whitehall.
4   Sir Thomas Wriothesley, Lord Chancellor and later Earl of Southampton (1505–50);
      Richard Rich, first Baron Rich (c.1496–1567). Both were pro-Catholic Privy Council-
      lors. Wriothesley later attended Anne Askew's execution.

52   Philip Sidney *An Apology for Poetry*

Sir Philip Sidney (1554–86) was born at Penshurst. He was the eldest son of Sir
Henry Sidney and Mary Dudley (the sister of the Earl of Leicester). Sidney was
educated at Shrewsbury School with Fulke Greville (Text 49), then at Christ
Church, Oxford. He travelled widely in Europe between 1572 and 1575. He was a
writer of both poetry and prose, his most famous works including the sonnet
sequence *Astrophil and Stella* and the romance *Arcadia*. In 1585 he went to the
Low Countries as part of an expedition against the Spanish, where he was made
governor of Flushing. He died three weeks after being wounded in a skirmish
outside Zutphen. None of his major works were published in his lifetime. *An
Apology* was published in 1595.

Source: *An Apology for Poetry or the Defence of Poesy*, ed. G. Shepherd,
Manchester University Press, Manchester, 1973, pp. 100–8

Only the poet, disdaining to be tied to any such subjection, lifted up with the
vigour of his own invention, doth grow in effect into another nature, in making
things either better than Nature bringeth forth, or, quite anew, forms such as
never were in Nature, as the Heroes, Demigods, Cyclops, Chimeras, Furies, and
such like: so as he goeth hand in hand with Nature, not enclosed within
the narrow warrant of her gifts, but freely ranging only within the zodiac of his
own wit.

     Nature never set forth the earth in so rich tapestry as divers poets have done;
neither with pleasant rivers, fruitful trees, sweet-smelling flowers, nor whatsoever
else may make the too much loved earth more lovely. Her world is brazen, the
poets only deliver a golden.[1]

     But let those things alone, and go to man – for whom as the other things are,

so it seemeth in him her uttermost cunning is employed – and know whether
she have brought forth so true a lover as Theagenes, so constant a friend as
Pylades, so valiant a man as Orlando, so right a prince as Xenophon's Cyrus, so
excellent a man every way as Virgil's Aeneas.[2] Neither let this be jestingly conceived, because the works of the one be essential, the other in imitation or fiction;
for any understanding knoweth the skill of the artificer standeth in that *Idea* or
fore-conceit of the work, and not in the work itself. And that the poet hath that
Idea is manifest, by delivering them forth in such excellency as he hath imagined
them. Which delivering forth also is not wholly imaginative, as we are wont to
say by them that build castles in the air; but so far substantially it worketh, not
only to make a Cyrus, which had been but a particular excellency as Nature might
have done, but to bestow a Cyrus upon the world to make many Cyruses, if they
will learn aright why and how that maker made him.[3]

Neither let it be deemed too saucy a comparison to balance the highest point
of man's wit with the efficacy of Nature; but rather give right honour to the heavenly Maker of that maker, who having made man to His own likeness, set him
beyond and over all the works of that second nature: which in nothing he showeth
so much as in Poetry, when with the force of a divine breath he bringeth things
forth far surpassing her doings, with no small argument to the incredulous of
that first accursed fall of Adam: since our erected wit maketh us know what perfection is, and yet our infected will keepeth us from reaching unto it. But these
arguments will by few be understood, and by fewer granted. Thus much (I hope)
will be given me, that the Greeks with some probability of reason gave him the
name above all names of learning.

Now let us go to a more ordinary opening of him, that the truth may be more
palpable: and so I hope, though we get not so unmatched a praise as the etymology of his names will grant, yet his very description, which no man will deny,
shall not justly be barred from a principal commendation.

Poesy therefore is an art of imitation, for so Aristotle termeth it in his word
mimesis, that is to say, a representing, counterfeiting, or figuring forth – to speak
metaphorically, a speaking picture – with this end, to teach and delight.

Of this have been three several kinds. The chief, both in antiquity and excellency, were they that did imitate the inconceivable excellencies of God. Such were
David in his Psalms; Solomon in his Song of Songs, in his Ecclesiastes, and
Proverbs; Moses and Deborah in their Hymns; and the writer of Job: which,
beside other, the learned Emanuel Tremellius and Franciscus Junius do entitle
the poetical part of the Scripture.[4] Against these none will speak that hath the
Holy Ghost in due holy reverence. In this kind, though in a full wrong divinity,
were Orpheus, Amphion, Homer in his Hymns, and many other, both Greeks
and Romans. And this poesy must be used by whosoever will follow St James's
counsel [*James* 5: 13] in singing psalms when they are merry, and I know is used
with the fruit of comfort by some, when, in sorrowful pangs of their death-
bringing sins, they find the consolation of the never-leaving goodness.

The second kind is of them that deal with matters philosophical: either moral,
as Tyrtaeus, Phocylides, and Cato; or natural, as Lucretius and Virgil's Georgics;
or astronomical, as Manilius and Pontanus; or historical, as Lucan:[5] which who

mislike, the fault is in their judgements quite out of taste, and not in the sweet food of sweetly uttered knowledge.

But because this second sort is wrapped within the fold of the proposed subject, and takes not the course of his own invention, whether they properly be poets or no let grammarians dispute, and go to the third, indeed right poets, of whom chiefly this question ariseth. Betwixt whom and these second is such a kind of difference as betwixt the meaner sort of painters, who counterfeit only such faces as are set before them, and the more excellent, who having no law but wit, bestow that in colours upon you which is fittest for the eye to see: as the constant though lamenting look of Lucretia, when she punished in herself another's fault; wherein he painteth not Lucretia whom he never saw, but painteth the outward beauty of such a virtue.[6] For these third be they which most properly do imitate to teach and delight, and to imitate borrow nothing of what is, hath been, or shall be; but range, only reined with learned discretion, into the divine consideration of what may be and should be. These be they that, as the first and most noble sort may justly be termed *vates*, so these are waited on in the excellentest languages and best understandings, with the foredescribed name of poets; for these indeed do merely make to imitate, and imitate both to delight and teach: and delight to move men to take that goodness in hand, which without delight they would fly as from a stranger, and teach, to make them know that goodness whereunto they are moved: which being the noblest scope to which ever any learning was directed, yet want there not idle tongues to bark at them.

These be subdivided into sundry more special denominations. The most notable be the Heroic, Lyric, Tragic, Comic, Satiric, Iambic, Elegiac, Pastoral, and certain others, some of these being termed according to the matter they deal with, some by the sorts of verses they liked best to write in; for indeed the greatest part of poets have apparelled their poetical inventions in that numbrous kind of writing which is called verse – indeed but apparelled, verse being but an ornament and no cause to Poetry, since there have been many most excellent poets that never versified, and now swarm many versifiers that need never answer to the name of poets. For Xenophon, who did imitate so excellently as to give us *effigiem justi imperii*, 'the portraiture of a just empire,' under the name of Cyrus (as Cicero saith of him), made therein an absolute heroical poem. So did Heliodorus in his sugared invention of that picture of love in Theagenes and Chariclea; and yet both these writ in prose: which I speak to show that it is not rhyming and versing that maketh a poet – no more than a long gown maketh an advocate, who though he pleaded in armour should be an advocate and no soldier. But it is that feigning notable images of virtues, vices, or what else, with that delightful teaching, which must be the right describing note to know a poet by, although indeed the senate of poets hath chosen verse as their fittest raiment, meaning, as in matter they passed all in all, so in manner to go beyond them: not speaking (table talk fashion or like men in a dream) words as they chanceably fall from the mouth, but peizing [weighing] each syllable of each word by just proportion according to the dignity of the subject.

Now therefore it shall not be amiss first to weigh this latter sort of Poetry by his works, and then by his parts, and if in neither of these anatomies [dissections] he be condemnable, I hope we shall obtain a more favourable sentence. This purifying of wit, this enriching of memory, enabling of judgment, and enlarging of conceit, which commonly we call learning, under what name soever it come forth, or to what immediate end soever it be directed, the final end is to lead and draw us to as high a perfection as our degenerate souls, made worse by their clayey lodgings, can be capable of. This, according to the inclination of the man, bred many formed impressions. For some that thought this felicity principally to be gotten by knowledge, and no knowledge to be so high and heavenly as acquaintance with the stars, gave themselves to Astronomy; others, persuading themselves to be demi-gods if they knew the causes of things, became natural and supernatural philosophers; some an admirable delight drew to Music; and some the certainty of demonstration to the Mathematics. But all, one and other, having this scope – to know, and by knowledge to lift up the mind from the dungeon of the body to the enjoying his own divine essence. But when by the balance of experience it was found that the astronomer looking to the stars might fall into a ditch, that the inquiring philosopher might be blind in himself, and the mathematician might draw forth a straight line with a crooked heart, then lo, did proof, the overruler of opinions, make manifest that all these are but serving sciences, which, as they have each a private end in themselves, so yet are they all directed to the highest end of the mistress-knowledge, by the Greeks called *architectonike*, which stands (as I think) in the knowledge of a man's self, in the ethic and politic consideration, with the end of well-doing and not of well-knowing only: even as the saddler's next end is to make a good saddle, but his farther end to serve a nobler faculty, which is horsemanship; so the horseman's to soldiery, and the soldier not only to have the skill, but to perform the practice of a soldier. So that, the ending end of all earthly learning being virtuous action, those skills, that most serve to bring forth that, have a most just title to be princes over all the rest.

Wherein if we can, show we the poet's nobleness, by setting him before his other competitors, among whom as principal challengers step forth the moral philosophers, whom, me thinketh, I see coming towards me with a sullen gravity, as though they could not abide vice by daylight, rudely clothed for to witness outwardly their contempt of outward things, with books in their hands against glory, whereto they set their names, sophistically speaking against subtlety, and angry with any man in whom they see the foul fault of anger. These men casting largesse as they go of definitions, divisions, and distinctions, with a scornful interrogative do soberly ask whether it be possible to find any path so ready to lead a man to virtue as that which teacheth what virtue is – and teacheth it not only by delivering forth his very being, his causes, and effects, but also by making known his enemy, vice, which must be destroyed, and his cumbersome servant, passion, which must be mastered, by showing the generalities that containeth it, and the specialities that are derived from it; lastly, by plain setting down, how it extendeth itself out of the limits of a man's own little world to the government of families, and maintaining of public societies.

The historian scarecely giveth leisure to the moralist to say so much, but that he, loaden with old mouse-eaten records, authorising himself (for the most part)

upon other histories, whose greatest authorities are built upon the notable foundation of hearsay; having much ado to accord differing writers and to pick truth
out of partiality; better acquainted with a thousand years ago than with the
present age, and yet better knowing how this world goeth than how his own wit
runneth; curious for antiquities and inquisitive of novelties; a wonder to young
folks and a tyrant in table talk, denieth, in a great chafe, that any man for teaching of virtue, and virtuous actions is comparable to him. 'I am *testis temporum,
lux veritatis, vita memoriæ, magistra vitæ, nuncia vetustatis.*[7] The philosopher', saith
he, 'teacheth a disputative virtue, but I do an active. His virtue is excellent in the
dangerless Academy of Plato, but mine showeth forth her honourable face in the
battles of Marathon, Pharsalia, Poitiers, and Agincourt.[8] He teacheth virtue by
certain abstract considerations, but I only bid you follow the footing of them
that have gone before you. Old-aged experience goeth beyond the fine-witted
philosopher, but I give the experience of many ages. Lastly, if he make the song-
book, I put the learner's hand to the lute; and if he be the guide, I am the light.'

Then would he allege you innumerable examples, conferring story by story,
how much the wisest senators and princes have been directed by the credit of
history, as Brutus, Alphonsus of Aragon,[9] and who not, if need be? At length the
long line of their disputation maketh a point in this, that the one giveth the
precept, and the other the example.

Now whom shall we find (since the question standeth for the highest form in
the school of learning) to be moderator? Truly, as me seemeth, the poet; and if
not a moderator, even the man that ought to carry the title from them both, and
much more from all other serving sciences. Therefore compare we the poet with
the historian and with the moral philosopher; and if he go beyond them both,
no other human skill can match him. For as for the divine, with all reverence it
is ever to be excepted, not only for having his scope as far beyond any of these
as eternity exceedeth a moment, but even for passing each of these in themselves.
And for the lawyer, though *jus* be the daughter of justice, and justice the chief
of virtues, yet because he seeketh to make men good rather *formidine poenae* [fear
of punishment] than *virtutis amore* [love of virtue];[10] or, to say righter, doth not
endeavour to make men good, but that their evil hurt not others; having no care,
so he be a good citizen, how bad a man he be: therefore as our wickedness maketh
him necessary, and necessity maketh him honourable, so is he not in the deepest
truth to stand in rank with these who all endeavour to take naughtiness away
and plant goodness even in the secretest cabinet of our souls. And these four are
all that any way deal in that consideration of men's manners, which being the
supreme knowledge, they that best breed it deserve the best commendation.

The philosopher therefore and the historian are they which would win the goal,
the one by precept, the other by example. But both, not having both, do both
halt. For the philosopher, setting down with thorny argument the bare rule, is
so hard of utterance and so misty to be conceived, that one that hath no other
guide but him shall wade in him till he be old before he shall find sufficient cause
to be honest. For his knowledge standeth so upon the abstract and general, that
happy is that man who may understand him, and more happy that can apply
what he doth understand. On the other side, the historian, wanting the precept,

is so tied, not to what should be but to what is, to the particular truth of things and not to the general reason of things, that his example draweth no necessary consequence, and therefore a less fruitful doctrine.

Now doth the peerless poet perform both: for whatsoever the philosopher saith should be done, he giveth a perfect picture of it in some one by whom he pre-supposeth it was done, so as he coupleth the general notion with the particular example. A perfect picture I say, for he yieldeth to the powers of the mind an image of that whereof the philosopher bestoweth but a wordish description, which doth neither strike, pierce, nor possess the sight of the soul so much as that other doth.

For as in outward things, to a man that had never seen an elephant or a rhi-noceros, who should tell him most exquisitely all their shapes, colour, bigness, and particular marks; or of a gorgeous palace, the architecture, with declaring the full beauties might well make the hearer able to repeat, as it were by rote, all he had heard, yet should never satisfy his inward conceits with being witness to itself of a true lively knowledge; but the same man, as soon as he might see those beasts well painted, or the house well in model, should straightways grow, without need of any description, to a judicial comprehending of them: so no doubt the philosopher with his learned definition – be it of virtue, vices, matters of public policy or private government – replenisheth the memory with many infallible grounds of wisdom, which, notwithstanding, lie dark before the imaginative and judging power, if they be not illuminated or figured forth by the speaking picture of poesy.

Tully taketh much pains, and many times not without poetical helps, to make us know the force love of our country hath in us. Let us but hear old Anchises speaking in the midst of Troy's flames, or see Ulysses in the fulness of all Calypso's delights bewail his absence from barren and beggarly Ithaca. Anger, the Stoics say, was a short madness: let but Sophocles bring you Ajax on a stage, killing and whipping sheep and oxen, thinking them the army of Greeks, with their chief-tains Agamemnon and Menelaus, and tell me if you have not a more familiar insight into anger than finding in the schoolmen his genus and difference.

NOTES

1   A reference to the literary tradition of the declining four ages of man: from golden down through silver, brass and iron, in which Sidney lived.

2   Theagenes, Thessalian hero in a Greek prose romance, *Aethiopica*, by the fourth-century bishop Heliodorus. It was one of Sidney's models for *Arcadia*; Pylades was a devoted friend of Orestes and assisted him in avenging the murder of his father; Orlando (the French Roland), hero of Ariosto's epic poem *Orlando Furioso* (1516); Cyrus the Great (559–529 BCE), founder of the Persian empire; humanist authors held Aeneas to be the perfection of manhood.

3   Xenophon's *Cyropaedia* was considered by sixteenth-century readers to constitute a manual for kings.

4   Emanuel Tremellius (1510–80) and Franciscus Junius the Elder (1545–1602) worked on a Protestant Latin translation of the Bible from the original languages. Here Sidney is referring to the Preface of Part 3, the Poetic Books, of their *Testamenti Veteris Biblia Sacra* of 1575–9.

5   These references are all to poets whose works would have been available in the sixteenth
      century. Tyrtaeus of Aphidnae (*fl.* 655–668 BCE) inspired the Spartans to victory through
      his warsongs; Phocylides of Miletus (*fl.* 560 BCE) was a gnomic poet; The *Distichs* of
      Dionysius Cato (fourth century BCE) was used as a school text from the Middle Ages
      and was used to teach both syntax and morality; Titus Lucretius Carus (*c.*99–55 BCE)
      was a Roman poet; Virgil's *Georgics* (*Art of Husbandry*) were admired for their know-
      ledge of agriculture; Manilius was a Roman poet who wrote an astronomical poem in
      five books; Pontanus is Giovanni Pontano (1426–1503), who wrote *Urania*, a five-book
      poem on the stars. He was viceroy to Ferdinand I of Naples and tutor to his son; Marcus
      Annaeus Lucanus (Lucan, 39–65), Roman poet and author of an unfinished epic,
      Pharsalia, on the civil wars between Pompey and Gaius Julius Caesar.

6   The story of Lucretia. Paintings by Paolo Veronese and Albrecht Dürer of Lucretia fit
      with Sidney's description.

7   'History is indeed the witness of the ages, the light of truth, the life of memory, the
      governess of life, the herald of antiquity', Cicero, *De Oratore* II, IX, 36.

8   Marathon (490 BCE), where the Athenians beat the Persians; Pharsalia (48 BCE) where
      Gaius Julius Caesar defeated Pompey; Poitiers (1356) and Agincourt (1415), both English
      victories in the Hundred Years War.

9   Marcus Junius Brutus (85–42 BCE), Roman politician. He sided with Pompey before the
      battle of Pharsalia but then submitted to Caesar. He was involved in the plot to kill
      Caesar; Alphonsus is Alphonso V of Aragon and I of Naples and Sicily (1416–58).

10   Horace, *Epistles*, I, xvi, 52–3.

53 George Puttenham *The Arte of Poesie* (1589)

George Puttenham (1529–90/1) was educated at Christ's College, Cambridge and
the Middle Temple. He wrote court poems and a defence of the execution of Mary
Queen of Scots. He was suspected of being a Catholic or an atheist and was
accused of plotting to assassinate Edmund Grindal, archbishop of Canterbury
(1519–83). Puttenham's *Arte* is in many ways a typical example of Elizabethan
treatises on poetry. It was published in 1589.

Source: *The Arte of Poesie, Elizabethan Critical Essays*, ed. G. G. Smith, Oxford
University Press, Oxford, 1937, vol. I (2 vols), pp. 3–9

WHAT A POET AND POESIE IS, AND WHO MAY BE WORTHILY SAYD THE MOST
EXCELLENT POET OF OUR TIME

A poet is as much to say as a maker. And our English name well conformes with
the Greeke word, for of ποιεῖν, to make, they call a maker *Poeta*. Such as (by
way of resemblance and reuerently) we may say of God; who without any trauell
to his diuine imagination made all the world of nought, nor also by any paterne
or mould, as the Platonicks with their Idees do phantastically suppose.[1] Euen so
the very Poet makes and contriues out of his owne braine both the verse and
matter of his poeme, and not by any foreine copie or example, as doth the translator, who therefore may well be sayd a versifier, but not a Poet. The premises
considered, it giueth to the name and profession no smal dignitie and prehemi-
nence, aboue all other artificers, Scientificke or Mechanicall. And neuerthelesse,
without any repugnancie at all, a Poet may in some sort be said a follower or

imitator, because he can expresse the true and liuely of euery thing is set before him, and which he taketh in hand to describe: and so in that respect is both a maker and a counterfaitor: and Poesie an art not only of making, but also of imitation. And this science in his perfection can not grow but by some diuine instinct – the Platonicks call it *furor*;[2] or by excellencie of nature and complexion; or by great subtiltie of the spirits & wit; or by much experience and obseruation of the world, and course of kinde; or, peraduenture, by all or most part of them. Otherwise, how was it possible that *Homer*, being but a poore priuate man, and, as some say, in his later age blind, should so exactly set foorth and describe, as if he had bene a most excellent Captaine or Generall, the order and array of battles, the conduct of whole armies, the sieges and assaults of cities and townes? or, as some great Princes maiordome and perfect Surueyour in Court, the order, sumptuousnesse, and magnificence of royal bankets, feasts, weddings, and enteruewes? or, as a Polititian very prudent and much inured with the priuat and publique affaires, so grauely examine the lawes and ordinances Ciuill, or so profoundly discourse in matters of estate and formes of all politique regiment? Finally, how could he so naturally paint out the speeches, countenance, and maners of Princely persons and priuate, to wit, the wrath of *Achilles*, the magnanimitie of *Agamemnon*, the prudence of *Menelaus*, the prowesse of *Hector*, the maiestie of king *Priamus*, the grauitie of *Nestor*, the pollicies and eloquence of *Vlysses*, the calamities of the distressed *Queenes*, and valiance of all the Captaines and aduenturous knights in those lamentable warres of Troy?[3] It is therefore of Poets thus to be conceiued, that if they be able to deuise and make all these things of them selues, without any subject of veritie, that they be (by maner of speech) as creating gods. If they do it by instinct diuine or naturall, then surely much fauoured from aboue; if by their experience, then no doubt very wise men; if by any president or paterne layd before them, then truly the most excellent imitators & counterfaitors of all others. But you (Madame) my most Honored and Gracious,[4] if I should seeme to offer you this my deuise for a discipline and not a delight, I might well be reputed of all others the most arrogant and iniurious, your selfe being alreadie, of any that I know in our time, the most excellent Poet; forsooth by your Princely purse, fauours, and countenance, making in maner what ye list, the poore man rich, the lewd well learned, the coward couragious, and vile both noble and valiant: then for imitation no lesse, your person as a most cunning counterfaitor liuely representing *Venus* in countenance, in life *Diana*, *Pallas* for gouernement, and *Iuno* in all honour and regall magnificence.[5]

CHAP. II.

THAT THERE MAY BE AN ART OF OUR ENGLISH POESIE, ASWELL AS THERE IS OF THE LATINE AND GREEKE.

Then as there was no art in the world till by experience found out, so if Poesie be now an Art, & of al antiquitie hath bene among the Greeks and Latines, & yet were none vntill by studious persons fashioned and reduced into a method of rules and precepts, then no doubt may there be the like with vs. And if th'art of Poesie be but a skill appertaining to vtterance, why may not the same be with

vs aswel as with them, our language being no lesse copious, pithie, and signifi-
catiue then theirs, our conceipts the same, and our wits no lesse apt to deuise
and imitate then theirs were? If againe Art be but a certaine order of rules prescribed by reason, and gathered by experience, why should not Poesie be a vulgar
Art with vs aswell as with the Greeks and Latines, our language admitting no
fewer rules and nice diuersities then theirs? but peraduenture mo[r]e by a peculiar, which our speech hath in many things differing from theirs; and yet, in the
generall points of that Art, allowed to go in common with them: so as if one
point perchance, which is their feete whereupon their measures stand, and in
deede is all the beautie of their Poesie, and which feete we haue not, nor as yet
neuer went about to frame (the nature of our language and wordes not per-
mitting it),[6] we haue in stead thereof twentie other curious points in that skill
more then they euer had, by reason of our rime and tunable concords or sim-
phonie, which they neuer obserued. Poesie therefore may be an Art in our vulgar,
and that verie methodicall and commendable.

CHAP. III.
HOW POETS WERE THE FIRST PRIESTS, THE FIRST PROPHETS, THE FIRST
LEGISLATORS AND POLITITIANS IN THE WORLD.

The profession and vse of Poesie is most ancient from the beginning, and not,
as manie erroniously suppose, after, but before, any ciuil society was among men.
For it is written that Poesie was th'originall cause and occasion of their first assemblies, when before the people remained in the woods and mountains, vagarant
and dispersed like the wild beasts, lawlesse and naked, or verie ill clad, and of all
good and necessarie prouision for harbour or sustenance vtterly vnfurnished, so
as they litle diffred for their maner of life from the very brute beasts of the field.
Whereupon it is fayned that *Amphion* and *Orpheus*, two Poets of the first ages,
one of them, to wit *Amphion*, builded vp cities, and reared walles with the stones
that came in heapes to the sound of his harpe, figuring thereby the mollifying of
hard and stonie hearts by his sweete and eloquent perswasion. And *Orpheus*
assembled the wilde beasts to come in heards to harken to his musicke, and by
that meanes made them tame, implying thereby, how by his discreete and whol-
some lesons vttered in harmonie and with melodious instruments he brought the
rude and sauage people to a more ciuill and orderly life, nothing, as it seemeth,
more preuailing or fit to redresse and edifie the cruell and sturdie courage of man
then it.[7] And as these two Poets, and *Linus* before them, and *Museus* also and
Hesiodus[8] in Greece and Archadia, so by all likelihood had mo Poets done in
other places and in other ages before them, though there be no remembrance left
of them, by reason of the Recordes by some accident of time perished and failing.
Poets therfore are of great antiquitie. Then forasmuch as they were the first that
entended to the obseruation of nature and her works, and specially of the Celestiall courses, by reason of the continuall motion of the heauens, searching after
the first mouer, and from thence by degrees comming to know and consider of
the substances separate & abstract, which we call the diuine intelligences or good
Angels (*Demones*), they were the first that instituted sacrifices of placation, with

inuocations and worship to them, as to Gods; and inuented and stablished all
the rest of the obseruances and ceremonies of religion, and so were the first Priests
and ministers of the holy misteries. And because for the better execution of that
high charge and function it behoued them to liue chast, and in all holines of life,
and in continuall studie and contemplation, they came by instinct diuine, and
by deepe meditation, and much abstinence (the same assubtiling and refining
their spirits) to be made apt to receaue visions, both waking and sleeping, which
made them vtter prophesies and foretell things to come. So also were they the
first Prophetes or seears, *Videntes*, for so the Scripture tearmeth them in Latine
after the Hebrue word, and all the oracles and answers of the gods were giuen in
meeter or verse, and published to the people by their direction. And for that they
were aged and graue men, and of much wisedome and experience in th'affaires
of the world, they were the first lawmakers to the people, and the first polititiens,
deuising all expedient meanes for th'establishment of Common wealth, to hold
and containe the people in order and duety by force and vertue of good and
wholesome lawes, made for the preseruation of the publique peace and tran-
quillitie: the same peraduenture not purposely intended, but greatly furthered by
the aw of their gods and such scruple of conscience as the terrors of their late
inuented religion had led them into.

CHAP. IV.
HOW POETS WERE THE FIRST PHILOSOPHERS, THE FIRST ASTRONOMERS AND
HISTORIOGRAPHERS AND ORATOURS AND MUSITIENS OF THE WORLD.

Vtterance also and language is giuen by nature to man for perswasion of others
and aide of them selues, I meane the first abilite to speake. For speech it selfe is
artificiall and made by man, and the more pleasing it is, the more it preuaileth
to such purpose as it is intended for: but speech by meeter is a kind of vtterance
more cleanly couched and more delicate to the eare then prose is, because it is
more currant and slipper vpon the tongue, and withal tunable and melodious,
as a kind of Musicke, and therfore may be tearmed a musicall speech or vtterance, which cannot but please the hearer very well. Another cause is, for that is
briefer & more compendious, and easier to beare away and be retained in
memorie, then that which is contained in multitude of words and full of tedious
ambage and long periods. It is beside a maner of vtterance more eloquent and
rethoricall then the ordinarie prose which we vse in our daily talke, because it is
decked and set out with all maner of fresh colours and figures, which maketh
that it sooner inuegleth the judgement of man, and carieth his opinion this way
and that, whither soeuer the heart by impression of the eare shalbe most affec-
tionatly bent and directed. The vtterance in prose is not of so great efficacie,
because not only it is dayly vsed, and by that occasion the eare is ouerglutted
with it, but is also not so voluble and slipper vpon the tong, being wide and lose,
and nothing numerous, nor contriued into measures and sounded with so gallant
and harmonical accents, nor, in fine, alowed that figuratiue conueyance nor so
great licence in choise of words and phrases as meeter is. So as the Poets were
also from the beginning the best perswaders, and their eloquence the first

Rethoricke of the world, euen so it became that the high mysteries of the gods should be reuealed & taught by a maner of vtterance and language of extraordinarie phrase, and briefe and compendious, and aboue al others sweet and ciuill as the Metricall is. The same also was meetest to register the liues and noble gests of Princes, and of the great Monarkes of the world, and all other the memorable accidents of time: so as the Poet was also the first historiographer. Then forasmuch as they were the first obseruers of all naturall causes & effects in the things generable and corruptible, and from thence mounted vp to search after the celestiall courses and influences, & yet penetrated further to know the diuine essences and substances separate, as is sayd before, they were the first Astronomers and Philosophists and Metaphisicks. Finally, because they did altogether endeuor them selues to reduce the life of man to a certaine method of good maners, and made the first differences betweene vertue and vice, and then tempered all these knowledges and skilles with the exercise of a delectable Musicke by melodious instruments, which withall serued them to delight their hearers, & to call the people together by admiration to a plausible and vertuous conuersation, therefore were they the first Philosophers Ethick, & the first artificial Musiciens of the world. [. . .]

NOTES

1   An allusion to the Platonic notion of an immaterial world of forms.
2   Fury, or inspiration.
3   Puttenham here summarises incidents from Homer's *Iliad*.
4   In this sentence, Puttenham addresses Queen Elizabeth I (1558–1603).
5   Venus is the goddess of love; Diana the goddess of chastity; Pallas the goddess of wisdom. Juno is the queen of the goddesses and the wife of Jupiter.
6   In this paragraph, Puttenham patriotically asserts the value of English poetry in comparison with the ancient poetry of the Greeks and Romans. He also recognises the different metrical qualities of English. In comparison, English verse does not have 'feete'. That is, English verse is accentual rather than quantitative – it observes the stress of syllables rather than their length as sounds.
7   Amphion and Orpheus are mythical figures whose poetry had the powers Puttenham describes here.
8   Linus and Museus were also mythical figures; Hesiod was an ancient Greek pastoral and religious poet.

54 Johannes de Witt **Remarkes on the London theatres (1596?)**

Johannes de Witt was a Dutch traveller who visited London, probably in 1596. He wrote a series of observations in Latin. His former fellow-student in Utrecht, Aernout (or Arend) van Buchel copied an excerpt from the *Observationes Londinenses* into his commonplace book where it is preserved. In this extract de Witt describes four London theatres, the Theatre and the Curtain north of the river Thames and the Rose and the Swan on Bankside to the south.

Source: *Shakespeare's Globe Rebuilt* ed. J. R. Mulryne and M. Shewring, Cambridge University Press in Association with Mulryne and Shewring Ltd., Cambridge, 1997, Appendix C, p. 189

There are four amphitheatres in London of notable beauty which from their different signs are given different names. In these each day a different play is performed for the people. The two more splendid of them are situated across the Thames to the south, and from the signs hanging before them are called the Rose and the Swan. There are two others outside the city to the north, on the road going through the Bishop's gate, called in the vernacular 'Biscopgat'. There is also a fifth, but of a different [use?] and structure, being given over to animal contests, in which many bears, bulls and dogs of huge size are reared in various dens and cages and kept for fighting, so providing a most entertaining spectacle for the people. The grandest and largest of all the theatres, however, is that whose sign is the Swan (in the vernacular 'the Swan theatre'), which in fact accommodates three thousand people in its seats. It is built of compacted flint stones (of which there is a huge supply in Britain) and furnished with wooden columns which are so painted as to deceive even the most prying. I have drawn it above since it appears to imitate in its shape the form of a Roman structure [theatre].

55 Thomas Platter **Visits to London Theatres (1599)**

Thomas Platter was a young Swiss, who visited London from 18 September to 20 October 1599. The Globe theatre was first erected in 1599 and Platter visited it to see Shakespeare's *Julius Caesar*. He gives a brief description of the performance, but provides interesting details of the Globe itself and two other theatres, one of which seems to have been the Curtain.

Source: *Shakespeare's Globe Rebuilt* ed. J. R. Mulryne and M. Shewring, Cambridge University Press in Association with Mulryne and Shewring Ltd., Cambridge, 1997 Appendix C, pp. 190–1

On the 21st of September, after the mid-day meal, about two o'clock, I and my company went over the water [i.e. across the Thames] and saw in the house with the thatched roof the tragedy of the first Emperor Julius Caesar quite aptly performed. At the end of the play according to their custom they danced quite exceedingly finely, two got up in men's clothing and two in women's [dancing] wonderfully together.

At another time, not far from our inn in the suburbs, at Bishopsgate according to my memory, again after lunch, I saw a play where they presented different nations with which each time an Englishman struggled over a young woman, and overcame them all, with the exception of the German who won the girl in a struggle, sat down beside her, and drank himself tipsy with his servant, so that the two were both drunk, and the servant threw a shoe at his master's head, and both fell asleep. In the meantime the Englishman crept into the tent, and carried off the German's prize, and thus outwitted the German in turn. In conclusion they danced in English and Irish fashion quite skilfully. And so every day at two o'clock in the afternoon in the city of London sometimes two sometimes three plays are given in different places, which compete with each other and those which perform best have the largest number of listeners. The [playing] places are so constructed that [the actors] play on a raised scaffold, and everyone can see everything. However there are different areas and galleries where one can sit more comfortably and better, and where one accordingly pays more. Thus whoever wants to stand below pays only one English penny, but if he wishes to sit, he enters through another door where he gives a further penny, but if he wants to sit in the most comfortable place on a cushion, where he will not only see everything but also be seen, he gives at another door a further English penny. And during each play things to eat and drink are brought round among the people, of which one may partake for whatever one cares to pay.

The actors are dressed in a very expensive and splendid fashion, since it is the custom in England when notable lords or knights die they bequeath and leave their servants almost the finest of their clothes which, because it is not fitting for them to wear such clothes, they offer [them] for purchase to the actors for a small sum of money.

How much time they can happily spend each day at the play, everyone knows who has seen them act or perform.

56 Christopher Marlowe **Extracts from *The Jew of Malta* (*c*.1589–92)**

These four extracts are from the popular play, *The Jew of Malta* by Christopher Marlowe (1564–93), one of the major influences on *The Merchant of Venice*. Marlowe, a shoemaker's son, wrote a number of plays including *Tamburlaine*, *Dr Faustus* and *Edward II*. He was stabbed to death in 1593 in a tavern brawl.

Extract i is the Prologue, in which Machiavel – Marlowe's demonic caricature of Machiavelli – presents the play's anti-hero Barabas as one of his 'climbing followers'.

Extract ii is a soliloquy from Act 1 Scene 1 in which Barabas outlines his devotion to material wealth and explains the success of Jews as venture capitalists.

Extract iii is part of Barabas's dialogue with his newly purchased Turkish slave Ithamore from Act 2 Scene 3: here Barabas itemises the villainies he claims to have performed against Christians.

Extract iv is a longer excerpt from Act 1 Scene 2, in which the Governor of Cyprus, Ferneze, levies the Turkish tribute money from the Jewish community.

Here we see Barabas isolated both from the Christian majority and his fellow Jews as he opposes this policy and apparently loses his wealth.

Source: *The Jew of Malta*, ed. D. Bevington, Manchester University Press, Manchester, Student Revels Editions, 1997, pp. 17–19, 24–6, 28–36, 57–8

Extract i) Prologue

[*Enter*] MACHIAVEL.

Machiavel. Albeit the world think Machiavel is dead,
    Yet was his soul but flown beyond the Alps,
    And, now the Guise is dead, is come from France
    To view this land and frolic with his friends.
    To some perhaps my name is odious,   5
    But such as love me guard me from their tongues;
    And let them know that I am Machiavel,
    And weigh not men, and therefore not men's words.
    Admired I am of those that hate me most.
    Though some speak openly against my books,   10
    Yet will they read me and thereby attain
    To Peter's chair, and, when they cast me off,
    Are poisoned by my climbing followers.
    I count religion but a childish toy,
    And hold there is no sin but ignorance.   15
    Birds of the air will tell of murders past?
    I am ashamed to hear such fooleries!
    Many will talk of title to a crown;
    What right had Caesar to the empery?
    Might first made kings, and laws were then most sure   20

2. *beyond the Alps*] i.e. from Italy into France and thence to England.

3. *the Guise*] Henry, third Duke of Guise, was assassinated on 23 December 1588 by order of the French king Henry III, an event dramatized by Marlowe himself in scene xxi of *The Massacre at Paris*. Guise was a bitter enemy of the French Protestants, or Huguenots, who regarded him as evil and ambitious, since he was the chief architect of the slaughter of many Huguenots at the Massacre of St Bartholomew in 1572.

4. *this land*] England (even though the play is set in Malta).

6.] 'But those who are my true followers refrain from naming me openly (lest those who hate me be alarmed).'

7. *them*] i.e. my true followers; or, my detractors.

8. *weigh not*] attach no value to, am not impressed by. Machiavel has no respect for conventional pieties.

12. *Peter's chair*] i.e. the papacy. Machiavel boasts that clerics who aspire to the papacy secretly use his methods of intrigue, and, when they then adopt a more pious pose as pope, are overthrown by other closet Machiavellians.

15. *ignorance*] either (1) ignorance of the rules for worldly success, or (2) the kind of superstition jeered at in ll. 16–17.

19. *empery*] empire, rule, dominion.

When like the Draco's they were writ in blood.
Hence comes it that a strong-built citadel
Commands much more than letters can import –
Which maxima had Phalaris observed,
He'd never bellowed in a brazen bull   25
Of great ones' envy. O' the poor petty wights
Let me be envied and not pitièd!
But whither am I bound? I come not, I,
To read a lecture here in Britany,
But to present the tragedy of a Jew,   30
Who smiles to see how full his bags are crammed,
Which money was not got without my means.
I crave but this: grace him as he deserves,
And let him not be entertained the worse
Because he favours me.   35

                                                       [*Exit.*]

Extract ii) Barabas' Soliloquy

Barabas. Thus trolls our fortune in by land and sea,
        And thus are we on every side enriched.
        These are the blessings promised to the Jews,
        And herein was old Abram's happiness.   105

21. *Draco*] an Athenian legislator who received in 621 BCE special authority to codify and promulgate laws for the city, replacing private vengeance with a code that became proverbial for its severity.

23. *letters*] erudition.

24. *maxima*] maxim.

Phalaris] tyrant of Acragas in Sicily in the sixth century BCE who is reported to have roasted his victims in a brazen bull invented by Perillus, and to have put Perillus himself to death as the bull's first victim. Machiavel appears to follow an account in Ovid's *Ibis* describing how Phalaris too died in the bull. Phalaris was allowed by Erasmus to have one redeeming feature, his love of letters; to Machiavel, this is his fatal weakness.

26. *Of . . . envy*] Machiavel may refer to an uprising among the aristocrats and people of Agrigentum that led to Phalaris' downfall, or else conflates the stories of Phalaris and Perillus in such a way as to reflect Perillus' outcry against his fate.

petty wights] commoners of no importance. Machiavel would rather be envied for his cunning than pitied as a loser, just as he thinks Phalaris would have been better off tending to his strong citadel rather than striving for a humane reputation as a man of letters.

28. *whither . . . bound*] i.e. 'Where am I going?' Machiavel has let his tongue run away with him.

29. *read*] give.

Britany] Britain; a form widely used in Elizabethan English.

33. *grace*] show favour to.

34. *entertained*] received, accepted.

35. *favours me*] (1) takes my part; (2) resembles me.

102. *trolls*] comes 'rolling in' abundantly.

105. *old Abram's happiness*] i.e. the covenant made between God and Abraham, giving Canaan to Abraham and his heirs for ever (Genesis, 15.13–21, 17.1–22; see also Exodus, 6.1–8, and Galatians, 3.16).

What more may heaven do for earthly men
Than thus to pour out plenty in their laps,
Ripping the bowels of the earth for them,
Making the sea their servant and the winds
To drive their substance with successful blasts?   110
Who hateth me but for my happiness?
Or who is honoured now but for his wealth?
Rather had I, a Jew, be hated thus
Than pitied in a Christian poverty.
For I can see no fruits in all their faith   115
But malice, falsehood, and excessive pride,
Which methinks fits not their profession.
Haply some hapless man hath conscience,
And for his conscience lives in beggary.
They say we are a scattered nation;   120
I cannot tell, but we have scambled up
More wealth by far than those that brag of faith.
There's Kirriah Jairim, the great Jew of Greece,
Obed in Bairseth, Nones in Portugal,
Myself in Malta, some in Italy,   125
Many in France, and wealthy every one –
Ay, wealthier far than any Christian.
I must confess we come not to be kings.
That's not our fault. Alas, our number's few,
And crowns come either by succession   130
Or urged by force; and nothing violent,
Oft have I heard tell, can be permanent.
Give us a peaceful rule; make Christians kings,
That thirst so much for principality.
I have no charge, nor many children,   135

110.] 'to propel their richly laden merchant ships with propitious winds'.

111. *happiness*] good fortune, prosperity.

117. *profession*] professed religious faith. (Pronounced in four syllables.)

118. *hapless*] unfortunate (playing on *Haply*, perchance). The man who chooses to live by his conscience, says Barabas, will live in beggary.

121. *I cannot tell*] I cannot say as to that.

scambled up] scraped together, struggled indecorously or rapaciously in order to amass wealth.

123. *Kirriah Jairim*] a city name ('Kiraith-iearim'), cited in Joshua, 15.9 and 60, and Judges, 18.12, perhaps mistakenly given to a person in 1 Chronicles, 2.50–3, Geneva version.

124. *Obed*] a not uncommon biblical name (1 Chronicles, 2.12; Ruth, 4.17–22).

Bairseth] not identified; possibly a distortion of a biblical name such as Baaseiah (1 Chronicles, 6.40).

Nones] Some figures bearing similar names were Portuguese maranos, or Christian converts, living in Constantinople and also in London, in the mid sixteenth century.

128. *come not to be*] do not succeed in becoming.

134. *principality*] sovereignty, supreme authority.

135. *charge*] financial burden.

But one sole daughter, whom I hold as dear
As Agamemnon did his Iphigen;
And all I have is hers. But who comes here?

Extract iii) Barabas' dialogue

Ithamore. Oh, brave, master, I worship your nose for this!
Barabas. As for myself, I walk abroad o' nights,
 And kill sick people groaning under walls;
 Sometimes I go about and poison wells;
 And now and then, to cherish Christian thieves,   180
 I am content to lose some of my crowns,
 That I may, walking in my gallery,
 See' em go pinioned along by my door.
 Being young, I studied physic, and began
 To practise first upon the Italian;   185
 There I enriched the priests with burials,
 And always kept the sexton's arms in ure
 With digging graves and ringing dead men's knells;
 And after that was I an engineer,
 And in the wars 'twixt France and Germany,   190
 Under pretence of helping Charles the Fifth,
 Slew friend and enemy with my stratagems.
 Then after that was I an usurer,
 And with extorting, cozening, forfeiting,
 And tricks belonging unto brokery,   195
 I filled the jails with bankrupts in a year,

137. *Agamemnon*] a dramatic irony, since Agamemnon, the leader of the Greek army in the Trojan war, was obliged to appease the goddess Artemis by sacrificing his daughter Iphigenia to her.

176. *nose*] The epithet here suggests that the actor playing Barabas wore a large false nose; see III.iii.10 and IV.i.25. On the other hand, James Shapiro, in *Shakespeare and the Jews* (1995), warns against too easy assumptions of such visual labelling of Jewish figures on the Elizabethan stage.

180–3.] Presumably, Barabas uses some of his money as a trap for thieves, so that they will be apprehended and executed.

182. *gallery*] balcony.

183. *pinioned*] with arms tied together or shackled.

184. *Being young*] when I was a young man.

physic] medicine.

185. *the Italian*] Italians.

187. *ure*] use, practice.

189. *engineer*] constructor of military works and devices.

191. *Charles the Fifth*] Habsburg emperor of Spain and Germany.

194. *cozening*] cheating.

forfeiting] subjecting a borrower to forfeiture or confiscation because of that person's inability to repay.

195. *brokery*] trafficking as a broker.

And with young orphans planted hospitals,
And every moon made some or other mad,
And now and then one hang himself for grief,
Pinning upon his breast a long great scroll   200
How I with interest tormented him.
But mark how I am blest for plaguing them:
I have as much coin as will buy the town!

Extract iv) Barabas' Trial Scene

Enter [FERNEZE,] *Governor of Malta*, Knights [, *and* Officers,]
met by Bashaws *of the Turk*, [*and*] CALYMATH.

Ferneze. Now, bashaws, what demand you at our hands?
First Bashaw.
        Know, Knights of Malta, that we came from Rhodes,
        From Cyprus, Candy, and those other isles
        That lie betwixt the Mediterranean seas –
Ferneze. What's Cyprus, Candy, and those other isles   5
        To us, or Malta? What at our hands demand ye?
Calymath. The ten years' tribute that remains unpaid.
Ferneze. Alas, my lord, the sum is over-great.
        I hope your highness will consider us.
Calymath. I wish, grave governor, 'twere in my power   10
        To favour you, but 'tis my father's cause,
        Wherein I may not – nay, I dare not – dally.
Ferneze. Then give us leave, great Selim Calymath.
                            [*Ferneze consults with his Knights.*]
Calymath. [*To his Bashaws*]
        Stand all aside, and let the knights determine,
        And send to keep our galleys under sail,   15
        For happily we shall not tarry here. –
        Now, governor, how are you resolved?

197.] 'and filled the orphanages'.
198. *moon*] month. (The moon was widely supposed to influence the insane.)
199. *one hang*] caused someone to hang.
201. *with interest*] with threats of foreclosure for interest payment due.
0.2. *Bashaws*] pashas, Turkish aristocrats and military leaders.
2. *Knights of Malta*] The Knights of St John of Jerusalem were stationed on Malta beginning in 1530.
9. *consider*] be considerate towards.
10. *grave*] a common form of respectful address.
11. *my father's*] i.e. Emperor of Turkey's; see l. 39. Selim succeeded his father, Suleman the
Magnificent, in 1566.
13. *give us leave*] 'A polite request for privacy for consultation' (Bennett).
15. *send*] send word.
16. *happily*] with good luck, if things go well.
17. *how . . . resolved?*] what have you decided?

Ferneze. Thus: since your hard conditions are such
            That you will needs have ten years' tribute past,
            We may have time to make collection   20
            Amongst the inhabitants of Malta for 't.
First Bashaw. That's more than is in our commission.
Calymath. What, Callapine, a little courtesy!
            Let's know their time; perhaps it is not long,
            And 'tis more kingly to obtain by peace   25
            Than to enforce conditions by constraint. –
            What respite ask you, governor?
Ferneze.   But a month.
Calymath. We grant a month, but see you keep your promise.
            Now launch our galleys back again to sea,
            Where we'll attend the respite you have ta'en,   30
            And for the money send our messenger.
            Farewell, great governor and brave knights of Malta.
Ferneze. And all good fortune wait on Calymath.
                        Exeunt [CALYMATH *and* Bashaws].
            Go one and call those Jews of Malta hither.
            Were they not summoned to appear today?   35
First Officer. They were, my lord, and here they come.

                    Enter BARABAS *and three* Jews.

First Knight. Have you determined what to say to them?
Ferneze. Yes, give me leave; and Hebrews, now come near.
            From the Emperor of Turkey is arrived
            Great Selim Calymath, his highness' son,   40
            To levy of us ten years' tribute past.
            Now then, here know that it concerneth us –
Barabas. Then, good my lord, to keep your quiet still,
            Your lordship shall do well to let them have it.
Ferneze. Soft, Barabas, there's more longs to 't than so.   45
            To what this ten years' tribute will amount,
            That we have cast, but cannot compass it
            By reason of the wars, that robbed our store;
            And therefore are we to request your aid.

    20. *We*] i.e. we ask that we.
    22. *commission*] instructions, authority as ambassadors.
    23. *Callapine*] the name, evidently, of the First Bashaw in this scene and perhaps of the
Bashaw in III.v.
    24. *their time*] what time they require.
    30. *attend*] await.
    43. *quiet*] peaceful state of affairs.
    still] always, continually.
    45. *there's . . . so*] there's more to it than that. (*Longs* = belongs, pertains.)
    47. *cast*] calculated.
    compass] encompass, achieve.

Barabas. Alas, my lord, we are no soldiers;   50
        And what's our aid against so great a prince?
First Knight. Tut, Jew, we know thou art no soldier;
        Thou art a merchant, and a moneyed man,
        And 'tis thy money, Barabas, we seek.
Barabas. How, my lord, my money?
Ferneze.   Thine and the rest.   55
        For, to be short, amongst you 't must be had.
First Jew. Alas, my lord, the most of us are poor!
Ferneze. Then let the rich increase your portions.
Barabas. Are strangers with your tribute to be taxed?
Second Knight.
        Have strangers leave with us to get their wealth?   60
        Then let them with us contribute.
Barabas. How, equally?
Ferneze.   No, Jew, like infidels.
        For through our sufferance of your hateful lives,
        Who stand accursèd in the sight of heaven,
        These taxes and afflictions are befall'n,   65
        And therefore thus we are determinèd:
        Read there the articles of our decrees.
Officer. (*Reads.*) 'First, the tribute-money of the Turks shall all be levied
        amongst the Jews, and each of them to pay one-half of his
        estate.'   70
Barabas. How, half his estate? [*Aside*] *I hope you mean not mine.*
Ferneze. Read on.
Officer. (*Reads.*) 'Secondly, he that denies to pay shall straight become a
        Christian.'
Barabas. How, a Christian? [*Aside*] *H'm, what's here to do?*   75
Officer. (*Reads.*) 'Lastly, he that denies this shall absolutely lose all he has.'
All three Jews. O, my lord, we will give half!
Barabas. O earth-mettled villains, and no Hebrews born!
        And will you basely thus submit yourselves   80
        To leave your goods to their arbitrament?
Ferneze. Why, Barabas, wilt thou be christened?

50–1.] Barabas, in pretended innocence, supposes that he and his fellow Jews are being asked
to take up arms against the Turks.

58. *increase your portions*] give extra money to bring the overall contributions to the required
amount.

59. *strangers*] aliens, foreigners.

64.] The Jews were held responsible for the crucifixion of Christ.

66. *are determinèd*] have resolved.

73. *denies*] refuses.
straight] immediately.

75. *what's . . . do*] what shall I do about this?

79. *earth-mettled*] having a dull or phlegmatic temperament.

81. *arbitrament*] decision, control.

Barabas. No governor, I will be no convertite.

Ferneze. Then pay thy half.

Barabas. Why, know you what you did by this device?   85
　　　　Half of my substance is a city's wealth.
　　　　Governor, it was not got so easily;
　　　　Nor will I part so slightly therewithal.

Ferneze. Sir, half is the penalty of our decree;
　　　　Either pay that or we will seize on all.   90

Barabas. Corpo di Dio! Stay, you shall have half;
　　　　Let me be used but as my brethren are.

Ferneze. No, Jew, thou hast denied the articles,
　　　　And now it cannot be recalled.

　　　　　　　　　[*Exeunt* Officers, *on a sign from* FERNEZE.]

Barabas. Will you then steal my goods?   95
　　　　Is theft the ground of your religion?

Ferneze. No, Jew, we take particularly thine
　　　　To save the ruin of a multitude;
　　　　And better one want for a common good
　　　　Than many perish for a private man.   100
　　　　Yet, Barabas, we will not banish thee,
　　　　But here in Malta, where thou got'st thy wealth,
　　　　Live still; and if thou canst, get more.

Barabas. Christians, what or how can I multiply?
　　　　Of naught is nothing made.   105

First Knight.
　　　　From naught at first thou camest to little wealth,
　　　　From little unto more, from more to most.
　　　　If your first curse fall heavy on thy head,
　　　　And make thee poor and scorned of all the world,
　　　　'Tis not our fault, but thy inherent sin.   110

Barabas. What? Bring you scripture to confirm your wrongs?
　　　　Preach me not out of my possessions.
　　　　Some Jews are wicked, as all Christians are;
　　　　But say the tribe that I descended of
　　　　Were all in general cast away for sin,   115
　　　　Shall I be tried by their transgression?
　　　　The man that dealeth righteously shall live;
　　　　And which of you can charge me otherwise?

88. *slightly*] easily, readily.

91. Corpo di Dio!] By God's body! (An ironic oath here, referring to the crucified Christ.)

96. *ground*] basis, fundamental principle.

99. *one want*] that one individual should go without. (Cf. John, 11.50.)

108. *your first curse*] i.e. the curse that the Jews accepted when they demanded Christ's crucifixion and said, 'His blood be on us, and on our children' (Matthew, 27.25).

115. *cast away*] rejected by God, damned.

117.] Compare Proverbs, 10.2 and 16 and 12.28, Romans, 4.13, and Galatians, 3.13–29.

Ferneze. Out, wretched Barabas!
    Shamest thou not thus to justify thyself,   120
    As if we knew not thy profession?
    If thou rely upon thy righteousness,
    Be patient, and thy riches will increase.
    Excess of wealth is cause of covetousness,
    And covetousness, Oh, 'tis a monstrous sin!   125
Barabas. Ay; but theft is worse. Tush, take not from me then,
    For that is theft; and if you rob me thus,
    I must be forced to steal, and compass more.
First Knight. Grave governor, list not to his exclaims.
    Convert his mansion to a nunnery;   130
    His house will harbour many holy nuns.

Enter Officers.

Ferneze. It shall be so. – Now, officers, have you done?
First Officer. Ay, my lord, we have seized upon the goods
    And wares of Barabas, which being valued
    Amount to more than all the wealth in Malta,   135
    And of the other we have seizèd half;
    Then we'll take order for the residue.
Barabas. Well then, my lord, say, are you satisfied?
    You have my goods, my money, and my wealth,
    My ships, my store, and all that I enjoyed,   140
    And having all, you can request no more –
    Unless your unrelenting flinty hearts
    Suppress all pity in your stony breasts,
    And now shall move you to bereave my life.
Ferneze. No, Barabas, to stain our hands with blood   145
    Is far from us and our profession.
Barabas. Why, I esteem the injury far less
    To take the lives of miserable men
    Than be the causers of their misery.
    You have my wealth, the labour of my life,   150
    The comfort of mine age, my children's hope;
    And therefore ne'er distinguish of the wrong.
Ferneze. Content thee, Barabas, thou hast naught but right.

---

119. *Out*] an expression of indignation or reproach.
121. *profession*] i.e. Old Testament religion and covetous ways.
128. *compass*] encompass; contrive an evil purpose.
129. *exclaims*] exclamations, outcries.
136. *other*] other Jews.
137.] i.e. 'then we'll make arrangements for the proper disposal of all the rest'.
152. *distinguish of the wrong*] make subtle distinctions intended to minimize the wrong you have done me.
153. *right*] justice.

Barabas. Your extreme right does me exceeding wrong.
    But take it to you, i' the devil's name!   155
Ferneze. Come, let us in, and gather of these goods
    The money for this tribute of the Turk.
First Knight. 'Tis necessary that be looked unto;
    For if we break our day, we break the league,
    And that will prove but simple policy.   160
                Exeunt [FERNEZE, Knights, *and* Officers].
Barabas. Ay, policy, that's their profession,
    And not simplicity as they suggest.   [*He kneels.*]
    The plagues of Egypt and the curse of heaven,
    Earth's barrenness, and all men's hatred,
    Inflict upon them, thou great Primus Motor!   165
    And here upon my knees striking the earth
    I ban their souls to everlasting pains
    And extreme tortures of the fiery deep
    That thus have dealt with me in my distress.
First Jew. Oh, yet be patient, gentle Barabas.   170
Barabas. Oh silly brethren, born to see this day!
    Why stand you thus unmoved with my laments?
    Why weep you not to think upon my wrongs?
    Why pine not I and die in this distress?
First Jew. Why, Barabas, as hardly can we brook   175
    The cruel handling of ourselves in this.
    Thou seest they have taken half our goods.
Barabas. Why did you yield to their extortion?
    You were a multitude, and I but one,
    And of me only have they taken all.   180
First Jew. Yet, brother Barabas, remember Job.
Barabas. What tell you me of Job? I wot his wealth
    Was written thus: he had seven thousand sheep,
    Three thousand camels, and two hundred yoke
    Of labouring oxen, and five hundred   185

154. *extreme*] harsh. Accented on the first syllable.
159. *break our day*] miss our deadline.
break the league] violate our treaty obligations.
160. *simple policy*] a foolish trick.
161. *policy*] trickery, duplicity.
162. *simplicity*] honesty, lack of guile.
163. *The plagues of Egypt*] See Exodus, 7–12.
165. *Primus Motor*] First Mover.
167. *ban*] curse.
171.] i.e. 'O foolish fellow Jews, destined from birth to behold this unhappiness!'
175–6. *as . . . this*] 'we find it as difficult as you to endure our harsh treatment'.
181–208.] See Job, especially 1.3, 3.1–10, 7.3, and 7.11.
182. *I wot*] I know.

> She-asses; but for every one of those,
> Had they been valued at indifferent rate,
> I had at home, and in mine argosy
> And other ships that came from Egypt last,
> As much as would have bought his beasts and him,   190
> And yet have kept enough to live upon;
> So that not he, but I, may curse the day,
> Thy fatal birthday, forlorn Barabas,
> And henceforth wish for an eternal night,
> That clouds of darkness may enclose my flesh   195
> And hide these extreme sorrows from mine eyes.
> For only I have toiled to inherit here
> The months of vanity and loss of time,
> And painful nights have been appointed me.
> *Second Jew.* Good Barabas, be patient.
> *Barabas.*   Ay, ay;   200
> Pray leave me in my patience. You that
> Were ne'er possessed of wealth are pleased with want.
> But give him liberty at least to mourn
> That in a field amidst his enemies
> Doth see his soldiers slain, himself disarmed,   205
> And knows no means of his recovery.
> Ay, let me sorrow for this sudden chance;
> 'Tis in the trouble of my spirit I speak.
> Great injuries are not so soon forgot.
> *First Jew.* Come, let us leave him in his ireful mood.   210
> Our words will but increase his ecstasy.
> *Second Jew.* On, then. But trust me, 'tis a misery
> To see a man in such affliction.
> Farewell, Barabas.   *Exeunt* [*three* Jews].
> *Barabas.* Ay, fare you well.   [*He rises.*]   215
> See the simplicity of these base slaves,
> Who, for the villains have no wit themselves,
> Think me to be a senseless lump of clay
> That will with every water wash to dirt!
> No, Barabas is born to better chance   220

187. *indifferent*] impartial.
189. *last*] most recently.
198. *vanity*] vain striving.
201. *patience*] stoical suffering (playing on *be patient*, l. 200).
202. *pleased with want*] content with having little.
206. *of*] for.
211. *ecstasy*] frenzy.
217.] 'who, since the base wretches have no sagacity themselves'.
219.] i.e. 'that will break apart at the first shock or crisis'.
220. *chance*] fortune.

And framed of finer mould than common men,
That measure naught but by the present time.
A reaching thought will search his deepest wits
And cast with cunning for the time to come,
For evils are apt to happen every day.   225

221. *framed . . . mould*] fashioned out of better quality materials.
223.] 'A person endowed with foresight will exercise his utmost ingenuity'.
224. *cast*] forecast, make arrangements in advance.

Section Five

The Reformation

57 Girolamo Savonarola **The Sermon on the Renovation of the Church (1495)**

The Dominican friar Girolamo Savonarola (1452–98) was one of a number of Italian churchmen particularly concerned with the wickedness of the age. Like other members of the Dominican order, he called for spiritual repentance and moral reform. It was, however, his prophetic utterances and their political resonances that led to his excommunication in 1497 and his execution the following year. In this sermon, given in the Duomo in Florence in 1495, he preached the renewal of the church on pain of God's retribution. Texts 57 to 60 are all concerned with the movement for reform and renewal within the Catholic Church before the Lutheran Reformation.

Source: *The Catholic Reformation: Savonarola to Ignatius Loyola: Reform in the Church 1495–1540*, ed. J. C. Olin, Harper and Row, New York, 1969, pp. 13–14

I know that this morning I am mad and that I am speaking all these things foolishly, but I want you to know that this light does not justify me, for only if I am humble and have charity will I be justified.[1] And this light was not given for me, nor because of my merit, but for you, Florence, was it given me. And therefore, Florence, this morning I have told you these things so openly, inspired by God to tell them to you in this way, so that you may know everything and will not have any excuse whatever when the flagellation comes and will not be able to say: 'I did not know it!' I cannot speak more clearly; and I know that this morning I shall be taken for a madman, for many have come here to accuse me. If you say that I am mad, I shall be patient. I have spoken to you in this way because God wished that I speak to you thus.

From the time that I began this Apocalypse we have had much opposition: some of this you know, some God knows, some His angels know. We must struggle against the lukewarm and against the two-fold wisdom, that is, against the wisdom of the New and Old Testament, against the two-fold knowledge, against the philosophy and knowledge of Sacred Scripture,[2] against the two-fold evil, that is, against the evil which the lukewarm commit today and which those commit who know they are doing evil and want to do it. It was not this way in the time of Christ, because only the Old Testament existed; and if they went astray, they thought they were doing good. And therefore I say to you that, if Christ were to return down here again, He would again be crucified. [. . .]

I have said to you: *Gladius Domini cito et velociter super terram* [The sword of the Lord comes soon and swiftly over the earth]. Believe me that the knife of God will come and soon. And do not laugh at this word *cito* [soon] and do not say that it is a *cito* as used in the Apocalypse, which takes hundreds of years to come. Believe me that it will be soon. Believing does not harm you at all, as a matter of fact it benefits you, for it makes you turn to penance and makes you walk in God's way; and do not believe that it can harm you rather than benefit you. Therefore believe that it is soon, although the precise time cannot be given, for God does not wish it, so that his elect remain always in fear, in faith and in charity, and continually in the love of God. And so I have not told you the appointed time, in order that you may always do penance and always please God. [. . .]

Lastly, I agree that this morning I have been a madman. You will say it, and I knew before I came up here that you would say it. God wanted it this way. Nevertheless I say to you in conclusion that God has prepared a great dinner for all Italy, but all the foods will be bitter, and He has served only the salad which consisted of a small quantity of bitter herbs. Understand me well, Florence: all the other foods are also to come, and they are all bitter, and the foods are to be many, for it is a great dinner. Therefore I conclude, and keep it in mind, that Italy is now at the beginning of her tribulations.

O Italy, O princes of Italy, O prelates of the Church, the wrath of God is over you, and you will not have any cure unless you mend your ways! [. . .]

NOTES

1   Savonarola quotes and refers here to St Paul's words in II *Corinthians* 11 and I *Corinthians* 13.
2   These are allusions to the opposition of certain preachers and theologians who used scripture against Savonarola.

58 The Introduction to the Rule of the Genoese Oratory of Divine Love (1497)

The Oratory of Divine Love was founded in Genoa in 1497 by Ettore Vernazza. It was an association of devout laymen influenced by the religious revival within the Catholic church and was intended to promote the spiritual development of the members of the fraternity and to encourage them to do charitable works. Comparable fraternities were founded elsewhere in Italy. An off-shoot of this one was established in Rome some time after 1514 and was influential in promoting the cause of spiritual renewal among the Catholic priesthood.

Source: *The Catholic Reformation: Savonarola to Ignatius Loyola: Reform in the Church 1495–1540*, ed. J. C. Olin, Harper and Row, New York, 1969, p. 18

In the name of the Lord Jesus Christ here begin the Chapters of the Fraternity of Divine Love under the protection of St. Jerome.

Brethren, this our fraternity is not instituted for any other reason than to root and implant in our hearts divine love, that is to say, charity; and thus it is called the Fraternity of Divine Love. And this is so because charity does not proceed from other than the gentle look of God, who, if He looks upon us, looks upon those who are humble in heart, according to the saying of the prophet: 'Whom do I regard if not the lowly and the man who trembles at my word?' [*Isaiah* 66:2] Thus let him who would be a brother in this company be humble of heart, to which humility tend all the customs and institutions of this fraternity; and let each direct his mind and hope toward God, placing in Him all his affection; otherwise he is a false brother and a hireling who would bring forth no fruit in this fraternity, which can bear no fruit other than that pertaining to the charity of God and of neighbor. And let this suffice for the title, and let it be understood at the outset that what is in the present Chapters or in others, if such be ordered in the future, is not binding under sin, above all mortal.

59 Giles of Viterbo **Address to the Fifth Lateran Council (1512)**

Giles (Antonini) of Viterbo (1469–1532) entered the Augustinian order of friars in 1488, becoming prior general 1507–1518 under the patronage of Pope Julius II (1503–13). He was elected a cardinal in 1517 and became bishop of Viterbo in 1523. In 1527 he gathered at his own expense a force of two thousand men to defend Rome against the French forces. He was closely connected with many of the leading literary and artistic movements and with individuals such as Marsilio Ficino (1433–99) and Johannes Reuchlin (1455–1522), while at the same time holding a central position in the administration of the church. He was interested in reconciling non-Christian thought with Christian orthodoxy in the service of the divine harmony of the universe. He was also, despite his concern with the sinful and worldly indulgence of Rome, much involved with the rebuilding of St Peter's. This address, given at the opening of the Council, was said to have moved some of its auditors to tears. The Lateran Council (1512–17) was called by Pope Julius II. It was not a representative body since delegates from France, England and Germany were prevented from attending because of continuing warfare in northern Italy. It achieved very little in the way of reform but it none the less represents the acknowledgement on the part of the papacy of the problems facing the church. Gianfrancesco Pico della Mirandola (see Text 88) also addressed the Council with an eloquent defence of the need for a moral crusade in the Catholic church.

Source: *The Catholic Reformation: Savonarola to Ignatius Loyola: Reform in the Church 1495–1540*, ed. J. C. Olin, Harper and Row, New York, 1969, pp. 44–53

There is no one here, I believe, who does not wonder, when there are so many men in the city who are famed indeed for their ability to speak with dignity and eloquence, why I, who can in no way be compared with these brilliant men, should be the one to appear before us and should dare to speak on so important a matter and in so great an assembly that the world has none more esteemed or more sacred. I might indeed say that something has intervened, and for this reason I have been preferred over the others, not because of any excellence but because of earlier times and activities. And so for this reason I seem to have been invited as the first to cast a spear in this conflict and to begin the Holy Lateran Council.

For about twenty years ago, as much as I was able and my meager strength allowed, I explained the Gospels to the people, made known the predictions of the prophets, expounded to nearly all of Italy John's Apocalypse concerning the destiny of the Church, and repeatedly asserted that those who were then listening would see great agitation and destruction in the Church and would one day behold its correction. Now it has seemed proper that he who had said these things would happen bears witness that they have happened, and he who had so often cried out, 'My eyes will see salutary times,' now at last cries out, 'My eyes have seen the salutary and holy beginning of the awaited renewal.' If only you be present, Renewer of the world, Child of a divine Father, Preserver and Savior of mortal men, you may grant to me the power to speak, to my address the power to persuade, to the Fathers the power to celebrate, not with words but with deeds, a true, holy, and full Council, to root out vice, to arouse virtue, to catch the foxes who in this season swarm to destroy the holy vineyard, and finally to call fallen religion back to its old purity, its ancient brilliance, its original splendor, and its own sources. Thus I shall say of a Council both how useful it is for the Church at all times and how necessary it is for our times, with the preface that I would not dare alter the prophetic writings, but would make use of the words and speeches in their entirety, as they are accustomed to be read, not only because men must be changed by religion, not religion by men, but because the language of truth is straightforward. And from the beginning this division came to mind: some things are divine, others celestial, others human.

Divine things certainly do not need correction because they are not subject to motion or change. But celestial and human things, being subject to movement, long for renewal. [. . .] For what food is for bodies that they may live and procreation for species that they may be perpetuated, correction, cultivation, instruction serve as the occasion demands for human souls. And, as no living thing can long survive without nourishment from food, so man's soul and the Church cannot perform well without the attention of Councils. If you should take rain from the meadows, streams from the gardens, tilling from the fields, pruning from the vines, and nourishment from living beings, these would soon dry up and grow wild, and the latter would cease living and die. Such was the case after the time of Constantine when, though much splendor and embellishment were added to religion, the austerity of morals and living was greatly weakened.

As often as the holding of Councils was delayed, we saw the divine Bride forsaken by her Spouse and that message of the Gospel accomplished which was recited yesterday. 'A little while and you shall not see me.' We saw Christ sleeping in a small boat, we saw the force of the winds, the fury of the heretics, raging against the bright sails of truth. We saw evil's desperate recklessness battering the laws, authority, and majesty of the Church. We saw wicked greed, the cursed thirsting for gold and possessions. We saw, I say, violence, pillage, adultery, incest, in short, the scourge of every crime so confound all that is sacred and profane, and so attack the holy bark, that this bark has been almost swamped by the waves of sin and nearly engulfed and destroyed.

Once again at the prompting of that Spirit to whom public prayers have this day been decreed, the Fathers have had recourse to a Council. As quickly as possible they have corrected and settled all matters. They have exercised their command over the winds and storms, and as though carried to the safest of ports they have compelled might to yield to reason, injustice to justice, vice to virtue, storms and waves to serenity and tranquility. [. . .]

In order to prove from experience what we assert as true by reason, we must consider that there are three fundamental articles of belief from which flows the Church's entire faith. The first is the unity of the divine nature. The second is the most blessed Trinity of parent, child, and love in the same nature. The third is the conception of the divine Child in the womb of the Virgin. On these, as on the highest peaks and most sacred mountains, the remaining nine parts of faith and all piety are founded. 'His foundation upon the holy mountains [the Lord loves].' [*Psalm* 87:1] Truly, unity is called the mountain of God because God's essence and nature consist precisely in unity. And in order that we may reflect upon the fact that this unity is not solitary and sterile, but rather endowed with the richest abundance, fertile mountain is added. And when indeed the Word is given body in the Virgin, the prophet describes the mountain as coagulated.[1] [. . .]

What I have just said about faith, which indeed would not exist without the establishment of a Council, I wish applied to temperance, justice, wisdom, and the other virtues. Certainly we all desire idleness rather than hard work, leisure rather than activity, pleasure rather than deprivation. But whenever we take notice of what is done at Councils, so that an evaluation may be made, the question of morals and living be investigated, and the wicked discovered, judged, and punished, while, on the other hand, the upright are attracted, encouraged, and praised, unbelievable incentives to cultivate virtue are inspired, with the result that men take courage, decide on the better course of action, undertake to give up vice and pursue virtue, and strive after nothing that is not honorable and lofty. It is this which has been the distinguishing characteristic of a Council, from which shone forth, as though from the Trojan horse, the brightest lights of so many minds. This approval of virtue, this condemnation of vice brought forth the Basils, Chrysostoms, Damascenes in Greece, the Jeromes, Ambroses, Augustines, Gregorys in Italy. And what books, writings, and memorials, what a wealth of learning, instruction, and divine wisdom have they not gathered into the Christian treasury? [. . .]

What should I say about that most serious and most dangerous matter of all, which everyone in our days deplores? I mean the wrongs inflicted by princes, the insolence of armies, the threats of armed force. For what can be heard or thought of that is more pitiable than that the queen of heaven and earth, the Church, is forced to be a slave to might, to surrender, or to shudder before the weapons of plunderers? This pestilence today spreads so far, rises to such a height, and gathers so much strength that all the authority of the Church and its freedom conferred by God seem overturned, struck to the ground, and completely destroyed. Therefore, beware, O Julius II, Supreme Pontiff, beware lest you believe that any man has ever conceived a better or more beneficial plan than you have conceived at the prompting of the Holy Spirit in convening a Council, whose decrees certainly no kings, no princes, can despise, nor can they disregard its commands or disparage its authority. For if there are some who by chance have dared to esteem lightly the pope alone, defenseless by himself, they have become accustomed to fear and respect him when he is provided, by the authority of a Council, with the support and devotion of princes and nations.

If we recall the accomplishments of Councils, we realize that there is nothing more effective, greater, or more powerful than these. [. . .]

For what else is a holy Council if not an object of fear for the evil, a hope for the upright, a rejection of errors, a seed-bed and revival of virtues, whereby the deceit of the devil is conquered, the allurements of the senses removed, reason restored to its lost citadel, and justice returned from heaven to earth? [. . .] Oh, those blessed times that have brought forth Councils! How foolish are the times that have not recognized their importance! How unhappy those that have not allowed them!

Since we have spoken summarily of the past benefits from Councils, let us now, as briefly as possible, touch upon those from our Council. Therefore I call upon you, Julius II, Supreme Pontiff, and Almighty God calls upon you, that God who has wished you to act as His vicar on earth, who long ago chose you alone from so great a senate, who has sustained you as bridegroom of His Church into the ninth year, who has given you a good mind for planning and a great facility for acting (to none of your predecessors has He ever given so much) so that you might drive away robbers, clear the highways, put an end to insurrections, and raise the most magnificent temple of the Lord ever seen by man, and so that you might do what no one before has been able to do, make the arms of the Church fearful to great kings that you might extend your rule and recover Rimini, Faenza, Ravenna, and many other places. Even though the enemy can seize these, he cannot prevent you as Pope from accomplishing all this. For the excellence of great princes must be appraised not on the basis of chance or accident, but from plans and actions. Now two things remained for you to do, that you convene a Council and that you declare war on the common enemy of Christians. And what from the beginning you always intended, pledged, and proposed, may you now perform for God, for the Christian flock, and for your own piety and fidelity. [. . .]

Many things, but especially the loss of the army, should prompt us to perform these deeds, for indeed I think that it was an act of divine Providence that relying on arms alien to the Church we suffered defeat, so that returning to our own arms we might become victors.[2] But our weapons, to use the words of the Apostle, are piety, devotion, honesty, prayers, offerings, the shield of faith, and the arms of light.[3] If we return to these with the aid of the Council, just as with arms that were not ours we were inferior to an enemy, so with our own weapons we shall be superior to every enemy. [. . .]

I see, yes, I see that, unless by this Council or by some other means we place a limit on our morals, unless we force our greedy desire for human things, the source of evils, to yield to the love of divine things, it is all over with Christendom, all over with religion, even all over with those very resources which our fathers acquired by their greater service of God, but which we are about to lose because of our neglect. For from extreme poverty these resources became most abundant in such a way that they seem not so long after about to perish, and, unless we sound the signal for retreat, unless we have regard for our interests, this most rich fillet,[4] which had served to decorate the heads of the priests, will be found hardly to cover them. Hear the divine voices everywhere sounding, everywhere demanding a Council, peace, that holy enterprise [against the Moslems]. When has our life been more effeminate? When has ambition been more unrestrained, greed more burning? When has the license to sin been more shameless? When has temerity in speaking, in arguing, in writing against piety been more common or more unafraid? When has there been among the people not only a greater neglect but a greater contempt for the sacred, for the sacraments, for the keys [of forgiveness of sins], and for the holy commandments? When has our religion and faith been more open to the derision even of the lowest classes? When, O sorrow, has there been a more disastrous split in the Church? When has war been more dangerous, the enemy more powerful, armies more cruel? When have the signs, portents, and prodigies both of a threatening heaven and of a terrified earth appeared more numerous or more horrible? When (alas, tears hold me back) has the slaughter and destruction been bloodier than at Brescia or at Ravenna? When, I say, did any day among accursed days dawn with more grief or calamity than that most holy day of the Resurrection?[5] [. . .]

The people pray, men, women, every age, both sexes, the entire world. The Fathers ask, the Senate entreats, finally the Pope himself as a suppliant implores you to preserve him, the Church, the city of Rome, these temples, these altars, these your own principal shrines, and to make strong the Lateran Council, proclaimed today in your presence by the Supreme Pontiff Julius II (may it be auspicious, happy and favorable for us, for your Church and for all of Christendom), that it may accomplish under the power of the Holy Spirit the surest salvation of the world. We beg you to see to it that the Christian princes are brought to peace and the arms of our kings turned against Mohammed, the public enemy of Christ, and that the fire of charity of the Church is not only not extinguished by these waves and storms, but that by the merits of the saving Cross and under the guidance of the Holy Spirit, which are jointly commemorated today, it is cleansed from every stain it has received and is restored to its ancient splendor and purity.

NOTES

1	The reference to the fertile mountain derives from *Isaiah* 5:1 and *Psalms* 68:16. The mountain is described as coagulated (*mons Coagulatus* in the Vulgate).
2	This is a reference to the defeat of Spanish–papal forces by the French at the battle of Ravenna on 11 April 1512 (Easter Sunday). The battle took place just before Giles of Viterbo's address.
3	*Ephesians* 6:13–17; *Romans* 13:12.
4	'Fillet' is used to signify the wealth and possessions of the church.
5	A further reference to the battle of Ravenna.

60 The *Consilium de Emendanda Ecclesia* (1537)

Pope Paul III (1534–49, formerly Cardinal Alessandro Farnese) was the first pope to recognise officially the need for reform within the Catholic church. Appointing Cardinal Contarini as chairman, he assembled a commission of nine churchmen to make recommendations for reform to be considered at a General Council in Mantua in 1537. For the first time senior churchmen addressed the corruption of the papal curia and the church's pastoral failings. Though little in the way of direct reform was to flow from it (it was necessary to wait for the Council of Trent for this), the document confirmed the criticism of German Protestants and both Martin Luther and Johannes Sturm published commentaries on it.

Source: *The Catholic Reformation: Savonarola to Ignatius Loyola: Reform in the Church 1495–1540*, ed. J. C. Olin, Harper and Row, New York, 1969, pp. 187–91, 196–7.

[. . .] You, Most Holy Father, and truly Most Holy, instructed by the Spirit of God, and with more than that former prudence of yours, since you have devoted yourself fully to the task of curing the ills and restoring good health to the Church of Christ committed to your care, you have seen, and you have rightly seen, that the cure must begin where the disease had its origin, and having followed the teaching of the Apostle Paul you wish to be a steward, not a master, and to be found trustworthy by the Lord, having indeed imitated that servant in the Gospel whom the master set over his household to give them their ration of grain in due time [*Luke* 12:42], and on that account you have resolved to turn from what is unlawful, nor do you wish to be able to do what you should not. [. . .]

We have therefore made, in obedience to your command and insofar as it can be briefly done, a compilation of those diseases and their remedies – remedies, we stress, which we were able to devise given the limitations of our talents. But you indeed according to your goodness and wisdom will restore and bring to completion all matters where we have been remiss in view of our limitations. [. . .]

The first abuse in this respect is the ordination of clerics and especially of priests, in which no care is taken, no diligence employed, so that indiscriminately the most unskilled, men of the vilest stock and of evil morals, adolescents, are admitted to Holy Orders and to the priesthood, to the [indelible] mark, we stress, which above all denotes Christ. From this has come innumerable scandals and a contempt for the ecclesiastical order, and reverence for divine worship has not only been diminished but has almost by now been destroyed. Therefore, we think that it would be an excellent thing if your Holiness first in this city of Rome appointed two or three prelates, learned and upright men, to preside over the ordination of clerics. He should also instruct all bishops, even under pain of censure, to give careful attention to this in their own dioceses. Nor should your Holiness allow anyone to be ordained except by his own bishop or with the permission of deputies in Rome or of his own bishop. Moreover, we think that each bishop should have a teacher in his diocese to instruct clerics in minor orders both in letters and in morals, as the laws prescribe.

Another abuse of the greatest consequence is in the bestowing of ecclesiastical benefices [church offices], especially parishes and above all bishoprics, in the matter of which the practice has become entrenched that provision is made for the persons on whom the benefices are bestowed, but not for the flock and Church of Christ. Therefore, in bestowing parish benefices, but above all bishoprics, care must be taken that they be given to good and learned men so that they themselves can perform those duties to which they are bound, and, in addition, that they be conferred on those who will in all likelihood reside. A benefice in Spain or in Britain then must not be conferred on an Italian, or vice versa. [. . .]

Another abuse, when benefices are bestowed or turned over to others, has crept in in connection with the arrangement of payments from the income of these benefices. Indeed, the person resigning the benefice often reserves all the income for himself. [. . .]

It is a great abuse when all revenues are reserved and everything is taken away which should be allotted to divine service and to the support of him who holds the benefice. And likewise it is certainly a great abuse to make payments to rich clerics who can live satisfactorily and respectably on the income they have. Both abuses must be abolished. [. . .]

Another abuse has become prevalent, that bishoprics are conferred on the most reverend cardinals or that not one but several are put in their charge, an abuse, most Holy Father, which we think is of great importance in God's Church. In the first place, because the offices of cardinal and bishop are 'incompatible.' For the cardinals are to assist your Holiness in governing the universal Church; the bishop's duty however is to tend his own flock, which he cannot do well and as he should unless he lives with his sheep as a shepherd with his flock.

Furthermore, Holy Father, this practice is especially injurious in the example it sets. For how can this Holy See set straight and correct the abuses of others, if abuses are tolerated in its own principal members? [. . .] [T]he life of these men ought to be a law for others, nor should they imitate the Pharisees who speak and do not act, but Christ our Savior who began to act and afterwards to teach. [. . .]

[M]ost blessed Father, the abuse that first and before all others must be reformed is that bishops above all and then parish priests must not be absent from their churches and parishes except for some grave reason, but must reside, especially bishops, as we have said, because they are the bridegrooms of the church entrusted to their care. For, by the Eternal God, what sight can be more lamentable for the Christian man travelling through the Christian world than this desertion of the churches? Nearly all the shepherds have departed from their flocks, nearly all have been entrusted to hirelings. [. . .]

Having set forth in brief all those matters which pertain to the pontiff of the universal Church as far as we could comprehend them, we shall in conclusion say something about that which pertains to the bishop of Rome. This city and church of Rome is the mother and teacher of the other churches. Therefore in her especially divine worship and integrity of morals ought to flourish. Accordingly, most blessed Father, all strangers are scandalized when they enter the basilica of St. Peter where priests, some of whom are vile, ignorant, and clothed in robes and vestments which they cannot decently wear in poor churches, celebrate mass. This is a great scandal to everyone. Therefore the most reverend archpriest or the most reverend penitentiary must be ordered to attend to this matter and remove this scandal. And the same must be done in other churches. [. . .]

These are the abuses, most blessed Father, which for the present, according to the limitations of our talents, we thought should be compiled, and which seemed to us ought to be corrected. You indeed, in accord with your goodness and wisdom, will direct all these matters. We certainly, if we have not done justice to the magnitude of the task which is far beyond our powers, have nevertheless satisfied our consciences, and we are not without the greatest hope that under your leadership we may see the Church of God cleansed, beautiful as a dove, at peace with herself, agreeing in one body, to the eternal memory of your name. You have taken the name of Paul; you will imitate, we hope, the charity of Paul. He was chosen as the vessel to carry the name of Christ among the nations [*Acts* 9:15]. Indeed we hope that you have been chosen to restore in our hearts and in our works the name of Christ now forgotten by the nations and by us clerics, to heal the ills, to lead back the sheep of Christ into one fold, to turn away from us the wrath of God and that vengeance which we deserve, already prepared and looming over our heads.

> Gasparo, Cardinal Contarini
> Gian Pietro [Carafa], Cardinal of Chieti
> Jacopo, Cardinal Sadoleto
> Reginald [Pole], Cardinal of England
> Federigo [Fregoso], Archbishop of Salerno
> Jerome [Aleander], Archbishop of Brindisi
> Gian Matteo [Gilberti], Bishop of Verona
> Gregorio [Cortese], Abbot of San Giorgio, Venice
> Friar Tommaso [Badia], Master of the Sacred Palace[1]

NOTE

1   The authorship of the *Consilium* has been debated. It was probably a collective work, although it is likely that Contarini and Carafa were the main authors.

61   Conrad Celtis **Inaugural address to the University of Ingolstadt (1492)**

Conrad Celtis (1459–1508), known as the 'German arch-humanist', was a celebrated lyric poet who became poet laureate to the emperor Maximilian I (1486–1519). He received his humanist education in Germany before travelling to

Italy in 1487, where he objected to the condescension with which his German humanist education was received. He then held positions at Cracow and Nuremberg, before being appointed in 1492 to the chair of poetry and rhetoric at the University of Ingolstadt, delivering this address on his appointment there. In 1497 he was invited by the emperor to the University of Vienna, where he remained until his death.

Source: *The Northern Renaissance*, ed. L. W. Spitz, Prentice Hall, Englewood Cliffs, New Jersey, 1972, pp. 15–23, 25–7

I would not have considered it something special, most excellent fathers and distinguished youths, that I, a German and your fellow countryman, can speak to you in Latin, if those ancient talents of our Germany still flourished, and if that age had returned in which our ambassadors are said to have spoken Greek rather than Latin. But, since through the adverseness of the ages and the change of the times, not only amongst us but even in Italy, the mother and ancient parent of letters, all the past splendor of literature has perished or been extinguished, and all the noble disciplines have been driven away and ruined by barbaric tumults, I am not at all confident that, given the slowness of my mind and the poverty of my powers, I can speak to you adequately in Latin. This is especially true since I have not lacked industry or good teaching, which many of you have up till now experienced and deplored in yourselves. However, lest I be accused of coming in total silence to this place, so richly adorned by your presence, I would rather offend by stammering than lightly pass over by silence your love for me and for the commonwealth of letters. I shall hope for your indulgence if you consider that a little man born in the midst of barbarity and drunkenness, as they say, cannot speak so sensibly as is required by your most sagacious ears and by this auditorium, assigned to me for oratory and poetry by the most illustrious prince, our [Duke] George [the Rich of Bavaria Landshut], and by you most distinguished gentlemen who are privy to all his counsels.

I have decided, moreover, that I can say nothing to you more worthy and pleasant, or more appropriate for me and fitting for you to hear, than to exhort your minds to virtue and the study of the liberal arts. For through them true glory, immortal fame, and happiness can be attained even in this brief life of ours. None of you should be found so sluggish and lazy that you do not regard it as a beautiful, excellent, and magnificent thing to strive toward these lofty goals which can make one truly happy. [. . .]

I shall regard it as enough, and more than enough, men of Germany and illustrious youths, if by my presentation today, such as it is, I shall have added, impressed, and as it were, branded upon your spirits some stimulus to glory and virtue, so that you keep ever before your eyes that immortality which you must seek only from the fountain of philosophy and the study of eloquence. I cannot easily declare with what great labors and vigils you must linger and sweat over these two things – that is to say, over the writings of the ancient philosophers, poets, and orators. For they alone have prescribed for us the way to live well and happily and have set before us Nature which is both the parent of the human race and the cause of all things (as it were), as an example and mirror of life to be imitated. From them you will learn to praise good deeds and to detest evil deeds, and from them you will learn to console yourselves, to exhort, to impel, and to hold back. You will strive to contemplate the Ruler of all things and Nature itself, which is the summit of human happiness. [. . .]

But to you, excellent gentlemen and noble youths, I now direct my address, to whom, thanks to ancestral virtue and invincible German strength, the empire of Italy has passed and who frequent this university rather than all the other centers of study in our Germany, make it fruitful, and serve as a great adornment and elegance. I exhort you to turn first to those studies that can render your minds gentle and cultured and call you away from the habits of the common crowd, so that you dedicate yourselves to higher studies. Keep before your eyes true nobility of mind, and consider that you are bringing not refinement but dishonor to our empire if you merely feed horses and dogs and pursue ecclesiastical prebends rather than the study of letters. As you seek splendor for your dignities with virtue, knowledge, and erudition, reflect on how to add honor to your holy morals so that men may esteem you worthy of those honors, so that they pursue you, and not you them, like fowlers a flock of birds. Noble men, emulate the ancient Roman nobility who, after they had taken over the empire of the Greeks, combined all their wisdom and eloquence so that it is a question as to whether they equalled or actually surpassed all the Greek faculty of invention and apparatus of learning. So you, too, having taken over the rule of the Italians and having cast off your vile barbarity, must strive after the Roman arts. Take away that infamy of the Germans among the Greek, Latin, and Hebrew writers, who ascribe to us drunkenness, barbarism, cruelty, and whatever is bestial and foolish. Regard it as a great shame for yourselves not to know the histories of the Greeks and the Latins, and beyond all shamelessness not to know the situation, the stars, rivers, mountains, antiquities, peoples of our region and land – briefly, all that foreigners have shrewdly gathered together concerning us. It seems a great miracle to me how the Greeks and Romans with such precise diligence and exquisite learning surveyed our land – 'the greatest part of Europe,' to use their own words, but rough and crude, I think, compared with the South; and they expressed our morals, affections, and spirits with words like paintings and the lineaments of bodies. Cast out, noble men, cast out and eliminate those villanies which they relate were bestowed among us as proofs of manly excellence. It is a wonder that this native sickness has endured for nearly fifteen hundred years in some parts of Germany. [. . .]

O men of Germany, assume those ancient passions by which you were so often a dread and terror to the Romans, and turn your eyes to the wants of Germany and consider her lacerated and divided borders. What a shame to have a yoke of servitude imposed on our nation and to pay tributes and taxes to foreign and barbaric kings. O free and strong people, O noble and brave nation, clearly worthy of the Roman Empire, your renowned seaport [Danzig] is held by the Pole and your ocean gateway is occupied by the Dane! In the east the most vigorous tribes are held as slaves; the Marcomanni [Bohemians], Quadi [Moravians], and Bastarnae [Slovaks] live, as it were, separate from the body of our Germany.

I do not even speak of the Transylvania Saxons, who also use our national culture and native language. In the west, however, upper Gaul [France] is so friendly and munificent toward us, thanks to the immortal virtue and incredible wisdom of Philipp of the Rhenish Palatinate, who rules the shore on either side of its renowned river and ever will rule with an auspicious reign, 'As long as the pole rotates the stars, as long as the breezes strike the shores.' But to the south we are burdened with a kind of distinguished servitude, for new colonies are continually being established, thanks to that ancient and detestable avarice for fostering luxuries by which our land is being emptied of its wonderful natural resources, while we pay from the public treasury to others what we need for ourselves [papal exploitation]. So determined is fortune or fate to pursue and destroy the Germans, the remnants of the Roman Empire. [. . .]

And these are the reasons – I say with great bitterness – why our princes despise learning and always remain unlearned, why they are regarded with derision by others and are ridiculed as 'barbarous,' because, even in these otherwise prosperous times, they neglect the liberal arts and their proponents. There is nothing more vile and abject at their courts than those who profess with a word or gesture a knowledge of letters – so greatly our barbarity pleases us and the sickness of an intractable mind. Even among our high churchmen and, to use an ancient term, the 'sacred flames,' to whom the care and protection of letters rightly belongs, they have been so contemptuous of the trifling value of letters and of those devoted to them that they prefer the wild animals of the forests, the long-eared dogs, the snorting and spirited horses, and other pleasures and amusements like Rhea, the wife of Mars [mother of Romulus and Remus], [Emperor] Claudius, and Sardanapalus [effeminate king of Assyria]. We know some bishops, come up from obscure origins, who, when they receive studious men from abroad at their courts, refuse to speak to them to show their knowledge, to such an extent does the silence of Pythagoras please them, lest they seem to be dishonored in their barbarous majesty by the parsimony of the Roman language. Meanwhile they pant with greed like rapacious hawks for money or for the approbations of kings, which they dare exhibit before their doors like common eager whores. So much has Italian luxury and savage cruelty in extorting pernicious silver corrupted us that it would clearly have been more godly and holy had we lived that rude and silvan life of olden times, when we lived within the limits of moderation, rather than bringing in so many instruments of gluttony and luxury, and adopting foreign manners. So it happens that our rulers take those men into their familiar circle who are similarly inclined and exclude those who cherish learning and wisdom. The founders of the Greek and Roman Empire, in contrast, so honored wise men that they bestowed upon them imperial honors and called their secretaries friends. [. . .] I will give no other reason for Italy's flourishing than that they excel us in no other felicity than the love and study of letters. With these they intimidate other nations as though with weapons and lead others to admire them by their talent and industry. [. . .]

Meanwhile in the heart of our Germany we tolerate the reign of a pertinacious religion most sumptuous in its use of a foreign tongue [Hussites in Bohemia]. Although their university [Charles University in Prague] weeps and sighs over the ruin of its ancient felicity, they must nevertheless render thanks to the gods because an Italian is their leader [Augustinus Lucianus of Vicenza]. Because the university had no cultivators of true philosophy, it left behind a strong proof by its fall that the foundations of religion can be strengthened and preserved by no one better than by a true philosopher, rather than by those who regard the highest wisdom as ignorance and who merely accommodate themselves by habit to ostentation for the common crowd and set forth only a small shadow of learning and virtue. [. . .]

We are able to attain nothing magnificent, high and excellent, while we seek only inferior things, as though certain basic teachings of our religion were not to be found in Plato and Pythagoras, in whom the most beautiful association of the light of nature and of grace may be perceived. But concerning this another time.

For that reason turn, O Germans, turn about to the more gentle studies, which philosophy and eloquence alone can teach you. Consider well that it is not without reason that the Greek and Roman founders of the Empire devoted such great efforts and watchful attentions to those matters and decorated the teachers of those subjects with the highest honors, for they understood that by the power of language and the lessons of wisdom the assemblies of men, cities, religions, the worship of the gods, the most holy morals and the broadest empires could be preserved and governed. [. . .]

[T]he states of Greece and now of Italy wisely educated their boys from the very beginning with the hymns of poets. In those hymns they learned to perceive musical tunes and the sweetest modulations of harmony, on which that age is very keen; and they provided for those tender spirits, inclined to inertia and laziness, a stimulant to industry so that they were excited to learning with a cheerful zeal, a lively spirit, and eagerness. The gravity of words and meanings imbibed by tender minds will thus endure to a more advanced age and until death, and will continually sprout forth again through an entire lifetime. Aristotle prescribes this plan when he stipulates that adolescents should be educated in musical hymns. Because it – that is, harmony – stirs up the talents of boys and impels them to the acumen of oratory and the production of song. That discipline is very well adapted for relaxing the spirit and for consoling and uplifting minds; it sounds forth in sacred hymns their praises of the gods and carries them off in divine meditations. For this reason Pythagoras and Plato, the loftiest philosophers, named poetry the first philosophy and theology, which uses hymns for its demonstrations and arouses with melodious speech. But the other discipline – that is, oratory – spreads out with humble, loose, and free speech. Poetry is more concise in rhythm and a bit more free with words, but similar and almost equal in many kinds of embellishment. Neither the one nor the other must be neglected; but from the very beginning, O men of Germany, the minds of the boys must be instructed in and, if I may say so, allured with songs. And when the sublime admiration of things resides in these, the beauty and polish of words, the spirits of the youths easily gain strength from them. In an intellectually stronger age, when the youthful spirit has already been hardened by those beginnings, and thought has been invigorated, they are better instructed and better prepared to lead themselves to the reading of more serious philosophers and orators. From these they can finally rise to their own inventions and to the sublimity of the poetic discipline and its figures, attaining to the praises of illustrious authors in writing histories and poems. They will then procure immortality for themselves and glory and praise for the fatherland. I have spoken.

62 Martin Mair **Summary of a letter to Cardinal Enea Silvio Piccolomini (1457)**

Martin Mair was chancellor to the Archbishop of Mainz. When Enea Silvio Piccolomini (later pope Pius II, see Text 41) was elevated to the rank of Cardinal, Mair wrote to congratulate him and to set out some of the continuing grievances of the German nation against the papal curia. The letter itself does not survive, but Piccolomini summarised it in his lengthy reply which was published in 1457 under the title *De ritu, situ, moribus et conditione Germaniae* (*On the Customs, Morals, Condition and Place of the German People*) as a defence of the papacy, dismissing Mair's complaints.

Source: *Manifestations of Discontent in Germany on the Eve of the Reformation: A Collection of Documents*, ed. G. G. Strauss, Indiana University Press, Bloomington, 1971, pp. 37–8

Martin Mair, chancellor to the Archbishop of Mainz, sends warmest greetings to the venerable Father Enea, Cardinal of Siena.

Letters from friends have brought me the news of your elevation to the cardinalship. My congratulations go to both of us: to you because a fitting reward has now been bestowed upon one of your ability, and to myself whose friend has attained a position and dignity which may upon occasion be useful to me and to those close to me.

One thought alone clouds my joy in your elevation. It is that you have been born into a time fraught with dangers for the Holy See. The Archbishop, my master, receives daily accusations and complaints against the Roman pontiff [Calixtus III, 1455–58], who, it is charged, keeps neither the decrees of the Council of Basel nor the agreements made by his predecessor [Nicholas V]; who, moreover, despises the German nation and seems bent on sapping it of its strength and substance. To wit: Elections of prelates are set aside. Benefices and incomes of all kinds are reserved[1] to cardinals and protonotaries; you yourself are the holder of reservations of benefices in three German provinces. Expectancies[2] are granted in unlimited numbers. Annates or semi-annual revenues are collected without thought of respite, and everyone knows how much more is squeezed out of us than we owe. Clerical positions are given not to those best qualified to hold them but to the highest bidders. New indulgences are approved day after day for one purpose only: their profits to Rome. Turkish tithes are levied without so much as a by-your-leave to our own prelates. Law suits that should plainly be heard in our own courts are summarily transferred to Rome. A thousand subtle tricks are invented to cheat us 'barbarians' out of our money.

As a result of these abuses, our proud nation, once renowned for the ability and courage with which it gained the Roman imperium and became lord and master over the world, has been reduced to beggary, subjected to humiliating exactions, and left to cower in the dust, bemoaning its misery. Now, however, our leaders have been, so to speak, awakened from their sleep and have begun to ponder what means they might take to oppose their misfortunes, shake off their yoke, and regain the ancient freedom they have lost. Consider what a blow it will be to Rome if the German princes should succeed in their design! Thus, joyful as I am in the thought of your new dignity, I am saddened that your service as cardinal should come at so troublesome a time. God's plan may be otherwise, however, and His will is sure to prevail.

Be of good cheer, then, and let your wisdom reflect on the measures that must be taken to keep the raging stream safely in its bed. Farewell!

From Aschaffenburg, August 31, 1457[3]

NOTES

1   Papal reservation was the right of the pope to reserve the nominations of some benefices to himself. Originally this applied to clerics who died in Rome but was expanded in the thirteenth and fourteenth centuries.

2   Expectancy was appointment to an ecclesiastical post before it became vacant. This had been forbidden by canon law but had been used in the fourteenth and fifteenth centuries, particularly by popes in the appointment of bishops.

3   This date was added by Cardinal Piccolomini. He is likely to have received the letter before this date.

63   Martin Luther **Autobiographical fragment on his conversion (1545)**

Martin Luther (1483–1546) studied law at the University of Erfurt, then joined the order of Augustinian friars or hermits. In 1508–9 he taught moral philosophy at the University of Wittenberg and spent a brief period in Erfurt, returning to Wittenberg in 1511, where he remained for most of the rest of his life, apart from a period of enforced exile. In 1545, shortly before his death, he wrote the preface to an edited collection of his Latin writings in which he reflected upon the process of his spiritual enlightenment. Texts 63 to 72 are writings by Luther on the essentials of his beliefs and his development from a critic of corrupt practices within the Catholic church to a reformer outside it, supporting new congregations in their development of a distinctive theology and liturgy.

Source: K. Leach, *The German Reformation: Documents and Debates*, Macmillan, Basingstoke, 1991, pp. 21–2.

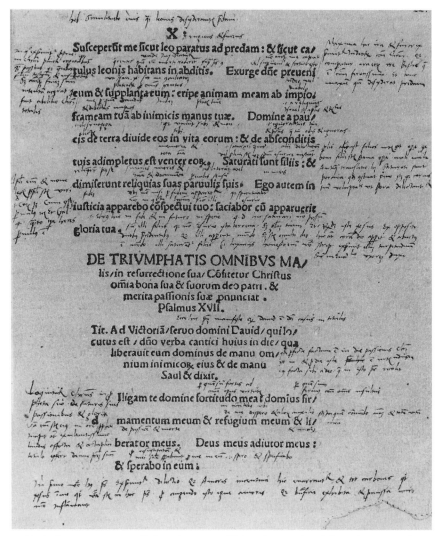

21 Luther's commentary on Psalms 16.12–17.3a (Vulgate), reproduced from the manuscript of his first lectures on the Book of Psalms 1513–15, Herzog August Bibliothek, Wolfenbüttel.

Meanwhile in that year [1519] I had once again turned to the task of interpreting the Psalms, relying on the fact that I was in better training for it since I had handled in the schools the epistles of St. Paul to the Romans and Galatians, and the epistle to the Hebrews. I had certainly been seized with a wondrous eagerness to understand Paul in the epistle to the Romans, but hitherto I had been held up – not by a 'lack of heart in my heart's blood', but by one word only, in ch.1: 'The Righteousness of God is revealed in [the Gospel].' For I hated this word 'righteousness of God', which by the customary use of all the doctors I had been taught to understand philosophically as what they call the formal or active righteousness whereby God is just and punishes unjust sinners.

For my case was this: however irreproachable my life as a monk, I felt myself in the presence of God to be a sinner with a most unquiet conscience, nor could I believe him to be appeased by the satisfaction I could offer. I did not love – nay I hated this just God who punishes sinners, and if not with silent blasphemy, at least with huge murmuring I was indignant against God, as it were really not enough that miserable sinners, actually ruined by original sin, should be crushed with every kind of calamity through the law of the Ten Commandments, but that God through the Gospel must add sorrow to sorrow, and even through the Gospel bring his righteousness and wrath to bear on us. And so I raged with a savage and confounded conscience.

At last, as I meditated day and night, God showed mercy and I turned my attention to the connection of the words, namely – 'The righteousness of God is revealed, as it is written: the righteous shall live by faith' – and there I began to understand that the righteousness of God is the righteousness in which a just man lives by the gift of God, in other words by faith and that what Paul means is this: the righteousness of God, revealed in the Gospel, is *passive*, in other words that by which the merciful God justifies us through faith, as it is written, 'The righteous shall live by faith. At this stage I felt myself straightway bound afresh to have entered into the open gates into paradise itself. There and then the whole face of scripture was changed.

64 Martin Luther **Preface to the complete edition of A German Theology (1518)**

During his formative years, Luther had been much impressed by the writings of the late medieval German mystics which emphasised what later came to be known as 'the conversion experience', the process whereby the believer came to certainty of his or her salvation. In 1516 he had published an incomplete version of one of these works, *A Spiritually Noble Little Book*, by an unknown German mystic. Finding a more complete version of it, he published it in 1518 as *A German Theology*, adding a foreword emphasising the value of such spiritual insights over the authority of scholastic writers.

Source: *Luther's Works, vol. 31, The Career of the Reformer I*, ed. H. J. Grimm, Muhlenberg Press, Philadelphia, 1957, pp. 75–6

One reads that St. Paul, although he was an unimportant and a despised person, nevertheless wrote powerful and courageous letters [II Cor. 10:10] and gloried in the fact that his language was not embellished with ornate and flowery words [I Cor. 1:17], yet was richly endowed with literary art and wisdom. When one contemplates God's wonders it is obvious that brilliant and pompous preachers are never chosen to spread his words. As it is written, *Ex ore infantium*, 'By the mouth of babes and infants,' that is, of those who are not eloquent, 'thou hast chanted thy glory in the best manner' [Ps. 8:2]. Likewise, 'The wisdom of God makes the tongues of the inarticulate most articulate' [Cf. Prov. 10:20]. Furthermore, God punishes persons with high opinions of themselves who become offended and angered by those simple people, *Consilium inopis*, etc.: 'You have dishonored good counsel and doctrine because they were given you by poor and unprepossessing persons' [Cf. Ps. 14:6], etc.

I say the above because I wish to warn everyone who reads this book not to harm himself and become irritated by its simple German language or its unadorned and unassuming words, for this noble little book, poor and unadorned as it is in words and human wisdom, is the richer and more precious in art and divine wisdom. To boast with my old fool,[1] no book except the Bible and St. Augustine has come to my attention from which I have learned more about God, Christ, man, and all things. I now for the first time become aware of the fact that a few of us highly educated Wittenberg theologians speak disgracefully, as though we want to undertake entirely new things, as though there had been no people previously or elsewhere. Indeed, there have been others, but God's wrath, aroused by our sin, has prevented us from being worthy enough to recognize or hear them. It is obvious that such matters as are contained in this book have not been discussed in our universities for a long time, with the result that the holy Word of God has not only been laid under the bench but has almost been destroyed by dust and filth.

Let anyone who wishes read this little book, and then let him say whether theology is original with us or ancient, for this book is certainly not new. But some may say, as in the past, that we are German theologians. We shall let that stand. I thank God that I hear and find my God in the German tongue, whereas I, and they with me, previously did not find him either in the Latin, the Greek, or the Hebrew tongue. God grant that this little book will become better known. Then we shall find that German theologians are without a doubt the best theologians. Amen.

Doctor Martin Luther,
Augustinian at Wittenberg

NOTE

1   Faith in Christ, Luther maintained with St Paul, makes one a fool in Christ.

65   Martin Luther **Letter to Eobanus Hessus (1523)**

On 29 March 1523, Luther wrote to the celebrated humanist poet Eobanus Hessus (Eoban Koch, 1488–1540), congratulating him on a poem he had written. At the time, Hessus was studying medicine at Erfurt, having earlier espoused Luther's doctrines while professor of Latin there. The following year he was appointed Professor of History at Philipp of Hesse's new University of Marburg.

Source: *The Religious Renaissance of the German Humanists*, ed. L. W. Spitz, Harvard University Press, Cambridge, Mass., 1963, p. 243

Do not give way to your apprehension lest we Germans become more barbarous than ever we were by reason of the decline of letters through our theology. I am persuaded that, without a skilled training in literary studies, no true theology can establish and maintain itself, seeing that in times past it has invariably fallen miserably and fallen prostrate with the decline of learning. On the other hand it is indubitable that there has never been a signal revelation of divine truth unless first the way has been prepared for it, as by a John the Baptist, by the revival and pursuit of the study of languages and literature. Assuredly there is nothing I should less wish to happen than that our youth should neglect poetry and rhetoric. My ardent vow is that there should be as many poets and rhetoricians as possible, because I see clearly that by no other methods is it possible to train men for the apt understanding, the apt and felicitous treatment of sacred things. Wherefore I beg that you may incite the youth of Erfurt to give themselves strenuously to this study. I am often impatient that in this age of enlightenment time will not permit me to devote myself to poetry and rhetoric, though I formerly bought a Homer in order that I might become a Greek.

66 Martin Luther *To the Councilmen of all Cities in Germany That They Establish and Maintain Christian Schools (1524)*

The early years of reform in Germany led to the expropriation by laymen of many endowments intended by pious benefactors for Christian schooling. Luther attacked the education given at cathedral and monastic schools. This work, written in early 1524 as an appeal to all members of town councils, was intended to offer practical advice on providing a suitable Christian education for young people. It was less an educational manifesto than a call to city rulers to provide adequate education for the populace in the face of the decline in the number of schools and the corruption of the remainder.

Source: *Luther's Works, vol. 45, The Christian in Society II*, ed. W. J. Brandt, Muhlenberg Press, Philadelphia, 1962, pp. 348–70

We are today experiencing in all the German lands how schools are everywhere being left to go to wrack and ruin. The universities are growing weak, and monasteries are declining. . . . The carnal minded masses are beginning to realise that they no longer have either the obligation or the opportunity to thrust their sons, daughters and relatives into cloisters and foundations, and to turn them out of their own homes and establish them in others' property. For this reason no-one is any longer willing to have his children get an education. 'Why', they say, 'should we bother to have them go to school if they are not to become priests, monks or nuns?' 'Twere better they should learn a livelihood to earn.'

[. . .] It is my earnest purpose, prayer and desire that these asses' stalls and devil's training centers should either sink into the abyss or be converted to Christian schools. [. . .]

In ancient Rome . . . boys were so taught that by the time they reached their fifteenth, eighteenth or twentieth year they were well versed in Latin, Greek and all the liberal arts (as they were called), and then immediately entered upon a political or military career. Their system produced intelligent, wise and competent men, so skilled in every art and rich in experience that if all the bishops, priests and monks in the whole of Germany were rolled into one, you would not have the equal of a single Roman soldier. As a result their country prospered and they had capable and trained men for every position. [. . .]

Although the gospel came and still comes to us through the Holy Spirit alone, we cannot deny that it comes through the medium of languages, was spread abroad through that means, and must be preserved by the same means. . . . In proportion as we value the gospel, let us zealously hold onto the languages. For it was not without purpose that God caused his Scripture to be set down in these two languages alone – the Old Testament in Hebrew, the New in Greek. Now if God did not despise them but chose them above all others for his word, then we ought to honour them above all the others.

[. . .] A saintly life and right doctrine is not enough. Hence, languages are absolutely and altogether necessary in the Christian church, as are the prophets and interpreters, although it is not necessary that every Christian or every preacher be such a prophet. [. . .]

[. . .] it is also a stupid undertaking to attempt to gain understanding of Scripture by laboring through the commentaries of the fathers and a multitude of books and glosses. Instead of this, men should have devoted themselves to the languages. [. . .]

Now if (as we have assumed) there were no souls, and there were no need at all of schools and languages for the sake of the scriptures and of God, this one consideration alone would be sufficient to justify the establishment everywhere of the very best schools for both boys and girls, namely that in order to maintain its temporal estate outwardly the world must have good and capable men and women, men able to rule well over land and people, women able to manage the household and train children and servants aright. Therefore it is a matter of properly educating our boys and girls to that end. [. . .]

For my part, if I had children[1] and could manage it, I would have them study not only languages and history, but also singing and music, together with the whole of mathematics. [. . .] The ancient Greeks trained their children in these disciplines; yet they grew up to be people of wondrous ability, subsequently fit for everything. How I regret now that I did not read more poets and historians, and that no-one taught me them! Instead, I was obliged to read at great cost, toil and detriment to myself, that devil's dung, the philosophers and sophists, from which I have [done] all I can do to purge myself.

[. . .] My idea is to have the boys attend a school for one or two hours during the day, and spend the remainder of time at home, learning a trade, or doing whatever is expected of them.

[. . .] In like manner, a girl can surely find time enough to attend school for an hour a day, and still take care of her duties at home.

NOTE

1   He later had three sons and three daughters.

67   Martin Luther **Article 32 from his *Explanations of the 95 Theses* (1518)**

In his *Explanations*, first published in 1518 in Latin, Luther explained how his doctrine of justification by faith and his evangelical convictions led inexorably to a new theology which defied the authority of the church. Apart from elaborating his position on indulgences he also questioned the primacy of the pope and the authority of the Church fathers' writings over the word of the scriptures. The work did much to precipitate the initiation of formal proceedings for heresy against Luther. In Article 32 Luther argues against indulgences on the grounds that those who purchased them felt assured of their salvation.

Source: *Luther's Works, vol. 31, The Career of the Reformer I*, ed. H. J. Grimm, Muhlenberg Press, Philadelphia, 1957, pp. 79–83

ARTICLE 32

Those who believe that they can be certain of their salvation because they have indulgence letters will be eternally damned, together with their teachers.

I maintain this thesis and prove it in the following way:

Jeremiah 17 [:5] says: 'Cursed is the man who trusts in man and makes flesh his arm.' We have no other hope of salvation except in Jesus Christ alone, 'nor is there any other name given under heaven, by which we must be saved' [Acts 4:12; cf. Acts 15:11]. May the hope that is based upon dead letters and on the name of indulgences and intercessions perish!

Secondly, as I have said, letters and indulgences do not confer salvation, but only take away punishments, that is, canonical punishments, and not even all of these. Oh that the earth and all its fulness would cry out and weep with me over the manner in which Christian people are seduced who have no other understanding of indulgences except that they are useful for salvation and for the fruits of the spirit! It is no wonder that this is so, since the plain truth of the matter is not made clear to them.

Oh unhappy Christians, who can trust for their salvation neither in their merits nor in their good conscience! They are taught to put their confidence in a signed parchment and sealing wax. Why should I not speak in such a manner? What else, I ask, is conferred by indulgences? Not contrition, not faith, not grace, but only the remission of punishments of the outer man which have been established by the canons.

To digress just a little: I myself have heard that there are many who, after their money was given and their letters purchased, placed their complete confidence in these indulgences. For (as they said) either they heard these things about indulgences or else (I believe this to their credit) they must have understood that the preachers of indulgences taught these things. I am not censuring anyone, for I should not do so since I have not heard the indulgence preachers. As far as I am concerned, they may excuse themselves until they become whiter than snow. Surely these people must be reproved for having wax in their ears that they hear only pernicious things when these preachers tell them salutary things. This occurs when these preachers say, for example, 'Above all, brothers, believe in Christ, trust in him and repent, take up your cross, follow Christ, mortify your flesh, learn not to be afraid of punishments and death. Above all else, love one another, serve one another even by neglecting indulgences. Minister first to the needs of the poor and the destitute' [I Pet. 4:8–11]. I say that when they are preaching these and similar pious, religious, and holy matters, the gullible populace, turned aside as it were by a strange miracle, hears entirely different things, namely, things like these: 'Oh you senseless and stupid people, almost more like beasts than men, who are not aware of such a great outpouring of grace! See now how heaven is open on all sides! If you do not enter now, when will you ever enter? See how many souls you can redeem! O hard-hearted and indifferent people! For twelve denarii you can release your father from purgatory, and are you so ungrateful that you would not come to the aid of your parent who is in the midst of such great punishment? I myself deserve to be excused at the final judgment, but you stand accused all the more since you have neglected such great salvation [Cf. Heb. 2:3]. I tell you, that if you had only one tunic, in my judgment you should tear it from your body and sell it piece by piece in order that you might obtain such great favors.' But then when the point has come to discuss those who speak against the grace given through indulgence, while they gush forth with nothing but benedictions, the crowd stands trembling and is afraid that heaven will crash to the ground and that the earth will open up.

The people hear that punishments far worse than those of hell threaten them, so that it is probably true that when those preachers curse, God blesses by means of their curses, and when they bless, God curses. For how else could it happen that these preachers speak things that are so different from what the people hear? Who can understand it? Where, I ask, do those hobgoblin words come from? I still do not believe all the things which the populace says it has heard here and there. Otherwise I would consider the ideas which they preach heretical, wicked, and blasphemous.

I do not believe it is true that one of them prohibits burials of the dead and the invitation of the priests to be made until those who want funeral rites, masses, and festivals for the dead to be conducted drop more money into the chest. The people make up these things also. I do not believe that story which is said to have been brought back by a certain person and embellished with lies, namely, that in a certain place thousands of souls (I don't know how many; if I remember correctly, it was either three or five thousand) were redeemed by means of these indulgences. Of these thousands of people only three were condemned; and they were condemned because they withheld indulgence money. No one actually said this, but while the preachers were telling the story of Christ's passion the crowd heard such things, or else they afterwards imagined that they had heard it. I do not believe it is true that these preachers of indulgences indiscriminately grant to coachmen, landlords, and servants indulgences for four, five, or as many souls as they want instead of paying them with money.

I do not believe it when the people say that, after the preachers have poured forth their exhortations with violent bellowing from their pulpits that the people put their money in the chest, they shout, 'Deposit, deposit, deposit' (for the people imagine that this is the head and the tail [Isa. 9:14], indeed even the very heart, of the sermon and almost the whole sermon itself). And I do not believe that then, in order that the apostolic preachers may teach the message of indulgences not only with words but also by example, they come down from their pulpits, go first of all to the collection box so that everyone can see, all the while stirring up and provoking the simple and foolish people in the hope of sucking out their very marrow, then deposit their own coin in a magnificent gesture with a resounding ring, wonder whether all the others will let their whole lifesavings flow in, smile at those who do deposit their coins, and become indignant at those who refuse to do so. I myself do not say that they have a corner on the soul-market. I am indignant at the people who because of their ignorance not only interpret such pious efforts as an appearance of greed but as a greed that reaches frenzy. Nevertheless it appears to me that the people who accept from these new spirits either a new interpretation or error perhaps deserve to be pardoned, although they have in former times been accustomed to hearing those things which pertain to love and humility.

But if I wanted to draw up a catalogue of all the monstrosities I have heard about, a new volume would be necessary. My own opinion is that even if indulgences were enjoined and salutary, nevertheless, because they have now been so terribly abused and reduced to such a scandal, this would be reason enough for abolishing them altogether. If they are permitted to thrive much longer, those who preach them will, because of their love for money, finally become insane. I honestly believe that the indulgence preachers have not said all the things which have been reported about them here and there. But at least they should have set the people right and expressed themselves more clearly, or, better still, they should speak moderately about indulgences in accordance with the wording of the canons.

68 Martin Luther *The Bondage of the Will* (1525)

Luther and Erasmus had each respected the views and scholarship of the other, although following Luther's publication of *The Babylonian Captivity* in 1520 Erasmus rejected Luther's position. It was not, however, until 1524 that Erasmus published his critique of Luther in *De Libero Arbitrio* (*Of Free Will*) (1524). He argued that Luther's wholesale criticism of the church was too radical, but he still hoped that a solution could be mediated on the idea that humankind should have freedom of choice. Initially, Melanchthon and others of Luther's supporters favoured Erasmus's position, but Luther was stung by the criticism and produced a point-by-point refutation of Erasmus in *De Servo Arbitrio* (*The Bondage of the Will*) which led to a complete breach between the two men.

Source: *Luther's Works, vol. 33, The Career of the Reformer III*, ed. P. S. Watson, Fortress Press, Philadelphia, 1972, pp. 270–7

Let us take a look here at what Paul says later about the example of Abraham [Rom. 4:1–3]. 'If Abraham,' he says, 'was justified by works, he has something to boast about, but not before God. For what does the Scripture say? "Abraham believed God, and it was reckoned to him as righteousness."' Please notice here too the distinction Paul makes by referring to a twofold righteousness of Abraham.

First, there is the righteousness of works, or moral and civil righteousness; but he denies that Abraham is justified in God's sight by this, even if he is righteous in the sight of men because of it. With this righteousness, he has indeed something to boast about before men, but like the rest he falls short of the glory of God. Nor can anyone say here that it is the works of the law, or ceremonial works, that are being condemned, seeing that Abraham lived so many years before the law was given. Paul is speaking simply about the works Abraham did, and the best ones he did. For it would be absurd to argue as to whether anyone is justified by bad works. If, therefore, Abraham is not righteous because of any works, and if both he himself and all his works remain in a state of ungodliness unless he is clothed with another righteousness, namely, that of faith, then it is plain that no man is brought any nearer to righteousness by his works; and what is more, that no works and no aspirations or endeavors of free choice count for anything in the sight of God, but are all adjudged to be ungodly, unrighteous, and evil. For if the man himself is not righteous, neither are his works or endeavors righteous; and if they are not righteous, they are damnable and deserving of wrath.

The other kind of righteousness is the righteousness of faith, which does not depend on any works, but on God's favorable regard and his 'reckoning' on the basis of grace. Notice how Paul dwells on the word 'reckoned,' how he stresses, repeats, and insists on it. 'To one who works,' he says, 'his wages are not reckoned as a gift but as his due. And to one who does not work but has faith in him who justifies the ungodly, his faith is reckoned as righteousness, according to the plan of God's grace' [Rom. 4:4 f.]. Then he quotes David as saying the same about the 'reckoning' of grace: 'Blessed is the man against whom the Lord will not reckon his sin,' etc. [Rom. 4:6 ff.]. He repeats the word 'reckon' nearly ten times in this chapter. In short, Paul sets the one who works and the one who does not work alongside each other, leaving no room for anyone between them; and he asserts that righteousness is not reckoned to the former, but that it is reckoned to the latter provided he has faith. There is no way of escape for free choice here, no chance for it to get away with its endeavoring and striving. It must be classed either with the one who works or with the one who does not work. If it is classed with the former, so you are told here, it does not have any righteousness reckoned to it, whereas if it is classed with the latter – the one who does not work but has faith in God – then it does have righteousness reckoned to it. But in that case it will no longer be a case of free choice at work, but of a being created anew through faith.

Now, if righteousness is not reckoned to the one who works, then clearly his works are nothing but sins, evils, and impieties in the sight of God. Nor can any impudent Sophist break in here with the objection that a man's work need not be evil, even if the man himself is evil. For Paul purposely speaks, not simply of the man as a man, but of the man as a worker, in order to make it unmistakably plain that the man's works and endeavors themselves are condemned, no matter what their nature, name, or sign may be. It is, however, with good works that he is concerned, since he is arguing about justification and merit. Hence although with the phrase 'one who works' he refers quite generally to all workers and all their works, it is particularly of their good and virtuous works that he is speaking. Otherwise, there would be no point in his distinction between the 'one who works' and the 'one who does not work.'

I will not here elaborate the very strong arguments that can be drawn from the purpose of grace, the promise of God, the meaning of the law, original sin, or divine election, any one of which would be sufficient by itself to do away completely with free choice. For if grace comes from the purpose or predestination of God, it comes by necessity and not by our effort or endeavor, as we have shown above. Moreover, if God promised grace before the law was given, as Paul argues here and in Galatians, then grace does not come from works or through the law; otherwise the promise means nothing. So also faith will mean nothing – although Abraham was justified by it before the law was given – if works count for anything. Again, since the law is the power of sin [I Cor. 15:56] in that it serves only to reveal and not to remove sin, it makes the conscience guilty before God, and threatens it with wrath. That is what Paul means when he says: 'The law brings wrath' [Rom. 4:15]. How, then, could there be any possibility of attaining righteousness through the law? And if we receive no help from the law, what help can we expect from the power of choice alone?

Furthermore, seeing that through the one transgression of the one man, Adam, we are all under sin and damnation, how can we attempt anything that is not sinful and damnable? For when he says 'all,' he makes no exception either of the power of free choice or of any worker, but every man, whether he works or not, endeavors or not, is necessarily included among the 'all.' Not that we should sin or be damned through that one transgression of Adam if it were not our own transgression. For who could be damned for another's transgression, especially before God? It does not, however, become ours by any imitative doing of it ourselves, for then it would not be the one transgression of Adam, since it would be we and not Adam who committed it; but it becomes ours the moment we are born – a subject we must deal with some other time. Original sin itself, therefore, leaves free choice with no capacity to do anything but sin and be damned.

These arguments, I say, I will not elaborate, both because they are so very obvious and so very substantial, and also because we have already said something about them earlier in the book. But if we wished to list all the points made by

Paul alone by which free choice is overthrown, we could not do better than make a running commentary on the whole of Paul, showing how the much vaunted power of free choice is refuted in almost every word. I have already done this with the third and fourth chapters [of the *Epistle to the Romans*], on which I have chiefly concentrated in order to expose the inattentiveness of all these friends of ours who have a way of reading Paul that enables them to find, even in his clearest passages, anything but these very strong arguments against free choice. I also wanted to show the foolishness of the confidence they repose in the authority and writings of the ancient doctors, and to leave them to consider what the effect of these most evident arguments must be if they are treated with due care and judgment.

For my own part, I confess to being greatly astonished. Paul again and again uses these universal terms, 'all,' 'none,' 'not,' 'nowhere,' 'apart from' – for example: 'All have turned aside'; 'None is righteous'; 'No one does good, not even one'; 'All are sinners and damned through one man's transgression'; 'We are justified by faith, apart from law, apart from works' – so that although one might wish to put it differently, he could not speak more clearly and plainly. Hence I am, as I say, astonished that in face of these universal words and sentences, contrary and even contradictory ideas have come to prevail, such as: 'Some have not turned aside, are not unrighteous, not evil, not sinners, not damned,' and 'There is something in man that is good and strives after the good' – as if the man that strives after the good, whoever he may be, were not included in the words 'all,' 'none,' 'not'!

I should not myself find it possible, even if I wished, to make any objection or reply to Paul, but should have to regard my power of free choice, endeavors and all, as included in those 'alls' and 'nones' of which Paul speaks, unless a new kind of grammar or a new use of language were introduced. It might have been possible to suspect a trope and give a twist to the words I have cited if Paul had used this kind of expression only once or in only one passage; but in fact he uses it continually, both in the affirmative and the negative form, treating his theme through a polemical partition of categories which on both sides have universal application. In consequence, not only the natural sense of the words and the actual statement he makes, but both the immediate and wider context and the whole purpose and substance of his argument lead alike to the conclusion that what Paul means to say is that apart from faith in Christ there is nothing but sin and damnation – it was in this way that we promised we would refute free choice, so that all our opponents would be unable to resist; and I think I have done it, even though they will neither admit defeat and come over to our view, nor yet keep silence. That is not within our power; it is the gift of the Spirit of God.

However, before we hear John the Evangelist, let us add a crowning touch from Paul – and if that is not enough, we are prepared to bring out the whole of Paul against free choice, commenting on him verse by verse. In Romans 8[:5]: where he divides the human race into two types, namely, flesh and spirit (just as Christ does in John 3[:6]), he says: 'Those who live according to the flesh set their minds on the things of the flesh, but those who live according to the Spirit set their minds on the things of the Spirit.' That Paul here calls carnal all who are not spiritual is evident both from this very partition and opposition between spirit and flesh, and from his own subsequent statement: 'You are not in the flesh but in the Spirit if the Spirit of God really dwells in you. Anyone who does not have the Spirit of Christ does not belong to him' [Rom. 8:9]. What else is the meaning of 'You are not in the flesh if the Spirit of God is in you' but that those who do not have the Spirit are necessarily in the flesh? And if anyone does not belong to Christ, to whom else does he belong but Satan? Clearly, then, those who lack the Spirit are in the flesh and subject to Satan.

Now let us see what he thinks of the endeavor and power of free choice in those he calls carnal. 'Those who are in the flesh cannot please God' [Rom. 8:8]. And again: 'The mind of the flesh is death' [v. 6]. And again: 'The mind of the flesh is enmity toward God' [v. 7]. Also: 'It does not submit to God's law, indeed it cannot' [v. 7]. Here let the advocate of free choice tell me this: how something that is death, displeasing to God, hostility toward God, disobedient to God, and incapable of obedience can possibly strive toward the good? For Paul did not choose to say simply that the mind of the flesh is 'dead' or 'hostile to God,' but that it is death itself, hostility itself, which cannot possibly submit to God's law or please God, just as he had said a little before: 'For what was impossible to the law, in that it was weak because of the flesh, God has done,' etc. [v. 3].

I, too, am familiar with Origen's fable about the threefold disposition of flesh, soul, and spirit, with soul standing in the middle and being capable of turning either way, toward the flesh or toward the spirit. But these are dreams of his own; he states but does not prove them. Paul here calls everything flesh that is without the Spirit, as we have shown. Hence the loftiest virtues of the best of men are in the flesh, that is to say, they are dead, hostile to God, not submissive to the law of God and not capable of submitting to it, and not pleasing to God. For Paul says not only that they do not submit, but that they cannot. So also Christ says in Matthew 7[:18]: 'A bad tree cannot bear good fruit,' and in Matthew 12[:34]: 'How can you speak good when you are evil?' You see here not only that we speak evil, but that we cannot speak good. And although he says elsewhere that we who are evil know how to give good gifts to our children [Matt. 7:11], yet he denies that we do good even when we give good gifts, because although what we give is a good creation of God, we ourselves are not good, nor do we give these good things in a good way; and he is speaking to all men, including his disciples. Thus the twin statements of Paul are confirmed, that the righteous live by faith [Rom. 1:17], and that whatsoever is not of faith is sin [Rom. 14:23]. The latter follows from the former, for if there is nothing by which we are justified but faith, it is evident that those who are without faith are not yet justified; and those who are not justified are sinners; and sinners are 'bad trees' and cannot do anything but sin and 'bear bad fruit.' Hence, free choice is nothing but a slave of sin, death, and Satan, not doing and not capable of doing or attempting to do anything but evil.

Take also the example in chapter 10 [Rom. 10:20], quoted from Isaiah: 'I have been found by those who did not seek me; I have shown myself to those who did not ask for me' [Isa. 65:1]. He says this with reference to the Gentiles, because it has been given to them to hear and to know Christ, though previously they could not even think of him, much less seek him or prepare themselves for him by the power of free choice. From this example it is clear enough that grace comes so freely that no thought of it, let alone any endeavor or striving after it, precedes its coming. It was the same also with Paul when he was Saul. What did he do with his wonderful power of free choice? He certainly gave his mind to very good and virtuous things from the point of view of reason. But observe by what endeavor he finds grace! Not only does he not seek it, but he receives it even while raging furiously against it. On the other hand, he says concerning the Jews in chapter 9 [Rom. 9:30]: 'Gentiles who did not pursue righteousness have attained it, that is, righteousness through faith; but Israel who pursued the righteousness which is based on law did not succeed in fulfilling that law.' What murmur can any defender of free choice raise against this? The Gentiles, just when they are full of ungodliness and every kind of vice, receive righteousness freely by the mercy of God, while the Jews, who devote themselves to righteousness with the utmost zeal and endeavor, are frustrated. Does not this simply mean that the endeavoring of free choice is in vain, even when it strives after the best, and that of itself it rather 'speeds toward the worse, and backward borne glides from us?' [Virgil *Georgics.* i. 200] Nor can anyone say that they did not strive with the utmost power of free choice. Paul himself bears them witness in chapter 10, 'that they have a zeal for God, but it is not enlightened' [Rom. 10:2]. Therefore, nothing is lacking in the Jews that is attributed to free choice, and yet nothing comes of it, or rather, the opposite comes of it. In the Gentiles there is nothing to be found of what is attributed to free choice, and yet the righteousness of God results. What is this but a confirmation by the unequivocal example of the two nations and the clearest possible testimony of Paul that grace is given freely to those without merits and the most undeserving, and is not obtained by any efforts, endeavors, or works, whether small or great, even of the best and most virtuous of men, though they seek and pursue righteousness with burning zeal?

69 Martin Luther *An Appeal to the Ruling Class of German Nationality as to the Amelioration of the State of Christendom* (1520)

The *Appeal* was published in response to attacks made on Luther for having challenged the notion of the papacy's absolute power. He appears to have written it with the help of members of the Elector of Saxony's court, jurists and members of the Wittenberg faculty. Luther called for the laity to reform the church since it seemed incapable of reforming itself, advice which, in the event, was largely followed in German cities and with the support of rulers such as Elector Frederick the Wise of Saxony. Luther argues that the state or secular power rather than the church has the authority to act to curb evil, that the pope alone does not have sole authority to interpret scripture, and that the decisions of church councils were not invalid without papal sanction.

Source: *Martin Luther: Selections from his Writings,* ed. J. Dillenberger, Anchor Books, New York, 1961, pp. 428–31

[. . .] The Romanists traffic in livings more disgracefully than the Gentiles under the cross trafficked with Christ's garments.

But the whole of the above is almost ancient history at Rome, and has become a custom. Yet Avarice has devised one thing more, perhaps the last, for I hope it will choke him. The pope possesses a refined device called *pectoralis reservatio*, i.e., his mental reservation, *et properius motus,* i.e., and his own free will and power. This is how it works. A certain candidate comes to Rome seeking a specified benefice. It is duly assigned under seal to him in the customary manner. Then comes another applicant who either offers to purchase the same benefice, or makes his claim in consideration of services rendered to the pope in a way which we shall not recount. The pope thereupon annuls the appointment already made, and gives it to the second applicant. If anyone were to protest that this transaction was an injustice, the Most Holy Father has to offer some explanation, lest he be accused of having flagrantly violated the law. He therefore declares that he had made reservations in his heart and conscience about that particular benefice, and had retained his control of it undiminished – and this, though in fact he had never given it another thought, or heard another word about it. Such an instance shows that the pope has discovered a worthy little 'gloss', by using which he can tell lies and play tricks without incurring censure, and can deceive and fool everybody publicly without a blush. Yet all the time he claims to be the head of the Christian Church, although he is a barefaced liar letting the Evil One dominate him.

This arbitrary and deceptive 'mental reservation' on the part of the pope creates a state of affairs in Rome that beggars description. You can find there a buying and selling, a bartering and a bargaining, a lying and trickery, robbery and stealing, pomp, procuration, knavery, and all sorts of stratagems bringing God into contempt, till it would be impossible for the Antichrist to govern more wickedly. There is nothing in Venice, Antwerp, or Cairo to compare with the fair which traffics in Rome. In those cities, right and reason enjoy some respect; but here things go on in a way that pleases the devil himself. This kind of morality flows like a tide into all the world. Such people rightly fear a reformation, or an unfettered council. They would rather set kings and princes at odds than that these should unite and bring a council together. No one could bear to have villainies of this kind come to the light of day.

Finally, the pope has built a market-house for the convenience of all this refined traffic, viz.: the house of the *datarius*[1] in Rome. This is where all those resort who deal in this way in benefices and livings. From him they must buy these 'glosses' and transactions, and get power to practise their archvillainy. In former days, Rome was still gracious enough to sell or suppress justice for a moderate price. But to-day, she has put her prices so high that she lets no one act the villain before he has paid a huge sum. If that is not more like a den of iniquity than any other den one can imagine, then I do not know what a den of iniquity is.

But, if you bring money to this ecclesiastical market, you can buy any of the goods I have described. Here any one can pay and then legally charge interest on loans of any sort. You can get a legal right to goods you have stolen or seized. Here vows are annulled; here monks receive liberty to leave their orders; here marriage is for sale to the clergy; here bastards can become legitimate, and any form of dishonour and shame can achieve dignity; all kinds of iniquity and evil are knighted and ennobled. Here a marriage is permitted which is within the forbidden degrees, or which is otherwise objectionable. O what a jugglery and extortion go on here! until it would seem that all the laws of the canon were only given to produce gilded nooses, from which a man must free himself if he would become a Christian. Indeed, here the devil becomes a saint and a god: what cannot be done anywhere else in heaven or earth, can be done in this house. They call the process *compositiones*. Yes, compositions, really confusions. O how light a tax is the Rhine-toll compared with the exactions of this sacred house!

Let no one imagine I am overdrawing the picture. Everything is public, and people in Rome have to acknowledge that it is terrible beyond the power to describe. I have not yet touched, nor do I intend to touch, upon the hellish dregs of the personal vices; I am dealing only with commonplace things, and yet I have not space to name them all. The bishops and priests, and especially the university doctors, whose salaries are given for the purpose, ought to have done their duty and, with one accord, written and declaimed against these things; but they have done the very opposite.

I must come to an end and have done with this section. Because the whole immeasurable greed which I have recounted is not satisfied with all this wealth, enough probably for three mighty kings, the business is now to be transferred, and sold to Fugger of Augsburg.[2] Henceforward bishoprics and livings for sale or exchange or in demand, and dealings in the spiritualities, have arrived at their true destination, now that the bargaining for spiritual or secular properties has become united into a single business. But I would like to hear of a man who is clever enough to discover what Avarice of Rome might do which has not already been done. Then perhaps Fugger would transfer and sell to someone else these two lines of business which are now to be combined into one. In my view, we have reached the limit.

For to describe what they have stolen in all countries, and are still stealing, and extorting, by indulgences, bulls, letters of confession, butter letters, and other *confessionalia*[3] – to describe all this is work for the odd-job man, and is like playing pitch and toss with a devil in hell. Not that it brings in little profit: it is enough to supply ample revenues for a mighty king; but it is not to be compared with the swelling flood of treasure described above. For the time being, I shall hold my tongue, and not say where the Indulgence-money has gone. Later I shall inquire about it. The Campofiore and Belvedere and a few more places probably know something about it.[4]

This wicked régime is not only barefaced robbery, trickery, and tyranny appropriate to the nether regions, but also a destruction of the body and soul of Christendom. Therefore we ought to make every effort to protect Christendom from this hurt and damage. If we are willing to make war on the Turks, let us begin here where they are most iniquitous. If we are right in hanging thieves and beheading robbers, why should we leave Avarice of Rome unpunished? Here is the greatest thief and robber that has ever come or is likely to come on earth, and the scandal is perpetrated in the holy names of Christ and St. Peter. Who can go on tolerating it or keeping silence? Almost all he possesses has been got by theft and robbery. Everything recorded in the histories tells the same story. The pope has never bought properties so great that his income from his ecclesiastical offices should amount to ten hundred thousand ducats, apart from the mines of treasure as already described, and his landed estates. Neither is it that which Christ and St. Peter bequeathed to him, nor that which any one has given or loaned to him; nor has it been acquired by prescription or ancient right. Tell me where he got it? On this point watch what they are seeking for and aiming at when they send out legates to gather funds against the Turks.

NOTES

1   A datary was an officer of the Papal court in Rome who registered and dated all documents issued by the Pope. By the early sixteenth century they were responsible for representing the Pope in the grant of dispensations, etc.
2   The Fuggers were bankers to the Papal *Curia*.
3   Letters of confession allowed the choice of confessor and of items to confess; butter letters allowed certain foods to be eaten on fast days; *confessionalia* were letters which excused the recipient from various burdensome duties. A fee was payable for this.
4   The Campo dei Fiori was one of Rome's oldest and most popular open markets; the Belvedere was a vast enclosed courtyard commissioned by Julius II in 1504 and constructed by Bramante (1444–1514).

70   Martin Luther **Article 25 from *Defence and Explanation of all the Articles of Dr Martin Luther which were unjustly condemned by the Roman Bull* (1521)**

On 15 June 1520 Pope Leo X (1513–21) issued the bull *Exsurge Domine* which condemned as 'heretical or scandalous, or false and offensive to pious ears, or as dangerous to simple minds, or subversive of catholic truth' forty-one theses extracted from Luther's writings. Luther was given sixty days to recant or else face excommunication. In September the bull was published in Germany and on 10 December Luther burned his copy of it outside the gates of Wittenberg with the words, 'Because you have destroyed God's truth, may the Lord destroy you in this fire'. He published four defences of his position of which this was the last, appearing in German in March 1521.

Source: *Luther's Works, vol. 32, The Career of the Reformer II*, ed. G. Forell, Muhlenberg Press, Philadelphia, 1958, pp. 67–71

THE TWENTY-FIFTH ARTICLE

The Roman bishop, the successor of St. Peter, is not by Christ's appointment vicar of Christ over all the churches of the world.

This is another of the key teachings which abolish the holy gospel and replace Christ with an idol in Christendom. Against it I have proposed this article. I stand by it and can prove it as follows:

First, since everything that is done in the church is proclaimed in clear and plain passages of Scripture, it is surely amazing that nothing is openly said in the whole Bible about the papacy. This is especially strange since my opponents consider the papacy the most important, most necessary, and most unique feature in the church. It is a suspicious situation and makes a bad impression that so many matters of lesser importance are based upon a multitude of reliable and clear passages of Scripture, while for this one doctrine no one has been able to produce a single clear reason. It is clearly stated in the gospel that St. Peter is a fisherman and an apostle, which they consider a matter of small importance compared with the papacy; yet there is not one single letter which states that St. Peter is above all the churches in the world.

At this point I would like to have it understood that I do not propose this article because I wish to repudiate the pope. Let him have as much power as he will, it makes no difference to me, and he is welcome to it. But there are two things I can neither tolerate nor keep silent about. First, he and his supporters torture, violate, and blaspheme the holy Word of God in order to establish their power. Second, they revile, slander, and anathematize the Greeks, and all others who do not submit to the pope, as though these were not Christians. They act as if being a Christian meant being bound to the pope and to Rome, while St. Paul and Christ have bound it only to faith and to God's Word, of which no one knows less or has less than the pope and his followers. And yet, though without faith and God's Word, he wants to be not only a Christian, but the god of all Christians and condemn all those who do not worship him, no matter how sound their faith and their gospel.

Moreover, if the pope were sensible, he would welcome less trouble, and he would not load all the affairs of the world on his own shoulders. It is surely impossible to tie the whole world to one place and transact all its business there.

But watch how they torture and insult the holy words of God in order to establish their prevaricated power. Christ says to St. Peter in Matt. 16 [:18], 'You are Peter' – that is a rock – 'and on this rock I will build my church, . . . I will give you the keys of the kingdom of heaven . . . and whatever you loose on earth shall be loosed in heaven.' Here they interpret the rock to mean St. Peter, and pretend that it is the papal power on which Christ builds his church, and that, therefore, all churches ought to be subject to the pope's power. According to the teaching of these experts the church built on the rock means the church subject to the pope: an interpretation of his words Christ has had to suffer all these years.

Now, in order to bring their lies and guile clearly into the open, and to make them blush for shame, let us examine Christ's words. If to build the church upon a rock means nothing but to be subject to the pope, as they say, it follows that the church can be built and exists without faith, without the gospel, and without any sacraments (for what is built is built and needs no further building). The power and authority of the pope are one thing; faith, sacraments and gospel are quite another thing. If, therefore, the church is built on the pope's power, it is evident that for the building of it the pope's power and authority are sufficient, and faith is not necessary, or anything else. Especially since the pope and his followers live, as a rule, without faith or the gospel and the sacraments, indeed, they despise them like heathen, and yet his power remains rock, building, and church, as they say. Isn't this a fine explanation of Christ's word! If the papists have the power to interpret Christ's word any way they please, who will stop someone else from saying that the rock and the building of the church are an ass and a cow, or whatever else his nightmares tell him?

Again, in this same passage, Christ speaks of this rock and of his church and says, 'the gates of hell shall not prevail against it' [Matt. 16:18]. Here Christ says clearly that against his rock and building and church the very devils shall not prevail. If, then, the rock is papal power and the building represents submission to this authority, how does it happen that this building and authority have in fact collapsed and the gates of hell have prevailed against it? For all Christendom has fallen away from the pope; for example, the Greeks, the Bohemians, Africa, and the whole Orient! Or to be more accurate, they never were built upon this rock. Now, if Christ, who cannot lie, promises that the gates of hell shall not prevail against his building, and no one can deny that the Orient has fallen away, it follows that Christ speaks the truth and the pope lies, and the building is not obedience to his power but something else, which the gates of hell have not been able to break down.

And it cannot be said that these people are no longer Christians because they do not obey the pope and are not built on him, since the pope himself and all his followers wish to be considered Christians, though they do not obey God in a single letter, and live, for the most part, without faith. So far they have been successful with their lies in maintaining that those who do not agree with them on this point are heretics and they themselves good Christians, though they do not take their stand with God and Christ on any point. Thus they make monkeys and fools of all the world, and define the terms 'Christian' and 'heretic' to suit themselves.

But let us leave their false interpretation and take up the true meaning of these words. To say that the gates of hell cannot prevail against this building must mean that the devil has no power over it; and this happens when the building is based on firm faith and stands without sin. Where faith is lacking or sin is present, there the devil rules and prevails against the building. Thus St. Peter teaches us [I Pet. 5:9] that we are to fight the devil with a strong faith, for the devil centers his attack on faith. From this it follows that this rock is Christ himself, for this is what St. Paul calls him in I Cor. 10 [:4]. The building is the believing church, in which there is no sin, and to build is nothing but to become a believer and free from sin, as St. Peter also teaches in I Pet. 2 [:5] that we are to be built into a spiritual house on Christ the rock.

Now, since the pope and his authority and those who obey him walk in sin and horrible perversions and are the devil's henchmen, as everyone can see, it must be a lying invention that the rock and the building, which Christ puts beyond the reach of the gates of hell, mean the papal power and rule. This power the devil has brought into subjection to himself. If the power of the pope were the 'rock' in Christ's words it could not do any evil, for Christ does not lie. But before our very eyes papal power has become the devil's power, a power for evil now as in the past.

Come on, you papists, crack this nut! This Scripture passage won't do any more, the citadel has been conquered, the pope has fallen, and he has nothing to stand on. For this saying of Christ has been the only basis on which the papacy has relied and built its claims all these many years. Now its lies and falsehoods have been revealed. If we have gained nothing else from the pope in this controversy we have at least liberated this passage of Scripture. In fact, this wins the war and decapitates the papacy, for this passage speaks stronger against the pope than for him. He who tells a single lie is assuredly not of God and everything else he says is suspect. But since the pope has lied about this fundamental doctrine and this key passage of Scripture on which it is based, and since he has perverted God's word and deceived the world with his false rule, what St. Paul says of him is certainly true, that the coming of the Antichrist shall be through the activity of the evil spirit, who enters only through lies and false interpretations of Scripture [II Thess. 2:9].

71 Martin Luther **Fragment of a letter to Philipp Melanchthon (1521)**

Luther relied upon Melanchthon to translate his ideas into practical propositions. In many matters, especially details of liturgy and practice, Luther was content to let believers do as they pleased, adopting new practices and verbal formulations as appropriate. To a large extent it was Melanchthon who developed a systematic and usable version of Luther's theology that might form the basis for the establishment of a new church. It was at this time, too, that the necessity for such work became evident as Luther's one-time follower, Andreas Karlstadt (c.1480–1541) developed Luther's ideas in directions which Luther himself could not accept. By 1521, for example, Karlstadt was arguing that those who received only the bread at communion were not true Christians. Luther had been content up until then to argue that communion should be administered to the laity in both kinds but would not say that to withhold the wine was a sin. This fragment is dated 1 August 1521.

Source: *Luther's Works, vol. 48, Letters*, ed. G. G. Krodel, Fortress Press, Philadelphia, 1963, pp. 277–82

[. . .] Paul speaks very openly concerning the priests. He says demons have forbidden them to marry. [*Timothy* 4:1] Since the voice of Paul is the voice of the Divine Majesty, I do not doubt that it must be trusted in this matter. Therefore even if they have consented to the devil's prohibition at the time of their initiation, then now, knowing the true state of the case and with whom they made their pact, the contract should be boldly broken.

God's Word clearly establishes that the prohibition [of marriage] originates with the devil; this puts me under considerable pressure. [. . .]

Why then do you hesitate to yield to this statement of God, even against the gates of hell? [The vow of celibacy] is not the same as the oath the children of Israel swore to the Gibeonites. [*Joshua* 9]. For they were commanded both to offer peace and accept it if offered them, and to gain proselytes [who] would comply with their religious observances. All this took place with the Gibeonites. Nothing happened there which was against the Lord or at the instigation of the 'spirits of error.' Although the [Israelites] murmured in the beginning, they finally accepted it [*Joshua* 9:16–18].

Moreover, celibacy is merely a human institution. Man, who has instituted it, can also abolish it; therefore any Christian can abolish it. I would say this even if it had been instituted by a good man instead of by demons.

I have no such declaration of God concerning the monks; therefore it is not safe to make the same assertion about them. I myself would not dare to comply with it [i.e. that the vow of monastic celebacy is to be abolished]; therefore I will not counsel anyone else to do so. If only we could achieve that henceforth no one would become a monk, or that a monk would not withdraw in the years of physical desire. We must avoid offense, even in the things that are permitted, unless we have a clear word of Scripture on our side. [. . .]

Concerning the argument that it is better to marry than to burn, or that they should enter the estate of matrimony in the sin of a broken promise in order to avoid the sin of fornication[1] – what is this other than quibbling rationalization? We are looking for a word of Scripture and a testimony of the divine will. Who knows if he who 'burns' today will 'burn' tomorrow?

I would not have allowed priests to marry merely because of the 'burning' if Paul did not call the prohibition of marriage erroneous, demonic, hypocritical, and condemned by God [1 *Timothy* 4:1]. Thus even without the 'burning' he compels us to give up celibacy for the sake of the fear of God. But it will be good to argue this matter at somewhat greater length. For I, too, would want to help the monks and nuns more than anything else, so greatly do I pity these wretched men and boys and girls who are vexed with pollutions and burnings.

Concerning 'both kinds' in the Eucharist, I am not arguing on the basis of the example [of the early church] but of the word of Christ. He[2] did not show that those who receive only the 'one kind' either have or have not sinned. But it is important that Christ did not require either kind, just as he does not absolutely require baptism, when a tyrant or the world prevent the use of water. The violence of persecution puts asunder a husband and wife (whom God has forbidden being put asunder) [*Matthew* 19:6], but they do not consent to the separation. In the same way pious hearts do not consent to being deprived of the 'other kind.' Who will deny, however, that they who do consent to it and approve of it – I mean the papists – are not Christians and are guilty of sin?

Since, then, Christ does not absolutely require 'both kinds,' and the tyrant prevents them, I do not see how those who receive only the 'one kind' commit sin. For who can take the 'other kind' by force, against the will of the tyrant? We are under no compulsion here, therefore, except that of reason, which declares that Christ's institution is not being observed; Scripture, however, does not make any decision, and without a word of Scripture we cannot declare it [i.e. the with-holding of the cup] sin. The Lord's Supper is Christ's institution, to be used in freedom, and it cannot be imprisoned in whole or in part. For what would happen in a situation similar to that of the martyr Donatus,[3] when some could not partake of the wine because the chalice was broken and the wine spilled, and no other wine was at hand? And I could quote many similar cases. In summary: since Scripture does not force [us to say] that [communion with] only 'one kind' is sin, I cannot claim it.

I am greatly pleased, of course, that you are restoring Christ's institution [i.e. the giving of bread and wine to communicants]. I had especially intended to work for this, had I returned to you; for now we recognize this tyranny and can resist it, and are no longer forced to receive only 'one kind.' But I also will never say another private mass in all eternity. Let us pray to the Lord, I beseech you, that he hasten to give us a larger portion of his Spirit, for I suspect that the Lord will soon visit Germany, as its unbelief, impiety, and hatred of the gospel deserve. But of course this plague will then be charged to us on the grounds that we heretics have provoked God, and we will be scorned by men and despised by the people [*Psalms* 22:6]. [The papists], however, will find excuses for their sins, and will justify themselves; [God will thus prove] that the wicked cannot be made good, either by kindness or by wrath, and that many will be tempted to do evil. The Lord's will be done. Amen.

If you are a preacher of grace, then preach a true and not a fictitious grace; if grace is true, you must bear a true and not a fictitious sin. God does not save people who are only fictitious sinners. Be a sinner and sin boldly, but believe and rejoice in Christ even more boldly, for he is victorious over sin, death, and the world. As long as we are here [in this world] we have to sin. This life is not the dwelling place of righteousness, but, as Peter says [*II Peter* 3:13], we look for new heavens and a new earth in which righteousness dwells. It is enough that by the riches of God's glory we have come to know the Lamb that takes away the sin of the world [*John* 1:29]. No sin will separate us from the Lamb, even though we commit fornication and murder a thousand times a day. Do you think that the purchase price that was paid for the redemption of our sins by so great a Lamb is too small? Pray boldly – you too are a mighty sinner.

August 1, 1521

NOTES

1   Both arguments were among Karlstadt's 21 June theses. They were based on 1 *Corinthians* 7:9 and 7:2.
2   Luther's meaning is unclear here. He could be referring either to Christ or to Karlstadt.
3   This refers to a story from the *Golden Legend*. While St Donatus was celebrating the

Lord's Supper, one of his deacons broke the chalice. Since it could not be replaced, Donatus picked up the pieces, and by his prayers, the pieces were joined together and the chalice could be used again.

72 Martin Luther *The Babylonian Captivity of the Church* (1520)

The Babylonian Captivity of the Church (also known as *The Pagan Servitude*) marked Luther's move from outlining the abuses of the Catholic church to criticism of its very substance. In particular he discussed the seven sacraments, their validity and purpose, arguing that there were properly only three: baptism, penance and communion. However, later in the work he argues that strictly speaking only baptism and communion were sacraments since they were divinely instituted signs, whereas penance lacked such authority and was really only a way of reaffirming baptism.

Source: *Luther's Works, vol. 36, Word and Sacrament II*, ed. A. R. Wentz, Muhlenberg Press, Philadelphia, 1959, pp. 18–19, 21–3, 34–9, 51–2, 54

To begin with, I must deny that there are seven sacraments, and for the present maintain that there are but three: baptism, penance, and the bread.[1] *All three have been subjected to a miserable captivity by the Roman curia, and the church has been robbed of all her liberty.* Yet, if I were to speak according to the usage of the Scriptures, I should have only one single sacrament, but with three sacramental signs, of which I shall treat more fully at the proper time.

Now concerning the sacrament of the bread first of all.

I shall tell you now what progress I have made as a result of my studies on the administration of this sacrament. For at the time when I was publishing my treatise on the Eucharist,[2] I adhered to the common custom and did not concern myself at all with the question of whether the pope was right or wrong. But now that I have been challenged and attacked, nay, forcibly thrust into this arena, I shall freely speak my mind, whether all the papists laugh or weep together. [. . .]

But imagine me standing over against them and interrogating my lords, the papists. In the Lord's Supper, the whole sacrament, or communion in both kinds, is given either to the priests alone or else it is at the same time given to the laity. If it is given only to the priests (as they would have it), then it is not right to give it to the laity in either kind. For it must not be given rashly to any to whom Christ did not give it when he instituted the sacrament. Otherwise, if we permit one institution of Christ to be changed, we make all of his laws invalid, and any man may make bold to say that he is not bound by any other law or institution of Christ. For a single exception, especially in the Scriptures, invalidates the whole. But if it is given also to the laity, it inevitably follows that it ought not to be withheld from them in either form. And if any do withhold it from them when they ask for it they are acting impiously and contrary to the act, example, and institution of Christ.

I acknowledge that I am conquered by this argument, which to me is irrefutable. I have neither read nor heard nor found anything to say against it. For here the word and example of Christ stand unshaken when he says, not by way of permission, but of command: 'Drink of it, all of you' [Matt. 26:27]. For if all are to drink of it, and the words cannot be understood as addressed to the priests alone, then it is certainly an impious act to withhold the cup from the laymen when they desire it, even though an angel from heaven [Gal. 1:8] were to do it. [. . .]

If, however, either kind may be withheld from the laity, then with equal right and reason a part of baptism or penance might also be taken away from them by this same authority of the church. Therefore, just as baptism and absolution must be administered in their entirety, so the sacrament of the bread must be given in its entirety to all laymen, if they desire it. I am much amazed, however, by their assertion that the priests may never receive only one kind in the mass under pain of mortal sin; and that for no other reason except (as they unanimously say) that the two kinds constitute one complete sacrament, which may not be divided. I ask them, therefore, to tell me why it is lawful to divide it in the case of the laity, and why they are the only ones to whom the entire sacrament is not given? Do they not acknowledge, by their own testimony, either that both kinds are to be given to the laity or that the sacrament is not valid when only one kind is given to them? How can it be that the sacrament in one kind is not complete in the case of the priests, yet in the case of the laity it is complete? Why do they flaunt the authority of the church and the power of the pope in my face? These do not annul the words of God and the testimony of the truth. [. . .]

But what carries most weight with me, however, and is quite decisive for me is that Christ says: 'This is my blood, which is poured out for you and for many for the forgiveness of sins.' Here you see very clearly that the blood is given to all those for whose sins it was poured out. But who will dare to say that it was not poured out for the laity? And do you not see whom he addresses when he gives the cup? Does he not give it to all? Does he not say that it is poured out for all? 'For you' [Luke 22:20], he says—let this refer to the priests. 'And for many' [Matt. 26:28], however, cannot possibly refer to the priests. Yet he says: 'Drink of it, all of you' [Matt. 26:27]. I too could easily trifle here and with my words make a mockery of Christ's words, as my dear trifler does. But those who rely on the Scriptures in opposing us must be refuted by the Scriptures. [. . .]

But now I ask, where is the necessity, where is the religious duty, where is the practical use of denying both kinds, that is, the visible sign, to the laity, when everyone concedes to them the grace of the sacrament without the sign? If they concede the grace, which is the greater, why not the sign, which is the lesser? For in every sacrament the sign as such is incomparably less than the thing signified. [. . .]

[. . .] Let us not dabble too much in philosophy, [. . .] Does not Christ appear to have anticipated this curiosity admirably by saying of the wine, not *Hoc est sanguis meus*, but *Hic est sanguis meus*? [Mark 14:24]. He speaks even more clearly when he brings in the word 'cup' and says: 'This cup [*Hic calix*] is the new testament in my blood' [Luke 22:20; I Cor. 11:25]. Does it not seem as though he desired to keep us in a simple faith, sufficient for us to believe that his blood was in the cup? For my part, if I cannot fathom how the bread is the body of Christ, yet I will take my reason captive to the obedience of Christ [II Cor. 10:5], and clinging simply to his words, firmly believe not only that the body of Christ is in the bread, but that the bread is the body of Christ. My warrant for this is the words which say: 'He took bread, and when he had given thanks, he broke it and said, "Take, eat, this (that is, this bread, which he had taken and broken) is my body"' [I Cor. 11:23–24]. And Paul says: 'The bread which we break, is it not a participation in the body of Christ?' [I Cor. 10:16]. He does not say 'in the bread there is,' but 'the bread itself is the participation in the body of Christ.' What does it matter if philosophy cannot fathom this? The Holy Spirit is greater than Aristotle. Does philosophy fathom their transubstantiation? Why, they themselves admit that here all philosophy breaks down. That the pronoun 'this,' in both Greek and Latin, is referred to 'body,' is due to the fact that in both of these languages the two words are of the same gender. In Hebrew, however, which has no neuter gender, 'this' is referred to 'bread,' so that it would be proper to say *Hic* [bread] *est corpus meum*. Actually, the idiom of the language and common sense both prove that the subject ['this'] obviously points to the bread and not to the body, when he says: *Hoc est corpus meum, das ist meyn leyp*, that is, 'This very bread here [*iste panis*] is my body.'

Thus, what is true in regard to Christ is also true in regard to the sacrament. In order for the divine nature to dwell in him bodily [Col. 2:9], it is not necessary for the human nature to be transubstantiated and the divine nature contained under the accidents of the human nature. Both natures are simply there in their entirety, and it is truly said: 'This man is God; this God is man.' Even though philosophy cannot grasp this, faith grasps it nonetheless. And the authority of God's Word is greater than the capacity of our intellect to grasp it. In like manner, it is not necessary in the sacrament that the bread and wine be transubstantiated and that Christ be contained under their accidents in order that the real body and real blood may be present. But both remain there at the same time, and it is truly said: 'This bread is my body; this wine is my blood,' and vice versa. Thus I will understand it for the time being to the honor of the holy words of God, to which I will allow no violence to be done by petty human arguments, nor will I allow them to be twisted into meanings which are foreign to them. At the same time, I permit other men to follow the other opinion, which is laid down in the decree, *Firmiter*, only let them not press us to accept their opinions as articles of faith (as I have said above).

[. . .] [T]here is no opinion more generally held or more firmly believed in the church today than this, that the mass is a good work and a sacrifice. And this abuse has brought an endless host of other abuses in its train, so that the faith of this sacrament has become utterly extinct and the holy sacrament has been turned into mere merchandise, a market, and a profit-making business. Hence participations, brotherhoods, intercessions, merits, anniversaries, memorial days[3] and the like wares are bought and sold, traded and bartered, in the church. On these the priests and monks depend for their entire livelihood. [. . .]

In the first place, in order that we might safely and happily attain to a true and free knowledge of this sacrament, we must be particularly careful to put aside whatever has been added to its original simple institution by the zeal and devotion of men: such things as vestments, ornaments, chants, prayers, organs, candles, and the whole pageantry of outward things. We must turn our eyes and hearts simply to the institution of Christ and this alone, and set nothing before us but the very word of Christ by which he instituted the sacrament, made it perfect, and committed it to us. For in that word, and in that word alone, reside the power, the nature, and the whole substance of the mass. All the rest is the work of man, added to the word of Christ, and the mass can be held and remain a mass just as well without them. Now the words of Christ, in which he instituted this sacrament, are these:

'Now as they were eating, Jesus took bread, and blessed, and broke it, and gave it to his disciples and said, "Take, eat; this is my body, which is given for you." And he took a cup, and when he had given thanks he gave it to them, saying, "Drink of it, all of you; for this cup is the new testament in my blood, which is poured out for you and for many for the forgiveness of sins. Do this in remembrance of me."' [. . .]

Let this stand, therefore, as our first and infallible proposition – the mass or Sacrament of the Altar is Christ's testament, which he left behind him at his death to be distributed among his believers. For that is the meaning of his words, 'This cup is the new testament in my blood' [Luke 22:20; I Cor. 11:25]. Let this truth stand, I say, as the immovable foundation on which we shall base all that we have to say. For, as you will see, we are going to overthrow all the godless opinions of men which have been imported into this most precious sacrament. Christ, who is the truth, truly says that this is the new testament in his blood, poured out for us [Luke 22:20]. Not without reason do I dwell on this sentence; the matter is of no small moment, and must be most deeply impressed on our minds.

Thus, if we enquire what a testament is, we shall learn at the same time what the mass is, what its right use and blessing, and what its wrong use.

A testament, as everyone knows, is a promise made by one about to die, in which he designates his bequest and appoints his heirs. A testament, therefore, involves first, the death of the testator, and second, the promise of an inheritance and the naming of the heir. Thus Paul discusses at length the nature of a testament in Rom. 4, Gal. 3 and 4, and Heb. 9. We see the same thing clearly also in these words of Christ. Christ testifies concerning his death when he says: 'This is my body, which is given, this is my blood, which is poured out' [Luke 22:19–20]. He names and designates the bequest when he says 'for the forgiveness of sins' [Matt. 26:28]. But he appoints the heirs when he says 'For you [Luke 22:19–20; I Cor. 11:24] and for many' [Matt. 26:28; Mark 14:24], that is, for those who accept and believe the promise of the testator. For here it is faith that makes men heirs, as we shall see.

You see, therefore, that what we call the mass is a promise of the forgiveness of sins made to us by God, and such a promise as has been confirmed by the death of the Son of God. For the only difference between a promise and a testament is that the testament involves the death of the one who makes it. A testator is a promiser who is about to die, while a promiser (if I may put it thus) is a testator who is not about to die. [. . .] Now God made a testament; therefore, it was necessary that he should die. But God could not die unless he became man. Thus the incarnation and the death of Christ are both comprehended most concisely in this one word, 'testament.'

From the above it will at once be seen what is the right and what is the wrong use of the mass, and what is the worthy and what the unworthy preparation for it. If the mass is a promise, as has been said, then access to it is to be gained, not with any works, or powers, or merits of one's own, but by faith alone. For where there is the Word of the promising God, there must necessarily be the faith of the accepting man. It is plain therefore, that the beginning of our salvation is a faith which clings to the Word of the promising God, who, without any effort on our part, in free and unmerited mercy takes the initiative and offers us the word of his promise. 'He sent forth his word, and thus [sic] healed them,'[4] not: 'He accepted our work, and thus healed us.' First of all there is God's Word. After it follows faith; after faith, love; then love does every good work, for it does no wrong, indeed, it is the fulfilling of the law [Rom. 13:10]. In no other way can man come to God or deal with him than through faith. That is to say, that the author of salvation is not man, by any works of his own, but God, through his promise; and that all things depend on, and are upheld and preserved by, the word of his power [Heb. 1:3], through which he brought us forth, to be a kind of first fruits of his creatures [Jas. 1:18]. [. . .]

Now there is yet a second stumbling block that must be removed, and this is much greater and the most dangerous of all. It is the common belief that the mass is a sacrifice, which is offered to God. Even the words of the canon[5] seem to imply this, when they speak of 'these gifts, these presents, these holy sacrifices,' and further on 'this offering.' Prayer is also made, in so many words, 'that the sacrifice may be accepted even as the sacrifice of Abel,' etc. Hence Christ is termed 'the sacrifice of the altar.' Added to these are the sayings of the holy fathers, the great number of examples, and the widespread practice uniformly observed throughout the world. [. . .]

When he instituted this sacrament and established this testament at the Last Supper, Christ did not offer himself to God the Father, nor did he perform a good work on behalf of others, but, sitting at the table, he set this same testament before each one and proffered to him the sign. Now, the more closely our mass resembles that first mass of all, which Christ performed at the Last Supper, the more Christian it will be. But Christ's mass was most simple, without any display of vestments, gestures, chants, or other ceremonies, so that if it had been necessary to offer the mass as a sacrifice, then Christ's institution of it was not complete.

Not that any one should revile the church universal for embellishing and amplifying the mass with many additional rites and ceremonies. But what we contend for is this: No one should be deceived by the glamor of the ceremonies and entangled in the multitude of pompous forms, and thus lose the simplicity of the mass itself, and indeed practice a sort of transubstantiation by losing sight of the simple 'substance' of the mass and clinging to the manifold 'accidents'of outward pomp. For whatever has been added to the word and example of Christ is an 'accident' of the mass, and ought to be regarded just as we regard the so-called monstrances and corporal cloths in which the host itself is contained. Therefore, just as distributing a testament or accepting a promise differs diametrically from offering a sacrifice, so it is a contradiction in terms to call the mass a sacrifice, for the former is something that we receive and the latter is something that we give. The same thing cannot be received and offered at the same time, nor can it be both given and accepted by the same person, any more than our prayer can be the same thing as that which our prayer obtains, or the act of praying be the same thing as the act of receiving that for which we pray. [. . .]

Therefore, let the priests who offer the sacrifice of the mass in these corrupt and most perilous times take heed, first, that they do not refer to the sacrament the words of the greater and lesser canon, together with the collects, because they smack too strongly of sacrifice. They should refer them instead to the bread and the wine to be consecrated, or to their own prayers. For the bread and wine are offered beforehand for blessing in order that they may be sanctified by the word and by prayer [I Tim. 4:5], but after they have been blessed and consecrated they are no longer offered, but received as a gift from God. And in this rite let the priest bear in mind that the gospel is to be set above all canons and collects devised by men, and that the gospel does not sanction the idea that the mass is a sacrifice, as has been shown. [. . .]

NOTES

1   'The bread' was a common designation for Communion where the laity were given bread but not wine.
2   *A Treatise Concerning the Blessed Sacrament* (1519).
3   Participations allowed spiritual 'participation' in masses even if one were not present; brotherhoods were confraternities which paid to have masses said for them and engaged in devotional exercises for gaining merit. This gave members the benefits accruing from prayers and attendance at masses of all the other members; anniversaries were masses said on behalf of the soul of a deceased person daily for a year or annually on the anniversary of their death; masses for the dead were read on memorial days.
4   *Sic* is Luther's own interpolation into the Vulgate text.
5   The canon of the mass is the part of the liturgy of the mass where the bread and wine are consecrated. Luther translated the canon from Latin in his treatise *On The Abomination of the Secret Mass* (1525).

73   Philipp Melanchthon **Inaugural address to the University of Wittenberg (1518)**

Philipp Melanchthon (1497–1560) was great-nephew of the celebrated humanist scholar Johannes Reuchlin and received from him his early education. He was subsequently educated at the universities of Heidelberg and Tübingen where he became an expert in Greek and published a Greek grammar in 1518. On the strength of this, he was appointed by Elector Frederick the Wise of Saxony to be first professor of Greek at the University of Wittenberg. Four days after his arrival he gave his inaugural address, speaking about curricular reform and his belief that true learning would bring about moral reformation. This text and Text 74 show how Melanchthon's thought developed and how he made Luther's ideas systematic.

Source: *The Reformation in its own Words*, ed. H. J. Hillerbrand, SCM Press, London, 1964, pp. 58–60

It appears impudent and presumptuous indeed to speak in this illustrious gathering, since both my temperament and the nature of my studies keep me from such a place and such a laudatory gathering of orators. The difficulties of the subject-matter, which I am about to consider, could also frighten me, if my respect for true studies and my office would not exhort me to recommend to you to the best of my ability sound scholarship and the newly awakening muses. Their cause I have pledged to guard against the barbarians, who in barbaric fashion, that is, with might and deception, demand in vulgar fashion the titles and rights of learned teachers and to this very day with evil cunning frustrate men. Some stop with sly arguments the German youth which for several years attempts to enter the arena of scholarly competition. They claim that to study the newly awakening literary sciences was more difficult than profitable; that to learn Greek was a matter of idle minds and nothing but boasting; that Hebrew had little to commend itself. In the meantime the true sciences were allowed to decay, philosophy made into an orphan.

Certain men, be it because of intellectual immoderation or quarrelsomeness, jumped upon Aristotle, a crippled Aristotle who for the Greeks themselves was as mysterious as Apollo's 'Delphic oracle'. . . . Noble studies were more and more neglected, the knowledge of Greek was lost, and the bad was being taught instead of the good. From thence arose Thomas, Scotus, Durandus,[1] the seraphic and cherubinic doctors and their followers in greater number than even the offspring of Kadmos.[2] . . . Such studies were prevalent for about three hundred years in England, France, and Germany – and I will not speak further about what transpired during that time. The inevitably unprofitable results must be obvious from what I have said. To make it very clear, listen carefully:

First of all, the neglect of the old disciplines and the introduction of this bold way of commentating and philosophizing caused both Greek and mathematics to be forgotten and religion to suffer. What worse, more raging evil could one think of? And yet none was ever more widespread. Until that time philosophy had been altogether Greek, and only Cyprian, Hilary, Ambrose, Jerome, and Augustine[3] had excelled in Latin. Greek had been in the West virtually the language of religion. By despising Greek, the inestimable benefit of philosophy for humanistic studies was lost. With this disappeared the participation in religion. This development brought decay for Christian morals and the customs of the Church as well as for literary studies. Alleviation easily might have been

22 Albrecht Dürer,
Philipp Melanchthon, 1526
engraving, 17.6 × 12.7 cm,
Germanisches
Nationalmuseum,
Nuremburg.

possible, if only one thing had not perished. The decay of erudition might have
been halted had the ecclesiastical ritual not been touched. With the help of good
erudition one could have done away with the corruption in the Church, raised
up the fallen spirit of man, strengthened this spirit and called it back to order.
Through our guilt or through fate, noble erudition turned into its opposite, and
old piety turned into ceremonies, and was put into the hands of human traditions, human decisions, decretals, regulations, moods and the glosses of the
scribes. . . .

In theology, too, it is important how education is performed. If any field of
studies, then theology requires especially talent, training, and conscientiousness.
The aroma of God's salve supersedes all the aromas of human knowledge. Led
by the Holy Spirit, but accompanied by humanist studies, one should proceed
to theology. . . . But since the Bible is written in part in Hebrew and in part in
Greek – as Latinists we drink from the stream of both – we must learn these
languages, unless we want to be 'silent persons' as theologians. Once we understand the significance and the weight of the words, the true meaning of Scripture will light up for us as the midday sun. Only if we have clearly understood
the language will we clearly understand the content. All the dry glossaries, con-
cordances, disconcordances and the like, which have been manufactured without

number, are only hindrances for the spirit. If we put our minds to the sources, we will begin to understand Christ rightly. Then his commandments will become understandable, and we will have tasted from the blessed nectar of sacred wisdom. And, if we 'harvest the grapes in the vineyards of Engedi', as we read in the Song of Songs, the beloved will encounter us 'jumping over hills and mountains', and sweet odours will lead us into the Garden of Eden . . . in death we will receive the kiss of the beloved: woven into his limbs will we live and die, immersed into Zion's sight. . . . These are the fruits of the heavenly wisdom. Let us adore them purely and untouched by our sophistication – as Paul often admonishes us, especially in his letter to Titus; let the Christian teaching be pure, free from all corruption. Doctrine is to be pure. This means: we are not to dirty the sacred Scripture with unprofitable foreign writings. If we mingle the profane with the sacred, we must know that all the profane desires, hatred, quarrelsomeness and factions, division and anger will appear. Whoever wishes to penetrate into religion, must take off the old Adam and put on a new, incorruptible one. That is, he must shake off and break with human desires and with the yoke of the sly serpent with superior power. . . .

This is what I meant when I said that the Church has decayed by a lack of education and that true and genuine piety was perverted by human additions. Once there was a delight in man's commentaries, one ate instead of the divine manna baal-peor and men ceased to be Christians. This I want to say the way I mean it. I mean nothing but what the order of the Church recognizes as evangelical truth. That will be my 'might and power', as the Hebrews say.

NOTES

1   Thomas Aquinas, Johannes Duns Scotus and Durandus of Alvernia (fl. *c.*1205), an early translator of Aristotle.

2   Cadmus was the legendary founder of Mycenean Thebes. Before the town could be established he had to kill a dragon. After death its teeth were scattered on the earth and were transformed into savage warriors, *Spartoi.*

3   These were all early Fathers of the church (Patristics).

74 Philipp Melanchthon *Loci Communes* (1521)

Melanchthon soon became an enthusiastic admirer of Luther's teachings and in 1519 edited his commentaries on the Psalms and Paul's Epistle to the Galatians. Developing further his study of Paul's work, Melanchthon was able to offer a systematic critique of scholastic philosophy, preferring the word of scripture to 'scholastic trifling'. He was particularly concerned to summarise the outlines of Lutheran reform in a clear, comprehensible and systematic form, which he did in *Loci Communes* [*Common places*].

Source: *Melanchthon and Bucer*, ed. W. Pauk, Library of Christian Classics, vol. 19, SCM Press, London, 1969, pp. 86–9, 133–6, 145–7

GRACE

Just as the law is the knowledge of sin, so the gospel is the promise of grace and righteousness. Therefore, since we have spoken of the word of grace and righteousness, that is, the gospel, the principles of grace and justification should be included here. For in this way the nature of the gospel can be more fully understood.

At this point one may rightly remonstrate with the Scholastics. They have shamefully misused that sacred word 'grace' by using it to designate a quality in the souls of the saints. The worst of all offenders are the Thomists who have placed the quality 'grace' in the nature of the soul, and faith, hope, and love in the powers of the soul. How old-womanish and stupid is the way they dispute about the powers of the soul! But let these godless men demean themselves and pay the penalty for their trifling with the gospel and despising it. You, dear reader, pray that the Spirit of God may reveal his gospel to our hearts. For the gospel is the word of the Spirit which cannot be taught except through the Spirit. Isaiah says this in ch. 54:13: 'All your sons shall be taught by the Lord.'

1. In the writings of the New Testament the word 'grace' (*gratia*) is commonly used for the Hebrew word *hēn*. This the translators of the LXX often changed to *charis*, as in Ex. 33:12: 'You have also found favor (*gratia*) in my sight.' But it means plainly what *favor* means in Latin, and would that the translators had preferred to use the word *favor* to *gratia*! For then the Sophists would have lacked the occasion for going foolishly astray on this topic. Therefore, just as the grammarians say that Julius favors Curio when they mean that in Julius is the favor with which he has befriended Curio, so in Holy Writ 'grace' means 'favor,' and it is the 'grace' or 'favor' in God with which he has befriended the saints. Those Aristotelian figments about qualities are tiresome. Grace is nothing else, if it is to be most accurately defined, than God's goodwill toward us, or the will of God which has mercy on us. Therefore, the word 'grace' does not mean some quality in us, but rather the very will of God, or the goodwill of God toward us. [. . .]

[W]e have made the terminology of the word 'grace' as simple as possible, following the phraseology of Scripture, which says that grace is the favor, mercy, and gratuitous goodwill of God toward us. The gift is the Holy Spirit himself, whom he pours into the hearts of those on whom he has had mercy. The fruits of the Holy Spirit are faith, hope, love, and the remaining virtues. So much for the term 'grace.' To sum it all up, grace is nothing but the forgiveness or remission of sins. The Holy Spirit is the gift that regenerates and sanctifies hearts, in accordance with Ps. 104:30: 'When thou sendest forth thy Spirit, they are created; and thou renewest the face of the ground.' The gospel promises grace as well as the gift of grace. The Scriptures are plain on this, and therefore it seems enough to cite one passage, Jer. 31:33: 'After those days, says the Lord, I will put my law within them, and I will write it upon their hearts.' These words certainly refer to the gift of grace, and the words following them to grace itself (v. 34): 'They shall all know me, from the least of them to the greatest of them, says the Lord; for I will forgive their iniquity, and I will remember their sin no more.'

JUSTIFICATION AND FAITH

1. Therefore, we are justified when, put to death by the law, we are made alive again by the word of grace promised in Christ; the gospel forgives our sins, and we cling to Christ in faith, not doubting in the least that the righteousness of Christ is our righteousness, that the satisfaction Christ wrought is our expiation, and that the resurrection of Christ is ours. In a word, we do not doubt at all that our sins have been forgiven and that God now favors us and wills our good. Nothing, therefore, of our own works, however good they may seem or be, constitutes our righteousness. But FAITH alone in the mercy and grace of God in Christ Jesus is our RIGHTEOUSNESS. This is what the prophet says and what Paul discusses so often. 'The righteous shall live by faith' (Rom. 1:17). Rom. 3:22 speaks of 'the righteousness of God through faith in Jesus Christ.' There has now been made manifest not the hypocrisy of works, which men count as righteousness, but a righteousness has been revealed of such a kind that God reckons it as righteousness. Rom. 4:5: 'To one who . . . TRUSTS . . . , his faith is reckoned as righteousness.' Gen. 15:6: 'And he [Abraham] BELIEVED the Lord; and he reckoned it to him as righteousness.' I commend these two passages to you very highly so that you may understand that faith is properly called righteousness. For the Sophists are offended by this kind of speech – when we say that faith is righteousness. [. . .]

SIGNS

We have said that the gospel is the promise of grace. This section on signs is very closely related to the promises. The Scriptures add these signs to the promises as seals which remind us of the promises, and definitely testify of the divine will toward us. They testify that we shall surely receive what God has promised. In the use of signs there have been most shameful errors. For when the Schools argue the difference between the sacraments of the Old and New Testaments, they say that there is no power to justify in the sacraments of the Old Testament. They attribute the power to justify to the sacraments of the New Testament, which is surely an obvious mistake, for faith alone justifies. [. . .]

Run through all Scripture, if you care to, and dig out the meaning of signs from sacred history, not from the godless Sophists. [. . .] Why seek many examples, since Scripture is full of instances of this kind? From them I believe the function of signs can be learned.

Signs do not justify. [. . .] So Baptism is nothing, and participation in the Lord's Supper is nothing, but they are testimonies and seals of the divine will toward you which give assurance to your conscience if it doubts grace or God's goodwill toward itself. Hezekiah could not doubt that he would recover when he had not only heard the promise but had also seen the promise confirmed by a sign. Gideon could not doubt the promise that he would be victorious, since he had been strengthened by so many signs. In like manner you ought not to doubt that you have experienced mercy when you have heard the gospel and received the signs of the gospel, baptism, and the body and blood of the Lord. Hezekiah could have been restored without a sign if he had been willing to believe the bare promise of God, and Gideon would have overcome without a sign if he had believed. So you can be justified without a sign, provided you believe.

Therefore, signs do not justify, but the faith of Hezekiah and Gideon had to be buoyed up, strengthened, and confirmed by such signs. [. . .]

Those things which others call 'sacraments' we call 'signs,' or, if you please, 'sacramental signs.' For Paul calls Christ himself a 'sacrament' (Col. 1:27; I Tim. 3:16, Vulg.). If you do not like the term 'sign,' you may call the sacraments 'seals,' for by this term the nature of the sacraments is more closely approximated. Those are to be commended who have compared these signs with symbols or military passwords, because signs were only marks by which those to whom the divine promises pertained could be known. Although he had already been justified, Cornelius was baptized that he might be reckoned in the number of those to whom the promise of the Kingdom of God and eternal life pertained. I have given this instruction on the nature of signs that you may understand what a godly use of the sacraments is, lest anyone follow the Scholastics, who have attributed justification to the signs by a terrible error.

There are two signs, however, instituted by Christ in the Gospel: Baptism and participation in the Lord's Table. For we judge that sacramental signs are only those which have been divinely handed down as signs of the grace of God. For we men can neither institute a sign of the divine will toward us nor can we adapt those signs which Scripture has employed otherwise as signifying that will. Therefore, we marvel the more how it ever came into the minds of the Sophists to include among the sacraments things which the Scriptures do not mention by so much as a word, especially when they attributed justification to signs. From what source has their doctrine of ordination been fabricated? God did not institute marriage to be a special sign of grace. Extreme unction is more an ancient rite than a sign of grace. Luther disputed at length on this subject in his *Babylonian Captivity*, and from this work you will get a more precise argument. This is the core of the matter: grace is not definitely and properly revealed except by those signs which have been handed down by God. Therefore, nothing can be called a sacramental sign except what has been added to the divine promises. For this reason, it was said by the ancients that sacraments consist of things and words. The thing is the sign and the words are the promise of grace. [. . .]

PARTICIPATION IN THE LORD'S TABLE

Participation in the Lord's Table, that is, eating the body and drinking the blood of Christ, is a certain sign of grace. For He says in Luke 22:20: 'This cup . . . is the new covenant in my blood,' etc. In I Cor. 11:25 we read: 'Do this as often as you drink it, in remembrance of me.' This means that when you celebrate Communion, you should be reminded of the gospel or the remission of sins. It is not, therefore, a sacrifice if it was given only as a sure reminder of the promise of the gospel. Nor does participation in the Supper destroy sin, but faith destroys it, and faith is strengthened by this sign. The sight of Christ did not justify Stephen when he was on the point of death, but it strengthened the faith through which he was justified and made alive. Likewise, participation in the Supper does not justify, but it strengthens faith, as I have said above. All Masses are godless, therefore, except those by which consciences are encouraged for the strengthening of faith. A sacrifice is what we offer to God, but we do not offer Christ to God. But he himself offered up himself once for all. Therefore, those who perform Masses in order to do some good work or offer Christ to God for the living and the dead with the idea that the oftener this is repeated, the better they become, are caught in godless error. I think that for the most part these errors must be blamed on Thomas who taught that a Mass benefits others besides the one who partakes.[1]

The function of this sacrament, however, is to strengthen us whenever our consciences totter and whenever we have doubts concerning God's will toward us. These times come often in life, but especially when we are about to die. Particularly those about to die, therefore, must be strengthened by this sacrament. Nor are we living a true Christian life unless we die continually. Confirmation, in my opinion, is the laying on of hands. Unction, I think, is what Mark 6:13 mentions. But I cannot see that these two have been given as sure signs of grace. It is certain that marriage was not instituted for this purpose either. And what came into the minds of those who numbered ordination among the signs of grace? For ordination is nothing else than choosing from the Church those who are to teach, baptize, bless the Supper, and share alms with the needy. Those who taught, baptized, and blessed the Supper were called 'bishops' or 'presbyters.' Those who distributed alms to the needy were known as 'deacons.' The functions of these men were not so specialized that it was sacrilege for a deacon to teach, to baptize, or to bless the Supper. On the other hand, these duties are for all Christians, for the keys belong to all (Matt. 18:18). But the administration of these things was put in the hands of certain men that there might be those who knew that it was their special duty to superintend ecclesiastical affairs, and that there might be those to whom matters could be duly referred if anything came up.

In passing, I should like to remind you that the words 'bishop,' 'presbyter,' and 'deacon,' have nothing to do with the word 'priest.' For Scripture uses the word 'priest' in connection with sacrifice and intercessory prayer. We Christians are all priests because we offer a sacrifice, namely, our body. Apart from this, there is no place for sacrifice in Christianity, and we have the right to pray to God and even to placate him. [. . .]

NOTE

1   Thomas Aquinas, *Summa theologica*, III, q.79, a.7.

75   Ulrich Zwingli *On the Lord's Supper* (1526)

On the Lord's Supper was the first, clear expression of Ulrich Zwingli's belief that both the Catholic and Lutheran positions on the real presence were wrong. He denied that Christ was either literally or corporeally present in or with the elements (the bread and the wine). The bread could not be Christ's flesh, nor the resurrected body of Christ; nor could the presence of Christ be in and with the bread even if the bread remained itself. He did not deny Christ's spiritual presence but believed the words 'This is my body' to be symbolical. He was anxious to distinguish between the sign and the thing itself that was signified.

Source: *Zwingli and Bullinger*, ed. G. W. Bromiley, Library of Christian Classics, vol. 24, SCM Press, London, 1953, pp. 222–3

In the first article, God willing, it was made clear from the nature of Christ's works that the saying, 'This is my body,' cannot be taken literally, otherwise we tear his flesh with our teeth in the very same way as it was pierced by the nails and the spear [at the crucifixion]. In the second [article] we considered the clear Scriptures which will not permit of the literal presence of his flesh and blood in this sacrament, a necessary procedure if we are not to rush to the details of the Holy Scripture, but in everything to test the meaning which Scripture as a whole will bear. For if Scripture is spoken by God, as is taught by Peter and Paul, then it cannot contradict itself. If it appears to do so, it is because we do not rightly understand it, comparing Scripture with Scripture [. . .] Our present task is to indicate that interpretation of the words 'this is my body' which will best harmonize with the rest of Scripture and the three articles of the creed.

76   Ulrich Zwingli *An Exposition of the Faith* (1531)

An Exposition of the Faith was written by Zwingli in 1531 but was not actually published until after his death, appearing in 1536 with the First Helvetic Confession. It provides a clear amplification of some of Zwingli's beliefs about the Lord's supper. He also wrote in the same work against the revolutionary social and political implications of some Protestant teaching.

Source: *Zwingli and Bullinger*, ed. G. W. Bromiley, Library of Christian Classics, vol. 24, SCM Press, London, 1953, pp. 254–65

In the Lord's supper the natural and essential body of Christ in which he suffered and is now seated in heaven at the right hand of God is not eaten naturally and literally, but only spiritually, and that the papist teaching that the body of Christ is eaten in the same form and with the same properties and nature as when he was born and suffered and died is not only presumptuous and foolish but impious and blasphemous.

[. . .] When you come to the Lord's Supper to feed spiritually upon Christ, and when you thank the Lord for this great favour, for the redemption whereby you are delivered from despair, and for the pledge whereby you are assured of eternal salvation, when you join with your brethren in partaking of the bread and wine which are the tokens of the body of Christ, then in the true sense of the word you eat him sacramentally. You do inwardly that which you represent outwardly, your soul being strengthened by the faith which you attest in the tokens.

But of those who publicly partake of the visible sacraments or signs, yet without faith, it cannot properly be said that they eat sacramentally.

[. . .] Whether we like it or not, we are forced to concede that the words: 'This is my body' cannot be taken naturally or literally, but have to be construed symbolically, sacramentally, metaphorically or as a metonomy, that: 'This is my body,' that is, 'This is the sacrament of my body,' or, 'This is my sacramental or mystical body,' that is, the sacramental and representative symbol of the body which I readily assumed and yielded over to death.

77 Venetian diplomatic report **Description of the religious situation in Augsburg (1530)**

To support their trade and banking the Venetians maintained an extensive network of ambassadors and envoys all over Europe for the purposes of reporting on current affairs. This report was sent from Augsburg at the time of the imperial diet of 1530 which was called to try to settle the religious differences within the Holy Roman Empire.

Source: *The Reformation in its Own Words*, ed. H. J. Hillerbrand, SCM Press, London, 1964, pp. 402–3

This city is divided into three factions, viz. the papists who still have here their churches, images, masses, canonical hours, and bells, though they are in very small number as compared with the other inhabitants. . . .

The second faction is that of the Lutherans, who are numerous, and complain greatly of the dismissal by the Government of some of their preachers, because they did not agree with certain other preachers of the faction of Zwingli in the matter of the eucharist; but the Government acted thus for the public peace.

The third faction, which is that of Zwingli, is the greatest, and it comprises beyond comparison many more of the citizens, so that yesterday they celebrated the communion *more Zwinglij*, and side with him in all things as you know, and all the Evangelical preachers are unanimously in his favour. . . .

On holidays, the aforesaid preachers preach '*la scriptura sacra*' in five places, some of them expounding Matthew, some Paul . . . before the sermon, there being present a very great concourse of people evincing much devotion; and they go without much ringing of bells, which merely strike the hours. All the people sing the Psalms of David, most melodiously, causing great spiritual joy and consolation to the hearers; so that after the sermon, they always sing a psalm; and then the preacher exhorts them to give alms, which are most abundant, in such wise that the need of such as are unable to help themselves is provided for. He

23 *Jakob Fugger and his*
bookkeeper Matthaus Schwarz,
Herzog Anton Ulrich-
Museum, Brunswick.

also exhorts them to pray for all sorts and conditions of men, as likewise for the propagation of the Gospel. They live very frugally, with regard both to apparel, household furniture, and daily food; and they administer exemplary justice.

They also give daily lectures in Hebrew, Greek and Latin; and attend more than ever was the practice formerly to the education of youth, both as concerns literature and sound Christian morality.

78 Johannes Wildenauer Egranus **Letter to Martin Luther (1521)**

Egranus was a humanist scholar and preacher at the church of St Mary in Zwickau, Saxony. He was a moderate reformer whose criticisms of the old church were largely restricted to indulgences and the cult of saints. Thomas Müntzer (*c.*1489–1525) had received a humanist education but later rejected book-learning. He argued that every individual had the right to interpret the scripture as they pleased, subject to the guidance of the Holy Spirit. Müntzer preached in Zwickau for some months in 1520 and 1521. However, Müntzer fell out with

Egranus and left Zwickau after causing discord there. Egranus wrote to Luther in May 1521 about his experience.

Source: S. Karant-Nunn, *Zwickau in Transition 1500–47: the Reformation as an Agent of Change*, Ohio State University Press, Columbus, 1987, p. 103

Your Thomas – for so he styles himself – came here and made everything topsy-turvy with his insane noise and his teachings. The stubbornness and shamelessness of the man are great. He directs himself in accordance with neither the advice of friends nor the authority of scripture, but supported only by his [purported] revelations he causes nothing but factionalism. This is a person who is born to schism and heresy. But in the end the evil falls upon his own head and he into the pit that he has dug for others. In a disgraceful manner he has taken flight. As is his nature, he has (to the disgrace of this otherwise famous city) had fellow conspirators among the people, folk encumbered with debts, law-breakers, persons given to revolt, whom in the main he attracted to himself through his confessional office and through private conventicles. His poison is the heritage he left behind, for the day laborers scream even yet against every person of rank, every preacher and priest. I hear that the wild beast strews about all sorts of lies concerning me. I must bear that; my conscience and my innocence comfort me. I do not believe that any good and educated man can trust this most mendacious human being.

79 Philipp Melanchthon **Letter to Elector Frederick the Wise of Saxony (1521)**

While Melanchthon was responsible for turning Luther's inspiration into practical liturgical and organisational terms to facilitate the development of Lutheran churches, he was also more influenced than Luther by the radical reformers. He was initially impressed by the Zwickau prophets and their conviction that the Holy Spirit worked in them, though uncertain about their assertion that the Spirit did not require the application of the Scriptures as a test of its merits. This letter was written to the Elector Frederick the Wise of Saxony (1486–1525) on 27 December 1521. The Elector was the protector and patron of Luther during the years of the break with Rome. However, he never committed himself to following Luther's theological position, much to Luther's frustration.

Source: *Melanchthon in English: a Memorial to William Hammer*, ed. L. C. Green and C. D. Froelich, Center for Reformation Research, Sixteenth Century Bibliography 22, St Louis, 1982, p. 1

I have conversed with them [the Zwickau prophets] myself, and they declare most wonderful things about themselves, namely that God with a loud voice sent them forth to teach, that they enjoy the most intimate conversations with God, behold future events, and that they are, in short, prophetic and apostolic men. I cannot describe how all this moves me. That spirits possess them seems to be established

24 *Prophetic Dream of Frederick the Wise*, Herzog August Bibliothek, Wolfenbüttel.

by many reasons, about which no-one can easily form an opinion but Martin [Luther]. If the Gospel and the honour and peace of the Church are in danger, it is absolutely necessary that these people should have an interview with Martin, especially as they appeal to him.

80 Martin Luther **Letter to Nicholas Hausmann (1522)**

At the time of writing this letter (17 March 1522), Luther was in hiding at the Elector of Saxony's castle at Wartburg, but had been told of the visit of the Zwickau prophets to Wittenberg. Hausmann was town preacher at Zwickau and a long-standing associate of Luther. He had also been informed by Melanchthon (13 January 1522) that the Zwickau prophets were citing *Mark* 16:16, a key text for Luther, in order to challenge infant baptism.

Source: *Luther: Evidence and Commentary*, ed. I. D. Kingston Siggins, Oliver and Boyd, Edinburgh, 1972, pp. 105–6

To the faithful evangelist of the church at Zwickau, lord Nicholas Hausmann, his dearest brother in Christ.

Jesus.

Greetings. Although I have been occupied in various ways by our great disturbances here, my Nicholas in Christ, yet I could not fail to write to you, especially when the occasion itself prompted it and the friend of yours who bears this letter requested it. And I hope that you are firm in the faith and are growing daily in the knowledge of Christ. These 'prophets' of yours who have come from Zwickau are in labour and giving birth to monsters I do not like. If they come to birth, the harm they do will not be mild. This spirit of theirs is extremely insidious and specious, but the Lord be with us. Amen.

Satan has attempted great evils here in my fold, to such an extent that it will be difficult to counteract him without scandalising both sides. You should certainly see that you do not permit any innovation to be made by popular decree or force. The things which our people attempted by violence and force are to be withstood only by the Word, overthrown by the Word, destroyed by the Word. It is Satan who makes them act thus. I condemn masses regarded as sacrifices or good works. But I am unwilling to lay a hand on those who are reluctant or unbelieving, or to prohibit them by force. With the Word alone do I condemn; he who believes it, let him believe and follow it, he who does not believe it, let him not believe and go his way. For a person is not to be constrained to faith and the things which are of faith, but is to be drawn by the Word so that he comes spontaneously in willing belief. I condemn images, but with the Word, not so that they will be burned, but so that trust will not be placed in them, as has happened so far and still happens. They would fall of their own accord if an instructed people knew that they were nothing in God's eyes. I similarly condemn the laws of the pope on confession, communion, prayer, and fasting, but with the Word, so that I may free consciences from them. When their consciences are free, then they can use these laws for the sake of others who are weak and still entangled in them, and in turn not use them when people become strong, and in this way love will reign in such external works and laws. But now no one disgusts me more than this mob of ours which has abandoned the Word, faith, and love, and boasts that it is Christian only because they can eat meat, eggs, milk before the eyes of the weak, use both elements [in the sacrament], and give up fasting and prayer.

I beg that you, too, will adopt this position in your teaching. Certainly everything is to be proved by the Word, but hearts are to be led on a little at a time, like the flocks of Jacob [Gen. 33: 14], so that first they take up the Word gladly, and later, when they are strong, do all things. But perhaps it is superfluous to tell you this, all of which you know. Yet concerned love prompted this duty. Farewell in Christ, and aid the gospel with your prayers. Wittenberg, March 17, 1522.

Your Martin Luther.

81 Sebastian Lötzer **The Twelve Articles of the Peasants of Swabia (1525)**

The Twelve Articles were composed at Memmingen in Swabia by a journeyman and lay preacher, Sebastian Lötzer, in late February 1525. They were compiled out of a list of 300 or so grievances produced by peasants of the region. The

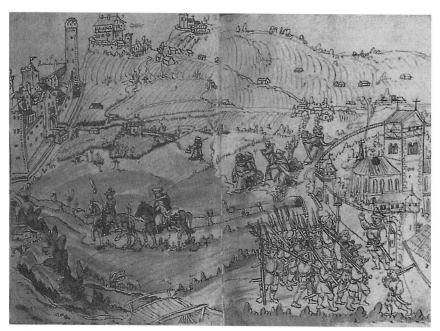

25 *Peasant Army at the Gates of a Monastery*, pen and ink drawing, Weissenar Chronicle of Abbot Jakob Murer, 1525, Fürstlich Waldburger-Zeil'sches Gesamtarchiv Schloss Zeil, Leutkirch, Germany.

introduction and biblical references were added by the Memmingen preacher, Christoph Schappeler, to demonstrate how the peasants' demands were consonant with the word of God, though individual groups of peasants had been referring to the word of God since 1524. These articles formed the basis for numerous documents produced in other parts of Germany and, as a blueprint for radical social reform, provided the ideological basis for the Peasants' War (1525).

Source: *The German Peasants' War: A History in Documents*, ed. T. Scott and R. W. Scribner, Humanities Press International, Atlantic Highlands, New Jersey, 1991, pp. 253–7

> *The just and fundamental chief articles of all peasants and subjects of ecclesiastical and secular authorities in which they consider them-selves aggrieved*

The Antichrists   To the Christian reader, peace and the grace of God through Christ. There are many Antichrists who have recently used the assemblies of peasants as a reason for pouring scorn on the The fruit of the Gospel, saying: 'These are the fruits of the new Gospel: to be obe-new Gospel dient to no one, to rebel and rise in revolt everywhere, to rally and band together with great force, to reform and overthrow ecclesiastical and secular authorities, indeed, perhaps even to slay them.' The following articles are a reply to all these godless and malicious critics. First, they will refute this calumny on the Word of God, and secondly provide a Christian justification for the disobedience, indeed, the rebellion, of all the peasants. In the first place, the Gospel is not the cause of disturbance or rebellion, since it speaks of Christ the promised Messiah, whose Word and life teach nothing but love, peace, patience, and concord, so that all who believe in this Christ become loving, peaceful, patient, and of one mind. Therefore the purpose of all the peasants' articles (as will clearly be seen) is to hear the Gospel and live according to it. How then can the Antichrists call the Gospel a cause of disturbance and disobedience? That some Antichrists and enemies of the Gospel object to and bridle at this intention and desire is not due to the Gospel but to the devil, the most harmful enemy of the Gospel, who has awakened such opposition in his followers through unbelief, so that the Word of God (which teaches love, peace, and concord) will be suppressed and abolished.

The reply of the articles
The articles' justification,
Romans 1:3

Secondly, it follows clearly that the peasants who ask for this Gospel as their teaching and rule of life should not be called disobedient or rebellious. But if God deigns to hear the peasants (who plead anxiously to live according to his Word), who shall reproach the will of God? Who shall meddle in his judgement? Yea, who shall oppose his majesty? Did he not hear the children of Israel when they cried out to him and deliver them from the hand of Pharoah? Shall he not also save his own today? Yea, he will save them, and speedily! Therefore, Christian reader, read the following articles with care, and then decide.

Romans 11:33
Isaiah 40:13
Romans 8:31
Exodus 3:7–8 and 14:10ff
Luke 18:7–8

Here follow the articles
The first article

First, it is our humble plea and request, as it is also the will and intention of all of us, that we should henceforth have the power and authority for the whole community to choose and elect its own pastor, and also to have the power to depose him should he conduct himself improperly. The same elected pastor shall preach the holy Gospel to us purely and clearly, without any human additions to doctrines and commandments. For constant preaching of the true faith impels us to ask God for his grace that he may instill in us the same true faith and confirm it. For if his grace is not instilled in us, we remain always mere flesh and blood, which is worth nothing. As Scripture clearly says, we can only come to God through true faith, and can be saved only through his mercy. That is why we need such a guide and pastor; and thus our demand is grounded in Scripture.

1 Tim 3:1ff
Titus 1:6–9
Acts 14:23

Deut 17:7–10
Exodus 31:6, 10
Deut 10:8
John 6:63

Gal 2:3ff., 11ff

The second article

As the entire
epistle to the
Hebrews says [cf.
7:4ff]
Psalm 109
[110:4]
Gen 14:20
Deut 18:1; 12:6
Deut 26:2ff. 12ff
1 Tim 5:18
Matth 10:9–10
1 Cor 9:9

Secondly, although the true tithe is ordained in the Old Testament and discharged in the New, nonetheless we will gladly pay
the true grain tithe, only in just measure. Since it should be given
to God and distributed to his servants, it belongs to a pastor who
proclaims the Word of God clearly. We wish this tithe in future
to be collected and received by our churchwarden, elected by the
community. From it he will give the pastor who is elected by
the entire community his adequate and sufficient sustenance
for himself and his dependants, according to the judgement of
the whole community. The remainder shall be distributed to the
needy poor present in the same village, according to circumstances and the judgement of the community. Any further
remainder should be retained against the need to provide military
service in defense of the country, which should be paid for from
this surplus, so that no territorial tax will be laid upon the poor

A Christian offer

man. Should it be that one or more villages have sold the tithe
because of some need, whoever can prove he has purchased it with
the consent of the whole village shall not suffer loss, for we will

Luke 6:29
Matth 5:40

reach a proper settlement with him according to the circumstances of the case to redeem the tithe within a suitable time and

One should take
no man's goods
from him

in suitable instalments. But whoever has not purchased the tithe
from a village, but rather their forefathers have appropriated it for
themselves, we will not, we should not, and we are not obliged
to pay him any more, but only, as stated above, to maintain our
elected pastor with the tithe, to collect what remains or dis-
tribute it, as is written in holy Scripture, to the needy, be they
clerical or lay. The small tithe we will not pay at all, for the Lord

Genesis 1:20

God created cattle for the free use of man, and we regard it as an
improper tithe, invented by men. Therefore we will no longer pay
it.

The third article

Isaiah 53:4–5
1 Pet 1:18–19
1 Cor 7:22–23
Romans 13:1
Wisdom 6:3
1 Pet 2:13
Deut 6:13
Matth 4:10
Luke 4:8
Luke 6:31
Matth 7:12
John 13:34

It has hitherto been the custom for the lords to treat us as their
serfs, which is pitiable since Christ has redeemed and bought us
all by the shedding of his precious blood, the shepherd just as the
highest, no one excepted. Therefore it is demonstrated by Scripture that we are free and wish to be free. Not that we wish to be
completely free and to have no authority, for God does not teach
us that. We should live according to his commandments, not the
free license of the flesh; but we are to love God, recognize him as
our Lord in our neighbor, and do all that God commanded us at
the Last Supper, as we would gladly do. Therefore we ought to
live according to his commandment, which does not show and
teach us not to obey authority, but rather that we should humble
ourselves before everyone, not just authority, so that in this way

we will gladly obey our elected and appointed rulers (whom God   Romans 13:1
has ordained over us) in all reasonable and Christian matters. We   Acts 5:29
have no doubt that, as true and genuine Christians, you will
gladly release us from serfdom, or else show us from the Gospel   A Christian offer
that we are serfs.

The fourth article

It has hitherto been the custom that no poor man has been   Genesis 1:11
empowered or permitted to catch game, wildfowl, or fish in   Acts 10:12–13
flowing water, which we consider quite improper and unbroth-   1 Tim 4:3
erly, indeed selfish and contrary to the Word of God. In some   1 Cor 10:26ff
places the lords keep game in defiance of [our wishes] and to our Col 2:16
great detriment, for we must suffer the dumb animals wantonly
and unnecessarily to devour our crops (which God has caused to
grow for the use of man), not to mention that this is contrary to
God and love of one's neighbor. For when the Lord God created
man he gave him dominion over all creatures, over the birds in   A Christian offer
the air and the fish in the water. Therefore it is our request that
whoever has waters for which he has adequate documents to prove
that they have been unwittingly bought by him, should not have   A Christian offer
them taken from him by force, but rather that Christian consideration be shown for the sake of brotherly love; but whoever
cannot provide adequate proof, should surrender them to the
community in a reasonable manner.

The fifth article

We are also aggrieved about woodcutting, for our lords have   As indicated
appropriated the woods to themselves alone, and when the poor   above, in the first
man has need of timber he must buy it at twice the price. It   book of Moses
is our opinion that all woods held by ecclesiastical or secular   [Genesis 1:29]
lords who have not bought them, should revert to the entire   Thus there will be
community. The community should be free to allow everyone   no forest clearance
in an orderly manner to take home without charge whatever   except with
he needs for firewood, and also to take timber for building free   agreement of the
of charge, but only with the knowledge of the official elected   officials
by the community for that purpose. If there are no woods
available other than those which have been properly purchased,
a brotherly and Christian agreement should be reached with
the owner. But if the property has first been arbitrarily expropriated and then sold, agreement should be reached according to
the facts of the matter in the light of brotherly love and holy
Scripture.

The sixth article

The sixth concerns our grievous burden of labor services, which   A Christian offer
are increased from day to day in amount and variety. We request

Romans 10:3–4 that a proper investigation be made in order that we be not so
heavily burdened, but to have consideration for us with regard to
how our forefathers performed services, but only according to the
Word of God.

The seventh article

Seventh, in future we will not allow a lord to oppress us further.
Rather, as the lord has conferred a holding on [a peasant] on
proper terms, so shall the latter possess it according to the agree-
Luke 3:14 ment between lord and peasant. The lord should not force or
1 Thess 4:6 compel him further in any way by asking for more services or
other dues without recompense, so that the peasant may use and
enjoy his property unburdened and in peace. But if the lord
requires services, the peasant should willingly serve his lord before
others, but at a time and day which is not to the disadvantage of
the peasant, and for a proper wage.

The eighth article

Eighth, we are aggrieved, especially the many of us who have
farms, that these cannot bear the rents, whereby the peasants
Matth 10:10 lose their property and are ruined. The lords should have honorable men inspect these properties and fix a fair rent, so that the
peasant does not work for nothing, for every laborer is worthy of
his hire.

The ninth article

Isaiah 10:1
Ephes 6:9 Ninth, we are aggrieved about cases of felony, where new laws
Luke 3:14 are constantly being passed, for punishments are not imposed
Jer 26:4 according to the facts of the case, but sometimes out of ill-will,
As above, sometimes out of partiality. In our opinion, punishment should
Luke 6:31 be imposed according to the old written penalties, according to
the circumstances, and not with partiality.

The tenth article

Christian offer Tenth, we are aggrieved that some have appropriated meadows or
arable that once belonged to the community. We wish to restore
these to common ownership, unless they have been properly purchased. If they have been improperly purchased, an amicable and
brotherly agreement should be reached by the parties according
to the facts of the case.

The eleventh article

Deut 18:[1] Eleventh, we wish to have the custom called heriot totally abol-
Matth 8:22 ished, for we shall never tolerate or permit widows and orphans
Matth 23:14 to be shamefully deprived and robbed of their property, contrary
to God and to honor, as has happened in many places and in
various forms, where those who should protect and guard them

have instead flayed and them us; and if they had the slightest Isaiah 10:1–2
pretext they would have taken it all. God will tolerate it no longer
and it should be completely abolished. Henceforth, no one should
be obliged to pay anything, either small or great amounts.

Conclusion

Twelfth, it is our conclusion and final opinion that if one or more Since all articles
of the articles presented here be not in accordance with the Word are contained in
of God (which we would doubt), and such articles be demon- the Word of God
strated to us to be incompatible with the Word of God; then we
will abandon them, when it is explained to us on the basis of
Scripture. If any articles be conceded to us which are later found
to be unjust, they shall be null and void from that moment, and
no longer valid. Similarly, if further articles are found in Scrip- A Christian offer
ture to be in truth contrary to God and a burden to our
neighbor, we shall reserve the right to have them included. We
will exercise and apply Christian doctrine in all its aspects, for
which we shall pray to the Lord God, who alone (and no one
else) can give it to us. The peace of Christ be with us all.

82 The Federal Ordinance (1525)

The Federal Ordinance, concluded at Memmingen on 7 March 1525, provided a
more practical manifesto for the rebels. On 5 March a peasant parliament had met
at Memmingen, leading to the formation of the Christian Union of Upper Swabia,
one of the most powerful forces of the war. The ordinance formed the basis for
the conduct of the union and parallel versions were produced elsewhere in
Germany. Indented clauses represent the aims of separate groups of rebels active
at this time.

Source: *The German Peasants' War: A History in Documents*, ed. T. Scott and R. W.
Scribner, Humanities Press International, Atlantic Highlands, New Jersey, 1991, pp.
130–2.

Agenda and articles concluded on Tuesday after Invocavit [7 March] by all the
captains of the troops who have pledged themselves to each other in the name
of the holy and indivisible Trinity.

This Christian Union and alliance has been founded to the praise and honor
of Almighty God, invoking the holy Gospel and Word of God, also to assist
justice and godly laws, without prejudice or harm to any spiritual or secular
person, in so far as is contained in and may be demonstrated by the Gospel and
godly law, and especially to increase brotherly love.

[1] First, the honorable commons of the region [*Landschaft*] of this Christian
Union undertakes in no way to refuse, but obediently to abide by, whatever it is
obliged to render to spiritual or secular authority under godly law.

[2] Item, it is the commons' will and intention that a common public peace

[*Landfrieden*] be observed and that no one should injure another. If it should arise, however, that one party starts warfare and rebellion against another, no one should rush to arms or take sides in any way; rather their neighbor, of whatever estate he may be, should be empowered to make and command peace. The first command or call to peace shall immediately be heeded. Whoever infringes such a command to peace shall be punished according to his [degree of] blame.

[3] All debts should be paid when they fall due if they are recognized or may be authenticated by sealed deed. But if anyone enters a plea of defense, his rights should be reserved at his own cost without prejudice to the commons of this Christian union. But ongoing debts such as tithes and other rente-charges and annuities shall be suspended until the issue has been resolved.

[4] Item, unrecognized innovations in debt which some have hitherto demanded and received without any foundation in godly justice, likewise tithes, rente-charges and annuities, shall be suspended until the issue has been resolved.

[4] Where there are castles situated in this region which are not allied to this Christian union, the owners of the same castles shall be requested by friendly exhortation not to keep in their castles more provisions than they reasonably require, and not to garrison the same castles with artillery and persons not belonging to this union. If they wish henceforth to garrison more than previously they should do so with persons who are allied and belong to this union, at their own cost and risk. Likewise the convents.

[5] All persons in the service of princes and lords should relinquish and renounce their oaths [of allegiance]. Once they have done so, they shall be admitted to this union. Whoever will not do so, however, shall gather up his wife and children and not darken this region again. If a lord should summon an official [*Amtmann*] or anyone else in this league, he shall not [present himself] alone but take with him two or three persons as witnesses to what transpires.

[5] ... in order that the common man is not, as previously, thrown into jail and on trying to set himself free [is required to] confess and swear an affidavit of his guilt, even though innocent.

[6] Item, all rectors and vicars shall graciously be enjoined and requested to proclaim and to preach the holy Gospel. The parishes of those who agree to do so shall then be given a reasonable competency. But those who refuse shall be suspended and the parish placed in the hands of another.

[6] Item, all rectors (for we refuse to have vicars) shall graciously be enjoined and requested henceforth to proclaim the holy Gospel and to confess and put an end to the error of their ways. The parishes and benefices of those who agree to do so shall then be given a reasonable competency. But those who refuse shall be suspended and the parish placed in the hands of another who will.

[7] In order that all dissension and discord in spiritual matters be laid to rest and that no one declare or denounce another from the pulpit as a heretic, as previously, the Word of God only, as aforementioned, shall be preached, without

human addition. Should, however, a dispute arise, the priests of the same region or place shall be convoked with their Bibles and the matter resolved according to the content of the holy Scripture and not according to human judgement, and be finally proclaimed in the presence of the common soldiery of those parts.

[7] Item, whoever wishes to enter into a treaty with his overlord shall not conclude such a treaty without the advance knowledge and consent of the commons of the region. Even though such be concluded with the consent of the same commons, the same [parties to the treaty] shall nevertheless agree to join and to remain in the eternal alliance and Christian union.

[8] Item, in each troop of this union a commander and four captains shall be detailed and appointed, who shall be empowered to negotiate as appropriate with other commanders and captains, in order that the commons [as a whole] is not constantly obliged to assemble.

[9] Item, no booty purloined from any associate [of this union] shall be kept or appropriated.

[10] . . . rather, as soon as such [an incident] is reported, the commons [*Volk*] shall be summoned by flying pickets or by [sounding the] alarm to set off in hot pursuit, so that the injured person's property is restituted. Whoever gives shelter to the robbers or the booty or who disposes of it nefariously shall be dealt with on the same footing as the robbers themselves.

[10] Item, all craftsmen who, to ply their trade, wish to emigrate from this region shall swear to the captain of their parish not to allow themselves to be recruited against this Christian union; rather, should they hear or get wind of any adversity threatening this region, they should inform this union and, if it proves necessary, immediately return to their fatherland and come to its defense. The mercenaries [*Kriegsleute*] shall be likewise pledged.

[11–12] . . . The mercenaries [*Kriegsleute*] shall be likewise pledged, who should reserve their entire service and hire themselves out [only] to this Christian union.

[11] The courts and justice shall flourish as before.

[13] . . . and no one who seeks justice shall be denied recourse to it.

[14] Item, overlords shall cause no one to be arrested, thrown into prison, or placed in the stocks unless accused of a capital crime.

[12] Item, gambling, blasphemy, and drunkenness are forbidden. Whoever transgresses shall be punished according to [the degree of] his blame.

[16] Each shall allow the other to retain his dialect [*Sprache*] and [mode of] dress, or else they shall be punished for disobedience to this Christian union.

[17] Item, all who pledge themselves to this Christian union shall pay from each hearth [*Herdstatt*, i.e. farmstead] two kreutzers, the money to cover the cost of couriers, etc.

[18] Item, in order that this Christian union, founded through God's grace, shall the more steadfastly and unshakably be upheld, first and foremost sealed deeds incorporating the aforementioned articles shall, wherever possible, be drawn up by towns, villages [*Flecken*], and communities [*Landschaften*] and deposited in a safe place.

83 Martin Luther **Letter to John Rühel (1525)**

John Rühel was councillor to Count Albrecht of Mansfeld. In April 1525 Luther had written *Admonition for Peace* in reply to the Twelve Articles of the Swabian peasants. He knew little of the uprising then and urged rulers to listen to the peasants' grievances. As he learned more of the events of the rising, he spoke out against violence and finally came round to opposing the rebels altogether. The letter was written, on 4 May, 1525, as a warning to the count to quell immediately any incipient revolt in his territories.

Source: *Luther's Works 49, Letters II*, ed. G. G. Krodel, Fortress Press, Philadelphia, 1972, p. 109

If there were thousands more of the peasants, they would still be altogether robbers and murderers, who would take the sword simply because of their own insolency and wickedness, and who want to expel sovereigns [and] lords, and [to destroy] everything, and to establish a new order in this world. But for this they have neither God's commandment, authority, right or injunction, as the lords have it now. In addition, the peasants are faithless and are committing perjury towards their lords. Above all this, they borrow the authority of the divine word and gospel [for covering up] their great sins, and thus disgrace and slander [God's name] [. . .] I still firmly hope that the peasants will not be victorious, or at least not remain so.

84 **The Erfurt 'Peasant Articles' (1525)**

The Erfurt articles were composed at the beginning of May 1525 by the urban opposition and peasants of the Erfurt region. They represented the grievances of townspeople more than the preceding documents. Luther was invited by the town council to comment upon them; his comments, made on 21 September, are shown in italics.

Source: *The German Peasants' War: A History in Documents*, ed. T. Scott and R. W. Scribner, Humanities Press International, Atlantic Highlands, New Jersey, 1991, pp. 174–6

Here follows the list of articles that all quarters of the city of Erfurt, and the guilds belonging thereto, have discussed for further improvement.
1. Concerning the parishes, it is thought good that these should be redivided into parishes [of a size] more suitable for the town, and that the community of each parish should appoint and dismiss its own pastor. These appointed pastors should present the pure Word of God clearly and without addition of any human commands, regulations, or doctrines affecting the conscience.
But the town council should have ultimate authority over who holds office in the town.
2. On intolerable interest payments, by which we mean the redeemable loans or

usury, where the sum repaid often exceeds the capital: these we will pay no longer. Where the capital sum has not yet been repaid, the balance outstanding shall be settled within a period to be agreed, so that a fair mean may be found. We also request that the exchange rates and the coinage be investigated.

Indeed, nothing better than that one should pay interest on the sum with which it is secured in Erfurt.

4. On property removed from the commune, such as wood, water, etc. This should be returned to the use of the commune at once and a control instituted so that nothing further can be done without the consent of the commune.

That is not to be, but [if so] the authorities should do it, or purchase it for the common good of the town.

5. On legacies and endowments of altars. Where these are already established, the clergy should no longer receive them, but the heirs and the descendants of those who founded them. Where the heirs and descendants can no longer be traced, such endowments should be placed in a common chest.

The persons who now hold them should be allowed to enjoy them until they die, where such persons and monies stand under the town council's control, or else let one entrust them to God [i.e. put them in the common chest], [except] in so far as the heirs are quite poor and needy.

6. On the town council: we should have an eternal council, which should present an annual accounting to the guardians [acting] on behalf of the quarters and the commune, in so far as this can be seen to be useful.

If one does not trust the town council, why set one up? Why have one at all?

7. The current council should present an account of all income and expenditure.

Indeed, that the council should not be a council, but that the mob should rule everything.

8. All forms of commercial activity should be free to every citizen who so desires.

So that no poor man should [be able to] stand before the rich or be able to nourish himself.

9. Every citizen who has a house and home and resides therein should be free to brew.

So that the rich alone can be brewers!

10. The full quarter-measure [of beer or wine] should be given for the money.

Has that not always been the case?

11. Each person who fulfils civic duties and who conducts himself honorably and decently should be freely permitted to work at his trade unhindered by the guilds.

I leave that to the decision of the town council.

12. All matters placed before the town council for judgement according to the town statutes should be settled without delay within fourteen days, at the citizen's plea presented in person. Where the citizen is unable to plead his own case, the town council should appoint someone from its own ranks to plead his cause, without further cost to the citizen.

That is also a secular matter, and does not fall within my competence.

13. The city chancery should be investigated, so that no one will be deceived, as has hitherto occurred.

Likewise.

14. Negotiations should be held with the house of Saxony to obtain a gracious remission of the protection fees [paid to the princes of Saxony in return for their military protection of the town].

Indeed, so that no one will defend the city of Erfurt, or that the princes should outlay cash in its defense. I should like to know if Erfurt will then spend the money to buy peace and protection!

15. Since the citizens and countryfolk are heavily burdened with the safe conduct [fees], the matter should graciously be reviewed.

Indeed, may God allow us to injure princes and cities, as long as we have our own way!

16–17. Henceforth notorious knaves and wenches of all classes should no longer be tolerated, nor the house of common women. Also, all those who are in arrears to the town council, whoever they are, should be firmly requested [to pay up].

Both go well together.

18. In all earnest we request and desire, as do the countryfolk, that no sworn citizen should be imprisoned without a hearing, unless it be for a capital offense.

Where the town council sees that as desirable.

19. All citizens held in Erfurt should be released on verbal sureties.

According to the pleasure of the town council.

20. Where some citizens have been exiled during and after the rebellion, and protest their innocence, they should be allowed to put their case.

That is fair.

21. The town council should henceforth levy no imposts without the will and knowledge of the entire commune and countryfolk.

It would then be necessary to pay the people!

22. Those living [in the suburbs] before the gates request permission to sell their home-grown wine in the suburbs.

The town council will see to whatever is best.

23. It is our request that one should consider whether the illustrious university, such as it was until now, might not be revived.

That is the best of all.

24. No one should be placed in jeopardy by this [revolt].

That is also good, for many perhaps mean well; the others should be given the benefit of the doubt and be admonished to desist from their designs.

25. Although all excises and impositions are [declared to be] abolished, the council should see to it that meat and bread are sold at fair prices.

The council should normally do this as a duty of their office.

26. Foreign bakers and butchers should be allowed to sell twice weekly.

The council will see to it.

27. All properties taken from the common city and the town council – i.e. taxation, rents, labor services, or whatever – should be returned to the city as before, namely, such as [those from the villages of] Melchendorf, Gispersleben, half of Kiliani.

God help the council thereto.

28. Every citizen should be able to use the common without hindrance to his neighbor.

That is up to the town council.

But one article has been left out, that the council may do nothing, have no power entrusted to it, but must sit there like a ninny and kowtow to the commune like a child, govern with hands and feet tied, and pull the wagon like a horse while the driver reins in and pulls the horses [back]. Thus it would be according to the illustrious model of these articles.

85 Hermann Mühlpfort, Mayor of Zwickau **Letter to Stephen Roth at Wittenberg (1525)**

Mühlpfort, who was mayor of Zwickau, had been an associate of Luther's, but voiced his doubts in this letter of 4 June 1525 about Luther's (by now) implacable opposition to the rebels in both town and country, fearing that Luther's stance would damage the moderate Protestant cause.

Source: *The German Peasants' War: A History in Documents*, ed. T. Scott and R. W. Scribner, Humanities Press International, Atlantic Highlands, New Jersey, 1991, pp. 322–4

God be praised, there is peace in and around the city of Zwickau. God help us with his grace. Doctor Martin has fallen into great disfavor with the common people, also with both learned and unlearned; his writing is regarded as having been too fickle. I am greatly moved to write to you about this, for the pastor [Nicholas Hausmann] and the preachers here have been greatly disconcerted and amazed by the tracts recently issued, since one is clearly contrary to the other. First, [in his *Admonition to Peace: A Reply to the Twelve Articles of the Peasants in Swabia*] that Christian man Dr Martin certainly wrote well, addressing both sides about the danger of princes and peasants jeopardizing their souls' salvation; with God's grace, he certainly expressed a sound judgement with his proposal about how the matter could be mediated, for I, with my limited understanding, knew of no better counsel. But, as I know, the great and powerful would remit to the poor none of their ruinous and intolerable burdens, and may God in heaven take pity on it, for such burdens were contrary to God and all justice.

Afterwards, in a second tract [*A Shocking History and God's Judgement on Thomas Müntzer*], written after he had received a letter from Thomas Müntzer, who so pitiably misled the poor folk, he [Luther] became instead the hammer of the poor, without regard for their need, by calling for the poor alone to be quickly destroyed. In the third tract [*Against the Robbing and Murdering Hordes of Peasants*], which I do not consider theological, he called for the private and public murder of the peasants: as long as strength coursed through one's veins, they should be sent to their judgement before God. Is the devil, and those who do this, to be our Lord God? Here I do not agree. In my opinion, there was no pressing need for this hasty tract. There was enough murdering of peasants, burghers, women, and children taking place; not only were the poor folk being killed, but also their goods and possessions were being taken from their innocent wives and children and burnt. God knows, these same knights are supposed to be the children of God! But we should have more pity for the poor, needy, and simple folk who were misled by Thomas and others, and when Thomas Müntzer's letter arrived, [Luther] might well have reacted more thoughtfully.

It is true, as Martin writes, that rebellion should be put down, and it is entirely fitting that secular authority should punish, though they do it without being asked; but, contrary to his first tract, he conceded too much to one side – indeed, far too much, for the poor were to be strangled. I find that incomprehensible. I know what is happening in towns and villages, such that one should complain to God in heaven . . . But Martin's remedy is said to be the best: that the peasants should bear more, while the nobility [receive] the lion's share and yet concede the least. There is no lack of peasants and burghers. God knows, the matter cannot be done otherwise, but the merciful God will punish sin with sin. See how violently the nobility will impose all their burdens on the people with the sword and [shed] the blood of the suffering poor, who cannot protect themselves from hunger because of their poverty. But they [the nobility] will rely on Martin's tract, that this will gain them eternal salvation. If my gracious lord [the elector of Saxony] and other princes had issued a public edict calling for regard for the need of the peasantry, and they had not then disbanded, I would not have had so much pity, but no such thing happened.

Dear Christian brother, who will now speak out about the need of the commons in town and village? Who will have the strength of spirit not to hold back from doing so? Whoever speaks out will be accused of being a rebel and everyone will have to keep silent for fear of tyrants, lest it be said that one is speaking against authority. I know already that in several places more has been imposed upon the poor than before, and they are told openly: 'You owe me this; if you do not do it, you are opposing me who am your lord and have sovereign authority over you.' It is said that complaints should be laid before the princes; [but], yea, I know no one [who] will be a just judge. Who can see an end to the matter? I know of matters that were complained about forty years ago; what has been achieved other than trouble, care, labor, and expenditure of money? Christ's sheep must suffer and leave things to God. The poor lack instruction because they are provided with poor preachers. Why did the authorities not act in time? The poor folk are to be pitied in their ignorance. I fear God will not let it go unpunished. We can see how some of the nobility kill, stab, and shoot whenever they catch sight of the peasantry . . . Now I believe that Doctor Martin has good cause to reprove all rebels, for otherwise things would turn out badly. But if the self-interested and the greedy would remit a little to the poor all this would cease . . .

What has moved me to write to you, besides Martin's rash tract, is that poverty has been so much forgotten. I also believe that my pious, Christian territorial princes, young and old, who were certainly innocent of this rebellion and of the bloodshed, could have averted rebellion in their lands if they had exercised control over the nobility, for they have always avoided shedding blood and have not ceased to protect the pious from the wicked. But I fear there will be more disobedience . . . I fear truly that more violence will erupt and the nobility will increase their arrogance further. There is such boasting and thumping. No one I have seen speaks of kindness and forgiveness; they say that everyone will simply be killed, burnt, beheaded who now refuses what they had to render before, whether justly or unjustly, in the way of labor service, grazing, and the like.

. . . Oh God, if only the princes had followed Martin's advice and allowed some commissioners from the nobles and the towns to negotiate in God's name. But they would not concede this honor to the towns, which are not regarded as fit to advise a prince. This bloodshed was done without the will and knowledge of the towns. May God grant that some heed will still be taken. I also believe that there is no fault in the pious princes, whom I love as my father, except that those near and around them will not give up their proud incomes . . . God knows, I had five weeks' trouble and care to prevent disturbance in this town, and I believe that with God's aid I have helped to prevent it and continue to do so as far as I am able. But I do not agree with Doctor Martin, as I have said, that the need of the poor should be forgotten, murder be called for, and the middle way ignored so that no cordial negotiations are undertaken . . . If both sides concede something it would be pleasing to God, and from it would grow the fruits of faith: obedience, love of authority, and [brotherly love] towards subjects . . . Martin has not done well in Zwickau and in the countryside and towns; he has written the truth in condemning rebellion, but the poor have been greatly forgotten . . . Dated on Whitsun, in the year '25.

[Enclosure:] Monks and nuns have moved back into Mühlhausen again, they hold and celebrate the papist Mass and other human ceremonies again. God be praised, it means the war is at an end. You Wittenbergers have gained honor from those who call for bloodshed . . . Now you reject everything which you once regarded as Christian, and since you praise murder and killing, that also has to be good.

The rumor among the people is that Doctor Martin has lost the [support of] the elector [of Saxony] unless he sells foxes' brushes to the other princes and the nobility.[1] Some towns, lords, and nobles who previously held German Masses now abandon them and revert to the old Latin rites.

NOTE

1   This implies that Luther will lose support unless he indulges in hypocritical flattery.

86 Martin Luther **Letter to Nicholas Hausmann (1524)**

For several years Luther corresponded with his long-standing associate Nicholas Hausmann (see Text 80) about how to translate doctrinal changes implied by

26 The last portrait of Luther, drawn by his valet Reifenstein, in a book by Melanchthon. Melanchthon added the following words:

Doctor Martin Luther
Alive I was your plague, o pope,
Dead I shall destroy you.
He died in the year 1546
He lived for 63 years
The 64th year was the year of his death
It was the 18th of February when he
    encountered death,
    at night between two
    and three o'clock.
On the 22nd of the month he was
    buried in the Castle Church of
    Wittenberg.

He is dead, yet he lives.

Stiftung Luthergedenkstätten in Sachsen-Anhalt, Wittenberg.

Luther's theology into church services. Hausmann had urged Luther to produce new forms of service for use in reformed congregations and in his replies to Hausmann, Luther set out a good many of his ideas about the reformed liturgy. This letter was written in Wittenberg on 17 November 1524.

Source: *Luther's Works 49, Letters II,* ed. G. G. Krodel, Fortress Press, Philadelphia, 1972, p. 90

I desire a German mass more than I can promise [to work on an order for it]. I am not qualified for this task, which requires both a talent in music and the gift of the Spirit. Meanwhile I charge each one to use his judgment (*sic*) until Christ gives us something different. I do not consider it sufficiently safe to call a council of our party for establishing unity in ceremonies [. . .] If in these external matters one congregation does not voluntarily want to follow another, why should it be compelled to do so by decrees of councils, which are soon converted into laws and snares for the souls. Of its own accord the congregation should, therefore, follow another one, or else be allowed to enjoy its own customs; only the unity of the Spirit should be preserved in faith and the Word, however great might be the diversity and variety in respect to the flesh and elements of the world.

87 Martin Luther *Against the Heavenly Prophets in the Matter of Images and Sacraments* (1525)

This work was written as Luther's defence against the claims of Andreas Bodenstein von Karlstadt. (*c*.1480–1541) who opposed both Luther's theology of the mass and his beliefs about the place of images and ceremonies in the reformed communion service.

Source: *Luther's Works 40, Church and Ministry II*, ed. C. Bergendoff, Muhlenberg Press, Philadelphia, 1958, p. 99

I have myself seen and heard the iconoclasts read out of my German Bible. I know that they have read out of it, as one can easily determine from the words they use. Now there are a great many pictures in those books, both of God, the angels, men and animals, especially in the Revelation of John and in Moses and Joshua. So now we would kindly beg them to permit us to do what they themselves do. Pictures contained in these books we would paint on walls for the sake of remembrance and better understanding, since they do no more harm on walls than in books. It is to be sure better to paint pictures on the walls of how God created the world, how Noah built the ark, and whatever other good stories there may be, than to paint shameless worldly things.

Section Six

Renaissance Science

88 Galileo Galilei *The Starry Messenger* (1610)

Galileo Galilei (1564–1642) was born in Pisa, the son of the court musician and composer, Vincenzo Galilei. Originally intended for either a clerical or medical career, Galileo left university without a degree in order to pursue his interest in mathematics, mechanics and hydrostatics. He eventually obtained the chair of mathematics at the university of Pisa where he grew sceptical of traditional Aristotelian views on motion and began to develop his own approach to physics based largely on his considerable skill in mathematics. From Pisa he moved to the university of Padua where there was greater academic freedom for him to explore his original research. While here, he began experimenting with the telescope. The results of his research are contained in *Siderius Nuncius* (*The Starry Messenger*) which he dedicated to the young Cosimo de' Medici. In this work, Galileo successfully demonstrated the potential virtues of the telescope, particularly its usefulness in undermining ancient science and providing further evidence for the Copernican world-view. Shortly after its publication, he became philosopher and mathematician to Cosimo II, now Grand Duke of Tuscany (1610–20), and returned to Florence where he was increasingly drawn into disputes with other courtiers and churchmen culminating in his infamous appearance before the Inquisition in 1633.

Source: *Telescopes, Tides, and Tactics: A Galilean Dialogue about the Starry Messenger and the Systems of the World*, ed. S. Drake, University of Chicago Press, Chicago and London, 1983, pp. 12–16

To the Most Serene Cosimo II d' Medici
Fourth Grand Duke of Tuscany:

Surely a distinguished public service has been rendered by those who have pro-tected from envious hatred the noble achievements of men excelling in virtue, and have thus preserved from oblivion and neglect names that deserve immor-tality. So likenesses sculptured in marble or cast in bronze have been handed down to posterity; to that we owe our statues, both pedestrian and equestrian; so we have columns and pyramids whose cost (as the poet says) is astronomical; and last, so entire cities have been built to bear the names of men deemed by posterity worthy of commendation through the ages. For the nature of the human mind is such that, unless stimulated by images of things acting on it from outside, remembrance of the originals quickly passes away.

Looking to things still more stable and enduring, some have entrusted the immortal fame of illustrious men not to marble and metal, but to the custody of the Muses and to imperishable literary monuments. But why dwell on these things as if human ingenuity were satisfied with earthly regions and dared not advance farther? Seeking farther, and well understanding that all human monuments eventually perish through violence of the elements or by great age, ingenuity has in fact found monuments still more incorruptible, over which voracious time and envious ages have been unable to assert their rights.

Turning heavenward, man's wit has thus inscribed on the familiar and ever-lasting orbs of most bright stars the names of those whose famous and godlike deeds have caused them to be accounted worthy of eternity in the companion-ship of the stars. Thus the fame of Jupiter, of Mars, of Mercury, Hercules, and other heroes whose names are borne by stars will not fade until the extinction of the stars themselves.

Yet this invention of human ingenuity, noble and praiseworthy though it is, has been out of fashion for many centuries. Primeval heroes are in possession of those bright abodes and hold them in their own right. In vain did the piety of Augustus attempt to elect Julius Caesar into their number, for when he tried attaching the name 'Julian' to a star that appeared in his time (one of those bodies that the Greeks call *comets* and the Romans also named for their hairy appearances), it vanished in a short time and mocked his too-ambitious wish. But we, most serene prince, are able to read Your Highness into the heavens far more correctly and auspiciously; for scarce have the immortal graces of your spirit begun to shine on earth when bright stars appear in the heavens as tongues to tell and celebrate your surpassing virtues for all time. Behold, then, four stars reserved to bear your famous name – bodies that belong not to the inconspicuous multitude of the fixed stars, but to the bright ranks of the planets. Variously moving around most noble Jupiter as children of his own, they com-plete their orbits with marvelous speed, executing at the same time, with one harmonious accord, mighty revolutions every dozen years about the center of the universe – that is, the Sun.

The Maker of the stars Himself has indeed seemed by clear indications to direct me to assign to these new planets Your Highness's famous name in preference to all others. For just as these stars, like children worthy of their sire, never leave Jupiter's side through any notable distance, so – and indeed who does not know this? – clemency, kindness of heart, gentleness of manner, splendor of royal blood, nobility in public affairs, and excellency of authority and rule have all fixed their home and habitation in Your Highness. And who – I ask again – does not know that all those virtues emanate from the benign star of Jupiter, next after God the source of all good things? Jupiter; Jupiter, I say, at the instant of Your Highness's birth, having lately emerged from the turbid mists of the horizon to occupy the middle of the heavens, illuminating the eastern sky from his own royal house, looked out from that exalted throne on your auspicious birth, pouring forth all his splendor and majesty in order that your tender body and your mind (already adorned by God with most noble ornaments) should imbibe with the first breath that universal influence and power.

But why should I employ mere plausible arguments when I can prove my con-clusion absolutely? It pleased almighty God that I should instruct Your Highness in mathematics four years ago, at that time of year when it is customary [for pro-fessors] to rest from the most exacting studies. Now, since it was clearly mine by divine will to serve Your Highness and thus to receive from near at hand the rays of your surpassing clemency and beneficence, what wonder is it that my heart is so inflamed as to think day and night of little else than how I, who am indeed your subject not only by choice but by birth and lineage, may make myself known to you as most grateful and most desirous of your glory? Therefore, most serene Cosimo, having discovered under your patronage these stars unknown to any astronomer before me, I have with good right decided to designate them by your august family name. And if I am the first to have investigated them, who can justly blame me if I also name them, calling those the Medicean stars in the hope that this name will bring them as much honor as the names of other heroes have bestowed on other stars? For – to say nothing of Your Highness's most serene ancestors, whose everlasting glory is testified to by the monuments of history – your virtue alone, most worthy Sire, can confer upon these stars a name immortal. No one can doubt that you will fulfill the expectations, high though they be, that you have aroused at the beginning of your auspicious reign, and not only meet but far surpass those. For when you have conquered your peers you may still vie with yourself, and you and your greatness will increase with every day.

Accept then, most clement prince, this noble glory reserved for you by the stars. May you long enjoy those blessings sent to you not so much by the stars as by God, their creator and their governor.

Your Highness's most devoted servant,

Galileo Galilei

Padua, March 12, 1610

89 Paracelsus **On Medical Reform (1529/1533)** (i) *Das Buch Paragranum* (1529–30)[1] (ii) *De Ordine Doni* (1533)

Theophrastus Philippus Aureolus Bombastus von Hohenheim, more generally known as Paracelsus (1493–1541), was born at Einsiedeln in Switzerland, the son of a physician. His early education was in botany, mining and metallurgy and is most notable for the early introduction which it provided for Paracelsus to engage in practical science in local mines and laboratories. As a young man, he travelled widely in Europe, studying briefly at the university of Ferrara where he would have come into contact with the latest developments in medical humanism. He does not appear to have gained any official qualifications, however, and for the remainder of his career he consistently denounced the medicine of the 'schools', and in particular the dominance of the curriculum by the ancient Greek physician, Galen. Though Paracelsus published little in his own life-time, he rapidly acquired a reputation as both a medical iconoclast and a critic of contemporary society. After his death, however, his radical approach to medicine – in particular his advocacy of chemical drugs and new theories of disease – won widespread support despite the continuing opposition of many university-trained physicians, clerics and others to various aspects of his life, work and thought.

Source: *Paracelsus: Essential Readings*, ed. and trans. N. Goodrick-Clarke, Crucible Press, Wellingborough, 1990, pp. 72–4, 167–70

i) *Das Buch Paragranum*

And because I write from the true source of medicine, I must be rejected, and you who are born neither of the true origin nor of the true heredity must adhere to the spurious art which raises itself beside the true. Who is there amongst the instructed who would not prefer what is grounded on a rock to what is grounded on sand? Only the abandoned academic drunkards who bear the name of doctor must suffer no deposition! They abide, painted doctors, and if they were not painted with this title, who would recognize them? Their works would certainly not reveal them. Outwardly they are beautiful, inwardly they are squalid dunces. What instructed and experienced man desires a doctor who is only an outward show? None. Only the simpletons desire him. What, then, is the origin of that medicine which no instructed man desires, from which no Philosophy issues, in which no Astronomy can be noted, in which no Alchemy is practised, and in which there is no vestige of Virtue? And because I point out these things essential in a physician, I must needs have my name changed by them to Cacophrastus [guided by evil] when I am really called Theophrastus [guided by God], both for my art's sake and by my christening.

Understand then thoroughly that I am expounding the basics of medicine upon which I stand and will stand: namely, Philosophy, Astronomy, Alchemy, and Virtue. The first pillar, Philosophy, is the knowledge of earth and water; the second pillar, Astronomy together with Astrology, has a complete knowledge of the two elements, air and fire; the third pillar, Alchemy, is knowledge of the experiment and preparation of the four elements mentioned; and the fourth pillar, Virtue, should remain with the physician until death, for this completes and preserves the other three pillars. And note well, for you too must enter here and come to understand the three pillars, otherwise it will be known by the very peasants in the villages that your trade is to treat princes and lords, towns and countries through lies and deception only and that you know neither your trade nor the truth, for the education which prepares you fits you for fools and hypocrites, all you supposed physicians. And as I take the four pillars, so must you take them too and follow after me, not I after you. [. . .]

You are serpents and I expect poison from you. With what scorn have you proclaimed that I am the Luther of physicians, with the interpretation that I am a heretic. I am Theophrastus and more so than him to whom you compare me. I am that and am a monarch of physicians as well, and can prove what you are not able to prove. I will let Luther justify his own affairs, and I will account for mine, and will rise above the charges which you level against me: the arcana will raise me up to that height. Who are Luther's foes? The very rabble that hates me. And what you wish him you wish me – to the fire with us both. The heavens did not make me a physician, God made me one: it is not the business of the heavens but a gift from God. I can rejoice that rogues are my enemies, for the truth has no enemies except liars. I need wear no armour nor shield against you, for you are neither very learned nor experienced enough to refute one word of

27 Cosmè Tura, Francesco del Cossa, Ercole de'Roberti and others, *Hall of the Months*, detail of *April* and *May*, 1469–70, fresco, 4m wide each, commissioned by Borso d'Este, Palazzo Schifanoia, Ferrara. Photo: Alinari.

mine. I wish I could protect my bald head against the flies as efficiently as I can defend my monarchy. I will not defend my monarchy with empty talk but with arcana. And I do not take my medicines from the apothecaries, their shops are just foul sculleries which produce nothing but foul broths. But you defend your-selves with belly-crawling and flattery. How long do you think it will last? . . . Let me tell you this, the stubble on my chin knows more than you and all your scribes, my shoebuckles are more learned than your Galen and Avicenna,[2] and my beard has more experience than all your high colleges.

ii) *De Ordine Doni*

Self-interest makes mendacious people out of you noblemen and authorities. Your food and needs are provided by the three other 'monarchies'. You owe money to nobody for anything in the three monarchies, neither to the cobbler nor to the tailor . . . In order to cover your needs you must buy corn, meat, and salt for money and so you raise taxes . . . Buying increases, prices rise, and cereals and bread are dearer . . . But you can prevent this by not settling with money but with that which the money is supposed to buy, namely with corn, meat, salt, and bread. How much milder and better you would govern if you were rid of money. For wherever there is money, there is worry. That is what causes murders; bread and meat do not cause them. You become profiteers, gamblers, debauchees, and whores from money, and your money does no one any good. You do not invest it in the country but give it to the whores and the Pharisees, and there is only bad feeling, dishonour, mischief, and evil, wealth, dancing, tournaments, and banqueting. These represent no virtue on the part of the authorities. But seek your triumph in the wisdom of doing what is sufficient, the virtue of justice and truth.

Outside the four monarchies there is yet another livelihood created by God – namely the hunting of birds, fish, and wild animals. No one but God feeds them, but they come to us and nourish us. Therefore this livelihood shall belong to the poor, because it is superfluous to the hierarchy of masters and servants: the poor folk may learn how to fish, catch birds, and hunt wild animals in the woods and the fields . . . Thus, you outside the four monarchies, support yourselves in a communal 'landscape', each concerned with the other and not with himself. Thus God gives us peace, rest, health, and food in many ways with much joy among neighbours, parents and children, strangers and local people. But if we do not act in this way, there is plague, inflation, hunger, war, wrangling, and strife, and each is against all. And neither the sun nor the moon is favourable to us and none to another, [even] the beasts on the road hate us. Such is the reign of the devil.

There are several gangs outside the monarchies which make a living on the paths of unrighteousness, such as the merchants, interest brokers, money-lenders, buying agents, rag-and-bone men, hucksters, and many others, who all make a living out of the other four [monarchies], neither as masters nor as servants. They have an alien ungodly livelihood which is forbidden in the Ten Commandments. Lending money and earning interest destroys commonality. Agency creates inflation and comes from the devil and his own. For these people behave like false prophets towards the common man. They talk glibly, and the common man knows no better. Satan draws his authority from them . . . You will know them by their works. They lie and trick, lend on interest, against security . . . why do you tolerate them among you? You may think they are on your side, but they are only on their own side and respect neither God nor His kingdom. They take the highest chair and the highest place at the table, and the whole world defers to them.

They call a disgrace a clever move, a deception a masterpiece. There can be no greater deception of one's neighbour than the doings of businessmen. Their whole life is devilish. They seduce rich and poor . . . They steal the land and labour from princes and lords with cunning and polite deception. They seduce all estates and want to be the best, they are the greatest favourites of the princes and are held in high regard. They mix with the nobility and the princes only to swindle them hugely . . . What is their luxury, what is their belief, what is their whole

Christian life? Nothing, for it is all deception and a devilish life. They are pepper-traders and deal in spices. What good is it? Whom does it benefit? . . . Does not a peasant live as well on turnips as someone who eats spices? All traders in spices are full of the devil and his servants, through whom he disgraces the people . . . They are whores and rogues, thieves and scoundrels . . . Where does their wealth come from? From lies, deceptions, and unjust takings.

Then there are the merchants' hirelings, the factors and the bookkeepers. Look what kind of people they are . . . They cannot eat, drink, and whore enough, tempting youth with all their tricks, inventing all sorts of rubbish and luxury. It all comes from idleness. What is the use of their services to the poor and the faithful? Is there any honesty, courage, or justice in them? They have all the power in the town and the country. Whoever has no wealth, has no honour and is worthless in their league. Thus the poor man is swindled out of his standards and his trust and picks up their attitudes and learns to deceive in order not to lose face . . . The cleverer a businessman, the greater his deceit.

NOTES

1   The title of *Das Buch Paragranum* does not translate into English. It is a treatise on the Four Pillars of Medicine (Philosophy, Astronomy, Alchemy, The Virtues).
2   Galen was a Greek physician of the second century CE whose writings formed the basis of the medical curriculum of the Renaissance; Avicenna (or ibin Sini, d.1037) was an Arabic commentator on Galen whose works were highly influential throughout the Renaissance.

90 Gianfrancesco Pico della Mirandola *The Witch or On the Deception of Demons* (1523)

Gianfrancesco Pico della Mirandola (1469–1533) is perhaps better known today as the nephew and biographer of the celebrated humanist Giovanni Pico della Mirandola (1463–94). He was, however, a formidable scholar in his own right who wrote extensively on a number of subjects and corresponded with some of the most celebrated humanist intellectuals of his age. Despite his great learning, he was led, under the influence of his spiritual mentor, Girolamo Savonarola, to renounce all forms of classical learning, particularly the pagan teachings of Aristotle, in favour of Christian simplicity based upon faith in the Church and the Scriptures. Consequently, in the sixteenth century, he became a fierce advocate of religious reform and spiritual regeneration based on the model outlined by Savonarola before his death at the stake in 1498. At the Lateran Council in 1515, Pico outlined before Pope Leo X his vision of how this might be achieved, voicing in the process similar concerns to those which were expressed by Luther just two years later. Failure to implement a programme of clerical and ecclesiastical reform, Pico warned, would lead to divine retribution. Pico, however, was no Lutheran. Though he continued to defend Savonarola's image and shelter his disciples, he was scathing in his condemnation of Luther's schism. A loyal son of the Church, Pico remained at heart a conservative reformer whose aversion to classical learning and literature was confirmed by his pronounced religious faith and, ironically, his attachment to the revival of the philosophical scepticism of the ancients.

   Strix (*The Witch*) first appeared in Latin in 1523 at Bologna where it was published alongside other works by Pico, including his address to Leo X at the Lateran Council. The original (not included here) contains a dedication to the author by the poet, Giovanni Antonio Flaminio; an address by Pico to his friend, the celebrated medical humanist, Giovanni Manardi; and a dedicatory epistle by the Dominican scholar, Leandro Alberti, to the bishop of Bologna. All three men seem to have shared Pico's religious and spiritual concerns. Flaminio, for example, in the same year as *Strix*'s publication, sought papal support for a crusade against the Turks. Alberti, who translated *Strix* into Italian in 1524, edited a life of the medieval mystic and prophet, Joachim of Fiore. The text itself, composed in the form of a dialogue and divided into three books, is here heavily edited, representing approximately half the length of the original.

Source: Gianfrancesco Pico della Mirandola, *Strix*, 1523, Bologna, translated for this edition from the copy in the British Library by Rod Boroughs

Speakers: Apistius (Doubter); Phronimus (Prudent); Strix (Witch); Dicastes (Judge)

Book One

Apistius:	Phronimus – look at that great crowd rushing through the vegetable market. Where can they be going?
Phronimus:	Let's approach and find out the reason for so large a gathering. We've nothing to lose by taking a short stroll.
Apistius:	It won't be short if we go as far as the newly built church dedicated to the Virgin Mother of God and named 'Of the Miracles', which lies beyond the first mile-stone. I imagine all these people are heading there since I think I can see some members of the Order which has elected to serve at that holy shrine.[1]
Phronimus:	I think you're right. If I'm not mistaken, I noticed among the crowd of youths the attendants who assist the inquistor in conducting trials of evil-doers. But, after all, what harm can there be in taking ourselves along there? In fact, I think we'll profit from the walk [. . .]. It might also be worthwhile if it enables us to learn something new; for I've a feeling that a witch has been caught and that this motley crowd [. . .] is hurrying to catch a glimpse of her.
Apistius:	Do witches live in these parts? I wouldn't object to travelling ten miles to see one of those.
Phronimus:	If you've never set eyes on a witch before, then perhaps your wish will be granted today.
Apistius:	If only I might discover that bird I've so eagerly searched for but never found![2]
Phronimus:	What 'bird' are you talking about?

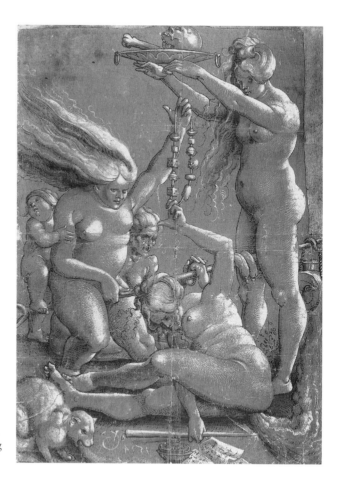

28 Urs Graf, *The Witches' Sabbath*, 1514. Graphische Sammlung Albertina, Vienna.

Apistius:	The screech-owl.
Phronimus:	Are you joking, Apistius?
Apistius:	Believe me, I'm speaking not in jest but in earnest. For to learn about something that antiquity was ignorant of is most agreeable, especially to a curious man.
Phronimus:	Do you, then, suffer from ignorance of something that everyone else knows about?
Apistius:	Do you, then, believe that I would wish to claim for myself knowledge of something which great and highly learned men of the past have not claimed to have understood, or, if they have understood it, have never seen it?
Phronimus:	What's that?
Apistius:	The 'bird-witch'. For though I have read the following: '. . . the wings of the infamous screech-owl together with the flesh'; '. . . the complaint of the restless owl and the nocturnal screech-owl'; '. . . the sad omen of the unfortunate screech-owl sounds'; and '. . . the heart of a gloomy owl and a hoarse screech-owl's vitals cut

out alive';[3] and also that the screech-owl was invoked in ancient curses, yet there is no agreement as to what it is, nor what its nature is. The Elder Pliny thought that what had been written on the subject of screech-owls – that they put their breasts into the mouths of infants and suckle them – was a fable, and, in fact, he clearly stated that he did not know what kind of bird the screech-owl was.[4]

Phronimus: I'm surprised that you, who I perceive to be well versed in the poets, have not read that in ancient times screech-owls were repelled from the doors with a stick of whitethorn; and that 'there are greedy birds . . . which have huge heads, bulging eyes, curved beaks mottled with grey, and hooked talons';[5] and that they were called by that name because they screech horribly at night.[6] So you see that the screech-owl, the origin of its name, its nature and appearance have all been recorded in literature.

Apistius: I understand what you say, but perhaps such screech-owls are diverse in type and varied in their nature. For it's also written that, rather than suckling their infants, they suck out their blood. Thus Ovid: 'They fly by night, and attack children who do not have nurses, and they defile their bodies snatched from their cradles'.[7] And indeed, the following verses persuade me to believe that these things have been observed as far back as heroic times: 'They came into Procas's bed-chamber. The five-day-old child was a fresh prey for the birds. They sucked his infant breast with their greedy tongues. And the unfortunate boy cried and craved help. Terrified by his scream, the nurse rushed to her charge and found his cheeks lacerated by harsh talons'.[8] Don't such mutually contradictory functions appear to you to demonstrate the varied and contrary nature and condition of screech-owls? It seems right to regard those birds which perform the function of a nurse as benevolent, and these others which drain the blood of infant children and kill them as extremely harmful.

Phronimus: Well, I think that both are fables; or else, if there is any real truth in the tale, I don't believe that 'they are either born birds, or made such by spells which evil old women use to transform themselves into birds'.[9] Rather, I believe that it was brought about through the assistance of wicked demons [. . .]. And so, I'm all the more amused by the defence against witchcraft prescribed by that demon who adopted the appearance of Janus: 'Touch the doors three times with an arbutus twig, mark the threshold three times with the same twig and sprinkle water at the entrance',[10] and he further enjoined them to do other things which were not sacred but rather abominable portents, though even learned physicians refer to them. 'Moreover, if the black screech-owl goes after babies, for example, dropping milk from its slimy breasts into their extended lips . . .'[11] And, in fact, this is what witches in our own time do, for it is said that when they are conveyed to the 'Game of Diana', they defile new-born infants crying in their cradles, and then apply remedies to them. I think these events have their origin in the screech-owls of old, just as their name is also derived from them: for women who commit such wickedness are now given the name *strix*, not only here but everywhere.

Apistius: So, Phronimus, you seem to be deluded by the same error that sways most of our countrymen, in that you think what the crowd says is true – that there are certain wretched women who fly together to banquets and carnal unions with spirits in the dead of night, and who bewitch infants.

Phronimus: Come now. You can't call it an error when so many erudite, worldly wise and virtuous men know and openly declare the truth of these things.

Apistius: Well, I for one could never be persuaded to believe them.

Phronimus: And why not?

Apistius: Because it seems so ridiculous that these harlots, by making a circle, applying unguent to their bodies and muttering certain words, can meet with infernal demons and ride at night on a piece of wood used for beating flax and hemp, or on a she-goat, or a he-goat, or a ram; that they are conveyed through the air and fly on the winds to join in the dances of Diana and Herodias,[12] playing, eating, drinking and delighting in lewd pleasures. What's more, I understand that they themselves don't even agree about all this: some of them say they are lifted up through the highest regions of the heavens, while others claim they are carried down nearer the earth. Some even testify that they travel only in their minds and not their bodies [. . .]. Furthermore, it is said that they have carnal unions with demons who, unless I'm mistaken, have no bodies. So what contact can there be with such demons? What passion? How can carnal women gain pleasure from some empty spirit? I've read that phantoms fight with the dead, not with the living.

Phronimus: If I counter your arguments, you will yield to me, I hope.

Apistius: Of course.

Phronimus: Truly, it is the mark of the prudent man that he allows himself to be influenced, guided and led by his ancestors' judgements, examples and authority [. . .]. And this is even more true of the man who's endowed with natural talents and accomplished in letters [. . .]. It seems to me from the conversation so far that you're very knowledgeable about the pagan poets and not averse to the philosophers either.

Apistius: I don't claim to be well versed in the poets: that's a claim that should not be made lightly. In the first place, one needs to know both the Greek and Latin tongues. Then one must know the profound meanings – frequently drawn from the store of philosophy –

in which poets and, above all, Homer, abound. I've heard that Homer is illuminated in great commentaries by Aristotle and certain Stoic philosophers. I also understand that Plutarch claimed in a mighty tome that that blind poet [i.e. Homer] was possessed of all science and art, and that, in short, he knew all things human and divine. For this reason, while I deny that I have a great knowledge of the poets, none the less I admit that I have engaged in studying them now and then – but only in order to learn about languages and to imbibe certain precepts befitting our way of life [. . .]. Also, I didn't want to appear ignorant of literature when the occasion arose in gatherings of friends. And if I have not drunk in all the philosophy that's said to be hidden in literature, then at least I've touched upon it, and, as they say, 'taken a sip'.

Phronimus: I don't consider you to be led by boastfulness or self-deprecation, but rather by truthfulness, the virtue which Aristotle locates midway between those two vices.[13] For you neither pretend that you know nothing, nor boast that you grasp everything. And what you say about the knowledge of poets is true. Indeed, Plato himself and Aristotle frequently cite Homer, Hesiod, Simonides, Pindar, Euripides and other poets. Consequently, despite what you say, I suspect that you are concealing the fact that you have embraced this philosophy and have more knowledge than you are prepared to admit.

              [. . .]

              Have you ever read in Homer how Ulysses came to the Cimmerians?

Apistius: Yes I have, and how the air where this people lived was thick and dark, impervious to the sun's rays.

Phronimus: And what did he do there?

Apistius: Many things.

Phronimus: Aren't these his words? 'Immediately I myself drew my sword from beside my thigh and began to dig a pit of a cubit's length this way and that, and around it poured a libation to the shades of the dead.'[14]

Apistius: You've translated the sense as well as the words excellently.

Phronimus: I imagine you've also read more than once about the games of Diana and the dances with her companion nymphs.

Apistius: Yes, indeed I have.

Phronimus: And I suppose you've also read about Venus's union with Anchises,[15] and how many heroes of ancient times were born from those false gods.

Apistius: Yes, frequently.

Phronimus: In wondrous ways these false gods deluded men who dedicated themselves to rustic and pastoral cares [. . .]. Thus, as the poet Ovid relates, a demon in the form of Thetis (who was believed by the pagans to be a sea-goddess) deceived the shepherd Peleus.[16] Also, in order that Peleus would not discover the trick, he was instructed by another demon – the multiformed Proteus – how Thetis might be captured, 'even though she counterfeited a hundred forms'.[17] [. . .] Therefore demons would adopt various forms, sometimes of beings who were believed to be goddesses, sometimes of nymphs of the earth, sometimes of nymphs of the sea [. . .]. Demons also appeared as clouds, as Juno did to Ixion, from whose union the centaurs were born. And they prepared other illusions with which they deceived the pagans, and double deceits with which they tricked the learned and the unlearned alike. Every image of false divinity oppressed that simple age with lewdness. What's more, even Diana (whose Game we are revealing, to the anger of the demon), who pretended to prize virginity in order, perhaps, to seduce those who abhorred foul lasciviousness, is known to have prostituted herself. Thus they say that Diana, under the name of the moon (as she was also known) was violated by Endymion. Similarly, Firmicus tells how Hippolytus had carnal union with her in her guise as Diana, and how, after he died, the place where he was buried was assiduously searched for and the healing hands of Aesculapius applied to his wounds. Thus returned to life, he assumed the name of Virbius.

If there is any basis to these tales, they should all be ascribed to demonic magic. Aesculapius was well rewarded for his magical powers – that is, with a horrendous death – for all the ancient authors agree that he was struck dead by lightning, though there are different opinions as to which particular sacrilege provoked this [*There follows a lengthy discussion of the various reasons given by classical authors for the death of Aesculapius, the Roman god of medicine*].

[. . .]

Thus we find that the narrative of Aesculapius's death is more varied than the story of Romulus' murder. Both men, however, were made gods by the pagans, despite the fact that the former was a magician and the latter a robber. I am all the more amazed, therefore, that that famous man, in the time of our grandfathers, was not more circumspect when he promised to reveal to an important prince, in return for a large sum of money, the entire Trojan War and the siege of Ilium. For while he was drawing the circle to show where Achilles and Ulysses were encamped, he was carried off by demons and never seen again.

Apistius: These are extraordinary things you're telling me.

Phronimus: Yes, extraordinary, but also true. The prince ordered that this magician be searched for in various parts of Italy, Germany, and many other places. And after the master died, one of his disciples came to this town, which bears the traces of his wickedness to this day. A man who had been robbed asked him to help find the thief. So he painted a likeness of the thief, recited certain sacrilegious things, and revealed in a saucer of water his appearance, dress and complete method of robbery. I know of another man who was revealed by this disciple to have stolen amulets when no one was around and put them in a strongbox in his own home. I recall the man renounced superstition thereafter and abjured the practice of magic.

If we were to walk together for ten days, I don't think it would be long enough for me to describe all the deceptions of demons, manifested in various ways, which I have observed. With very good reason is he called 'Satan',[18] for he is always plotting against mankind in all manner of ways, particularly in the realm of carnal pleasure, which we have determined to discuss. Anyone who denies this has to contend with numerous opponents. Augustine writes in *The City of God*, Book XV: 'Since there is such abundant testimony, and since those who have had no experience of it attest that they have heard about it from others who have experienced it, it would be impudent to deny that silvans and fauns, which are commonly called *incubi*, were often outrageous to women, and that they desired and performed carnal union with them, and that certain demons (which the Gauls called *dusii*) both attempted and effected this impurity continually.'[19]

Apistius: Please, go on.

Phronimus: As regards travelling through the air, I think you've also heard (if you've not read) how Abaris rode on an arrow from Phoebus's Hyperborean temple to Pythagoras in Italy.

Apistius: Yes, and I know that a Platonic philosopher wrote about this.[20]

Phronimus: If you recall this, you won't have difficulty agreeing to the following. You will know that all of Ulysses's necromancy began with the circle. Consequently, you may easily see that these tales of creating circles are not new but are ancient tricks or illusions [. . .]. Conversations with spirits do not, however, originate with Homer but are far more ancient, as those who know the hymns of Orpheus will attest [. . .].[21]

While they may have used different rites, each of these men sought to have commerce with the dead and, it was said, descended below. Long after Orpheus and Homer, it was said that Pythagoras did this, that he saw the souls of Hesiod and Homer being punished on account of the things they had said about the gods; and that, because of this, he himself was held in great honour by the people of Croton, especially when he related that he had observed below men being tortured because they had not wished to have intercourse with their own wives.

Furthermore, as regards travelling through the air, I don't know why you are so sceptical. To me, it doesn't seem to make any difference whether one flies on the winds by means of an arrow, or a bench, or a she-goat. It isn't recorded by what means Pythagoras and Empedocles were transported . . . Both, however, were deceived by Pallas Athene, that is, by the demon's cunning.

Apistius: I also remember hearing, if I'm not mistaken, about Simon Magus, who caused his own destruction by attempting to fly through the air.[22]

Phronimus: Perhaps you have also heard about certain Ethiopians who harness dragons and fly to Europe sitting on their backs. Roger Bacon is said to have written about this[23] [. . .]. But if you concede that there were *succubi* and *incubi* spirits in antiquity, why is it that you will not admit that they also exist in our times, when their existence is confirmed by so many and such weighty testimonies? [. . .] As for the unguent, you must know, I think, what Lucian of Syria and Apuleius the African wrote, the one in Greek, the other in Latin [. . .]. Thus [Lucian] says, 'As soon as the woman applied the oil to herself, she began to turn into a bird, starting with her toenails'; and a little later he adds that she had become nothing less than [. . .] 'a night raven'.[24] And so it seemed to those who saw her, or who pretended to see her, that she had become a night raven. I certainly don't believe that anything can transform itself into another shape by means of some perfume, or spell, or magic. Those witches, however, wanted to be seen smearing themselves with certain unguents so that they might seem – either to themselves or others – to have been transformed into a form different from their own. And though this false and vapid orator [i.e. Lucian] pretended to have transformed himself, he did not pretend to have mutated into a bird but rather an ass, even though he had used the same potion [. . .]. With this tale, Lucian indicates that it is the image and not the essence of the thing that changes, and he proves this most clearly when he asserts that the character and intellect of Lucius were preserved in the ass.

But it is impossible to believe that this fantasy of a human changing his form would have come into Lucian's mind if it had not been well known that such transformations were peculiar to Thessalian women. And the Platonic writer Apuleius, who later imitated Lucian, confirmed this, too. He made up a story of his journey to Thessaly, where he shrugged off his old form and assumed a new one by, if I remember his words correctly, 'putting on a little more of the ointment'.[25] Thus it seems that Apuleius wanted to imitate Lucian in nearly every respect, especially given that he made mention of the Thessalian spell, the magic oil that transforms, and the rose-remedy that returns one to normal.

Apistius: Why do you think they said roses were an antidote?

Phronimus: If there is any basis to it, I believe it is derived from Aristotle, in whom I have read, among many other marvellous things, that the smell of roses is fatal to asses.[26] Both Lucian and Apuleius knew this and imagined that this was how they lost the ass's form [. . .]. Or perhaps some other magic was involved. For the Thessalian and Thracian women were once notorious for their sorcery [. . .]. I think that, although these things appear to be false, they may have originated in some semblance of truth. And it seems more likely that these tales grew out of the prodigies of demons and are not without some basis in true history (albeit coloured by a great many falsehoods), rather than originating in dreams, as Synesius writes.[27]

[. . .]

But come, let us discuss the remaining subjects so that we may reach a decision about those, too. Countless things have been written about sorcery – the potions, spells and philtres, the Sabine cries and the Marsian incantations. Even though Ulysses's oarsmen were said to have grunted with the swine, having been transformed by that woman's charms; even though, according to the famous tale, Hercules, soaked with the blood of Nessus the centaur, burned with passion; even though loves were inflamed by Colchian philtres;[28] and even though it is well known that the illicit commerce of lust is indicated by such things, yet this was not just lust, but lust combined with sorcery, to which no one submits unless he so desires. This is why Homer relates that Ulysses sought Circe not with a kiss but with a sword;[29] for just as he was not enthralled by love, so he was not ensnared by sorcery, which is impotent without the malevolent guile of demons.

Thus, the demon possesses those who want to be possessed, and to make them desire it he employs various arts. He captivates the crowd by lust; those devoted to the civil life he captivates with wealth; and those very few who have dedicated themselves to philosophical study, he captivates with renown [. . .].

Demons insinuate themselves with men in various forms. Philostratus calls them 'spirits', 'sorceresses' and 'hobgoblins'.[30] In Isaiah, where the carnal union of demons is mentioned, we learn about the sorceress's bed.[31] Some people think that demons are *incubi* and believe that the upper parts of sorceresses appear in human form, while the lower parts are in the form of a beast. Indeed, some Hebrews understand sorceresses to be *furies*, although in the Lamentations of the prophet Jeremiah the sorceress is said to have breasts.[32] [. . .]. However, demons are not motivated by lascivious desire, but rather by malice, for they seek to bring ruin on mankind. They do not seek blood to drink, nor flesh to devour. Rather, they seek to lead the soul and body into everlasting torment. Demons breathe in a hidden flame, but they themselves are not inflamed by it, a fact which did not escape the excellent poet, when he said, 'You will breathe in a hidden fire'.[33] I recall that a witch once stated that when demons presented themselves to the senses in different forms, she could distinguish them from real beings because a fire burned in her chest at the same time. She also related that fire suddenly appeared when they cooked meat [during the Game]. I think that you'll understand this better when you hear the Judge, who I think I see in the distance engaged in combat with the witch if my eyes don't deceive me.

[. . .]

[After a brief exchange in which both men compliment each other on their learning, Phronimus returns to the task of convincing Apistius as to the reality of witches and witchcraft.]

Phronimus: It may be fear or lapses of memory that cause witches to give such differing accounts of the Game, for they are mostly uneducated, rustic women. It's also possible that the discrepancies are to be ascribed to the demon's deception, which does not affect them all in the same way [. . .].

As regards the movement by which they are conveyed by the demon and the place where they are set down, these matters should not surprise you at all. What is false in nature is very often multiplex and diverse; what is truthful is founded on simplicity. This can be seen from what we've been saying. It can also be observed in works of poetry, which are variable and inconsistent, and very frequently in histories in which two, three or more traditions are recorded. It is seen, too, in the ideas of philosophers and lawyers' responses. But you will never observe this in the writings of theologians [. . .] for there are never any discrepancies when theologians discuss those subjects which are their preserve – that is, the precepts and decrees that relate to faith and morality which are essential to our salvation. In works of theology, these things are always consonant and consistent in every respect. And so the malign demon, the friend of dissension, is as lying and deceitful as he is varied and changeable in appearance . . . Just as the demon would beguile certain ancient philosophers under the cloak of learning – for example, Pythagoras, Empedocles, Apollonius and others of that kind [. . .] – so he once would lure wretched women with revels and licentiousness (and today he also seduces wretched men with such things). But many philosophers, as is well known, abhorred such wickedness, so he enticed them to worship him in other ways: with the pretence of wisdom and under the veil of superstition masquerading as religion. Instructed by the demon, philosophers devoted themselves to prayers, hymns, and oracles, whereby they thought they might know the future and be conveyed through the air to various places. It was by the agency of demons that philosophers became esteemed as gods among men. How else could Pythagoras' disciples have seen him disputing at one moment in Taormina in Sicily, and in Metapontum the next, after the briefest of intervals? And how else could Empedocles have journeyed through the air? [. . .]. Anyone who believes that Apollonius could foresee the future and command demons is very much mistaken. The evil demon only pretended to be tormented by him in order to seduce him under the cloak of a false divinity and thereby entrap others readily. This is evident from these philosophers' deaths. The demon sought to destroy Pythagoras first by insurrection, then by fire, and finally he had him put to death by the sword. The manner in which he destroyed Empedocles is infamous, for the philosopher was impelled to such a pitch of insanity that he thought he had become divine [. . .] But whether he died in this manner [by throwing himself into the volcano], or [. . .] by putting a noose around his neck and hanging himself from a tall cherry tree, one must suppose that it was the demon who incited him to kill himself [. . .]. Perhaps the demon also seized Apollonius together with his soul, leading him down to eternal damnation. His death seems suited to the magic arts, for there are different traditions of the way he died [. . .]. [However,] the oracles, which had ensnared almost the whole world with the same deceits, ceased after the Incarnation. And he who once openly poured forth oracles [i.e. Satan], now babbles in dark byways, seeking carnal unions which people nowadays regard as infamous, though they were formerly considered glorious [. . .].

In this way, the demon would lure those who desired carnal pleasure into wickedness, embellishing the illusion with superstition. Likewise, he seduced those who desired glory, by enabling them, through commerce with him, not only to predict the future while they lived, but also to continue giving out oracles when they were dead. In this way, they say, Orpheus, who was esteemed as a prophet in his own life-time, continued to make prophecies after his death [. . .]. Similarly, they said that kings engaged in warfare after their deaths [. . .]. According to Philostratus, Achilles appeared to Apollonius of Tyana and Protesilaus, together with the other commanders who had gone to war against Priam [. . .]. But the fact that their appearance, conduct and actions are different from those described by Homer, and do not concur with what either Dares of Phrygia or Dictys of Crete wrote in their histories, should be a warning to you of the magnitude of the deceptions of demons and of the lies with which they assail our knowledge, as well as the poisonous nonsense with which they infect our customs.[34]

Why is it, then, that you are so amazed at the many inane and absurd things (most of them mutually contradictory) observed of witches in our own age, when the demon was able to deceive those who considered themselves wise and deluded them into believing things that were contradictory, inconsistent, and quite contrary to reason? You should rather be amazed at the wisdom and power of Christ. For before the Incarnation the evil demon convinced kings, orators, and philosophers throughout the world so that his power was supreme and deserving of all praise and wisdom; yet now he is scarcely able to persuade the most wretched men and women to worship him and carry out his commands. And what used to be practised openly in every nation, throughout the world as something glorious, is now done in secret by a few people in isolated and obscure places. Moreover, today it is regarded as something full of shame and ignominy. And consider this, which, above all, befits divine glory: so firm is the foundation of the Christian faith that the evil demon does not allow witches to have commerce with him unless they first abjure our faith, reject the sacraments and scorn the saving host. Thus the enemy of God and mankind enjoins those who have abandoned our religion to be initiated into his sacrilegious rites. And clearly this is because false-hood cannot stand together with truth, nor darkness with light, nor superstition with religion. But I think you have already become more certain about these matters which we have been discussing on our journey.

Look! There's the witch speaking with the judge at the entrance of the church.

[. . .]

[Enter the judge, Dicastes, who proceeds to introduce himself and the miserable witch. The three men agree to meet the following morning when the judge will continue his public examination of the witch.]

Book Two
[Apistius begins the discussion by asking the witch if she has ever taken part in the Game of Diana.]

[. . .]

Phronimus: It's my belief that the Game of Diana is partly derived from the ancient game, and partly the product of modern superstitions; or, speaking in the neoteric style [i.e. in the language of Aristotelian scholasticism], that it is ancient in its substance, but new in its accidents.

Dicastes: You've come up with an excellent distinction, which could help to resolve many of the uncertainties that surround the subject. For example, some people make the great mistake of supposing that

	these wretched women are always conveyed to the Game in their minds and imaginations, not in their bodies.
Apistius:	So, do you believe that witches are always physically transported to the Game?
Dicastes:	Not at all. Sometimes they are found sitting on beams, overcome with such torpor that they are unable to feel blows. And sometimes they are found with their brooms gripped so tightly between their thighs that the brooms cannot be prised from them, even though they are asleep. But they themselves believe they have been transported on these brooms.
Apistius:	What's the reason, do you suppose, that they are sometimes physically transported to the Game, yet at other times, despite their claims to be physically present, it is only in their imaginations that they attend?
Dicastes:	Sometimes it's a trick and cunning delusion of the demon; sometimes it's a matter of the witch's own choice. The German theologians, Heinrich and Jakob, have written about this, as I recall. They tell of a witch who used to traverse space by one method or the other, as she pleased – that is, awake and in her body or occasionally, when she wearied of the journey, in her imagination only. Then she would recline on her bed and when she had uttered some accursed words, a simulacrum of the whole Game would be represented on a dark cloud, as if on a stage.[35]
Phronimus:	What would you say to those who opposed you on this?
Dicastes:	First, I'd say that I am amazed that, on the basis of one method of making this journey – one sometimes used by sacrilegious women in a certain part of the world – they seek to judge all other kinds of sacrilege, superstition and magical vanities, and seek to extend this one method to every part of the world. Likewise, I'm amazed that they think they know so much that they can confine the enormous power which the demon has wielded since the Creation to a pounding-mill, as they say.[36] Furthermore, I'm amazed that they do not allow the text of the laws to be expounded, as others who have far better judgement do, in such a way as to separate the things that pertain to nature from those that pertain to the Catholic faith. Finally, I'm dumbfounded that they openly try to say that it does not occur; for it is extremely ignorant of them to deny it is possible, and extremely impudent of them, and in contradiction to thousands of witnesses to say that it has not happened on occasions.

But perhaps someone bolder than I will say that he desires to see the true exemplar of the laws of the Council, and a higher authority than that of the compiler. For Gratian distorts very many things, and this is one of the reasons, perhaps, that his compilation has never been generally approved or accepted in place of the laws, which it is a sin to challenge.[37]

But while I concede all this, it seems that my opponent's mouth has been closed by your distinction, through which it is evident that this 'Hunt' of wretched men and women in our time is in part similar to, and in part different from, the Game of Diana. For Diana is not adopted here, and there is no belief in the goddess of the pagans, and those other things condemned by the Council in that region are not seen here. Nevertheless, many things happen here which, from what we read, have never happened there, and which have much in common with other pagan superstitions and the illusions of malevolent demons: the pernicious unguents, the innocent blood of children, the circle, the magic incantations, the numerous sorceries and the physical journeys through the air. Moreover, in my opinion anyone who asserts that this super-human movement through the air cannot be effected by the demon ought to be put on trial as a heretic. For [. . .] it is written in the Gospel that our Lord Jesus Christ was placed on the mountain top and on the pinnacle of the temple.[38] All theologians cite this as evidence that, as far as moving from place to place is concerned, bodies are obedient to the will of disembodied spirits. And so it is a matter for the law to decide whether these witches are transported in reality or not. For when it is known that something is possible, we can only learn whether or not it has been done from witnesses – and we have plenty of those.

Phronimus: It isn't surprising that they draw such a ridiculous interpretation from the text of the laws, while others perceive truth in it. For just as God draws good from bad, so men who are wrongly instructed try to draw bad from good. Consequently, every heresy drawn from the scriptures is due to man's malice. The scriptures themselves are not at fault.

[. . .]

Dicastes: The demon can move bodies as he pleases.
Phronimus: Yes, but it doesn't follow that he can transport witches to the banks of the River Jordan in so short a time [. . .].
Dicastes: Why is this not possible?
Phronimus: Because your teachers say it isn't.
Dicastes: How do they preclude it?
Phronimus: Thomas Aquinas asserts that the whole mass of the world cannot be moved by the demon as this is against nature, which does not permit the integral order of matter and the elements to be dispersed and destroyed.[39] Indeed, it is against the nature of the human body – that which both preserves and destroys it – for it to be conveyed at such great speed. Since these women are alive, the impact of the air would be bound to destroy them. Because the nature of the air remains unchanged, it would prove an immense obstacle. If, however, the air were to become rarefied, it

would quickly turn into fire; and if it were to become denser, it would impede the speed of their journey. Even if you were to move all the air with your thoughts, as Aristotle supported the heavens with his, then you would still be opposed by both Philoponus among the Greeks and Johannes Scotus among his countrymen.[40] They would object by adducing the intrinsic nature of quantity, which demands that a body must move one part of itself after another, even through the great void where there is no air. So that, even if all opposing winds were removed, the journey from here to Asia would still have taken much longer than they said it did.

Apistius:	Please leave your investigation of these subtleties until another day. [*To the witch*] Tell us about the Game.
Strix:	As soon as we arrive, we see the Lady sitting with her lover.
Apistius:	Who is her lover?
Strix:	I don't know. I know only that he is a handsome man dressed in gold.
Apistius:	Go on.
Strix:	Then we take the consecrated host to the Lady. She accepts it gratefully and with a cheerful expression, and then she orders that it be placed on a stool and trampled and urinated on.
Apistius:	Who gave you the host to take to the Game?
Strix:	The priest, Bernio, a native of this town.
Dicastes:	The most wicked and worthless man I have ever known – or anyone else has known, judging from what I've read! After his countless outrages had been discovered, I divested him of his priestly authority and handed him over to the magistrate, who immediately imposed on him the punishment decreed by the laws.
Apistius:	[*To the witch*] Continue with your account.
Strix:	We eat, drink, and enjoy carnal pleasures. What more do you want to know?
Apistius:	I want you to explain in detail what you eat.
Strix:	Meat and the other foods people like to eat.
Apistius:	Where do you get this meat from?
Strix:	We slaughter oxen, but they come back to life.
Apistius:	Whose oxen are they?
Strix:	They belong to the people we hate. We also drink together, drawing wine from casks. Finally, each woman summons her own demon to satisfy her desires, and each of the male demons engages in intercourse.
Dicastes:	What you say about the oxen sounds ridiculous.
Phronimus:	They're like the oxen in Lucian's tale [. . .]
Apistius:	They are indeed similar. For there's little difference between an 'ox's hide crawling and its half-cooked flesh bellowing',[41] and this illusion in which the folded-up skin of a devoured ox rises to its feet.
Phronimus:	Like marvels occurred when the Argives believed that the

Argonauts' beechwood ship spoke,[42] and when Achilles's horse, Xanthus, foretold the future.[43] But in my opinion, while one might believe that Xanthus spoke, one should not believe the flights of Pegasus, or those of Daedalus, or of him that 'brought back the famous spoils of that Lybian monster, cleaving the thin air on whirring wings'.[44]

Apistius: But if you can accept that a witch can fly, why do you laugh when you read that 'Parrhasian wings carried Perseus aloft'?[45]

Phronimus: I don't laugh at that – if, that is, you mean that such things were brought about by the demon's art. If, on the other hand, you believe that they were brought about by man's power or ingenuity, then, yes, I laugh. For I don't consider a man or a horse with wings that can fly, and a horse with a tongue that can speak, to be prodigies of the same order. It's no miracle that so many small birds can repeat with articulate voices the words they frequently hear, so how much easier must it be for a horse to be rendered capable of speech, through some spirit, be it good or evil.

Apistius: Are you saying that this can happen?

Phronimus: Of course – nature being consistent.

Apistius: Could you give an example to support this?

Phronimus: Yes, here's just one example. It's written in the Book of Numbers that Balaam's ass spoke.[46] According to the theologians, it was the power of the angel that brought this about. And though the ass herself did not know what she was saying, her tongue was made to utter things useful to the Hebrew army, which, it is written, was guided by the good spirit [. . .].

Apistius: [*To the witch*] We know that demons have neither flesh nor bones. How, then, do they eat and how do they perform carnal union?

Strix: The particles they assume are similar to flesh and bones, but are denser than those of mortals [. . .]. When our lust was satisfied, we were taken home again.

Apistius: Did he ever come to visit you there?

Strix: Yes, very frequently, and sometimes he would accompany me when I travelled to and from the market. I remember one evening when I was returning home from the town, he had carnal union with me three times before we got back.

Apistius: How far beyond the town walls is your house?

Strix: About a mile.

[. . .]

Apistius: It's impossible for me to imagine what pleasure these women derive from this union.

Phronimus: They report that they are filled with a pleasure so great they say there's no pleasure like it on earth. There are several reasons for this, I think. First, there are the beautiful visages those forsaken spirits adopt; then, there is the uncommon size of their members.

They charm their eyes with the former and fill up their hidden parts with the latter. Moreover, the demons pretend to be in love with them, and nothing is more gratifying to these wretched women than this. Also, perhaps, the demons are able to excite them inwardly, giving the women more delight than they experience by sleeping with men. The same thing occurs, I believe, to men who use demon *succubi*.[47] That most wicked priest I mentioned earlier said that he got far more pleasure from sleeping with a demon called Armellina than from any of the women he'd slept with [. . .]. By her command, the infants he had undertaken to baptise according to the rite of the Church, he would take back unclean to their homes; and he would raise before the people unconsecrated host to be worshipped, pretending with words and gestures to consecrate it so as to conceal his iniquity. And if ever he did consecrate it according to rite, he would raise it on high and keep it back to give to the witches so that they might take it to the Game [. . .].

But you shouldn't suppose that those who are seized by such love – some of whom are atheists, some despisers of God and deserters from the faith – act solely against religion: they also carry out acts of extreme wickedness against the state. They steal the property of others, contaminate everything with their sorcery, and they immerse themselves totally in adulteries and other impurities. They murder children and suck out their blood, they provoke violent storms, and they lay waste to the fields with hail-storms [. . .].

Apistius: [*To the witch*] Have you ever summoned up thunder?

Strix: Yes, often.

[. . .]

Apistius: Did you plot this ruin to repay someone?

Strix: No, I did it out of hatred.

Phronimus: [. . .] These witches also seduce the minds of men into wickedness with charms that allure their senses [. . .]

We've seen this repeated here in our town. There was that priest who was seventy-two years old when we extinguished the flames of his passion with the flames generated by the piled-up faggots – the self-same faggots he used to travel to his *succuba*. Another man, who was more than seventy-five, and another, who had seen eighty summers, used to attend the same Game together, eight times a month. Thus, it is well known from the testimonies of very many men that there is not one witch, or two, or three, but many; and that there are not three or four men who use demon *succuba*, but a great number. They themselves claim that around two thousand men assemble at the Game.

Apistius: Antiquity has handed down the names of three or four famous enchantresses. So, in our own age, most enchantresses are called Medea, many are called Canidia, and there is more than one Erichtho.[48]

Phronimus: Are you surprised that there are six hundred Medeas, when you are well aware – and not at all shocked – that twelve thousand Circes can be found in one city alone?

Apistius: I understand.

Phronimus: Consequently, I believe it is the work of divine providence that in these times, when everything seems to be getting worse and worse, God Himself has sought to strengthen belief in the hearts of the faithful in many ways, and thus to extend religion far and wide.

Apistius: What ways are those?

Phronimus: Three in particular: by prophecies coming to pass, by divine miracles, and by the revelation of the wickedness of these abominable rites. We have discovered that war, famine and pestilence have come to pass exactly as divinely foretold so many years ago. If faith had not been so strong in this town, those who disbelieved the prophecies might have imagined that the dreadful calamity which destroyed them had come about by chance or fate. Faith has recently been awakened in this town, however, by the many miracles performed by the Virgin Mother of God. And just as these miracles in themselves confirm our Christian faith, so the witches' confessions act as a further source of corroboration; for it is through their confessions, made by very many witnesses of both sexes, that we have learned how malign demons oppose Christian truth. And the more these demons exert themselves in plotting to obscure and destroy that truth, the more exalted it becomes and the brighter it shines far and wide.

Apistius: Well spoken. Now, good witch, have you also murdered children?

Strix: Yes, many.

[. . .]

[*There follows a description of the methods used by the witch in murdering and killing children.*]

Apistius: What promises do your lovers make to you? What hopes do they give you?

Strix: Life, riches, and pleasures – our enjoyment of these things is unceasing.

Apistius: Did he ever bestow money on you?

Strix: He gave me some once but it disappeared – I've only a few pennies left.

[. . .]

[*At this point in the interrogation, Dicastes leaves in order to make preparations for the three men's supper, after which they promise to speak more on the subject. In Dicastes's absence, Phronimus and Epis-*]

*tius question the witch further. On his return Dicastes, together with
Phronimus, enquire whether Apistius has changed his mind with
respect to the existence of witches. Apistius is still not fully convinced
and eagerly awaits further discussion with the expert, Dicastes.*]

Book Three

Apistius: Now that your feast has removed our hunger, Inquisitor Dicastes, let me ask you first about something that has inserted into my mind not so much a doubt as a lance[49] – if, that is, we concede that what we have heard from the witch is true.

Dicastes: Ask whatever you like.

Apistius: I'm not satisfied by those who say that, though these monstrous vices are tolerated, those who immerse themselves in wickedness eventually have judgement passed upon them in Hell, and thus pay the due penalty. Surely, it would be better if their vices were prohibited rather than permitted and then punished?

Dicastes: It would be better, certainly, if you made that point to the perpetrator of the vice, who, had he abstained from it, would have done himself much more good.

Apistius: But why is he allowed to commit the vice? Don't we agree it would have been a more divine act if the crime had been prohibited by God?

Dicastes: It is prohibited by law, but people are not prevented from doing it.

Apistius: Why are they not prevented from doing it?

Dicastes: Because it's left to man's free will.

Apistius: Wouldn't it have been better if the man, who God knew would plunge headlong into impiety, had never been born?

Dicastes: It would indeed have been better for the man who persists in the vice right to the end of his life if he had died in his mother's womb.

Apistius: Do you think it would have been better if he'd never lived?

Dicastes: Better for whom?

Apistius: For the man himself.

Dicastes: That is a foolish question since *the man* and *nothing* are so contrary that the one is cancelled out by the other, and there isn't anything that can conceivably be good or bad for *nothing*.

Apistius: So why did God, in his consummate goodness, create a man he knew would be condemned to everlasting torment?

Dicastes: Because of his consummate goodness.

Apistius: How so?

Dicastes: In order that God's infinite goodness should not be defeated by man's evil. This is how the Apostle Peter is said to have answered when Simon Magus asked almost the same question (if their discussion is accurately recorded by St Clement).[50] Do you really think that God ought to have ceased from his work of infinite power, his sublime favour of creating souls, just because man was going to abuse that favour? Moreover, if you consider all the other virtues that God has shown to the world, you will see that justice stands out in that it binds men who would rather flee than follow His gifts of goodness and clemency. Mercy is, therefore, neither extinguished nor diminished, and exacts a less severe punishment than that demanded by the rigour of justice. And frequently something arises from this wickedness and from these vices which is brought forth by God Himself. For, as Augustine declares, God is so good that He would not permit anything evil to happen unless He wished to produce from it a greater good.[51] Learned men often, if not always, understand that a greater good is drawn from evil, but the common people do not discern this. There are many examples I could give you; here are just a few. The righteous Joseph was sold by his brothers, which was a terrible crime.[52] The ignorant masses don't seek to know anything more than this. But learned and pious men know that, as a result of such an evil transaction, Joseph became king of Egypt and saved from death his father, brothers, and all his family [. . .]. Similarly, the virtue and glory of the martyrs shone through the torments and deaths they suffered at the hands of tyrants. And finally – and what other examples are necessary besides this one? – through the death of Christ, God reveals his outstanding goodness, redeems mankind from eternal death, and opens the gate to piety and justice.

Apistius: You have removed the doubt that was troubling me. Now explain to me, as you earlier promised you would, why it is we should regard this Game as something historical rather than as a piece of fiction.

Phronimus: Would you believe every history?

Apistius: Certainly not. For though that work of Lucian of Samosata is the purest fable, yet it is circulated as if it were a true narrative. Moreover, there is so much uncertainty in most histories, with their two-fold and sometimes manifold versions, that they scarcely seem any different from fables.

Phronimus: You understand this very well. For just as some truth occasionally shines out from the obscurity of fables, so you may find among the many mutually contradictory historical narratives one that is true. The others, since they waver with falsehood, must be deemed to be fables. For, assuredly, truth cannot conflict with truth. So, Dicastes, I think I know what Apistius means.

Dicastes: What's that?

Phronimus: That a history should be confirmed by a great number of witnesses and not be contradicted by any other history of equal or greater authority.

Apistius: Yes, exactly.

Dicastes: I promise to show how our conviction that this Game takes place, and our attempts to procure its eradication, pertain to the Christian religion. I'll produce a great number of histories, which do not contradict each other but are wholly consistent. And I'll have the witch brought back here for you. Prison guard! Bring her here at once and put her on oath again to make her confess the truth. Also, many of the testimonies I'll adduce for you have been given by men bound by the sacrament, and have been written down for posterity in order that the truth may be established.

Apistius: Begin then.

Dicastes: I could refer you to books on the subject, which have been composed with great diligence. But while this would not be unwelcome to Phronimus, who has shown that he's well versed in all the kinds of writers we have been discussing, it would not, however, satisfy Apistius, who appears to have read a lot of literature of the more refined kind and to shun all books that lack elegance and polish.[53]

Apistius: Could it be, Dicastes, that you are hereby condemning elegance of speech in verse and prose?

Dicastes: Not at all.

Apistius: But it does appear that some people who know only 'Parisian-style' writing – that is, writing set out in questions – detest continuous oration composed in a smooth, elegant and ornate style [. . .].[54]

Dicastes: Am I to be included in their number, when I am perfectly well aware that John Chrysostom, Basil, and the three Gregorys wrote in an elegant fashion in Greek, as did Jerome, Augustine, Cyprian, Ambrose and others in Latin?

Apistius: Did they also write in verse?

Dicastes: Most of them did, certainly. So it's untrue to say that that kind of writing was unknown in those times. They even used to oppose enemies of the faith in verse. And in our own age, too, there are those who are drawn to our rites by eloquence – eloquence that is virtuous and thus certainly not to be condemned, just as an outstanding good among men, which is supported by the reason and authority of our ancestors, cannot be condemned.

Apistius: What books are they and when were they produced?

Dicastes: There are many – some of them were written sixty years ago, though one has been produced in our own age.

Apistius: Who were the authors?

Dicastes: I think they were Belgian or German, but the authors of the one written in our own age were both German. These have sought to pound the sorceresses with a hammer, and have done so with more force and justice than Nicocreon the Cypriot displayed in executing Anaxarchus of Abdera.[55]

Apistius: In what style were these books composed?

Dicastes: In what is commonly called the 'Parisian style' – that is, set out in questions – but written with great subtlety (as much as the subject allows) and, as it seems to me, truthfulness. And it is not only I who think this – many theologians do as well. The preface of this last volume begins with the Pope, and at the end is sanctioned by the authority of the Emperor. And I know that the book was publicly praised by the professors of divinity in Cologne.[56]

Apistius: I'd rather you told me things relevant to the subject under discussion, Dicastes. And whether you decide to take them from this book or another, please relate them in language with which I am familiar [. . .].

Dicastes: I shall do as you ask, but I preface my reply with the plea that you will forgive me if I should say something which your ears are unaccustomed to. For while I am very interested in Greek and Latin letters, I have applied myself with no less dedication to the studies of theologians, who, because they hold the refinement of words in less esteem, are able to devote themselves to the knowledge of things as they really are.

Phronimus: To lack refinement of words is less serious than to lack knowledge of things. I've always contended that the man who is distinguished in both is superior to those who depend on either one or the other. But if it were necessary to do without one of them, I don't believe that the knowledge of things should ever be valued less than words (though, as I have gathered from your conversation, you have no need to ask for forgiveness on this score).

Dicastes: I'll speak in Latin to the best of my ability. First of all, it's well known that anyone who would deny the existence of demons would place themselves outside the Catholic Church, since he would oppose many parts of sacred Scripture and the Gospel in particular.

Apistius: I concede that this is undoubtedly the absolute truth.

Phronimus: The same man would also have to be thrown out of the Academy and the Lyceum since Plato and all the Platonic philosophers regularly mention demons, and Aristotle, too, did not shrink from mentioning them by name in the *Ethics*, *Politics* and *Rhetoric*, and well as other places.

Dicastes: But they differ from us in that they considered demons to be good and bad. We maintain that they are all malign, and although we refer to them by the appellations of 'Devil' and 'Satan', they are also known by the name 'demon'. Hence those words of the Prophet: 'All the pagan gods are demons'.[57] And the Apostle says, 'I do not want you to become the partners of demons'.[58] And further: 'The demons believe and tremble with fear'.[59] Besides this, when sorceries were devised to charm away the crops, to annul marriage or bind it with torments – events out of the ordinary course of nature – no sane man doubted but that these things were brought about through pacts with demons. And hence we can learn many things in the works of theologians, both ancient and modern, in sacred literature, in the canons of the Roman Church,

and in the imperial laws. In Deuteronomy it is commanded that sorcerers and enchanters be put to death.[60] In Leviticus it is stipulated by law that soothsayers and those who employ prophetic spirits shall be stoned to death.[61] And many more examples can be found in Questions 24 and 26 of the *Decretals* compiled by Gratian.

Apistius: So much can be read on the subject of the doctrines of Christianity in Augustine's *City of God* that one needs little else besides them. I hardly need cite more modern theologians who have argued in many places against sorcery. In civil law, too, in the *Codex* of Justinian many laws were established against sorcerers and astrologers [. . .]. I do not deny the existence of demons, nor that much can be accomplished by their malice, but I would like to be shown the things which pertain particularly to this subject. Do they go, or are they conveyed, to the Game in their bodies, rather than merely in spirit?

[There follows further discussion of this point, drawing on the evidence of the witch, who confessed to having travelled to the sabbat in both 'body and soul'. Apistius, however, remains sceptical.]

Phronimus: [*to Apistius*] Do you believe that in those ancient and heroic times demons appeared which, according to our religion, you would not hesitate to call a type of evil spirit?

Apistius: Of course.

Phronimus: Then why don't you believe that these demons, in the guise of men, sought carnal union with women, and that, in the guise of women, they sought carnal union with men?

Apistius: Because they are not of flesh and so cannot derive pleasure from carnal love.

Phronimus: It's been stated many times that they don't do it for its own sake, but rather in order to deceive.

Apistius: Yes, it's said that the gods and goddesses had children, and I recall that the day before yesterday you said that fables have some force to them. Where, then, does the semen in the males come from? And where do the embryos in the females come from? How are the infant children produced?

Phronimus: You're right to have doubts. For when Moses mentioned 'the sons of God and men' in the holy book of Genesis, some took it to mean carnal unions of this kind, while others thought it referred to just and unjust progeny.[62] But it must not, on this account, be supposed that we are to regard those who are said to be the sons of Jove and Apollo as having sprung from the seed of demons; for demons do indeed lack seed. Rather, we should regard them as the sons of man whose seed was taken and used by the demon. For that 'she-demon' (as I might put it: that is, a demon in the guise of a woman) lies under a man, and when that same demon, in the form of a man, lies upon a woman, he puts the semen into her private parts. And so we should judge that the woman who conceives by that seed becomes pregnant by the man from whom the seed flowed. And we should judge that, in the case of those who were falsely believed to be the offspring of goddesses, the demon stole the real embryos from other women and gave them to the women they were deceiving [. . .].

[*There follows a brief discussion of demons who incite homosexual love, and the origins of this 'execrable vice' in ancient times. Apistius, who would like to relegate such occurrences to the ancient world, is refuted by Dicastes who insists that they still take place.*]

Apistius: Why, then, are the instances of this vice not made famous?

Dicastes: Two reasons come to mind. The first is that after the malign demon had been cast out from the dominion of the world through the blood and death of Christ, he no longer deceived men so frequently or so publicly. For once he was worshipped in the guise of a deity, but now he lives, like a deserter or fugitive, in abandoned and hidden places. The second reason is that he used to spread his nets of love for all kinds of men, but now he particularly sets out to ensnare with carnal pleasure just two kinds of men – the best and the worst. By the best, I mean those who have dedicated themselves to God with all their might [. . .]. The demon frequently attacks these men, but because these things happen in secret, they are not revealed, except occasionally as an example and help to others. By the worst, I mean this breed of witches we are presently discussing – and you know we have to use threats and torture to extort their loves from them since they do not speak openly about such things except with their followers.

[. . .]

Apistius: Sorcery would seem to be the only subject left to discuss now.

Dicastes: What do you wish to know?

Apistius: Whether sorcery is really performed or whether it is merely a trick of the imagination. For the force of divine providence – ever just and inscrutible – has plainly revealed why God sometimes permits it to happen and at other times prohibits it.

Phronimus: Do you recall Lucian of Samosata and Apuleius of Madauros?

Apistius: Of course. I've read them on occasion, and I heard you discussing them the day before yesterday. But I think the things contained in the story of the ass, both the Greek and Latin versions, are fictitious and didn't really happen.

Phronimus: While I don't doubt that many of those things – or most, or even all of them, if you prefer – are made up, I contend that they are not created from nothing. Similarly, our Augustine does not consider the transformations described by Varro (the transformations of Diomede's companions into birds, Circe's transformation of Ulysses's companions into beasts, and the transformation of Arcadians into wolves) to have been wholly without foundation. In Book XVIII of *The City of God*, he relates that even in his own time a great many things went on in Italy which were similar to those reported, or fabricated, by Apuleius.[63] However, he asserts that demons can accomplish nothing by their own natural power which is not permitted by almighty God, whose judgements, though frequently mysterious, are never unjust. Thus, he argues that, if demons do perform anything of this kind, it is merely in appearance that beings created by the one true God are transformed, so that they appear to be what they are not. All this he attributes to the imaginative faculty or to demons substituting one thing for anther. Augustine also believes that man's imaginative faculty is able to take on, as it were, the physical form of an animal and present itself in this form both to others' senses and to the man's own senses. And so Augustine judges that the deeds of those asses [. . .], the transformation of the Arcadians into wolves, and Circe's spell that transformed the companions of Ulysses, should all be attributed to that same imaginative faculty [. . .].

Dicastes: Phronimus has given a very concise and, in my opinion, very accurate account of Augustine's views. Theologians are in universal agreement that man's senses and his imaginative faculty are by their nature subject to the demon's power [. . .]. Truly, many things can be counterfeited through the trickery of demons and many things can appear to be different from what they are [. . .]. Moreover, the eyes of those seeing can be deceived and the keenness of their minds confounded when the imaginative power is disturbed [. . .]. Thus it follows that those who have not undertaken a thorough examination of these things are easily deceived. For they do not comprehend the written texts well or discern the great difference between nature and that which might be produced from the nature of things [. . .], between what is true and what has the appearance of the truth, and between that which manifests its true self and that which manifests the form of another. Such people belittle the force of universal nature and the power of demons. And, finally, they fail to appreciate that the justice of God is frequently mysterious and always most equitable.

Phronimus: But now, Dicastes, the evening twilight approaches, bidding us return home. If this discussion has not satisfied you, Apistius, I fail to see what will. For you have been able to learn both from antiquity and the present that this Game is no empty fable [. . .]. It has, of course, changed in accordance with the demon's will – and perhaps he will change it again, so subtle in his deceptions is the ancient enemy of mankind. I've shown you that circles, unguents, magical words, journeys through the air and the coition of demons are found as much in our own age as they were in heroic times. I've shown you how, from the beginning of antiquity, malign demons have devised tricks against mankind – how they have deluded with their utterances, deceived with their intimacy, and attempted to inveigle every epoch, and both sexes, with their various simulacra and apparitions; how they have counterfeited divinity and provided mortals with noxious feasts; and how, in the form of pack animals with wings, they have transported mortals, and have sought abominable carnal unions with them. So now [. . .] will you consent to return home with me?

Apistius: Yes, I shall, for now I am satisfied.

[*Phronimus and Apistius take their leave of Dicastes, with Apistius now resolved to change his name to Pisticus, 'Believer', in recognition of his new found faith in the existence of witches and demons.*]

NOTES

1   The Dominican monastery of Santa Maria de Miracoli, founded in 1522.
2   In this opening exchange, Apistius intentionally misunderstands Phronimus by taking the word 'strix' in its original meaning of 'screech-owl', the bird which came to be regarded as the magical embodiment of the witch.
3   Ovid, *Metamorphoses* VII.269; Lucan, *Pharsalia* VI.689; Seneca, *Hercules Furens* 688; *Medea* 733.
4   Pliny, *Natural History* XI.39.95.
5   Ovid, *Fasti* VI.131–4.
6   *Strix* derives from a Greek word meaning 'to screech'.
7   Ovid, *Fasti* VI.135–8.
8   Ovid, *Fasti* IV.143–8.
9   Ovid, *Fasti* VI.141–3.
10   Such measures against witchcraft, usually referred to as 'white witchcraft' in early modern Europe, were increasingly subject to official disapproval, particularly by those in authority who wished to see all forms of magical practice proscribed.
11   Quintus Serenus, *Liber Medicinalis* LVIII.1035–6. This was a Latin medical poem written in the third century CE.
12   The figure of Herodias, the wife of Herod Antipas (22 BCE–c.40 CE) and mother of Salome, was first associated with Diana in the early eleventh-century text, the *Canon Episcopi*. She appears frequently alongside Diana in medieval accounts and trials of witchcraft in Italy.
13   Aristotle, *Nicomachean Ethics* IV.vii.1–17.
14   Homer, *Odyssey* XI.24–25. In the original, Phronimus cites Homer in Greek.
15   Aeneas the Trojan was born as a result of Venus' union with Anchises.
16   Ovid, *Metamorphoses* XI.276f.
17   Ovid, *Metamorphoses* XI.253.
18   The word Satan derived from the Hebrew word for an adversary, opponent or plotter.
19   Augustine, *City of God* XV.23.
20   Iamblichus, *Life of Pythagoras* 19.
21   Orpheus was an ancient Greek figure who was the centre of an ascetic cult which preached the virtues of spiritual redemption. One way in which this might be achieved was through the singing of hymns or poems reputedly written by Orpheus. They acquired something of a vogue in the Renaissance, particularly among those, such as Ficino, attracted to the revival of Neoplatonism.

22   *Acts* 8: 9.

23   Roger Bacon (*c*.1214–94) was a celebrated English scholar whose interests included magic and alchemy.

24   Pseudo-Lucian, *The Ass* 12.

25   Apuleius, *Metamorphoses* III.24.

26   It has not been possible to trace the source of this reference which may derive from a work falsely attributed to Aristotle in the Renaissance.

27   Synesius of Cyrene, a Christian Platonist of the fifth century CE, was the author of the treatise *On Dreams*.

28   Sabines were renowned for their knowledge of herbs and incantations; Marsians were famed for their wizardry; Colchis was the legendary home of Medea. This section draws on Horace, *Epode* 17.

29   Homer, *Odyssey* X.321–2.

30   Philostratus, *Life of Apollonius* IV.25.

31   *Isaiah* 34: 14.

32   *Lamentations* 4: 3.

33   Virgil, *Aeneid* I.688.

34   Philostratus, *Life of Apollonius* IV.16; cf. Eusebius, *Treatise against the Life of Apollonius* 14–15. The histories of the Trojan War, attributed to Dares of Phrygia and Dictys of Crete, achieved great popularity in the Middle Ages. Apollonius of Tyana, a contemporary of Christ, received widespread acclaim in the Renaissance as a magus and worker of wonders. Pico reserved special criticism for Apollonius, along with other ancient *magi*, in his *De Rerum Praenotione* (*c*.1507), a work dedicated to exposing the follies and deceits of those who claimed to be able to tell the future.

35   Heinrich Kramer [Institoris] and Jakob Sprenger, *Malleus Maleficarum* (*The Hammer of Witches*, 1486), Pt.2,Qn.1.Ch.3.

36   A proverbial place of drudgery.

37   The judge is here referring to the *Decretals* of Gratian (*c*.1140) which constituted the first major attempt to codify the canon laws of the early medieval church. On the subject of witchcraft, they followed the 'sceptical' tone of the *Canon Episcopi* and have subsequently been seen by scholars as providing one reason for the relative lack of interest in witch-hunting in the medieval period. Not surprisingly, Renaissance demonologists were critical of their tone and content and, as here, sought to subvert their influence upon contemporary demonological thought.

38   *Luke* 4.

39   See e.g. Thomas Aquinas, *De malo*, Qu.16.Art.10.

40   Pico here plays devil's advocate, pointing out the inconsistencies of philosophy and its inability to provide answers to theological, or other, questions. John Philoponus was a sixth-century CE Christian Aristotelian. John Duns Scotus (*c*.1265–1308) was a Franciscan scholar and early disciple of Aquinas.

41   Lucian, *Gallus* 2.

42   Apollonius Rhodius, *Argonautica* IV.580–91.

43   Homer, *Iliad* XIX.404–24.

44   Ovid, *Metamorphoses* IV.618; i.e. Perseus with the gorgon's head.

45   Lucan, *Pharsalia* IX.660.

46   *Numbers* 22: 28–30.

47   Phronimus' account of the sexual encounters between witches and demons is largely drawn from the *Malleus Maleficarum* which goes into great detail on the subject.

48   In the story of the Argonauts, Medea used magic to help Jason and become his lover. Canidia was a sorceress frequently mentioned by the poet Horace; see e.g. *Epode* 5 and 17. Erichtho was a Thessalian woman, famous for her knowledge of poisonous herbs and medicines; see e.g. Lucan, *Pharsalia* VI.507; Ovid, *Heroides* 15.139.

49   Play on words: *scrupulus* = 'doubt' or 'small sharp stone'.

50   Clement of Alexandria, *Miscellanies* VII.107.

51   This was a commonplace of Augustinian thinking, repeated throughout his writings.

52   *Genesis* 37.

53   Dicastes is clearly referring here to Apistius's strong humanist credentials.

54   Pico here refers to the style of scholastic debate which continued to dominate the universities of Renaissance Europe. Pico himself remained extremely ambivalent about the validity of the 'Parisian style' which he discussed in his *De studio humanae et divinae philosophiae libri duo* (*On the Study of Human and Divine Philosophy in Two Books*, Bologna, 1497).

55   Anaxarchus of Abdera, a philosopher of the fourth century BCE, was put into a stone mortar and pounded to death with iron hammers on the orders of Nicocreon, tyrant of Cyprus. The allusion is to *Malleus maleficarum*; see note 34.

56   The *Malleus Maleficarum* begins with the Bull of Innocent VIII (1484), in which the Pope commissioned the authors, two Dominican monks, to root out witches in various parts of Germany. It ends with a letter of approbation from the Theology faculty at the University of Cologne.

57   The source of this biblical reference is uncertain.

58   1 *Corinthians* 10: 20.

59   *James* 2: 19.

60   *Deuteronomy* 18: 10–12.

61   *Leviticus* 19: 31.

62   *Genesis* 6: 4.

63   Augustine, *The City of God* XVIII.16–18.

Section Seven
Montaigne

91 Michel de Montaigne **from his *Travel Journal* (1581)**
(i) Montaigne witnesses a ceremony (ii) At a medicinal bath

Michel de Montaigne (1533–92), one of the greatest writers of the French
Renaissance, was author and reinventor of the *Essays* (first edition 1580; second,
much enlarged edition, 1588; third editions, on which he was working at the time
of his death, published posthumously 1595). The *Travel Journal* is the account of
his journey to Italy through France, Switzerland, Germany and Austria 1580–81.
While his ostensible purpose was to take the waters in an attempt to relieve
'the stone' (kidney-stones) from which he began to suffer in 1578, Montaigne
valued the journey – his sole venture outside France – principally as a unique
opportunity to satisfy his curiosity and enlarge his experiences of life. The *Travel
Journal*, half of which was written by a secretary, half by Montaigne himself (and
half of that in Italian) was forgotten after his death and first published only in
1774. In the first extract Montaigne witnesses a ceremony (Rome, January 1581);
in the second Montaigne records his experiences at the medicinal baths (La Villa,
near Lucca, August 1581).

Source: *Travel Journal*, trans. and with an introduction by D. M. Frame, North Point
Press, San Francisco, 1983 pp. 80–3, 152–5.

i) Montaigne witnesses a ceremony

On January 28th [1581] Monsieur de Montaigne had the colic, which did not
keep him from any of his ordinary actions, and passed a rather biggish stone and
other smaller ones.

On the 30th he went to see the most ancient religious ceremony there is among
men, and watched it very attentively and with great profit: that is, the circumcision of the Jews.

He had already seen their synagogue at another time, one Saturday morning,
and their prayers, in which they sing without order, as in the Calvinist churches,
certain lessons from the Bible in Hebrew, that are suited to the occasion. They
sing the same songs, but with extreme discord, because they do not keep time
and because of the confusion of so many voices of every sort of age; for the children, even the very youngest, take part, and all without exception understand
Hebrew. They pay no more attention to their prayers than we do to ours, talking
of other affairs in the midst of them and not bringing much reverence to their
mysteries. They wash their hands on coming in, and in that place it is an
execrable thing to doff one's hat; but they bow the head and knees where their
devotions ordain it. They wear over their shoulders or on their head a sort of
cloth with fringes attached: the whole thing would be too long to describe. After
dinner their doctors each in turn give a lesson on the Bible passage for that day,
doing it in Italian. After the lesson some other doctor present selects some one
of the hearers, and sometimes two or three in succession, to argue with the reader
about what he has said. The one we heard seemed to him to argue with great
eloquence and wit.

But as for the circumcision, it is done in private houses, in the most convenient and lightest room in the boy's house. Where he was, because the house was inconvenient, the ceremony was performed at the entrance door. They give the boys a godfather and a godmother, as we do; the father names the child. They circumcise them on the eighth day from their birth. The godfather sits down on a table and puts a pillow on his lap; the godmother brings him the infant there and then goes away. The child is wrapped in our style; the godfather unwraps him below, and then those present and the man who is to do the operation all begin to sing, and accompany with songs all this action, which lasts a short quarter of an hour. The minister may be other than a rabbi, and whatever he may be among them, everyone wishes to be called to this office, for they hold that it is a great blessing to be employed at it often: indeed, they pay to be invited to do it, offering, one a garment, another some other commodity for the child; and they hold that he who has circumcised up to a certain number, which they know, when he is dead has this privilege, that the parts of his mouth are never eaten by worms.

On the table where this godfather is seated there is also a great preparation of all the instruments necessary for this operation. Besides that, a man holds in his hands a phial full of wine and a glass. There is also a brazier on the ground, at which brazier this minister first warms his hands, and then, finding this child all stripped, as the godfather holds him on his lap with his head toward him, he takes his member and with one hand pulls back toward himself the skin that is over it, with the other pushing the glans and the member within. To the end of this skin which he holds toward the said glans he applies a silver instrument which stops the said skin there and keeps the cutting edge from injuring the glans and the flesh. After that, with a knife he cuts off this skin, which they immediately bury in some earth which is there in a basin among the other preparations for this mystery. After that the minister with his bare nails plucks up also some other particle of skin which is on this glans and tears it off by force and pushes the skin back beyond the glans.

It seems there is much effort and pain in this; however, they find no danger in it, and the wound is always cured in four or five days. The boy's outcry is like that of ours when they are baptized. As soon as this glans is thus uncovered, they hastily offer some wine to the minister, who puts a little in his mouth and then goes and sucks the glans of this child, all bloody, and spits out the blood he has drawn from it, and immediately takes as much wine again, up to three times. This done, they offer him, in a little paper cup, some red powder which they say is dragon's blood,[1] with which he salts and covers the whole wound; and then he very tidily wraps this boy's member with cloths cut specially for this. That done, they give him a glass full of wine, which wine they say he blesses by some prayers that he says. He takes a swallow of it, and then dipping his finger in it he three times takes a drop of it with his finger to the boy's mouth to be sucked; and afterward they send this glass, in the same state, to the mother and the women, who are in some other part of the house, to drink what wine is left. Besides that, another person takes a silver instrument, round as a tennis ball, held by a long handle (which instrument is pierced with little holes, like our cassolettes), and carries it to the nose, first of the minister, and then of the child, and then of the godfather: they suppose that these are odors to confirm and enlighten minds for devotion. He meanwhile still has his mouth all bloody.

On the 8th, and then again on the 12th, he had a touch of colic and passed some stones without great pain.

The Shrovetide that took place in Rome that year was more licentious, by permission of the Pope, than it had been for several years before: we found, however, that it was not much of a thing. Along the Corso, which is a long street in Rome that gets its name from this very thing, they race, now four or five boys, now some Jews, now some old men stark naked, from one end of the street to the other. You have no pleasure in it except in seeing them pass in front of the place where you are. They do the same with horses, on which are little boys who drive them with whips, and with donkeys and buffaloes driven with goads by men on horseback. For each race there is a prize offered which they call *il palio*: pieces of velvet or cloth. The gentlemen, in a certain part of the street where the ladies have a better view, run at the quintain on fine horses, and have good grace at it; for there is nothing that this nobility so commonly knows how to do well as exercises on horseback. The stand which Monsieur de Montaigne had made cost them three crowns. It was indeed situated in a very fine place in the street.

On those days all the beautiful gentlewomen of Rome were seen at leisure: for in Italy they do not mask themselves as in France, and show themselves with faces quite uncovered. As for perfect and rare beauty, there is no more of it, he said, than in France, and except in three or four he found no excellence; but commonly they are more attractive, and you do not see so many ugly ones as in France. Their heads are without comparison more advantageously dressed, and the lower part below the girdle. The body is better in France: for here they are too loose around the girdle and carry that part like our pregnant women. Their countenance has more majesty, softness, and sweetness. There is no comparison between the richness of their apparel and of ours: all is full of pearls and precious stones. Wherever they let themselves be seen in public, whether in a coach, at a festival, or in the theater, they are apart from the men; however, at dances they intermingle freely enough, where there are occasions for talking and touching hands.

The men are very simply dressed, for all occasions, in black and Florentine serge; and because they are a little darker than we are, they somehow do not look like dukes, counts, and marquises, which they are, but have a rather mean appearance; for the rest, they are as courteous and gracious as possible, whatever the common run of Frenchmen say, who cannot call people gracious who find it hard to endure their excesses and their ordinary insolence. In every way we do all we can to get a bad reputation here. However, they have an ancient affection or reverence for France which makes those people very respected and welcome who deserve the least bit to be, and who merely control themselves without offending them.

On Thursday before Lent he went to the feast of the Castellano. A good deal of preparation had been made, notably an amphitheater very artfully and richly disposed for combat in the lists, which combat took place at night, before supper, in a square barn with an oval-shaped entrenchment in the middle. Among other singularities, the pavement was painted in an instant with various designs in red: having first coated the pavement with some sort of plaster or lime, they laid over it a piece of parchment or leather cut into a stencil of the devices they wanted; and then they passed a brush dipped in red over this piece and printed through the openings what they wanted on the pavement, and so quickly that in two hours the whole nave of a church would be painted so.

At supper the ladies are served by their husbands, who stand about them and give them drink and what they ask for. They served a great deal of roast fowl dressed in its natural feathers as if alive; capons cooked entire in glass bottles; quantities of hares, rabbits, and live birds in pasties; admirably folded linen. The ladies' table, which was of four dishes, could be taken off in pieces, and underneath there was another all served and covered with sweetmeats.

The men do not wear masks when they go visiting. They do wear inexpensive masks when they walk about town in public or set up teams for tilting at the ring. There were two fine rich companies got up in this fashion on Shrove Monday to run at the quintain; they surpass us above all in abundance of very handsome horses. [. . .]

ii) At a medicinal bath

Tuesday August 15th [1581] I went to the bath early and stayed there a little less than an hour. I again found it rather cold than otherwise. It did not start me sweating at all. I arrived at these baths not only healthy, but I may further say in all-round good spirits. After bathing, I passed some cloudy urine; and in the evening, after walking a good bit over alpine and not at all easy roads, I passed some that was quite bloody; and in bed I felt something indefinably wrong with the kidneys.

On the 16th I continued the bathing, and I went to the women's bath, where I had not yet been, in order to be separate and alone. I found it too hot, either because it was really so or indeed because my pores, being opened from the bathing of the day before, had made me get hot easily. At all events I stayed there an hour at most and sweated moderately. My urine was natural; no gravel at all. After dinner my urine again came turbid and red, and at sunset it was bloody.

On the 17th found this same bath more temperate. I sweated very little. The urine rather turbid, with a little gravel; my color a sort of yellow pallor.

On the 18th I stayed two hours in the aforesaid bath. I felt I know not what heaviness in the kidneys. My bowels were reasonably loose. From the very first day I felt full of wind, and my bowels rumbling. I can easily believe that this effect is characteristic of these waters, because the other time I bathed I clearly perceived that they brought on the flatulence in this way.

On the 19th I went to the bath a little later to give way to a lady of Lucca who wanted to bathe, and did bathe, before me; for this rule is observed, and reasonably so, that the ladies may enjoy their own bath when they please. I again stayed there two hours. There came over me a little heaviness in my head, which had been in the best of condition for several days. My urine was still turbid, but in different ways, and it carried off a lot of gravel. I also noticed some sort of commotion in the kidneys. And if my feelings are correct, these baths can do much in that particular; and not only do they dilate and open up the passages and conduits, but furthermore they drive out the matter, dissipate and scatter it. I voided gravel that seemed really to be stones broken up into pieces.

In the night I felt in the left side the beginning of a very violent and painful colic, which tore me for a good while and yet did not run its ordinary course: it did not reach the belly and the groin, and ended in a way that made me believe it was wind.

On the 20th I was two hours in the bath. The wind in my lower intestines gave me much annoyance and discomfort all day. I continually voided very turbid, red, thick urine with some little gravel. I felt bad in my head. My bowels were rather livelier than usual.

Feast days are not observed here as religiously as we observe them, especially Sunday. The women do most of their work after dinner.

On the 21st I continued my bathing. After taking my bath I had a lot of pain in my kidneys. My urine was very turbid. I voided gravel, but not much. The pain I suffered then in the kidneys, as far as I could judge, was caused by wind, which was stirring all over. From the turbidity of the urine I guessed that some large stone was about to descend. I guessed only too well.

After writing this up in the morning, I came to be greatly afflicted with colicky pains immediately after dinner. And in order not to leave me too relaxed, one of these spasms attacked me together with a very acute toothache in the left jaw, which I had not felt before. Not being able to endure this discomfort, after two or three hours I went to bed, where in a short time this pain in the jaw left me.

Since the colic still tormented me, and I finally sensed (from feeling it move from place to place and occupy different parts of my body) that it was rather wind than a stone, I was forced to ask for an enema, which was administered to me at nightfall very comfortably, made of oil, camomile, and anise, and nothing else, by the prescription of the apothecary alone. Captain Paulino served me with it artfully in this way: feeling the wind rushing out against it, he stopped and drew back; and then continued very gently, so that I took in the whole thing without trouble. He did not need to remind me to retain it as long as I could, for it did not give me any desire to move my bowels. I stayed this way for as long as three hours, and then I tried to void it by myself. Being out of bed, I took a mouthful of marzipan with great difficulty, and four drops of wine. After going back to bed and sleeping a bit, I felt an inclination to go to the toilet; and by daybreak I had gone four times, though still keeping some part of the said enema that was not voided.

In the morning I felt much relieved, having got rid of an infinite amount of wind. I was left very tired, but with no pain. I ate a little dinner, without appetite; I drank without relish, although I felt very thirsty. After dinner that pain in my left jaw attacked me once again, from which I suffered very much from dinner to supper time. Considering it certain that this flatulence was caused by the bath, I let the bath alone. I got through the night with a good sleep.

In the morning on waking I found myself again weary and short of breath, my mouth dry, with a sharp bad taste, and my breath as if I had a fever. I did not feel any pain, but I continued passing this extraordinary and very turbid urine, which all the time carried with it sand and reddish gravel, but not in great quantity.

On the 24th, in the morning, I pushed down a stone that stopped in the passage. I remained from that moment until dinnertime without urinating, in order to increase my desire to do so. Then I got my stone out, not without pain and bleeding, both before and after: as big and long as a pine nut, but as thick as a bean at one end, and having, to tell the truth, exactly the shape of a prick. It was a very fortunate thing for me to be able to get it out. I have never ejected one comparable in size to this one. I had guessed only too truly from the quality of my urines that this would be the result. I shall see what is to follow.

There would be too much weakness and cowardice on my part if, finding myself every day in a position to die in this manner, and with every hour bringing death nearer, I did not make every effort toward being able to bear death lightly as soon as it surprises me. And in the meantime it will be wise to accept joyously the good that it pleases God to send us. There is no other medicine, no other rule or science, for avoiding the ills, whatever they may be and however great, that besiege men from all sides and at every hour, than to make up our minds to suffer them humanly, or to end them courageously and promptly.

On August 25th my urine regained its usual color, and I found my body in the same condition as before; except that many times, both day and night, I suffered in my left cheek; but it was a sort of pain that did not last at all. I remember that this pain bothered me at other times in my home.

On Saturday the 26th I was in the bath for an hour in the morning

On the 27th after dinner I was cruelly tormented by a very acute toothache, so that I sent for the doctor, who, when he had come and considered everything, and especially that my pain had left me in his presence, judged that this defluxion had no body unless a very subtle one, and that it was wind and flatulence that mounted from the stomach to the head and, mingling with a little humor, gave me that discomfort. This indeed seemed to me very likely, considering that I had suffered similar accidents in other parts of the body.

On Monday, August 28th, at dawn, I went to drink at Bernabò's spring, and drank seven pounds four ounces of the water, at twelve ounces to the pound. It made my bowels move once. I voided a little less than half of it before dinner. I clearly felt that it sent vapors to my head and made it heavy.

On Tuesday the 29th I drank at the ordinary spring nine glasses, which each contained one ounce less than a pound. Immediately my head felt bad. To tell the truth, my head was of itself in bad condition, and it had never fully recovered from the bad state it had fallen into in my first season of bathing. I was troubled by it more rarely and in a little different way than a month before, because my eyes were not weakened or dazzled. I suffered more in the back, and

never in the head without the pain passing immediately to the left cheek, affecting the whole of it, the teeth, even the lower ones, the ear, part of the nose. The
pain was brief, but most of the time very acute, and seized me very many times,
day and night. Such was the condition of my head this season.

I do believe that the fumes of this water, from drinking and also from bathing
(though more so in the former case than in the latter), are very bad for the head,
and, I can say with assurance, even worse for the stomach. And therefore their
custom is generally to take medicine to provide against this.

During that whole day and night I passed all but a pound of the water, counting what I drank at table, which was very little, and less than a pound. After
dinner, toward sunset, I went to the bath and stayed there three-quarters of an
hour. I sweated a little.

On Wednesday, August 30th, I drank nine glasses, eighty-one ounces. I passed
half of it before dinner.

On Thursday I discontinued the drinking, and in the morning went on horseback to see Controne, a very populous municipality in these mountains. There
are many beautiful fertile plains, and pastures at the top of the mountains. This
municipality has many little villas, comfortable stone lodgings, their roofs covered
with stone. I made a long tour around these hills before returning home.

I did not like the way I had got rid of the water I had taken lately. Therefore
I thought of giving up drinking it. I was displeased because I did not pass it all,
and the count of what I urinated did not match with what I had drunk. More
than three glasses of the water of the bath must have remained inside me. Besides,
I had an attack of constipation, in contrast with my ordinary state.

Friday, September 1st, 1581, I bathed for an hour in the morning. I sweated
some in the bath, and voided with the urine a large quantity of red gravel. When
drinking, I had voided none, or little. My head remained still in the same state,
that is to say bad.

I began to find these baths unpleasant. And if news had come from France,
which I was expecting, having been four months without receiving any, I would
have been ready to leave at the first opportunity, and do my autumn cure at any
other baths whatever. [. . .]

NOTE

1   A red resin used as an astringent.

Index